Lecture Notes in Artificial Intelligence 7004

Subseries of Lecture Notes in Computer Science

LNAI Series Editors

Randy Goebel
University of Alberta, Edmonton, Canada
Yuzuru Tanaka
Hokkaido University, Sapporo, Japan
Wolfgang Wahlster
DFKI and Saarland University, Saarbrücken, Germany

LNAI Founding Series Editor

Joerg Siekmann
DFKI and Saarland University, Saarbrücken, Germany

W0193312

Hepu Deng   Duoqian Miao   Jingsheng Lei
Fu Lee Wang (Eds.)

Artificial Intelligence and Computational Intelligence

Third International Conference, AICI 2011
Taiyuan, China, September 24-25, 2011
Proceedings, Part III

 Springer

Series Editors

Randy Goebel, University of Alberta, Edmonton, Canada
Jörg Siekmann, University of Saarland, Saarbrücken, Germany
Wolfgang Wahlster, DFKI and University of Saarland, Saarbrücken, Germany

Volume Editors

Hepu Deng
RMIT University, School of Business Information Technology
City Campus, 124 La Trobe Street, Melbourne, VIC 3000, Australia
E-mail: hepu.deng@rmit.edu.au

Duoqian Miao
Tongji University, School of Electronics and Information
Shanghai 201804, China
E-mail: miaoduoqian@163.com

Jingsheng Lei
Shanghai University of Electronic Power
School of Computer and Information Engineering
Shanghai 200090, China
E-mail: jshlei@126.com

Fu Lee Wang
Caritas Institute of Higher Education, Department of Business Administration
18 Chui Ling Road, Tseung Kwan O, Hong Kong, China
E-mail: pwang@cihe.edu.hk

ISSN 0302-9743   e-ISSN 1611-3349
ISBN 978-3-642-23895-6   ISBN 978-3-642-23896-3 (eBook)
DOI 10.1007/978-3-642-23896-3
Springer Heidelberg Dordrecht London New York

Library of Congress Control Number: 2011936133

CR Subject Classification (1998): I.2, H.3-4, F.1, I.4-5, J.3, K.4.4, D.2

LNCS Sublibrary: SL 7 – Artificial Intelligence

Typesetting: Camera-ready by author, data conversion by Scientific Publishing Services, Chennai, India

Printed on acid-free paper

Springer is part of Springer Science+Business Media (www.springer.com)

Preface

The 2011 International Conference on Artificial Intelligence and Computational Intelligence (AICI 2011) was held during September 24–25, 2011 in Taiyuan, China. AICI 2011 received 1,073 submissions from 20 countries and regions. After rigorous reviews, 265 high-quality papers were selected for publication in the AICI 2011 proceedings. The acceptance rate was 24%.

The aim of AICI 2011 was to bring together researchers working in many different areas of artificial intelligence and computational intelligence to foster the exchange of new ideas and promote international collaborations. In addition to the large number of submitted papers and invited sessions, there were several internationally well-known keynote speakers.

On behalf of the Organizing Committee, we thank Taiyuan University of Technology for its sponsorship and logistics support. We also thank the members of the Organizing Committee and the Program Committee for their hard work. We are very grateful to the keynote speakers, session chairs, reviewers, and student helpers. Last but not least, we thank all the authors and participants for their great contributions that made this conference possible.

September 2011

Hepu Deng
Duoqian Miao
Jingsheng Lei
Fu Lee Wang

Organization

Organizing Committee

General Co-chairs

Wendong Zhang   Taiyuan University of Technology, China
Qing Li   City University of Hong Kong, Hong Kong

Program Committee Co-chairs

Hepu Deng   RMIT University, Australia
Duoqian Miao   Tongji University, China

Steering Committee Chair

Jingsheng Lei   Shanghai University of Electric Power, China

Local Arrangements Co-chairs

Fu Duan   Taiyuan University of Technology, China
Dengao Li   Taiyuan University of Technology, China

Proceedings Co-chairs

Fu Lee Wang   Caritas Institute of Higher Education,
                                       Hong Kong
Ting Jin   Fudan University, China

Sponsorship Chair

Zhiyu Zhou   Zhejiang Sci-Tech University, China

Program Committee

Adi Prananto	Swinburne University of Technology, Australia
Adil Bagirov	University of Ballarat, Australia
Ahmad Abareshi	RMIT University, Australia
Alemayehu Molla	RMIT University, Australia
Andrew Stranier	University of Ballarat, Australia
Andy Song	RMIT University, Australia
An-Feng Liu	Central South University, China
Arthur Tatnall	Victoria University, Australia
Bae Hyeon	Pusan National University, Korea
Baoding Liu	Tsinghua University, China
Carmine Sellitto	Victoria University, Australia
Caroline Chan	Deakin University, Australia
CheolPark Soon	Chonbuk National University, Korea
Chowdhury Morshed	Deakin University, Australia
Chung-Hsing Yeh	Monash University, Australia
Chunqiao Tao	South China University, China
Costa Marly	Federal University of Amazonas, Brazil
Craig Parker	Deakin University, Australia
Daowen Qiu	Zhong Shan University, China
Dat Tran	University of Canberra, Australia
Dengsheng Zhang	Monash University, Australia
Edmonds Lau	Swinburne University of Technology, Australia
Elspeth McKay	RMIT University, Australia
Eng Chew	University of Technology Sydney, Australia
Feilong Cao	China Jiliang University, China
Ferry Jie	RMIT University, Australia
Furutani Hiroshi	University of Miyazaki, Japan
Gour Karmakar	Monash University, Australia
Guojun Lu	Monash University, Australia
Heping Pan	University of Ballarat, Australia
Hossein Zadeh	RMIT University, Australia
Ian Sadler	Victoria University, Australia
Irene Zhang	Victoria University, Australia
Jamie Mustard	Deakin University, Australia
Jeff Ang Charles	Darwin University, Australia
Jennie Carroll	RMIT University, Australia
Jenny Zhang	RMIT University, Australia
Jian Zhou T.	Tsinghua University, China
Jingqiang Wang	South China University, China
Jinjun Chen	Swinburne University of Technology, Australia
Joarder Kamruzzaman	Monash University, Australia
Kaile Su	Beijing University, China
Kankana Chakrabaty	University of New England, Australia

Table of Contents – Part III

Machine Vision

Natural Language Processing

Nature Computation

Neural Computation

Neural Networks

Particle Swarm Optimization

Pattern Recognition

Rough Set Theory

Support Vector Machine

An Algorithm of Determining the Plane Based on Monocular Vision and Laser Loop

Xinglong Zhu, Ying Zhang, Luyang Li, Longqin Gao, and Jiping Zhou[*]

School of Mechanical Engineering, Yangzhou University,
Huayang West Road 196, 225127, Yangzhou, Jiangsu, China
{xlzhu,yzhang,lyli,lqgao,jpzhou}@yzu.edu.cn

Abstract. Since the spot is elliptical when the cylindrical laser irradiates on the spatial plane, the pose of the spatial plane can be described by the elliptical spot. At the same time, the laser spot in the CCD plane is also elliptical. The information of the spatial plane will include in the image ellipse. The monocular vision has been established, and the boundary equation is obtained by image processing, and the relationship is derived between the boundary equation and the pose parameters of the spatial plane by minimum mean-square method. In order to obtain the depth information of the spatial plane, the boundary equation of the cylinder laser is introduced as the constrained condition. Because the constrained condition is transcendental equation set which includes trigonometric function, SWIFT (sequential weight increasing factor technique) is adopted for solving the parameters of the spatial plane. The simulation results show that the algorithm proposed is effective and feasible.

Keywords: monocular vision, cylinder laser spot, searching algorithm, position and pose.

1 Introduction

The stereo vision measurement technology based on the triangulation measurement principle has some special advantages, such as non-contact, fast, good flexibility, medium precision and so on. So it is widely used in online testing of modern manufacturing, contour measurement of three-dimensional objects, etc [1].

Pose determination of parameterized object models plays an important role in verification of model based recognition systems and real-time tracking of objects in images. Described herein is a data structure that models 3D parametric objects. Algorithms are presented for obtaining analytical partial derivatives of distance functions from projected model edges and endpoints to corresponding image segments, with respect to changes in model and camera parameters. These parameters include rotational, translational, scale and dilation in camera and object model. Solving for camera and model parameters in a 2D image (pose determination) is a nonlinear least squares paradigm. Weights are considered for line-to-line and point-to-point matching

---

[*] Xinglong Zhu: Prof., Ying Zhang: Master, Luyang Li: Associate Prof.,
Longqin Gao: Associate Prof., Jiping Zhou: Prof.

H. Deng et al. (Eds.): AICI 2011, Part III, LNAI 7004, pp. 1–11, 2011.
© Springer-Verlag Berlin Heidelberg 2011

to allow for the applicability of the methods to images with noisy data [2]. The orientation disparity field from two orthographic views of an inclined planar surface patch (covered by straight lines) is analyzed, and a new tool to extract the patch orientation is provided. That is, the function coupling the average orientation of each pair of corresponding surface contours with their orientation disparity. This function allows identifying the tilt of the surface, and two indeterminacy functions describing the set of surface inclinations (around the vertical and horizontal axes) over convergence angle values compatible with the orientation disparity field [3]. K Achour presents a new approach for 3D scene reconstruction based on projective geometry without camera calibration. Previous works use at least six points to build two projective reference planes. Their contribution is to reduce the number of reference points to four by exploiting some geometrical shapes contained in the scene. The first implemented algorithm allows the reconstruction of a fourth point on each reference plane. The second algorithm is devoted to the 3D reconstruction [4]. Perceived depth was measured for three-types of stereogram with the color/texture of half-occluded (monocular) regions either similar to or dissimilar to that of binocular regions or background. In a two-panel random dot stereogram the monocular region was filled with texture either similar or different to the far panel or left blank. In unpaired background stereogram the monocular region either matched the background or was different in color or texture and in phantom stereogram the monocular region matched the partially occluded object or was a different color or texture. In all three cases depth was considerably impaired when the monocular texture did not match either the background or the more distant surface. The content and context of monocular regions as well as their position are important in determining their role as occlusion cues and thus in three-dimensional layout [5]. A model-based method for indoor mobile robot localization is presented herein; this method relies on monocular vision and uses straight-line correspondences. A classical four-step approach has been adopted (i.e. image acquisition, image feature extraction, image and model feature matching, and camera pose computing). These four steps will be discussed with special focus placed on the critical matching problem. An efficient and simple method for searching image and model feature correspondences, which has been designed for indoor mobile robot self-location, will be highlighted: this is a three-stage method based on the interpretation tree search approach. During the first stage, the correspondences pace is reduced by virtue of splitting the navigable space into view-invariant regions. In making use of the specificity of the mobile robotics frame of reference, the global interpretation tree is divided into two sub-trees; two low-order geometric constraints are then defined and applied directly on 2D–3D correspondences in order to improve pruning and search efficiency. During the last stage, the pose is calculated for each matching hypothesis and the best one is selected according to a defined error function [6]. Li-Juan QIN etc presented a method that can determine the pose of objects from three lines in a general position. The configuration of three non-coplanar lines that intersect at two points has some particular characteristics, which three lines in a general position do not have. Here, they present a new method of determining object pose using this particular line configuration. In theory, this method enriches the pose estimation methods from three line correspondences. In addition, it provides guidance for practical applications. Furthermore, they propose a method to deal with multi-solution phenomenon and a new iterative method [7]. The present state-of-the-art in computing the error statistics in three-dimensional reconstruction from video concentrates on estimating the error covariance. A different source of error which has not received much attention is the fact that the reconstruction estimates are often significantly statistically biased. In this paper, they derive a precise expression for the bias in the depth estimate, based on the continuous (differentiable) version of structure from motion (SfM). Many SfM algorithms, or certain portions of them, can be posed in a linear least-squares (LS) frame-work. Examples include initialization procedures for bundle adjustment or algorithms that alternately estimate depth and camera motion. It is a well-known fact that the LS estimate is biased if the system matrix is noisy. In SfM, the matrix contains point correspondences, which are always difficult to obtain precisely; thus, it is expected that the structure and motion estimates in such a formulation of the problem would be biased. Existing results on the minimum achievable variance of the SfM estimator are extended by deriving a generalized Cramer–Rao lower bound [8]. S Frintrop and P Jensfelt are centered around landmark detection, tracking, and matching for visual simultaneous localization and mapping using a monocular vision system with active gaze control. They present a system that specializes in creating and maintaining a sparse set of landmarks based on a biologically motivated feature-selection strategy. A visual attention system detects salient features that are highly discriminative and ideal candidates for visual landmarks that are easy to redetect. Features are tracked over several frames to determine stable landmarks and to estimate their 3-D position in the environment. Matching of current land-marks to database entries enables loop closing. Active gaze control allows us to overcome some of the limitations of using a monocular vision system with a relatively small field of view. It supports 1) the tracking of landmarks that enable a better pose estimation, 2) the exploration of regions without landmarks to obtain a better distribution of landmarks in the environment, and 3) the active redetection of landmarks to enable loop closing in situations in which a fixed camera fails to close the loop [9]. Xinglong Zhu presents a quickly matching method, which enables to solve the corresponding points about the same point on the objective matter in the different CCD images by adding the laser on the cameras. The deepness message can be conveniently obtained by laser token [10].

In this paper, as the application of industrial robot vision system in the background, a new spatial plane determining algorithm is proposed. This paper is divided into the following sections: (1) Introduction of monocular vision model. (2) The spacial plane is described by ellipse; (3) The algorithm design is introduced. Finally, the numerical example verifies the feasibility of the method and it gives a summary of the study.

2 Monocular Vision Model

When the actor is performing in the stage, the spotlight is turned on. When the stage is irradiated by the spotlight, the spot shape is elliptical. With movement, the elliptical shape is changing. It shows the relative between the stage and the spotlight. Therefore, if the spotlight is fixed, and the pose of the stage plane is changed, the spot shape will take place change. When laser loop irradiates on the spacial plane, a few of shape will appear on the plane irradiated, sees Fig.1.

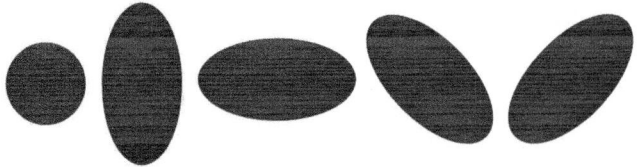

Fig. 1. The spot shape

The model, which uses monocular vision system to determine the pose of spatial plane, is shown in Fig.2. In this model, the relationship between the camera coordinate system and the world coordinate system and the camera's intrinsic parameters are known, the pinhole camera model is a useful model that enables simple mathematical formulation. The axis of cylindrical light source is parallel to cameras' optical axis.

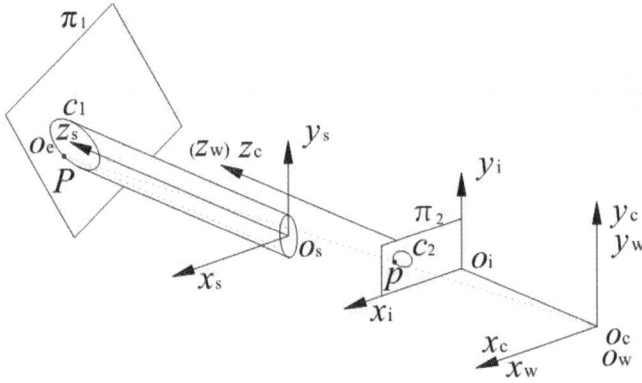

Fig. 2. Monocular vision system model

Define the camera coordinate system $o_c x_c y_c z_c$, the light source system $o_s x_s y_s z_s$, the imaging coordinate system $o_i x_i y_i z_i$ and its imaging plane π_2. Among them, z_c axis coincides with the camera optical axis, o_i is located in the camera optical axis. In general, it takes the camera coordinate system origin o_c as the absolute origin. So, the imaging coordinate system origin o_i is $[0 \quad 0 \quad f]^T$, f is the focal length. The center o_s coordinates of the cylindrical light source relative to camera coordinate system are $[e_x \quad e_y \quad 0]^T$. e_x and e_y are the relative offsets of the center of the cylindrical light source in x and y direction.

When the spatial plane π_1 is irradiated by cylindrical laser, the spot shape is elliptical. Its contours is expressed by c_1. Long half-axis length is R, short half-axis length is r, the center o_e coordinates is $\begin{bmatrix} e_x & e_y & z_L \end{bmatrix}^T$, z_L is the depth from ellipse center to the right camera coordinate system origin.

3 Spacial Plane Described with Ellipse

The spatial plane π_1 is described as follows,

$$\frac{x}{a} + \frac{y}{b} + \frac{z}{c} = 1. \tag{1}$$

In (1), a, b, and c are intercept at the x_c axis, y_c axis, and z_c axis, respectively.

From (1), determining the spatial plane need obtain three unknown parameters a, b, and c. When the spatial plane π_1 is irradiated by cylindrical laser, the spot shape is elliptical, its contour is denoted by c_1 curve, and its center is o_e. The spatial plane described is convenient by elliptical parameters, so we select laser spot to denote the pose of the spatial plane.

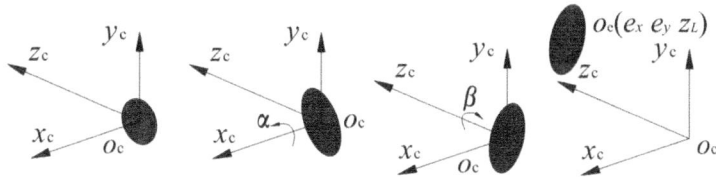

Fig. 3. The formation process of elliptical spot

The formation process of elliptical spot in spatial plane π_1: elliptical spot rotates α degrees around x_c axis firstly, then β degrees around z_c axis and finally ellipse center will pan $\begin{bmatrix} e_x & e_y & z_L \end{bmatrix}^T$, see Fig.3.

Therefore, the problem which determines the parameters of a, b and c may be transform into solving the elliptical pose and depth information parameters of α, β and z_L. That is,

$$(a,b,c) \rightarrow (\alpha, \beta, z_L). \tag{2}$$

In (2), elliptical pose α, β can be characterized on the CCD plane.

Select an arbitrary point P on the edge of ellipse, after rotation and translation, the coordinates are as follows:

$$\begin{bmatrix} x_e \\ y_e \\ z_e \end{bmatrix} = \begin{bmatrix} e_x + Rc\,\theta c\beta - rs\theta s\beta c\alpha \\ e_y + Rc\,\theta s\beta + rs\theta c\beta c\alpha \\ z_L + rs\theta s\alpha \end{bmatrix}. \tag{3}$$

Where $\begin{bmatrix} x_e & y_e & z_e \end{bmatrix}^T$ express an arbitrary point P's coordinates of the ellipse edge relative to the camera coordinate system. c , s denotes cos and sin respectively. The value of θ is $0-2\pi$. This shows that the elliptic laser spot edge can be expressed by (3).

The spatial straight line equation is constructed by point p and o_c:

$$\frac{x-x_e}{x_e-0} = \frac{y-y_e}{y_e-0} = \frac{z-z_e}{z_e-0} . \tag{4}$$

Let us denote $z = f$ and an arbitrary point's coordinates of imaging edge curve C_2 are obtained from (4):

$$\begin{bmatrix} x_i \\ y_i \\ z_i \end{bmatrix} = \begin{bmatrix} x_e f / z_e \\ y_e f / z_e \\ f \end{bmatrix} . \tag{5}$$

Then, the trigonometric functions about θ can be derived by (3) and (5).

$$\cos\theta = \frac{a_1 x_i + a_2 y_i + a_3}{R(a_7 x_i + a_8 y_i + a_9)}$$

$$\sin\theta = \frac{a_4 x_i + a_5 y_i + a_6}{r(a_7 x_i + a_8 y_i + a_9)}$$

$a_1 = z_L \cos\beta \cos\alpha - e_x \sin\alpha \quad a_2 = z_L \sin\beta \cos\alpha + e_y \sin\alpha$

$a_3 = -f(e_x \cos\beta + e_y \sin\beta)\cos\alpha$

$a_4 = -z_L \sin\beta$

$a_5 = z_L \cos\beta$

$a_6 = f(e_x \sin\beta - e_y \cos\beta)$

$a_7 = \sin\beta \sin\alpha$

$a_8 = -\cos\beta \sin\alpha$

$a_9 = f \cos\alpha$

From $\sin^2\theta + \cos^2\theta = 1$, two variables and 2nd order equation can be obtained:

$$b_0 x_i^2 + b_1 x_i y_i + b_2 y_i^2 + b_3 x_i + b_4 y_i + b_5 = 0 . \tag{6}$$

$b_0 = a_1^2 r^2 + a_4^2 R^2 - a_7^2 R^2 r^2$

$b_1 = 2(a_1 a_2 r^2 + a_4 a_5 R^2 - a_7 a_8 R^2 r^2)$

$$b_2 = a_2^2 r^2 + a_5^2 R^2 - R^2 r^2 a_8^2$$

$$b_3 = 2(a_1 a_3 r^2 + a_4 a_6 R^2 - a_7 a_9 R^2 r^2)$$

$$b_4 = 2(a_2 a_3 r^2 + a_5 a_6 R^2 - a_8 a_9 R^2 r^2)$$

$$b_5 = a_3^2 r^2 + a_6^2 R^2 - a_9^2 R^2 r^2$$

Equation (6) is the ellipse equation.
From (3) again, we can obtain

$$x_e = e_x + Rc\theta c\beta - rs\theta s\beta c\alpha. \tag{7}$$

$$y_e = e_y + Rc\theta s\beta + rs\theta c\beta c\alpha. \tag{8}$$

Form (7) and (8),

$$\cos\theta = \frac{(x_e - e_x)\cos\beta + (y_e - e_y)\sin\beta}{R}$$

$$\sin\theta = \frac{(y_e - e_y)\cos\beta - (x_e - e_x)\sin\beta}{r\cos\alpha}$$

Then,

$$d_0 x_e^2 + d_1 x_e y_e + d_2 y_e^2 + d_3 x_e + d_4 y_e + d_5 = 0. \tag{9}$$

In (9),

$$d_0 = R^2 \sin^2\beta + r^2 \cos^2\alpha\cos^2\beta$$

$$d_1 = (r^2 \cos^2\alpha - R^2)\sin 2\beta$$

$$d_2 = R^2 \cos^2\beta + r^2 \cos^2\alpha\sin^2\beta$$

$$d_3 = [e_y(R^2 - r^2 \cos^2\alpha)\sin 2\beta - 2e_x(R^2 \sin^2\beta + r^2 \cos^2\alpha\cos^2\beta)]$$

$$d_4 = [e_x(R^2 - r^2 \cos^2\alpha)\sin 2\beta - 2e_y(R^2 \cos^2\beta + r^2 \cos^2\alpha\sin^2\beta)]$$

$$d_5 = (r^2 \cos^2\alpha\cos^2\beta + R^2 \sin^2\beta)e_x^2 + (r^2 \cos^2\alpha\sin^2\beta + R^2 \cos^2\beta)e_y^2 +$$
$$(r^2 \cos^2\alpha - R^2)e_x e_y \sin 2\beta - R^2 r^2 \cos^2\alpha$$

Substituting (7) and (8) to (10),

$$(x - e_x)^2 + (y - e_y)^2 = r_1^2. \tag{10}$$

In (10), r_1 is radius of the laser cylinder, it equals r.
In comparison with (9) and (10), we may obtain the following equations,

$$d_1 / d_0 = 0. \tag{11}$$

$$d_2/d_0 = 1. \tag{12}$$

$$d_3/d_0 = -2e_x. \tag{13}$$

$$d_4/d_0 = -2e_y. \tag{14}$$

$$d_5/d_0 = -r^2. \tag{15}$$

4 Algorithm Design

Figure 4 shows that the spot shape is elliptical when the spatial plane is irradiated by cylindrical laser, which is equivalent to the formation: the plane $o_c x_c y_c$ rotates 60° around the x-axis firstly, then rotates 30° around the z-axis and finally pans $[30 \quad 40 \quad 75]^T$ mm. Take the camera coordinate system origin o_c as the absolute origin. The origin o_i coordinates of the imaging coordinate system are $[0 \quad 0 \quad 25]^T$ mm. The center o_s coordinates of the cylindrical laser relative to camera coordinate system are $[30 \quad 40 \quad 0]^T$ mm. The ellipse center o_e coordinates are $[30 \quad 40 \quad 75]^T$ mm. The radius of cylindrical laser is 10 mm. Figure 5 shows the images in the imaging plane.

Fig. 4. Simulative spot   Fig. 5. Images in imaging plane

According to the above known parameters and (3)-(5), we can obtain the data of image edge on CCD plane. The data shows in table 1.

Table 1. CCD Imaging Ellipse fitting

$\theta/°$	X_i/mm	Y_i/mm	$\theta/°$	X_i/mm	Y_i/mm
0	12.8868	15.0000	180	7.1132	11.6667
18	11.4158	14.7573	198	8.3666	11.6905
36	9.9986	14.4209	216	10.0019	11.9041
54	8.7194	14.0276	234	11.8691	12.3201
72	7.6309	13.6055	252	13.7026	12.9079
90	6.7699	13.1770	270	15.1700	13.5836
108	6.1681	12.7610	288	15.9889	14.2279
126	5.8600	12.3767	306	16.0424	14.7295
144	5.8859	12.0465	324	15.4064	15.0244
162	6.2906	11.7983	342	14.2795	15.1043

Assuming that elliptical equation on CCD plane is as follows,

$$x^2 + B_1 xy + B_2 y^2 + B_3 x + B_4 y + B_5 = 0 . \tag{16}$$

According to the data in table 1, we can determine the elliptical parameters on CCD plane by minimum mean-square elliptical algorithm. After fitting process, the elliptical parameters on CCD plane shows in table 2.

Table 2. Elliptical Parameters on Ccd Plane

B_1	B_2	B_3	B_4	B_5
-3.9899	8.8868	31.4459	-194.0465	1111.1111

Therefore, $b_i / b_0 = B_i$, (i=1,2,3,4,5), that is, the following of five equal equation can be obtained,

$$b_1/b_0 = -3.9899 . \tag{17}$$

$$b_2/b_0 = 8.8868 . \tag{18}$$

$$b_3/b_0 = 31.4459 . \tag{19}$$

$$b_4/b_0 = -194.0465 . \tag{20}$$

$$b_5/b_0 = 1111.1111 . \tag{21}$$

Through (11)-(15) and (17)-(21), we can solving the unknown parameters R, z_L, α and β. Because (11)-(15) and (17)-(21) are equation set which include trigonometric function, it is difficult to solve the R, z_L, α and β by analytic solution. Therefore, we adopt a searching method to solve the above problem. The original problem transforms to solve the minimum question,

$$\min J = 0. \tag{22}$$

s.t.

$$h_i = b_i / b_0 - B_i. \quad (i=1,2,3,4,5) \tag{23}$$

That is, it must satisfy (17)-(21).And at the same time, it must satisfy (11)-(15), that is,

$$h[6] = d_1/d_0. \tag{24}$$

$$h[7] = d_2/d_0 - 1. \tag{25}$$

$$h[8] = d_3/d_0 + 2e_x. \tag{26}$$

$$h[9] = d_4/d_0 + 2e_y. \tag{27}$$

$$h[10] = d_5/d_0 + r^2. \tag{28}$$

The above solving the minimum problem will translate into the following penalty function question,

$$P(\Theta, r_k) = \min J + r_w \sum_{i=1}^{10} h_i^2. \tag{29}$$

In (29), r_w is the penalty factor. $\Theta = [R \quad z_L \quad \alpha \quad \beta]$ is optimize variable.

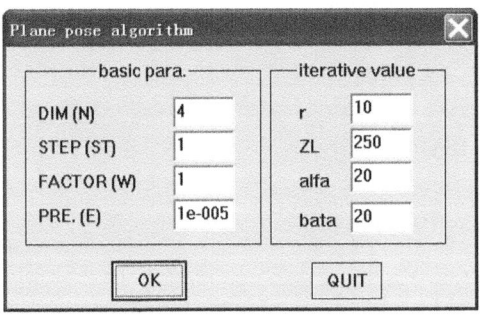
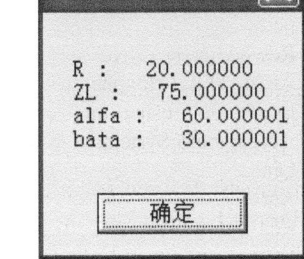

Fig. 6. Dialogue box   Fig. 7. The searching result

Figure   6   is   the   dialogue   box.   The   initial   iterative   values $\Theta = [R \quad z_L \quad \alpha \quad \beta] = [10\text{mm} \quad 250\text{mm} \quad 20° \quad 20°]$. Figure 7 is the searching results.

$\Theta^* = [R^* \ z_L^* \ \alpha^* \ \beta^*] = [20\text{mm} \ 75\text{mm} \ 60.000001° \ 30.00001°]$. The searching result is next to the known values. It test that the algorithm proposed is feasible.

5 Conclusions

An algorithm that can determine the depth and pose information of the spatial plane is proposed. The algorithm adopts the monocular vision image in CCD plane and the boundary equation of the cylinder laser spot. Because of only the monocular vision, the vision model is simpler, the arithmetic speed is faster, and the system cost is cheaper. Because the boundary equation of the cylinder laser is introduced, the algorithm can obtain the depth information, as well as the pose parameters of the spatial plane. The simulation results show that the method is effective and feasible.

Acknowledgment. This work is supported by National Science Foundation of China under Project 60977071, by Science and Technology Department of Jiangsu Province under Project BK2010323, by "333 Talents Engineering" of Jiangsu Province under Project BRA2010131 and by Innovation Fund for Small and Medium-Sized Technology-Based Firms of Jiangsu Province under Project BC2009242.

References

1. Yamada, H., Togasaki, T., Kimura, M., et al.: High density 3-D packaging technology based on the sidewall interconnection method and its application for CCD micro camera visual inspection system. IEEE Transactions on Advanced Packaging 26(2), 113–121 (2003)
2. Goldberg, R.R.: Pose determination of parameterized object models from a monocular image. Image and Vision Computing 11(1), 49–62 (1993)
3. Fantoni, C.: 3D surface orientation based on a novel representation of the orientation disparity field. Vision Research 48(25), 2509–2522 (2008)
4. Achour, K., Benkhelif, M.: A new approach to 3D reconstruction without camera calibration. Pattern Recognition 34(12), 2467–2476 (2001)
5. Grovea, P.M., Gillamb, B., Onoa, H.: Content and context of monocular regions determine perceived depth in random dot, unpaired background and phantom stereograms. Vision Research 42(15), 1859–1870 (2002)
6. Aider, O.A., Hoppenot, P., Colle, E.: A model-based method for indoor mobile robot localization using monocular vision and straight-line correspondences. Robotics and Autonomous Systems 52(2,3), 229–246 (2005)
7. Qin, L.-J., Zhu, F.: A New Method for Pose Estimation from Line Correspondences. Acta Automatic Sinica 34(2), 130–134 (2008)
8. Roy-Chowdhury, A.K., Chellappa, R.: Statistical Bias in 3-D Reconstruction From a Monocular Video. IEEE Transactions on Image Processing 14(8), 1057–1062 (2005)
9. Frintrop, S., Jensfelt, P.: Attentional Landmarks and Active Gaze Control for Visual SLAM. IEEE Transactions on Robotics 24(5), 1054–1064 (2008)
10. Zhu, X.: Quick measurement algorithms of position and pose of spatial object by CCD images based on stereo vision and laser token. Chinese Journal of Mechanical Engineering 40(7), 161–165 (2004)

A Novel Content-Based Image Retrieval Approach Using Fuzzy Combination of Color and Texture

Mohsen Fathian and Fardin Akhlaghian Tab

Department of Computer Engineering, University of Kurdistan, Sanandaj, Iran
{mohsen.fathian,f.akhlaghian}@gmail.com

Abstract. A novel content-based image retrieval approach using fuzzy combination of color and texture image features is expressed in this paper. To accomplish this, color histogram and autocorrelogram of the partitioned image as color features and Gabor wavelet as texture feature are used. Color and texture features are separately extracted and kept as feature vectors. In comparing images similarity stage, the difference between feature vectors is computed. Since center of image is more important, higher weight is considered for it in the comparison of autocorrelograms, and due to this fact the retrieval performance is improved; and also finding the most similar regions using autocorrelogram of the other regions, makes the algorithm more invariant to rotation and to somehow to changing the viewing angle. To make the final decision about images similarity ratio, a fuzzy rule-based system is utilized. Experimental results show this method improved the performance of content-based image retrieval systems.

Keywords: content-based image retrieval, color, texture, fuzzy system.

1 Introduction

With the rapid growth of the digital technology and accessibility of it, huge amount of digital images are easily produced and therefore image databases are becoming larger and wider. Consequently, the need for efficient tools to retrieve image from databases becomes crucial. Since, for huge image databases, manually annotating and indexing of text-based retrieval systems, are cumbersome and practically impossible [1,2], automatic content-based image retrieval systems are required.

Content-based image retrieval systems use low-level visual features such as color, texture, shape and spatial information [1,2]. Most of these systems utilize combination of these features to retrieve images [3].

Color and texture are among the more expressive and important of the visual features [4]. Since in some images with similar content, colors are different while textures are similar, using the texture feature in addition to color feature improve the performance of retrieval systems and become more robust against changing color or lightening condition. In this work, color histogram and color autocorrelogram of partitioned image are used as color descriptor whereas Gabor wavelet is used as texture descriptor.

H. Deng et al. (Eds.): AICI 2011, Part III, LNAI 7004, pp. 12–23, 2011.

Color autocorrelogram of partitioned image intuitively includes local more than global information. On the other hand, histogram is a global color feature and does not present any spatial correlation information of image's color. By combining these two features, color feature is growing up. Gabor wavelet is efficient tool in image retrieval as texture feature. By using this feature in addition to color feature the feature vectors that represent images content are improved.

For estimating distance of every two images, at first three feature vectors of each image are extracted, and then their difference are computed. Difference of color autocorrelogram feature, is computed based on the regions of the partitioned images. Considering the importance of the center region of images, they are compared with doubled weight. In comparison of each remains region, the most similar region in the other image is found and then the difference of their autocorrelogram is computed.

In order to estimate the final distance of any two images, differences of the three feature vectors are converted to fuzzy sets, and then a fuzzy rule base is applied which incorporates expert knowledge in final result. The output value of this fuzzy system indicates images similarity ratio. Based on this measure, images are retrieved and final rank of the similar images is obtained. Emphasizing on the comparison of the proposed color autocorrelogram method in fuzzy rule-base, makes the algorithm invariant against translation, rotation and to somehow changing the viewing angle.

The paper is organized as follows: In section 2, color features include color histogram and color autocorrelogram of partitioned image are expressed. In section 3, a brief review of Gabor wavelet is given. Similarity measure to evaluate the similarity of feature vectors of images is expressed in section 4. The method for combining color and texture features using fuzzy system is presented in section 5. Experimental results are given in section 6 and finally, conclusions are drawn in section 7.

2   Color Feature

Color as the most important visual feature is widely used in content-based image retrieval systems [4,5]. Large variety of techniques to extract this feature is presented [6,7,8]. Among them that can be pointed out: color histogram [8], color coherent vector [9], color correlogram [10] and morphological description of color [11].

Any attempt on color description has to address certain issues first: the choice of color space and quantization levels. A good choice results in a system working properly against variations due to different illumination conditions. Extensive researches show that selection of the proper color space in combination with other descriptors can give great result [4].

In this study, color histogram and color autocorrelogram of partitioned image are used as two color descriptors. In both of them RGB color space is used, and each channel of red, green and blue are mapped to 8 bins.

2.1   Color Histogram

Color histogram is commonly used as a color feature descriptor to retrieve images [8,12], and indicate total color scattering in an image. Advantages of this method are as follow: It is effective, implemented easily and small size memory is required.

Histogram is invariant to translation and rotation of the image plane, and change slowly under change of angle of view [8].

Computing color histogram is as follow: Suppose I be a color image. Colors in I are quantized into m colors: $c_1, c_2, ..., c_m$. For a pixel $p = (x, y) \in I$, assume that $I(p)$ represents it's quantized color. Let $I_c = \{p \mid I(p) = c\}$, So the notation $p \in I_c$ means: $I(p) = c$.

Color histogram of image I at particular color c_i, is defined by (1):

$$h_{c_i}(I) = \{n_p \mid p \in I_{c_i}\} . \tag{1}$$

In this equation, n_p is the number of pixels in the image that their colors are c_i. Therefore, histogram H of an image I is defined as a vector according to the (2):

$$H = \{h_{c_1}(I), h_{c_2}(I), ..., h_{c_i}(I), ..., h_{c_m}(I)\} . \tag{2}$$

Histogram of each color channel can be used as a feature vector.

2.2 Color AutoCorrelogram of Partitioned Image

Another color feature used in this work is color autocorrelogram, which is a subset of color correlogram. A color correlogram expresses how the spatial correlation of pairs of colors changes with distance [13]. Any scheme that is based on only global properties may be sensitive to changes in appearance, while the correlogram is more stable against these changes.

Suppose I be an $n \times n$ image (for simplicity we assume that the image is square). Using the distance $d \in \{1, 2, ..., n\}$, the correlogram of I for $i, j \in \{1, 2, ..., m\}$ and $k \in \{1, 2, ..., d\}$ as (3) is defined [10]:

$$\gamma_{c_i, c_j}^{(k)}(I) = Pr_{p_1 \in I_{c_i}, p_2 \in I} \left[p_2 \in I_{c_j} \mid |p_1 - p_2| = k \right] . \tag{3}$$

The color correlogram is a table indexed by color pairs; Where the k-th entry for (i,j) determines the probability of finding a pixel with color j at a distance k from a pixel with color i in the image. This feature makes image retrieval systems robust against large changes at appearance in the same scene [10]. The outstanding feature of color correlogram is that it includes spatial color information and can improve this shortcoming of color histogram method.

The autocorrelogram of image I capture spatial correlation between identical colors only and is defined in (4):

$$\alpha_c^{(k)} = \gamma_{c,c}^{(k)}(I) . \tag{4}$$

Regarding high computational cost and large size of color correlogram feature vector, practically, color autocorrelogram is used as a feature vector. In this paper color autocorrelogram with $d \in \{1, 2, ..., 10\}$ is used.

To make a more efficient autocorrelogram comparison, a new region-based approach is proposed in this paper. The method is started by partitioning the input $m \times n$ image to nine fixed regions that is identified in Fig. 1. An important and vital part of image is generally located in the center of it and with larger weighting of the comparison of center region of image, performance of image comparison and retrieval algorithms are greatly increased.

In the next stage and after partitioning images, for each region of the images, color autocorrelogram is separately computed. Then, in evaluation image similarity stage, for any two images, the weight of difference of center regions autocorrelogram is doubled. In comparison of each remains region, the most similar region in the other image is found and then the difference of their autocorrelogram is computed. The main reason of comparing the most similar regions is that image plane is rotate or translate occasionally, and also sometimes viewing angle is changed. In Fig. 2 two instances of these cases are shown; although, the main subject of the pair images in the center regions are similar, but the position of some other regions are changed. By comparing similar regions of any two images, rather than corresponding regions, the system performance is more improved [14].

Finally, for computing the distance between any two images based on color autocorrelogram, by summing the similar regions difference and also doubled center regions difference based on similarity measure, a number is obtained which gives the two images similarity ratio.

3   Texture Feature

Texture is another important low-level feature that widely used in content-based image retrieval. This feature is commonly combined with other features to form feature vectors of images. Many techniques have been developed for representing and measuring texture similarity. Most techniques measure the image texture by features such as the degree of contrast, coarseness, directionality and regularity [15]; or periodicity, directionality and randomness [16]. Alternative methods of texture analysis for image retrieval include the use of Gabor wavelets [17,18].

The Gabor wavelets can be considered as orientation and scale tunable edge and line detectors. Statistics of Gabor wavelet responses in a given image are used to characterize the underlying texture information.

$(1,1)$		$(1,m)$
1	2	3
$(n/3, m/3)$		$(n/3, 2m/3)$
4	5	6
$(2n/3, m/3)$		$(2n/3, 2m/3)$
7	8	9
$(n,1)$		(n,m)

Fig. 1. image partitioning method

Fig. 2. Two pairs of image; similar in center region, some other regions are replaced

A two dimensional Gabor function is a Gaussian modulated by a complex sinusoid [19]. It can be specified by the standard deviations σ_x and σ_y of the Gaussian envelope as (5):

$$\psi(x,y) = \frac{1}{2\pi\sigma_x\sigma_y} \exp\left[-\frac{1}{2}\left(\frac{x^2}{\sigma_x} + \frac{y^2}{\sigma_y}\right) + 2\pi j\omega x\right]. \tag{5}$$

Where ω is called the modulation frequency.

The Gabor wavelets are obtained by dilation and rotation of the generating function $\psi(x,y)$ as (6):

$$\psi_{mn}(x,y) = a^{-m}\,\psi(x',y'). \tag{6}$$

Where $x' = a^{-m}(x\cos\theta + y\sin\theta)$, $y' = a^{-m}(-x\sin\theta + y\cos\theta)$. And also $\theta = n\pi/N$, m and n specify the scale and orientation of the wavelet respectively, with $m=0,1,...,M-1$ and $n=0,1,...,N-1$.

The a, ω, σ_x and σ_y are defined as (7):

$$a = (U_h/U_l)^{\frac{1}{M-1}}$$

$$\omega_{m,n} = a^m U_l$$

$$\sigma_{x,m,n} = \frac{(a+1)\sqrt{2\ln 2}}{2\pi a^m(a-1)U_l} \tag{7}$$

$$\sigma_{y,m,n} = \frac{1}{2\pi \tan\left(\frac{\pi}{2N}\right)\sqrt{\frac{U_h^2}{2\ln 2} - \left(\frac{1}{2\pi\sigma_{x,m,n}}\right)^2}}$$

Where U_h and U_l are the upper and lower bound of the designing frequency band.

The response of Gabor wavelet is the convolution of Gabor window with image $I(x,y)$ which is given by (8):

$$G_{mn}(x,y) = \sum_s \sum_t I(x-s, y-t)\psi_{mn}^*(s,t). \tag{8}$$

Where, s and t are the filter mask size variables, and ψ_{mn}^* is the complex conjugate of ψ_{mn}.

In this work, $U_l = 0.05$, $U_h = 0.49$, s and t range from -30 to +30 which commonly used in the literature, are employed.

It is assumed that we are interested in images that have homogenous texture. After applying Gabor wavelets with different orientation at different scale on each image of database, an array of magnitudes is obtained. For forming feature vector f that represents image texture, mean μ_{mn} and standard deviation σ_{mn} of magnitude of transformed coefficients are used as (9) and (10) respectively:

$$\mu_{mn} = \sum_x \sum_y G_{mn}(x,y). \tag{9}$$

$$\sigma_{mn} = \sqrt{\sum_x \sum_y (|G_{mn}(x,y)| - \mu_{mn})^2}. \tag{10}$$

In this study, tree scales and four orientations are used and texture feature vector for each image is represents as (11):

$$f = (\mu_{00}, \sigma_{00}, \mu_{01}, \sigma_{01}, ..., \mu_{23}, \sigma_{23}) . \tag{11}$$

4 Similarity Measure

To evaluate the similarity between images, any measurement that can evaluate similarity between two feature vectors can be used. In this paper, Canberra (d_l) measure is used to indicate how similar the two images are, in both color and texture features cases [20]. Suppose $X = (x_1, x_2, ..., x_n)$ and $Y = (y_1, y_2, ..., y_n)$ are two n-dimensional vectors, and $D(X,Y)$ indicate their distance. Canberra distance measure for X and Y is defined by (12):

$$D(X,Y) = \sum_{i=1}^{p} \frac{|x_i - y_i|}{1 + x_i + y_i} . \tag{12}$$

The reason of using this measure to evaluate the similarity of images is to weight the difference values in comparison with the feature vectors size.

5 Combine Color and Texture Using Proposed Fuzzy System

Color autocorrelogram intuitively includes local more than global information. In addition computing the autocorrelogram over partitioned image amplifies the locality of the feature. On the other hand, histogram is a global color feature and does not present any spatial correlation information of image's color. While each alone color autocorrelogram or histogram feature has some weaknesses in description of image content, combination of these two features will produce a more effective hybrid feature. However, the short come of all the color based methods is retrieving of images with similar content and dissimilar colors (e.g. white flower and red flower). In this case, we require different features like texture which in combination with color features improves the performance of image retrieval systems.

For combining these three features and estimating the distance of every two images, a fuzzy rule-based system is utilized. Fuzzy system enters human knowledge in the algorithm and consequently, the accuracy of final results is improved.

In order to create the proposed fuzzy system, at the first step, the amount of distances of three expressed features for every two images are computed and normalized. In other words, for every two images three distances corresponding to color autocorrelogram, color histogram, and texture features are computed and normalized from 0 to 1 as described in the previous sections. These distances as the inputs of the fuzzy system should be converted to fuzzy values. For this purpose, for each feature vectors distance of compared pair images, triangular membership functions are defined as Fig. 3, in which three members include very similar (VS), similar (S) and not similar (NS) are presented.

In the next step, for all combinations of these three vectors and according to the membership functions, the fuzzy rules base is experimentally defined as Table 1.

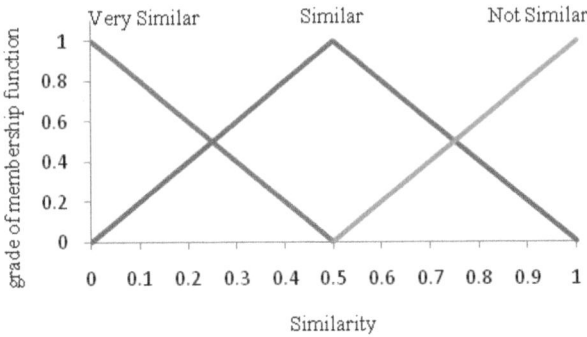

Fig. 3. Membership functions of system inputs

Table 1. IF–THEN rules for combining similarities measure

Rule	Fuzzy input variables of similarity (IF)			Fuzzy output (THEN)	Rule	Fuzzy input variables of similarity (IF)			Fuzzy output (THEN)
	Color Histogram	*Color Auto- Correlogram*	*Gabor wavelet*	*Similarity*		*Color Histogram*	*Color Auto- Correlogram*	*Gabor wavelet*	*Similarity*
1	VS	VS	VS	1	15	S	S	NS	8
2	VS	VS	S	2	16	S	NS	VS	7
3	VS	VS	NS	4	17	S	NS	S	8
4	VS	S	VS	2	18	S	NS	NS	10
5	VS	S	S	3	19	NS	VS	VS	6
6	VS	S	NS	5	20	NS	VS	S	8
7	VS	NS	VS	4	21	NS	VS	NS	10
8	VS	NS	S	5	22	NS	S	VS	8
9	VS	NS	NS	7	23	NS	S	S	9
10	S	VS	VS	3	24	NS	S	NS	11
11	S	VS	S	5	25	NS	NS	VS	10
12	S	VS	NS	7	26	NS	NS	S	11
13	S	S	VS	5	27	NS	NS	NS	12
14	S	S	S	6					

Output of this fuzzy system is a number which indicate final image similarity measure. For this reason, 12 membership functions have been introduced as shown in Fig. 4. The first member indicates a large amount of similarity, the second indicates less similarity, and so the rest of the membership functions follow this rule.

The proposed fuzzy system is based on the Mamdani fuzzy inference approach which is appropriate for decision making and control [21]. In the proposed fuzzy system, to compute *and* function, the average of operands is used and also to compute aggregation of outputs, the *probabilistic or* is applied. Finally, in defuzzification stage and to achieve a crisp number to compare images similarities, the *Centroid* method is applied. This method finds the point where a vertical line would slice the aggregate set into two equal masses [22]. Mathematically this center of gravity (COG) can be expressed as (13):

$$COG = \frac{\int_a^b \mu_A(x)x\,dx}{\int_a^b \mu_A(x)\,dx}.$$
(13)

Where $\mu_A(x)$ is the aggregated membership function, and x is the output variable.

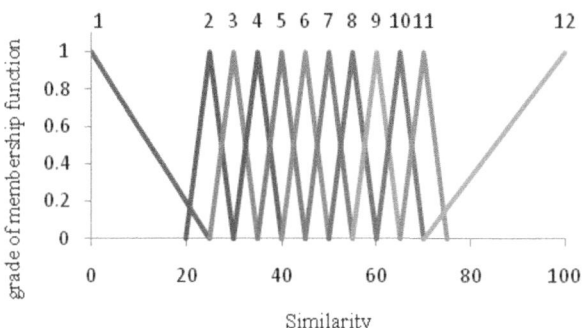

Fig. 4. Membership functions of system output

6   Experimental Results

In this section, the proposed method has been tested on a database which included 1000 images from the COREL image database [23]. This database consists of 10 semantic categories and each category contains 100 images. All images in each category have the same semantic features, although there might be difference in low-level features. Semantic groups are defined as follow: Africa, beach, building, bus, dinosaur, elephant, flower, horse, mountain and food.

In order to evaluate the system performance, different criteria have been proposed. Precision and recall are the most common criteria of efficiency evaluation for image retrieval systems. Precision can be seen as a measure of exactness or fidelity, whereas recall is a measure of completeness [24]. Precision *P* and recall *R* for the query image I_k (k=1,2,...,1000) are calculated with (14) and (15) respectively:

$$P = \frac{No.of\ relevant\ images\ retrieved}{Total\ no.of\ images\ retrieved(N)}.$$
(14)

$$R = \frac{No.of\ relevant\ images\ retrieved}{Total\ no.of\ relevant\ images\ in\ the\ collection}.$$
(15)

The average precision for images belonging to the qth semantic category (A_q) by (16) is defined as follows:

$$\bar{P}_q = \sum_{k \in A_q} P(I_k)/|A_q| , q=1,2,...,Q .$$
(16)

Where, Q is number of semantic groups in the database. Finally, the total average of precision by (17) is defined as follows:

$$\bar{P} = \sum_{q=1}^{Q} \bar{P}_q/Q .$$
(17)

The average recall is computed in the same manner.

In order to obtain reliable estimates, each image of the 10 categories served as the query subject in turns, making a total of 1000 queries. The average recall and precision of each query are computed.

For forming precision versus recall chart, for each distance, the following operations are performed: for each query, the average of precision $\bar{P}$ and recall $\bar{R}$ for all the retrieved images of the database are computed. The pair $(\bar{P}, \bar{R})$ makes a point of the chart. By changing the distance value, different points are obtained and the graph is drawn.

The precision versus recall chart of proposed method is shown in Fig. 5 and compared to the results of three expressed features. In Table 2 and Table 3, the average precision of the 10 and the 50 first retrieved images are shown, respectively. As can be observed, the proposed method in both of precision and recall performed better than color histogram, color autocorrelogram and Gabor transform methods.

Table 2. Results of $\bar{P}\%(N=10)$ for expressed methods

S. No:	Category	Color Histogram	Color Auto-Correlogram	Texture Gabor	Color Auto-Correlogram of partitioned images	Fuzzy Combination
1	Africa	76	77.70	43	78.30	79.70
2	Beach	50.70	46.70	37.90	48.10	52.50
3	Building	47.70	46.90	29.50	50.40	52.10
4	Bus	63.70	65.10	73	62.60	70
5	Dinosaur	99.80	99.70	99.40	100	100
6	Elephant	63.20	63.50	54.90	68.60	71.70
7	Flower	81	81.30	74.10	89.80	89.90
8	Horse	88.10	85.80	48.20	88.90	91.90
9	Mountain	39	41.60	31.10	44.50	48.70
10	Food	67.40	66.50	39.60	69.70	71.50
	Total	**67.66**	**67.48**	**53.07**	**70.09**	**72.80**

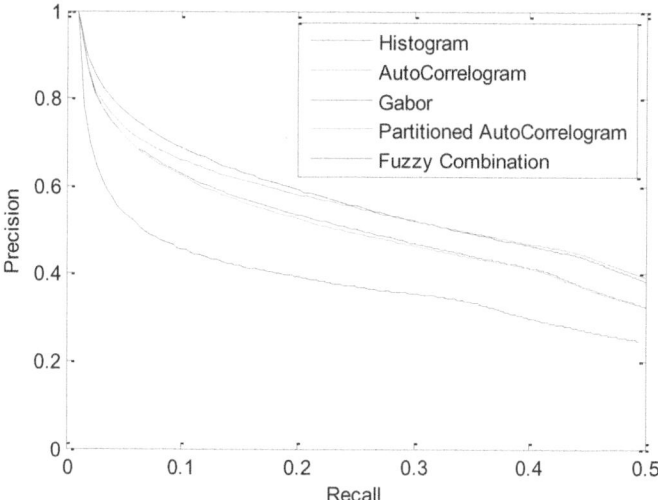

Fig. 5. Precision versus recall chart of the expressed methods

Table 3. Results of $\bar{P}\%(N=50)$ for expressed methods

S. No:	Category	Color Histogram	Color Auto-Correlogram	Texture Gabor	Color Auto-Correlogram of partitioned images	Fuzzy Combination
1	*Africa*	54.92	57.38	27.64	62.18	58.66
2	*Beach*	30.72	30.52	27.94	33.32	33.48
3	*Building*	29.32	27.10	19.42	30.68	30.64
4	*Bus*	51.64	52.28	50.96	46.16	54.86
5	*Dinosaur*	99.52	99.20	98.84	99.72	99.68
6	*Elephant*	43.58	43.66	39.7	44.86	49.76
7	*Flower*	64.78	63.62	55.44	76.48	74.44
8	*Horse*	58.86	52.60	30.72	67.74	65.22
9	*Mountain*	25.90	25.20	19.98	30.08	29.30
10	*Food*	41.14	41.78	23.92	47.20	44.38
	Total	**50.04**	**49.33**	**39.46**	**53.84**	**54.04**

7   Conclusions

A new method for content-based image retrieval using color and texture features was presented in this paper. Color histogram and color autocorrelogram of partitioned image were used as color features, whereas Gabor wavelet used as texture feature.

At first, each of three expressed feature was separately computed for all images of database and images similarities based on them were defined. Then, for combining these results and make final decision about images similarities, a fuzzy system were used which include human knowledge about similarities of images.

The results shown the combination of the three expressed features to evaluate the images similarities is better than results from individual of them. By using such as fuzzy systems, any kind of low-level image features can be combined very well, and consequently, the performance of image retrieval systems is improved.

References

1. Liu, Y., Zhang, D., Lu, G., Ma, W.: A survey of content-based image retrieval with high-level semantics. Elsevier Pattern Rec. 40, 262–282 (2007)
2. Oussalah, M.: Content-Based Image Retrieval: Review of State of Art and Future Directions. In: IEEE Image Processing Theory, Tools & Application, pp. 1–10. IEEE Press, Sousse (2008)
3. Chen, Z.: Semantic Research on Content-Based Image Retrieval. In: IEEE International Conference on Multimedia Technology, pp. 1–4. IEEE Press, Ningbo (2010)
4. Manjunath, B.S., Ohm, J.R., Vasudevan, V.V., Yamada, A.: Color and texture descriptors. IEEE Trans. Circuits Syst. Video Technol. 11(6), 703–715 (2001)
5. Sun, J., Zhang, X., Cui, J., Zhou, L.: Image retrieval based on colour distribution entropy. Elsevier Pattern Rec. Lett. 27(10), 1122–1126 (2006)
6. Plataniotis, K.N., Venetsanopoulos, A.N.: Color Image Processing and Applications. Springer, Berlin (2000)
7. Lu, T., Chang, C.: Color image retrieval technique based on color features and image bitmap. Info. Processing and Management 43, 461–472 (2007)
8. Swain, M.J., Ballard, D.H.: Color indexing. Computer Vision 7(1), 11–32 (1991)
9. Pass, G., Zabih, R., Miller, J.: Comparing images using color coherence vectors. In: Fourth ACM Multimedia Conference, New York, pp. 65–74 (1996)
10. Huang, J., Kumar, S., Mitra, M., Zhu, W., Zabih, R.: Image indexing using color correlograms. In: IEEE Computer Society Conference on Vision and Pattern Recognition, pp. 762–768. IEEE press, San Juan (1997)
11. Aptoula, E., Lefèvre, S.: Morphological Description of Color Images for Content-Based Image Retrieval. IEEE Trans. on Image Processing 18(11), 2505–2517 (2009)
12. Ogle, V., Stonebraker, M.: Chabot: Retrieval from a relational database of images. IEEE Computer 28(9), 40–48 (1995)
13. Huang, J., Kumar, S., Mitra, M., Zhu, W., Zabih, R.: Spatial Color Indexing and Applications. Computer Vision 35(3), 245–268 (1999)
14. Fathian, M., Akhlaghian Tab, F.: Content-Based Image Retrieval Using Color Features of Partitioned Images. In: IEEE International Conference on Graphic and Image Processing, pp. 235–239. IEEE Press, Manila (2010)
15. Tamura, H., Mori, S., Yamawaki, T.: Texture features corresponding to visual perception. IEEE Trans. on Systems, Man and Cybernetics. 6(4), 460–473 (1976)
16. Liu, F., Picard, R.W.: Periodicity, directionality and randomness: Wold features for image modeling and retrieval. IEEE Trans. on Pattern Analysis and Machine Intelligence 18(7), 722–733 (1996)
17. Manjunath, B.S., Ma, W.Y.: Texture features for browsing and retrieval of large image data. IEEE Trans. on Pattern Analysis and Machine Intelligence 18(8), 837–842 (1996)
18. Randen, T., Husøy, J.H.: Filtering for texture classification: A comparative study. IEEE Trans. on Pattern Analysis and Machine Intelligence 21(4), 291–310 (1999)

19. Murala, S., Gonde, A.B., Maheshwari, R.P.: Color and Texture Features for Image Indexing and Retrieval. In: IEEE International Advance Computing Conference, pp. 1411–1416. IEEE press, Patiala (2009)
20. Androutsos, D., Plataniotis, K.N., Venetsanopoulos, A.N.: A Novel Vector Based Approach to Color Image Retrieval Using a Vector Angular-Based Distance Measure. Computer Vision and Image Understanding 75, 46–58 (1999)
21. Kruse, R., Gebhardt, J., Klawon, F.: Foundations of Fuzzy Systems. Wiley, Chichester (1994)
22. Ross, T.J.: Fuzzy Logic with Engineering Applications. McGraw-Hill, Inc., New York (1995)
23. Corel Corporation, Corel Gallery Images, http://www.corel.com
24. Muller, H., Muller, W., Squire, D.M., Maillent, S.M., Pun, T.: Performance Evaluation in Content-Based Image Retrieval: Overview and Proposals. Elsevier Pattern Rec. Lett. 22, 593–601 (2001)

Control System of the Explosive Ordnance Disposal Robot Based on Active Eye-to-Hand Binocular Vision[*]

Lei Cai[1], Faliang Chang[1], Shaowen Li[3], and Xuexia Zhang[2]

[1] School of Control Science and Engineering, Shandong University, Jinan 250061, China
[2] College of Animal Science, Henan Institute of Science and Technology,
Xinxiang 453003, China
[3] Troops 94569, PLA of China, Jinan 250023, China
cailei1998@sohu.com

Abstract. Aiming at the disadvantages of manual operation and remote control of the EOD robot and to meet the demand of the technology and tactics, we propose a mobile robotic manipulation system equipped with an active eye-to-hand binocular vision sensor. The active vision system is able to observe arm gesture of a user by visually recognizing features on the arm and reconstructing the arm pose in Cartesian space. The target that is suspicious can thus be identified based on the arm pose. If confirmed, a vision based control law is able to drive the robot toward the target position and to fetch the target by the robotic arm. Experiments indicate that the proposed design of automatic control system is effective.

Keywords: explosive disposal robot, active eye-to-hand binocular vision, control system.

1 Introduction

The research of explosive ordnance disposal (EOD) robot is a hot spot in robot field currently, involving in knowledge in different fields, including mechanic design, the image processing, kinetic control, sensor technology, mechanics of communication etc. EOD robot is a robot that can replace man to reconnoiter, remove and deal with explosives or other dangerous articles in the dangerous environment directly; it can also attack terrorists effectively [1]. It is important to improve the power of antiterrorism and to safeguard the state development of politics and economy.

The EOD robots have been developed for many years in some countries, but for most of the current EOD robots, operator has to operate the buttons on the control panel in order to control and operate every freedom of motion of joints; it is very hard to operate [2]. A robot operating expert has to be familiar with the status of EOD and then judge which motions have to been taken in order to get the manipulator of the robot to a accurate position, a series of buttons have to be operated to realize the

* This work was supported by China Natural Science Foundation Committee (60775023, 60975025), Natural Science Foundation Committee of Shandong Province of China (Z2005G03), and SRF for ROCS, SEM.

H. Deng et al. (Eds.): AICI 2011, Part III, LNAI 7004, pp. 24–31, 2011.

motions of the arm of the robot, the speed and the continuity lies on familiarity of the operator, which reduces the efficiency greatly [3].

In this paper, we focus on designing and implementing a mobile robot which can help users to retrieve household items. Aiming at the disadvantages of manual operation and remote control of the EOD robot and to meet the demand of the technology and tactics, we propose a mobile robotic manipulation system equipped with an active eye-to-hand binocular vision sensor. Experiments indicate that the proposed design of automatic control system is effective.

2   The Feature and Design of Active Eye-to-Hand Binocular Vision System

2.1   The Feature of Active Eye-to-Hand Binocular Vision System

Visual system works as eyes in an EOD robot; it captures real-time images and passes them to the console. With the images processing, EOD robot computes the position of the suspicious objects accurately, controls itself to be close to the objects and grasp it automatically. At the same time, the visual system lays a solid foundation for the research such as visual navigation and obstacle avoidance; it can also record the process of explosive handling, provide evidence for the police to crack criminal cases. Some features are as follows.

1. *Complexity:* To a general images processing system, cameras are fixed usually, and the distance between the object and cameras is fixed also. But, in EOD robot, cameras are fixed on the paw, because of the unceasing movement of the robot, the paw moves unceasingly too, but the position of cameras and the angle of observation are changing all the time, which gives some difficulties to the processing of images, some ordinary means can not be used [4].

2. *Real-time performance:* The result of images processing is the control information of EOD robot, and visual navigation is based on it [5]. So, the images processing system must be real-time, its speed of processing must be as quick as possible to meet the demand of the system.

2.2   Design of the Control System of EOD

The EOD robot control system is composed of multilayer structures; it comprises main control computer as control system layer, embedded PC/104 computer as motion control layer and DC motor servo control as low layer. We adopt PC, embedded PC/104 computer, ADT650 data acquisition card and 4-route DC motor servo control system in hardware control structure, while adopt Matlab RTW (Real-time Workshop) rapid control prototyping (RCP) method and apply PC target application environment to develop control system model for the EOD robot.

The processing flow of control system is as follows: after obtains the 3D coordinates of the object with binocular vision system, sends the 3D coordinates to the control system in the console, and then sends them to the PC/104 motion control layer by data transmitter-receiver, computes the motion angle of every joint, corresponding pulse count, rotating angle of the motors and the object position, finally, the control system drives the paw to grasp the object.

3   Key Technologies of Active Eye-to-Hand Binocular Vision System

The active binocular vision system is capable of identifying the target by observing the gesture of a user. Specifically, image preprocessing, target and head tracking, and reconstruction of the arm direction are employed as follows.

3.1   Image Preprocessing

The image preprocessing of the proposed vision system consists of two parts, color filtering with connected component labeling and edge detection [6]. Combining with connected component labeling, color filtering can be used to detect the target in the image plane under different lighting conditions according to the color difference between the target and the background. In order to locate the precise target position, edge detection has been further used by

$$g(x, y) = \sum_{i=-a}^{a} \sum_{j=-b}^{b} w(i, j) f(x+i, y+j) \tag{1}$$

where $g(x, y)$ is the edge image, $w(i, j)$ is an $m \times n$ soble mask, $f(x, y)$ is the input image, $a = (m-1)/2$, and $b = (n-1)/2$.

3.2   Target and Head Tracking

Because the target is defined as a green mug, a rectangle template has been created for template matching. Therefore, the target can be detected by finding the smallest d in Eq. (2).

$$d = \sum_{i=-1}^{m} \sum_{j=-1}^{n} T_r(i, j) - f(x, y) \tag{2}$$

where $T_r(i, j)$ is the rectangle template. m and n are the template size.

During the target detection process, the size of the target may be changing due to the movement of the robot. Therefore, the template is also scaled into different sizes for effective matching result.

Similarly, the head detection also uses image preprocessing to filter out the skin color and the edge image. Then, the head can be detected in image space by using ellipse template to find the smallest differences between the template and the real image. The detection system flowchart is shown in Fig. 1.

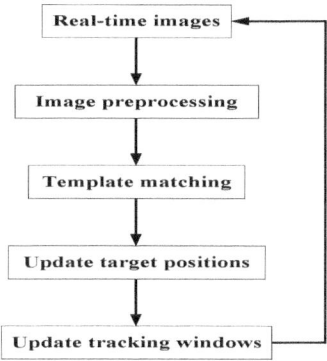

Fig. 1. Flowchart for target and head detection

3.3   Reconstruction of Arm Direction

In this paper, two feature centers of the blue and red segments on the arm of the user are used for identifying the arm pose. Since the position of these features in image space can be detected, the position of the features in Cartesian space, rR (red segment) and rB (blue segment), can thus be calculated by using Eqs. (3) and (4) based on calibrated camera model.

$$A(\theta)r = B(\theta) \tag{3}$$

$$r = \left[A^T(\theta)A(\theta) \right]^{-1} A^T B(\theta) \tag{4}$$

where

$$A(\theta) = \begin{bmatrix} u_1 k_1^T - f_1 i_1^T \\ v_1 k_1^T - f_1 i_1^T \\ u_2 k_2^T - f_2 i_2^T \\ v_2 k_2^T - f_2 i_2^T \end{bmatrix}, B(\theta) = \begin{bmatrix} \left(u_1 k_1^T - f_1 i_1^T \right) c_1 \\ \left(v_1 k_1^T - f_1 i_1^T \right) c_1 \\ \left(u_2 k_2^T - f_2 i_2^T \right) c_2 \\ \left(v_2 k_2^T - f_2 i_2^T \right) c_2 \end{bmatrix},$$

θ denote camera extrinsic parameter vector, c_i is the coordinate of the optical center with respect to the base frame, f_i denotes the focal length, $[u_i, v_i]^T$ denotes the feature's image coordinate, and i_i, j_i and k_i are the columns of the rotation matrix of camera i, $j = 1, 2$.

With the positions of the two features r_R and r_B in Cartesian space, the target searching region in image space can be determined based on the projection of the two features in binocular image space using Eq. (5).

$$G(r) = \begin{bmatrix} u_1 \\ v_1 \\ u_2 \\ v_2 \end{bmatrix} = \begin{bmatrix} f_1 \dfrac{i_1^T (r - c_1)}{k_1^T (r - c_1)} \\[2ex] f_1 \dfrac{j_1^T (r - c_1)}{k_1^T (r - c_1)} \\[2ex] f_2 \dfrac{i_2^T (r - c_2)}{k_2^T (r - c_2)} \\[2ex] f_2 \dfrac{j_2^T (r - c_2)}{k_2^T (r - c_2)} \end{bmatrix} \tag{5}$$

Since the arm and the target may not both appear in the binocular images, the target searching region determined based on the arm pose must be updated according to the initially detected arm pose and the motion of the active cameras and the mobile robot it self. The system can thus effectively locate the target within the searching region to reduce redundant computation. The procedure to determine target searching region is illustrated in Fig. 2.

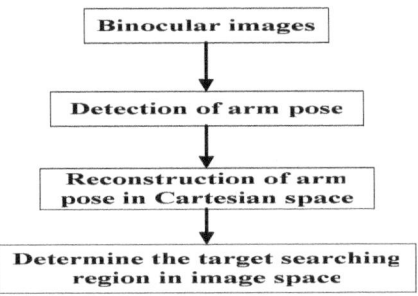

Fig. 2. Procedure to determine target searching region

4   Experiments and Results Analysis

We test the EOD robot with the mode of horizontal grasp which is run automatically, that is to say, the crossing angle between the small arm the robot and the horizontal is zero. When several test points on the X, Y and Z directions are chosen, we can get the trend of the error on the three directions. The best grasp space can be got in the meantime.

4.1   X-Axis Direction

On the X direction, we place some objects before the EOD robot from near to far every 10 cm. Table 1 and fig.3 show that the far the manipulator is on the X direction, the more the error is, therefore, we reach the conclusion that it is better to get near to the object in the course of grasping. On the other hand, because of the field of vision, the value of X can not be too small; otherwise, the robot may not grasp the object or beyond its vision.

Table 1. Experiment data of auto grasp in X-axis

Test No.	Actual coordinates of object(cm)		Final coordinates of paw(cm)		Error of location(cm)		
	X	Y	X	Y	DX	DY	DZ
1	58.2	23.1	55.3	24.6	-0.5	-3.1	1.5
2	65.3	24.1	68.7	23.8	-1.4	-3.4	1.2
3	74.5	19.8	76.8	21.8	-1.9	-2.1	2.1
4	87.3	19.7	86.4	20.6	-2.5	-1.2	1.4
5	92.2	21	97.8	22	-2.6	-1.9	0.9
6	105.3	18.9	112	20	-3.4	-0.3	0.9

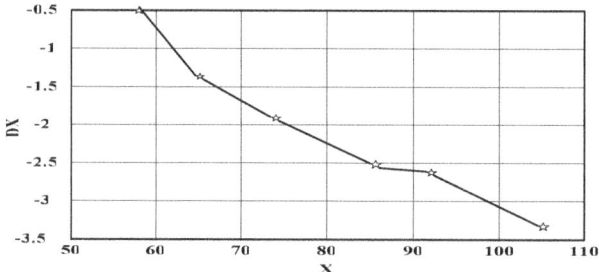

Fig. 3. Error analysis chart in X-axis

4.2 Y-Axis Direction

On the Y direction, we place some objects before the EOD robot from low to high and select 7 test points. Table 2 and fig.4 show that it has the least error when the value of Y is between -10cm and 30cm, the lower or the higher the test point is, the more the error is.

4.3 Z-Axis Direction

On the Z direction (Z direction means that the arm move from left to right or in reverse order), we place some objects right in front of the EOD robot on the line parallel with Z direction every 20 cm and select 7 test points. Table 3 and fig.5 show that the error changes from big to small when move the object from left to right or in reverse order, and after passing the middle position when it is right in front of the robot, the error changes from small to big. Therefore, we arrive at a conclusion that, in the course of grasping, there is the least error when the manipulator is just in front of the robot, otherwise, the error increases.

Table 2. Experiment data of auto grasp in X-axis

Test No.	Actual coordinates of object(cm)		Final coordinates of paw(cm)		Error of location(cm)		
	X	Y	X	Y	DX	DY	DZ
1	58.2	23.1	55.3	24.6	-0.5	-3.1	1.5
2	65.3	24.1	68.7	23.8	-1.4	-3.4	1.2
3	74.5	19.8	76.8	21.8	-1.9	-2.1	2.1
4	87.3	19.7	86.4	20.6	-2.5	-1.2	1.4
5	92.2	21	97.8	22	-2.6	-1.9	0.9
6	105.3	18.9	112	20	-3.4	-0.3	0.9

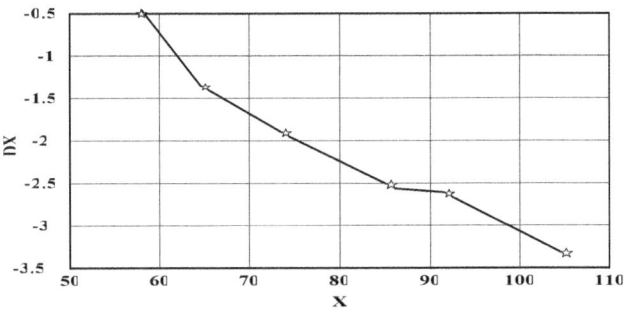

Fig. 4. Error analysis chart in X-axis

Table 3. Error analysis chart in Z-axis

Test No.	Actual coordinates of object(cm)		Final coordinates of paw(cm)		Error of location(cm)		
	X	Y	X	Y	DX	DY	DZ
1(-60)	102.6	20.9	106.4	21.2	-4	-1.6	2.4
2(-40)	92.8	20.8	94.6	23.5	-2	-2.4	2.1
3(-20)	86.7	21	88.2	25.7	-1.5	-4.7	1.7
4(0)	85.1	22.4	85.6	25.8	-0.5	-3.5	1
5(20)	86.5	21.3	87.5	24.1	-1.2	-3	0.5
6(40)	95.2	20.8	98.3	23.3	-3	-2.6	0.9
7(60)	106.3	21.2	110	23	-4	-1.7	1.6

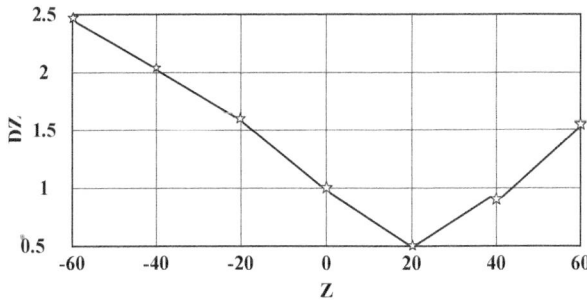

Fig. 5. Error analysis chart in Z-axis

5   Conclusion

Aimed at the disadvantages of manual operation and remote control of the EOD robot, a control system design of a EOD robot based on the binocular vision location is pretended. Apply binocular vision location to EOD robot, the location precision is high and the error is less the 5mm, there is nothing to intervene in the course of grasp. The control system adopts real-time system based on PC target; the method has the advantages such as it is rapid to develop and easy to debug, and it is a strong tool in the development and test of a control system. The successfully and automatically grasp experiments indicates the control system is valid.

In addition, the motion of the manipulator is a control of point to point; our next work is to research the problem such as the track planning of the manipulator and the path planning of robot, so as to solve the problem of speed plan control of the manipulator and obstacle avoiding.

References

1. Russell, T., Dan, S.: Medical robotics in computer integrated surgery. IEEE Tran. On Robotics and Automation 19(5), 765–781 (2003)
2. Shen, J., Dong, Z., Hao, Y., et al.: Research on a virtual training simulator for explosive-handling robot. Robot 27(5), 426–430 (2005)
3. Chen, X.: The feature analysis of robot using for antiterrorism. Robot technique and application 6, 15–18 (2005)
4. Ning, K., Yang, R., Weng, X.: Development on embed control firmware based TRX51 for explosive handling robot. Application of Electronic Technique 3, 17–20 (2005)
5. Fu, W., Zhou, C.: The Develop of the Bomb disposed Robot Control System Base on Image Identification. In: 3rd International Congress on Image and Signal Processing, pp. 2691–2695. IEEE Press, New York (2010)
6. Yang, G., Kong, L., Wang, J.: A new calibration approach to hand-eye relation of manipulator. Robot 28(4), 400–405 (2006)

Obstacles Detection in Dust Environment with a Single Image

Yuanyu Wang[1] and Yuanzong Li[2]

[1] Department of Computer Fundamental Education,
TaiYuan University of Technology, China
w_m7372@yahoo.com.cn
[2] College of Mechanical Engineering, TaiYuan University of Technology, China
liyuanzong@tyut.edu.cn

Abstract. Because of light scattering and absorbing in dust environment, it is difficult to detect obstacles with camera. In order to solve this problem, a method of obstacles detection in dust environment from a single image was presented. The method realized distance detection and contour detection for obstacle in dust environment. First, depth map of dust image and geometric reasoning approach based on imaging model of a camera were combined to detect the distance between camera and obstacle of any shape. Then, depth map was applied to detect the contour of the obstacle in dust environment. Namely, edges belonging to contours were selected by using depth map. The validity and feasibility of the method was fully demonstrated by the experiments. The method provides a simple and economical way to detect obstacles in dust environment.

Keywords: dust, obstacle detection, image restoration, depth map, geometric reasoning.

1 Introduction

Because visual sensors are inactive, they are less dependent on the environment, and vision sensors often provide better resolution data, longer ranges at faster rates than other range sensors, recently, vision-based obstacle detection is becoming popular. Stereo vision and optical flow are vision-based techniques for obstacle detection [1],[2]. However, if the working environment is the dust environment, these approaches are not hard to implement.

Due to light scattering and absorption, dust results image degradation, features of the image in dust are hard to detect. It seems dust environment is an obstacle to vision based obstacle detection. So far, the studies on this problem are very limited.

As we known, the extent of image degradation in dust environment is related with distance [3],[4]. So we can use the method of image restoration in the environment of dust [5] to obtain depth map from a single image in dust. Depth map reveals the distance ratio of two different pixels. In order to get the real distance value we need a reference distance with exact value.

H. Deng et al. (Eds.): AICI 2011, Part III, LNAI 7004, pp. 32–38, 2011.
© Springer-Verlag Berlin Heidelberg 2011

Geometric reasoning method has been used to measure distance between obstacles and a robot with a single camera [6]. But the method is invalid for detecting hanging obstacles.

Taking the advantage of depth map of dust image and geometric reasoning method, a new obstacle detection method was proposed. It is monocular vision based obstacle detection method. It could not only detect the distance between obstacles of various shapes at any time with a single image, but also the outline of the obstacles. According to the experimental results, the method works well in dust environment.

2   The Depth Map of Image in Dust Environment

According to the image degradation model in dust environment [4], the intensity reaches camera can be expressed as the following:

$$I = I_0 t[1 - \frac{p(0,0)}{4\pi} \ln t] + A[1-t]$$
(1)

Where, I_0 is the incident intensity, A is the global atmosphere light, t is transmission, $p(0,0)$ is phase function, it indicates the ratio of the energy entering the camera and the energy lost. Since $t = exp(-\beta d)$, where β is scattering coefficient. d is the depth of view. so (1) shows that the light intensity attenuates exponentially as the depth of field increases. So, the degradation of the image is spatially various.

Based on the image model in dust environment, the transmission t can be got by dark channel prior algorithm [4] as (2) shown:

$$t = 1 - \min_{c}(\min_{y \in \Omega(x)} (\frac{I^c(y)}{A^c}))$$
(2)

Where, I^c refers to a color channel of I, $\Omega(x)$ is a local patch centered at x.

Although we have obtained t, there are block effects since the transmission is not always constant in a patch. The transmission process needs to be refined further. so we made use of the image matting algorithm proposed by Levin [7]. Then, the refined transmission t was obtained [5].

For $t = exp(-\beta d)$, so the distance d of pixel i can be expressed as (3).

$$d_i = -\frac{\ln t_i}{\beta}$$
(3)

Thus we got depth map of the image in dust environment. Where, β is an unknown constant.

If an exact distance d_r is given, then the distance of any pixel of the image can be obtained as (4) shown:

$$d_i = d_r \frac{\ln t_i}{\ln t_r}$$
(4)

3   Distance Detection for Obstacles

3.1 Geometric Reasoning Method

Based on the small hole imaging model, a monocular vision system can be simplified to a projection model of the camera as Fig.1 shown. Where, m and n represent the width and height of the image respectively, v and u represent image coordinates component.

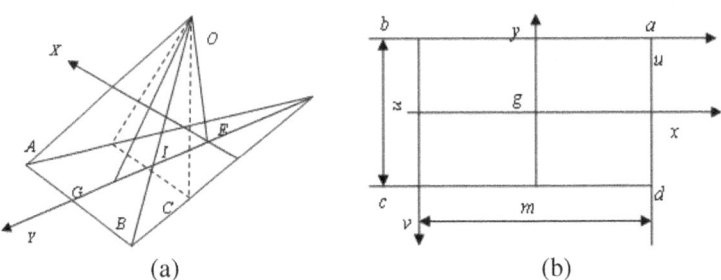

Fig. 1. Geometic model of camera. (a) projection relation of camera; (b) coordinates in image plane.

Then, a coordinate system was established as Fig.2 shown. The relationship between image coordinate and ground coordinate is:

$$\begin{cases} \alpha'+\beta'+\delta'= 90^\circ \\ \tan\beta'= b/h \\ \tan(\alpha'+\beta') = (b+d')/h \\ \tan\gamma'= w/(b+d') \end{cases} \tag{5}$$

Where, h is the height of camera, b is distance of blind area, d' is the distance between the optical center and the intersection of the optical axis and the ground plane, w is half width of horizontal view field, which can be measured directly, α' is half angle of vertical view field, γ' is half angle of horizontal view field, δ' is the pitch angle of the camera.

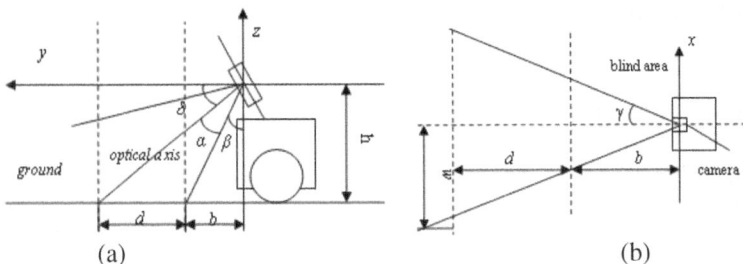

Fig. 2. Coordinate system of geometric reasoning. (a) Coordinate on vertical plan; (b) Coordinate on horizontal plane.

Let dr be the distance between optical center and center point of the blind area as Fig.3 shown, then dr can be expressed as the following:

$$d_r = \sqrt{b^2 + h^2} \qquad (6)$$

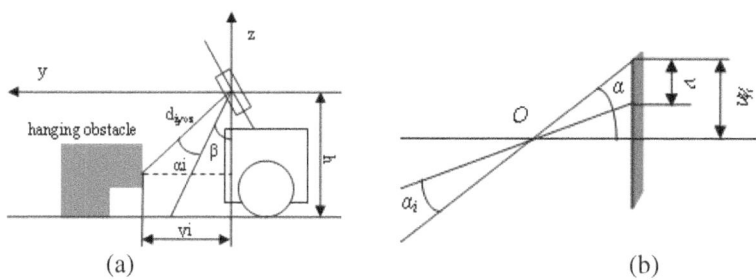

(a)   (b)

Fig. 3. Distance detection for obstacle by our method. (a) Geometric reasoning on YOZ plane; (b) Geometric reasoning on XOY plane.

Substitute (13) into (11), di is obtained:

$$d_i = \sqrt{b^2 + h^2}\, \frac{\ln t_i}{\ln t_r} \qquad (7)$$

Thus, the projection of di on YOZ plan is:

$$d_{iyoz} = d_i \cdot \sqrt{\frac{n^2 + ((\frac{n}{2} - v)\tan\alpha')^2}{n^2 + ((\frac{n}{2} - v)^2 + (\frac{m}{2} - u)^2)\tan^2\alpha'}} \qquad (8)$$

3.2 Coordinates of the Obstacle

According to (5), (7), and (8), the y-axis component of obstacle can be deduced as Fig. 3 shown.

$$y_i = d_{iyoz} \cdot \sin(\alpha_i' + \beta') \qquad (9)$$

Where, $\alpha_i' = \alpha' - \arctan((1 - \frac{2v}{n})\tan(\alpha'))$. Similarly, the z-axis component of obstacle is.

$$z_i = d_{iyoz} \cos(\alpha_i' + \beta') \qquad (10)$$

Finally, the x-axis component of obstacle is.

$$x_i = d_{ixoy} \cdot \sin \gamma_i' \tag{11}$$

Where,

$$d_{ixoy} = d_i \cdot \sqrt{\frac{n^2 + ((\frac{m}{2} - u)\tan \alpha')^2}{n^2 + ((\frac{n}{2} - v)^2 + (\frac{m}{2} - u)^2)\tan^2 \alpha'}} \quad ,$$

$$\gamma_i' = \arctan(\frac{m - 2u}{m}\tan \gamma') .$$

4 Contour Detection for Obstacles

Contours detection is important features for obstacles detection. Here we proposed a contour detection method based on depth edge recognition. There are many kinds of edges, for example reflectance edges, illumination edges, and depth edges. A reflectance edge is an edge where the reflectance of two surfaces changes. The border between different materials is a reflectance edge because they reflect different amounts of light. An illumination edge is an edge where the lighting changes. The border of shadow is an illumination edge [8]. Depth edge is an edge where two parts with different image depth. Closed depth edge can be treated as contour of obstacle. So it is important for obstacle detection to recognize depth edges from reflectance edges and illumination edges. The depth edges can be recognized with three steps. Step 1: using canny algorithm to detect edges of the restored image. Step 2: getting depth map of original image in dust. Step 3: comparing the depth value of both sides according to depth map, if the difference is greater than a threshold, then the edge is a depth edge; else the edge is of other edges. Thus the contour of the obstacles can be extracted from canny edge detected result.

5 Experiments

A hanging obstacle in the experiment was built as Fig. 4(a) shown. The upper red-box protruded 0.1m than lower yellow-box. Then, a camera was mounted as Fig.2 shown. The height of the camera h=0.6m, the half angle of vertical field of the camera α' =18°, the half angle of horizontal field of the camera γ' =21°, the blind zone b=0.7m, the angle of blind zone β'=50°, the horizontal distance between upper part of the obstacle and the camera yh=1m, while the distance between lower part of the obstacle yu=1.1m,

Thereafter a dust environment was produced. The size of the dust particles were approximate 20μm. An image of the obstacle in the dust environment was taken. We selected three points on the image as Fig. 4(b) shown. Those points are on horizontal

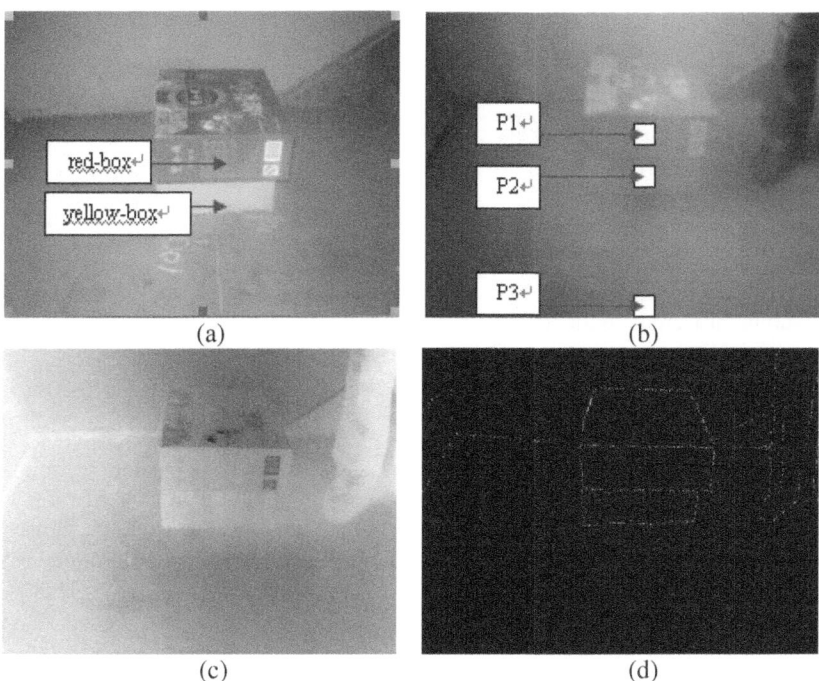

Fig. 4. Experimental results.(a)Hanging obstacle,(b) Obstacle in dust, (c) Depth map, (d) Contour of obstacle.

axis of symmetry. P1 and P2 are the points to be measured, while P3 is a reference point whose horizontal distance was b. Fig. 4(c) is the depth map.

Because the distance between image plane of camera and obstacle is not very easy to measure, so we have to prove the method indirectly by measuring the coordinates of P1 and P2. According to (9), (10), and (11), we were able to get the three coordinates of P1 and P2. The results of calculation and results of actual measurement were listed in Table 1.

The contour of the obstacle was extracted according to depth edge information, for the same reason, we measure the size of obstacle to prove contour detection method

Table 1. Points of three dimension coordinates on obstacle

The test point	Calculated x-coordinate of point	Calculated y-coordinate of point	Calculated z-coordinate of point	Actual x-coordinate of point	Actual y-coordinate of point	Actual z-coordinate of point
P1	2.2	101.1	-38.3	2	100	-40
P2	2.6	111.8	-58.9	2	110	-60

Table 2. Size of obstacle

Test object	Actual height (cm)	Calculated height (cm)	Actual width (cm)	Calculated width (cm)
Red-box	11.3	10.2	28.2	27.3
Yellow-box	15.2	14.2	29.2	28.1

indirectly, as Fig. 4(d) shown. The results of calculation and results of actual measurement were listed in Table 2.

6 Conclusion

Dust degrades the quality of image, and causes troubles for obstacle detection with vision. But the image taken in dust environment implies depth information with a single image. The paper takes advantage of this attribute and combined with geometric reasoning method to realize obstacle detection in dust environment with a single image. Experiments have proven the validity of our method.

References

1. Qiang, Z., Jia, W.: Monocular vision based navigation algorithm for mobile robots in unknown environments. Journal of Beijing University of Aeronautics and Astronautics 34, 614–617 (2008)
2. Ulrich, I., Nourbakhsh, I.: Appearance-Based Obstacle Detection with Monocular Color Vision. In: Proceedings of the AAA I National Conference on Artificial Intelligence, pp. 866–871. AAAI Press, Menlo Park (2000)
3. Narasimhan, S.G., Nayar, S.K.: Vision and the atmosphere. International Journal on Computer Vision 48, 233–254 (2002)
4. He, K., Sun, J., Tang, X.: Single Image Haze Removal Using Dark Channel Prior, Computer Vision and Pattern Recognition, pp. 1956–1963. IEEE press, Los Alamitos (2009)
5. Wang, Y., Li, Y., Zhang, T.: Method to restore dust degraded images. Huazhong Univ. of Sci. & Tech (Natural Science Edition) 38, 42–44 (2010)
6. Guo, L., Xu, Y.-C., Li, K.-Q., Lian, X.-M.: Study on Real-time Distance Detection Based on Monocular Vision Technique. Journal of Image and Graphics 11, 74–81 (2006)
7. Levin, A., Lischinski, D., Weiss, Y.: A closed form solution to natural image matting. Computer Vision and Pattern Recognition 1, 61–68 (2006)
8. Bruce Goldstein, E.: Sensation and Perception, 8th edn. Wadsworth Publishing Co. Inc., Belmont (2009)

An Object Recognition Strategy Base upon Foreground Detection

Jifei Chen, Yafei Zhang, Yulong Tian, and Jianjiang Lu

Institute of Command Automation,
PLA University of Science and Technology
miipl606@163.com

Abstract. Unmanned aerial vehicles equipped with surveillance system have begun to play an increasingly important role in recent years, which has provided valuable information for us. Object recognition is necessary in processing video information. However, traditional recognition methods based on object segmentation can hardly meet the system demands for running online. In this paper, we have made use of SVM based upon HOG feature descriptors to achieve online recognizing passersby in an UAV platform, and designed an object recognition framework based on foreground detection. In order to accelerate the processing speed of the system, our scheme adopts recognizing objects only in the foreground areas which largely reduces searching scope. In conclusion, our methods can recognize specified objects and have a strong anti-jamming capability to the background noise.

Keywords: Object Recognition, UAV, HOG, Foreground Detection.

1 Introduction

Nowadays, many countries in the world are actively developing target recognition technology which has been widely applied everywhere including fingerprint recognition, iris recognition, and motor vehicles detection and so on. However, there are plenty of objects belonging to various categories. What's more, objects themselves may be sheltered, of different posture, defect and blurred. So the problem of object recognition is very complex. Even in one category, the distinction existing among species and population, and among their shape and appearance, leads to the difficulty of recognition.

The problem of object recognition can be divided into instance recognition and category recognition [1]. The method of instance recognition recognizes objects according to the difference between target images and sample images while the method of category recognition needs recognize a special classification, taking pedestrians and vehicles for example. In the process of object recognition, the description of image feature is necessary. Images can be represented by feature sets including color, brightness, and noises and so on. In order to get the optimal detection effect, we need utilize the most related feature to detect objects, and make sure the feature is stable when visual angle or objects' shape changes.

H. Deng et al. (Eds.): AICI 2011, Part III, LNAI 7004, pp. 39–46, 2011.
© Springer-Verlag Berlin Heidelberg 2011

The feature description methods can be divided into scattering description method and density description method. Scattering description method needs extract interesting feature points from an image and extract local feature from it, and finally build object detection classifier based on such features. The most general scattering descriptors contain Laplace detector, Harris detector and SIFT point detector and so on. Scattering description method can detect some special objects and they are often used in instance recognition. In recent years, density description method is increasingly becoming popular, which extracts image features densely from detection window and combines these features into a high dimensional description vector, so as to make sure that whether a special object is contained in the window. These features often include brightness, gradient and high order partial differential operator and so on. Familiar image gradient description methods mainly contain HOG description method, shape context and so on.

HOG feature belongs to gradient description methods, which was firstly proposed by Dalal in 2005 [2], and continuously improved by researchers. Pedro improved original HOG algorithm at SVM's solution step and built a multi-scale deformable objects mixture model [3]. Their system got a 20% higher precision than the average precision in VOC2006 test set and outperformed the best result in VOC2007.

On the whole, good object recognition technology in UAV videos should have the capability to detect and recognize objects in complex background and various weather conditions. In UAV videos, pedestrians and vehicles are main moving objects, so it is important to recognize the two categories. Dalal got a high recognition precision to recognition pedestrian in MIT dataset [4] and INTRIA dataset [5] using HOG. At the same time, HOG feature is competitive in PASCAL VOC competion in recent years. In addition, Dalal and other researchers found the feature descriptors were still well used in recognizing other categories. We mainly utilize HOG-based SVM to recognize moving pedestrian and have designed a foreground detection based object recognition framework. Although HOG feature descriptor can adapt to video monitoring in aerial scenario [6],it seems inefficient in a real-time system. In order to improve system's efficiency, our paper only recognizes objects in the foreground detection regions, so the searching regions are much reduced. In the rest part of this paper, we will firstly introduce some knowledge about how to build a training set in a recognition system, and then talk about how the HOG is used in our recognition framework in UAV videos, and finally exhibit our experiment results, from which we can see that our method can recognize objects in UAV videos online and is robust to background noises.

2   Our Object Recognition Strategy

2.1   The Problem of Building Training Sets

A good nature dataset is very important in each phase of object recognition including learning objects' visual template, the category of scenarios, the detection and location of instances in images and testing the efficiency of recognition algorithms. Therefore, it is much concerned about how to build a good nature dataset in recent years.

However, any dataset cannot cover all the instances even in one category, so the test images should be sampled equably as far as possible to catch the essence of categories. At the same time, the work of building datasets is a huge project which is labor cost, so people have proposed many automatically label tools, taking [7] as an example.

In addition to this kind of open label approach, many organizers have developed universal test datasets including UIUC [8], Caltech [9, 10] and Pascal VOC [11]. These datasets are generally built according to such rules: firstly, make sure there are plenty of category numbers to exclude the randomicity; secondly, make sure that there are plenty of instances in one category to enlarge the covering region of instances and increase the difficulty of recognition. These datasets have provided a public reference to evaluate various algorithms.

2.2   The Introduction of HOG

The recognition strategy that we designed is based on the moving region marked by foreground detection as Fig. 1 illustrated. At the same time, HOG feature based method has excluded the effect of background when the module is training. So our strategy has certain ability to counteract interference of background.

Fig. 1. Illustration of objects recognition based on foreground detection

The method of density grid based image local gradient histogram was constantly used in the last ten years [12-14] for the reason that objects' local appearance and shape could often be described well through pixels' local density distribution or edge orientation. The idea of HOG feature comes from SIFT feature description method and improves on it. It outperforms existing feature sets for human detection and many other shape-based categories [2]. The method is based on evaluating well-normalized local histograms of image gradient orientations in a dense grid.

The details of HOG implementations can be found in paper [2] and [15], which have expatiated how to use fine scale derivatives, how to select the number of orientation bins and how to normalize overlapping descriptor blocks and so on.

2.3   Our Work

We proposed an object recognition framework based upon the result of foreground detection as illustrated by Fig. 2. For each current frame, we use a motion compensation technology [16] to calculate an affine transformation matrix from last frame to current frame, and align the successive frames to extract moving blobs using the method of frame-differencing. The recognition work is based on such blobs. Each of the recognition region is much reduced, so the time efficiency is improved.

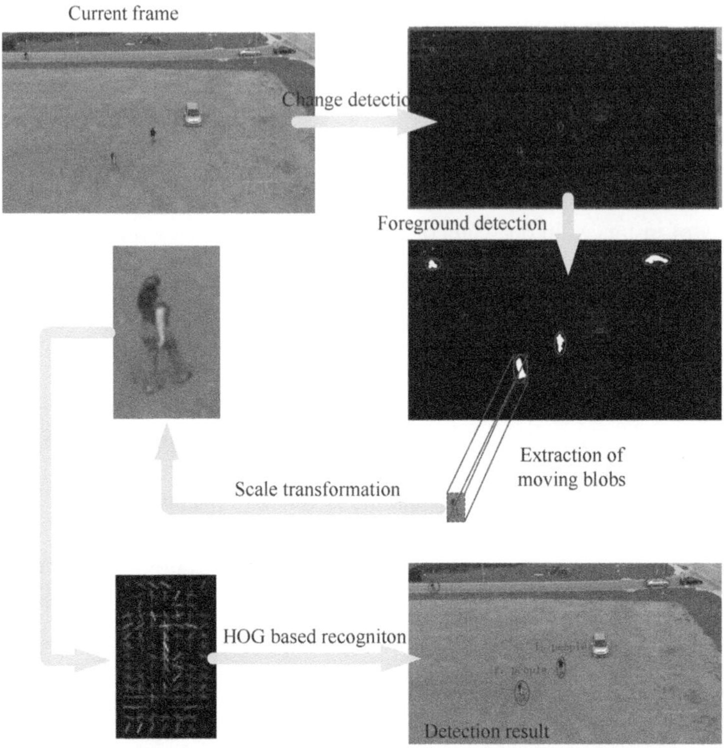

Current frame

Change detection

Foreground detection

Extraction of moving blobs

Scale transformation

HOG based recogniton

Detection result

Fig. 2. The logical graph of objects recognition based on blob detection

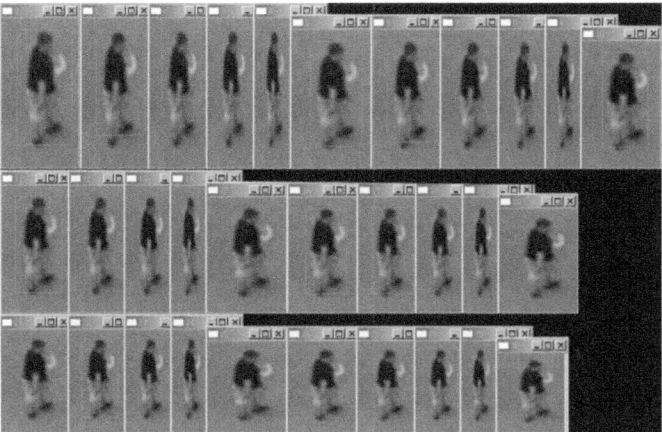

Fig. 3. Hit distribution based on various scale transformation

The size of pedestrian HOG template designed by Dalal is 64×128. However, most moving objects in high aerial UAV videos are less than 64×128 in the imaging plane. In order to balance the hit rate and detection efficient, we should properly scale the blobs before they were recognized. Fig. 3 exhibits the hit distribution using different height-width rate to scale a moving blob. Because HOG feature uses the objects' gradient information, a linear interpolation to scale an image will not destroy their gradient information severely.

Not only should the detection size of moving blobs be considered, but also the position of objects in a detection window deserves special attention. Dalal had pointed out in paper [2] that their 64×128 detection window included about 16 pixels of margin around the person on all four sides. Decreasing it from 16 to 8 pixels decreases performance by 6% at 10-4 FPPW. Keeping a 64×128 window but increasing the person size within it causes a similar loss of performance, even though the resolution of the person is actually increased. So in an ideal situation, we should try to adjust the objects to the center of a detection window and satisfy that there are more than 16 pixels around the interesting objects. Of course, the more pixels around the interesting objects, the lower efficiency will the detection system make.

3   Experiment and Conclusion

In order to improve the recognition speed and keep the recognition precision, we have made some trials. Firstly, we randomly selected an image with a standing people in the center of it, and kept some margins around the people. Secondly, we took the step length 16 to traversal size 48×80 to 112×208, which contained 31 situations. Finally, we used a linear SVM to classify these images and observed the results' distribution as table 1 illustrated in which the measure time was by millisecond. From experiment result we find out that if the width of an image is less than 64 or the height of an image is less than 128, the objects will not be checked out. As Fig. 4 illustrated, if the height to width ratio is between 1.57 and 2.17, most of the result is correct, and the average of recognition time is 60.0ms, the fastest time is 19.74 of the size 80×144 and the slowest time is 99.37ms of the size 112×208.

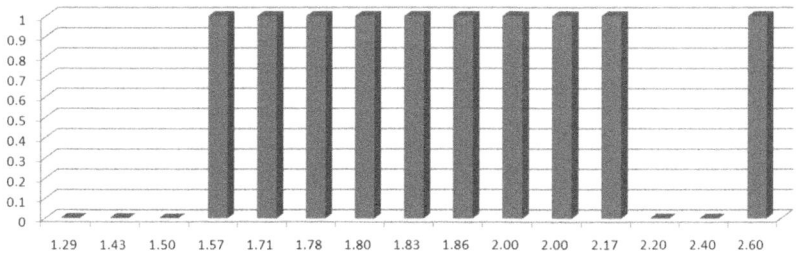

Fig. 4. The relationship between height-width ratio and hit ratio

Although the recognition time in each frame is very short, there may be many moving foreground objects in one frame. Assuming there are 10 moving objects in one frame, and the average time cost in each frame is 600ms, which can hardly meet the demand of an online system. Many researchers had proposed improved strategy of HOG. They used cascade method to optimize the search path of detection window so as to improve recognition efficiency [17]. Another way to enhance the recognition efficiency is to take the strategy of jumping recognition. The recognition module we designed is illustrated by Fig. 5 which can be plugged into the UAV video analysis system in the end.

Table 1. The Resulst Using Different Width-Height Ratio

ID	Width (Pixel)	Height (Pixel)	Recognition Time	Is it hit?	ID	Width (Pixel)	Height (Pixel)	Recognition Time	Is it hit?
1	112	208	99.370	Yes	11	112	176	60.260	Yes
2	96	208	78.690	Yes	12	96	176	56.410	Yes
3	80	208	44.320	Yes	13	80	176	38.170	No
4	64	208	9.022	No	14	64	176	7.640	No
5	48	208	7.472	No	15	48	176	7.077	No
6	112	192	79.880	Yes	16	112	160	42.850	No
7	96	192	72.600	Yes	17	96	160	38.280	Yes
8	80	192	40.600	No	18	80	160	35.020	Yes
9	64	192	8.045	No	19	64	160	6.716	No
10	48	192	6.865	No	20	48	160	6.196	No

ID	Width (Pixel)	Height (Pixel)	Recognition Time	Is it hit?	ID	Width (Pixel)	Height (Pixel)	Recognition Time	Is it hit?
21	112	144	24.480	No	31	96	112	6.465	No
22	96	144	22.180	No	32	80	112	6.593	No
23	80	144	19.740	Yes	33	64	112	5.084	No
24	64	144	6.057	No	34	48	112	4.313	No
25	48	144	5.401	No	35	80	96	4.807	No
26	112	128	7.915	No	36	64	96	4.287	No
27	96	128	7.257	No	37	48	96	3.880	No
28	80	128	6.294	No	38	64	80	3.742	No
29	64	128	5.780	Yes	39	48	80	3.520	No
30	48	128	4.974	No					

Fig. 5. Illustration of automatically recognition of moving objects

4 Future Work

Although our foreground based object recognition strategy has accelerated our system to some extent, there is still room for optimizing the position and the size of detection window. On the other hand, our module can only recognize a minority of categories which can hardly meet practical demand, so we need to train more templates to achieve this goal. What's more, we propose to find a more proper SVM other than a linear one to expect a better recognition precision in the future.

References

1. Szeliski, R.: Computer Vision: Algorithms and Applications. Electronic Draft, Unpublished (2010)
2. Dalal, N., Triggs, B.: Histograms of Oriented Gradients for Human Detection. In: Proceeding of the IEEE Conference on CVPR, pp. 886–893. IEEE Computer Society, Washington (2005)
3. Felzenszwalb, P., McAllester, D., Ramanan, D.: A Discriminatively Trained, Multiscale, Deformable Part Model. In: IEEE Conference on Computer Vision and Pattern Recognition (2008)
4. Papageorgiou, C., Poggio, T.: A trainable System for Object Detection. International Journal of Computer Vision 38 (2000)
5. LEAR – Data Sets and Images, http://lear.in-rialpes.fr/data
6. Oreifej, O., Mehran, R., Shah, M.: Human Identity Recognition in Aerial Images. In: IEEE Conference on Computer Vision and Pattern Recognition (2010)
7. Von, A.L., Liu, R., Blum, M.: Peekaboom: a Game for Locating Objects in Images. In: ACM SIGCHI, pp. 55–64 (2006)
8. DiCarlo, J.J., Cox, D.D.: Untangling Invariant Object Recognition. Trends in Cognitive Sciences 11, 333–341 (2007)

9. Gallant, J.L., Connor, C.E., Van, E.D.C.: Neural Activity in Areas V1, V2, and V4 during Free Viewing of Natural Scenes Compared to Control Images. Neuroreport. 9, 85–89 (1998)
10. Griffin, G., Holub, A., Perona, P.: Caltech-256 Object Category Dataset. In: Caltech Technical Report. Pasadena, California (2007)
11. PASCAL Object Recognition Database Collection, Visual Object Classes Challenge, http://www.pascal-network.org/challenges/VOC
12. Lowe, D.: Distinctive Image Features from Scale-invariant Key Points. International Journal of Computer Vision 60, 91–110 (2004)
13. Freeman, W.T., Roth, M.: Orientation Histograms for Hand Gesture Recognition. In: International Workshop on Automatic Face and Gesture Recognition, IEEE Computer Society, Zurich (1995)
14. Mikolajczyk, K., Schmid, C.: Scale and Afine Invariant Interest Point Detectors. International Journal of Computer Vision 60 (2004)
15. Dalal, N.: Finding People in Images and Videos. PhD thesis, Institut National Polytechnique de Grenoble (2006)
16. Keller, Y., Averbuch, Y.: A.: Fast Gradient Methods Based on Global Motion Estimation for Video Compression. IEEE Transactions on Circuits and Systems for Video Technology 13, 300–309 (2003)
17. Felzenszwalb, P., Girshick, R.B., McAllester, D.: Cascade Object Detection with Deformable Part Models. In: Proceedings of IEEE Conference on Computer Vision and Pattern Recognition (2010)

Camera Self-calibration Based on the Vanishing Points*

Dongsheng Chang[1], Kuanquan Wang[2], and Lianqing Wang[1,2]

[1] School of Computer Science and Technology, Harbin Institute of Technology,
Harbin 150001, China
dongshengchang@gmail.com, wangkq@hit.edu.cn, lianqingw@gmail.com
[2] Xi'an Communication Institute Xi'an 710106, China

Abstract. In this article, a new method for camera self-calibration is presented. A correspondent matrix can be built by matching the corresponding vanishing points between two images and the proposed method must use at least two of these matrices for calibration. The images are all taken from different orientations in any locations for the same object in space. The vanishing points in the image are the projective points of the infinity points in space. So in the calibration, it has no constraints about the location and the orientation of the camera and the calibration procedure is easy. Since when the internal parameters of camera are changed during the task, the camera can be easily and effectively calibrated if the vanishing points can be conveniently gotten from the task images or the camera can insert three or more images about the same object during the ongoing task. Compared with the traditional methods of camera self-calibration, this method is an easier and more effective calibration method and also it is an online calibration with accurate results.

Keywords: vanishing points, online self-calibration, projection matrix.

1 Introduction

The camera self-calibration is a method that only uses self-constraints of cameras to estimate their internal parameters. It has been widely applied in the mobile robot navigation, machine vision, biomedical and visual surveillance.

The camera calibration techniques can be divided into two categories: online calibration and offline calibration. The online camera calibration means that the camera can be re-calibrated without stopping the ongoing task when its parameters change when being used. In other words, online camera self-calibration is a method which doesn't limit locations and orientations of the camera and doesn't need to know any projective geometry or epipolar structure. However, the offline calibration is on a contrary that it must interrupt the ongoing task for re-calibration.

There are many self-calibration methods. And the common method of camera self-calibration is based on the projective geometry theory and epipolar structure [1, 2].

* Supported by NSFC project (grant no 60872099).

H. Deng et al. (Eds.): AICI 2011, Part III, LNAI 7004, pp. 47–53, 2011.

And Zhengyou Zhang proposed a method which was based on plane precise template [3]. However, these kinds of methods need a complex process of calibration.

Some other methods of camera self-calibration on active vision are based on knowing the moving or rotation of the cameras [4, 5, 6]. And another method had been proposed by Richard that requires the camera at the same location take the images of the same object in different orientations [7, 8]. For these methods have constraints to the camera, they are not suitable for online re-calibration.

In this article, the proposed calibration method is not essential to interrupt the task for re-calibration. And it does not need to know the camera's location or to track the motion of the camera. This method uses at least three views for calibration with three steps. Firstly, it extracts the corner points, and then the vanishing points of the specific direction are computed in every image. Secondly it uses the vanishing points to compute the correspondent matrix between any two images. Finally, it can use at least two of these correspondent matrixes to compute the calibration matrix.

In specific application areas, as long as there is a method for conveniently computing the vanishing points or the camera can insert at least three images for the same object in the ongoing task, the proposed method can be calibrated online.

This paper is organized as follows: the section 2 simply introduces the camera model. The section 3 shows the proposed algorithm of self-calibration. And the experiment results are given in section 4. Section 5 gives the conclusion.

2   The Camera Model

The camera model is pinhole, as indicated in Figure 1. It is a linear mapping from 3D projective space points to 2D projective space points. The points are parameterized by homogeneous coordinate, and the projection transformation can be represented by a matrix $M = 3\times4$, the rank of which is 3. The matrix M may be decomposed as $M = K(R\ t)$, wherein t is a 3×1 vector, representing the location of the camera, R is a 3×3 rotation matrix, representing the orientation of the camera with respect to an absolute coordinate frame, and K is the internal parameter of the camera, which is the purpose of camera self-calibration.

The real camera has uncertain principal point. And in the manufacturing process of the CCD camera, the pixel of the camera is not exactly square. So the coordinate of the image is has a skew and the magnifications of the horizontal and the vertical directions are not exactly equal. The matrix K can be written as

$$K = \begin{pmatrix} k_u & s & u_0 \\ 0 & k_v & v_0 \\ 0 & 0 & 1 \end{pmatrix} \tag{1}$$

wherein k_u and k_v the indicate the magnification in the u and v coordinate directions, u_0 and v_0 are the coordinates of the principal point, and s is the skew of the image coordinate axes.

3 Algorithm of Camera Self-calibration

3.1 The Projection Matrix

The vanishing point is an important feature in the projective geometric. B. Caprile and V. Torre firstly provided the calibration method based on vanishing points [9]. They proved three properties of vanishing points about camera calibration. The first two properties are useful for the determination of the extrinsic parameters, and the third property is useful for estimating the internal parameters.

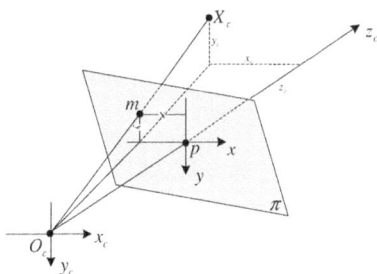

Fig. 1. Pinhole camera model

In the proposed method, the first property will be used. It says the parallel planes are correspondent to the same infinity line in space and the parallel lines are correspondent to the same infinity point in space. So either the infinity line or the infinity point has no relation with the location of the camera in space.

Let $m = (u, v, 1)$ be the point of image coordinate and $X = (x, y, z, 0)$ be the infinity point of space coordinates. The projective transformation can be written as

$$w \begin{bmatrix} u \\ v \\ 1 \end{bmatrix} = \begin{bmatrix} p_{11} & p_{12} & p_{13} & p_{14} \\ p_{21} & p_{22} & p_{23} & p_{24} \\ p_{31} & p_{32} & p_{33} & p_{34} \end{bmatrix} \begin{bmatrix} x \\ y \\ z \\ 0 \end{bmatrix} = KR \begin{bmatrix} x \\ y \\ z \end{bmatrix} \tag{2}$$

wherein w is a non-zero factor and m is a vanishing point. The displacement vector is eliminated and the calibration matrix is only related to the rotation matrix and the internal parameters. The rank of the matrix KR is 3, so it is invertible.

3.2 Calculation of Vanishing Points

In space, the infinity point represents the direction of the line. For the linear camera model, the vanishing point correspondent to the infinity point in space is the intersection of a set of lines in image which is in correspondence with the parallel lines. In this paper, the corner points should be extracted firstly. And then it uses the corner points to fit the straight lines in different directions.

Let $\varepsilon = [\varepsilon_1, \varepsilon_2, \varepsilon_3]$ and $\mu = [\mu_1, \mu_2, \mu_3]$ be two lines in image, then the intersection of the two lines can be calculated by

$$\varepsilon \times \mu = \begin{bmatrix} \dfrac{\varepsilon_2}{\mu_2} & \dfrac{\varepsilon_3}{\mu_3} & , & \dfrac{\varepsilon_3}{\mu_3} & \dfrac{\varepsilon_1}{\mu_1} & , & \dfrac{\varepsilon_1}{\mu_1} & \dfrac{\varepsilon_2}{\mu_2} \end{bmatrix} \tag{3}$$

In order to obtain and maintain higher accuracy of vanishing points, a set of lines which are correspondence to a set of parallel lines in space are used to compute the intersection of them which is the vanishing point.

3.3 Determining the Calibration Matrix

Two images are taken from different orientation for the same target. Let $M_1 = KR_1$ and $M_2 = KR_2$ be the projection matrix of the two images, taking any point x in the world coordinate, its corresponding points in two images are $m_1 = KR_1 x$ and $m_2 = KR_2 x$. The relationship between m_1 and m_2 is

$$m_2 = KR_2 (KR_1)^{-1} m_1 = KR_2 R_1^{-1} K^{-1} m_1 = KRK^{-1} m_1 \tag{4}$$

By the equation above, it can skillfully and reasonably eliminate the displacement of the camera between two images. Let $P = KRK^{-1}$, which is a conjugate rotation matrix, wherein K is the conjugating element[7, 8], and P is normalized, so its determinant is 1.

A pair of points can provide two equations for the camera calibration, since it must use four pairs of points at least to compute the projective transformation P, and any three of them can't be at a line. The experiment uses the same camera with the same internal parameters to take two views. Since there is only the rotation matrix is the variable in the projection transformation.

For $P_j = KR_j K^{-1}$ and K is the calibration matrix, so $K^{-1} P_j K = R_j$. For a rotation matrix R, it meets the relation that $R = R^{-T}$, wherein R^{-T} is the inverse transpose of R. From the relation $R_j = K^{-1} P_j K$, it can be attained that $R_j = K^T P_j K^{-T}$. So an equation about R can be expressed that

$$(KK^T) P_j^{-T} = P_j (KK^T) \tag{5}$$

Let $C = KK^T$, then C can be written that

$$C = KK^T = \begin{pmatrix} a & b & c \\ b & d & e \\ c & e & f \end{pmatrix} \tag{6}$$

The equation (5) gives nine linear equations in six independent entries of C. However, the nine linear equations are redundant, which are not sufficient to solve C. If two or more of such P_j are known, then the C can be found by using least-squares to compute an over-determined set of equations. When C has been got, the calibration matrix K can be unique computed by the Cholesky factorization.

Attention, the Cholesky factorization must require C to be positive-definite. However, for the noisy input data, the C is not positive-definite when the points matching have gross errors. So as long as the vanishing points are computed accurately, the matrix C almost is positive-definite and an accurate calibration result can be obtained.

3.4 Algorithm Idea

1. Extract points of the images and compute the vanishing points with 4 directions
2. Compute the correspondent matrix P between two images with vanishing points.
3. Use at least two different matrices P to solve the equation (5).
4. Find the calibration matrix K by using Cholesky factorization to decompose C.

4 Experiment Result

In the experiment, Canon EOS 500D camera is used to take a set of images. The size of all images is 2352×1568 pixels. The checkerboard grid map was employed as the calibration object, just because it was easy to find the vanishing points in different directions. The images were all taken by the camera with different locations and orientations, as shown in Figure 2. The calibration object should contain at least two checkerboard grid maps (neither two of these maps is parallel).

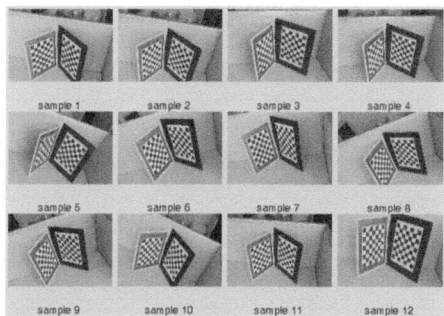

Fig. 2. Calibration images of proposed method

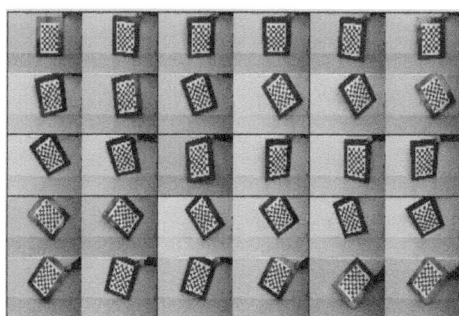

Fig. 3. Calibration images of zhang's method

In order to compare the performances of the proposed method, the same camera with the same internal parameters was calibrated by Zhengyou Zhang's method [10], because this method has been proved an effective method with acceptable errors in practice. The calibration results of these two methods are summarized in table 1.

30 images were used for calibration in Zhang's method, and just 4 images were used in the proposed method every time. By comparing the calibration results of these two methods from table 1, it can be seen that the proposed method has achieved a very good accuracy. If the result data of Zhang's method were marked the ideal data, the relative error of the proposed method can be computed, as shown in table 2.

As illustrated in table 2, the data are the relative errors of every element of calibration matrix in each experiment. It also proves that the proposed method has achieved a good accuracy.

Table 1. The results of the calibration

Method	Sample	k_u	k_v	p_u	p_v	s
Zhang	Figure 3	3068.902	3070.454	1155.647	703.864	0.000
This paper	1 7;2 10	3054.143	3164.292	1129.025	698.296	4.861
	1 9;6 10	3076.504	3148.625	1154.059	667.750	3.482
	2 6;3 12	3060.566	3068.440	1073.419	674.346	2.204
	3 12;4 9	3041.077	3008.468	1142.384	736.239	9.117
	5 8;6 11	3029.147	2985.174	1137.528	737.249	2.985

Table 2. The errors of the proposed method

Experiment Samples	k_u	k_v	p_u	p_v
1 7; 2 10	0.00481	-0.03056	0.02303	0.00791
1 9; 6 10	-0.00248	-0.02545	0.00137	0.05131
2 6; 3 12	0.00271	0.00065	0.07115	0.04194
3 12; 4 9	0.00907	0.02187	0.01147	-0.04607
5 8; 6 11	0.01295	0.02777	0.01568	-0.04743

5 Conclusions

In this article, the proposed method uses the vanishing points for camera calibration which can make the camera freely move and rotate in space. It is also independent on the projective geometry and epipolar structure. The calibration result accuracy is depended on the corner extraction accuracy. With the increase of experimental images, the experimental results are more stable and accurate. Besides, if there is a method for conveniently computing the vanishing points or inserting three or more images about the same object during the ongoing task, the proposed method will be an online camera self-calibration approach.

References

1. Maybank, S.J., Faugeras, O.D.: A theory of self-calibration of a moving camera. International Journal of Computer Vision 8(2), 123–151 (1992)
2. Faugeras, O.D., Luong, Q.-T., Maybank, S.J.: Camera Self-calibration: Theory and experiments. In: Sandini, G. (ed.) ECCV 1992. LNCS, vol. 588, pp. 321–334. Springer, Heidelberg (1992)
3. Zhang, Z.: A flexible new technique for camera calibration. IEEE Transactions on Pattern Analysis and Machine Intelligence 22, 1330–1334 (2002)
4. Dron, L.: Dynamic camera self-calibration from controlled motion sequences. In: Proc. IEEE Conf. on Computer Vision and Pattern Recognition, pp. 501–506 (1993)
5. Basu, A.: Active calibration: Alternative strategy and analysis. In: Proc. IEEE Conf. on Computer Vision and Pattern Recognition, pp. 495–500 (1993)
6. Du, F., Brady, M.: Self-calibration of the intrinsic parameters of cameras for active vision systems. In: Proc. IEEE Conf. on Computer Vision and Pattern Recognition, pp. 477–482 (1992)
7. Hartley, R.I.: Self-calibration of stationary cameras. International Journal of Computer Vision 22, 5–23 (1997)
8. Hartley, R.I.: Self-calibration from multiple views with a rotation camera. In: Proc. of the 3rd, European Conference on Computer Vision, vol. I, pp. 471–478 (1994)
9. Caprile, B., Torre, V.: Using Vanishing Points for Camera Calibration. International Journal of Computer Vision 4(2), V127–V140 (1990)
10. Bouguet, J.Y.: Complete camera calibration toolbox for matlab [EB/OL], (2002), Retrieved from the World Wide Web
    http://www.vision.caltech.edu/bouguetj/calibdoc/index.html

Lane Detection in Critical Shadow Conditions Based on Double A/D Convertors Camera

Bin Yang, Yangchang Wang, and Jilin Liu

Zhejiang University, Institute of Information and Communication Engineering,
Xindian Building. 317,
310027 Hangzhou, China
ryanyoung.soloy@gmail.com

Abstract. Lane detection in unstructured environments is the basis for navigation of mobile robots. A method for detecting lane in critical shadow conditions is proposed. Based on the color information of the unstructured lane, an improved region-growing algorithm is employed to segment the image. To enhance the image quality and the accuracy of the algorithm, a double A/D convertors camera is used to recover the color space information of the environments in critical shadow conditions. The results demonstrate that proposed method segments the lane effectively, and is robust against shadows, noises and varied illuminations.

Keywords: Lane detection, shadow, double A/D convertors camera.

1 Introduction

For automatic guided mobile robot lane detection in unstructured environments is considered as an important basic module. Many approaches have been applied to lane detection in the literature, which can be generally classified into two main categories, i.e. feature-based methods and model-based methods. Feature-based methods always rely on low-level features as painted lines [1]-[3], edges [4] or combined image features [5], these methods depend heavily on the lane marks and lane edges, and the features are always not visible or being confused with shadows in complex environments. Some model-based methods are developed on prior knowledge of the road shape [6]-[7], they are more robust to noise, but they still tend to detect error candidates of the road edges when shadow condition is critical.

Kuo-Yu Chiu presented a lane detection method using color-based segmentation algorithm [8]. The algorithm chooses a region of interest to find out a threshold using statistical method, the threshold then will be used to distinguish possible lane boundary. This method is more robust against noise, shadows comparing to the previous algorithms, but the light intensity in the scene is varying, single threshold will cause misjudgment of the boundary especially when the shadow condition is critical, and this method also suffers from limit dynamic range of the camera.

Fig. 1 shows images under strong sunlight, both the shadows on the road and the wayside are confused and cannot be recognized clearly.

H. Deng et al. (Eds.): AICI 2011, Part III, LNAI 7004, pp. 54–62, 2011.

Fig. 1. Images under strong sunlight

To recover the details of the color information of the image, we use double A/D convertors camera to capture the scene [9], and an improved region-growing algorithm is employed to detect the lane with critical shadows.

2 Double A/D Convertors Camera

The dynamic range of traditional imaging device is about 60dB-70dB while the nature of scene covers about 100dB. Double A/D convertors camera was developed to extend the dynamic range of the imaging device, the architecture can be seen in Fig. 2.

Fig. 2. CCD sensor system with double A/D convertors

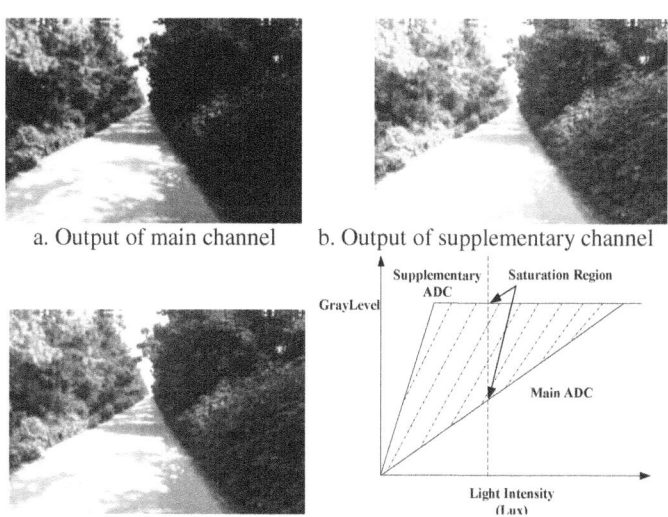

a. Output of main channel   b. Output of supplementary channel

c. Output of the camera   d. Response curve of the two channels

Fig. 3. Outputs of CCD sensor system with double A/D convertors

A supplementary A/D channel is added which is dedicated for the low intensity part of the scene to recover the details of the distortion region. And the image can be composed by an on-chip interpolation module for real time application.

Fig. 3 shows the example image. Fig.3.a represents the original image with critical shadow captured by the main channel. Fig.3.b shows the image captured by the supplementary channel which recovers the region with low intensity. Fig.3.c is the final output of the camera system. We plot the response curve of the system in Fig.3.d, both of the two channels with different slopes enclose a shadow region which is accessible by on-chip interpolation algorithm, thus the dynamic range of the system is extended.

3   Preliminaries of Lane Detection

We use HSV color model for the processing because the gray image is sensitive to noise, lighting changes, occlusions and so on. Fig. 4 is the HSV color space model: we use a column to depict the color space of a pixel. Hue is the attribute of a visual sensation according to which an area appears to be similar to one of the perceived color. Saturation is the colorfulness of a stimulus relative to its own brightness. Value equals to the brightness of a similarly illuminated white.

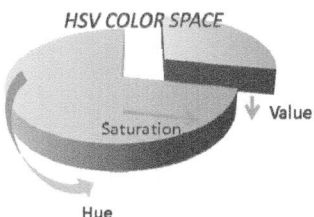

Fig. 4. HSV color space model

The converting formula from RGB to HSV model can be expressed as below.

$$H = \begin{cases} \dfrac{G-B}{\max-\min} & if \quad \max = R \\ 2 + \dfrac{B-R}{\max-\min} & if \quad \max = G \\ 4 + \dfrac{R-G}{\max-\min} & if \quad \max = B \end{cases}$$

$$S = \frac{\max-\min}{\max} \tag{1}$$

$$V = \frac{\max}{256}$$

We use gridding matrix for the segmentation algorithm because there are lots of correlationships between adjacent regions and pixels. Single pixel is unreasonable as it is much sensitive to noise, halation and so on. The gridding matrix is shown in Fig. 5.

Minimum Unit

Fig. 5. Gridding matrix for lane segmentation

The gridding block is selected as the minimum unit which means that every calculation, estimation and judgment would be operated basically on the single block.

4   Region Growing Algorithm

We use improved region-growing algorithm to segment the lane. Each single block can be classified into three clusters: Lane, Shadow and Wayside. The features of HSV color space of each cluster are concluded in Table 1.

Table 1. HSV color space features of clusters

	Hue	Saturation	Brightness
Lane	Converging	Converging	High
Shadow	Converging	Low	Relative low
Wayside	Converging	High	Low in general

These basic features of the clusters in HSV color space provide us a thread to set the blocks apart with K-Mean Clustering method.

Each block may contain multi-elements of different clusters, as seen in Fig. 6.

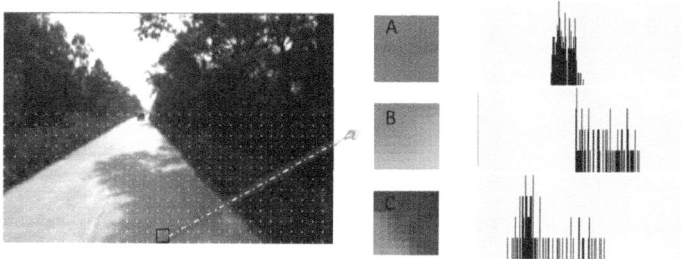

Fig. 6. Composition of gridding blocks

Block A has simplex elements which all belong to one cluster while block B and block C have multi-clusters elements. In order to simplify the processing we use standard deviation for the estimation of the blocks in brightness space, and an OTSU algorithm is employed to filter the minor cluster elements of the blocks. The standard deviation is expressed below:

$$\sigma(B) = \sqrt{\frac{1}{N}\sum_{i=1}^{N}(B_i - B)^2} \qquad (2)$$

Where B is the mean of the brightness of the block and B_i is the brightness of each pixel. We set a threshold window for $\sigma(B)$ to apply OTSU method to those blocks with high standard deviation in brightness space.

OTSU is a method automatically performing a histogram shape-based image thresholding. It assumes that there are two classes of pixels contained in the image and then it calculates the optimum threshold separating those two classes. So in our processing the goal is to maximize the inter-class variance, which can be expressed as:

$$\sigma_b^2(t) = \sigma^2 - \sigma_w^2(t) = \omega_1(t)\omega_2(t)[\mu_1(t) + \mu_2(t)]^2 \qquad (3)$$

$\omega_i(t)$ is the probability of class i with threshold t and $\sigma_i^2(t)$ is the variance of class i. $\mu_i(t)$ is the mean of brightness of class i. So the algorithm can be depicted as:

(1)   Compute histogram and probabilities of each brightness level.
(2)   Set up initial variables for $\omega_i(t)$ and $\mu_i(t)$.
(3)   Step through all thresholds t, update $\omega_i(t)$, $\mu_i(t)$ and $\sigma_b^2(t)$.
(4)   Desired threshold corresponds to the maximum $\sigma_b^2(t)$.

After OTSU algorithm the block is simplified to be a simplex block with minor class elements filtered. Then we try to classify the blocks into certain cluster.

Since the scene of the lane is non-homogeneous structure with the light intensity varying along the image. We divide the whole image into two processing parts: left side and right side. The sunlight situation is quite different at these two sides as the sun moves its position relative to the ground all the time. We assume that there is a seed area inside which blocks belong to cluster Lane. Then the searching sequence would be from middle to left for the blocks at the left side and from middle to right for the ones at the right side. After the marginal block, the processing steps into the line above, as seen in Fig. 7.

Left side   Right side

Fig. 7. Searching sequence of region-growing

For each cluster, we use a global First-In First-Out (FIFO) structure to reserve the last fifteen recognized blocks to calculate the global color space value. Fig. 8 is the example of the FIFO structure for the saturation of cluster Lane.

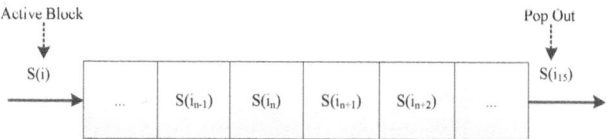

Fig. 8. FIFO structure for the saturation

S(i) is the saturation of the active block which is recognized as cluster Lane, pushed into the FIFO, with $S(i_{15})$ popping out of the structure. Then the system would update the value of the saturation for cluster Lane by averaging the last 15 Lane blocks' saturation. This mechanism makes a more accurate and dynamic estimation on the scene's color space.

For a single block, a Three Level Estimation Process would be applied to decide which cluster the block belongs to. A clustering energy function is presented for the judgment of the blocks:

$$E_j(i) = \alpha * (B(i) - B_j(i))^2 + \beta * (S(i) - S_j(i))^2 + \sigma * (H(i) - H_j(i))^2 \qquad (4)$$

α, β and σ is the weighting factor for the components of the HSV color space while $B(i)$, $S(i)$ and $H(i)$ correspond to brightness, saturation and hue of the active block respectively. $B_j(i)$, $S_j(i)$ and $H_j(i)$ correspond to the HSV color space value of the reference cluster. This energy function demonstrates how close that the active block is from the reference cluster, and the active block would be recognized as the cluster with a minimum energy function result.

1) Slipping window:
We apply a slipping window to the active block in the first level estimation as seen in Fig. 9. The white frame is the slipping window for the active block (black frame). The blocks inside the slipping window all have been recognized except the active one. We choose the recognized blocks to be the reference, substituting their color space value into the energy function and the active block belongs to the cluster with the minimum energy function result.

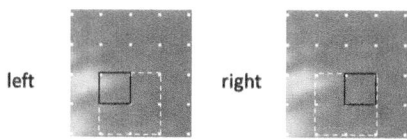

Fig. 9. Slipping window for the active block

2)   Global cluster color space:

We have mentioned in Fig. 8 that for each cluster, there will be three global FIFOs to reserve the value of their color space. The global FIFOs update all the time since the light intensity varies at different region. When some cluster does not exist in the slipping window for the active block, we choose the corresponding global value from the FIFO to substitute in the energy function.

3)   Feature based estimation:

We would apply a third level estimation based on the HSV color space features to the active block when the former estimations are invalid. If the energy function's result is quite high with cluster Lane as the reference cluster, we use the features in Table.1 to make estimation for the active block.

Fig. 10 is the experiment result of the Three Level Estimation on some region of the scene. Yellow blocks correspond to the cluster Lane while gray blocks correspond to Shadow and black blocks correspond to Wayside.

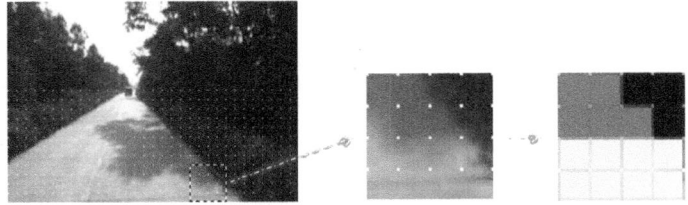

Fig. 10. Experiment result for Three Level Estimation

5   Experiment Results

Table 2 is the experimental platform and system parameters of our program. We take images from unstructured lane under critical shadow conditions, as seen in Fig.11.

Table 2. Experimental platform and system parameters

Automobile	Sport Utility Vehicle
Height of Camera	2.2m
Angle of Inclination	30°
CCD Sensor	ICX205AK
Chip Size	7.6mm*6.2mm
ADC Resolution	10-bit
Image Resolution	320×240

The images in the first column are captured from the main channel of the camera. The high dynamic range of the scene results in a high contrast of the image. The images in the second column are the outputs of the double A/D convertors camera.

Outputs from two channels are composed through on-chip interpolation module. The dynamic range of the image is enhanced with more legible wayside. Images from third column are the lane detection results. Red points correspond to blocks belong to lane or shadow while black points correspond to wayside. We use least squares algorithm to find the best fitting of the marginal red points to plot the lane edge.

Fig. 11. Experiment results under critical shadow conditions

6   Conclusion

We have presented a lane detection algorithm based on double A/D convertors camera to solve critical shadow conditions in unstructured environments. The camera with on-chip pixel-level interpolation module output images with high dynamic range, which helps to retain the details of the color space of high contrast scene. An improved region-growing method is presented to classify the images into three clusters for further processing, and a three level estimation process is employed for the segmentation. The experimental results justify that the method is much effective and robust against shadows and varied light conditions.

References

1. Kim, Z.: Robust Lane Detection and Tracking in Challenging Scenarios. IEEE Transactions on Intelligent Transportation Systems 9, 16–26 (2008)
2. Mastorakis, G., Davies, E.R.: Improved Line Detection Algorithm for Locating Road Lane Markings. Electronics Letters 47, 183–184 (2011)
3. Nuthong, C., Charoenpong, T.: Lane Detection using Smoothing Spline. In: 2010 3rd International Congress on Image and Signal Processing (CISP), vol. 2, pp. 989–993 (2010)
4. Gong, J., Wang, A., Zhai, Y., Xiong, G., Zhou, P., Chen, H.: High Speed Lane Recognition under Complex Road Conditions. In: Intelligent Vehicles Symposium, pp. 566–570. IEEE Press, Los Alamitos (2008)

5. Jeong, P., Nedevschi, S.: Efficient and Robust Classification Method using Combined Feature Vector for Lane Detection. IEEE Transactions on Circuits and Systems for Video Technology 15, 528–537 (2005)
6. Asif, M., Arshad, M.R., Irfan Zia, M.Y., Yahya, A.: An Implementation of Active Contour and Kalman Filter for Road Tracking. Laeng International Journal of Applied Mathematics 37 (2007)
7. Cheng, H.Y., Yu, C.C., Tseng, C.C., Fan, J.C., Hwang, J.N., Jeng, B.S.: Environment Classification and Hierarchical Lane Detection for Structured and Unstructured Roads. Computer Visions 4, 37–49 (2010)
8. Chiu, K.-Y., Lin, S.-F.: Lane Detection using Color-based Segmentation. In: IEEE Symposium on Intelligient Vehicles, pp. 706–711. IEEE Press, Los Alamitos (2005)
9. Yang, B., Wang, Y., Liu, J.: HDR CCD Image Sensor System through Double-A/D Convertors. In: 2011 International Conference on Machine Learning and Artificial Intelligence (2011)

Image Selection Based on Grayscale Features in Robotic Welding

Zhen Ye[1,2], Gu Fang[1], Shanben Chen[2], and Ju Jia Zou[1]

[1] School of engineering, University of Western Sydney, Australia, 2751
17191207@student.uws.edu.au, {G.Fang,J.Zou}@uws.edu.au
[2] Institute of Welding Engineering, Shanghai Jiao Tong University, China, 200240
{ruan,sbchen}@sjtu.edu.cn

Abstract. In robotic welding seam tracking based on visual information has been studied in the recent years. However, it is difficult to ensure the quality of images obtained in the welding process because it is easily affected by spattering, fuming and electromagnetic noise. The paper introduces a method to select useful images before further processing. Experimental tests are conducted to verify its accuracy.

Keywords: Pulsed MIG, Vision Sensor, Image selection, Grayscale.

1 Introduction

Currently, most of the robots used in arc welding applications are of the "teach and playback" type. However, such robotic welding systems are rigid and cannot adjust to errors in the weld seam coordinates caused by natural welding environmental factors. Therefore sometimes these robotic welders cannot meet the high quality requirement of the welding process. To address this issue, some seam tracking systems are developed to solve the problem [1-6]. In these systems, visual sensors have been adopted because of their non-contact to the weld pool and rich information of the welding process. In some studies [7-9], camera was designed with filters to view the welding process directly. This direct observation of the welding process helped to realize the seam tracking based on the size and the position of the seam and the welding pool. However, it is difficult to ensure that welding images obtained during the welding process are clear and contain useful information. Furthermore, welding images are more easily spoiled in MIG welding due to its less stable process than the TIG welding.

In this paper, a method is developed to select images based on image's grayscale and histogram features. This selection process will allow only those images deemed 'useful' to be further processed. This selection process not only avoids the unnecessary image processing, but also provides reference for future adaptive edge detection.

The rest of this paper is organized as follows: the robotic welding system used in image acquisition is described in Section 2. In section 3, a method to select images is developed and in Section 4 a series of tests are conducted to confirm the effectiveness and accuracy of the method. Finally, Section 5 summarizes the finding of the paper.

H. Deng et al. (Eds.): AICI 2011, Part III, LNAI 7004, pp. 63–70, 2011.

2 The Experiment System

The welding robot system in our research includes a "teach and playback" robot, a visual sensor composed of a CCD camera and the optical filters, a current sensor, welding source and a computer. The schematic diagram of the system is shown in Fig.1.

Q235 steel sheet is welded by pulsed MIG welding. And shielding gas is 92% Ar +8% CO_2. Some other welding conditions are listed in Table 1.

Table 1. Welding parameters

Groove type	Wall thickness	Diameter of welding wire	Root gap	Root face	Welding current	welding voltage	Flow rate	Wire feed rate	Welding speed
V	4.5mm	1.2mm	0	1mm	146A	25V	15L/min	4m/min	5mm/s

By performing the spectrum analysis of the welding scenes under the above welding conditions, it is found that the light spectrum from 620nm to 680nm is composed of continuous line, and the intensity of this light spectrum is lower than others. Consequently an optical filter is chosen with the central wavelength of 660nm. Furthermore, a dimmer glass is also selected for the visual sensor to reduce the exposure light going into the camera. Another factor that affects the quality of the image is the welding current [10]. Therefore the image capturing is controlled to take place when the welding current is at its minimum.

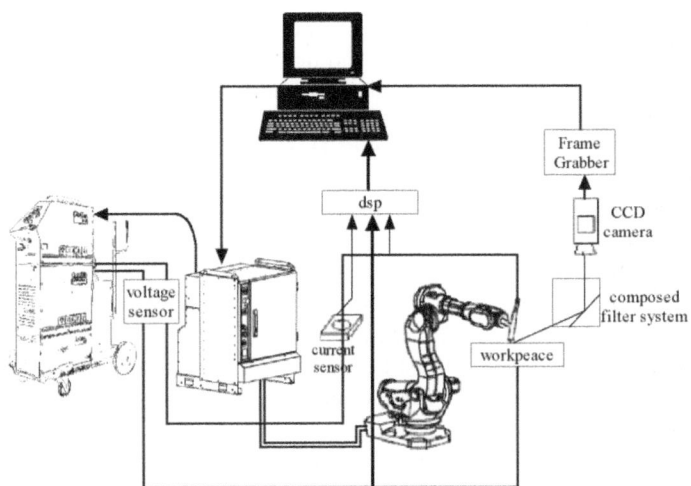

Fig. 1. The schematic diagram of the welding robot system

3 A Method for Image Selection

Since welding images are affected by droplet transfer, spattering, fuming and electromagnetic noise, it is difficult to ensure that every image captured is clear even when we control the capturing moment. Processing an image without useful information not only is a waste of time but also could potentially lead to wrong results being derived. Therefore, an easy and fast method is required to determine which images are 'useful' for further processing.

According to the analysis of images, they can be divided into three classes: dark, good, and bright. The criteria to discriminate these classes are shown in Table 2, and typical images in these categories are shown in Figure 2.

Table 2. The criteria for discriminating images

Dark	Brightness is too low and edge of the groove, electrode or welding pool cannot be seen clearly.
Good	Brightness is appropriate and edge of the groove, electrode and welding pool can all be seen clearly.
Bright	Brightness is too high and edge of the groove, electrode or welding pool cannot be seen clearly.

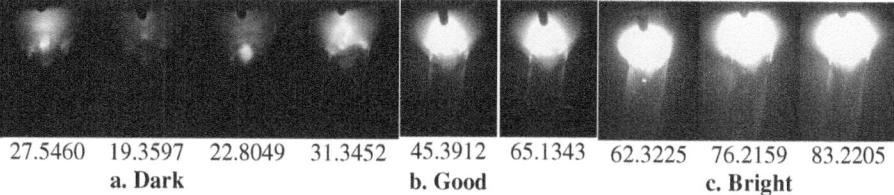

| 27.5460 | 19.3597 | 22.8049 | 31.3452 | 45.3912 | 65.1343 | 62.3225 | 76.2159 | 83.2205 |
| **a. Dark** | | | | **b. Good** | | **c. Bright** | | |

Fig. 2. Three classes of images (numbers under the images are the average grayscale value of each image): a. Dark. b. Good. c. Bright

3.1 Average Gray Value

The biggest difference between these three classes of images is the variety of their brightness, which can be represented by average gray value as shown in Equation (1).

$$Agv = \frac{\sum\limits_{x=1,y=1}^{x=m,y=n} f(x,y)}{m \times n} \tag{1}$$

Where:

Agv is the Average Gray Scale Value of the image;
f(x,y) is the pixel value of the xth row and the yth column in an image;
m is the number of rows in an image;
n is the number of columns in an image.

The average gray scale values of images in Fig 2 are shown under each image. During the experiments, 350 images were captured. Amongst these, 70 are regarded as dark images, 200 are good images and 80 are bright images as determined by human observation. To develop the image selection method, we used half of these images, i.e., 35 dark images, 100 good images and 40 bright images to determine the selection criteria. The rest of them are used to test the accuracy of our selection method.

By analyzing average gray scale values of three classes of images, the threshold of Agv is acquired, as shown in Table 3.

Table 3. The threshold of the average grayscale value

Class	Average gray value
Dark	Agv≤30
Good	39≤Agv≤60
Bright	Agv>70

It can be seen from the figures in Table 3 that there are gaps between 30 ~ 39 and 60 ~ 70. In these gaps, the images cannot be classified correctly. This is because there are both Dark and Good images with Agvs between 30 and 39 and Good and Bright images with Agvs between 60 and 70. This 'overlap' phenomenon could be shown in Fig 3. Thus additional criterion is needed.

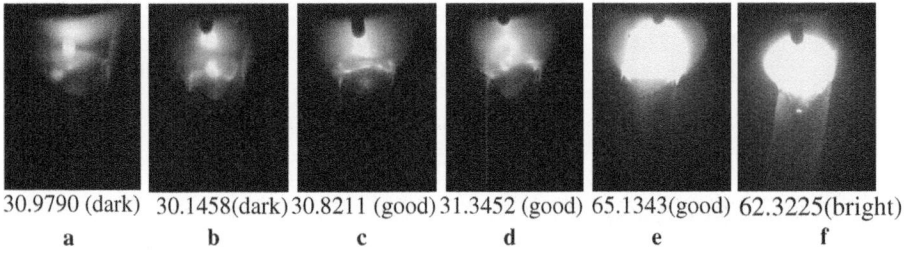

30.9790 (dark)	30.1458(dark)	30.8211 (good)	31.3452 (good)	65.1343(good)	62.3225(bright)
a	b	c	d	e	f

Fig. 3. The images which cannot be discriminated easily

3.2   Histogram Features

By analyzing Figure 3.a~b and Figure 3.c~d, it is found that the biggest difference between them is the clarity of the weld seam. So the area occupied by the seam is separated from the original image, and its average gray value is calculated, as shown in Fig 4. However, the result shows that it is impossible to discriminate them in this way.

According to these images, the intensity of the arc light has a great impact on the definition of the seam. Therefore features of the arc light can indirectly affect the clarity of the seam. Observing the pixel values around the weld zone, it is found that the different ranges of their magnitude reflect corresponding parts of the welding image. A typical image and its grayscale distribution are shown in Figure 5.

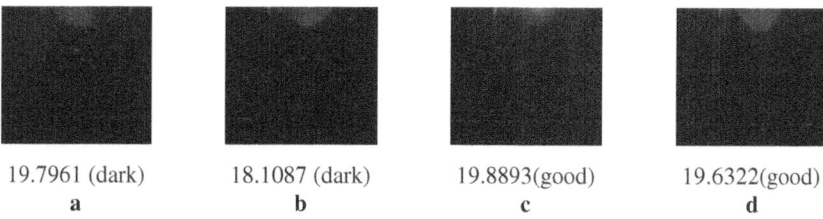

| 19.7961 (dark) | 18.1087 (dark) | 19.8893(good) | 19.6322(good) |
| a | b | c | d |

Fig. 4. The seams of the images in Fig. 3.a~d and their average gray values

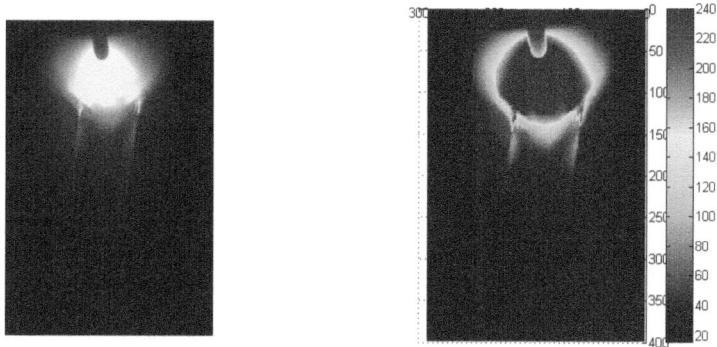

Fig. 5. A typical welding image and its grayscale distribution

From Figure 5 it is clear that the arc light mainly contains the pixels on the range of gray value from 235 to 240, and the area that arc light may influence has the pixel intensity value from 180 to 240. Therefore, this range of 180 to 240 is a good representation of the arc light. To count the area with this 'good lighting' conditions, Equation 2 is developed.

$$g(x, y) = \begin{cases} 1 & 180 \le f(x, y) \le 240 \\ 0 & others \end{cases}$$

$$IAR = \sum_{x=1, y=1}^{x=m, y=n} g(x, y) \tag{2}$$

Where:

IAR is the area that arc light may influence and $g(x,y)$ is the modified intensity of the pixel. All other notations are the same as those in Equation 1.

However, this measure will fail when the object of the camera is moving faster, which could enlarge the area of the range from 180 to 240 and reduce that of the range from 235 to 240. Therefore, it is worthwhile to count the intensity contents in the range of 235 to 240. This measure is calculated using Equation 3.

$$g(x, y) = \begin{cases} 1 & 235 \le f(x, y) \le 240 \\ 0 & others \end{cases}$$

$$AL = \sum_{x=1, y=1}^{x=m, y=n} g(x, y) \tag{3}$$

where:

AL is the area of the arc light. All other notations are the same as those in Equation 2.

It is found, by the analysis of the Figure 3.e~f, that the biggest distinction between them is the clarity of the welding pool. Since the gray value of the welding pool is quite different from that of the arc light, we can use this difference to discriminate this situation. From Figure 5 it is observed that the welding pool mainly contains pixels on the range of gray value from 100~180. Therefore, Equation 4 is developed to count the welding pool area in the image.

$$g(x, y) = \begin{cases} 1 & 100 \le f(x, y) \le 180 \\ 0 & others \end{cases}$$

$$WPL = \sum_{x=1, y=1}^{x=m, y=n} g(x, y)$$

$$(4)$$

Where:

WPL is the welding pool area where gray values range from 100~180. All other notions are the same as those in Equations 2 and 3.

The selection criteria that incorporate all three measures expressed in equations 2 – 4 are shown in Tables 5 and 6.

Table 4. Threshold of AL and IAR

Class	Criteria
Good	IAR>1400 && AL>600
Dark	Others

Table 5. Threshold of WPL

Class	Criteria
Good	WPL>6000
Bright	Others

3.3 Selection of Images

By combining the selection criteria presented above, the overall selection process is done as:

- Calculating the average gray value of the image and classifying it by Table 3;
- If the AGV of the image is among 30~39, IAR and AL should be calculated and the image is classified by Table 4.
- If the AGV of the image is among 60~70, WPL should be calculated and the image is classified by Table 5.

4 Results and Discussions

The method developed in Section3 is used to recognize the remaining 175 images, and the results are shown in Table 7.

Table 6. The result of recognition

Recognition Results / Human observation results	Dark	Good	Bright	Recognition Accuracy
Dark	35	1	0	97.2%
Good	0	96	4	96%
Bright	0	2	38	95%

From Table 7, it can be seen that the images are being selected with an accuracy rate of more than 95%. Although misjudgements still occur occasionally, the situations that lead to these misjudgements are discussed below.

Dark images are judged as Good ones
In some images, droplets cover a part of arc light, as shown in Figure 6.a. It happens to affect the arc light as a source for the seam. However, it does not have a great impact on IAR.

Good images are judged as Bright ones
Sometimes the edge of the arc light and that of the welding pool almost coincide, as shown in Figure 6.b. This results in WPL smaller than normal, and causes mistakes.

Bright images are recognized as Good ones
This happens when the arc deviates from the centre of the welding pool, as shown in Figure 6.c. From the image, a side of the welding pool can be seen clearly, therefore the image meet the criteria in section 3.2. However, the other side is covered by the deviated arc, which leads to an incomplete welding pool and therefore makes the information useless.

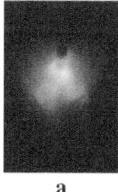
a

b

c

Fig. 6. Images which is misjudged

Overall, the probability of misjudgment due to situations discussed above is very small, less than 5% Therefore, the method provided in this paper is effective for image selection.

5 Conclusion

The paper defines three general classes of images in the welding process. To select good images, the paper analyzes the relationship between images and their gray scale distributions, and finds that average gray value and histogram features can be used to discriminate images. A method is developed to select Good images using these criteria. It is found using experiments that the recognition accuracy is above 95%.

Acknowledgement. This work is partly supported by the Australian Research Council under project ID LP0991108 and the Lincoln Electric Company (Australia).

References

1. Kim, J.W., Na, S.J.: Study on arc sensor algorithm for weld seam tracking in gas metal arc welding of butt joints. In: Proceedings of the Institution of Mechanical Engineers, Part B: Journal of Engineering Manufacture, vol. 205(B4), pp. 247–255 (1991)
2. Suga, Y., Naruse, M., Tokiwa, T.: Application of neural network to visual sensing of weld line and automatic tracking in robot welding. Welding in the World 34, 275–282 (1994)
3. Kuo, H.-C., Wu, L.-J.: An image tracking system for welded seams using fuzzy logic. J. Mater. Process. Technol. 120(1), 169–185 (2000)
4. Lee, S.K., Na, S.J.: A study on automatic seam tracking in pulsed laser edge welding by using a vision sensor without an auxiliary light source. J. Manuf. Syst. 21(4), 302–315 (2002)
5. Lee, S.K., Chang, W.S., Yoo, W.S., Na, S.J.: A tudy on a vision sensor based laser welding system for bellows. J. Manuf. Syst. 19(4), 249–255 (2007)
6. Micallef, K., Fang, G., Dinham, M.: Automatic Seam Detection and Path Planning in Robotic Welding. In: Tarn, T.J., Chen, S.B., Fang, G. (eds.) Robotic Welding, Intelligence and Automation, pp. 23–32. Springer, Heidelberg (2011)
7. Bae, K.Y., Lee, T.H., Ahn, K.C.: An optical sensing system for seam tracking and weld pool control in gas metal arc welding of steel pipe. J. Mater. Process. Technol. 120(2), 458–465 (2002)
8. Shen, H.Y., Li, L.P., Lin, T., Chen, S.B.: Real-time Seam Tracking Technology of Welding Robot with Visual Sensing. Journal of Intelligent and Robotic systems 59, 283–298 (2010)
9. Ma, H., Wei, S., Sheng, Z.: Robot welding seam tracking method based on passive vision for thin plate closed-gap butt welding. International Journal of Advanced Manufacturing Technology 48, 945–953 (2010)
10. Yan, Z.H., Zhang, G.J., Gao, H.M., Wu, L.: Weld pool boundary and weld bead shape reconstruction based on passive vision in P-GMAW. China Welding 15(2), 20–24 (2006)

A New Shape from Shading Approach for Specular Surfaces

Guohui Wang, Wei Su, and Yugui Song

School of Optoelectronic Engineering, Xi'an Technological University
Xi'an 710032, China
booler@126.com, leitin@126.com, petersong96@yahoo.com.cn

Abstract. Shape recovery is a basic problem in computer vision. Shape from shading (SFS) is an approach to get the 3D shape from a single shading image. Diffuse model is usually used to approximate the surface reflectance property. For specular surfaces, however, it is not suitable. In this paper, we propose a new SFS approach for specular surfaces. The Blinn-Phong reflectance model is applied to characterize the specular reflection property. The image irradiance equation for specular surfaces is obtained under the assumptions that the camera performs an orthographic projection and its direction is the same as the light source. Then, it is formulated as an Eikonal PDE which includes the shape of the surfaces. The viscosity solution of the resulting PDE is approximated by using the high-order Godunov fast sweeping method. Experiments are performed on both sphere and vase images and the results show the efficiency of the proposed approach.

Keywords: shape from shading, specular surfaces, Eiknoal PDE, high-order fast sweeping method.

1 Introduction

Shape recovery is a basic problem in computer vision. Shape from shading (SFS), presented by Horn [1], is an approach to get the 3D shape from one single shading image. Horn firstly derived an image irradiance equation expressing the relationship between the shape of a surface and its corresponding brightness variations. There are mainly two steps in solving SFS problem [2]. The first step is to formulate the image irradiance equation based on the certain assumption, which is the modeling of the image formation process and is determined by three factors: the camera, the light source and the reflectance property of the surface. The second step is to design a numerical algorithm to obtain a solution of the image irradiance equation, which is the shape of the given intensity image.

Since Horn's work, a large number of different SFS approaches have come out [2, 3]. Horn and Brooks [4] used the variational approach to solve the SFS problem. The shape was recovered by minimizing an energy function which consists of several constrains such as smoothness constraint and integrability constraint. To obtain a unique solution, Rouy and Tourin [5] presented a viscosity solution approach to SFS based on the Hamilton-Jacobi-Bellman equation and the viscosity solution theories.

H. Deng et al. (Eds.): AICI 2011, Part III, LNAI 7004, pp. 71–78, 2011.

Tsai and Shah [6] applied the linear approximation to the reflectance function in terms of the depth directly. Their method reconstructed the shape with a Jacobi iterative scheme. Lee and Kuo [7] proposed an iterative SFS algorithm with perspective projection. They approximated a smooth surface by the union of triangular surface patches which involved only the depth variables. The shape was reconstructed by linearizing the reflectance map and minimizing a quadratic cost functional. With the work of Rouy and Tourin [5], Kimmel and Sethian [8] presented a novel orthographic SFS algorithm. They formulated the image irradiance equation as an Eikonal PDE and computed it by using the fast marching method [9]. Yuen et al. [10] proposed a perspective SFS through extending the SFS method of Kimmel and Sethian [8]. Tankus et al. [11] derived the image irradiance equation under the perspective projection and solved it by using the iterative fast marching method. They suggested the orthographic fast marching method [8] as the initial solution, and then solved the perspective problem with an iterative method. It is well worth mentioning that Prados had made a great contribution to the SFS field [12]. They generalized the problem of orthographic and perspective SFS and associated the image irradiance equation with a Hamiltonian and approximated its viscosity solution using optimal control strategy.

Although the above work make a great deal of research, most of them concentrate on the diffuse surfaces and use Lambertian model to approximate the reflectance property. For specular surfaces, obviously, it is not suitable. Recently, Lee and Kuo [13] proposed a generalized reflectance map model, where the camera performs a perspective projection and the reflectance model is a linear combination of Lambertian and Torrance-Sparrow model [14] for the diffuse reflection and specular reflection. Ahmed and Farag [15] used Ward model [16] to express the specular surfaces. Both Torrance-Sparrow and Ward model, however, are complicated to be used in SFS problem and not easy to solve the corresponding image irradiance equation.

In this paper, we propose a new SFS approach for specular surfaces. The Blinn-Phong reflectance model [17] is applied to characterize the reflectance property of the specular reflection. The image irradiance equation for specular surfaces is obtained under the assumptions that the camera performs an orthographic projection and its direction is the same as the point light source. Then, the equation is formulated as an Eikonal PDE which includes the shape of the specular surfaces. The viscosity solution of the resulting Eikonal PDE is approximated by using the high-order Godunov fast sweeping method which is developed in our preceding work [18].

2   Image Irradiance Equation Base on the Blinn-Phong Model

With the basis that the optical axis of the camera is $z-$ axis and the image plane is $x-y$ plane, the SFS problem can be considered as that of recovering a smooth surface, z, satisfying the image irradiance equation [4]:

$$I(x, y) = R(p(x, y), q(x, y)), \qquad (1)$$

where $I(x, y)$ is the image irradiance and equals to the image brightness. R is the reflectance map conducted by the reflectance model. $p \equiv z_x(x, y)$ and $q \equiv z_y(x, y)$ denote the first partial derivatives of z with respect to x and y respectively.

Assuming that the camera performs an orthographic projection, we can use the following equation to express the normal vector **n** at the point $(x, y, z(x, y))$:

$$\mathbf{n} = [p, q, -1]^T. \tag{2}$$

Figure 1 shows the reflection geometry model of a surface. **L** is the incident direction of the light source, **R** is the reflection direction, **V** is the direction of the camera, and **h** is the angular bisector of **L** and **V**. θ_i, ϕ_i and θ_r, ϕ_r are the incident slant, tilt angles and the camera slant, tilt angles, respectively. δ is the angle between **n** and **h**.

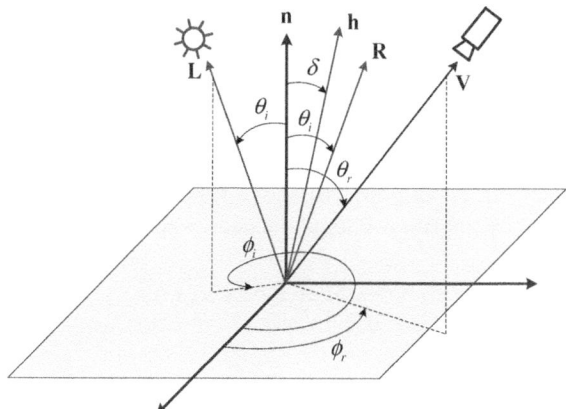

Fig. 1. Reflection geometry model

For a specular surface, Torrance and Sparrow [14] used the following equation to compute the surface reflected radiance:

$$L_s = E_0 \frac{1}{\cos \theta_r} \exp(-\frac{\delta^2}{\sigma^2}), \tag{3}$$

where E_0 is the intensity of the light source. The parameter σ is used as a measure of the surface roughness.

In order to get rid of the complicacy resulting from Torrance-Sparrow model, Phong [19] proposed a mathematically simple model to express the specular reflection:

$$L_s = E_0 (\frac{\mathbf{R}}{\|\mathbf{R}\|} \cdot \frac{\mathbf{V}}{\|\mathbf{V}\|})^N, \tag{4}$$

where N is a power which models the specular reflected light and can also be applied as a measure of shininess of the surface. Obviously, it is not convenient to compute the surface radiance in terms of $(\mathbf{R} \cdot \mathbf{V})$.

For convenience, Blinn [17] presented another mathematically simple model (5) by substituting $(\mathbf{n} \cdot \mathbf{h})$ into $(\mathbf{R} \cdot \mathbf{V})$ of Eq. (4).

$$L_s = E_0 (\frac{\mathbf{n}}{\|\mathbf{n}\|} \cdot \frac{\mathbf{h}}{\|\mathbf{h}\|})^N = E_0 (\cos \delta)^N. \tag{5}$$

Assuming that the direction of the light source is the same as the direction of the camera, we have $\theta_i = \theta_r$, $\phi_r = \phi_i$. As a result, Eq. (5) has been transformed into

$$L_s = E_0 (\cos \theta_i)^N. \tag{6}$$

If we define that the direction vectors of the light source and the camera are also $[0,0,-1]^T$ and because θ_i is the angle between $\mathbf{n}$ and $\mathbf{L}$, in this case, we have

$$\cos \theta_i = \frac{\mathbf{n}}{\|\mathbf{n}\|} \cdot \frac{\mathbf{L}}{\|\mathbf{L}\|} = \frac{1}{\sqrt{1 + p^2 + q^2}} = \frac{1}{\sqrt{1 + \|\nabla z\|^2}}. \tag{7}$$

The substitution of Eq. (7) into Eq. (6), the reflectance map and the image irradiance equation conducted by the Blinn-Phong model are expressed as

$$R(p,q) = (\frac{1}{\sqrt{1 + \|\nabla z\|^2}})^N = I(x, y). \tag{8}$$

The Eq. (8) is also derived as

$$\|\nabla z(x, y)\| = \sqrt{I(x, y)^{-2/N} - 1} = F(x, y). \tag{9}$$

Now the SFS problem (8) can be derived as the following standard Eikonal PDE:

$$\begin{cases} \|\nabla z(x, y)\| = F(x, y) & \forall x \in \Omega \\ z(x, y) = \varphi(x, y) & \forall x \in \partial\Omega \end{cases}, \tag{10}$$

where Ω is the image domain and $\varphi(\mathbf{x})$ is a real continuous function defined on $\partial\Omega$.

3   A Numerical Algorithm to Approximate the Solution of the Resulting Eikonal PDE

In order to approximate the viscosity solution of the resulting Eikonal PDE (10), we use the numerical algorithm developed in our preceding work [18], which is the high-order Godunov fast sweeping method [20].

Consider a uniform discretization $\{(x_i, y_j) = (ih, jh), i = 1, 2, \cdots, m, j = 1, 2, \cdots, n\}$ of the domain Ω. By definition, $Z_{i,j} \equiv Z(x_i, y_j)$. A high-order Godunov upwind difference scheme is used to discretize the Eikonal PDE (10):

$$\left\{ \max\left[\frac{z_{i,j}^{new} - z_1}{h}, 0 \right] \right\}^2 + \left\{ \max\left[\frac{z_{i,j}^{new} - z_2}{h}, 0 \right] \right\}^2 = F_{i,j}^2, \tag{11}$$

where

$$z_1 = \min[(z_{i,j}^{old} + hp_{i,j}^+), (z_{i,j}^{old} - hp_{i,j}^-)],$$
$$z_2 = \min[(z_{i,j}^{old} + hq_{i,j}^+), (z_{i,j}^{old} - hq_{i,j}^-)],$$

$$(12)$$

with

$$p_{i,j}^+ = (1-\alpha_+)\left(\frac{z_{i+1,j} - z_{i-1,j}}{2h}\right) + \alpha_+\left(\frac{-z_{i+2,j} + 4z_{i+1,j} - 3z_{i,j}}{2h}\right),$$

$$p_{i,j}^- = (1-\alpha_-)\left(\frac{z_{i+1,j} - z_{i-1,j}}{2h}\right) + \alpha_-\left(\frac{3z_{i,j} - 4z_{i-1,j} + z_{i-2,j}}{2h}\right),$$

$$(13)$$

where

$$\alpha_+ = \frac{1}{1+2\beta_+^2}, \quad \beta_+ = \frac{\varepsilon + (z_{i+2,j} - 2z_{i+1,j} + z_{i,j})^2}{\varepsilon + (z_{i+1,j} - 2z_{i,j} + z_{i-1,j})^2},$$

$$\alpha_- = \frac{1}{1+2\beta_-^2}, \quad \beta_- = \frac{\varepsilon + (z_{i,j} - 2z_{i-1,j} + z_{i-2,j})^2}{\varepsilon + (z_{i+1,j} - 2z_{i,j} + z_{i-1,j})^2}.$$

$$(14)$$

Here, ε is a small constant to prevent the denominator from being zero. Similarly, q^- and q^+ are defined.

Now the viscosity solution of the PDE (10) is:

$$z_{i,j}^{new} = \begin{cases} \dfrac{z_1 + z_2 + \sqrt{2h^2 F_{i,j}^2 - (z_1 - z_2)^2}}{2} & |z_1 - z_2| < hF_{i,j} \\ \min[z_1, z_2] + hF_{i,j} & |z_1 - z_2| \geq hF_{i,j} \end{cases}$$

$$(15)$$

The algorithm can be summarized as follows:

1) *Initialization:* Set the grid points on the boundary $\partial\Omega$ to be exact values, i.e., $z_{i,j}^0 = \varphi_{i,j}$, which are fixed during the iterations. The solution from the first-order Godunov fast sweeping scheme is used as the initial values at all other grid points.

2) *Alternating Sweepings:* At iteration $k+1$, we compute $z_{i,j}^{new}$ according to the update formula (15) by Gauss-Seidel iterations with four alternating direction sweepings:

- From upper left to lower right, i.e., $i = 1:m$, $j = 1:n$;
- From lower left to upper right, i.e., $i = m:1$, $j = 1:n$;
- From lower right upper to left, i.e., $i = m:1$, $j = n:1$;
- From upper right to lower left, i.e., $i = 1:m$, $j = n:1$.

3) *Convergence Test:* If $\left\|z^{k+1} - z^k\right\|_{L^1} \leq \mu$, where μ is a given stopping criterion, the algorithm converges and stops; otherwise returns to 2). Here, we take $\mu = 10^{-3}$.

4 Experimental Results

4.1 Experimental Results on Sphere Image

In these experiments, we employ a synthetic sphere image which is generated by the formula:

$$z(x, y) = \sqrt{R^2 - x^2 - y^2},\tag{16}$$

where $(x, y) \in [-49, 50] \times [-49, 50]$ and $R = 40$ is the radius.

The ground truth of the vase and the synthetic image generated by the Eq. (8) are shown in Fig. 2(a) and Fig. 2(b), respectively. The parameter K is set as 5. The reconstructed surface using the presented algorithm is shown in Fig. 2(c), while the error surface with the ground truth is shown in Fig. 2(d). The algorithm stopped after 95 iterations. The mean absolute error (MAE) and the root mean square error (RMSE) are 1.2724 pixels and 1.3637 pixels, respectively.

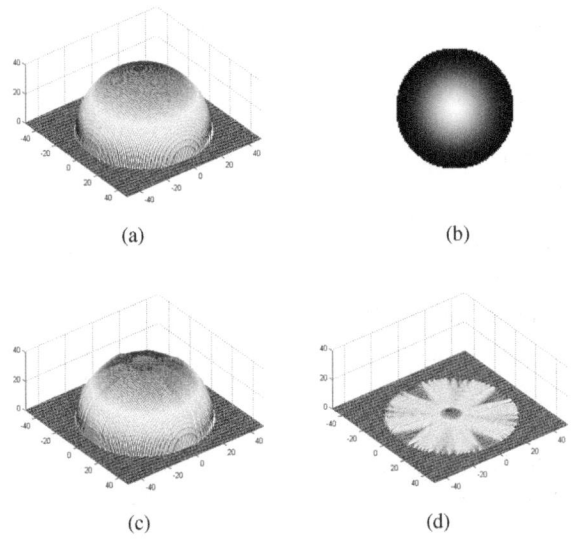

(a)   (b)

(c)   (d)

Fig. 2. Experimental results for the sphere

4.2 Experimental Results on Vase Image

In these experiments, we employ a synthetic sphere image which is generated by the formula:

$$z(x, y) = \sqrt{R^2 - x^2 - y^2},\tag{17}$$

where $f(x) = 0.15 - 0.025(2x+1)(3x+2)^2(2x-1)^2(6x-1)$ and $(x, y) \in [-0.5, 0.5]$ $\times[-0.5, 0.5]$. We map the x and y ranges to $[-49, 50]$ and scale $z(x, y)$ by a factor of 100. This yields a maximum depth value of approximately 28.55.

The ground truth of the vase and the synthetic image generated by the Eq. (8) are shown in Fig. 3(a) and Fig. 3(b), respectively. The parameter K is also set as 5. The reconstructed surface using the presented approach is shown in Fig. 3(c), while the error surface with the ground truth is shown in Fig. 3(d). The algorithm stopped after 126 iterations. The MAE and RMSE are 1.0057 pixels and 1.1157 pixels, respectively.

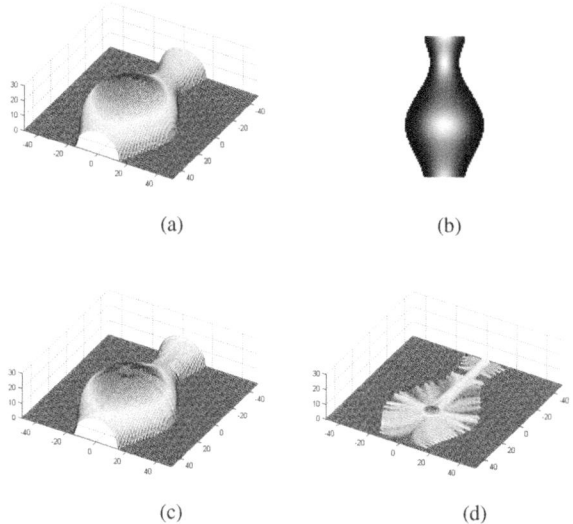

(a)   (b)

(c)   (d)

Fig. 3. Experimental results for the vase

5   Conclusion

This paper proposes a new SFS approach for specular surfaces. We apply the Blinn-Phong reflectance model to characterize the reflectance property of the specular reflection. The image irradiance equation for specular surfaces is obtained under the assumptions that the camera performs an orthographic projection and its direction is the same as the point light source. Then, the equation is formulated as an Eikonal PDE which includes the shape of the surfaces, and we approximate the solution of the resulting Eikonal PDE by using the high-order Godunov fast sweeping method. Experiments are conducted on both sphere and vase images and the results show that the proposed approach is effective and accurate.

Acknowledgments. This work is supported by the program of The Project Supported by Natural Science Basic Research Plan in Shaanxi Province of China (Program No. 2011JQ8004). At the same time, this work is supported by the Scientific Research Program Funded by Shaanxi Provincial Education Department (Program No. 11JK0996) and is also supported by the Program for Innovative Science and Research Team of Xi'an Technological University.

References

1. Horn, B.K.P., Brooks, M.J.: Shape from Shading. MIT Press, Cambridge (1989)
2. Zhang, R., Tsai, P.-S., Cryer, J.E., Shah, M.: Shape from Shading: A Survey. IEEE Trans. Pattern Anal. Mach. Intell. 21, 690–706 (1999)
3. Durou, J.-D., Falcone, M., Sagona, M.: Numerical Methods for Shape-from-shading: A New Survey with Benchmarks. Comput. Vis. Image Underst. 109, 22–43 (2008)
4. Horn, B.K.P., Brooks, M.J.: The Variational Approach to Shape From Shading. Comput. Vis. Graph. Image Process. 33, 174–208 (1986)
5. Rouy, E., Tourin, A.: A Viscosity Solutions Approach to Shape-from-shading. SIAM J. Numer. Anal. 29, 867–884 (1992)
6. Tsai, P.-S., Shah, M.: Shape from Shading Using Linear Approximation. Image Vis. Comput. 12, 487–498 (1994)
7. Lee, K.M., Kuo, C.-C.J.: Shape from Shading with Perspective Projection. Comput. Vis. Graph. Image Process. 59, 202–212 (1994)
8. Kimmel, R., Sethian, J.A.: Optimal Algorithm for Shape from Shading and Path Planning. J. Math. Imaging Vision 14, 237–244 (2001)
9. Sethian, J.A.: Fast Marching Methods. SIAM Rev. 41, 199–235 (1999)
10. Yuen, S.Y., Tsui, Y.Y., Leung, Y.W., Chen, R.M.M.: Fast Marching Method for Shape from Shading under Perspective Projection. In: The 2nd IASTED International Conference on Visualization, Imaging and Image Processing, pp. 584–589. Malaga, Spain (2002)
11. Tankus, A., Sochen, N., Yeshurun, Y.: Shape-from-Shading Under Perspective Projection. Int. J. Comput. Vis. 63, 21–43 (2005)
12. Prados, E., Faugeras, O.: A generic and provably convergent Shape-From-Shading Method for Orthographic and Pinhole Cameras. Int. J. Comput. Vis. 65, 97–125 (2005)
13. Lee, K.M., Kuo, C.-C.J.: Shape from Shading with a Generalized Reflectance Map Model. Comput. Vis. Image Underst. 67, 143–160 (1997)
14. Torrance, K.E., Sparrow, E.M.: Theory for Off-Specular Reflection From Roughened Surfaces. J. Opt. Soc. Am. 57, 1105–1114 (1967)
15. Ahmed, A.H., Farag, A.A.: Shape from Shading for Hybrid Surfaces. In: The 14th IEEE International Conference on Image Processing, vol. II, pp. 525–528. IEEE, San Antonio (2007)
16. Ward, G.J.: Measuring and modeling anisotropic reflection. ACM SIGGRAPH Comput. Graph. 26, 265–272 (1992)
17. Blinn, J.F.: Models of light reflection for computer synthesized pictures. ACM SIGGRAPH Comput. Graph. 11, 192–198 (1977)
18. Wang, G., Liu, S., Han, J., Zhang, X.: A Novel Shape from Shading Algorithm for Non-Lambertian Surfaces. In: The 3rd International Conference on Measuring Technology and Mechatronics Automation, vol. 1, pp. 222–225. IEEE, Shanghai (2011)
19. Phong, B.T.: Illumination for computer generated pictures. Comm. ACM 18, 311–317 (1975)
20. Zhang, Y.-T., Zhao, H.-K., Qian, J.: High Order Fast Sweeping Methods for Static Hamilton-Jacobi Equations. J. Sci. Comput. 29, 25–56 (2006)

Image Feature to Take the Edge of the Research Methods by Anisotropic Diffusion

Qi Wang[1] and Shaobin Ren[2]

[1] College of Mechanical Engineering, Taiyuan University of Technology,
No. 79 West Yingze Street, Taiyuan 030024, Shanxi, China
wqmngp@sina.com
[2] College of Science, Taiyuan University of Technology, No. 79 West Yingze Street,
Taiyuan 030024, Shanxi, China
rsb_long@126.com

Abstract. Like to raise the inspection as the quality of the picture, noise and enhance the image of the test is the image of the main objective. Its main objective is to reinforce the edge of specific characteristics for the measurement. This article against partial differential equations(PDE) in image processing the application of the study and learn and form the operator combines to form, based on the gradient and the edge of the detection methods, and simulations validate the test.

Keywords: component, anisotropic diffusion, partial differential equations, mathematical morphological, Visual Basic.

1 Introduction

The PDE (partial differential equations), research has been 300 years of history. However, it is only used in image processing research focus in recent years. Treatment of partial differential equations has the advantage of computational mathematics there are many numerical methods can be used. For example, the image of a model to be able to effectively change their image; hot proliferation of partial differential equations, which can simulate image from the physical to the process to degenerate; reverse the spread of partial differential equations can be successfully conducted image of the standards set; function structure of the equation can be better implementation of step-wise tracking, and was used in the image of the division [1].

2 Partial Differential Equations Theory

Partial differential equations arising in mechanics, geometry, physics and theoretical study of subjects. Mainly used in image processing is denoising content [2]. Gabor First, in 1960 the system of partial differential equations are considered, the original image and the blurred image is proportional to the difference between the approximation of its Laplace transform them to the relevant classification.

H. Deng et al. (Eds.): AICI 2011, Part III, LNAI 7004, pp. 79–85, 2011.
© Springer-Verlag Berlin Heidelberg 2011

Let the original image is u0, The blur process can use the following linear heat equation: (Equation 1)

$$\frac{\partial u}{\partial t} = \varepsilon \Delta u, u(0) = u_0 \tag{1}$$

The Δ is the Laplace operator. It can be expressed as discrete: (Equation 2)

$$u_{n+1} = u_n + \varepsilon \Delta u_n \tag{2}$$

On the contrary, the process of image ambiguity can use the following formula: (Equation 3)

$$\frac{\partial u}{\partial t} = -\varepsilon \Delta u \tag{3}$$

Its input is the inspection images u_0, Discrete form of the type: (Equation 4)

$$u_{n+1} = u_n - \varepsilon \Delta u_n \tag{4}$$

Discrete form of these two different representatives of the two completely opposite physical meaning, in which formula (1) represents the heat transfer process, commonly known as the heat equation; the formula (3) indicates that the heat transfer of the anti-process, often called the reverse heat equation. It is based on two different equations, PDE method is divided into two large branches. Linear heat equation for anisotropic diffusion for edge detection and image denoising; and the nonlinear inverse diffusion processing for image restoration.

3 Anisotropic Diffusion Filtering Theory

Image restoration filtering results in the output signal to noise ratio increased at the same time, inevitably leads to blurred edges. So Perona and Malik proposed a method of nonlinear image smoothing - Anisotropic Filtering [3]: (Equation 10,Equation 5)

$$\frac{\partial u}{\partial t} = div(c \cdot \nabla u) \tag{5}$$

In the above formula, u is the input signal, div is the gradient operator, said the gradient, c is the diffusion coefficient. Usually c is the image gradient function, which increases monotonically with the gradient decreased. The range [0,1]. The diffusion system determines the direction of diffusion, provides a proliferation of local adaptive control strategies, the spread of the location in the noise as much as possible, and stop at the edges of the image. Diffusion coefficient is commonly used: (Equation 6)

$$c_1 = e^{-(\frac{\|\nabla_i u_i\|}{\lambda})^2} \tag{6}$$

In the above formula, ∇_i is the gradient in the direction of i, λ is the gradient threshold, which determines the edge to be retained is. Another commonly used diffusion operator is: (Equation 7)

$$c_2 = \frac{1}{1 + (\|\nabla_i u_i\| / \lambda)^{1+\alpha}} \qquad (\alpha > 0) \tag{7}$$

The traditional idea is to detect the image low-pass filtering, and then calculated on the basis of gradient changes, as the image edge detection. Many scholars proposed a variety of different situations the diffusion coefficient of the program [4][5][6][7], their common feature is the first image with different pre-treatment, but this approach often leads to image edge of the drift . Morphological gradient operator is calculated corrosion is calculated directly on the original first difference, and then use the edge enhancement morphological gradient operator corrosion and reduce noise. Morphological operations will not bring the edge because of the location of the offset, so using this method can accurately locate the edge of the image, but also has strong anti-noise ability.

Corrosion in the morphology of a feature than the structural elements can be eroded by a small image details. This is combined into the erosion and dilation morphological opening operation to remove the root causes of image noise. However, computing the minimum criteria for corrosion of operation makes the image details are often not retained. PDE is the use of corrosion morphology after the extraction of image edge gradient image, it can get a good noise immunity and precise positioning, but also has strong anti-noise ability.

Morphological transformation is the most basic form of expansion and corrosion. Suppose a function $f : R^d \to R$ represents a d-dimensional signal (when d = 2 that an image). $g : B \to R$ That defined in the compactly supported function on a structure. The input f function is the structure function g multi-scale expansion $f \oplus g$,and corrosion $f \Theta g$ can be defined as: (Equation 8,Equation 9)

$$(f \oplus g_s)(x) = \sup_{v \in sB}\{f(x-v) + sg(\frac{v}{s})\} \tag{8}$$

$$(f\Theta g_s)(x) = \inf_{v \in sB}\{f(x-v) - sg(\frac{v}{s})\} \tag{9}$$

$g_s :_s B \to R$ is the structure function of the multi-scale representation, $sB = \{sb : b \in B\}$, $s \geq 0$, $gs(x) = sg(x/s)$, s>0。 When the structure function is a constant equal to zero, it is usually referred to as flat structure function g, Multi-scale dilation and erosion at this time reduced to the following formula: (Equation 10,Equation 11)

$$(f \oplus gs)(x) = \sup_{v \in sB}(x-v) \tag{10}$$

$$(f\Theta \ gs \ )(\ x \ ) = \inf_{v \in sB} \ (x + v)$$
(11)

The operator is applied to solve partial differential equations. Which use flat structuring elements: $B = \{(x, y) : \sqrt{x^2 + y^2} \le 1\}$. The image f (x, y) expansion of (corrosion) of the result: (Equation 12)

$$\begin{cases} \partial_t u = \pm | \nabla u | \\ u_0 = f(x, y) \end{cases}$$
(12)

Osher and Sethian's description of the unilateral use of upwind difference for corrosion PDE algorithm is one relatively simple formula (Equation 13).

$$\frac{u_{ij}^{n+1} - u_{ij}^n}{\nabla t} = -((\min(\frac{u_{i-ij}^n - u_{ij}^n}{h_1}, 0))^2 + (\min(\frac{u_{i+ij}^n - u_{ij}^n}{h_2}, 0))^2$$
$$+ (\min(\frac{u_{ij-i}^n - u_{ij}^n}{h_3}, 0))^2 + (\min(\frac{u_{ij-i}^n - u_{ij}^n}{h_4}, 0))^2)^{\frac{1}{2}}$$
(13)

Morphological erosion operator defined as equation 14:

$$u_{ij}^{n+1} = E\left(u_{ij}^n\right) = c \bullet \left(u_{ij}^n + \Delta t \varepsilon_{ij}^n\right)$$
(14)

4   New PDE-Based Morphological Erosion Operator

Gradient edge detection method based on the calculation usually original edge gradient was smoothed before, the purpose is to reduce the noise impact of the edge gradient. Usually the first low-pass filter, and then the gradient calculations. But it actually only consider if the signal is noisy, directly calculate the gradient will generate a lot of nothing to do with the great value of the edge, the first low-pass filter can be the maximum inhibition. The actual result is the original image from fine to coarse scale space reduced scale space, it often will affect the exact location of the edge. Many solutions have been proposed for this program. Optimization of the frequency domain, such as edge detection, wavelet edge detection methods.

Fig. 1. Lenaa adding noise2%

Fig. 2. Canny operator results

Morphological erosion operator based on the gradient image can not directly change the image edge denoising. Therefore, after considering the corrosion noise directly applied to the edge gradient image feature extraction. This means there is more than the original method of positioning the edge of capacity and robustness. New approaches in the calculation of the original image smoothing difference do before, but the application of PDE morphological erosion operator to do noise reduction on the difference image.

Fig. 3. LOG operator results   **Fig. 4.** Morphological results

4.1 Morphological Erosion Operator Edge Detection Algorithm

Define horizontal and vertical multi-scale operators as equation 15 and 16.

$$d_\sigma^h(f) = \frac{f(x+\sigma, y) - f(x-\sigma, y)}{2\sigma} \tag{15}$$

$$d_\sigma^w(f) = \frac{f(x, y+\sigma) - f(x, y-\sigma)}{2\sigma} \tag{16}$$

Where σ is the scale factor, input image in the σ scale gradient vector can be expressed as equation 17:

$$M_\sigma = \sqrt{(d_\sigma^h)^2 + (d_\sigma^w)^2} \tag{17}$$

Gradient direction angle is expressed as equation 18:

$$A_\sigma = \arg(d_\sigma^h + i d_\sigma^w) \tag{18}$$

4.2 Algorithm Steps

- at a certain scale to solve the input image vertical and horizontal gradient images.
- respectively, horizontal and vertical gradient image using the formula (11), the morphological erosion operation.
- the use of formula (17) Calculate the edge of the image.

Calculation process in the experiment, for an image of the morphological operation can be repeated, so as to constitute an iterative process. Determined according to the image signal to noise ratio the number of iterations, the number of multi-effect, but also the corresponding computation increases linearly. Therefore, in the process of calculating the image analysis needs to select the appropriate number of iterations.

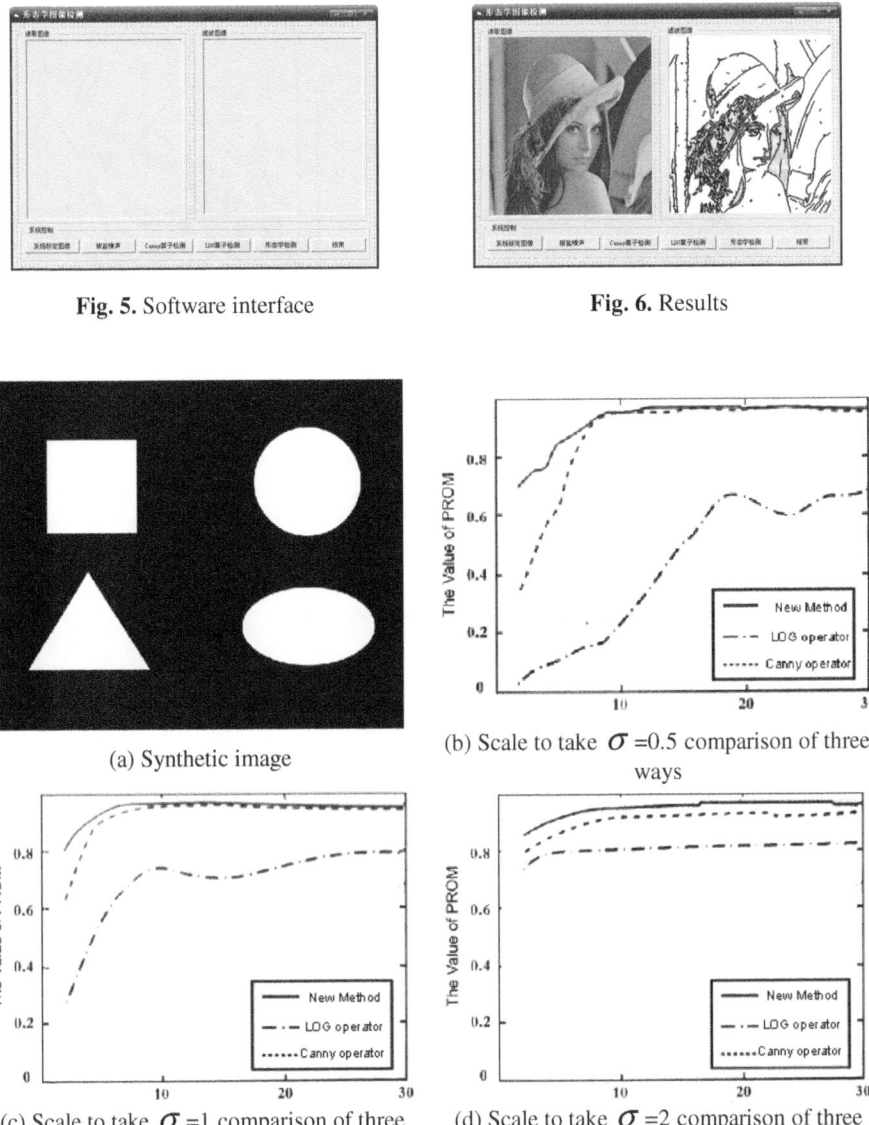

Fig. 5. Software interface   **Fig. 6.** Results

(a) Synthetic image

(b) Scale to take σ =0.5 comparison of three ways

(c) Scale to take σ =1 comparison of three ways

(d) Scale to take σ =2 comparison of three ways

Fig. 7. Image edge detection methods with different accuracy compared

Experiment calculated according to each generated image to determine whether to continue the calculation, a process similar to the detection of the calibration process, comparing the new image with the original image, the edge of the key position to determine whether the circumstances meet the requirements.

4.3 Experimental Comparison

PDE-based edge to verify the accuracy of detection methods, refer to Pratt's evaluation curve [8] criteria, programming, using the Canny operator, respectively, LOG operator on Lena image after treatment compared with the algorithm. The results shown in Fig.7. From the results, Canny operator and LOG operator is very sensitive to salt and pepper noise, when the noise ratio greater than 2%, these two operators in the detection process has basically been unable to confirm the exact location of the edge. PDE algorithm is of such noise has a strong anti-jamming capability.

5 Conclusion

Using morphological edge detection algorithm of corrosion is the biggest characteristic of the original image without noise reduction but directly in the original image to obtain the finest scale gradient image. Using the gradient of the image edge detection, image smoothing can effectively avoid the edge caused by drift. Therefore, this method can effectively solve the detection process, the noise caused by sensor detection mechanism of difficult problems, in terms of automatic identification will have broad application prospects.

References

1. Ding, M., Chai, C.: Medical Image Processing. Higher Education Press, BeiJing (2010)
2. Caselles, V., More, J.: Introduction to the special issue on partial differential equations and geometry-driven diffusion in image processing and analysis. IEEE Transaction on Image Processing 7(3), 269–273 (1998)
3. Pernoa, P., Malik, J.: Scale-space and edge detection using anisotropic diffusion. IEEE Trans. Pattern and Machine Intelligence 12(7), 629–639 (1990)
4. Liang, P., Wang, Y.F.: Local scale controlled anisotropic diffusion with local noise estimate for image smoothing and edge detection. IEEE Computer Society, Washington, DC, USA (1998)
5. Elder, J.H., Zucker, S.W.: Local scale control for edge detection and blue estimation. IEEE Transaction on Pattern Analysis and Machine Intelligence 20(7), 699–716 (1998)
6. You, Y.L., Xun, W.Y., Tannenbaum, A.: analysis of anisotropic diffusion in image processing. IEEE Transaction on image Processing 5(11), 1539–1553 (1996)
7. Segall, C.A., Acton, S.T.: Moorphological anisotropic diffusion. In: IEEE International Conference on Image Processing, vol. 3, pp. 348–351 (1997)
8. Pratt, W.K.: Digital Image Process, pp. 20–23. John Wiley & Sons, Chichester (1991)

Fabric Defect Detection Based on Computer Vision

Jing Sun and Zhiyu Zhou

College of Information and Electronics, Zhejiang Sci-Tech University, Hangzhou, China
{jings531,zhouzhiyu1993}@163.com

Abstract. Broken ends, missing picks, oil stain and holes are the most common fabric defects. To deal with the situation that manual fabric detection will affected by the subjective factors of inspectors, an automatic computer vision based fabric defect detection method is introduced in this paper. The system uses threshold segmentation method to identify if there are any defects existed in the fabric, adopts image feature based approach to recognize oil stain and holes, and uses training based technique to detect broken ends and missing picks. Experimental results show that the proposed approach has the advantage of easy implementation, high inspection speed, good noise immunity, greatly meeting the needs for automatic fabric defect inspection.

Keywords: fabric detect, computer vision, automatic detection.

1 Introduction

Fabric defect detection is a crucial process of quality control in the textile production, fabric inspection by human sight easily affected by the physical quality and mental status of the inspectors. Under the fierce competition in textile industry recently, quality assurance being an essential premise to promote competitive advantage of product, therefore automatic fabric defect detection has become one of the most enlivened areas in the domain of textile industry. Ref. [1] derived a method of fuzzy label co-occurrence matrix set. In this method, gray levels with same tone are classified into one class, and using categories instead of gray level to decrease dimension as well as taking the "abnormal" gray level as one class so as to formulate a larger component, resulting the highlighted features of fabric defect. Chi-ho Chan et al. [2] developed a method for defect detection by means of Fourier analysis. Gabor filters are a set of narrow ban-pass filters, which not only have ideal discriminate abilities both in spatial and frequency domains, but also have obvious characteristics of direction and frequency selection, thus can achieve optimal joint localization in spatial and frequency domains. In view of this, [3-4] utilized Gabor filter transformation which is highly suitable for texture image analysis to attain the goal of defect inspection and recognition. Neural network means the simulation of the function of biological neurons whose most distinguishing characteristic being the capability to approximate to any complicated linear relations as well as dynamically adjust network parameters by learning, so [5-6] applied this method in defect inspection. In this paper, computer vision technology is exploited to complete the

H. Deng et al. (Eds.): AICI 2011, Part III, LNAI 7004, pp. 86–91, 2011.

detection of the common fabric defects such as broken ends, missing picks, oil stain and holes.

2   Image Acquisition

The nature of real-time fabric detection requires not only rapid inspection speed but also intense clarity and high resolution of the captured images, which makes it necessary for computer vision system to employ high quality graphic grabbing card. First, we use CCD camera to capture images of the weaving cotton grey fabric, then segment them into frames with 512*512 pixels in size, and the number of ends and picks are 340*160 threads/100cm2. Finally, we convert them into binary images.

3   Experimental Method

For the captured fabric images, different kind of defect leads to different distribution on gray level. In the case of defects such as broken ends, missing picks and holes, there exist larger gaps in the fabric resulting in more backlighting transmission, so these types of defects in the fabric image showing higher intensity. With the similar reason, those types of defects such as oil stain revealing smaller intensity for there are less backlighting transmission. In the mean time, the four classes of defects such as broken ends, missing picks, oil stain and holes appear drastic spatial distribution feature with clear direction which helps to distinguish the four types. Broken picks can be judged as horizontal defects, broken ends as vertical defects, oil stain and holes as regional distributed defects but they are quite different in the distribution of intensity.

Generally speaking, what a computer vision inspection system analyzes and manipulates is that of specific objects. Therefore, we can choose adequate technology and simplify the execution process based on the prior knowledge of the performed objects which is also sufficiently understood to achieve the goal of automatic operation. According to the prior knowledge extracted from the shape of fabric defect, we introduced an approach based on local fabric defect inspection and recognition described as follows: first, carry out binary segmentation to get two-level image which is then taken a morphological opening operation to remove noise, second, extract parameters such as shape characteristic factor. Through local analysis, we effectively distinguish the common defects such as oil stain and holes. As for the other kind of defects aside from the discussed ones we use training based methodology which does like this: first, run binary segmentation to get two-level image, then extract parameters such as shape characteristic factor, after that, acquire classification parameter by training to make classification and as a result we can distinguish broken ends and missing picks.

3.1   Image Segmentation

Image segmentation means that to partition target image into several interested regions corresponding to various targets, intrinsically speaking, it is a process to make classification by means of various characteristic of pixels. For the reason that the effect of image segmentation will directly affect the extracting of the target characteristic and inspection accuracy, image segmentation ought to be the crucial process in computer vision inspection.

Here we use threshold segmentation combined with experiential value for there are great difference in the intensity between defects and normal fabric. The intensity of defects with the kind of oil stain are less than that of normal defects, so let the variation area of gray level be [0, Tmin]; While the intensity of defects with the kind of holes are greater than that of normal defects, so let the area be [Tmax, 255]. Then we get binary images as follows:

$$B(i, j) = \begin{cases} 0 & T_{min} \leq I[i, j] \leq T_{max} \\ 1 & otherwise \end{cases}$$

Where Tmin, Tmax denote the experiential values which are set to 125 and 195 respectively. Meanwhile, label the intensity variation area [0, Tmin] and [Tmax, 255] to RGB (255, 0, 0) and RGB (0, 0, 255) respectively.

3.2   Filter Based on Mathematic Morphology

The Mathematic morphology refers to a technology dealing with shape features of image, which is to describe the nature attribute of image through designing a whole set of transformations (calculations), ideas and algorithms. Unlike the normal spatial and frequency domain algorithms, this method is based on differential geometry and stochastic theory. This is because differential geometry can get measurement of all kinds of geometry parameters indirectly, and can reflect the stereo property of the image. Motivated by the above reasons, we employ various kinds of transformation and calculation in mathematic morphology to depict the essential attribute or key structure of the image, that is, the relationship between elements or components in the image.

Firstly, we take morphological opening operation:

$$A \circ B = (A \ominus B) \oplus B$$

to eliminate discrete dots and "blur" to implement smoothness for binary image. Normally, the image after segmentation would embedded with some noise which are formed by the backlighting transmit from the gaps of weft and wrap yarns with uniform distribution, and similar intensity to the defects such as broken picks and taking up small area (usually one to two pixels) . However, when we take the former morphological operation, the isolated dots can be removed by the erosion manipulation and then the dilatation operation is carried to restore what the original image likes before erosion and smooth it. In this situation, the key factor is to choose appropriate structure element to ensure the elimination of noise but also to keep the original shape of image roughly.

3.3   Filter Based on Mathematic Morphology

The algorithm is performed by using a 6*6 matrix to match the output image, that is, every pixel in the image is presented to see whether the corresponding 6*6 pixel matrix around it can match the given template matrix. If the match occurs, the pixel with RGB(255, 0, 0) is judged as oil stain defect and similarly the one with RGB(0, 0, 255) is identified as holes defect. Otherwise, we pass it to the feature-based training process to determine whether there exist defects such as broken ends and picks.

After threshold the captured holes defective image, as shown in Fig. 1(a), there are many noises embedded in the image, caused by backlighting transmitting through the gaps between the weft and wrap yarn of the grey cloth. Fig. 1(b) illustrates the image after opening operation. The result of oil stain image after threshold is given in Fig. 2(a). And the image after opening operation is shown in Fig. 2(b).

(a)   (b)

Fig. 1. Example of hole defects inspection: (a) image after binalization (b) image after opening operation

(a)   (b)

Fig. 2. Example of oil stain defects inspection: (a) image after binalization (b) image after opening operation

3.4 Broken Ends, Missing Picks Detection Based on Direction Feature Training

Generally speaking, computing vision detecting system conducts analysis and implementation specific to a particular object, hence we can choose adequate technique and simplify the detecting procedure based on the prior knowledge of the discussed object coupled with sufficient understanding of which, and finally achieve the goal of automatic processing.

Once the binary image obtained as a result of threshold operator, the intensity property of broken ends and missing picks are extremely approximate, the only discrepancy lies in their direction: continuous white color emerge in vertical direction of the intensity of broken ends defect, while for mission picks defect it appears in horizontal direction. In view of this, detecting algorithm extracts this specific feature of broken ends and missing picks and applies to the training and identification procedures, which is described in detail as follow:

First we make summation of the intensity values of the two level output image in the horizontal direction, then take the row which reveals the largest summation value as the feature of the image and simultaneously record the characteristic value. After doing these the feature and output value are shown in Fig. 3:

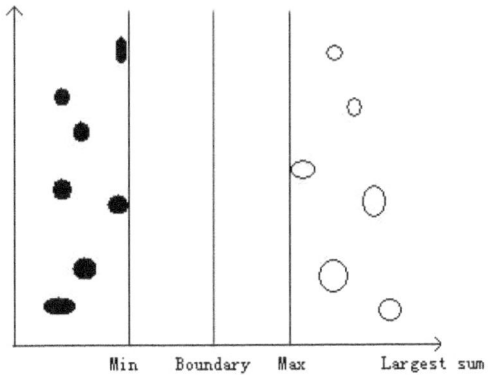

Fig. 3. Features and output values

As seen in Fig. 3, we set the maximum feature value in broken ends as Min, and the least feature value in broken picks as Max. From the fig, we can conclude that they are linear separable, so the line used for segmentation is set: X=MIN + (MAX-MIN)/2.

Through the above mentioned stages the classifier was trained, which can be devoted to perform recognition described as several steps. First we extract the maximum summation in the horizontal direction of the fabric to be performed, then carry out classification using the trained classifier, that is: when the feature lies in the left of the line, it can be judged as broken ends defect, while at right to be broken picks defect, as a result, the detection performance of broken ends and broken picks defects is completed.

4 Experimental Method

In our study, we choose cotton grey fabric as the detection object from which we obtain the original image with 512*512 pixels in size for each frame. Due to the intensive spatial distribution feature in direction shown in the four kinds of defects such as broken ends, missing picks, oil stain and holes, a simple but also practical detection algorithm is suggested in our paper. A simple interactive strategy adopting threshold to get binary defect image under practical circumstance is utilized to meet the need of real time inspection. Rely on the prior knowledge of defect shape, the fabric image is performed segmentation and mathematic morphologic opening operation to eliminate noise, which is afterwards manipulated rest on extracted local feature and the fabric shape factor is calculated to be taken as recognition parameters.

5   Conclusions

Computer vision based fabric defects inspection has been a challenging yet hard research area in nowadays automation of textile industry, so seeking an inspection algorithm with high detection speed and good accuracy has been the subject of study currently. This paper is narrowly focused on a detecting method including these procedures as segmentation and filtering of the defect image, feature extracting of the fabric defect, detecting based on local feature and training. Experimental results show that it is effective under common fabric defects such as broken ends, missing picks, oil stain and holes. However, in practical application, there are more types of fabric defect such as wrinkles generated by cloth self-weight resulting false defect, which will increase the difficulty of inspection. Thus, more reliability and stronger self-adaptation is needed and intensive study in automatic fabric defect inspection should be taken.

References

1. Zou, C., Wang, B., Sun, Z.: Detection of Fabric Defects with Fuzzy Label Co-occurrence Matrix Set. Journal of Donghua University (English Edition) 26(5), 549–553 (2009)
2. Chan, C.-h., Pang, G.K.H.: Fabric Defect Detection by Fourier Analysis. IEEE Transactions on Industry Applications 36(5), 1267–1276 (2000)
3. Bodnarova, A., Bennamoun, M., Latham, S.: Optimal Gabor Filters for Textile Flaw Detection. Pattern Recognition 35, 2973–2991 (2002)
4. Mak, K.L., Peng, P.: An Automated Inspection System for Textile Fabrics Based on Gabor Filters. Robotics and Computer-Integrated Manufacturing 24(3), 359–369 (2008)
5. Yuen, C.W.M., Wong, W.K., Qian, S.Q., et al.: Fabric Stitching Inspection Using Segmented Window Technique and BP Neural Network. Textile Research Journal 79(1), 24–35 (2009)
6. Shi, M., Jiang, S., Wang, H., et al.: A Simplified Pulse-coupled Neural Network for Adaptive Segmentation of Fabric Defects. Machine Vision and Applications 20(2), 131–138 (2009)

A New Answer Analysis Approach for Chinese Yes-No Question

Lei Xu, Yong Ren, and Wangyi Ye

Department of Electronic Engineering, Tsinghua University, Beijing 100084, China
xul04ster@gmail.com, reny@tsinghua.edu.cn,
ywy04@mails.tsinghua.edu.cn

Abstract. The accumulated question-answer archives in community-based question answering (CQA) services have produced a valuable repository for knowledge discovery. The yes-no question is a common type of question which has not been well studied in previous work. This paper proposed a novel approach to analyze answers to Chinese yes-no questions in CQA services. The analysis task was innovatively formed as a sentence selection problem: sentences that best expressed the answerer's opinion were selected. First, a conditional random field (CRF) based annotation model was proposed to split the question into several segments. Then a new score function, which combined position information of the sentence and segmentation information of the question, was designed to score all sentences of one answer. Experiment results validated the effectiveness of the CRF-based question segmentation method. The proposed answer scoring function was also proved to be more appropriate than other approaches with respect to satisfying user's information need.

Keywords: community-based question answering, yes-no question, answer analysis, question segmentation, scoring function.

1 Introduction

Community-based question answering (CQA) has become a popular web service during recent years. Famous CQA services such as Baidu Zhidao[1], Yahoo! Answers[2] have accumulated very large archives of question and answer pairs, producing a valuable knowledge repository which implies many potential applications. Lots of studies have been conducted on CQA, including question retrieval ([1], [2], [3], [4]), question classification ([5], [6]), answer quality evaluation ([7], [8]), answer summarization ([5], [9], [10], [11]), etc.

Yes-no question is common type of question in CQA services, while previous research mainly focused on *Wh*-questions, namely questions raised by using interrogative pronouns such as what, where, when, etc. This paper aimed at finding an appropriate way for analyzing answers to Chinese yes-no questions. As the name

---

[1] http://zhidao.baidu.com/
[2] http://answers.yahoo.com/

H. Deng et al. (Eds.): AICI 2011, Part III, LNAI 7004, pp. 92–103, 2011.

"yes-no" suggests, the answer to a yes-no question is polar — positive or negative, support or against, true or false. A certain part of the answer shows the polarity. We call this part the *Assertion* of the answer. It can be a word, a phrase, or several sentences. The rest part of the answer just gives some explanations or detailed descriptions. The object of our work is to automatically determine which sentences of an answer should be the *Assertion* part. This problem can be seen as a variation of answer summarization. For a given yes-no question, by putting all *Assertion* parts of different answers together we get an answer summary. From this summary, the questioner can easily get a clear overview of other peoples' opinions.

Finding *Assertion* part in answers, especially in Chinese answers, is not trivial. In English, sentences staring with the word "yes" or "no" in most cases can be identified as the *Assertion*. While in Chinese, such cue words can hardly be found. This increases the difficulty of analyzing Chinese answers.

A novel sentence scoring algorithm was designed in this paper to pick out the *Assertion* sentences in one answer. Two factors were considered. One is the position of the sentence, and the other is the relevance between the sentence and the question. To some extent, the *Assertion* part of an answer can be seen as the repetition of the question. But not all the words in the question have the same probability to be repeated. Therefore, before measuring the relevance, the question needs to be analyzed first to determine which part of it has the most immediate influence on making an *Assertion*. We proposed a CRF (conditional random field) based method to reveal the structure of the question. Some heuristic rules were also applied to make the measurement much closer to people's intuition.

The rest of the paper is organized as follows: Section 2 gives a formalized description of the *Assertion* selection problem. Section 3 introduces the question segmentation method. Section 4 describes the proposed answer scoring algorithm. Experimental result is given in Section 5. Section 6 introduces some related work. Finally, conclusions and future directions are drawn in Section 7.

2   Problem Formalization

(q, A) denotes a question-answer pair in the Q&A archive. The question q consists of two fields: question title and question body. The question body describes the question title in more detail and it is an optional field. In this paper we only focused on the title field. More precisely, we focused on the interrogative sentence in the title. If not special specified, we use the term "question" to refer to the interrogative sentence of question title. The answer A can be expressed as a set of multiple sentences: $A = \{a_1, a_2, \cdots, a_{|A|}\}$ ($|A|$ denotes the cardinality of set A). The object of our work is to find the *Assertion* sentence from A for a given question q:

$$a_{ass} = \operatorname*{argmax}_a Score(a, q) . \tag{1}$$

The scoring function $Score(a, q)$ will be described in Section 4.

3 Question Segmentation

According to Chinese linguistics, the yes-no question is constructed by adding an interrogative modal particle to a declarative sentence. To some extent, the *Assertion* part of an answer can be seen as the repetition of the declarative sentence, more precisely, partial repetition. Some words of the question are more likely to be repeated than the rest. For example, the word "可以" ("can") in the question "仙人掌可以防电脑辐射吗?" ("Can cactus protect people from the computer radiation?") is most likely to be used in the *Assertion* part to this question. We divided a question into different segments and marked the segment which has the highest possibility to show in the *Assertion* part. Later this segment will be assigned higher weight when comparing the question with sentences in the answer.

A CRF-based method was developed to do the segmentation job. A question is first split into tokens by using a word segmentation software[3]. Then the tokens are annotated with different labels by the CRF model. Continuous tokens with same labels compose one segment. Some previous work ([12], [13]) has proved the effectiveness of CRF-based question annotation. Features used for training the CRF model are listed in Table 1.

Table 1. Features and templates for the CRF model

Words of current token and neighboring tokens
Word(-2), Word(-1), Word(0), Word(1), Word(2)
Part of speech tags of current token and neighboring tokens
POS(-2), POS(-1), POS(0), POS(1), POS(2)
combination of words
Word(-2)&Word(-1)&Word(0), Word(-1)&Word(0)&Word(1), Word(0)&Word(1)&Word(2), Word(-1)&Word(0), Word(0)&Word(1)
combination of part of speech tags
POS(-2)&POS(-1)&POS(0), POS(-1)&POS(0)&POS(1), POS(0)&POS(1)&POS(2), POS(-1)&POS(0), POS(0)& POS (1)
labels of previous token and current token
Tag(-1)&Tag(0)

The annotation result of previous example question is as follows (words in parentheses are corresponding English expressions):

仙人掌 (cactus)/S_1 可以 (can)/S_2 防 (protect)/S_3 电脑 (computer)/S_3 辐射 (radiation)/S_3 吗 /S_4 ?/S_5.

A question can have 5 segments at most. "S_4" denotes the modal particle at the end of the question. The question mark is annotated with "S_5". These two types of segments are not taken into account when analyzing answers. Tokens which have the highest possibility to shown in the *Assertion* part are labeled with "S_2". Typical words in S_2 include "可以/能" (can), "是" (be), "会" (will), "有" (have), etc. Tokens before and after

---

[3] http://ictclas.org/

segment S_2 are labeled with "S_1" and "S_3" respectively. We assume that segment S_2 is indispensable, while either S_1 or S_3 can be null. This assumption holds true for most Chinese yes-no questions.

4 Answer Scoring

For a given question q, the score of a sentence a in answer A is the product of two factors:

$$Score(a, q) = W_{pos}(a) \cdot qRelevance(a, q) . \tag{2}$$

4.1 Position Weight

$W_{pos}(a)$ denotes the position weight of sentence a:

$$W_{pos}(a) = 1 - (a.position - 1)/|A| . \tag{3}$$

Sentences in A are sorted in the order they appear and $a.position$ is the rank of a ($1 \leq a.position \leq |A|$). According to (3), leading sentences in one answer are assigned higher weight, which makes them more likely to be chosen as the *Assertion* part. It is consistent with people's language habit when answering a yes-no question.

4.2 Relevance to Question

$qRelevance(a, q)$ denotes the relevance between a and q:

$$qRelevance(a, q) = \sum_{k=1}^{3} W_{S_k} R_k(a) . \tag{4}$$

S_k denotes one segment in q. The parameter W_{S_k} is the weight of S_k. The value of W_{S_k} will be adjusted according to the segmentation result, which we will explain later. $R_k(a)$ denotes the relevance between S_k and a. The question q, the question segment S_k and the sentence a are all modeled as "bag of words" (punctuation, modal particles and auxiliary words are removed):

$$q = \{t_1^q, t_2^q, \cdots, t_{|q|}^q\},\ S_k = \{t_1^k, t_2^k, \cdots, t_{|S_k|}^k\},\ a = \{t_1^a, t_2^a, \cdots, t_{|a|}^a\} . \tag{5}$$

A simple definition of $R_k(a)$ is the proportion of word overlap between S_k and a:

$$R_k(a) = |SW_k|/|a| . \tag{6}$$

Where SW_k denotes the set of words appearing in both S_k and a.

For a Chinese yes-no question, words in S_2 can be analogous to the auxiliary verbs in English, such as "do", "will", "shall", etc. These words usually have no clear meaning unless some context information is provided by S_1 and/or S_3. People can choose words other than those in S_2 to express their opinions, as long as they can be understood correctly in context. For example, the S_2 part of the question

"仙人掌能防电脑辐射吗?" is "能" ("can"). But a possible response to this question is "可以的" (another way to say "Yes, it can"). If we only consider exact word matching between q and a, this sentence will be regarded as totally irrelevant to the question, since all the SW_k sets are null. In fact, this sentence is exactly the *Assertion* part we should pick out. To solve this problem, an additional set $\widetilde{SW}_2$ is constructed:

$$\widetilde{SW}_2 = \{t| \, t \in a \wedge (\textstyle\sum_q f^q_{S_2}(t) > 1) \, . \tag{7}$$

Where

$$f^q_{S_2}(t) = \begin{cases} 1, & \text{if } t \text{ appears in segment } S_2 \text{ of question } q \\ 0, & \text{otherwise} \end{cases} \, . \tag{8}$$

By gathering all the words which have shown in the S_2 part more than once, we created a "synonym" list for words in current S_2. This list can help to avoid missing such *Assertion* sentences as described in the example.

On the other hand, both the question title and the sentence in an answer are usually very short, there is often very little word overlap between them. To bridge this lexical gap, we use the co-occurrence of n-grams as a complement to measure the relevance between a and q. Inspired by intuitions from linguistics, many work have proved that word co-occurrence statistics can provide a natural basis for semantic representations ([15]).

Similar to W_{S_k}, the form of $R_k(a)$ is not fixed. How to measure the relevance depends on the characteristics of the question and the sentence itself. For convenience, we use a 3-bit code to represent question and answer respectively. The question q is encoded as $q_1 q_2 q_3$, where

$$q_k = \begin{cases} 1, & \text{if } |S_k| > 0 \\ 0, & \text{otherwise} \end{cases} \, . \tag{9}$$

The answer sentence a is encodes as $a_1 a_2 a_3$, where

$$a_k = \begin{cases} 1, & \text{if } |SW_k| > 0 \\ 2, & \text{else if } k = 2 \text{ and } |\widetilde{SW}_2| > 0 \\ 0, & \text{otherwise} \end{cases} \, . \tag{10}$$

According to the definitions of question segments we described in section 3, a question q belongs to one of the three types: 111, 110 and 011. Correspondingly, the relevance between a and q is measured in different ways.

1) $q_1 q_2 q_3 = 111$

For this type of question, the weights of different segments are set as: $W_{S_1} = 1$, $W_{S_2} = 5$, $W_{S_3} = 3$. W_{S_2} has the highest value according to the definition of segment S_2. W_{S_3} is higher than W_{S_1} because the focus of this type of question usually falls in the S_3 part.

There are 12 possible values of $a_1 a_2 a_3$. If $a_2 a_3 = 10$ or $a_2 a_3 = 20$, we consider the following three situations:

If $a = SW_2$ or $a = \widetilde{SW}_2$, which means sentence a just repeats the S_2 part of q. It is the simplest way to answer a yes-no question. This sentence must be the *Assertion* part. Thus, $R_k(a)$ is assigned a very large value, for example,100.

If the rest words in a other than those in SW_2 and $\widetilde{SW}_2$ are words with polarities, such as "肯定" ("definitely") and "不" ("not"), a should be *Assertion*. $R_k(a)$ is also assigned a very large value. Two lists of polarity words are manually created, one represents affirmative attitude and the other represents negative attitude.

If a does not meet the above two conditions, we measure the *Overlap* between n-grams:

$$Overlap(g^a, g^q) = cf(g^a, g^q)/min(f(g^q), f(g^a)) . \tag{11}$$

Where g^a and g^q denote the n-grams (bigrams and trigrams) in a and q:

$$g^a \in BG^{a2} \cup TG^{a2}, \; g^q \in BG^{q23} \cup TG^{q23},$$

$$BG^{a2} = \{t_i t_{i+1}\}, \; TG^{a2} = \{t_i t_{i+1} t_{i+2}\} \; (i \geq min\{k: t_k \in SW_2 \vee t_k \in \widetilde{SW}_2\}), \tag{12}$$

$$BG^{q23} = \{t_i t_{i+1}\}, \; TG^{q23} = \{t_i t_{i+1} t_{i+2}\} \; (i \geq min\{k: t_k \in S_2\}) .$$

$f(g)$ denotes the occurrence frequency of the n-gram g in the archive. $cf(g^a, g^q)$ denotes the co-occurrence frequency of g^a and g^q. $R_1(a)$ takes the simple form as defined in (6). $R_2(a)$ and $R_3(a)$ are defined as follows:

$$R_2(a) = \begin{cases} 1, & if \; max_{g^a, g^q} \, Overlap(g^a, g^q) > \theta_o \\ 0, & otherwise \end{cases} . \tag{13}$$

$$R_3(a) = \begin{cases} max_{g^a, g^q} \, Overlap(g^a, g^q), & if \; max_{g^a, g^q} \, Overlap(g^a, g^q) > \theta_o \\ 0, & otherwise \end{cases} . \tag{14}$$

Where θ_o is the threshold of the *Overlap* value. A sentence will be thought as irrelevant to a question segment if the maximum n-grams overlap between them is smaller than the threshold.

For other types of a, $R_k(a)$ is calculated as defined in (6).

2) $q_1 q_2 q_3 = 110$

For this type of question, the weights of different segments are set as: $W_{S_1} = 3$, $W_{S_2} = 5$, $W_{S_3} = 0$.

There are 6 possible values of $a_1 a_2 a_3$. If $a_1 a_2 a_3 = 010$ or $a_1 a_2 a_3 = 020$, we also consider 3 situations. The first two are same with 1). For the third situation, the n-grams used to measure *Overlap* are different:

$$g^a \in BG^{a12} \cup TG^{a12}, \; g^q \in BG^{q12} \cup TG^{q12},$$

$$BG^{a12} = \{t_{i-1} t_i\}, \; TG^{a12} = \{t_{i-2} t_{i-1} t_i\} \; (i \leq max\{k: t_k \in SW_2 \vee t_k \in \widetilde{SW}_2\}), \tag{15}$$

$$BG^{q12} = \{t_{i-1} t_i\}, \; TG^{q12} = \{t_{i-2} t_{i-1} t_i\} \; (i \leq max\{k: t_k \in S_2\}) .$$

$R_1(a)$ has the same form with $R_3(a)$ as defined in (14). $R_2(a)$ is defined by (13) and $R_3(a)$ is equivalent to zero.

98   L. Xu, Y. Ren, and W. Ye

For other types of a, $R_k(a)$ is defined by (6).

3) $q_1q_2q_3=011$

For this type of question, the weights of different segments are set as: $W_{S_1} = 0$, $W_{S_2} = 5$, $W_{S_3} = 3$.

There are 6 possible values of $a_1a_2a_3$. Except that $R_1(a)$ is equivalent to zero, we use the same way as described in 1) to define $R_2(a)$ and $R_3(a)$.

For each sentence a in A, we use (2) to compute its score. Then the sentences are ranked based on their scores. The top-ranked one or two sentences are selected as the *Assertion* part of answer A.

5 Experiments

We conducted several experiments to evaluate the performance of CRF based question segmentation and validate the feasibility of the proposed answer scoring algorithm.

5.1 Data Set

We crawled about 24600 resolved question pages from two famous Chinese CQA websites: Baidu Zhidao and Sina iask[4]. 24541 questions were extracted from these web pages. Some simple rules, such as the occurrence of interrogative pronoun and the modal particle at the end of the question, were employed to identify which questions are yes-no questions. Finally we got 4328 yes-no questions. We use these questions and their corresponding answers to carry out following experiments. For question that has multiple answers, multiple question-answer pairs were constructed for each answer. The final data set D is composed of 16802 question-answer pairs. The average length of question is 7.7 words, and the answer is 144.1 words. One question has 3.9 answers on average.

5.2 CRF-Based Question Annotation

We randomly chose 500 questions from D to conduct the annotation experiment on. After word segmentation and part-of-speech tagging, we manually annotated these questions. Some questions were chosen (randomly) for training the CRF model, the rest were used for testing. We altered the size of train set to see how the performance changed.

Similar to [12], we use 3 rates to measure the performance: Precision (*Pre*), Recall (*Rec*) and F-score (*F1*).

$$Pre = Match/Model, \ Rec = Match/Manual, \ F1 = 2*Pre*Rec/(Pre + Rec).\quad(16)$$

Match is the count of the tags that was predicted right. *Model* is the count of the tags that was predicted by the model. *Manual* is the count of the tags that was labeled manually.

---

[4] http://iask.sina.com.cn/

Table 2. Performances of different settings

Train Set	Test Set	Total Tags in Test Set	Pre (%)
400	100	798	96.24
300	200	1594	94.48
250	250	1867	94.59
200	300	2326	93.21
100	400	3126	91.97

Table 2 shows the performances of different train-test partitions. As the size of train set decreases and the size of test set increases, the performance declines. But the deterioration of the performance is not significant. Even if the size of train set is only one fourth that of test set, the precision still stays above 90%. This result shows that the CRF-based method is feasible and effective for the proposed question annotation task.

Table 3. Performances of S_2 segment

Train Set	Test Set	Manual	Model	Match	Pre (%)	Rec (%)	F1
400	100	114	112	107	95.5	93.9	0.947
300	200	223	220	198	90.0	88.8	0.894
250	250	278	276	250	90.6	89.9	0.903
200	300	334	327	284	86.9	85.0	0.859
100	400	459	418	359	85.9	78.2	0.819
average					89.9	87.2	0.884

The S_2 part of a question is very important for the following answer scoring task, so we took a further investigation of the performance on "S_2" annotation. As the results shown in Table 3, the average precision of different train-test partitions is about 90%. Hence, we can make the conclusion that as long as the size of train set is comparable with the test set, the performance of answer scoring will not be affected too much by the errors caused by question annotation.

5.3 Answer Assertion Selection

A CRF model was trained by using all the 500 questions in previous experiment. We applied this model to annotate all the questions in D. Answers in D were split into sentences. The average number of sentences in one answer is 32.3. We randomly chose 1206 questions and corresponding answers for evaluation. For each question-answer pair, three sentence rankings were produced. One is the position-based ranking (PosRank): sentences were ranked in the same order as they appeared in the answer. The second ranking was based on cosine similarity (CosRank): the given question and the answer sentence were modeled as TFIDF vectors. Sentences were ranked according to the cosine similarity between question and answer sentence vectors. The proposed scoring algorithm was used to produce the third ranking (ScoRank). For each ranking, the top 10 percent of the sentences were selected as *Assertion*.

The performance is measured with the following rate:

$$Satisfaction = C\_SuccessAnswer/C\_Answer .\qquad(17)$$

$C\_SuccessAnswer$ is the count of $SuccessAnswers$. A $SuccessAnswer$ means if we use selected $Assertion$ sentences to replace the original answer, the answerer's attitude can still be understood correctly. We manually checked each answer and counted the number of $SuccessAnswers$. C_Answer is the count of all answers. Table 4 shows the evaluation result. All of the three $Satisfaction$ rates are lower than 70%. This result can be ascribed to the dissatisfactory quality of answers in current CQA services. Sometimes the answerer just "copy-paste" an article (may be related) and doesn't give any direct $Assertion$ in his/her own words. For this type of answer, the $Assertion$ can only be inferred by users rather than directly picked out from the article. Compared to the first two ranking methods, the $Satisfaction$ rate rose about 8% percent when using the proposed scoring algorithm. The main reason of this improvement is that the proposed algorithm made better use of the information provided by the question. Not only the words but also the structure of the question is taken into account. Realizing that different parts of the question have different importance for making an $Assertion$ is the key to success.

Table 4. Performances of answer scoring

	PosRank	CosRank	ScoRank
C_SuccessAnswer	2286	2137	2596
C_Answer	4055	4055	4055
Satisfaction	0.564	0.527	0.640

Considering that the topic of the question may have some influence on the way how people answer it, we made a detailed comparison of the three methods on different topics. Questions in D belong to five topics: online shopping, radiation, train ticket, cold and losing weight. As shown in Fig. 1, the proposed scoring algorithm performed much better than the cosine similarity-based method over all topics. This result further confirmed the fact that users tend to use different expressions to make assertions rather than simply repeating the question sentence. The measures we took to bridge the lexical gap between question and answer, such as calculating the semantic overlap of n-grams, are quite necessary. On the other hand, the advantage of the proposed method over the position-based method was not so obvious. Two factors were responsible for this result. One is the short lengths of the answers. For an answer which only consists of one or two sentences, different ranking methods make no difference. This type of answer occupied a certain proportion of answers in D. Another possible reason is the language habit. People do prefer to give their assertions at the beginning of the answers. Thus the top positioned sentences also gained higher scores. The importance of the position factor still needs to be investigated in future work.

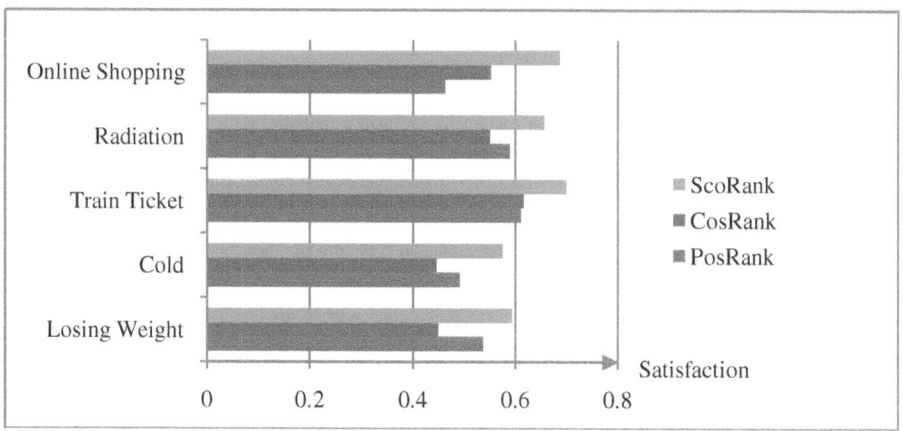

Fig. 1. Performances on different topics

6 Related Work

So far as we know, the answer analysis approach proposed in this paper is the first of its kind in the research field of CQA. Nevertheless, we have borrowed some ideas from previous work on question analysis and answer summarization.

Fan et al ([12], [13]) proposed a CRF model for semantic chunk annotation in a Chinese question and answering system. They defined five types of semantic chunks, such as Topic, focus, Restriction, etc. The features they used for training the CRF model are similar with ours, but their model is more applicable to *Wh*-questions.

Liu et al ([5]) carried out a comprehensive analysis of the question types in CQA services. They pointed out that for those *Open* and *Opinion* questions, they usually have multiple good answers. It can be a good support to our work. To summarize answers to *Opinion* questions, they use negative cue phrase such as "No, it isn't" and positive cue phrase such as "Yes, it is" to annotate the polar of the answer. As mentioned before, there is no such cue phrase in Chinese, so their method cannot be applied in our work.

Tang et al ([9]) proposed a probabilistic scoring model to distinguish high-quality answers from low quality answers and summarize answers for similar questions related to a given query. Four different probabilities were estimated to score a sentence: the prior probability of an answer, the similarity between the answer and the question, the relevance from question to query and the importance of a sentence for a given query. The position weight and the relevance to question in our scoring algorithm are analogous to the first two probabilities.

7 Conclusion and Future Work

A CRF-based question segmentation method and a new answer analysis approach for Chinese yes-no question were proposed in this paper. The notion of *Assertion* part of the answer and the scoring algorithm for selecting *Assertions* made our work different from previous studies on answer analysis. The proposed methods were proved to be feasible and effective by experiments on real data from CQA services.

The proposed scoring algorithm is essentially based on word matching between question and answer. Although some methods, such as making a gazetteer of S_2-labeled words and computing the co-occurrence frequency of n-grams, were employed to bridge the lexical gaps, the inherent limitations of word matching-based approach are still exist. For example, sometimes the *Assertion* part of the answer has no semantically similar words with the question and it cannot be identified by word-based methods, while humans can identify it based on the context, language habit or common knowledge. In future work, we will take these factors into account to improve the performance of the scoring algorithm. Also we will investigate whether the proposed answer analysis approach can be transplanted to other types of questions, such as *Wh*-questions.

Acknowledgement. This work was supported by National Natural Science Funding of China under Grant No. 60932005.

References

1. Jeon, J., Croft, W.B., Lee, J.H.: Finding Similar Questions in Large Question and Answer Archives. In: 14th Conference on Information and Knowledge Management, pp. 84–90. ACM Press, New York (2005)
2. Xue, X., Jeon, J., Croft, W.B.: Retrieval Models for Question and Answer Archives. In: 31st Annual International ACM SIGIR Conference, pp. 475–482. ACM Press, New York (2008)
3. Cao, X., Gao, C., Cui, B., Christian, S.J.: A Generalized Framework of Exploring Category Information for Question Retrieval in Community Question Answer Archives. In: 19th International Conference on World Wide Web, pp. 201–210. ACM Press, New York (2010)
4. Duan, H., Cao, Y., Lin, C.Y., Yu, Y.: Searching Questions by Identifying Question Topic and Question Focus. In: 46th Annual Meeting of the Association for Computational Linguistics, pp. 156–164. Association for Computer Linguistics, Stroudsburg (2008)
5. Liu, Y.J., Li, S.S., Cao, Y.B., Lin, C.Y., Han, D.Y., Yu, Y.: Understanding and Summarizing Answers in Community-based Question Answering Services. In: 22nd International Conference on Computational Linguistics, pp. 497–504. Association for Computational Linguistics, Stroudsburg (2008)
6. Blooma, M.J., Goh, D., Chua, A.: Question Classification in Social Media. International Journal of Information Studies 1(2), 101–109 (2009)
7. Wang, X.J., Tu, X., Feng, D., Zhang, L.: Ranking Community Answers by Modeling Question-Answer Relationships via Analogical Reasoning. In: 32nd Annual International ACM SIGIR Conference, pp. 179–186. ACM Press, New York (2009)
8. Lee, C.T., Rodrigues, E.M., Kazai, G.: Model for Voter Scoring and Best Answer Selection in Community Q&A Services. In: 2009 IEEE/WIC/ACM International Conference on Web Intelligence, pp. 116–123. IEEE Press, New York (2009)
9. Tang, Y., Li, F.T., Huang, M.L., Zhu, X.Y.: Summarizing Similar Questions for Chinese Community Question Answering Portals. In: 2nd International Conference on Information Technology and Computer Science, pp. 36–39. IEEE Press, New York (2010)

10. Tomasoni, M., Huang, M.: Metadata-Aware Measures for Answer Summarization in Community Question Answering. In: 48th Annual Meeting of the Association for Computational Linguistics, pp. 760–769. Association for Computational Linguistics, Stroudsburg (2010)
11. Li, S.S., Li, Z.J.: Answer Summarization via Term Hierarchical Structure. In: 7th International Conference on Fuzzy Systems and Knowledge Discovery, pp. 2349–2353. IEEE Press, New York (2010)
12. Fan, S.X., Ng, W.W.Y., Wang, X.L., Zhang, Y.Y., Wang, X.: Semantic Chunk Annotation for Complex Questions Using Conditional Random Field. In: Workshop on Knowledge and Reasoning for Answering Questions of Coling 2008, pp. 1–8. Association for Computational Linguistics, Stroudsburg (2008)
13. Fan, S.X., Wang, X., Wang, X.L., Zhang, Y.Y.: A New Question Analysis Approach for Community Question Answering System. International Journal on Asian Language Processing 19(3), 95–108 (2009)
14. Celikyilmaz, A., Hakkani-Tur, D.: A Graph-based Semi-Supervised Learning for Question Semantic Labeling. In: NAACL HLT 2010 Workshop on Semantic Search, pp. 27–35. Association for Computational Linguistics, Stroudsburg (2010)
15. Bullinaria, J., Levy, J.: Extracting Semantic Representations from Word Cooccurrence Statistics: a Computational Study. Behavior Research Methods 39(3), 510–526 (2009)
16. Schulte im Walde, S., Melinger, A.: An In-Depth Look into the Co-Occurrence Distribution of Semantic Associates. Journal of Italian Linguistics. Special Issue on From Context to Meaning: Distributional Models of the Lexicon in Linguistics and Cognitive Science, 89–128 (2008)

A Novel Pattern Matching Method for Chinese Metaphor Identification and Classification

Xiaoxi Huang[1,2], Huaxin Huang[1], Cihua Xu[1], Weiying Chen[1],
and Rongbo Wang[2]

[1] Center for the Study of Language and Cognition, Zhejiang University, China
[2] Institute of Computer Application Technology, Hangzhou Dianzi University, China
{itshere,rw211,xuch,chenweiying}@zju.edu.cn,
wangrongbo@hdu.edu.cn

Abstract. Metaphor is a pervasive phenomenon in natural language. This paper focuses on metaphor identification. Based on the linguistic definition, an improved classification system of Chinese metaphors is presented, classifying metaphorical language into two categories: referential metaphor with ten subclasses and collocational metaphor with five subclasses. Furthermore, a novel pattern matching algorithm on dependency tree is proposed for detecting potential metaphor occurrences and two quantified measures, referential adaptability degree (RA) and collocational adaptability degree (CA), are introduced for determining metaphor category. Finally, a computational model for Chinese metaphor identification and classification is developed.

Keywords: metaphor computation, pattern matching, natural language understanding, dependency tree.

1 Introduction

For most of us, metaphor is a figure of speech in which one thing is compared with another by saying that one is the other, as in "He is a pig". In the cognitive linguistics, metaphor is defined as understanding one conceptual domain in terms of another conceptual domain [1], which is called the Conceptual Metaphor Theory. As a pervasive phenomenon in natural language and a basic way of human thinking, metaphor has become the focus of linguistics, philosophy and cognitive science. Therefore, to build a human-like natural language processing (NLP) system, auto-processing of metaphor is an unavoidable task, which involves metaphor identification and metaphor interpretation [2]. In this paper, we focus on metaphor identification and classification in Chinese. Li and Yang proposed an embedded tree matching algorithm based on metaphorical dependency structure [3]. The main contribution of this paper is a novel pattern matching algorithm aimed to improve previous methods used in [3, 4].

The rest of this paper is organized as follows: Section 2 describes the formal representation of a metaphorical sentence based on dependency grammar. Section 3 displays the classification system of Chinese metaphor based on dependency tree schema. Section 4 develops the pattern matching algorithm, and Section 5 provides the quantified standard for metaphor identification. At last, the conclusion and future work are given in Section 6.

H. Deng et al. (Eds.): AICI 2011, Part III, LNAI 7004, pp. 104–114, 2011.
© Springer-Verlag Berlin Heidelberg 2011

2   Representation of Metaphorical Language

According to metaphorical utterance representation [3, 4], we call the primitives of metaphor the metaphor roles. In Chinese, the basic components of a metaphor utterance are target, source, grounding and mark. For example, in "小玲的脸红得像只苹果"(Xiaoling's face is as red as an apple), "Xiaoling's face" and "apple" are target concept and source concept respectively, "like" is the mark, and the grounding is described by "red".

In this work, we use the dependency grammar [5] to represent the structure of a sentence. In dependency grammar, a sentence is described as a dependency graph [6].

Definition 1 (Sentence). A sentence is a sequence of symbols, denoted as $S=w_0w_1...w_n$.

Here, w_0 = ROOT is a virtual root node inserted at the beginning of the sentence. Each symbol w_i represents a word.

Definition 2 (Dependency Relation Types). The finite set of the possible dependency relations held between any two words called dependency relation types, denoted as $R = \{r_1, r_2, \ldots, r_m\}$, a specific dependency relation $r \in R$ called an arc label.

Based on the above two definitions, we can define dependency graph as follow:

Definition 3 (Dependency Graph). A dependency graph is a labeled directed graph, and consists of nodes set V and label set A, denoted as $G = (V, A)$. For sentence S and dependency relation types set R, the following holds:

1) $V \subseteq \{w_0, w_1, ..., w_n\}$;
2) $A \subseteq V \times R \times V$;
3) For any arc label $r' \neq r$, if $(w_i, r, w_j) \in A$, then $(w_i, r', w_j) \notin A$.

The nodes in a dependency graph directly correspond to words in a sentence. We call a standard node set as spanning node set that contains all the words in the sentence [6], denoted as $V_S=\{ w_0, w_1, \ldots, w_n\}$. The arc label set A represents the dependency relations of G, such as $(w_i, r, w_j) \in A$ means there is a dependency relation r between the head word w_i and dependent w_j. The third condition makes sure that there can be no more than one relation within each word pair.

Using dependency relation types and dependency graph, we can further define the dependency tree.

Definition 4 (Dependency Tree). For an input sentence S and dependency relation types set R, if dependency graph $G=(V, A)$ is a directed tree with a unique initial node as w_0, and has a spanning node set V_S, then we call such dependency graph as dependency tree, where the node w_0 is a virtual node.

The state in the art of dependency parsing has been improved greatly in NLP, especially the methods based on machine learning. In our work, the Chinese dependency parser is LTP developed by Information Retrieval Lab, Harbin Institution of Technology (http://ir.hit.edu.cn).

Inspired by the work of Yang, Zhou et al [4], we also introduce the definition of dependency schema and its application in metaphorical language formalization.

Definition 5 (Dependency Schema). Given a dependency tree, if we replace the word in the tree with its part of speech (pos) tag, and remove the dependency arc, then the resulting tree is its dependency schema.

We can show the process of the schematization through an example from Yang et al[4]: "他巴望着毕业就像囚犯巴望重获自由。" (He looks forward to graduation just as prisoners look forward to regaining freedom). Fig. 1 shows the dependency graph of this Chinese metaphor. And the corresponding dependency tree is shown in Fig.2. Accordingly, with definition 5, the dependency schema is shown in Fig.3.

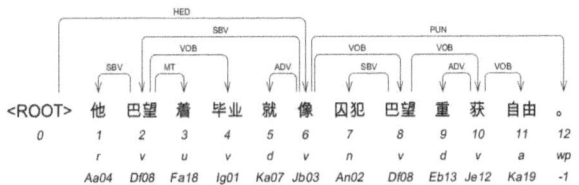

Fig. 1. The dependency graph

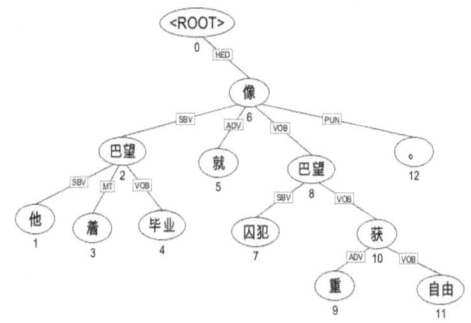

Fig. 2. The dependency tree

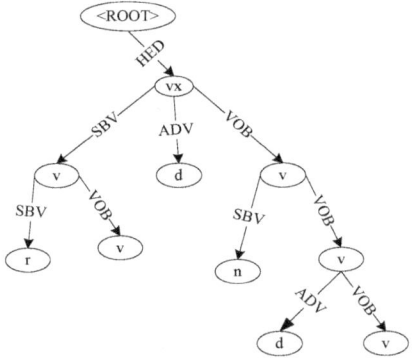

Fig. 3. The dependency schema

Dependency schema is helpful for us to analyze the constitution of sentences with different syntactic structures. As for metaphor utterances, we can tag the metaphor roles in the dependency schema. The dependency schema tagged with metaphor roles is called metaphor utterance dependency schema. We formalize the metaphor utterance dependency schema as M=(T, Met_T, Met_S, Met_G, Met_M), where T is the dependency tree of the metaphor utterance, and Met_* are metaphor roles, which are all sub trees of T. As shown in Fig.4, the sub trees with dashed circles are metaphor roles.

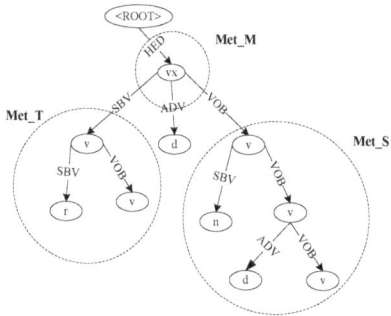

Fig. 4. The metaphor utterance dependency schema

3   The Classification System of Chinese Metaphors

Goatly[7] pointed out: "metaphor occurs when a unit of discourse is used to refer unconventionally to an object, process or concept, or colligates in an unconventional way". So, as to metaphorical language, metaphor can be triggered by unconventional denotation and unconventional collocation. According to this idea, Yang et al [4] classify Chinese metaphors into two main classes, namely unconventional referential metaphors with 21 subclasses and unconventional collocational metaphors with 11 subclasses. Their classification mainly depends on the linguistic constituents in a metaphor. For example, metaphors in structure like "A vx B" are categorized into 10 subclasses according to the linguistic constituents of A and B. This will bring out a problem: Because the constituents of A or B usually are very complicated, the classification is criticized for over-detailed with many subclasses [8].

Therefore, we reanalyze the metaphor dependency schemata used by [4], correct those unreasonable and wrong dependency relations, and merge the duplicated subclasses.

3.1   Referential Metaphors

At the conceptual level, referential metaphors can be classified into 4 basic classes: entity refers to entity; entity refers to event; event refers to entity; event refers to event. We regard entities as nouns and noun phrases in metaphor utterance dependency schema, and events as subject-predicate phrases or clauses.

(1) "A vx B" schema

In the classification system of Yang et al [4], according to the syntactic properties and constituents, schema "A vx B" is classified into 10 categories, the majority of which are decided for convenience of metaphor role tagging. In our view, they all can be boiled down to the following 4 basic classes:

a) *NP1 vx NP2*: In this class, both A and B are nominal phrases. It merges classes (1) and (2) in [4]. While tagging metaphor roles, the root of subtree NP1 is tagged as the target role Met_T of the metaphor, and NP2 as the source role Met_S, the indicating verb vx is tagged as the metaphor mark Met_M. At the conceptual level, this class belongs to "entity refers to entity".

b) *SP1 vx SP2*: In this class, SP1 and SP2 are subject-predicate phrases or clauses. At the conceptual level, SP1 and SP2 can be regarded as events, therefore, this class belongs to "event refers to event". As to metaphor roles tagging, SP1 is tagged as Met_T, SP2 as Met_S, and vx is still as Met_M.

c) *NP vx SP*: In this class, NP and SP represent nominal phrase and subject-predicate phrase respectively. Since NP can describe entities, and SP can describe events, this class can be regarded as "event refers to entity", where NP and SP are tagged as Met_T and Met_S respectively.

d) *SP vx NP*: This class means "entity refers to event".

The rest of referential metaphors with the form of "A vx B" in [4] can be put into the above 4 basic classes, and the additional constituents are treated as triggers of metaphor roles tagging.

(2) Indirect referential schema with indicating verbs as adverbial

In Chinese linguistics and rhetoric, there are a lot of researches on sentences with the form of "A 像B"(A is like B). Based on these achievements, combined with the properties of dependency grammar, we classify such metaphor schemata into 3 special indirect referential schemata.

a) A像B一样(**A is the same as B**): In this class, we treat "像..一样" as a frame which is tagged as metaphor mark role Met_M, then, according to the constituents of A and B, we can judge to which basic class it belongs.

b) *A 像B 一样P(A is as P as B)*: In this schema, P is the predicate constituent, which can be adjective phrase or verbal phrase. Here, A is Met_T, and B is Met_S. In general, P is salient features or actions of source domain(Met_S), therefore, we tag it as metaphor grounding(Met_G).

c) *A+P+得像+B(A is P as B)*: In this schema, the constituent "得像"(like as) is the complement of predicate P. The metaphor roles are similar to b).

The above three schemata can be further transformed as attributive structures, where the metaphor target role is the head word of the attributive structure.

After reorgnization in linguistic forms, the referential metaphors are classified into 10 subclasses. The details and examples of these schemata please refer to the Appendix B of [8].

3.2 Collocational Metaphors

Collocational metaphors are more perplexing than referential metaphors in linguistic forms. Referential metaphors usually are sentences or attributive structures with clauses as attributives, while collocational metaphors occur in any kind of linguistic unit, such as words, phrases and sentences etc. Wang [9] analyzed features of nominal phrase metaphors with the form of "n + n". Through the syntactic places where nominal metaphors appear in a sentence, she found nominal metaphors occur in object position, and seldom occur in subject position. Wang showed that we need conceptual knowledge to determine the source and target role of "n + n" nominal metaphors, otherwise, we cannot distinguish among metaphor roles [9, 10].

As to the types of collocation, collocational metaphors appear in subject-predicate collocation, predicate-object collocation, attributive-headword collocation, adverbial-headword collocation and verb-complement collocation.

In sum, we reorganize the current classification system of Chinese metaphor into 2 categories (referential metaphors and collocational metaphors) and 15 specific classes. All the class schemata are stored as metaphor role dependency schemata, and form a pattern knowledge base.

4   Pattern Matching Algorithm for Metaphor Identification

The pattern knowledge base contains the potential metaphor occurrences. In this section, we give the algorithm of metaphor identification based on pattern matching.

We denote a pattern tree as a 2-tuple T= (V, E) with root node as Root(T). Furthermore, T can be represented as $<t; T_1, T_2 \ldots T_k>$, where t=Root(T), k represents the out degree of T, namely the number of children of t, forest $< T_1, T_2 \ldots T_k>$ is the k subtree of T.

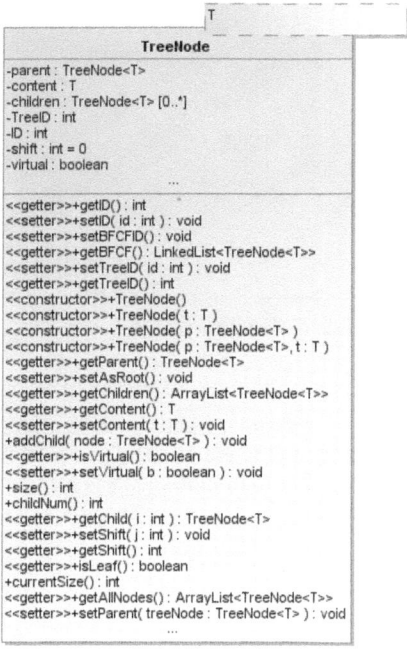

Fig. 5. Class diagram of TreeNode

A tree node is represented by class TreeNode, Fig.5 shows the class diagram of TreeNode. The field "content" is defined by CatItem which records the content of a node including word information such as POS, place, dependency relation, head etc. The comparison between two TreeNode is determined by POS and dependency relation, that is, if two nodes have the same POS and dependency relation, then they are identical.

Definition 6(Occurrence). Given tree T=(V, E) and pattern P=(Vp, Ep) with root as Root(T) and Root(P) respectively. Given $v \in V$ and $w \in Vp$, if v and w have the same content, namely v.getContent( )=w.getContent( ), we say that w has occurrence with v in T, denoted as <w, v>.

Definition 7(Tree Pattern Matching). Given tree T=(V, E) and pattern P=(Vp, Ep) with root as Root(T) and Root(P) respectively. For all $w \in Vp$, there is $v \in V$, such that <w, v> is an occurrence, and the following hold:

```
function NodeMatch
Input:Tree T=<V, E>, pattern P=<Vp, Ep>
Output: list of occurrences of nodes of P in T
1  tNodes=T.getAllNodes();
2  pNodes = P.getAllNodes();
3  for ( TreeNode pNode: pNodes )
4         inSubTree = false;
5         pList[pNode]= new ArrayList<TreeNode>();
6         for ( TreeNode tNode: tNodes)
7            if( tNode.getContent()==pNode.getContent())
8                inSubTree = true;
9                pList[pNode].add(tNode);
10        end if
11       end for
12       if (inSubTree == false )
13            pList=null;
14            break;
15       end if
16end for
17return pList;
```

Fig. 6. Pseudo codes of NodeMatch

(1) If <w, v> is an occurrence, and $w \neq Root(P)$, then the parents of w and v are also occurrence, namely <w.getParent(), v.getParent()> is an occurrence.
(2) If <w, v> is an occurrence, and w is not a leaf node, then for every child node p of w, there is a child node q of v, such that <p, q> is also an occurrence.

We say that tree T and pattern P are matching.

According to definition 6 and definition 7, we present the pattern matching algorithm. The algorithm involves two steps: the first step is processed by function NodeMatch, which finds all occurrences between nodes of pattern tree P and T based on definition 6; then according to definition 7, function MatchValidate executes the restrictions on the return value of NodeMatch, if all conditions are satisfied,

```
function MatchValidate
Input: List of occurrences of nodes of P in T, pList
Output: List of matching nodes between P and T
1  resultMatch=new TreeMap<TreeNode, TreeNode>;
2  for( TreeNode pNode: pList.keySet())
3     pMatches = pList[pNode];
4     for (TreeNode tNode: pMatches)
5       if ( pNode != Root(P))
6          parentMatches=pList[pNode.getParent()];
7             tParent = tNode.getParent();
8             if (tParent==null || parentMatches.contains(tParent)
9                pMatches.remove(tNode);
10            end if
11       else if (!pNode.isLeaf())
12            for(TreeNode pChild: pNode.getChildren())
13               childMatches = pList[pChild];
14               for(TreeNode tChild: childMatches)
15                  if(!tNode.getChildren().contains(tChild))
16                     pMatches.remove(tNode);
17                  end if
18               end for
19            end for
20       end if
21    end for
22 end for
23 for(TreeNode pNode: pList.keySet())
24    pMatches = pList[pNode];
25    for (TreeNode tNode: pMatches)
26       resultMatch[tNode] = pNode;
27    end for
28 end for
29 return resultMatch;
```

Fig. 7. Pseudo codes of MatchValidate

MatchValidate returns the set of all satisfied occurrences. The pseudo codes of NodeMatch and MatchValidate are shown in Fig.6 and Fig.7.

When a dependency tree is input and schematized, then through NodeMatch and MatchValidate, we can obtain the potential metaphor occurrence in the tree and the corresponding pattern number (namely the class id in the pattern knowledge base built in Section 3). Based on the result of this algorithm, the further processing of metaphor identification and tagging can proceed. As for the time complexity, we reduce the access time greatly by storing the parent node and child nodes of current tree node. According to the two steps, the time complexity is $O(2*k*m*n)$, where k is the number of patterns in the knowledge base, m is the node number of the input tree T, n is the average tree node number in the knowledge base, $n=(n_1+n_2+...+n_k)/k$. Comparred with the time complexity of $O(k*n*m^2)$ in reference [4], our algorithm is more efficient.

5   Metaphor Identification Process

The pattern matching algorithm detects all the possible metaphor occurrences and its category. In this section, we propose approaches to identify whether the input tree is a metaphor. We give quantified formulas for referential metaphors and collocational metaphors respectively.

5.1   Judgment for Referential Metaphors

After a tree is detected as a potential referential metaphor by matching algorithm, we use a variable called referential adaptability (RA) degree to determine whether it is a metaphor. Referential adaptability of a reference in form of "A vx B" means the reasonable degree of A referring to B. Frequently, a reference with higher RA is possibly a normal reference, while the one with lower RA is possibly an abnormal reference. According to the definition of metaphor in Goatly[7], RA can be used as a parameter to determine a metaphor. By applying research achievement in cognitive psychology, we use the hierarchical structure of concept to explain the normal and abnormal references. The hierarchical structure of concept is implemented by *isa* or *kindof* relation. In this paper, we use extended *Tongyici Cilin*[11, 12] as the resource of hierarchical structure. *Cilin* is a Chinese thesaurus, which includes about 77000 words that are structured as trees. The referential adaptability RA between two words is calculated by (1):

$$RA(w_1, w_2) = \frac{\left|level(w_1) - level(w_2)\right| + \sigma}{Dis(w_1, w_2) + \beta} \tag{1}$$

Where σ and β are smoothing parameters, $level(w)$ is the level of w in the hierarchy of *Cilin*, and $Dis(w_1, w_2)$ is the distance between w_1 and w_2 in *Cilin*, which is defined by (2):

$$Dis(w_1, w_2) = \sum_{i=1}^{level(w_1) - level(w)} \sigma_i + \sum_{j=1}^{level(w_2) - level(w)} \sigma_j \tag{2}$$

Where w is the least common parent of w_1 and w_2, σ_i is weight parameter for different level of *Cilin*, we set $\sigma = \beta = 1.2$, and σ_i $\{i=1,\ldots,5\}$ are $\{1, 1.1, 1.2, 1.4, 2.0\}$.

For example, we use (1) to calculate RA between "lawyer"(律师) and "fox" (狐狸) ,"occupation"(职业) respectively, namely RA("lawyer", "fox") and RA("lawyer", "occupation"). According to (2), we have Dis("lawyer", "fox")=1 and RA("lawyer", "fox")=10, then, according to (1), we obtain RA("lawyer", "fox")=1.0 and RA("lawyer", "fox")=0.2857. We set the threshold of RA as θ=0.7848, if $RA(w_1,w_2)$ >θ, then w_1 is normal referring to w_2, otherwise, we judge that there is a referential metaphor between w_1 and w_2. Therefore, "律师是狐狸"(lawyer is a fox) is a metaphor, while "律师是职业"(lawyer is an occupation) is not a metaphor.

5.2   Judgment for Collocational Metaphors

Collocation is an intricate issue in linguistics and NLP. Based on the definition of collocational metaphors given in section 3, we mainly focus on the collocation related to verbs. In Met*[13] and Meta5 [14], Fass proposed an approach to metaphor recognition based on the selectional restriction of verbs. Based on the idea of Fass[13, 14] and Yang et al.[15, 16], we present a case-based evaluation of collocation for recognition of collocational metaphors. We apply a variable called collocation adaptability (CA) degree to evaluate the reasonability of collocation between two words. CA is calculated by (3):

$$CA(w_1, w_2, r) = \max_{e_{w_1,r} \in S_{w_1,r}} sim(w_2, e_{w_1,r}) \tag{3}$$

Where, w_1 and w_2 are the head word and dependant word, r is the dependency relation, $S_{w_1,r}$ is the set of words which can be governed by w_1 through r. Words in $S_{w_1,r}$ are extracted from the collocation case base built by [16]. $sim(w, e)$ is the semantic similarity between w and e. We take the model proposed by Liu[17], which is based on Hownet[18]:

$$sim(S_1, S_2) = \sum_{i=1}^{4} \beta_i \prod_{j=1}^{i} sim_j(S_1, S_2) \tag{4}$$

Where S_1 and S_2 are the meanings of w and e respectively, $sim(w, e)$ selects the maximum similarity between their meanings. $Sim_j(S_1,S_2)$ is similarity between the j-th sememe, which is computed by (5):

$$sim(p_1, p_2) = \frac{\alpha}{d + \alpha} \tag{5}$$

Where $\alpha= 1.6, \beta_1=0.5, \beta_2=0.2, \beta_3=0.17, \beta_4=0.13$.

As an example, we show how to calculate the CA of a verb-object collocation "drinking mineral water"(喝矿泉水): firstly, we get the object set of "drink"(喝) from the collocation case base, S={tea(茶), soda water(汽水), spirit(白酒), plain boiled water(白开水), …,}, then compute similarity between "mineral water" and every word in S, and select the maximum $\max_{e \in S} sim("mineral water", e) = 1.0$ as the value of CA. As for the collocation "drinking ink"(喝 墨 水), we can obtain $CA = \max_{e \in S} sim("ink", e) = 0.2486$. We set the threshold of CA as $\rho=0.7$, if $CA(w_1,w_2) > \rho$, then w_1 and w_2 is a normal collocation, otherwise, we can judge that there is a collocational metaphor between w_1 and w_2.

6   Conclusions and Further Work

In this paper, we presented an improved classification system of Chinese metaphor based on dependency grammar, and proposed a novel tree pattern matching algorithm for detecting potential metaphor occurrences. Furthermore, we also proposed the detailed standards to determine the metaphor occurrences and classification.

In the future work, we will integrate this method of metaphor identification and classification into metaphor interpretation.

Acknowledgment. This research is supported in part by research grants from the Humanity and Social Sciences Foundation for Young Scholars of China's Ministry of Education (No.10YJCZH052), the Zhejiang Provincial Natural Science Foundation of China (NO.Y1080606), the Postdoctoral Science Foundation of China (No.20100481443), and the Humanity and Social Sciences Research Project of Zhejiang Provincial Educational Commission of China (NO.Y201010052).

References

1. Lakoff, G., Johnson, M.: Metaphors We Live By. The University of Chicago Press, Chicago (1980)
2. Shutova, E.: Models of Metaphor in NLP. In: Proceedings of the 48th Annual Meeting of the Association for Computational Linguistics, Uppsala, Sweden, pp. 688–697 (2010)
3. Li, J., Yang, Y., Zhou, C.: An Embedded Tree Matching Algorithm based on Metaphorical Dependency Structure. In: Proceedings of 2007 International Conference on Convergence Information Technology, pp. 607–611. IEEE Press, Los Alamitos (2007)
4. Yang, Y., Zhou, C., Ding, X., Chen, J., Shi, X.: Metaphor Recognition: CHMETA, A Pattern-based System. Computational Intelligence 25, 265–301 (2009)
5. Tesnière, L.: Elements de Syntaxe Structurale. Klincksieck, Paris (1959)
6. Kübler, S., McDonald, R., Nivre, J.: Dependency Parsing. Morgan & Claypool (2009)
7. Goatly, A.: The Language of Metaphors. Routledge, London (1997)
8. Huang, X.: Research on Some Key Issues of Metaphor Computation (in Chinese). Ph.D. Dissertation, Zhejiang University, Hangzhou (2009)
9. Wang, Z.: Chinese Noun Phrase Metaphor Recognition(in Chinese). Ph.D Dissertation. Beijing University, Beijing, China (2006)
10. Wang, Z.M., Wang, H., Duan, H., Han, S., Yu, S.-W.: Chinese Noun Phrase Metaphor Recognition with Maximum Entropy Approach. In: Gelbukh, A. (ed.) CICLing 2006. LNCS, vol. 3878, pp. 235–244. Springer, Heidelberg (2006)
11. Mei, J., Zhu, Y., Gao, Y., Yin, H.: Tongyici Cilin (in Chinese). Shanghai Lexicographic Publishing House, Shanghai (1996)
12. HIT-IRLab: TongYiCi CiLin (Extended_Version) (2005), http://ir.hit.edu.cn/
13. Fass, D.: Met*: A Method for Discriminating Metonymy and Metaphor by Computer. Computational Linguistics 17, 49–90 (1991)
14. Fass, D., Wilks, Y.: Preference Semantics, Ill-Formedness, and Metaphor. American Journal of Computational Linguistics 9, 178–187 (1983)
15. Yang, Y., Li, J., Zhou, C., Huang, X.: Example-based Discovery of Unconventional Chinese Semantic Collocations. Computer Science 35, 195–197 (2008)
16. Li, J., Yang, Y., Zhou, C.: Corpus Designing and Constructing for Metaphor Computation. Mind and Computation 1, 142–146 (2007)
17. Liu, Q., Li, S.: Word Similarity Computing Based on How-net. International Journal of Computational Linguistics & Chinese Language Processing 7, 59–76 (2002)
18. Dong, Z., Dong, Q.: Hownet And the Computation of Meaning. World Scientific Publishing Company, Singapore (2006)

A Decoding Method of System Combination Based on Hypergraph in SMT

Yupeng Liu, Sheng Li, and Tiejun Zhao

Machine Transaltion Lab, Harbin Institute of Technology
6F Aoxiao Building, NO.27 Jiaohua Street, Nangang District
Harbin, 150001, China
ypliu@mtlab.hit.edu.cn, lisheng@hit.edu.cn,
tjzhao@mtlab.hit.edu.cn

Abstract. The word level system combination, which is better than phrase level and sentence level, has emerged as a powerful post-processing method for statistical machine translation (SMT). This paper first give the definition of HyperGraph(HG) as a kind of compact data structure in SMT, and then introduce simple bracket transduction grammar(SBTG) for hypergraph decoding. To optimize the more feature weights, we introduce minimum risk (MR) with deterministic annealing (DA) into the training criterion, and compare two classic training procedures in experiment. The deoding approaches of n-gram model based on hypergraph are shown to be superior to conventional cube pruning in the setting of the Chinese-to-English track of the 2008 NIST Open MT evaluation.

Keywords: System combination, HyperGraph, N-gram model, Inside-outside Pruning.

1 Introduction

System combination[2][9][22] aims to find consensus translations among different statistical machine translation (SMT) systems. It has been proven that such consensus translations are usually better than the translation output of individual systems. Confusion network(CN) for word-level combination is a widely adopted approach for combining SMT output, which was shown to outperform sentence re-ranking methods and phrase-level combination[2]. In order to construct confusion network, word alignment between a skeleton (or backbone) and a hypothesis is a key technic in this approach. The important alignment methods include Translation Edit Rate (TER)[19] based alignment, which is proposed in Sim et al. (2007) and often taken as the baseline, and a couple of other approaches, such as the Indirect Hidden Markov Model (IHMM)[23] and the ITG-based alignment[6], which are recently proposed with better results reported. Joint optimization[24] integrates CN construction and CN-based decoding into a decoder without skeleton selection. Lattice-based system combination[10] model normalizes the alignment between the skeleton and the hypothesis CN into the lattice without breaking the phrase structure.

H. Deng et al. (Eds.): AICI 2011, Part III, LNAI 7004, pp. 115–125, 2011.
© Springer-Verlag Berlin Heidelberg 2011

In this paper, we start from the view of decoding, and introduce a hypergraph decoding algorithm of system combination which runs in a bottom-up manner. This algorithm parses the target words in the order of CN with reordered words and inserted *null* words. The hypergraph decoding based on system combination is different from the conventional decoding algorithm, in particular:

- The formal grammar is used in hypergraph-based system combination. Hypergraph is generally used by parsing and machine translation [17-18]. The algorithm produces the hypergraph by simple bracket transduction grammar (SBTG) with lexical and non-terminal rules.
- Two pass decoding algorithm is adopted in the framework. The first pass uses a 5-gram language model, and the resulting parse hypergraph is used in the second pass to guide search with the re-estimated n-gram probability. We can rescore the derivation through original viterbi model and re-estimated n-gram model, using the product of inside and outside probability.
- MR with/without DA, which attempts the solution of increasingly difficult optimization problem, is introduced in hypergraph decoding, because of fitting the curve of the probability distribute of log-linear model better and solving the large feature number.

This paper is structured as follows. We will first, in Section 2, give the definition of hypergraph; then in Section 3, we show decoding procedure including inside outside pruning, n-gram probablity re-estimation and decoding algorithm. In Section 4, experiment results and analysis are presented.

2   Hypergraph Definition

Formally, a hypergraph[17-18] in system combination is defined as a 4-tuple H=<V, E, G, R> , where V is a finite set of hypernode, E is a finite set of hyperedge, $G \in R$ is the unique goal item in H, and R is a set of weights. For a input sentence of target language $e_1^J = e_1, \ldots e_J$, each hypernode is in the form of X_i^j, which denotes the partial translation of target partial language $e_i, \ldots e_j$ spanning the substring from i-1 to j. Each hyperedge $e \in E$ is a triple tuple e=<T(e), h(e), w(e)>, where $T(e) \in V$ is a vector of tail nodes, $h(e) \in V$ is its head, and w(e) is a weight function from R|T(e)| to R.

Our hypergraph-based system combination is represented by simplified bracket transduction grammar (SBTG). Formally, the set of these hyperedges can be defined as a 3-tuple E=<T, N, P>, where T is a set of the terminal word symbol in target language, N is a set of the non-terminal symbol including three symbols N={S, X1, X2}, P is a set of production rules including two types:

- Lexical rule: X→w, w∈D
- Non-terminal rule : S→X1 X2,
                                     X→X1 X2

where D is a dictionary including null word (ε) for normalization in system combination, start symbol (G$\in$R) and single word. Non-terminal rule is like straight reordering in bracket transduction grammar [8].

2.1 Inside and Outside Prunning

The inside-outside algorithm is a way of re-estimating hyperedge probability in synchronous context-free grammar (SCFG). It was introduced as a generalization of the forward-backward algorithm for parameter estimation on Hidden Markov Models (HMM). It is used to compute expections, for example as part of the EM (expectation maximization) algorithm. Standard inside and outside recursion formulation is showed in Equation (1) and Equation (2), in which $I(v)$ and $O(v)$ is inside score and outside score in hypernode, $f(e)$ and $w(e)$ are feature and weight vector ,respectively, and $dim(f(e))$ is the dimension of feature vector. $IN(v)$ and $OUT(v)$ are incoming and outgoing hyperedge of v.

$$I(v) = \sum_{e \in IN(v)} \left[\sum_{dim(f(e))} f(e)w(e) \right] \cdot \left[\prod_{u \in T(e)} I(u) \right] \tag{1}$$

$$O(v) = \sum_{e \in OUT(v)} \left[\left(\sum_{dim(f(e))} f(e)w(e) \right) \times \left(O(h(e)) \prod_{\substack{u \in T(e) \\ u \neq v}} I(u) \right) \right] \tag{2}$$

Trough Equation (3), we can get the posterior probability of hyperedge including language model feature score, which is computed after its hypernode is generated. After coputing the posterior probability, we can prune these hyperedges whose probability is below the threshold. $P(e/F)$ is the posterior probability of specific hyperedge e, and p_e is the original weight of hyperedge e in hypergraph F, and Z is normalization factor that equals to the inside probability of the root node in F.

$$p(e \mid F) = \frac{1}{Z} p_e . O(h(e)) . \prod_{v \in T(e)} I(v) \tag{3}$$

The inside-outside algorithm for pruning and n-gram model is shown in Algorithm 1 and Algorithm 2.

Algorithm 1 Inside Recursion Algorithm
run from **bottom** to **top**
1: **for** $v \in F$
2:   $I(v) = 1$
3:   **for** $e \in IN(v)$

4:      $I_e(v) = p_e \cdot I_e(v)$

5:      **for** $u \in T(e)$

6:          $I_e(v) = I(u) \cdot I_e(v)$

7:      $I(v) = I(v) + I_e(v)$

8: **return** $I(v)$

Algorithm 2 Outside Recursion Algorithm
run from **top** to **bottom**
1: **for** $v \in F$
2. $O(v) = 1$
3:   **for** $e \in OUT(v)$
4:      $O_e(v) = p_e \cdot O(h(e))$
5:      **for** $u \in T(e)$
6:          **if** $u \neq v$
7:              $O_e(v) = I(u) \cdot O_e(v)$
8:      $O(v) = O(v) + O_e(v)$
9: **return** $O(v)$

2.2 N-Gram Probability

We adopt three types of n-gram estimation model and compare these models which are proposed by Li[26], which describes an algorithm for computing it through n-gram model, by Kumar[21],which describes an efficient approximate algorithm through the highest edge posterior probability relative to predecessors on all derivations in hypergraph, and by Dereno[12][13], which give the expectation count and exact algorithm. The n-gram estimation algorithm framework is shown in Algortihm 3.

Algorithm 3 N-gram Model/Posterior/Expectation Count Computation
run from **bottom** to **top**
1: run **inside** and **outside** algorithm
2: compute **hyperedge posterior probability** $P(e/F)$
3: for $v \in F$
3:   **for** $e \in IN(v)$
4:      **if** $w_n \in e$
5:          $ec_n(w) \mathrel{+}= p_w(e|F)$
6:          $ec_n(h(w)) \mathrel{+}= p_w(e|F)$

7: $p_n = \dfrac{ec_n(w)}{ec_n(h(w))}$

8: $q_n = \dfrac{ec_n(w)}{Z}$

9: **return** p_n as **n-gram model**

10: **return** $ec_n(w)$ as **n-gram expectation count**

11: **return** q_n as **n-gram posterior probability**

2.3 Decoding Algorithm

Different from conventional cube pruning[7], we use cube growing[16] to exploit the idea of lazy computation, which get n-best from top to bottom in hypergraph. Conceptually, complicate hypergraph decoding incorporates the following procedure:

1. Generating the hypergraph: generate all hypernodes and hyperedges inhypergraph F bottom-up in topological order. Every hypernode have many hyperedges with SBTG rule for phrase structure. According to the generating order of a target sentence, the decoding category is bottom-up[25]. Finally, the hypergraph has a distinguished goal item for convenient decoding.
2. Running inside recursion algorithm: for every hypernode, we compute the inside score from its hyperedges with tail nodes. The algorithm set the inside score of axiom item to zero, and run from bottom to top for the score through axiom item and inference rule[7].
3. Running outside recursion algorithm: for every hypernode, we compute the outside score of the hypernode, which might be the left or right branch of the parent hypernode(two non-terminal in SCFG).
4. Computing hyperedge posterior probability: according to inside and outside probability of hypernode and inside score of goal item and hyperedge weight, we compute the hyperedge posterior probability in hypergraph.
5. Inside-Outside pruning: to reduce the search space and improve the speed, pruning the hyperedges is important in the light of posterior probability. Our pruning strategy is including threshold and histogram. Pruning algorithm shows in above section.
6. Computing n-gram Probability: the method assume n-gram locality of the hypergraph, the property that any n-gram introduced by a hyperedge appears in all derivations that include the hyperedge and thus we apply the rule of edge e to n-grams on $T(e)$ and propagate n-1 gram prefixes or suffixes to $h(e)$.
7. Assigning scores to hyperedge: if the hyperedge introduce the ngram into the derivation, the n-gram probability is assigned to hyperedge for search k-best translation from hypergraph.
8. Reranking hyperedges in hypernode: we reestimate the n-gram model feature value by n-gram posterior probability and count expectation.
9. Finding the best path in the hypergraph: cube growing[16] compute the k-th best item in every cell lazily. But this algorithm still calculates a full k-th best item for

every hypernode in the hypergraph. We can therefore take laziness to an extreme by delaying the whole k-best calculation until after generating the hypergraph. The algorithm need two phases, which are forward that is same as viterbi decoding, but stores the hypergraph (keep many hyperedges in each hypernode) and backward phase that recursively ask what's your k-th best derivations from top to down.

The word posterior feature $f_s(arc)$ is the same as the one proposed by [2]. Other features used in our log-linear model include language model $f_{lm}=LM(e_i)$, real word count $f_{wc}=N_{word}(e_i)$ and ε word count $f_\varepsilon=N_{null}(e_i)$, where CN is confusion network. Equation (4) is decoding framework.

$$\log p(e \mid f) = \sum_{i=1}^{N_{arc}} \left[\log(\sum_{j=1}^{N_s} \lambda_j f_j (arc_i)) + \alpha LM(e_i) \right.$$

$$\left. + \beta N_{null}(e_i) + \gamma N_{word}(e_i) \right] \tag{4}$$

where f denote the source language, e denote the consensus translation generate by system combination. λ_i, α, β and γ is weight of other feature. Cube pruning algorithm with beam search is employed to search for consensus translation [16].

3 Experiments

In our chinese-english translation experiments, the candidate systems participating in the system combination are as listed in Table 1: Sys-1 uses a syntax-based decoder[1], informed by a source language dependency parse (Chinese); Sys-2 is a single-pass phrase-based system. The decoder uses a beam search to produce translation candidates left-to-right, incorporating future distortion penalty estimation and early pruning to limit the search[20]; Sys-3 is essentially the same as Sys-2 except that we apply a syntactic reordering system as a preprocessor to reorder Chinese sentences in training and test data in such a way that the reordered Chinese sentences are much closer to English in terms of word order. For a Chinese sentence, we first parse it using the Stanford Chinese Syntactic Parser [15], and then reorder it by applying a set of reordering rules, proposed by [3], to the parse tree of the sentence; Sys-4 is a syntax-based pre-ordering based MT system using a syntax-based pre-ordering model as described in [4]; Sys-5 is a hierarchical phrase-based system as described by [7]. It uses a statistical phrase-based translation model that uses hierarchical phrases; Sys-6 uses a lexicalized re-ordering model similar to the one described by [8]. It uses a maximum entropy model to predicate reordering of neighbor blocks (phrase pairs); Sys-7 is a two-pass phrase-based system with adapted LM proposed by Foster and Kuhn [11]. This system uses a standard two-pass phrase-based approach; Sys-8 is a hierarchical phrase-based system that uses a 4-gram language model in the first pass to generate n-best lists, which are rescored by three additional language models to generate the final translations via re-ranking.

Table 1. Performance of individual systems on the dev and test set

System ID	Dev(BLEU)	Test(BLEU)
Sys1	31.48	25.63
Sys2	31.41	26.78
Sys3	32.31	26.03
Sys4	30.55	27.38
Sys5	32.60	27.75
Sys6	28.99	22.86
Sys7	27.33	21.45
Sys8	28.91	22.67

3.1 Experimental Setup

The development set of experimental setup is NIST MT06 data set including 1099, and the test set of it is NIST MT08 data set including 1357 from both newswire and web-data genres. Both dev and test sets have four references per sentence. However, to save computation effort, the result on the dev and test set are reported in case insensitive BLEU score instead. The above system generates the 10-best of every sentence as input of system combination through the max-BLEU traning(MERT). The language model used for all models is a 5-gram model trained with Xinhua portion of LDC English Gigaword corpus version 3. We use incremental IHMM as baseline[5]. The parameter of incremental IHMM show in [5]. The lexical translation probabilities used in semantic similarity model are from a small portion (FBIS+GALE) of constrained track training data. The skeleton is select by MBR. The loss function used for incremental IHMM style is BLEU. As to incremental system, the default order of hypothesis is ascending according to BLEU score against the skeleton. We employ the distortion model in incremental IHMM[5]. When confusion network is built in training process, a set of word confident are added for decoding. Meanwhile, the decoder uses the features of word confident, language model, word penalty and null penalty.

We compare the system combination based on hypergraph decoding with conventional decoding style. The hypergraph decoder was implemented by modifying the classic CKY algorithm with cube growing[16].

3.2 Decoding Performance

During second-pass decoding, we use the same beam size as first pass decoding because the outside probability estimation of the second-pass decoding is discriminative enough to guide second-pass hypergraph decoding. We develop a unified algorithm of three n-gram probabilty which are n-gram model (denoted by ngram_1), n-gram count expection (denoted by ngram_2) and n-gram posterior probability (denoted by ngram_3), and then compare the performance of them.

The Effect of *n*-gram Model: as shown in Table 2, decoding with *1*-5-gram+*wp* (word penalty denoted by *wp*) model of different estimation methods improve (+0.94, +0.63 and +0.57 BLEU score) over baseline on the development set, and we achieve an absolute improvement (+1.16, +1.17 and +1.13 BLEU score) on the test set. The experimental result proves that n-gram feature is effective.

The effect of Viterbi model can be seen through comparing Table 3 with Table 2. The various interpolation models show an improvement of +0.25, +0.3 and +0.27 BLEU points over model without Viterbi on the development set, and +0.25, +0.13 and +0.04 BLEU point on test set. If we compare it with baseline (incremental IHMM), the best performance of three types of n-gram probability can be obtained when the setting is $Vi+1-5$gram_$1+wp$. It obtains +1.19 and +1.41 BLEU score on the development and test set respectively.

The experimental results prove the efficiency of n-gram and Viterbi+n-gram model.

Table 2. The quality of second-pass decoding on the development and test set

n-gram model	NIST06	NIST08
Baseline	39.34	32.82
*1-5*gram_$1+wp$	40.28	33.98
*1-5*gram_$2+wp$	39.97	33.99
*1-5*gram_$3+wp$	39.91	33.95

Table 3. The quality of second-pass decoding with Viterbi baseline on the development and test set

Viterbi+n-gram	NIST06	NIST08
$Vi+1-5$gram_$1+wp$	40.53	34.23
$Vi+1-5$gram_$2+wp$	40.27	34.12
$Vi+1-5$gram_$3+wp$	40.18	33.99

The Effect of MR with DA: MR with DA is introduces by [27], but it apply in SMT and don't compare performance of these scheme. We compare the five training schema: MERT vs. MR with different setting, which are with/without DA, with/without quenching scaling factor λ and on hypergraph. With the entropy constrains, starting temperature $T=1000$; quenching temperature $T=0.001$. The temperature is cooled by half at each step; then we double λ at each step. Once T is quite cool, it is common in practice to switch to rising λ directly and rapidly until some convergence condition. We optimize feature weight vector $\boldsymbol{\theta}$ and hyperparameter λ through BFGS optimization.

The configures of the experiment use the interpolation between $1-5$gram_1 and Viterbi model. We compare five settings on the development in Figure 1 and the test set in Table 4. MERT, MR without DA&quenching, MR&DA without quenching, MR&DA with quenching and MR&DA with quenching on HG achieve a BLEU score of 40.53, 40.17, 40.37, 40.50 and 40.50 on the development set. The best performance can be obtained by MERT on the development set, and meanwhile the worst performance can be obtained by it on test set. The fact proves the overfitting of MERT. The reason of decreased performance of 2-th iteration MR with DA is the initialization bias.

Table 4. The MERT and MR with/without DA performance of the test set

Training Criterion	NIST08
MERT	34.23
MR without DA&queching	34.24
MR&DA without quenching	34.28
MR&DA with quenching	34.29
MR&DA with quenching on HG	34.29

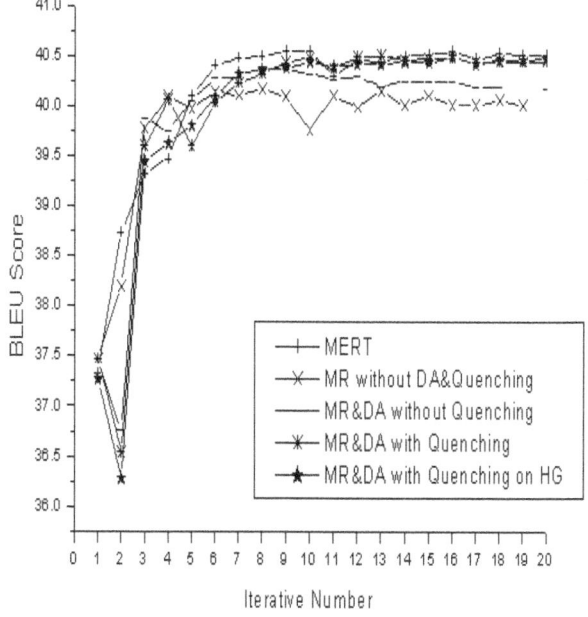

Fig. 1. The MERT and MR with/without DA performance on the development set

Compared to MERT, MR&DA on HG has almost the same performance on test set because of a small number of features[27] or a sparse feature of the non-terminal rule which only includes language model probability. In total, MR&DA on HG outperform baseline (incremental IHMM) using Cube Pruning up to +1.47 in BLEU score.

4 Conclusion

This paper proposed hypergraph_based decoding method in word–level system combination, and then compare a set of n-gram feature on hypergraph for two-pass decoding. The hypergraph decoding includes three types of n-gram probabilities, which are n-gram calculating style. The method is evaluated against state-of-the-art baselines including classic incremental IHMM on the NIST MT06 and MT08 C2E tasks. We also use HG-based MR with/without DA training, which solve the overfitting to objective function and a large number of features. The two-pass hypergraph decoding is shown to outperform cube pruning style decoding significantly. We ontain 1.28 and 1.59 BLEU score improvement in dev and test set through two-pass decoding using HG-based MR training.

Since our training algorithm can cope with a large number of features, in future work, we plan to incorporate more expressive features and hypergraph training in the model. We combine the different system combination model, which has the different expressive ability.

References

1. Menezes, A., Quirk, C.: Using Dependency Order Templates to Improve Generality in Translation. In: Proc. 2nd WMT at ACL, Prague, Czech Republic (2007)
2. Rosti, A.-V.I., Matsoukas, S., Schwartz, R.: Improved Word-level System Combination for Machine Translation. In: Proceedings of ACL (2007)
3. Wang, C., Collins, M., Koehn, P.: Chinese Syntactic Reordering for Statistical Machine Translation. In: EMNLP 2007 (2007)
4. Li, C.-H., Zhang, D., Li, M., Zhou, M., Li, C.-H., Li, M., Guan, Y.: A Probabilistic Approach to Syntax-based Reordering for Statistical Machine Translation. In: Proceedings of ACL (2007)
5. Li, C.-H., He, X., Liu, Y., Xi, N.: Incremental HMM Alignment for MT System Combination. In: Proceedings of ACL (2009)
6. Karakos, D., Eisner, J., Khudanpur, S., Dreyer, M.: Machine Translation System Combination using ITG-based Alignments. In: Proceedings of ACL (2008)
7. Chiang, D.: Hierarchical Phrase-based Translation. Computational Linguistics 33(2) (2007)
8. Xiong, D., Liu, Q., Lin, S.: Maximum Entropy based Phrase Reordering Model for Statistical Machine Translation. In: Proceedings of COLING/ACL 2006, Sydney, Australia, pp. 521–528 (July 2006)
9. Matusov, E., Ueffing, N., Ney, H.: Computing Consensus Translation from Multiple Machine Translation Systems using Enhanced Hypothesis Alignment. In: Proceedings of EACL (2006)
10. Feng, Y., Liu, Y., Mi, H., Liu, Q., Lu, Y.: Lattice-based System Combination for Statistical Machine Translation. In: Proceedings of ACL (2009)
11. Foster, G., Kuhn, R.: Mixture-Model Adaptation for SMT. In: Proc. of the Second ACL Workshop on Statistical Machine Translation, pp. 128–136 (2007)
12. Denero, J., Chiang, D., Knight, K.: Fast Consensus Decoding over Translation Forest. In: Proceedings of ACL (2009)

13. DeNero, J., Kumar, S., Chelba, C., Och, F.: Model Combination for Machine Translation. In: Proceedings of NAACL (2010)
14. Sim, K.C., Byrne, W.J., Gales, M.J.F., Sahbi, H., Woodland, P.C.: Consensus Network Decoding for Statistical Machine Translation System Combination. In: Proc. of ICASSP, pp. 105–108 (2007)
15. Levy, R., Manning, C.: Is It Harder To Parse Chinese, or The Chinese Treebank? Published in Proceedings of ACL 2003 (2003)
16. Huang, L., Chiang, D.: Better k-best Parsing. In: Proceedings of the International Workshop on Parsing Technologies (IWPT), pp. 53–64 (2005)
17. Huang, L., Chiang, D.: Forest Rescoring: Faster Decoding with Integrated Language Models. In: Proceedings of ACL, Prague, Czech Rep. (2007)
18. Huang, L.: Forest reranking: Discriminative parsing with Non-local Features. In: Proc. of (2008)
19. Snover, M., Dorr, B., Schwartz, R., Micciulla, L., Makhoul, J.: A Study of Translation Edit Rate with Targeted Human Annotation. In: Proceedings of AMTA (2006)
20. Moore, R., Quirk, C.: Faster Beam-Search Decoding for Phrasal Statistical Machine Translation. In: Proc. of MT Summit XI (2007)
21. Kumar, S., Macherey, W., Dyer, C., Och, F.: Efficient Minimum Error Rate Training and Minimum Bayes-Risk Decoding for Translation Hypergraphs and Lattices. In: Proceedings of ACL, pp. 163–171 (2009)
22. Bangalore, S., Bordel, G., Riccardi, G.: Computing Consensus Translation from Multiple Machine Translation Systems. In: Workshop on Automatic Speech Recognition and Understanding, Madonna di Campiglio, Italy, pp. 351–354 (2001)
23. He, X., Yang, M., Gao, J., Nguyen, P., Moore, R.: Indirect-HMM based Hypothesis Alignment for Combining Outputs from Machine Translation Systems. In: Proc. of EMNLP (2008)
24. He, X., Toutanova, K.: Joint Optimization for Machine Translation System Combination. In: Proc. of EMNLP (2009)
25. Liu, Y., Mi, H., Feng, Y., Liu, Q.: Joint Decoding with Multiple Translation Models. In: Proc. of ACL, pp. 576–584 (2009)
26. Li, Z., Eisner, J., Khudanpur, S.: Variational Decoding for Statistical Machine Translation. In: Proceedings of ACL (2009a)
27. Li, Z., Eisner, J.: First- and Second-order Expectation Semirings with Applications to Minimum-Risk Training on Translation Forests. In: Proceedings of EMNLP (2009b)

Automatically Ranking Reviews Based on the Ordinal Regression Model

Bing Xu, Tie-Jun Zhao, Jian-Wei Wu, and Cong-Hui Zhu

School of Computer Science and Technology,
Harbin Institute of Technology
Harbin, China
{xb,tjzhao,jwwu,chzhu}@mtlab.hit.edu.cn

Abstract. With the rapid development of Internet and E-commerce, the quantity of product reviews on the web grows very fast, but the review quality is inconsistent. This paper addresses the problem of automatically ranking reviews. A specification for judging the reviews quality is first defined and thus ranking review is formalized as ordinal regression problem. In this paper, we employ Ranking SVM as the ordinal regression model. To improve system performance, we capture many important features, including structural features, syntactic features and semantic features. Experimental results indicate that Ranking SVM can obviously outperform baseline methods. For the identification of low-quality reviews, the Ranking SVM model is more effective than SVM regression model. Experimental results also show that the unigrams, adjectives and product features are more effective features for modeling.

Keywords: Sentiment Analysis, Review Ranking, Ordinal Regression model, SVM Ranking.

1 Introduction

With the rapid development of Internet and E-commerce, the quantity of product reviews on the web grows very fast, but the review quality is inconsistent. Due to the fact that the number of reviews is too large, sometimes it is impossible for the users to read each comment by themselves. Especially, when some useful reviews locate at the end of all the reviews, the user may not be patient enough to find and read them. So it is very important to evaluate the quality of product reviews and rank reviews.

Ranking reviews is different from ranking search results. Because reviews are directly relevant to the product in the ranking reviews, assessing relevance is no longer important. Users want to browse the useful information such as product quality, service, etc. from reviews. Therefore, providing the detailed and multi-point subjective reviews is very valuable for users. A key problem of ranking reviews is how to determine which review is helpful and valuable, and then rank it to the top of review list.

Most websites can provide several ways of ranking reviews, including publication time, the number of voting according to the review helpfulness, the number of

H. Deng et al. (Eds.): AICI 2011, Part III, LNAI 7004, pp. 126–134, 2011.

responses reviews, product rating, etc. In contrast with other ways, manual voting is a more effective measure of providing valuable reviews for users. For example, on dangdang.com website, an interface allows customers to vote whether a particular book review is helpful or not. However, the issue of manual voting is that newly published reviews are always ranked at the bottom of the reviews and can not easily be found. The accumulation of votes takes time for a review to be listed at the front. So an automatically method for ranking reviews is very useful for ranking the new reviews and rarely voted reviews. Existing studies [1] [2] used these users' votes for training ranking models to assess the quality of reviews, which therefore are suffered from bias, including the imbalance vote bias, the winner circle bias, and the early bird bias.

In this paper, we propose a standard to assess the quality of book reviews and apply SVM Ranking to rank the book reviews. Firstly, the specification of reviews quality is defined, and then different classes of features are selected for modeling, including structural, lexical, syntactic, semantic features. Experiment results show that the proposed approach can rank high quality reviews to the front effectively.

The rest of the paper is organized as follows: Section 2 introduces the related work. In Section 3, we describe the specification of assessing the reviews quality and ordinal regression model. Section 4 reports experimental results and analysis. Section 5 summarizes our work in the paper and points out the future work.

2   Related Work

The task of ranking product reviews is related to a variety of research areas, including evaluation of reviews quality, opinion mining and learning to rank etc.

In the recent years, the evaluation of reviews quality attracts more and more researchers' attentions. Most researchers considered the problem as a ranking and solved it with classification, regression models etc. [1-7]. Liu et al. adopt SVM classification model to discriminate low-quality from high-quality reviews and define a standard specification to measure the quality of product reviews. Kim et al. and Zhang et al. presented SVM regression model to rank reviews and used the assessing information derived from users' votes of helpfulness provided by websites in the training and testing processing. Liu et al. proposed a nonlinear regression model for the helpfulness prediction and depended on three groups of factors to build model. The experimental results showed that their model is better than the SVM regression model. Zhang et al. proposed a linear model to predict the helpfulness of online product reviews. Lim et al. used scoring methods to measure the degree of spam for detecting users generating spam reviews or review spammers.

In domain of opinion mining, the focus is on distinguishing between subjective and objective texts, and mining polarity and opinions in product reviews [8-11]. Pang et al. examined several supervised machine learning methods for sentiment classification of movie reviews. Turney applied an unsupervised machine learning technique based on mutual information between document phrases and the words "excellent" and "poor" to find indicative words expressing opinions for classification. Liu and Popescu extracted and summarized users' opinions from product reviews. A sentence or a text segment in the reviews is considered as the basic unit that includes extracted opinion feature and its polarity of users' sentiments.

Learning to rank or machine-learned ranking is a type of supervised problem that is to automatically construct a ranking model from training data. Ranking models have been applied in many areas, such as information retrieval, sentiment analysis and machine translation [12] [13]. Herbrich et al. [14] proposed a new learning algorithm for the task of ordinal regression based on large margin rank boundaries. In his paper, this method is applied to the information retrieval task that is learning the order of documents according to an initial query. Joachims [15] proposed learning a ranking function for search as ordinal regression using click-through data. The Ranking SVM model is employed for ordinal regression.

In this paper, we formalize the ranking of review quality as ordinal regression and employed Ranking SVM model for implementation.

3   Modeling Review Quality

Firstly, let us formalize the problem of ranking of review quality. Given a training data set $D = \{x_i, y_i\}_{i=1}^{n}$, we construct a model that can minimize error in prediction of y given x. Here $x_i \in X$ and $y_i \in \{excellent, good, fair, bad\}$ represent a review and a label, respectively. When applied a new instance x, the model predicts the corresponding y and outputs the score of the prediction.

3.1   Ranking SVM Model

Classifying instances into the categories, "excellent", "good", "fair", "bad", is problem of a typical ordinal regression, for there is an order between the four categories.

Ranking SVM is employed as the model of ordinal regression. Given an instance x, Ranking SVM assigns a score to it based on

$$U(x) = \omega^T x \tag{1}$$

Where ω represents a vector of weights. The higher the value of $U(x)$ is, the better the quality of the instance x is. In ordinal regression, the value of $U(x)$ are mapped into intervals on the real line and the intervals correspond to the ordered categories. An instance that falls into one interval is classified into the corresponding ordered category. In our method of opinion ranking, we adopt scores output by a Ranking SVM.

3.2   Specification of Quality

In this section, four categories of review quality are defined, including "excellent review", "good review", "fair review" and "bad review". The different definitions of review quality represent different values of the reviews to users' purchase decision.

An excellent review is a comprehensive and detailed review or a relatively complete and detailed review on a product. It describes most aspects of a product and gives credible opinions with sufficient evidence. Usually an excellent review will be served as the main reference by users before making their purchase decision.

A good review presents some aspects of the product, but it is not a complete and detailed evaluation. It only supplies a brief description which can not offer users sufficient reference on a product.

A fair review contains a brief description on an aspect of the product. It often occurs with a short sentence and only provides less information.

A bad review is an unhelpful description that can be ignored on a product. It talks about some topic that is not related to the product. Sometimes users spend a lot of time to read, but do not get any valuable information.

3.3 Feature Selection

We experimented with seven features, including structural, lexical, syntactic and semantic features. Table 1 shows the list of the features.

Lexical feature captures the unigram feature of word. We calculate number of each word occurring in the review.

The number of sentences treated as the structural feature represents review length. This feature is considered to be related with information content of review.

Syntactic feature aims to capture the linguistic features of the review. In grammar, part-of-speech of a word is a linguistic category defined by its syntactic or morphological behavior. Common POS categories are: noun, verb, adjective, adverb .etc. In the syntactic features, the numbers of adjective and adverb tokens are calculated.

Table 1. Description of Feature Set

ID	Feature Set
1	The occurring frequency of each word in a review
2	The number of sentences in a review
3	The number of adverb in a review
4	The number of adjective in a review
5	The number of sentiment word in a review
6	The number of product features in a review
7	The occurring frequency of product features in a review

We hypothesized the high quality review will include the product features and sentiment words information, frequency and the number of product features are calculated and treated as the semantic features in the review. Product features in the review are better indicator of review quality. However, product feature extraction is not an easy task. In this paper, we adopt an unsupervised clustering approach to extract product features. Firstly, we adopt the shallow parser to identify noun phrases from reviews, and then k-means clustering approach is used to group noun phrase. To avoid the side effect of arbitrarily selecting the initial cluster centers, some representative product features are selected as the initial cluster centers. Experiment shows that supervised selecting of the cluster centers can increase precision of product attribute clustering. But there are many noise data in product features extracted by clustering. We remove these noun phrases that are far from cluster centers by setting the threshold. Finally, we check identification results manually for high performance.

Sentiment words are positive and negative words that correlate with product names and product features. We capture these features by extracting sentiment words using the publicly available list from the Hownet[1]. On one hand, the features of sentiment words help to distinguish subjective reviews from all reviews. On the other hand, the number of sentiment words is larger in a high quality review.

4 Experiment

In this section, we will describe our experimental setup, show our results and analyze performance.

4.1 Experiment Data

We use Ranking SVM model to verify the effectiveness of the proposed approach of review ranking. Because there is no standard data set for evaluation, we randomly collected 50 books as samples from a famous book-store website-dangdang.com.[2] After filtering the duplicated reviews, we got 2907 reviews and created a data set. Table 2 shows statistics on the data.

Table 2. Statistics of Review Quality

Review	Number
Number of reviews	2907
Number of excellent reviews	188
Number of good reviews	1592
Number of fair reviews	860
Number of bad reviews	330

Two annotators labeled the review independently with our definitions of review quality as their guideline. The value of kappa statistic is used to validate the effectiveness of labels by human. We found the two annotators achieved highly consistent results according to 0.8806 kappa value.

4.2 Measure of Evaluation

Evaluating the quality of ranking reviews is difficult. Five measures for evaluation of review ranking are adopted, including NDCG (Normalized Discounted Cumulative Gain), modified R-precision measures and Error_rate.

The following give the details.

$$NDCG @ n = Z_n \sum_{j=1}^{n} \begin{cases} 2^{r(j)} - 1, & j=1,2 \\ (2^{r(j)} - 1)/\log(1+j), & j > 2 \end{cases} \tag{2}$$

---

[1] http://www.keenage.com/

Where j is the position in the review list, r(j) is the score of the j-th review in the review list, and Zn is a normalizing factor.

R-precision is precision at rank R. Where R is the total number of same score reviews from the book. In the experiment, we calculate the three modified R-precision measures for different value of reviews.

$$R\text{-}precision\_E\,(book_i) = \frac{\left|\text{"excellent" reviews at R top ranked reviews}\right|}{R} \tag{3}$$

Where R is the number of "excellent"reviews from book$_i$.

$$R\text{-}precision\_E\,\&\,G\,(book_i) = \frac{\left|\text{"excellent" and "good" reviews at R top ranked reviews}\right|}{R} \tag{4}$$

Where R is the number of "excellent"and "good" reviews from book$_i$.

$$R\text{-}precision\_B\,(book_i) = \frac{\left|\text{"bad" reviews at R bottom ranked reviews}\right|}{R} \tag{5}$$

Where R is the number of "bad" reviews from book$_i$.

$$R\text{-}precision = \frac{\sum_{i=1}^{T} R\text{-}precision(book_i)}{T} \tag{6}$$

Where T is the number of books in data set. Using the formula (3), (4) and (5), we got R-precision_E, R-precision_E&G and R-precision_B.

Error_rate represents the error rate of all ranked pairs.

$$Error\_rate = \frac{\left|\text{error pairs at ranked reviews}\right|}{\left|\text{all pairs at ranked reviews}\right|} \tag{7}$$

4.3   System Performance and Analysis

In the experiment, we use 5-fold cross validation. The 50 books and their corresponding reviews are divided randomly into five subsets. One of the five subsets was treated as the test set and the other four subsets were combined to form a training set. The ranking model is trained on the training set and tested on the test set.

We use two baseline methods to compare performance of ordinal regression model for ranking review, including regression model and method of helpfulness voting from customers. For ordinal regression model and regression model, SVM ranking and SVM regression tool SVM^{light} is deployed. The linear, polynomial and radial basis function (RBF) kernels are tested on development data respectively. Finally, we find that the best results are shown using the linear kernel. Table 3 reports the average results of the five trials for all features combination with 95% confidence bounds.

In table 3, we find that both Ranking SVM and SVM regression outperform Voting method significantly. The results show that ordinal regression and regression models are significant and effective for review ranking. In particular, the results of Ranking SVM indicate that ordinal regression model is more effective than regression model with our all features in the five evaluation measures, but R-precision_E is different

Table 3. Results of Book Reviews Ranking

Evaluation Measures	Voting Method	SVM Regression	Ranking SVM
NDCG-10	0.6443	0.8708	**0.8840**
NDCG-20	0.6713	0.8847	**0.8959**
R-precision_E	0.1829	**0.4358**	0.4230
R-Precision_E&G	0.6281	0.8418	**0.8643**
R-precision_B	0.1443	0.3575	**0.5311**
Error_rate	0.4484	0.1492	**0.1266**

from other measures. Therefore we conclude that SVM regression is better to identify the excellent reviews, and Ranking SVM is more efficient to rank the top-10 and top-20 reviews. For bad reviews, Ranking SVM has more advantages over SVM regression.

To compare the effectiveness of individual features, we analyze the R-precision_E&G and the R-precision_B drop when each feature is removed from Ranking SVM and SVM regression in the Fig.1 and the Fig.2. The description of features is shown in Table 1.

From Fig.1 and Fig.2, we can find that the effectiveness of each feature is similar for Ranking SVM and SVM regression. The performance drops significantly when feature 1, 4, 6 and 7 is removed. So unigram features (feature 1) are very important for the ranking task. Comparing with unigram features, we didn't add bigram features since they are suffered from the data sparsity of short reviews. We can also find that the adjective feature (Feature 4) is an active feature, but the feature of sentiment word (feature 5) and the adverb feature (Feature 3) are negative features. The more adjectives a review has the more likely the review is good. On the other hand, negative effect of the sentiment word feature likely comes from adverb because the sentiment words include the adjectives and adverbs. The product feature (Feature 6 and 7) is an important semantic feature and their occurrence in a review correlate with review quality. In the high quality user-generated product review, the role of product feature becomes more effective.

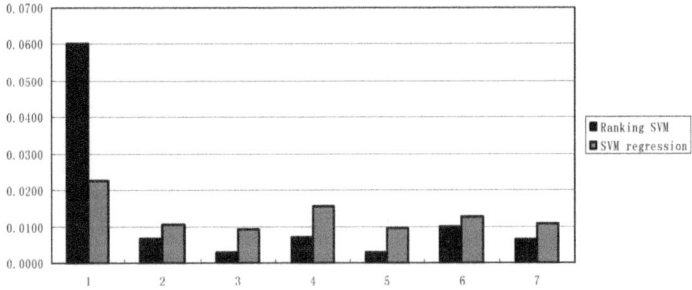

Fig. 1. The Results of R-precision_E&G Drop

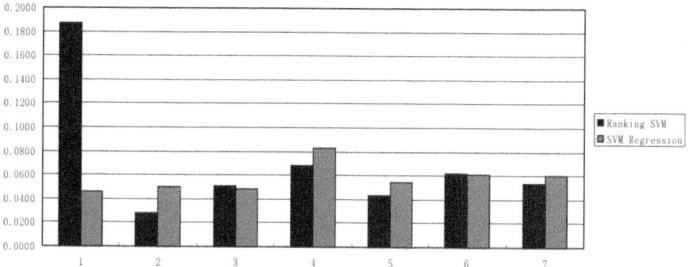

Fig. 2. The Results of R-precision_B Drop

Finally, we analyze the error results of Ranking SVM and SVM regression. We find that few subjective reviews sorted at the top are not associated with the book discussed. These reviews describe another book and were recommended to customers. In fact, these reviews should be labeled as "bad reviews". But this problem can not be solved using our proposed approach. Moreover, we also find that limitation of the features and annotation errors deteriorate the performance of ranking reviews.

5   Conclusion

For many online websites of product reviews, ranking review according to review quality is a key issue. But ranking of voting according to user helpfulness can not list these new and good reviews on the top in a short time. This paper proposed a new approach to automatically evaluate quality and rank review. Firstly, the specification of review quality is defined and a corresponding score is labeled. We trained a Ranking SVM system using the several effective features and then applied them to rank unlabeled reviews. For the task of ranking reviews, we use NDCG, three modified R-precision measures and proposed error rate to effectively assess the ranking results. Experimental results indicate that Ranking SVM outperforms the voting method significantly and is better than the SVM regression in the five measures. We also give a detailed analysis of effectiveness of each feature and conclude that unigrams, adjectives and product features are most useful.

In the future work, we hope to propose better discriminating standard for different reviews and validate the effectiveness of ranking reviews in other applications.

Acknowledgments. This work is supported by the National Natural Science Foundation of China (No. 61073130) and the National High-Tech Development 863 Program of China (No. 2006AA010108) and MOE-MS Key Laboratory Opening Funding of Natural Language Processing and Speech (HIT.KLOF.2009019).

References

1. Kim, S.M., Pantel, P., Chklovski, T., Pennacchiotti, M.: Automacically Assessing Review Helpfulness. In: Proceedings of the 2006 Conference on Empirical Methods in Natural Language Processing, pp. 423–430 (2006)

2. Liu, J.J., Cao, Y.B., Li, C.Y., Huang, Y.L., Zhou, M.: Low-Quality Product Review Detection in Opinion Summarization. In: Proceedings of the 2007 Joint Conference on Empirical Methods in Natural Language Processing and Computational Natural Language Learning, pp. 334–342 (2007)

3. Zhang, R.C., Thomas, T.: Helpful or Unhelpful: A Linear Approach for Ranking Product Reviews. Journal of Electronic Commerce Research 11(3), 220–230 (2010)

4. Zhang, Z., Varadarajan, B.: Utility Scoring of Product Reviews. In: CIKM 2006, pp. 52–57 (2006)

5. Liu, Y., Huang, X., An, A., Yu, X.: Modeling and Predicting the Helpfulness of Online Reviews. In: Proceedings of the 8th International Conference on Data Mining, pp. 443–452 (2008)

6. Lim, E.-P., Nguyen, V.-A., Jindal, N., et al.: Detecting product review spammers using rating behaviors. In: Proceedings of the International Conference on information and Knowledge Management (2010)

7. Lei, Z., Bing, L., Hwan, L.S., O'Brien-Strain, E.: Extacting and Ranking Product Features in Opinion Documents. In: Coling 2010, pp. 1462–1470 (2010)

8. Pang, B., Lee, L., Vaithyanathan, S.: Thumbs up? Sentiment Classification Using Machine Learning Techniques. In: EMNLP 2002, pp. 79–86 (2002)

9. Turney, P.: Thumbs up or Thumbs Down? Semantic Orientation Applied to Unsupervised Classification of Reviews. In: ACL 2002, pp. 417–424 (2002)

10. Liu, B., Hu, M., Cheng, J.: Opinion Observer: Analyzing and Comparing Opinions on the Web. In: Proc. International World Wide Web Conference, pp. 342–351 (May 2005)

11. Popescu, A.M., Etzioni, O.: Extracting Product Features and Opinions from Reviews. In: Proceedings of Empirical Methods in Natural Language Processing, pp. 339–346 (2005)

12. Xu, J., Cao, Y.-B., Li, H., Zhao, M., Huang, Y.-L.: A supervised Learning Approach to Search of Definations. Journal of Computer Science and Technology 21(3), 439–449 (2006)

13. Liu, T.-Y.: Learning to Rank for Information Retrieval. Foundations and Trends in Information Retrieval 3(3), 225–331 (2009)

14. Herbrich, R., Graepel, T., Obermayer, K.: Suppert vector learning for ordinal regression. In: Proceedings of 9th International Conference Artificial Neural Networks, pp. 97–102 (1999)

15. Joachims, T.: Optimizing Search Engines Using Click-through Data. In: Proceedings of the 8th ACM SIGKDD International Conference on Knowledge Discovery and Data Mining, pp. 133–142 (2002)

A Comparison of Whitespace Normalization Methods in a Text Art Extraction Method with Run Length Encoding

Tetsuya Suzuki

Department of Electronic Information Systems,
College of Systems Engineering and Science, Shibaura Institute of Technology,
Saitama, Japan
`tetsuya@sic.shibaura-it.ac.jp`

Abstract. Text based pictures called text art or ASCII art can be noise in text processing and display of text, though they enrich expression in Web pages, email text and so on. With text art extraction methods, which detect text art areas in a given text data, we can ignore text arts in a given text data or replace them with other strings. We proposed a text art extraction method with Run Length Encoding in our previous work. We, however, have not considered how to deal with whitespaces in text arts. In this paper, we propose three whitespace normalization methods in our text art extraction method, and compare them by an experiment. According to the results of the experiment, the best method in the three is a method which replaces each wide width whitespace with two narrow width whitespaces. It improves the average of F-measure of the precision and the recall by about 4%.

Keywords: Natural Language Processing, Pattern Recognition, Information Extraction.

1 Introduction

Text based pictures called text art or ASCII art enrich expression in text data such as Web pages and email text. Figure 1 shows a line-oriented text art, which is a cat-like character who stands around with smile.

They, however, can be noise in text processing and display of text. For example, they can be obstacle in text-to-speech software and natural language processing, and some of them lose their shape in small display devices.

Such problems can be solved by *text art extraction methods*, which detect text art areas in a given text data. Text art extraction methods can be constructed by *text art recognition methods*, which tell if a given fragment of text data is a text art or not. With a text art extraction method, we can ignore text arts in a given text data or replace them with other strings.

It is desirable that text art recognition methods and text art extraction methods are language-independent because a text data may include one or more kinds

H. Deng et al. (Eds.): AICI 2011, Part III, LNAI 7004, pp. 135–142, 2011.

```
      ∧＿∧
    (  ´∀`  )
    (         )
    |   |   |
    (＿_)＿_)
```

Fig. 1. A line-oriented text art

```
But perhaps we can run a scientific study of our own.
I'll volunteer for high IQ ('cause I'm an intellectual prick)
>>33 can volunteer for average IQ and
>>31 can volunteer for borderline-retarded IQ
Now let's go smoke dope.
    /
 |  ひさしぶりだな
 \
              \|/
    ＿＿＿＿＿＿＿＿＿＿＿＿
  ∧＿∧            /
 (  ・∀・)    ∧∧ <  いいじゃないか
 (    つ)   (´Д｀)  \
  ＿＿＿  (⊃_⊃
     日▽ ＼| BIBLO |＼
         ￣￣￣￣  \
U.S. House of Representatives:
http://www.internationalrelations.house.gov/110/lee021507.htm
In the autumn of 1944, when I was 16 years old, my friend, Kim Punsun, and I were
collecting shellfish at the riverside when we noticed an elderly man and a Japanese man
looking down at us form the hillside......
A few days later, Punsun knocked on my window early in the morning,
and whispered to me to follow her quietly. I tip-toed out of the house after her.
```

Fig. 2. An input text for our extraction method

```
>>31 can volunteer for borderline-retarded IQ
Now let's go smoke dope.
   /
 | ひさしぶりだな
 \
             \|/
    ＿＿＿＿＿＿＿＿＿＿＿＿
  ∧＿∧            /
 ( ・∀・)   ∧∧ <  いいじゃないか
 (   つ)  (´Д｀)  \
  ＿＿＿ (⊃_⊃
     日▽ ＼| BIBLO |＼
        ￣￣￣￣  \
U.S. House of Representatives:
http://www.internationalrelations.house.gov/110/lee021507.htm
In the autumn of 1944, when I was 16 years old, my friend, Kim Punsun, and I were
```

Fig. 3. A text art area candidate

```
    /
 | ひさしぶりだな
 \
             \|/
    ＿＿＿＿＿＿＿＿＿＿＿＿
  ∧＿∧            /
 ( ・∀・)   ∧∧ <  いいじゃないか
 (   つ)  (´Д｀)  \
  ＿＿＿ (⊃_⊃
     日▽ ＼| BIBLO |＼
        ￣￣￣￣  \
```

Fig. 4. A result of our text art extraction

of natural languages. Methods for text art recognition and text art extraction proposed in [1,3,4], however, are language-dependent.

We proposed a text art extraction method without any language-dependent text attribute [5]. Our method uses attributes of a given text data which represent how the text data looks like text art. One of the attribute is data compression ratio by Run Length Encoding (RLE). We use it to measure a characteristic of text arts that same characters often occur successively.

We, however, have not considered how to deal with whitespaces in text arts. We have the following three questions about it.

- There can be wide width whitespaces and narrow width whitespaces in a text data. Should we normalize their widths?
- Lengths of lines in a text art are not same in general. Should we add whitespaces to right ends of the lines to align them?
- Should we deal with left margins of text arts as parts of the text arts?

In this paper, we propose three whitespace normalization methods in our text art extraction method and compare them by an experiment.

The rest of the paper consists as follows. In section 2, we explain our text art extraction method. In section 3, we introduce whitespace normalization methods. In section 4, we explain our text art extraction test and evaluate the results. We finally state our conclusion in section 5.

2 A Text Art Extraction Method

In this section, we explain our text art extraction method which deals with line-oriented text arts. We first explain two parts of our extraction method: a procedure called scanning with window width k and a procedure called text area reduction. We then explain our text art extraction method. We finally explain a text art recognition machine used in the text art extraction method.

2.1 Scanning with Window Width k

We define a procedure called *scanning with window width k*. Given a text data T, the procedure watches successive k lines on T and move the area from the beginning to the end of T by one line. We call the successive k lines as *a window*, and call the k as *the window width*. During the scanning, it applies a procedure, which is for text attribute extraction or text art recognition, to each window.

2.2 Text Area Reduction

We define a procedure called *text area reduction* as follows. The procedure removes the following lines from a given text area represented by a pair of a start line and an end line of the entire text data.

– Successive lines from the start line which are recognized as non-text art
– Successive lines from the end line which are recognized as non-text art

This procedure uses a text art recognition machine for the recognition.

2.3 A Text Art Extraction Method

We define a text art extraction method with window width w. Given a text T, the procedure outputs a set of text art areas in T with the text art recognition machine M as follows.

1. It applies scanning with window width w to the text T with M. It means that the procedure applies M to the window in the scanning.
2. For each chunk of successive windows in which text data have been recognized as text arts, it records the text data in the chunk of the windows as a text art area candidate.
3. For each text art area candidate, it applies the text area reduction procedure with M.
4. It outputs the results of the text area reduction procedure as a set of text arts.

Figure 2 shows an example of input text data for our extraction method, where a text art is between English text. Figure 3 shows a text art area candidate obtained at the step 2 where there are redundant lines before and after the text art. Figure 4 shows the resulting text art extracted at the step 3.

2.4   A Text Art Recognition Machine

We use a text art recognition machine in our text art extraction method, which is constructed by a machine learning algorithm. It takes a set of text attributes as its input and outputs whether true or false. The true value and the false value represent that the text is a text art and that it is not respectively.

We construct training data for the machine learning as follows.

1. We prepare a set of text arts and a set of non-text arts.
2. We extract text attributes from them using the scanning with window width k $(= 1, 2, 3, \ldots, w)$.

The extracted text attributes are R, L and S. The attribute R is an attribute based on data compression ratio by RLE. Given a text T consisting of n lines, the attribute is defined as follow.

$$R \equiv \frac{\sum_{i=1}^{n} |RLE(l_i)|}{|T|} \tag{1}$$

where $|x|$ denotes the length of a string x, $RLE(x)$ denotes a string encoded from the string x by RLE, and l_i is the i-th line of T. The attributes L and S are the number of lines and the length of the text data respectively.

3   Whitespace Normalization Methods

We introduce whitespace normalization methods in our text art extraction method. These normalization methods are applied to a window just before we extract text attributes from the window or we use a text art recognition machine.

We explain some terminologies. We assume that text data is encoded in Unicode. Unicode characters are classified into some classes by their widths in [2]. We call characters in the classes F, W and A as *wide width characters*, and call characters in the other classes as *narrow width characters*. For example, Unicode white space characters U+0020 and U+3000 are *narrow width* and *wide width* respectively. We define *the width of a character* as follows: the width of a narrow width character is 1 and the width of a wide width character is 2. *The width of a line* is the sum of the widths of characters except its new line code.

We define the three whitespace normalization methods N1, N2, and N3 as follows.

N1. It replaces each wide width whitespace with two narrow width whitespaces.
N2. It adds narrow width whitespaces to the ends of lines in a window to make their widths w where w is the maximum width of lines in the window.
N3. It removes narrow width whitespaces in the left margin of a window after application of N1.

For the sake of convenience, we call a normalization method which never modify any given text as N0.

4   An Extraction Test

We compare the three whitespace normalization methods by an extraction test. We implemented our text art extraction method and the normalization methods in Perl. We used decision trees as text art recognition machines. The decision trees were constructed by the C4.5 machine learning algorithm implemented in the data mining tool Weka [6].

4.1   Text Data

We used two sets of text data E and J for the machine learning. The set of text data E consists of English text data with 289 text arts and 290 non-text arts, whose lines range from 1 to 118. The set of text data J consists of Japanese text data with 259 text arts and 299 non-text arts, whose lines range from 1 to 39. Their new line code is the sequence of CR LF.

We constructed training data and test data as follows. We divided the set of text data E and J into two groups A and B. Each of A and B consists of English text and Japanese text. We then made 800 text data from A as test data. Each of the 800 text data consists of three parts X, Y and Z where X and Z are randomly selected non-text art data from A and Y is randomly selected text art data from A. Each of X, Y and Z is English or Japanese text data. Figure 2 shows an example of such test data where X and Z are English text and Y is a Japanese text art. We also made 800 text data from B similarly.

4.2   Training and Testing

1. We constructed a recognition machine by the C4.5 machine learning algorithm with the attributes R, L and S extracted from A. We also constructed a recognition machine by C4.5 with the same attributes extracted from B.
2. For each case of N0, N1, N2, and N3, we had the following.
   (a) Changing window width from 1 to 10, we extracted text arts. We used the 800 text data constructed from B as test data and the recognition machine constructed from A.
   (b) We swapped A and B, and extracted text arts similarly.
   (c) For each window width, we calculated the average of the precision p, the average of the recall r, and the average of the inverse number of extracted text arts IT. In addition, we also calculated two F-measures using p, r, and IT as follows.

$$F_{p,r} \equiv \frac{2}{\frac{1}{p} + \frac{1}{r}} \tag{2}$$

$$F_{p,r,IT} \equiv \frac{3}{\frac{1}{p} + \frac{1}{r} + \frac{1}{IT}} \tag{3}$$

We explain the average of the inverse number of extracted text arts IT. As each test data contains one text art, IT should be 1.0. If the text art is averagely extracted as two text arts, the IT is 0.5. If the text art is averagely extracted as four text arts, the IT is 0.25.

4.3   Results

Tables 1 2, 3, and 4 show the results of the extraction test for N0, N1, N2 and N3 respectively. Each table has six columns: w (window width), p (average of precision), r (average of recall), IT (average of inverse number of text area), $F_{p,r}$ and $F_{p,r,IT}$. The overview of the results is as follows.

N0. $F_{p,r}$ takes the maximum 0.908 when the window width is 1 and $F_{p,r,IT}$ takes the maximum 0.834 when the window width is 7.

N1. $F_{p,r}$ takes the maximum 0.943 when the window width is 1 and $F_{p,r,IT}$ takes the maximum 0.924 when the window width is 7.

N2. $F_{p,r}$ takes the actual maximum 0.844 and $F_{p,r,IT}$ takes the maximum 0.862 when the window width is 10, though $F_{p,r}$ takes the maximum 0.908 in the Table 3. It is because our extraction method with N2 works as exactly same as that with N0 when the window width is 1.

N3. $F_{p,r}$ takes the maximum 0.908 when the window width is 1, and $F_{p,r,IT}$ takes the maximum 0.881 when the window width is 8.

Table 1. The results of the extraction test with N0

w	p	r	IT	$F_{p,r}$	$F_{p,r,IT}$
1	0.924	0.892	0.481	0.908	0.701
2	0.901	0.890	0.542	0.895	0.736
3	0.886	0.892	0.676	0.889	0.804
4	0.869	0.877	0.745	0.873	0.826
5	0.845	0.856	0.782	0.850	0.826
6	0.807	0.834	0.806	0.820	0.815
7	0.805	0.832	0.867	0.818	0.834
8	0.778	0.809	0.887	0.793	0.822
9	0.766	0.799	0.914	0.782	0.822
10	0.735	0.784	0.921	0.759	0.806

Table 2. The results of the extraction test with N1

w	p	r	IT	$F_{p,r}$	$F_{p,r,IT}$
1	0.952	0.934	0.595	0.943	0.789
2	0.937	0.937	0.677	0.937	0.831
3	0.936	0.934	0.785	0.935	0.879
4	0.923	0.920	0.820	0.921	0.885
5	0.905	0.907	0.895	0.906	0.902
6	0.874	0.888	0.914	0.881	0.892
7	0.899	0.930	0.943	0.914	0.924
8	0.880	0.913	0.950	0.896	0.913
9	0.840	0.879	0.956	0.859	0.889
10	0.815	0.852	0.958	0.833	0.871

4.4   Evaluation

The best normalization method in N1, N2 and N3 is N1 from the viewpoints of both $F_{p,r}$ and $F_{p,r,IT}$. The maximum $F_{p,r}$ of N1 is about 4% higher relative to that of N0, and the maximum $F_{p,r,IT}$ of N1 is about 11% higher relative to that of N0.

The second in the three methods is N3 from the viewpoints of both $F_{p,r}$ and $F_{p,r,IT}$. The maximum $F_{p,r}$ of N3 is equal to that of N0, and the maximum $F_{p,r,IT}$ of N3 is about 6% higher relative to that of N0.

Table 3. The results of the extraction test with N2

w	p	r	IT	$F_{p,r}$	$F_{p,r,IT}$
1	0.924	0.892	0.481	0.908	0.701
2	0.828	0.801	0.430	0.814	0.627
3	0.507	0.412	0.441	0.455	0.450
4	0.501	0.429	0.619	0.462	0.505
5	0.470	0.426	0.747	0.447	0.516
6	0.679	0.720	0.731	0.699	0.709
7	0.490	0.386	0.786	0.432	0.508
8	0.533	0.417	0.796	0.468	0.542
9	0.811	0.849	0.907	0.830	0.854
10	0.814	0.876	0.902	0.844	0.862

Table 4. The results of the extraction test with N3

w	p	r	IT	$F_{p,r}$	$F_{p,r,IT}$
1	0.923	0.894	0.439	0.908	0.670
2	0.909	0.906	0.512	0.907	0.722
3	0.901	0.905	0.654	0.903	0.801
4	0.877	0.890	0.732	0.883	0.826
5	0.881	0.934	0.810	0.907	0.872
6	0.846	0.886	0.836	0.866	0.855
7	0.828	0.877	0.874	0.852	0.859
8	0.851	0.910	0.885	0.880	0.881
9	0.840	0.913	0.858	0.875	0.869
10	0.809	0.875	0.857	0.841	0.846

Table 5. Cumulative percentages of the attribute R of Text arts with window width 2

Interval of R	N0	N1	N2	N3
0.0-0.2	0.4	1.7	0.4	0.7
0.0-0.4	2.7	11.3	3.3	6.0
0.0-0.6	7.7	27.1	10.3	15.8
0.0-0.8	15.5	48.4	20.3	32.0
0.0-1.0	29.7	66.1	38.1	50.6
0.0-1.2	46.3	79.4	57.5	65.0
0.0-1.4	63.3	90.2	76.4	79.6
0.0-1.6	83.0	95.9	90.9	90.7
0.0-1.8	95.7	98.5	98.1	97.6
0.0-2.0	100.0	100.0	100.0	100.0

Table 6. Cumulative percentages of attribute R of non-Text arts with window width 2

Interval of R	N0	N1	N2	N3
0.0-0.2	0.1	0.1	0.1	0.1
0.0-0.4	0.1	0.2	0.1	0.2
0.0-0.6	0.2	0.4	0.3	0.2
0.0-0.8	0.4	0.7	0.6	0.6
0.0-1.0	1.8	2.0	19.7	2.0
0.0-1.2	2.1	2.6	33.6	2.6
0.0-1.4	3.0	3.6	44.1	3.6
0.0-1.6	6.7	7.6	56.3	7.6
0.0-1.8	25.2	28.6	74.8	28.1
0.0-2.0	100.0	100.0	100.0	100.0

The worst in the three methods is N2 from the viewpoints of both $F_{p,r}$ and $F_{p,r,IT}$. The maximum $F_{p,r}$ of N2 is about 93% of that of N0, and the maximum $F_{p,r,IT}$ of N2 is about 3% higher relative to that of N0.

To explain both why N1 is the best and why N2 is the worst in our experiment, we show cumulative percentages of the attribute R of text data in Tables 5 and 6. In the following, we expect that R of text art is small and R of non-text art is large, and we focus on when the percentages become more than 20%.

The Table 5 shows the percentages of text art with window width 2.

- The cumulative percentage in N0 become more than 20% when the interval of data compression ratio is 0.0-1.0.
- The cumulative percentage in N1 become more than 20% when the interval of data compression ratio is 0.0-0.6.
- The cumulative percentage in each of N2 and N3 become more than 20% when the interval of data compression ratio is 0.0-0.8.

On the other hand, the Table 6 shows the percentages of non-text art with window width 2.

- The cumulative percentage in each of N0, N1 and N3 become more than 20% when the interval of data compression ratio is 0.0-1.8.
- The cumulative percentage in N2 become more than 20% when the interval of data compression ratio is 0.0-1.2.

From these observations, we can say that N1, N2, and N3 emphasized the characteristic of text art that same characters often occur successively. N2, however, gave the characteristic of text art to non-text art.

5   Conclusion

In this paper, we proposed three whitespace normalization methods in our text art extraction method, and compare them by a text art extraction experiment. Our extraction method uses data compression ratio of text data by Run Length Encoding to measure a characteristic of text art that same characters often occur successively. According to the results of our experiment, the best normalization method is a method which replaces each wide width whitespace in text data with two narrow width whitespaces. The best normalization method improves F-measure of the precision and the recall by about 4%.

References

1. EGG: AAscan (in Japanese),
   http://www11.plala.or.jp/egoo/download/download_index.html
   (retrieved on June 13, 2011)
2. Freytag, A.: Unicode Standard Annex #11 East Asian Width,
   http://www.unicode.org/reports/tr11/ (retrieved on June 13, 2011)
3. Hiroki, T., Minoru, M.: Ascii Art Pattern Recognition using SVM based on Morphological Analysis. Technical report of IEICE. PRMU 104(670), 25–30 (20050218),
   http://ci.nii.ac.jp/naid/110003275719/
4. Nakazawa, M., Matsumoto, K., Yanagihara, T., Ikeda, K., Takishima, Y., Hoashi, K.: Proposal and its Evaluation of ASCII-Art Extraction. Proceedings of the 2nd Forum on Data Engineering and Information Management (DEIM 2010), pp. C9–4 (2010)
5. Suzuki, T.: A Decision Tree-based Text Art Extraction Method without any Language-Dependent Text Attribute. International Journal of Computational Linguistics Research 1(1), 12–22 (2010)
6. The University of Waikato: Weka 3 - Data Mining with Open Source Machine Learning Software in Java, http://www.cs.waikato.ac.nz/ml/weka/
   (retrieved on June 13, 2011)

Decoding Optimization for Chinese-English Machine Translation via a Dependent Syntax Language Model[*]

Ying Liu[1], Zhengtao Yu[1,2], Tao Zhang[1], and Xing Zhao[1,2]

[1] School of Information Engineering and Automation, Kunming University of Science and Technology, Kunming 650051, China
[2] Key Laboratory of Intelligent Information Processing, Kunming University of Science and Technology, Kunming 650051, China
liuying_09@yeah.net, ztyu@hotmail.com,
ztbpf@126.com, zhaoxing2011@163.com

Abstract. Decoding is a core process of the statistical machine translation, and determines the final results of it. In this paper, a decoding optimization for Chinese-English SMT with a dependent syntax language model was proposed, in order to improve the performance of the decoder in Chinese-English statistical machine translation. The data set was firstly trained in a dependent language model, and then calculated scores of NBEST list from decoding with the model. According to adding the original score of NBEST list from the decoder, the NBEST list of machine translation was reordered. The experimental results show that this approach can optimize the decoder results, and to some extent, improve the translation quality of the machine translation system.

Keywords: Language model, Statistical machine translation, Decoding, Dependent syntax.

1 Introduction

In recent years, more and more syntactic information is incorporated into the machine translation process. As for formal grammar aspect, the ITG model [1], such as Wu Dekai was firstly utilized in synchronization syntax for statistical machine translation. Chiang proposed a hierarchical phrase model, and had the similar phrases with ITG model based on formal grammar [2], but more powerful than ITG model in its rearranging aspect. In linguistics and syntax, Yamda et al [3,4]. Presented and developed the string-tree model, Liu Yang also developed a tree-string model. After then, Lin's and Quirk et al. proposed a statistical translation model [5] based on path-based conversion model and dependent syntax, respectively [6]. In recent two years, the emerging forest-string model, such as Mi Haiao et al.'s research, was also based on syntactic analysis [7].

[*] This paper is supported by National Nature Science Foundation (60863011), Yunnan Nature Science Foundation (2008CC023), Yunnan Young and Middle-aged Science and Technology Leaders Foundation (2007PY01-11).

H. Deng et al. (Eds.): AICI 2011, Part III, LNAI 7004, pp. 143–150, 2011.

Optimization in the decoding, a Luo Yi's beam search algorithm by Dynamic Programming Thought, Beam Search algorithm based on the design and implementation of a beam search decoder [8]. But did not make the optimization of the language model. In syntactic aspects of linguistic-based, syntactic information only plays a role in the template extraction process in both dependent and phrase syntax after source or target language syntactic analysis. Since the word's syntax relation information is not included in the template, which causes mechanical splicing template in the process of decoding. Consequently, there is no contribution to the decoding due to no effective use of syntactic relation information.

Therefore, in this paper, based on dependent tree-string translation method, we firstly constructed a dependent syntax language model, and then calculated scores of NBEST list from decoding with the model. According to adding the original score of NBEST list from the decoder, the NBEST list of machine translation was reordered to optimize the decoder results.

2   Process of Translation Decoding

In SMT system, the purpose of decoding is to find the most likely translation according to the input source language sentence from a given language model, translation model and other models based on the information. No matter how the model decoding, the process will be a discrete optimal solution for solving NP problems. To current statistical machine translation based on syntax of research shows that, whether it is based on dependency grammar or phrase structure grammar, In terms of whether the template phrase-phrase model, tree-string model, string-tree model, or forest-string model ,templates are taken in the training, including the template of lexicalization and non-lexicalization, the syntactic relation information in the training, such as dependency syntax of subj and phrase structure grammar of NP, the syntactic relation information plays an important role in the extraction template.

After template training is completed, most adopts direct translation model in the decoding, such as formula (1)

$$Pr(s_1^I \mid t_1^J) = \frac{\exp[\sum_{m=1}^{M} \lambda_m h_m(s_1^I, t_1^J)]}{\sum_{\tilde{e}_1^I} \exp[\sum_{m=1}^{M} \lambda_m h_m(\tilde{e}_1^I, t_1^J)]} . \tag{1}$$

$h_m(s_1^I, t_1^J)$ is characteristic function ,Which $m = 1,...,M$, For each $h_m(s_1^I, t_1^J)$, model parameters corresponding λ_m . Our goal is to solve λ_m for making Chinese-English translation pair of the probability of each other's largest, namely $h_m(s_1^I, t_1^J)$ the largest. Where the denominator has no effect on the search results above formula, so our search model is(2):

$$\hat{\alpha} = \arg \max_{\alpha} \{ \sum_{m=1}^{M} \lambda_m h_m(s_1^I, t_1^J) \} . \tag{2}$$

When searching, the characteristic function as a constraint on the template stitching, in the normal decoding process produces NBEST candidate translation, the source language to dependency syntax parsing, from left to right, from bottom to top, changing NBEST candidate translation sequences. Because of containing variable in the template, the process of decoding change into derivation with probabilistic rules, the final selection with the maximum probability derivation. It can be seen for a same source language sentence, the design features of the same functions and decoding dependency syntax-based language model scores recalculated NBEST to try to get better translation results. Using the minimum Bayes risk decoding or re-scoring methods to compare the results of translation of multiple systems, after comparing the optimal sentences regard as the ultimate translation output.

3   Optimization of the Decoding Dependency Language Model

3.1   Statistical Language Model

In the field of statistical machine translation, dependency syntax for machine translation has some features, such as natural vocabulary, much closer to the semantic expression, and could better express the structural differences in languages, and because the dependency relationship is more than the phrase structure close to the significance of their expression between the words, so in this paper, dependency parsing in train the statistical language model.

Statistical language models are widely used to solve the problems of various natural language, such as speech recognition, machine translation, word segmentation, POS tagging, etc. It is the probability for the establishment of a language model, making the correct word sequence is more than the probability of word sequence error probability, $w_1, ..., w_m$ sentence for the word sequence. The probability by the formula (3) calculation

$$p(w_1, ..., w_m) = p(w_1) \prod_{i=2}^{m} p(w_i \mid w_1, ..., w_{i-1}) . \tag{3}$$

Assuming that the conditional probability of the current word with the previous n-1 only words related to (4),

$$p(w_1, ..., w_m) = p(w_1) \prod_{i=2}^{m} p(w_i \mid w_{i-n}, ..., w_{i-1}) . \tag{4}$$

Called Ngram model, this paper training is 3 per language model.

3.2   Dependency Language Model and Training

Statistical language model is used in various fields, such as natural language processing, speech recognition, intelligent input method, ORC recognition. The sequence is used to measure the compliance of a target level. To the English sentence. For example the following two English sentences:

S1: There is a cup on the table.
S2: There are a cup on the table.

From the perspective of English speakers, obviously, the first sentence is clearly more in line with the daily usage of English. But the computer does not know that knowledge, then the language model is to identify these knowledge. Language model is a Markov chain, Expression is a sequence of probability distribution, it can give the sample space of all possible sequences of class probability. In natural language, the language model that any word sequence is a sentence, but their probability are difference. In statistical machine translation, the decoding will match different templates, and ultimately the formation of many translations. Some of these translations the syntax used to meet the target language, while others do not match. Language model's job is to give the translation of sentences with different probabilities, and ultimately choose the best translation.

Dependency syntax language model based on dependency syntax module, including parts of speech and dependencies, dependency relationship which describes the relationship between two words, the potential of expressing a word binding with another word. In the field of statistical machine translation, dependency syntax for machine translation has some features, such as natural vocabulary, much closer to the semantic expression, and can better express the structural differences in languages, and because the dependency relationship is more than the phrase structure close to the significance of their expression between the words, so this paper to train the statistical dependency parsing language model, dependency language model training using the method of maximum likelihood estimation formula(5):

$$p(w_i \mid w_{i-n},...,w_{i-1}) = \frac{C(w_{i-n}...w_{i-1},w_i)}{C(w_{i-n}...w_{i-1})} . \tag{5}$$

Count(X) Said X in the training corpus that the number of occurrences. This is not the word sequence, but the sentence sequence dependencies. Using medical field to 3636 in English as the training set and Stanford parser for training tools, to the training set parsing each sentence in English, the following is an example:

Cold is caused by a virus.
Syntactic analysis of the dependency tree is as follows:
nsubjpass(caused-3, Cold-1)
auxpass(caused-3, is-2)
det(virus-6, a-5)
agent(caused-3, virus-6)

The mark indicates that the left parentheses dependencies between the words, the numbers behind words indicate the position of words in the sentence. To remove the dependency tree of the words, in order to retain syntax tree of the syntactic relations between words, from the training set by 3636 through the dependency syntax analysis and the extracted sentence contains only dependency relations between the words "sentence". For the above sentence, namely:

Nsubjpass auxpass det agent

Sequence of this kind of dependency as a "sentence", then, language model training parameters usually SRILM tools to srilm tool training 3 per dependency syntax language model. Language model output is the probability of a word sequence, that is, the probability of ternary grammar. In the training text, given any passage of the medicine field for consecutive words text, call interface provided SRILM, phrases can be easily obtained given the probability on the training text.

3.3   Optimized for Decoder Figures

Re-calculate the candidate translation scores and change the N-BEST candidate translation sequences based on dependency syntax relationship language model. Relative to the decoding process in Fig.1, After increasing the dependency syntax relationship language model constraints in the decoding stage, the whole process of translation system showed in Fig.1. The translation process of dependency tree-string:

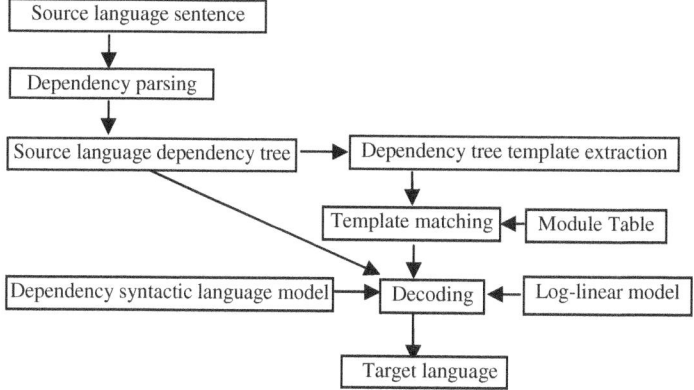

Fig. 1. Syntactic dependency relations role in the decoding stage

The task of the decoder is learned from the training text language model, translation model and the model of other additional information to determine the most the most similar translation of the source sentence. Based on dependency syntax relationship language model to re-calculate the candidate translation scores, and change NBEST candidate translation sequences. Relative to the decoding process of Fig.1, it's increasing the dependency syntax relationship language model constraints in the decoding stage, Fig.1 shows the translation process that whole process of translation system dependency tree-string.

From the struct tree of the source language to the string of the target language, the dependency tree-string, the translation model is used the role of randomization to describe the conversion of the relationship between the tree-tring, the decoding module framework showed in Fig.1. Input source language sentence, after dependent syntactic analysis, get the source language dependent tree. Then extracted template from the source language dependent tree, here we don't have to consider the target language, nor do word alignment constraints. The Process of extraction is bottom- up, first we get the child node's treelet, and then, the child node's assembled into parent node treelet. After getting the source language treelet, matching them with DTSC table which extracted from the modules table, if an extract of the source language side treelet is the same as the extracted treelet, we say that the template matching, and put it on the matching template table. After getting all the matching template table, we apply decoding algorithm to decode, and get the target language string.

Template table and template matching process played an important role in the whole translation process, and the translation efficiency mostly depends on whether the extracted templates is accurate. And for the medical domain, we use the template which defined in the artificial construct rules, it has many advantages such as translation accurate, adjustable sequence accurate and so on. This feature of the restricts areas avoid large-scale manual labor. Adding the template which defined in the artificial rules to the template extracted by generic domain, achieving template choice using the template matching algorithm in the decoding stage.

We selected 500 pairs of Chinese-English sentence pairs for test set, after producing N-BEST candidate translation during the normal decoding processes, record scores for each English sentence, analysis dependency syntax for each candidate translation, and get the dependency syntax sequence nodes, calculate the score of the node $DPni$ based on dependency syntax language model, so the i-sentence score of the NBEST candidate translation's final formula is (6):

$$scorei = Pni + DPni .   (6)$$

To re-sort the translation of the NBEST candidate using a new $scorei$, than output one or N translation results. Decoding process is similar to the process of analyzing a single language, which is the source language side of "syntactic analysis", with the transition rules to match the right side of the source language and generate the structure tree of the target language with the left. Using bottom-up method to traverse the source language structure tree for each node when decoding, for the child tree which use the current node as root node, the decoder searches all matching TAT, to obtain the corresponding candidate translation of these nodes through TAT, and store them to the corresponding stack. The higher-level translation obtained assembly by the lower-level child node which identified by the TAT.

We want improve the translation speed to reduce the search space, the paper made the following restrictions: Limit the match TAT number <= 20 for each node.

For the same N-word translation of the left and the right end, decoder combine them, and cut out the translation with a low probability using window function, only keeping of the highest probability one.

The results of experiment show that we re-calculate the candidate translation scores based on dependency syntax relationship language model, change the N-BEST candidate translation sequences. Increasing the dependency syntax relationship language model constraints in the decoding stage, we have a certain limit on the search algorithm.

3.4   Experimental Results and Comparative Analysis

The model's training and decoding is a key step in SMT, training of the model's including extraction template and parameters of training that the method of template extraction also determines the way of decoding. It was adopted the dependency tree-string's translation method to extract dependency trees for string template formed template library, and then training the parameters of the characteristic function, ultimately a final recursive paste and replace formed decoding process. Training set is 3636 Chinese-English sentence pairs of medical domain, test set is randomly selected 500 Chinese-English sentence pairs. That the conditions of training set and test set shown in Table 1.

Table 1. Case Training Set and Test Set

Set	Sentences	Chinese	English
Training set	Sentences	3636	
	Sentences	35374	37581
Test set	Sentences	500	
	Sentences	4015	4681

Table 2. NBEST Sequence Changes and the Score

Name	Sentences
Training set	500
Total change	23
Positive change	17
Negative change	6
System	BLEU4
Increase the language model	0.2312
Increase the language model	0.2323

We adopt common BLEU evaluation method, the results of translation rate, into a domain system of rules and resources—Based on Dependent Tree-String Translation System to compare experimental system, for each sentence generated NBEST candidate translation output the best translation results, Table 2 shows adopted based on dependency syntax relationship after constraints the language model training set after the translation of the best candidate for change.

Table 2 shown after produced NBEST candidates in the translation of increase language model, we adopt based on dependency syntax relationship language model re-calculated scores, the output of the best candidates for translation, and BLEU2 evaluation score results.

It can be seen in 500 of the training set, about 4.6% of the candidate translation changes, which occurred about a positive change in 74% and 16% of the sentences appeared negative changes. On the whole, take the sentence for the unit, and evaluation standards for BLEU calculation of score, about 3.4% of the translation effect of the sentence be enhanced, higher than the open fields and improve the accuracy of machine translation.

4 Conclusion and Outlook

This paper presents a training the dependency language model in medical data sets based on dependent tree-string translation method, and this model calculates scores of NBEST list generated from decoding which changes sequence of machine translation of NBEST and restricts search algorithm, in order to optimize results of decoder. The experimental results show that this approach can optimize the decoder results and improve the translational quality of the machine translation system to some extent. In the next work, we need to incorporate more syntactic features for machine translation.

References

1. Wu, D.: Stochastic inversion transduction grammars and bilingual parsing of parallel corpora. Computational Linguistics 23, 377–404 (1997)
2. Chiang, D.: A hierarchical phrase-based model for statistical machine translation. In: Proceedings of ACL, Ann Arbor, pp. 263–270 (2005)
3. Yamada, K., Knight, K.: A syntax-based statistical translation model. In: Proceedings of ACL 2001, pp. 523–530 (2001)
4. Galley, M., Hopkins, M., Knight, K., Marcu, D.: What's in a translation rule. In: Proceedings of HLT-NAACL 2004, pp. 273–280 (2004)
5. Lin, D., Cherry, C.: Word Alignment with Cohesion Constraint. In: Proceedings of HLT/NAACL 2003, Companion Volume, pp. 49–51. Edmonton, Canada (2003)
6. Quirk, C., Menezes, A., Cherry, C.: Dependency treelet translation: Syntactically informed phrasal SMT. In: Proceedings of ACL, Ann Arbor, Michigan, pp. 271–279 (June 2005)
7. Luo, Y.: Phrase-based statistical machine translation decoder beam search optimization and implementation. China University of Technology, Anhui (2007)
8. Deyi, X.: Research on Statistical Machine Translation Based on Bracketing Transduction Grammar and Dependency Grammar. Institute of Computing Technology Chinese Academy of Sciences, Beijing (2007)

Multi-task Learning for Word Alignment and Dependency Parsing

Shujie Liu

Harbin Institute of Technology
No. 92, West Da-Zhi Street, Nangang District
Harbin City, China
shujieliu@mtlab.hit.edu.cn

Abstract. Word alignment and parsing are two important components for syntax based machine translation. The inconsistent models for alignment and parsing caused problems during translation pair extraction. In this paper, we do word alignment and dependency parsing in a multi-task learning framework, in which word alignment and dependency parsing are consistent and assisted with each other. Our experiments show significant improvement not only for both word alignment and dependency parsing, but also the final translation performance.

Keywords: Multi-task learning, word alignment, dependency parsing, machine translation.

1 Introduction

Since noisy channel model is introduced by Brown et al. (1994), statistical methods are widely-used in machine translation. Och (2003) proposed a more generalized log-linear model with minimum error rate training (MERT) which has provided substantial improvements over the original noisy channel model. This method uses a discriminative framework to integrate several sub-models: translation model, language model, distortion model, and so on. The sub-models can be generative or discriminative, such as a generative translation model and a discriminative maximum entropy distortion model. The sub-models are usually trained separately and then integrated into a log-linear framework with weights tuned using MERT.

Among the sub-models, translation model plays a key role which measures the faithfulness of a candidate as the translation of a source language sentence. Translation model is usually a translation table which contains translation pairs with translation probabilities. Most systems discover translation pairs via phrase extraction and maximum likelihood estimation (MLE). Before phrase extraction, the sentence pairs in the training data must be word aligned.

There are two kinds of approaches for word alignment. One is generative models, such as Giza++ using IBM Models and HMM model, and generative ITG models for word alignment. The generative models usually use EM method to train the model parameters. Another one is discriminative model with kinds of features, such as log-linear models used in [1], CRF models used in [2], and discriminative ITG models

H. Deng et al. (Eds.): AICI 2011, Part III, LNAI 7004, pp. 151–158, 2011.

used in [3] and [4]. One disadvantage of generative models is that it is not very easy to integrate kinds of features which are not independent with each other, while it is very simple and easy for discriminative models. Another reason of popularity of discriminative model is the discriminative model can optimize the parameters with the final evaluation metrics oriented.

Dependency grammar (DG) is a class of syntactic theories developed by Lucien Tesnière. It is distinct from phrase structure grammars, as it lacks phrasal nodes. Structure is determined by the relation between a word (a head) and its dependents. Dependency parsing is a task trying to find the dependency relations between words in a sentence.

One modern approach to building dependency parsers, called data-driven dependency parsing, is to learn good and bad parsing decisions solely from labeled data, without the intervention of an underlying grammar.

Since word alignment focuses the relations of the words of sentence pairs, and dependency parsing focuses the relations of the words in one sentence, there are many works studying the relations between word alignment and dependency parsing. Some work use the word alignment result to generate dependency tree of the target sentence given the dependency tree of the source sentence using projection methods, and also dependency information can be used to generate better word alignment result.

In this paper, word alignment and dependency parsing are integrated in a multi-task learning framework, in which word alignment and dependency parsing can be consistent and assisted with each other by introducing common feature for them. By integrating three tasks (word alignment, source sentence dependency parsing, target sentence dependency parsing), we not only achieved better word alignment result, better dependency result for source and target sentences, and also, the final translation performance is improved significantly.

In the following of this paper, we will introduce related works in section 2, followed by the introduction of multi-task learning in section 3. Our method will be shown in section 4 in detail, and the experiments are conducted in section 5. The final conclusion and future work will be discussed in section 6.

2   Related Work

Reference [6] proposed a projection method to get the dependency parsing result for the target language sentence using the dependency parsing result of the source language sentence and the word alignment result of this sentence pair. With a post-projection transformation, the f-score for the target language sentences can achieve comparable result with the result of a clean target language parser.

Reference [7] presented an empirical study that quantifies the degree to which syntactic dependencies are preserved when parses are projected directly from English to Chinese. Their results show that the quality of the projected Chinese parses can achieve F-score of 76% with a small set of principled, elementary linguistic transformations.

Reference [5] proposed a word alignment procedure based on a syntactic dependency analysis of French/English parallel corpora, which is called "alignment by syntactic propagation": Both corpora are processed deeply with a dependency parser, and then starting with an anchor word pair which has high confident translation probability, the alignment link is propagated to the syntactically connected words. Based on their experiments, this approach can achieve a precision of 94.3% and 93.1% with a recall of 58% and 56%, respectively for each corpus.

Reference [8] presented a new statistical model for computing the probability of an alignment given a sentence pair using dependency cohesion constraint features. The added dependency cohesion constraint features can achieve AER reduction of 1.8 points. Reference [9] introduced soft syntactic constraints into a discriminative ITG word alignment framework trained with SVM, and produced a 22% relative reduction in error rate with respect to a strong flat-string model.

The most similar work with ours is reference [10], in which they jointly parsed a bitext, and got improved parse quality on both sides. In a maximum entropy bitext paring model, they defined a distribution over source trees, target trees, and node-to-node alignments between them using monolingual parse scores and various measures of syntactic divergence. The resulting bitex parser outperforms state-of-the-art monolingual parser baseline by 2.5 F1 at predicting English side trees and 1.8 F1 at predicting Chinese side trees, and also these improved trees yielded significant improvement in final machine translation.

Compared with reference [10], our work is different with them in following ways: one is that our work is a combination process for parsing and word alignment, not started from scratch; the other one is our syntactic parser trees for source and target sentences are dependency trees instead of constituent trees in reference [10]; the third one is that our features used are different with those in reference [10].

3   Multi-task Learning

As in [11, 12], multi-task learning (MTL) is an inductive transfer mechanism whose principle goal is to improve generalization performance. MTL improves generalization by leveraging the domain-specific information contained in the training signals of related tasks. It does this by training tasks in parallel while using a shared representation.

The performance improvement from MTL is due to the extra information in the training signals of related tasks. The traditional learning process tries to learn each task from scratch, while multi-task learning tries to share the common knowledge among the tasks. MTL prefers distributions that other tasks prefer, and MTL prefers not to use distributions other task prefers not to use. Consider two tasks T_1 and T_2 sharing common knowledge, optimization process is biased towards representations in the intersection of what would be learned for T_1 and T_2.

4   Our Method

4.1   Model

Log-linear models are used to do word alignment and dependency parsing for sentence pairs. The log-linear mode for word alignment is shown in equation (1), where (e, f) is the sentence pair to be aligned and a is the word alignment candidate, and $\widehat{a}$ is the best candidate given by the log-linear model. f is the feature vector used in log-linear model for predicting the word alignment for the sentence pair (e, f), and λ is the weight vector for feature vector f :

$$\hat{a} = \arg\max_{a}(\sum_{i=1}^{n} \lambda_i f_i(a, e, f)) \tag{1}$$

And the log-linear model for dependency parsing is shown in equation (2), where e is the sentence to be parsed, d is the dependency parsing tree candidates, and $\hat{d}$ is the best parsing candidate given by equation (2):

$$\hat{d} = \arg\max_{d}(\sum_{i=1}^{n} \lambda_i f_i(d, e)) \tag{2}$$

With the multi-task learning framework, we integrate the three tasks (word alignment, source dependency parsing and target dependency parsing) into one log-linear model, which is shown in equation (3):

$$(\hat{a}, \hat{d}_s, \hat{d}_t) = \arg\max_{(a, ds, dt)}(\sum_{i=1}^{n} \lambda_i f_i(a, ds, dt, e, f)) \tag{3}$$

where (ds, dt) are the dependency parsing trees for (e, f), and the features used in word alignment and source/target dependency trees are merged in to the new feature vector f with the feature weight λ .

Instead of starting from scratch to generate the word alignment matrix and dependency trees, here, we use the multi-task framework to do a combination task of results produced by other tools. For alignment, the alignment candidates for combination are generated by Giza++, an implementation of HMM alignment tool, and an implementation of a discriminative alignment in reference [13], and the dependency candidates for source and target sentences are generated from Berkeley parser and MST parser.

For the used word alignment tools, Giza++ is an implementation of IBM Models including IBM Model 1-5, the HMM alignment tool is an re-implement of HMM alignment, and the implementation of the discriminative alignment tool uses log-linear model and beam search to search a local optimized alignment result. The Berkeley parser is an un-lexicalized parser with hierarchically state-split PCFGs, with a coarse-to-fine method in which a grammar's own hierarchical projections are used to incremental pruning, and the MST parser is a non-projective dependency parser that searches for maximum spanning trees over directed graphs. Models of dependency structure are based on large-margin discriminative training methods.

With the output of initial alignment and dependency parsers, we use the intersection of the results as the start point link set of word alignment and dependency links, and then we perform a beam search process to add new links until the score of equation (3) is not improved. The added links must be links in one of the results for combining.

The used training method is minimum error rate training (MERT) as used in [15]. The objective function of the training target is defined as combination of F-score for word alignment and F-score for dependency parsing of source and target sentences.

4.2 Features for Word Alignment

- Translation probability

  The translation probability for a word pair (e_w, f_w) (e_w is a English word and f_w is Chinese word) is calculated using maximum-likelihood estimation (MLE), with the following equation:

$$P(e_w, f_w) = \frac{Count(e_w, f_w)}{\sum_{e_w'} Count(e_w', f_w)} \tag{4}$$

  where e_w' is any English word, $Count(e_w, f_w)$ is the count of times e_w is aligned to f_w. This count is calculated from the result of Giza++.

- Fertility probability

  The fertility probability depict the probability of a source word (English word) generates a number of Chinese words, as used in [14]. The fertility probability we used here are also calculated using MLE:

$$P(e_w, n) = \frac{Count(e_w, n)}{\sum_m Count(e_w, m)} \tag{5}$$

  where n and m are the number of fertility, and $Count(e_w, n)$ is the count of English word e_w are aligned to n Chinese words.

- Distortion probability

  The distortion probability is calculated in the same way as in [14].

4.3 Features for Dependent Parsing

- Dependency probability

  The dependency probability for a word pair is calculated using maximum-likelihood estimation (MLE), as similar as translation probability for word alignment.

- Root probability

  The root probability is the probability of a word as a root of a dependency tree, also calculated using MLE.

- Leaf probability

  The leaf probability is the probability of a word as a leaf of a dependency tree, which means this word can't be head of any words in the sentence, also calculated using MLE.

4.4 Features for Both Alignment and Parsing

●   Dependency propagation
    Supposing there are two words A,B in English sentence which have a X
    dependency relation, and there are two words C,D in Chinese sentence which
    also have a X dependency relation, and A and C have a alignment link, if there's
    a alignment link between B and D, we call it a good dependency propagation.
    The dependency propagation feature is the count of good dependency
    propagations.

●   Functional word links' suggestion
    For example in Figure 1, there is a Chinese functional "笔", and it's very hard to
    align it to the English word "that". But as we know there's dependency link
    between "那" and "笔", and this can be used to suggest a link of "that" and "笔".
    The functional word links' suggestion feature is the count of such phenomenon.

Fig. 1. An example of functional word links' suggestion

5   Experiments

5.1 Experiment Setting

The dependency tree for sentence pairs are LDC2007T02, we extracted 1000 sentence
pairs and annotated with word alignment result. The first 500 sentence pairs are used
as training data, and the left as the testing data. The original tree bank is constituent
syntactic trees, so we use Penn2Malt[1] to convert the constituent tree to dependency
tree.

5.2 Performance for Word Alignment and Dependency Parsing

The first experiment is to evaluate the word alignment performance and dependency
parsing performance. The word alignment results are shown in Table 1.
    From Table 1, we can find that the multi-task learning combination can improve the
word alignment performance about 2 points, not only for precision, but also for recall.
    The dependency parsing result are shown in Table 2.
    From Table 2, the improvement of our approach is about 3 points better compared
with the two baseline systems.

---

[1] http:// w3.msi.vxu.se/~nivre/research/Penn2Malt.html

Table 1. Word alignment performance using MTL. "Discrim" is the word alignment performance of the implementation of discriminative word alignment model as said in section IV.A. MTL is our approach with multi-task learning framework.

	Precision	Recall	F-Score
Giza++	0.84	0.82	0.83
HMM	0.79	0.84	0.82
Discrim	0.87	0.82	0.85
MTL	0.89	0.84	0.87

Table 2. Dependency parsing results using MTL combination. "Berkeley" stands for the dependency parsing result from Berkeley parser, and MST is the output of MST parser, while MTL is the dependency parsing result using MTL combination.

	Precision	Recall	F-Score
Berkeley	0.78	0.77	0.77
MST	0.79	0.80	0.89
MTL	0.81	0.83	0.82

5.3 Performance for Machine Translation

We also conduct an end-to-end evaluation of the alignment results with machine translation performance. The bilingual training dataset is the NIST training set excluding the Hong Kong Law and Hong Kong Hansard, and our 5-gram language model is trained from the Xinhua section of the Gigaword corpus. The NIST'03 test set is used as our development corpus and the NIST'05 and NIST'08 test sets are our test sets. We use our implementation of hierarchical phrase-based SMT (Chiang, 2007), with standard features. The SMT performance is shown in Table 3. From Table 3, we can find our method not only can improve the word alignment results and dependency parsing performance for source and target sentences, but also can improve the final machine translation performance on Nist'05 and Nist'06 significantly.

Table 3. Machine translation performance using the word alignment generated by MTL

	NIST'05	NIST'08
HMM	36.91	26.86
Giza	37.70	27.33
Discrim	37.51	27.42
MTL	38.32	27.95

6 Conclusion

In this paper, we do word alignment and dependency parsing in a multi-task learning framework, in which word alignment and dependency parsing are consistent and assisted with each other. Instead of starting from scratch to generate the alignment and dependency trees, we use the initial results from other tools to do a combination.

Our experiments show significant improvement not only for both word alignment and dependency parsing, but also the final translation performance.

References

1. Moore, R.C.: Sneddon, A discriminative framework for bilingual word alignment. In: HLT/EMNLP (2005)
2. Blunsom, P., Cohn, T.: Discriminative word alignment with conditional random fields. In: ACL (2006)
3. Cherry, C., Lin, D.: Soft Syntactic Constraints for Word alignment through discrinative training. In: ACL/COLING (2006)
4. Liu, S., Li, C.-H., Zhou, M.: Discriminative pruning for discriminative ITG alignment. In: ACL (2010)
5. Ozdowska, S.: Identifying correspondences between words: an approach based on a bilingual syntactic analysis of French/English parallel corpora. In: MLR 2004 Proceedings of the Workshop on Multilingual Linguistic Ressources (2004)
6. Hwa, R., Resnik, P., Weinberg, A.: Breaking the Resource Bottleneck for Multilingual Parsing. Technical report (2002)
7. Hwa, R., Resnik, P., Weinberg, A., Kolak, O.: Evaluating translational correspondence using Annotation Projection. In: ACL (2002)
8. Cherry, C., Lin, D.: A probability model to improve word aligment. In: ACL (2003)
9. Cherry, C., Lin, D.: Soft syntactic constraints for word alignment through discriminative training. In: COLING/ACL (2006)
10. Burkett, D., Klein, D.: Two languages are better than one (for syntactic parsing). In: EMNLP (2008)
11. Caruana, R.: Multitask Learning. In: Machine Learning (1997)
12. Pan, S.J., Yang, Q.: A survey on transfer learning. IEEE Transactions on Knowledge and Data Engineering
13. Liu, Y., Liu, Q., Lin, S.: Log-linear models for word alignment. In: ACL (2005)
14. Brown, P.F., Della Pietra, S.A., Della Pietra, V.J., Mercer, R.L.: The mathematics of statistical machine translation: parameter estimation. In: ACL (2003)
15. Fraser, A., Marcu, D.: Semi-supervised training for statistical word alignment. In: ACL (2006)

3D Human Motion Retrieval Based on ISOMAP Dimension Reduction

Xiaocui Guo, Qiang Zhang[*], Rui Liu, Dongsheng Zhou, and Jing Dong

Key Laboratory of Advanced Design and Intelligent Computing (Dalian University)
Ministry of Education, Dalian, 116622, China
zhangq@dlu.edu.cn

Abstract. In recent years, with the development and increasingly mature of motion capture technology, it has become one of the most widely used technologies to obtain realistic human motion in computer animation. With the increasing demands, motion dataset is becoming larger and larger. Due to motion feature data have the high-dimensional complexity, we first adopt nonlinear ISOMAP manifold learning algorithm to resolve the "curse of dimensionality" problem for motion feature data. In order to save the time of reducing dimension, we adopt the scarcity of neighboring-graph to improve ISOMAP algorithm for making it apply the massive human motion database. Then we build a motion string index for database, deploy Smith-Waterman algorithm to compare the retrieval samples' motion string with motion strings of candidate datasets, finally, we obtain the similar motion sequence. Experiment results show that the approach proposed in this paper is effective and efficient.

Keywords: Motion capture data, ISOMAP algorithm, Motion string indexing, Smith-Waterman algorithm, Retrieval.

1 Introduction

Human motion capture is a new rising technology for motion data collection in recent years. And many subjects are included in this technology, such as mathematics, computer graphics, image processing and data processing etc. The research of human motion capture not only has certain theoretical research significance, but also has wide application values. By now, human motion capture has been widely used in modern film and television animation, 3D game, intelligent control, virtual reality, tele-education, medicine scientific sports science research and sports training guidance etc. With the development and increasingly mature of motion capture technology, the captured motion data are becoming larger and larger, so it is a new challenge that how to process the massive motion data and apply motion captured databases efficiently. In these challenges, how to find the features which can exactly present motion information from complicated motions and how to retrieve the user

---

[*] Corresponding author.

H. Deng et al. (Eds.): AICI 2011, Part III, LNAI 7004, pp. 159–169, 2011.

needing motions from lots of motion data, and how to reuse the processed motion data effectively are all the hot issues in this field.

Motion capture is one of the most widely used techniques to obtain realistic human motion in computer animation. Motion capture data is usually high-dimensional, and it is laborious for large amounts of such data to classify and search manually. Therefore it needs an efficient motion data retrieval method to deal with it. Efficient retrieval needs an appropriate indexing scheme that can well organize the existing motion data. An effective similarity measure method is a necessary in organizing motion data. Due to the tree structure of human figure with many joints and a strong continuum in the posture sequence, 3D motion capture data shows its complexity both in space and time. Thus the processing of motion data usually requires high computational power [1].

Due to human motion exhibits its complexity both spatially and temporally, in essence, human motion is nonlinear. In this paper we adopt ISOMAP algorithm to reduce the dimensional of the original database, and adopt an improved method to raise the velocity of reducing dimension. In the process of reducing dimension, because of the characteristic of ISOMAP, it can still retain geometric structure of the original motion data. From the low-dimension motion data, we extract some presenting data to build a kind of motion string index for database. The time length and space complex of motion data with the motion string representation are greatly reduced in subsequent process. To evaluate the similarity of these motion clips, the Smith–Waterman algorithm is implemented to calculate the distance of the motion strings. As a local similarity metric of strings, the algorithm can discover semantically similar parts between two clips with unrelated data discarded, which is a common existence in motion data.

The paper is organized as follows. In Section 1 the related work in indexing and retrieval of motion capture data are discussed by us. In Section 2 we detail human motion. In Section 3 introduces our reducing dimensional algorithm. In Section 4 introduces our indexing and retrieval method. Experimental results are given in Section 5. Finally, in Section 6 we conclude this paper by discussing the advantages and limitations of our methods and providing directions for future work.

2 Related Work

In recent years, the researchers have conducted many meaning work at various aspects of human motion capture data such as features representation, feature extraction, indexing and retrieval. Yi et al. [2] realized a retrieval method for large human motion database, and proposed an indexing method based on geometric features, which used bone structure to tectonic indexed tree and with the geometric features of bone as branch as branch. Yamasaki et al. [3] proposed a scheme based on the content of the cross search for 3D human motion data retrieval, including time vary mesh (TVM) and shape geometric feature extraction for motion capture data. Muller et al. [4] defined a variety of qualitative geometric features to describe the specific body parts in a posture, and to derive motion data with these features. They through space-time invariant and the combination of geometric features with adaptive segmentation fragments adopt the indexing method to efficiently retrieval for the large motion database. The authors in [5] proposed a normalized algorithm to ensure motion data to have the same skeleton length, and also they improved the Muller's retrieval method. It makes the retrieval process have the function of sport reorganization and can automatically splicing to retrieve the motion that do not exist in a motion database by introducing automatic conversion strategy. The authors in [6] used hierarchical motion description for a posture, and then clustering-based key frame extraction for retrieving and compressing the motions, respectively. To extract key frames, they need to find similarity between each consecutive frame, which is time-consuming. Hachimura et al. [7] have investigated digital archiving of Japanese dance movements using motion capture system. Their researches and findings have related to motion segment, motion and/or player identification, extraction of characteristic poses, similarity retrieval of dance motions, and qualitative analysis of dance motion. Jian et al. [8] presented a motion retrieval method based on the two-way reference index (DRI). They first extracted human jointing 3D space-time features, and then selected representative motion clips form a smaller set to establish bidirectional index. Due to discard the most irrelevant motion clips, thus the movement similar matching computation is narrowed to a small range of candidate dataset, which improve the efficiency of retrieval.

Gaurav et al. [9] developed an efficient indexing approach for 3D motion capture data, supporting queries involving both sub-body motions as well as whole-body motions. The proposed indexing structure is based on the hierarchical structure of the human body segments consisting of independent index trees corresponding to each sub-part of the body. In the literature [10], they improved the above index methods, and solved mistake lost problem for the feature space division brings by improving index function. Zhigang et al. [11] presented a perceptually example-based human motion retrieval approach; they employed a motion pattern discovery and matching scheme that breaks human motions into a part-based, hierarchical motion representation. On the basis, they used KMP motion string matching algorithm and KD tree structure to retrieval the motion. In reference [1] Shuangyuan et al. presented an efficient motion data indexing and retrieval method based on self-organizing map and Smith–Waterman string similarity metric. But when the SOM converts high-dimensional data into low-dimensional space (typically 2D), it will lose some key information of motion posture to make primitive posture distortion, so it will reduce retrieval accuracy. Worawat et al. [12] proposed a new technique for dimensionality reduction based the average and variance of joint angles. The new dimensional reduction named Constant Approximation with Average and Variance (CAAV) exploiting simple comprehensible average and variance of the joint angles of a human body.

3 The Description of Human Motion

In this paper, we adopt the human skeleton model as shown in Figure 1. The model is comprised of 28 joints, each of which is organized in a tree-shape structure; the root is the root of the tree-shape human skeleton, and the sub trees of root are formed due to the root's extension to each end-joint of the human skeleton. The root joint is represented by 3 translation vectors and 3 rotation vectors, and each of the other non-root joints is represented with 3 translation vectors. The translation vector of root determines the current location of human motion, while the rotation vectors of root determines the direction of human body. The rotation vectors of other joint points represent the joint point's direction in the local coordinate where its father joint point is in, and the posture of human body is determined by them together.

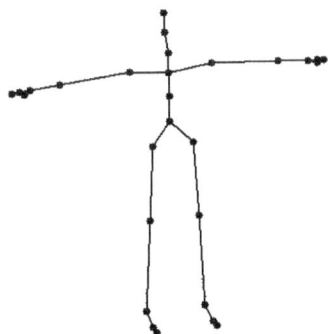

Fig. 1. The human skeleton model

The human motion data are regarded as body posture sequence which are derived from discrete time points sample, each sampled point as a frame, and each posture of which is decided by 28 joints together. So, at arbitrary time i, the human body posture can be represented as $F_i = (p_i^{(1)}, r_i^{(1)}, r_i^{(2)}, ..., r_i^{(28)})$, where $p_i^{(1)} \in R^3$ $r_i^{(1)} \in R^3$ separately represents the position and direction of root joint, namely the translation vectors and rotation vectors. $r_i^{(j)} \in R^3$, $j = 2, ..., 28$ is the direction of non-root joint.

According to the mutual relationship of each joint in human skeleton, at arbitrary time i, and the position of each non-root joint N_j in human skeleton can be obtained from formula (1).

$$p_i^{(j)} = T_i^{(root)} R_i^{(root)} .... T_0^{(grandparen\ t)} R_i^{(grandparen\ t)} (t) T_0^{(parent)} R_i^{(parent)} p_0^{(j)} \qquad (1)$$

where $P_i^{(j)}$ is the position of joint j at time i; $T_i^{(root)}$, $R_i^{(root)}$ are the position matrix and orientation matrix of root at time i; $T_0^{(k)}$ is position matrix of joint N_k in local coordinate system of its parent at start time; $R_i^{(k)}$ is orientation matrix of joint N_k, at time i, made by $r_i^{(k)}$, $P_0^{(j)}$ is position matrix of joint N_j, in local coordinate system of its parent at start time. So each frame of motion data is an 87-dimensional vector and a sequence of motion data can be represented by matrix $M \in \Re^{m \times n}$, where m is the number of frames, and n equals 87.

4   Dimension Reduction

Due to the high-dimensional complexity of motion features, we can't effectively directly deal with the motion features, so it is necessary to reduce dimension for them. We map the original high-dimensional data into a low-dimensional subspace by an effective and reasonable dimension reduction algorithm, then it reveals the internal structure of human motion and eliminate a number of related redundant information in high-dimensional feature through the low-dimensional space, thus it make the subsequent treatment directly on the low-dimensional subspace, which avoid the complex calculation of original data and a series of problems produced by "dimension disasters" and so on. Human motion is inherently nonlinear, just using linear dimension reduction methods is difficult to find out the inherent characteristics of some complicated motions, and it is probable to loss some important motion information. So in this paper we employ the nonlinear method to reduce dimension for motion data.

ISOMAP is a manifold learning method, and manifold is the concept of topology. Its principle is: firstly, it uses the shortest path in nearest diagram to get approximate geodesic distance to replace Euclidean distance that cannot express inner manifold structure, then they are inputted into the multidimensional dimension analysis (MDS) to process, and then it finds the low-dimensional coordinates that embedded in the high-dimension space.

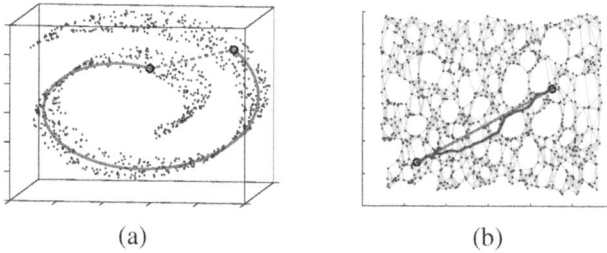

(a)   (b)

Fig. 2. The surveying distance estimation of ISOMAP dimension reduction

The dotted line indicates Euclidean distance of two points in three-dimensional space, the solid line means the actual distance of the two points on manifold, as shown in Fig.2 (a). We can see that Euclidian distance of the two points does not properly reflect the relationship in manifold. The ISOMAP dimension-reduction methods successfully reveals the manifold distance between two points, in blue line says the distance of the two points in the parameters space, the red line expressed the corresponding shortest path of two points on adjacency matrix as shown in Fig.2(b).

The specific steps of traditional ISOMAP algorithm are described as follows.

(1) Calculate neighbor points of each point (with K neighbor or ε neighborhood).

(2) Define an empowerment without directed graph the sample sets, if x_i and x_j are mutually neighbor point, the edge of weights will be $d_x(i, j)$.

(3)Employ *Dijkstra* or *Flyod* algorithm to calculate the shortest distance of between two points in chart, which define the distance matrix as $D_G = \{d_G(i, j)\}$.

(4) Use MDS for low-dimensional embedded manifold. The embedding low-dimensional is the second small to the d + 1 small eigenvalues corresponding eigenvectors of $\tau(D)$.

$$S = (S_{ij}) = (D_{ij}^{\ 2}), H = (H_{ij}) = (\delta_{ij} - 1/N), \tau(d) = -HSH / 2 \qquad (2)$$

Because the computational speed of the traditional ISOMAP algorithm is slower when it calculates the larger motion database, in order to reduce the time of dimension reduction to improve the overall retrieval efficiency, we use sparseness of adjacency graph to calculate the shortest path and build the low-dimensional embed with redundant distance to improve it, thus enhance the speed of dimension reduction. But the improved algorithms on storage rating of geometrical structure information of the original data also do not reduce. The specific improved algorithm is described as follows.

(1)Make D into sparse matrix with k = 7 neighbor.

(2)Use *Dijkstra* algorithm based on the Fibonacci heap data structure to calculate the shortest path.

(3)In *Dijkstra* algorithm call on "dijkstra.dll" which is compiled by "dijkstra.cpp" in the c + + environment.

The Fig.3 shows the human motion projection in low-dimensional subspace by ISOMAP dimension reduction.

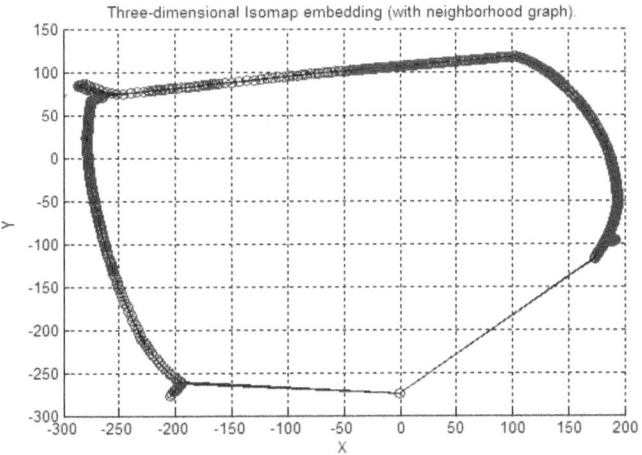

Fig. 3. A *Jump* motion projection in three-dimensional subspace

5   Index and Retrieval

Because human motion in the database not only has multiple attribute, but also has different lengths and speed, so obviously it is very difficult to directly retrieval the motion data, and the retrieval efficiency is very low. The purpose of establishing index is to exclude most irrelevant motion with retrieve samples from the motion database, which can avoid unnecessary traversal for large-scale database and the retrieval efficiency is improved.

5.1 Motion String Index

We extract a certain number of representative reference data from low dimensional data. For every motion clip, we calculate the distance between frames [8] to add the motion that has maximum variance to reference data, so we can get a motion string for each clip. Since human motion data exhibit intensive similarity in time axis, adjacent frames of a sequence are usually excluded. So we eliminate this redundancy to get a compact form of motion string, and every motion string is an index of a motion clip. Then we can eliminate most irrelevant data when retrieve and reach for the purpose of improving the calculation speed for the entire database index. From the Fig.4 we can see that the motion string indexing method can well preserve the motion information of original motion clips and reduce the complexity of the late process.

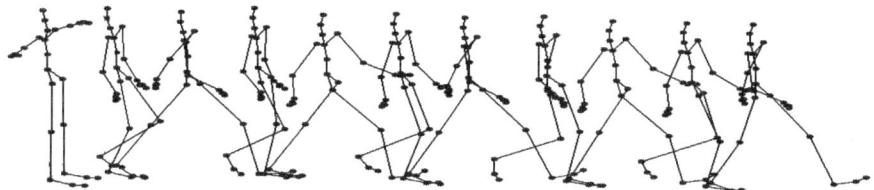

Fig. 4. A motion string of a Walk motion clip

Due to the time warping and spatial variations of human motion, motion clips with similar semantic meaning are usually not ideally aligned at the beginning. For example, comparing a short walking motion clip with a long one that contains only a walking subsequence, which is also called a segment, is a hard task on the original frame level because locating the match beginning requires a large computational cost, which is unaffordable when comparing a lot of clips. But when it comes to comparing the motion strings, the computation complexity is greatly reduced. Obviously, whether the selected motion string is appropriate and representative has greatly influence to the efficiency of the whole index system.

5.2 Clustering of Motions

Original motion data exist in high dimension space, so it is difficult to directly classify different motion. We employ ISOMAP method to map motion into low-dimensional manifolds, and as the characteristics of ISOMAP, it still can keep the geometrical structure of original data in the process of dimension reduction. Therefore the k-means clustering algorithms can be used to classify the database, and the motion clips are clustered into different group according to their motion types.

The K-means algorithm briefly described as follows.

(1)Determine an initial clustering center for each clustering, so that k clusters exists k clustering centers.

(2)Make each sample of the sample sets according to minimum distance principle assign to one of k clusters.

$$D_i = \min \left\{ \|x - c_i\| \right\} \quad x \in DataSet \qquad i=1, 2...k \qquad (3)$$

(3) Use the mean value of all samples in every clustering as a new clustering center.

(4) If clustering centers are changed, it will repeat the step 2 and 3, until clustering centers no longer changes.

(5) Finally, the k clustering centers are clustering results.

The criterion functions of K-means algorithm as follows.

$$J = \sum_{j=1}^{k} \sum_{i=1}^{n} \left\| x_i^{(j)} - c_j \right\|^2 \qquad (4)$$

where $x_i^{(j)} \in S_j$, C_j is the clustering center of clustering S_j.

5.3   Retrieval

After indexing and clustering the motion clips by the scheme described above, example-based motion retrieval can be performed. Given a motion database S and a retrieval sample Q, the goal of retrieval is to find all most similar motion data to Q. A retrieval sample is reduced dimension by ISOMAP algorithm to get a retrieval motion string. Then the motion string is compared to the motion motifs to get its nearest candidate group. The motion strings of the candidate group are on similarity calculation to that of the retrieval sample with Smith-Waterman algorithm to get retrieval results and retrieval results can be sorted by their degrees of similarity.

DTW is a matching method that used in time series of different lengths, but the greatest flaw is the quadratic athletic time consuming and storage space needs to limit its retrieval application in large-scale database. There have two algorithm are also most widely used in searching for the optimal similar compare algorithm of sequence. They are Blast algorithm and Smith-Waterman algorithm. The running speed of Blast algorithms is quicker than Smith-Waterman algorithm's, but Smith-Waterman algorithm is more accurate than Blast algorithm. Firstly, Smith-Waterman algorithm use iteration method to calculate all possible similarity score of two sequences, then to retrospectively seek optimum similarity comparison by the dynamic programming method.

Smith-Waterman algorithm is described as follows.

For two sequences S and T, $S[i]$ and $T[j]$, where $0 < i \leq |S|$, $0 < j \leq |T|$ belong to a character set Ω, to any of the elements and empty symbol, they have a score between them, which is represented with the scoring function $\sigma(x, y)$. $F(i, j)$ represents the optimal similarity compare scores between sequence S's prefixed $S[1]S[2]...S[i-1]S[i]$ and sequence T's prefix $T[1]T[2]...T[j-1]T[j]$. So has the following formula is

$$F(i, j) = \max \begin{cases} 0 \ (i = 0 \ or \ j = 0) \\ F(i-1, j-1) + \sigma(S[i], T[j]) \\ F(i-1, j) + \sigma(-, j) \\ F(i, j-1) + \sigma(i, -) \end{cases} \qquad (5)$$

By formula (5) we can get a score matrix M. Again to score matrix for dynamic programming method get back the similarity comparison algorithm.

Smith–Waterman algorithm compares segments of all possible lengths, instead of looking at each sequence in its entirety, and chooses whichever maximize the similarity measure. It is an effective local similarity measurement method. For example, DTW is a frame level distance metric method that can get ideal results only when there is good matching at beginning and end, with small distortions in the middle of two sequences. However, we can get optimal result with only parts of the motion strings considered by Smith–Waterman algorithm.

6 Experimental Results

Our experiment dataset is made up of 270 motion data clips, including 16 motion types such as walking, running, kicking, boxing, jumping, etc. The experimental data we adopted are from the Carnegie Mellon University motion capture database. All experiments were implemented in *Matlab* 7.1 on a PC with 2GB memory and a 2.70 GHz Dual-core processor.

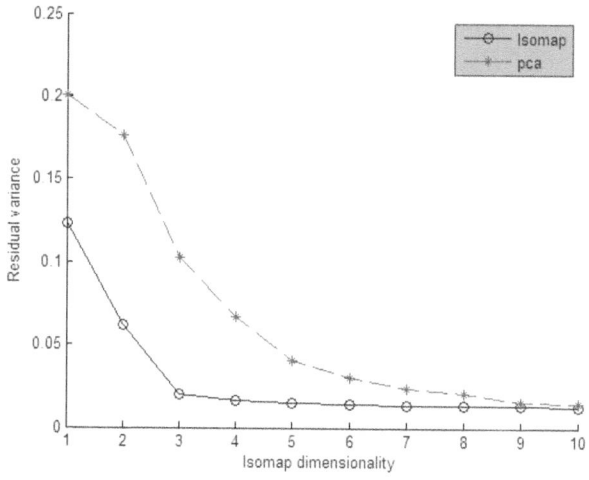

Fig. 5. The comparison of dimension-reduction methods

The dimensions of a Dance motion sequence from high-dimension to reduce 1-10 dimension of residual variance comparison are shown in Fig.5. For analyzing the data in graph we can see that PCA dimension-reduction methods obviously lost some key information of motion in reducing dimension process to complex human motion type, which will result in retrieval precision of decline. But due to the character of ISOMAP dovetails with the nonlinearity of human motion, we can see that it can well preserve the geometry information of original data, and from the Table 1 we can see that the ISOMAP algorithm on the reduced-dimension time also do not cause a big increase, while in this paper the time of improved ISOMAP algorithm by us is more faster. Therefore the adaptability of ISOMAP dimension reduction algorithm is better than the PCA algorithm.

Table 1. The comparison time of dimension-reduction methods

Example(frames)	PCA and ISOMAP(time/s)		Improved ISOMAP(time/s)
Walk (1034)	35	37	4
Run (1130)	51	55	5.4
Jump (826)	21	22	2.5
Dance (1830)	270	274	7

Table 2. The retrieval performance statistics

Example	Precision and Recall (%)		Retrieval time (s)
Walk	89.3	90	2
Run	87.2	88.5	3.2
Jump	86.3	87.3	4.1
Dance	84.8	85.9	4.8

From the Table 2 we can see that retrieval samples of different motion types obtain precision and the recall is also different. When the motion type changes complex, the precision and the recall also subsequently decline. But as a whole, our retrieval method achieves a pleasing result with good accuracy and efficiency.

7 Conclusion

With the development of motion capture technology and the establishment of large-scale 3D database, motion retrieval technology has come into being. In this paper, the ISOMAP algorithm is adopted to preprocess the original database, and improve the method to raise the velocity of reducing dimension. In the low-dimension space, we established a kind of motion string index to make the time length and space complex of motion data greatly reduce in subsequent process. We compare the motion strings of candidate group and the retrieval example with Smith-Waterman algorithm to obtain the similar motion sequence. Many unnecessary matching is avoided, so the retrieval efficiency is improved. Experimental results show that our method is effective.

Because k-means clustering algorithm can not necessarily get the optimal solution and often fall into local optimal rather than global optimal situation, and it needs to know quantity of classification in advance. Next, we will seek more appropriate clustering algorithm to improve the accuracy and efficiency of retrieval.

Acknowledgments. This work is supported by the National Natural Science Foundation of China (No.60875046), the Key Project of Chinese Ministry of Education (No.2009029,211036), the Program for Liaoning Excellent Talents in University (No.LR201003), the Program for Liaoning Science and Technology Research in University (No.LS2010008,2009S008, 2009S009), the Program for Liaoning Innovative Research Team in University(No. 2009T005,LT2010005).

References

1. Shuangyuan, W., Shihong, X., Zhaoqi, W.: Efficient motion data indexing and retrieval with local similarity measure of motion strings. Vis. Computer 25, 499–508 (2009)
2. Lin, Y.: Efficient Motion Search in Large Motion Capture Databases. In: Bebis, G., Boyle, R., Parvin, B., Koracin, D., Remagnino, P., Nefian, A., Meenakshisundaram, G., Pascucci, V., Zara, J., Molineros, J., Theisel, H., Malzbender, T. (eds.) ISVC 2006. LNCS, vol. 4291, pp. 151–160. Springer, Heidelberg (2006)
3. Yamasaki, T., Aizawa, K.: Content-Based Cross Search for Human Motion Data Using Time-Varying Mesh and Motion Capture Data. In: Proceeding of IEEE International Conference on Multimedia and Expo, ICME 2007, Beijing, China, pp. 2007–2009 (2007)
4. Muller, M., Roder, T., Clausen, M.: Efficient Content-Based Retrieval of Motion Capture Data. ACM Transactions on Graphics 24(3), 677–685 (2005)
5. Gao, Y., Ma, L., Chen, Y., Liu, J.: Content-Based Human Motion Retrieval with Automatic Transition. In: Nishita, T., Peng, Q., Seidel, H.-P. (eds.) CGI 2006. LNCS, vol. 4035, pp. 360–371. Springer, Heidelberg (2006)
6. Gu, Q., Peng, J., Deng, Z.: Compressions of human motion capture data using motion pattern indexing. Compute Graph Forum 28(1), 1–12 (2009)
7. Sonoda, M., Tsuruta, S., Yoshimura, M., Hachimura, K.: Segmentation of dancing movement by extracting features from motion capture data. Journal of the Institute of Image Electronics Engineers of Japan 37(3), 303–311 (2008)
8. Jian, X., Tongqiang, G., Tingyue, Z., Lv, Y.: Based on two reference index large human motion database index (in Chinese). Journal of Computer Research and Development 45(12), 2145–2153 (2008)
9. Pradhan, G.N., Li, C., Prabhakaran, B.: Hierarchical Indexing Structure for 3D Human Motions. In: Cham, T.-J., Cai, J., Dorai, C., Rajan, D., Chua, T.-S., Chia, L.-T. (eds.) MMM 2007, Part I. LNCS, vol. 4351, pp. 386–396. Springer, Heidelberg (2006)
10. Gaurav, N.P., Balakrishnan, P.: Indexing 3D Human Motion Repositories for Content-Based Retrieval. IEEE Transactions on Information Technology in Biomedicine 13(5), 802–809 (2009)
11. Zhigang, D., Qin, G., Qing, L.: Perceptually Consistent Example-based Human Motion Retrieval. In: I3D 2009, Boston, Massachusetts, Boston, Massachusetts, February 27-March 1, pp. 191–198. ACM, New York (2009)
12. Choensawat, W., Choi, W., Hachimura, K.: A quick filtering for similarity queries in motion capture databases. In: Muneesawang, P., Wu, F., Kumazawa, I., Roeksabutr, A., Liao, M., Tang, X. (eds.) PCM 2009. LNCS, vol. 5879, pp. 404–415. Springer, Heidelberg (2009)

Biomimetic Pattern Face Recognition Based on DCT and LDA

Jing Shao, Jia-fu Jiang, and Xiao-wei Liu

Institute of Computer and Communication Engineering
Changsha University of Science and Technology
Changsha, China
shaojing0514@163.com

Abstract. A new method of Biomimetic pattern face recognition theory based on DCT and LDA Transform is proposed. This method has solved the problem of the low recognition rate and the excessively high dimension problem. The features of human face on the training samples are extracted through DCT and LDA, mapping them into the high-dimensional space through Kernel function, and then use it to construct the cover region of each kind of sample. The person face is distinguished through the judgment that the person face characteristics belong to which kind of cover region or don't belong to any region. The experiment on the Yale and ORL face database demonstrated the efficiency and the feasibility of our algorithm.

Keywords: Discrete Cosine Transform(DCT), Linear Discriminant Analysis (LDA), biomimetic pattern recognition, high dimensional space cover.

1 Introduction

Face recognition is one of the most active research areas in computer vision and pattern recognition. Many face recognition algorithms have been developed, such as PCA [1], LDA [2] etc. However, they all set the "best division" as their goal whether the training sample classes belongs to a certain kind, which will causes the untrained sample class belong to some kind of trained sample class. As a consequence, mis-recognition exists. While the Biomimetic Pattern Face Recognition [3,4] is based on" things understand" to identify things, which is similar to human "know things" properties. The Biomimetic pattern recognition had been employed in face recognition [5, 8]. The discrete cosine transform has also been employed in face recognition [6, 7]. The DCT has several advantages over the PCA. Firstly, the DCT is data independent. Secondly, the DCT can be implemented using a fast algorithm.

Ju Sheng-Gen et al. [8] has presented a Biomimetic pattern face recognition method which is based on the K-L Transform .However, it has to calculate the eigenvalues of the covariance matrix in the progress of feature extraction, which will cause complex computation .To address this problem, Based on the idea of LDA and DCT, Yin Hong-tao et al.[7] has presented a method based on DCT and LDA, which employed the image projection technique, and has been developed for image feature extraction. The DCT+LDA method becomes an interesting technique in face recognition region,

H. Deng et al. (Eds.): AICI 2011, Part III, LNAI 7004, pp. 170–177, 2011.

since it can extract discriminative feature faster and better than the Karhunen-Loeve Transform.

In this paper, we propose a biomimetic pattern face recognition method based on DCT and LDA Transform. The effectiveness of the proposed method is verified using both the Yale database and the ORL database.

2 DCT, LDA, and Biomimetic Pattern Recognition

2.1 DCT

The DCT has been widely applied to solve numerous problems among the digital signal processing community. In particular, many data compression techniques employ the DCT, which has been found to be asymptotically equivalent to the optimal Karhunen-Loeve Transform (KLT) for signal decorrelation. Another merit of the DCT is that can be implemented efficiently using the Fast Fourier Transform (FFT). DCT has been widely used in image coding and face recognition. Signal after DCT transformation, energy could be concentrated in a few transform coefficient, signal the contribution of smaller coefficient will be deleted, using only reserved coefficient, it won't cause apparent distortion of signal. Given an input $m \times n$ image f (x, y) , its DCT coefficients, C(u,v) is obtained by the following formula:

$$C(u,v) = \alpha(u)\alpha(v) \times \sum_{x=0}^{m-1} \sum_{y=0}^{n-1} f(x,y) \cos\frac{(2x-1)u\pi}{2m} \cos\frac{(2y-1)v\pi}{2n} \tag{1}$$

where u=0,1,...,m-1 and v=0,1,...,n-1, $\alpha(u)$ and $\alpha(v)$ are defined by:

$$\alpha(u) = \begin{cases} \sqrt{1/m}, & u = 0 \\ \sqrt{2/m} & u = 1,2,\cdots,n-1 \end{cases} \tag{2}$$

$$\alpha(v) = \begin{cases} \sqrt{1/n}, & v = 0 \\ \sqrt{2/n} & v = 1,2,\cdots,n-1 \end{cases} \tag{3}$$

As the Fig.1 shows, after DCT transformation, we can get a coefficient matrix the same size of the original image .The low-frequency coefficients has concentrated in

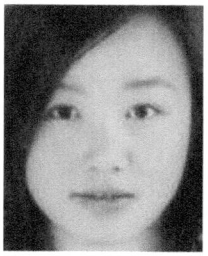

(a)RGB image   (b)Its DCT coefficient

Fig. 1. Face image and its DCT coefficients

the matrix of the top-left corner, which is image changes slower component; while the High frequency coefficients has concentrated in the down-right side of the matrix, which is the detail of the image and edge ingredients.

2.2 LDA

LDA is one of the best ways of feature extraction. It aims to extract the high-dimension feature space, and make the same category classes together, with different types of classes widely apart. Suppose that there are c kinds of classes, the numbers of total classes are N, The between-class scatter matrix S_b and the within-class scatter matrix S_w are defined as follows:

$$S_w = \frac{1}{N} \sum_{i=1}^{c} \sum_{j=1}^{N_i} (y_j^{(i)} - y^{(i)})(y_j^{(i)} - y^{(i)})^T \tag{4}$$

$$S_b = \frac{1}{N} \sum_{i=1}^{c} N_i (y^{(i)} - \bar{y})(y^{(i)} - \bar{y})^T \tag{5}$$

where N_i stands for the numbers of the i-th kind of classes, $y^{(i)}$ stands for the mean value of the i-th kind of classes, $y_j(i)$ stands for the j-th sample in the i-th classes, while $\bar{y}$ stands for the mean value of all the classes.LDA method tries to find a objective function $f(W_{fld})$ maximizing the ratio of determinant of the between-class scatter to the within-class scatter. And the $f(W_{fld})$ is defined as:

$$f(W_{fld}) = \frac{|W^T S_b W|}{|W^T S_w W|} \tag{6}$$

2.3 Biomimetic Pattern Recognition

Traditional Pattern Recognition aims at getting the optimal classification of different classes of sample in the feature space. However, the BPR intends to find the optimal covering of the samples in the same class. The case in two-dimensional space is illustrated by Fig. 2. the triangles represent samples in one class to be recognized. The circles and crosses represent samples in other different classes. Polygonal line represents the classification manner of traditional Back Propagation (BP) networks. Big circle represents the classification manner of Radial-Basis Function (RBF) networks. The ellipses as well as sausage-like curves represent "cognition" manner of BPR.

It can be seen that the basic method of BPR is to analyze the relation of training sample of the same class in feature space. And the PHC of sample distribution in the feature space makes it possible.

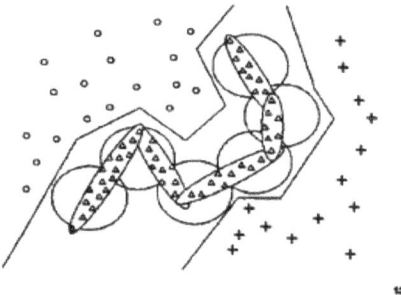

Fig. 2. The schematic diagram of the difference of BP, RBF, and BPR

3   Proposed Method

There are two steps to accomplish our goals, the first one is to extract the sample features of the face library, and the second one is to map the lower dimension of features to high dimension space, then recognize by Higher-dimensional space covers. Diagram of our face recognition system is showed in Fig. 3.

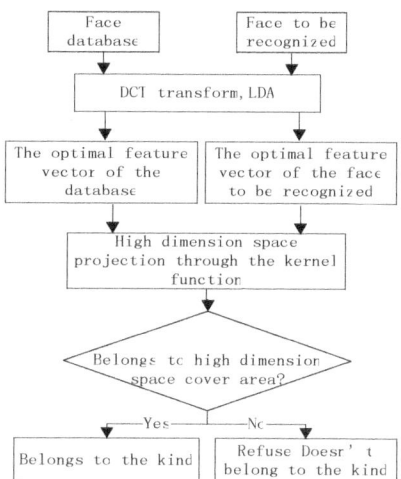

Fig. 3. Diagram of the proposed face recognition system

3.1   Extracting Sample Features of the Face Data-Base Using DCT and LDA

Given a face image training sets X, the number of total image is N. Firstly, we will classify all the image and set those who belongs to the same object as a kind, we marked X_i ;where the number of total image is N_i ,i=1,2,...c, c stands for the number of the kinds. And we can calculate the within-class average images m_i and the total average images m, and the difference image $\bar{x}$. And the total difference average images $\bar{m}$ by the following two formula:

$$\forall x \in X_i, m_i = \frac{1}{N_i}\sum x; \forall x \in X, m = \frac{1}{N}\sum x \tag{7}$$

$$\forall x \in X_i, X_i \in X, \bar{x} = x - m_i, \bar{m} = m_i - m \tag{8}$$

Then, we do Discrete Cosine Transform on training image and will get the DCT projection subspace W_{DCT} and mapping both within-class average images and the total average images into it the following formula.

$$\hat{x} = W_{DCT}^T \bar{x}, \hat{m}_i = W_{DCT}^T \bar{m}_i, \hat{m} = W_{DCT}^T \bar{m} \tag{9}$$

The following steps are calculation of the between-class scatter matrix S_b and the within-class scatter-matrix S_w using formula (4) and (5), calculating generalized eigenvalue and eigenvector, sorting according to the characteristic value from the large to the small. Keeping the former c-1 kinds, we can get the best classification subspace of LDA: W_{LDA} by keeping the former c-1 kinds. Combining the two subspace we will get the optimal cast shadow space:

$$W_{opt}^T = W_{LDA}^T W_{DCT}^T \tag{10}$$

3.2 High Dimensional Space Cover

We need the face image to identify the subtracted even face image, projecting their difference value into the optimal cast shadow space, so that we can get characteristic vector of the face image to identify:

$$z_i = W^T{}_{opt}(x - m) \tag{11}$$

We will use the polynomial kernel function [8], mapping z_i from low dimensionality space to high dimension space by the following formula.

$$k(z_i, z) = (z_i^T z + 1)^q, q > 0 \tag{12}$$

where z stands for the center of the similar sample. And then we can calculate similar sample's mean value C_i^H and variance ρ_i^H at all directions in the high dimension space. Judging whether it is satisfies the following inequality:

$\prod_{i=1}^{N} Exp\left[-\frac{(z_i^H - C_i^H)^2}{(\rho_i^H)^2}\right] \leq T$ where T stands for the size of face coverage, usually

T=0.95~0.975,and if they are satisfied, we can demonstrate that the face image to identify belongs to the kind. Otherwise, it doesn't belong to the kind.

3.3 Algorithm Process

Step1: Do Discrete Cosine Transform on training image and will get the DCT projection subspace W_{DCT} using LDA and we can get the best classification subspace of LDA: W_{LDA}, through combination of the two subspace we will get the optimal cast shadow space by equation (10).

Step2: Mapping z_i from low dimensionality space to high dimension space by using the polynomial kernel function $k(z_i,z)=(z_i^T z+1)^q, q>0$.

Step3: Select initial mean $C_i^H(0)$ at random, setting initial studying rate $\alpha(0)$;

Step4: Calculate the average minimum distance between similar face and the samples: $l^H(k)=\| Z_i^H(k)-C_i^H(k)\|$, find out the point that have the mini-distance: $q=\arg[\min l^H\{k\}]$.

Step5: updating:

$$C_i^H(k)=C_i^H(k-1)+\alpha(k)\Delta z_i^H(k); \Delta z_i^H(k)=z_i^H(k)-C_i^H(k-1);$$

$$\alpha(k)=\frac{\alpha(k-1)}{1+int[(k-1)/max\_ita]^{\frac{1}{2}}}$$ .where int[ ] stands for taking int, and max_ita

stands for the maximum iterating times.

Step6: Judging whether it is satisfying the inequality

$$\prod_{i=1}^{N} Exp\left[-\frac{(z_i^H-C_i^H)^2}{(\rho_i^H)^2}\right]\leq T$$; if it is satisfied, then exit the loop, otherwise go back
to step2.

4 Experimental Results

To test the performance of the proposed method, some experiments are performed on both the Yale face database and the ORL database.

4.1 Experiment on Yale Face Database

There are 15 people in Yale database, and each of them has 11 face images. We randomly select 5 face images from each subject to construct the training dataset, the remaining images are used as the test images. Each experiment is repeated 20 times. The average recognition rates on the test sets are showed in table 1.

Table 1. The recognition rates on Yale database (%)

DCT coefficients	9	16	25	36	49	64	81	100
Recognition rates	95.23	96.63	98.21	97.56	97.04	96.96	96.19	95.68

4.2 Experiment on ORL Face Database

There are 400 images of 40 individuals in this database. We randomly select 5 face images from each subject to construct the training dataset, the remaining images are used as the test images. Each experiment is repeated 20 times, the average recognition rates on the test sets is showed in table 2.

Table 2. The recognition rates on ORL database(%)

DCT coefficients	9	16	25	36	49	64	81	100
Recognition rates	95.10	96.54	98.1	97.44	96.92	96.67	96.08	95.56

We have compared our results with two recognition algorithms: DCT+PCA[6],and DCT+LDA[7].Here are the experiments performed on ORL face database.

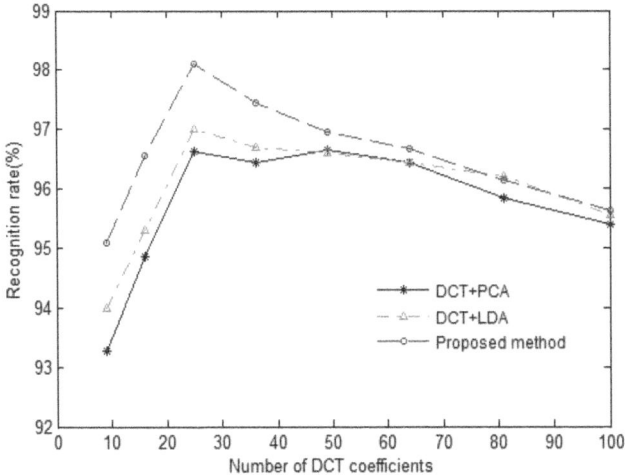

Fig. 4. Recognition accuracy versus different number of DCT coefficients.

We randomly select 5 face images from each subject to construct the training dataset, the remaining images are used as the test images. Each experiment is repeated 20 times.

We can clearly see that using more DCT coefficients cannot obtain the best recognition rate. We also compared our results with face recognition based on bionic pattern face recognition based on Karhunen-Loeve Transform[8], as table 3 shows.

Table 3. Recognition rate comparison on ORL database(%)

Methods	Recognition rate
Bionic pattern face recognition	97.5
Proposed method	98.1

5 Conclusions

In this paper, we have proposed a biomimetic pattern face recognition method based on DCT and LDA Transform .The experiment on the Yale and the ORC face database demonstrated that our method is better than the bionic pattern face recognition based on K-L Transform ,the PCA+DCT, and the DCT+LDA methods.

Acknowledgment. Project supported by Hunan Provincial NSF of China (Project No. 10JJ2050).

References

1. Sirovich, L., Kirby, M.: Application of Karhunen-Loeve procedure for the characterization of human faces. IEEE Trans Pattern Analysis and Machine Intelligence 3, 71–79 (1990)
2. Belhumeur, P.N., Hespanha, J.P.: Eigenfaces vs Fisher-faces: recognition using class specific linear projection. IEEE Trans Pattern Analysis and Machine Intelligence 19, 711–720 (1997)
3. Wang, S.-J., Chen, X.: Biomimetic Pattern Recognition-A new Model of Pattern Recognition Theory and Its Application. IEEE Trans Pattern Analysis and Machine Intelligence. 3, 2258–2262 (2003)
4. Wang, S.-J.: Analysis and Theory of High Dimension Space Geometry for Artificial Neural Networks. Journal of Electronic 30, 1–4 (2002)
5. Wang, S.-J.: Face Recognition: Biomimetic Pattern Recognition vs. Traditional Pattern Recognition. Journal of Electronic, 1057–1060 (2004)
6. Samir, A., Amine, S.M., Chahir, Y.: Face Recognition Using PCA and DCT. In: 2009 IEEE Fifth International Conference on MEMS NANO, and Smart Systems, pp. 15–19 (2009)
7. Yin, H.-T., Fu, P.: Face Recognition Based on DCT and LDA. Journal of Electronic 10, 2211–2214 (2009)
8. Ju, S.-G., Zhou, J.-L.: Face recognition based on bionic pattern. Journal of Sichuan University 45, 65–70 (2008)
9. Zhang, Y.-K., Liu, C.-Q.: A Novel Face Recognition Method Based on LDA. Journal of Infrared Millim 22, 327–330 (2003)
10. Azam, M.: Discrete Cosine Transform Based Face Recognition in Hexagonal Images. IEEE Trans. Pattern Analysis and Machine Intelligence, 474 –479 (2010)

Model Identification of Coal Main Fans in Mine Based on Neural Network

Xinhui Du, Ruifeng An, and Zhimei Chen

College of Electrical and Power Engineering
Taiyuan University of Technology, Shan Xi Electric Power Corporation
Taiyuan 030024
duxinhui211@163.com,
lovearf@163.com

Abstract. The parameters of main fans in coal mine such as air flow, wind speed, gas concentration and other conditions are closely related, for its complexity, it's difficult to establish the nonlinear mathematic model, and it's hard to describe the model properties by traditional identification method. Neural network is used in mine ventilator model identification. BP-Neural network based on L-M algorithm and RBF-Neural network based on K-mean algorithm are used in Neural network. The simulation results show that the two methods can satisfy the needs of identification precision, convergence rate, stability and tracking ability simultaneous.

Keywords: Main fans model, System identification, Neural network, BP, RBF.

1 Introduction

Gas accidents in China's coal mines major accident more than 70%, however coal face was a risk regions about gas and coal seam accident. About 80 percent of gas explosion accidents and local-ventilator were concerned.

The amount of wind in the coal face is a dynamic system that was closely related to gas concentration, wind resistance, tunnel length. These parameters are constantly changing, so be very difficult to establish the mathematical model. The traditional methods to gain the object properties and model were the following: step response method, the impulse response method, least square parameter identification methods and so on. Control accuracy is not high, the lack online self-learning or self-adjustment ability. Taking into account the nonlinear, multi-coupled, multi-interference of the system, using neural network can avoid the difficult of modeling, a better control performance. This paper based on Back Propagation (BP) algorithm Radial Basis Function (RBF) neural network identification to obtain the characteristics of the object, a mathematical model of the mine ventilation system was established, and its advantage was that the object does not need to add additional stimulus, only use the object input and output data that produced in normal operation condition can be more precise object model, will not adversely affect the system. Those two identification methods can be seen that a good description of the actual system

H. Deng et al. (Eds.): AICI 2011, Part III, LNAI 7004, pp. 178–185, 2011.

through the simulation, high precision identification, good robustness, tracking ability and stability, a good ventilation system to overcome the nonlinear , uncertainty, strong coupling and other factors.

2 The Main Fans System's Model Identification

The problem which is the description of system mathematics, using system identification has been resolved. The system was described through model to express, so the system identification is also called model identification, mainly including the confirmation model structure, estimation model unknown parameters and testing model effect.

There are a lot of identification methods, such as function simulating, artificial intelligence identification. Back Propagation (BP) neural network and Radial Basis Function (RBF) neural network identification were used in the paper.

2.1 Neural Network System Identification Theory

If the status of the system are unable to get, only the input and output data X (k), Y (k), then must adopt input/output model of identification method of system. Using neural network model identification system, the three contents are corresponding into neural network topology structure of choice, neural network learning training and network generalization ability test.

Based on neural network identification controlled object characteristics and model of simple principle and algorithm were introduced as follows:

Be collected to the object input/output data according to certain methods organized learning samples, providing with a delay unit network for learning. After a lot of training and after study, the network can be a very good approximation actual object's output.

Neural network for the essence of system identification was chosen a suitable neural network model to approximate the actual system. Compared with the traditional identification methods, application of neural networks for the advantages of system identification was don't need the actual system established beforehand to identify format, it was by the identification system of direct study system to input/output data, the purpose of the study was make the function of required deviation rule to the minimum by fixed network parameters (weights). In this way summarized that implicit in the system input/output data relationships. The relationship was described dynamics the dynamic property of the system operator P. P implicit in neural network, it was unknowable for the actually performance what kind of form in outside, namely the neural network identification was a black box.

2.2 Error (BP) Neural Network Model Identification

BP neural network model identification of mine fans.

BP network establishment attributed to BP algorithm, BP algorithm belong to the δ algorithm, was a kind of supervised learning algorithm. Its main ideas: for q learning samples: $x^1, x^2 \cdots, x^q$, known for its corresponding output samples $y^1, y^2 \cdots, y^q$. The purpose of study was using the error between the actual output of the network $A^1, A^2 \cdots, A^q$ and the target vector $y^1, y^2 \cdots, y^q$ to modify its value, and make $A^l (l = 1, 2, \cdots, q)$ with expectations of as close as possible, that is, make the network output layer error sum of squares was minimized. It makes through continuously relative to the error function in the direction of the slope drop calculation of network weights and deviation of change and gradually approximation targets. Every weights and deviation of changes and network error is proportional to the influence, and with back propagation style to deliver to each layer .

L - M algorithm
The original BP algorithm is along the gradient descent method, the parameters with error gradient in the opposite direction moving, reduce the error function until obtain minimum values, its computational complexity is mainly caused by the calculation partial derivative. This based on gradient descent method was linear convergence, speed very slowly.

The L-M algorithm in the thesis was a kind of using standard numerical optimization method fast algorithms, it was the gradient descent method and Gaussian-Newton method combination, also can called as Gaussian Newton improvement form, it not only has the Gauss – Newton local convergence, but also but also has the global properties gradient descent method. L - M algorithm about approximate second derivatives of information, was much fast than gradient method. L - M algorithm theory was as follows:

$x(k)$ mean both vectors the kth iterations of the weights and threshold, new weights and threshold value can be composed of vector $x^{(k+1)}$ obtained according to the following rules:

$$x^{(k+1)} = x^{(k)} + \Delta x \tag{1}$$

L - M algorithm was a kind of improved Gaussian - Newton method, its form for:

$$\Delta x = -\left[J^T(x)J(x) + \mu \right]^{-1} J(x)e(x) \tag{2}$$

$$J(x) = \begin{bmatrix} \dfrac{\partial e_1(x)}{\partial x_1} & \dfrac{\partial e_1(x)}{\partial x_2} & \cdots & \dfrac{\partial e_1(x)}{\partial x_n} \\[2mm] \dfrac{\partial e_2(x)}{\partial x_1} & \dfrac{\partial e_2(x)}{\partial x_2} & \cdots & \dfrac{\partial e_2(x)}{\partial x_n} \\[2mm] \vdots & \vdots & \cdots & \vdots \\[2mm] \dfrac{\partial e_N(x)}{\partial x_1} & \dfrac{\partial e_N(x)}{\partial x_2} & \cdots & \dfrac{\partial e_N(x)}{\partial x_n} \end{bmatrix} \tag{3}$$

In equation (2) scaling factor $\mu > 0$ is a constant, I is the identity matrix. L - M algorithm used approximate the second derivatives of information than gradient descent method, was much faster, practice shows that L-M algorithm than the original method using gradient descent method speed much fast about dozens or even hundreds of times. Plus, the $\left[J^T(x)J(x) + \mu I \right]$ is positive, therefore (2) always has its solution, in this sense, L-M algorithm is also superior to other algorithms.

In (2) scaling factor $\mu > 0$ is a constant, I is the identity matrix. L - M algorithm used approximate the second derivatives of information than gradient descent method, was much faster, practice shows that L-M algorithm than the original method using gradient descent method speed much fast about dozens or even hundreds of times. Plus, the $\left[J^T(x)J(x) + \mu I \right]$ is positive, therefore (2) always has its solution, in this sense, L-M algorithm is also superior to other algorithms.

2.3   Radiate Basis Function (RBF) Neural Network Model Identification

Radial basis function method was a technology for interpolation in high dimensional space. The basic RBF neural network was composed of three layers, each layer has a totally different effect. Input layer was composed by some perception of neurons, they connect the network with the external environment; The second layer was the only hidden layer in network, its role was provide non-linear conversion from the input space into the hidden layer space. In most cases, hidden layer had a higher dimension; Output layer is linearly layer, it provides the response for the input layer of activation patterns. It's topological structure shown as shown in figure 1.

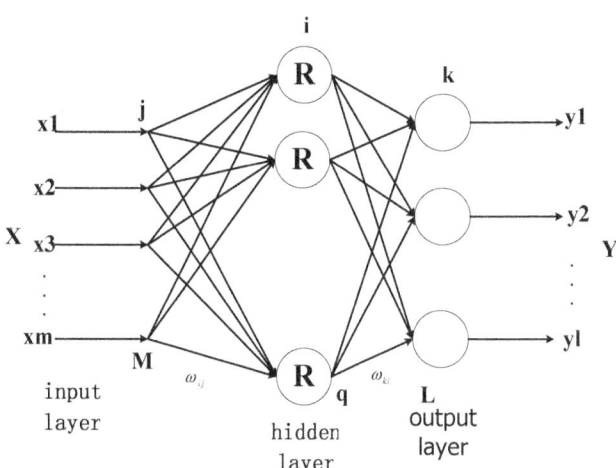

Fig. 1. RBF neural network structure

RBF network was partial approaches network with arbitrary precision, it can approximate any continuous function. Its working principle can be understood as a special fuzzy system.

The output calculation of the RBF network

Suppose the input n-dimension vector X, output m-dimension vector Y, input/output samples length L, then RBF network hidden layer the output of the ith node for:

$$q_i = R\|X - c_i\| \tag{4}$$

Among, the X n-dimension input vector; the c_i center of the ith hidden nodes, $i = 1, 2, \cdots \|\bullet\|$ usually the Euclidean norm; $R(\cdot)$ RBF function with the characteristics of local experience. It has many forms, embodies the RBF neural network nonlinear mapping capabilities.

The kth node of network output layer was linear combination of the hidden nodes output:

$$. \; y_k = \sum_i w_{ki} q_i - \theta_k \tag{5}$$

Among, w_{ki} the connection weights $q_i \to y_k$, θ_k of the kth node.

RBF learning algorithm.

Have p group with input and output samples x_p / d_q, $p = 1, 2, \cdots L$, to define target function:

$$J = \frac{1}{2}\sum_p \|d_p - y_p\|^2 = \frac{1}{2}\sum_p \sum_k (d_{kp} - y_{kp})^2 \tag{6}$$

The purpose of the study was to make $J \le \varepsilon$, in this type E_q was output vector of input x_p, RBF network learning algorithm was generally includes two stages:

In the center determination of hidden layer RBF self-organization choose law center was used in the paper.

Radial basis function weight learning, some like the center supervision and selection method were often been used.

Center self-organization selection method was a nonteacher learning, also called unsupervised learning, was for all samples input to cluster, was used to obtain the central node of hidden layer in the RBF. Here only introduced the k-means clustering algorithm that was common been used, the procedure as follows:

initialization: given all the hidden nodes initial center $c_i(0)$.

similar marching: calculating distance (Euclidean space) and get the smallest distance node:.

$$d_i(t) = \|x(t) - c_i(t-1)\|, \; 1 \le i \le h, \quad d_{\min}(t) = \min d_i(t) = d_r(t) \tag{7}$$

adjust center.

$$c_i(t) = c_i(t-1) \ 1 \leq i \leq h, \ i \neq r, c_r(t) = c_r(t-1) + \beta(x(t) - c_r(t-1)) \quad (8)$$

Among, β *learning speed,* $0 < \beta < 1$.

continue: make t add 1, back to the second step, and repeat the process until center C_r *almost the same end.*

RBF neural network and multi-layer perceptron (MLP) were layered feed-forward networks of nonlinear, they were approximator, but RBF neural network algorithm more simple, practical, and modeling quickly, sometimes need not repeated training process, thus in the system for on-line identification field had been widely used.

3   The Simulation Test Analysis of Experimental Results

3.1   BP Neural Network Simulation Test Results of the Experiment

The system neural network models include four layers: input layer, two hidden layer and output layer. Among them, there are two nodes input layers representing the test in two locations of wind speed; Hidden number of nodes were uncertain, need to adjust at the training process; The output layer contains three node, represent three different test point of gas concentration. Target accuracy was taken as 0.001, the maximum number of cycles for the 8000.

The sample of training model come from data collected at the scene, acquisition several sets of data sample, choose the half data to trained for neural network, because the data were too crowded, using MATLAB simulation software for input/output data first normalized mapping to the data between [-1, 1], so it was easy to improve neural network training speed. Using forecast result to evaluate ANN prediction performance.

The data that selected from different training sample data using the trained neural network model for MATLAB simulation tests, the gas concentration in the upper corner of the actual output and neural network output curve shown in figure 2, the error curve shown in figure 3.

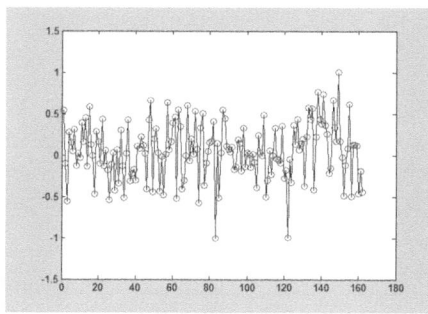
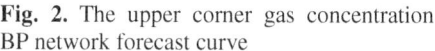
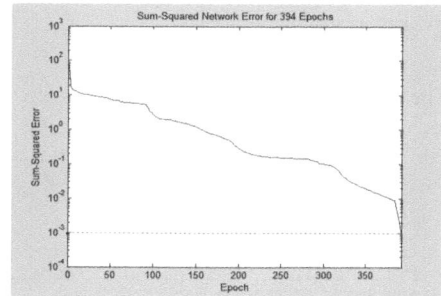

Fig. 2. The upper corner gas concentration BP network forecast curve

Fig. 3. The upper corner gas concentration BP nets training error curve

3.2   RBF Neural Network Simulation Test Results of the Experiment

Neural network models include: input layer, hidden and output layer. There are two nodes of input layers, respectively represent two site testing wind; number of nodes in the hidden layer had same number with input of each sample; the output layer contains three node, shows three different test point of gas concentration. Target accuracy was taken as 0.001, the maximum number of cycles for the 3000.

The BP neural network Settings same with the training and test sample data .The Input also need the normalized, not repeated .The upper corner gas concentration graph of actual output and neural network output as shown in figure 4 .Error curve as shown in figure 5.

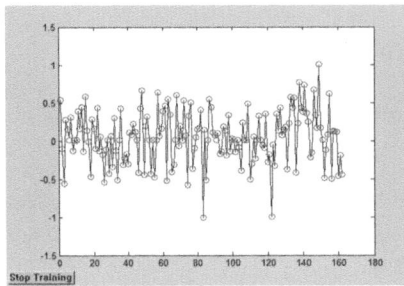   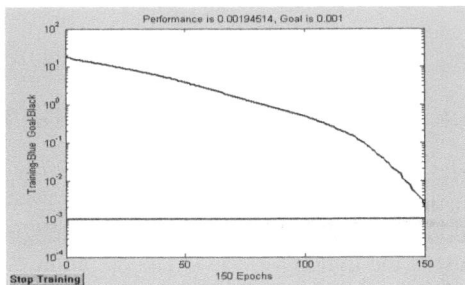

Fig. 4. The upper corner gas concentration RBF network forecast curve

Fig. 5. The upper corner gas concentration RBF nets training error curve

Two kinds of identification method compared the results shown in table 1.

Table 1. Performance comparison

performance	BP neural network	RBF neural network
error SSE	0.015%	0.00085%
identification time (s)	41.2190	5.4380
training times	394	140

4   Conclusion

The simulation tests show that both L - M algorithm of BP neural network and k-means clustering method of RBF neural network can be well applied in mine main fans mathematical model recognition u. Compared with the actual curve prediction curve, error are less than 0.1%. Neural network for mine main fans model identification has the following advantages:

- For nonlinear system (cannot been described linear model system) can been identified .And this identification was through network exterior fitting in the input/output of system, network internal inductive implied in the system input/output data accomplished the system characteristics, so the identification was realized by neural network itself.

- Identification convergence speed is not dependent on the dimension of unidentified system, only with neural network itself and its related to the algorithm. The traditional identification algorithm with the increase of model parameter dimension becomes complicated;
- Generalization ability and fault tolerance are advantages of neural network.

The simulation results also indicate that the using the RBF neural network method for identify the precision and time better than L - M algorithm of BP neural network. In mine main fans mathematical model recognition, identification method of RBF neural network will get more and more attention and application.

References

1. Hao, J.: BP algorithm and the application of coal and gas outburst prediction. Journal of Liaoning Technical University 1(23), 9–11 (2004)
2. Li, G.: Intelligent control and MATLAB simulation. Publishing house of electronics industry, Beijing (2005)
3. Sun, F., Shi, X.: Based on the MATLAB BP neural network design. Computer & Digital Engineering 8(35), 124–126 (2007)
4. Li, R.: Intelligent control theory and method. Xian University of electronic science and technology press (1999)
5. Chongzhi, F., Xiao, D.: Process identification. Tsinghua university press, Beijing (1998)
6. Kaili, Z., Kang, Y.: Neural network model and its MATLAB simulation program design. Tsinghua university press, Beijing (2006)
7. Akpan, V.A., Hassapis, G.: Adaptive predictive control using recurrent neural network identification. In: 17th Mediterranean Conference on Control and Automation, MED 2009 (2009)
8. Rhaman, M.K., Endo, T.: Recurrent neural network Classifier for Three Layer Conceptual. Network and Performance Evaluation 5(1), 40–48 (2010)
9. Albidewi, A., Ann, Y.T.: Combination of Subtractive Clustering and Radial Basis Function in Speaker identification, vol. 2(4) (April 2010)
10. Manjula, M., Sarma, A.V.R.S.: Classification of Voltage Sag Causes using Probabilistic neural network and Hilbert – Huang Transform 1(20) (2010)
11. Valarmathi, K., Devaraj, D., Radhakrishnan, T.K.: Intelligent techniques for system identification and controller tuning in pH process. Brazilian Journal of Chemical Engineering 26(1), 99–111 (2009)

Multiscale Finite Element Methods for Heat Equation in Three Dimension Honeycomb Structure

Xiao-qi Liu

Institute of Mathematics and Physics,
Central South University of Forestry and Technology, Changsha, China, 410004
xqliu2008@126.com

Abstract. Honeycomb structure is a kind of useful typical cellular solid. It has good physics, mechanism and heat properties because of its characteristics of cavity. The difficult to study the heat problem in honeycomb structure is the complexity of the geometric configuration. It is difficult to solve the problem by using directly finite element method because the subdivision is very difficult to obtain and very large scale computing and memory capacity. In this paper, we shall overcome above difficulties and study the heat equation in three dimensional honeycomb structure. A multiscale finite element method with high accuracy is presented. We derive the rigorous proofs of all convergence results.

Keywords: homogenization, multiscale asymptotic method, heat equation, honeycomb structure.

1 Introduction

Honeycomb structure is a kind of typical cellular solid. Because of its characteristics of cavity, it has good physics, mechanism and heat properties.Therefore, it has uses which compact solid hard to competent.

The difficult to study the heat problem in honeycomb structure is the complexity of the geometric configuration[4]. For example, since the cavity walls of the cellular solid of the space shuttle are very thin, it is not easy to solve the problem by using analytic method. In general, it is also difficult to solve the problem by using directly finite element method because the subdivision is very difficult to obtain and very large scale computing and memory capacity. There is good accuracy to find the effective coefficients of heat conduction in many cases by using the effective heat conduction method and common heat exchange equivalent method in engineering, but there is lower accuracy to compute the temperature field of the cavity surfaces and the interfaces of the different medias. Liqun Cao etc. studied the multiscale method of heat equation for the periodic or stochastic structure composite materials with non-cavities or solid small cavities [3, 4, 6], respectively. In the above problems, there is only one small periodic parameter $\varepsilon, 0 < \varepsilon = \frac{l}{L} << 1$, where l and L denote the sizes of the cell and

H. Deng et al. (Eds.): AICI 2011, Part III, LNAI 7004, pp. 186–194, 2011.

entire domain, respectively. The problem in this paper deal with two small parameters ε and δ, where ε denotes the size of the cell, and δ denotes the average thickness of the cavity walls. We suppose that the cavities are closed-celled and there are not convention and radiation.

The Einstein summation convention is used: summation is taken over repeated indices.

Let $\Omega \subset R^3$ be an open domain, $Y = (0,1)^3$,

$$Y_\delta = \{y \in Y|\ \texttt{dist}(y, \partial Y) < \delta/2\},\ T_\delta = Y\backslash Y_\delta$$

$\Omega_{\varepsilon\delta} = \Omega\backslash\overline{T}_{\varepsilon\delta}$ denote the domain containing the cavities, where $\overline{T}_{\varepsilon\delta}$ denotes the union of all periodic cavities. The boundary $\partial\Omega_{\varepsilon\delta}$ is composed by two parts. One is the union of all boundaries of cavities which are rigorous contained in the domain Ω denoted by $T_{\varepsilon\delta}$, the another is the boundary $\partial\Omega$. For the sake of convenience, we suppose that the boundary $\partial T_{\varepsilon\delta}$ is piecewise smooth and does not intersect with the boundary $\partial\Omega, \partial Y$. In Figure 1, $\Omega = (0,1)^3$, $\varepsilon = \frac{1}{3}, \delta = \frac{1}{24}$.

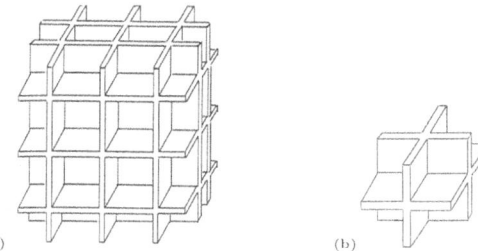

(a)   (b)

Fig. 1. (a) A honeycomb structure;   (b) Cell Y_δ

Consider the following heat equation in three dimension honeycomb structure:

$$\begin{cases} -\frac{\partial}{\partial x_i}\left(a_{ij}\left(\frac{x}{\varepsilon}\right)\frac{\partial u^{\varepsilon\delta}}{\partial x_j}\right) = f(x) \text{ in } \Omega_{\varepsilon\delta}, \\ u^{\varepsilon\delta} = 0 \text{ on } \partial\Omega, \\ \sigma(u^{\varepsilon\delta}) \equiv -a_{ij}\left(\frac{x}{\varepsilon}\right)\frac{\partial u^{\varepsilon\delta}}{\partial x_j}\tau_i = 0 \text{ on } \partial T_{\varepsilon\delta}, \end{cases} \quad (1.1)$$

where $\overrightarrow{\tau} = (\tau_1, \tau_2, \tau_3)$ denotes the unit outer normal vector of the cavities boundaries.

We make the following assumption for the coefficient matrix $\left(a_{ij}\left(\frac{x}{\varepsilon}\right)\right)$:
(A_1) $y = \varepsilon^{-1}x$, $a_{ij}(y)$ is 1-periodic in y.
(A_2) $a_{ij} \in L^\infty(R^3)$, $i, j = 1, 2, 3$.
(A_3) There exists $\gamma_0, \gamma_1 > 0$, such that

$$\gamma_0|\xi|^2 \leq a_{ij}(y)\xi_i\xi_j \leq \gamma_1|\xi|^2,\ \forall\xi \in R^3,\ |\xi|^2 = \xi_i\xi_i.$$

The function $a_{ij}\left(\frac{x}{\varepsilon}\right)$ is rapidly oscillating in the domain $\Omega_{\varepsilon\delta}$ as ε become smaller and smaller. The walls of the cavities shall become thinner and thinner as $\delta \to 0$.

It is very difficult to solve the problem if we subdivide the walls of the cavities into small elements since the mesh must be very thin leading a large scale computing. In this paper, we shall propose a multiscale algorithm for the problem.

2 Multiscale Asymptotic Expansion of the Temperature Field

In this paper, we suppose that the materials of the cavities walls are homogeneous. In fact, the solid of the walls are equivalent to a kind of homogeneous materials treated by homogenization method[7] and the problem (1.1) change into the following equation:

$$
\begin{cases}
-\frac{\partial}{\partial x_i}\left(a_{ij}\frac{\partial u^{\varepsilon\delta}}{\partial x_j}\right) = f(x) \text{ in } \Omega_{\varepsilon\delta}, \\
u^{\varepsilon\delta} = 0 \text{ on } \partial\Omega, \\
\sigma(u^{\varepsilon\delta}) \equiv -a_{ij}\frac{\partial u^{\varepsilon\delta}}{\partial x_j}\tau_i = 0 \text{ on } \partial T_{\varepsilon\delta},
\end{cases}
\tag{2.1}
$$

where $\Omega_{\varepsilon\delta}$ is the same as (1.1) and $a_{ij}(i,j=1,2,3)$ are constants.

Let $y = \varepsilon^{-1}x$. Formally set

$$
u^{\varepsilon\delta}(x) \cong \sum_{l=0}^{\infty} \varepsilon^l \sum_{\alpha_1,\cdots,\alpha_l=1}^{3} N_{\alpha_1\cdots\alpha_l}^{\delta}(y)D^\alpha u^{0,\delta}(x),
\tag{2.2}
$$

where $D^\alpha u^{0,\delta}(x)$ denotes the high order partial derivatives of $u^{0,\delta}(x)$, denotes by $D^\alpha u^{0,\delta}(x) = \frac{\partial^l u^{0,\delta}(x)}{\partial x_{\alpha_1}\cdots\partial x_{\alpha_l}}$, where $\alpha = \{\alpha_1,\cdots,\alpha_l\}$, $<\alpha> = l$, $\alpha_j = 1,2,3$, $j = 1,2,\cdots,l$. Putting (2.2) into (2.1), noticing that $\frac{\partial}{\partial x_i} \to \frac{\partial}{\partial x_i} + \varepsilon^{-1}\frac{\partial}{\partial y_i}$, and equating the coefficients of the same powers of ε, we obtain the following systems of equation[2, 5]: $N_0^\delta(y) \equiv 1$,

$$
\begin{cases}
\frac{\partial}{\partial y_i}\left(a_{ij}\frac{\partial N_{\alpha_1}^\delta(y)}{\partial y_j}\right) = -\frac{\partial}{\partial y_i}(a_{i\alpha_1}) & \text{in } Y_\delta, \\
\sigma_y(N_{\alpha_1}^\delta) = -\tau_i a_{i\alpha_1} & \text{on } \partial T_\delta, \\
N_{\alpha_1}^\delta(y) = 0 & \text{on } \partial Y,
\end{cases}
\tag{2.3}
$$

$$
\begin{cases}
\frac{\partial}{\partial y_i}\left(a_{ij}\frac{\partial N_{\alpha_1\alpha_2}^\delta(y)}{\partial y_j}\right) = -\frac{\partial}{\partial y_i}\left(a_{i\alpha_1}N_{\alpha_2}^\delta(y)\right) \\
-a_{\alpha_1 j}\frac{\partial N_{\alpha_2}^\delta(y)}{\partial y_j} - a_{\alpha_1\alpha_2} + \hat{a}_{\alpha_1\alpha_2}^\delta & \text{in } Y_\delta, \\
\sigma_y(N_{\alpha_1\alpha_2}^\delta) = -\tau_i a_{i\alpha_1}N_{\alpha_2}^\delta(y) & \text{on } \partial T_\delta, \\
N_{\alpha_1\alpha_2}^\delta(y) = 0 & \text{on } \partial Y,
\end{cases}
\tag{2.4}
$$

where (a_{ij}) is constant matrix, $\partial T_\delta, \partial Y$ denote the boundary of the cavity in $Y = (0,1)^3$ and the boundary of Y, respectively, $\hat{a}_{ij}^\delta = \frac{1}{|Y_\delta|}\int_{Y_\delta}\left(a_{ij}+a_{ik}\frac{\partial N_j^\delta(y)}{\partial y_k}\right)dy$, $|Y_\delta| = 3\delta(1-\delta+\delta^2/3)$.

For $< \alpha >= l \geq 3$, define

$$
\begin{cases}
\frac{\partial}{\partial y_i}\left(a_{ij}\frac{\partial N_{\alpha_1\cdots\alpha_l}^{\delta}(y)}{\partial y_j}\right) = -\frac{\partial}{\partial y_i}\left(a_{i\alpha_1}N_{\alpha_2\cdots\alpha_l}^{\delta}(y)\right) \\
-a_{\alpha_1 j}\frac{\partial N_{\alpha_2\cdots\alpha_l}^{\delta}(y)}{\partial y_j} - a_{\alpha_1\alpha_2}N_{\alpha_3\cdots\alpha_l}^{\delta}(y) \quad \text{in } Y_\delta, \\
\sigma_y(N_{\alpha_1\cdots\alpha_l}^{\delta}) = -\tau_i a_{i\alpha_1}(y)N_{\alpha_2\cdots\alpha_l}^{\delta}(y) \quad \text{on } \partial T_\delta, \\
N_{\alpha_1\cdots\alpha_l}^{\delta}(y) = 0 \quad \text{on } \partial Y.
\end{cases}
\tag{2.5}
$$

Remark 2.1. Using the uniforming ellipticity condition (A_3), Poincaré-Friedrichs inequality and Lax-Milgram Lemma, there exist an unique $N_{\alpha_1}^{\delta}(y)$, $N_{\alpha_1\alpha_2}^{\delta}(y), \cdots, N_{\alpha_1\cdots\alpha_l}^{\delta}(y)$. Then they can extend into $\Omega_{\varepsilon\delta}$ by periodicity. $u^{0,\delta}(x)$ is the solution of the following equation:

$$
\begin{cases}
-\frac{\partial}{\partial x_i}\left(\hat{a}_{ij}^{\delta}\frac{\partial u^{0,\delta}(x)}{\partial x_j}\right) = f(x) \text{ in } \Omega, \\
u^{0,\delta}(x) = 0 \text{ on } \partial\Omega.
\end{cases}
\tag{2.6}
$$

For $s \geq 1$, define following truncation function:

$$
u_s^{\varepsilon\delta}(x) = u^{0,\delta}(x) + \sum_{l=1}^{s}\varepsilon^l \sum_{\alpha_1,\cdots,\alpha_l=1}^{3} N_{\alpha_1,\cdots,\alpha_l}^{\delta}(y)D^{\alpha}u^{0,\delta}(x).
\tag{2.7}
$$

In order to obtain error estimates of the truncation function $u_s^{\varepsilon\delta}(x)$, we need to make the following assumptions for the geometry configuration and materials parameters [1]:

(B_1) The cavity T_δ is symmetric with respect to middle superplanes $\triangle_1, \triangle_2, \triangle_3$ of Y;

(B_2) $a_{ii}(y), i = 1, 2, 3$ is symmetric with respect to middle superplanes $\triangle_1, \triangle_2, \triangle_3$ of Y, $a_{ij}(y) = 0, i \neq j$.

Lemma 2.1.[1] Under the assumptions (B_1)–(B_2), $\sigma_y(N_{\alpha_1}^{\delta})$, $\sigma_y(N_{\alpha_1\alpha_2}^{\delta})$, $\sigma_y(N_{\alpha_1\alpha_2\alpha_3}^{\delta})$ are continuous on the boundary ∂Y.

From above arguments, we can obtain following convergence theorem.

Theorem 2.1. Let $\Omega_{\varepsilon\delta}$ be an entire periodic domain,i.e.

$$
\Omega_{\varepsilon\delta} = \bigcup_{z \in T_\varepsilon} \varepsilon(z + \overline{Y}), \quad z = (z_1, z_2, z_3), z_i \in Z,
$$

where T_ε is the index set and Z is the integer set, $u^{\varepsilon\delta}(x)$ is the weak solution of problem (2.1), $u_s^{\varepsilon\delta}(x)$ is its truncation function defined in (2.7). Under the assumptions condition (A_1)–$(A_2), (B_1)$–(B_2), if $f \in H^s(\Omega), u^{0,\delta} \in H^{s+2}(\Omega)$, then

$$
\|u^{\varepsilon\delta} - u_s^{\varepsilon\delta}\|_{1,\Omega_{\varepsilon\delta}} \leq
\begin{cases}
C(\delta) \cdot \varepsilon^{1/2}, \text{ if } s = 1, \\
C(\delta) \cdot \varepsilon^{s-1}, \text{ if } 2 \leq s \leq 4,
\end{cases}
\tag{2.8}
$$

where $C(\delta)$ is constant independent of ε but depend on δ.

3   The Limit Case of the Average Thickness δ of the Cavity Walls $\to$ 0

Take notice that in the error estimate (2.8), constant $C(\delta)$ is independent of ε, but depend on small parameter $\delta > 0$ (the average thickness of the solid cavity walls. In the following, we consider the case of $u^{0,\delta}(x)$ as $\delta \to 0$.

Lemma 3.1.[4] Let $u^{0,\delta}(x)$ be the weak solution of problem (2.6), as $\delta \to 0$, we have

$$u^{0,\delta} \to u^* \text{ strongly in } H_0^1(\Omega), \tag{3.1}$$

where u^* is the weak solution of the following equation:

$$\begin{cases} -\frac{\partial}{\partial x_i}\left(a_{ij}^* \frac{\partial u^*}{\partial x_j}\right) = f(x) \text{ in } \Omega, \\ \qquad\qquad u^* = 0 \text{ on } \partial\Omega, \end{cases} \tag{3.2}$$

where the constant matrix (a_{ij}^*) can be directly obtained by algebra method:$a_{ij}^* = a_{ij} - \frac{1}{3}\sum_{l=1}^{3} \frac{a_{il}a_{lj}}{a_{ll}}$, the constant matrix (a_{ij}) is made up of the effective heat conduction coefficients.

Similarly to (2.7), we define the following truncation function:

$$U_s^{\varepsilon\delta}(x) = u^*(x) + \sum_{l=1}^{s} \varepsilon^l \sum_{\alpha_1,\cdots,\alpha_l=1}^{3} N_{\alpha_1\cdots\alpha_l}^{\delta}(y)D^{\alpha}u^*(x), \tag{3.3}$$

where $N_{\alpha_1\cdots\alpha_l}^{\delta}(y)$ is the same as (2.7), but $u^*(x)$ is the weak solution of limit equation (3.2) as $\delta \to 0$.

Lemma 3.2.[4] Under the assumption conditions $(A_1) - (A_3)$, if $f \in H^s(\Omega), u^* \in H^3(\Omega)$, then

$$\|u^{\varepsilon\delta} - u^*\|_{0,\Omega_{\varepsilon\delta}} \leq C\delta^{1/2}(\delta^{1/2} + \varepsilon^{1/2}), \tag{3.4}$$

where C is a constant independent of ε, δ.

Using theorem 2.1, we can obtain the following convergence theorem.

Theorem 3.1. Let $\Omega_{\varepsilon\delta}$ be an entire periodic domain, $u^{\varepsilon\delta}$ be the weak solution of equation (2.1), $U_s^{\varepsilon\delta}$ is as in (4.4), under the assumption conditions $(A_1) - (A_3), (B_1) - (B_2)$, if $f \in H^s(\Omega), u^* \in H^{s+2}(\Omega)$, then

$$\|u^{\varepsilon\delta} - U_s^{\varepsilon\delta}\|_{1,\Omega_{\varepsilon\delta}} \leq C(\delta^{3/2} + \delta^{3/2}\varepsilon + \delta), \tag{3.5}$$

where C is a constant independent of ε, δ.

4   Finite Element Computation of the Cell Function $N_\alpha^\delta(y)$ in Y_δ

Let $\mathcal{J}^{h_0} = \{e\}$ be a family of regular tetrahedrons in Y_δ, $h_0 = \max_e h_e$. Define a linear finite element space:

$$V_{h_0} = \{v \in C(\overline{Y}_\delta) : v|_{\partial Y} = 0, v|_e \in P_1(e), e \in \mathcal{J}^{h_0}\} \subset H^1(Y_\delta) \qquad (4.1)$$

The discrete variational forms of (2.3), (2.4) and (2.5) are the following, respectively: $A(N^{\delta,h_0}_{\alpha_1}, v_{h_0}) = F^{h_0}_{\alpha_1}(v_{h_0})$, $\forall v_{h_0} \in V_{h_0}$; $A(N^{\delta,h_0}_{\alpha_1\alpha_2}, v_{h_0}) = F^{h_0}_{\alpha_1\alpha_2}(v_{h_0})$, $\forall v_{h_0} \in V_{h_0}$. For $l \geq 3$, $A(N^{\delta,h_0}_{\alpha_1\cdots\alpha_l}, v_{h_0}) = F^{h_0}_{\alpha_1\cdots\alpha_l}(v_{h_0})$, $\forall v_{h_0} \in V_{h_0}$, where the bilinear form: $A(w,v) = \int_{Y_\delta} a_{ij}(y)\frac{\partial w}{\partial y_j}\frac{\partial v}{\partial y_i}dy$, and linear functionals: $F^{h_0}_{\alpha_1}(v_{h_0}) = 0$,

$$F^{h_0}_{\alpha_1\alpha_2}(v_{h_0}) = -\int_{Y_\delta} a_{i\alpha_1}(y)N^{\delta,h_0}_{\alpha_2}\frac{\partial v_{h_0}}{\partial y_i}dy + \int_{Y_\delta}(a_{\alpha_1 j}\frac{\partial N^\delta_{\alpha_2}}{\partial y_j} + a_{\alpha_1\alpha_2} - \hat{a}^{h_0}_{\alpha_1\alpha_2})v_{h_0}dy,$$

where $\hat{a}^{h_0}_{\alpha_1\alpha_2} = \frac{1}{|Y_\delta|}\int_{Y_\delta}(a_{\alpha_1\alpha_2} + a_{\alpha_1 j}\frac{\partial N^{\delta,h_0}_{\alpha_2}(y)}{\partial y_j})dy$. For $l \geq 3$,

$$F^{h_0}_{\alpha_1\cdots\alpha_l}(v_{h_0}) = -\int_{Y_\delta} a_{i\alpha_1}N^{\delta,h_0}_{\alpha_2\cdots\alpha_l}\frac{\partial v_{h_0}}{\partial y_i}dy$$
$$+ \int_{Y_\delta}(a_{\alpha_1 j}\frac{\partial N^{h_0}_{\alpha_2\cdots\alpha_l}}{\partial y_j} + a_{\alpha_1\alpha_2}N^{\delta,h_0}_{\alpha_3\cdots\alpha_l})v_{h_0}dy.$$

We can obtain the following result by induction:

Theorem 4.1. Let $N^\delta_{\alpha_1\cdots\alpha_j}(y)$, $j = 1, \cdots$, be the weak solutions of (2.3), (2.4) and (2.5),respectively, $N^{\delta,h_0}_{\alpha_1\cdots\alpha_j}(y)$ be the corresponding finite element solutions, if $N^\delta_{\alpha_1\cdots\alpha_j} \in H^3(Y_\delta)$, $j = 1, \cdots, l$, then

$$\|N^\delta_{\alpha_1\cdots\alpha_j} - N^{\delta,h_0}_{\alpha_1\cdots\alpha_j}\|_{1,Y_\delta} \leq Ch_0\left(\sum_{k=1}^j \|N^\delta_{\alpha_1\cdots\alpha_k}\|_{2,Y_\delta}\right). \qquad (4.2)$$

5   Finite Element Computation of the Homogenized Equations

Let $\mathcal{J}^{h_1} = \{\tau\}$ be a family of regular tetrahedrons in Ω, $h_1 = \max_e h_\tau$. Define a linear finite element space:

$$V_{h_1}(Q) = \{v \in C(Q) : v|_{\partial Q} = 0, v|_\tau \in P_1(\tau), \tau \in \mathcal{J}^{h_1}\} \subset H^1(Q).$$

Let $\chi^{h_1}_j(y)$ be the finite solution of $\chi_j(y)$ in $V_{h_1}(Q)$. When we solve the homogenized equations (3.2) by using finite element method, in fact, we need to solve the modified equation as follows:

$$\begin{cases} \mathcal{L}^*_{h_1}\tilde{u}^* \equiv -\frac{\partial}{\partial x_i}(a^{*,h_1}_{ij}\frac{\partial \tilde{u}^*}{\partial x_j}) = f(x) & \text{in } \Omega, \\ \tilde{u}^*(x) = 0 & \text{on } \partial\Omega, \end{cases} \qquad (5.1)$$

where $a^{*,h_1}_{ij} = a^{h_1}_{ij} - \frac{1}{3}\sum_{l=1}^3 \frac{a^{h_1}_{il}a^{h_1}_{lj}}{a^{h_1}_{ll}}$.

Lemma 5.1.[4] The partial differential operator $\mathcal{L}^*_{h_1}$ satisfies the following condition:

$$a_{ij}^{*,h_1}\xi_i\xi_j \geq \lambda|\xi|^2, \quad \forall\, (\xi_1,\xi_2,\xi_3) \in R^2, \tag{5.2}$$

where $\lambda > 0$ is a constant independent of h_1.

From (3.2) and (5.1), we can derive following result.

Theorem 5.1. Let $u^*(x), \tilde{u}^*(x)$ be the weak solutions of (3.2) and (5.1), respectively, then

$$\|u^* - \tilde{u}^*\|_{1,\Omega} \leq Ch_1^2\|\chi\|_{2,Q}^2\|f\|_{0,\Omega}, \tag{5.3}$$

where $\|\chi\|_{2,Q}^2 = \|\chi_1\|_{2,Q}^2 + \|\chi_2\|_{2,Q}^2 + \|\chi_3\|_{2,Q}^2$, χ_i is the solution of problem (2.1).

Further more, it is easy to obtain following result.

Corollary 5.1. Suppose that $\tilde{u}^* \in H^{s+2}(\Omega)$, $0 \leq l \leq s$, then

$$\|D^l(u^* - \tilde{u}^*)\|_{1,\Omega} \leq Ch_1^2\|\chi\|_{2,Q}^2\|\tilde{u}^*\|_{s+2,\Omega}. \tag{5.4}$$

Similar to (3.3), we define following truncation function:

$$\tilde{U}_s^{\varepsilon\delta}(x) = \tilde{u}^*(x) + \sum_{l=1}^{s}\varepsilon^l \sum_{\alpha_1,\cdots,\alpha_l=1}^{3} N_{\alpha_1\cdots\alpha_l}^{\delta}(y)D^\alpha\tilde{u}^*(x). \tag{5.5}$$

From Corollary 3.1, we can obtain following theorem.

Theorem 5.2. Let $u^*(x), \tilde{u}^*(x)$ be the weak solutions of (3.2) and (5.1), respectively, $u^*, \tilde{u}^* \in H^{s+2}(\Omega)$, $0 \leq l \leq s$, Truncation functions $U_s^{\varepsilon\delta}(x), \tilde{U}_s^{\varepsilon\delta}(x)$ are determined by (3.3) and (5.5), respectively, then

$$\|U_s^{\varepsilon\delta} - \tilde{U}_s^{\varepsilon\delta}\|_{1,\Omega_{\varepsilon\delta}} \leq Ch_1^2\big(\|f\|_{0,\Omega} \\ + \|\tilde{u}^*\|_{s+2,\Omega}\sum_{l=1}^{s}\varepsilon^{l-1}\sum_{\alpha_1,\cdots,\alpha_l=1}^{3}\|N_{\alpha_1\cdots\alpha_l}^{\delta}\|_{1,Y_\delta}^2\big)\|\chi\|_{2,Q}^2. \tag{5.6}$$

6   Multiscale Finite Element Algorithm Scheme and Error Estimates

Let $\mathcal{J}^h = \{e\}$ be a family of regular tetrahedrons in Ω. Define finite element space

$$S_h^2(\Omega) = \{v \in C(\overline{\Omega}): \ v|_{\partial\Omega} = 0, v|_e \in P_2(e), \forall e \in \mathcal{J}^h\}.$$

Let $\tilde{u}^*, \tilde{u}_h^*$ be the weak solution and the finite element solution of (5.1) in $S_h^2(\Omega)$, respectively. If $\tilde{u}^* \in H^3(\Omega)$, then

$$\|\tilde{u}^* - \tilde{u}_h^*\|_{1,\Omega} \leq Ch^2\|\tilde{u}^*\|_{3,\Omega} \tag{6.1}$$

In this section, we shall give the multiscale finite element method with high accuracy and error estimates for solving numerically problem (2.1). To begin with, we introduce the higher-order difference quotients for calculating the partial derivatives of $\tilde{u}^*(x)$. We first define the first-order difference quotients as follows:

$$\delta_{x_i}\tilde{u}_h^*(M) = \frac{1}{\tau(M)}\sum_{e\in\sigma(M)}\left[\frac{\partial\tilde{u}_h^*}{\partial x_i}\right]_e(M),$$

where $\sigma(M)$ denotes the set of all elements relative to nodal point M, $\tau(M)$ is the number of elements of $\sigma(M)$, $\tilde{u}_h^*(x)$ denotes the finite solution of $\tilde{u}^*(x)$ in $S_h^2(\Omega)$, $\left[\frac{\partial \tilde{u}_h^*}{\partial x_i}\right]_e(M)$ is the value of $\frac{\partial \tilde{u}_h^*}{\partial x_i}$ on M. Similarly, we define the higher-order difference quotients:

$$\delta_{x_i \cdots x_l x_k}^m \tilde{u}_h^*(M) = \frac{1}{\tau(M)} \sum_{e \in \sigma(M)} \left[\sum_{j=1}^d \delta_{x_i \cdots x_l}^{m-1} \tilde{u}_h^*(P_j) \frac{\partial \psi_j}{\partial x_k} \right]_e (M), \qquad (6.2)$$

where d is the number of nodal points of e, $\psi_j(x)$ denotes the corresponding Lagrange interpolation function, $j = 1, 2, \cdots, d$.

A multiscale finite element method for the solution $u^{\varepsilon\delta}(x)$ can be written as follows: $\forall M \in \overline{\Omega}_{\varepsilon\delta}$,

$$U_{s,h_1,h}^{\varepsilon\delta,h_0}(M) = \tilde{u}_h^*(M) + \sum_{l=1}^s \varepsilon^l \sum_{\alpha_1,\cdots,\alpha_l=1}^2 N_{\alpha_1\cdots\alpha_l}^{\delta,h_0}(\xi(M)) \delta_{x_{\alpha_1}\cdots x_{\alpha_l}}^l \tilde{u}_h^*(M), \qquad (6.3)$$

where s is an integer, $2 \le s \le 4$, h_0, h_1, h are the mesh size of Y_δ, Q, Ω, respectively.

Theorem 6.1. Let $\Omega_{\varepsilon\delta}$ be an integer periodic domain, $u^{\varepsilon\delta}(x)$ be the solution of problem of (2.1), then

$$\|u^{\varepsilon\delta}(x) - U_{s,h_1,h}^{\varepsilon\delta,h_0}(x)\|_{1,\Omega_{\varepsilon\delta}} \le C(\delta + \delta^{3/2}\varepsilon^{s-1} + h_1^2 + h_0 + h), \qquad (6.4)$$

where $C > 0$ is a constant independent of ε, δ, h_1, h, h_0, h_1, h_0, h are the mesh size of Q, Y_δ, Ω, respectively, $2 \le s \le 4$.

Proof. For $x \in \Omega_{\varepsilon\delta}$,

$$\begin{aligned} u^{\varepsilon\delta}(x) - U_{s,h_1,h}^{\varepsilon\delta,h_0}(x) &= u^{\varepsilon\delta}(x) - U_s^{\varepsilon\delta}(x) \\ &+ U_s^{\varepsilon\delta}(x) - \tilde{U}_s^{\varepsilon\delta}(x) + \tilde{U}_s^{\varepsilon\delta}(x) - U_{s,h_1,h}^{\varepsilon\delta,h_0}(x). \end{aligned} \qquad (6.5)$$

$$\begin{aligned} \tilde{U}_s^{\varepsilon\delta}(x) - U_{s,h_1,h}^{\varepsilon\delta,h_0}(x) &= \tilde{u}^*(x) - \tilde{u}_h^*(x) \\ &+ \sum_{l=1}^s \varepsilon^l \sum_{\alpha_1,\cdots,\alpha_l=1} \left(N_{\alpha_1\cdots\alpha_l}^\delta - N_{\alpha_1\cdots\alpha_l}^{\delta,h_0}(y)\right) D^\alpha \tilde{u}^*(x) \\ &+ \sum_{l=1}^s \varepsilon^l \sum_{\alpha_1,\cdots,\alpha_l=1} N_{\alpha_1\cdots\alpha_l}^\delta(y) \cdot \left(D^\alpha \tilde{u}^*(x) - \delta_{x_{\alpha_1}\cdots x_{\alpha_l}}^l \tilde{u}_h^*(x)\right). \end{aligned} \qquad (6.6)$$

From (6.1),(4.2),(5.6) and (6.6), we have

$$\|\tilde{U}_s^{\varepsilon\delta} - U_{s,h_1,h}^{\varepsilon\delta,h_0}\|_{1,\Omega_{\varepsilon\delta}} \le C(h_0 + h). \qquad (6.7)$$

Finally from (6.5),(3.5),(6.2) and (6.7), we obtain (6.4).

References

1. Cao, L.Q.: Multiscale asymptotic expansion and finite element methods for the mixed boundary value problems of second order elliptic equation in perforated domains. Numer. Math. 103, 11–45 (2006)

2. Cao, L.Q., Cui, J.Z., Luo, L.J.: Multiscale asymptotic expansion and a post-processing algorithm for second order elliptic problems with highly oscillatory coefficients over general convex domains. J. Comp. and Appl. Math. 157, 1–29 (2003)
3. Cao, L.Q., Luo, J.L.: Multiscale numerical method for heat conduction and mass transfer problem in period structure of perforated composite materials. J. Engineering and Heat Physics 21(5), 610–614 (2000)
4. Cioranescu, D., Paulin, J.S.J.: Homogenization of Reticulated Structures. Applied Mathematics Sciences, vol. 139. Springer, Heidelberg (1999)
5. Gibson, L.J., Ashby, M.F.: Cellular solid: Structure and Properties, 2nd edn. University of Cambridge (1977)
6. Lin, R.T.: Introduction to Heat and Mass Transfer with Cavities. Science Press, Beijing (1995) (in chinese)
7. Liu, X.Q., Cao, L.Q., Zhu, Q.D.: Multiscale algorithm with high accuracy for the elatic equqtions in three-dimensional honeycomb structure, J. Comp. Appl. Math. 233, 905–921 (2009)

Outlier-Tolerant Fitting and Online Diagnosis of Outliers in Dynamic Process Sampling Data Series

Shaolin Hu[1,2], Xiaofeng Wang[2], Karl Meinke[3], and Huajiang Ouyang[4]

[1] State Key Laboratory of Astronautics,
Xi'an Satellite Control Center, Xi'an 710043, China
huf@mail.xjtu.edu.cn
[2] Xi'an University of Technology, Xi'an 710048, China
hfkth@126.com
[3] NADA, Royal Institute of Technology, Stockholm, 100 44 Stockholm, Sweden
[4] Liverpool University, Liverpool L69 3GH, UK

Abstract. Outliers as well as outlier patches, which widely emerge in dynamic process sampling data series, have strong bad influence on signal processing. In this paper, a series of recursive outlier-tolerant fitting algorithms are built to fit reliably the trajectories of a non-stationary sampling process when there are some outliers arising from output components of the process. Based on the recursive outlier-tolerant fitting algorithms stated above, a series of practical programs are given to online detect outliers in dynamic process and to identify magnitudes of these outliers as well as outlier patches. Simulation results show that these new methods are efficient.

Keywords: Outlier-Tolerance, Outlier Detection, Magnitude Identification, Non-stationary Signals, Sensors Fault.

1 Introduction

In many fields such as process safety and dynamic system surveillance, it is a valuable and widely applicable task to detect whether there exist any faults in a running process or not and to determine the magnitudes of these faults. In order to detect and diagnose faults in a process or a system, there are many kinds of approaches, such as detecting filters, analysis of influence function, residual analysis, parity equation and parity space, probability ratio or generalized likelihood ratio, innovation analysis of Kalman filter and classical statistical diagnosis. Patton et al (1989) and Isermann (1984) and paper [3] have reviewed the evolution of fault detection and diagnosis (FDD) from different viewpoints.

In summing up recent references on FDD, we may find that most of the approaches are based on the least squared (LS) estimators of process parameters, the LS fitting of process trajectories, likelihood ratio function, or equivalent transformations of process models, etc. Generally, these approaches stated above possess excellent properties when the process runs properly. Therefore these detection algorithms can be efficiently used to detect online the first fault and to detect offline more than one faults arising at different times for a dynamic process with faults.

H. Deng et al. (Eds.): AICI 2011, Part III, LNAI 7004, pp. 195–203, 2011.
© Springer-Verlag Berlin Heidelberg 2011

But, a lot of theoretical research and practical calculation in recent years reveal that some classical statistical tools (such as the LS estimators, the Kalman filter and the likelihood ratio, etc) lack the fault-tolerance against the bad influence from faults arising before the monitoring time. In other words, these detection algorithms have poor performance and may make a false prediction [2,4] in online monitoring the process that has historical faults. In this case, it is important to discuss how to online monitor the state of the dynamic process with historical faults.

In practical engineering fields, performance of the pulse-type faults in sensors is very similar with outlier in sampling data series. When a dynamic process runs for a long time, it is possible that there are some faults as well as outliers arising at different times. In paper [5], Dose and Linden brought forward a new concept outlier-tolerance in parameter estimation. Chatzis and Kosmopoulos used this term in data modeling [6]. Recently, Gadhok and Kinsner used a similar term outlier-robustness in clustering [7], Henri Pesonen set up an outlier-robust Bayesian filter in Integrity Monitoring of GNSS Positioning [8].

Along with these approaches stated above, a uniform frame will be built in this paper to detect abnormality including pulse-type faults as well as outliers online and to estimate magnitudes of them. It will be shown that these algorithms have strong tolerance to these kinds of abnormality and are reliable in monitoring process. At the end of this paper, some simulation results will be given to display that these new algorithms are valid.

2   Outlier-Tolerant Recursive Fitting

Assume that the output of a continuous-variable dynamic system is a measurable stochastic process $\{y(t), t \in T\}$ and that the expectant trajectory $\{\mu(t), t \in T\}$ of the output is square integrable and piecewise smooth in all finite intervals. Based on Weierstrass theorems and their generalized results [9], the function $\mu(t)$ ($t \in [t_a, t_b] \subseteq T$) can be approximated by the linear combination of a series of reasonably selected base functions $\{x_j(t) \in L^2[t_a, t_b], j = 1,2,3,\cdots\}$ with unknown constants $\{a_j \in R, j = 1,2,3,\cdots,s\}$

$$\sum_{j=1}^{s} a_j x_j(t) \rightarrow \mu(t) \quad (s \rightarrow +\infty) \tag{1}$$

Considering the compensating error principle and using $\{\varepsilon(t), t \in T\}$ to denote the integration of stochastic noise as well as the fitted model error, formula (1) can be expressed as following

$$y(t) = \sum_{j=1}^{s} a_j x_j(t) + \varepsilon(t) \tag{2}$$

2.1   The Recursive LS Fitting

In many engineering fields, dynamic processes run for a long time generally and involve complicated dynamic properties. In order to online analyze and online predict the state of such a process, recursive fitting is very necessary.

Now, let's construct a coefficient vector $\vec{\alpha} = (a_1, \cdots, a_s)^\tau$ and build a series of recursively gliding LS estimators for $\vec{\alpha}$ of the fitted model. Using the following notation

$$H_{(i \to j)} = \begin{bmatrix} x_1(t_i) & \cdots & x_s(t_i) \\ \vdots & & \vdots \\ x_1(t_j) & \cdots & x_s(t_j) \end{bmatrix}, \quad \vec{h}_i = \begin{bmatrix} x_1(t_i) \\ \vdots \\ x_s(t_i) \end{bmatrix}, \quad Y_{(i \to j)} = \begin{pmatrix} y(t_i) \\ \vdots \\ y(t_j) \end{pmatrix},$$

it can be proved that the LS estimators on $D_{(i+1 \to i+n)} = \{y(t_{i+1}), \cdots, y(t_{i+n})\}$ of $\vec{\alpha}$ can be expressed as the following

$$\hat{\vec{\alpha}}_{LS(i+1 \to i+n)} = J_{(i+1 \to i+n)} H^\tau_{(i+1 \to i+n)} Y_{(i+1 \to i+n)} \tag{3}$$

where $J_{(i+1 \to i+n)} = (H^\tau_{(i+1 \to i+n)} H_{(i+1 \to i+n)})^{-1}, \; n \geq s$.

As the process moves forward in time domain, formula (3) satisfies a recursive algorithm as following

$$\hat{\vec{\alpha}}_{LS(1 \to n+1)} = \hat{\vec{\alpha}}_{LS(1 \to n)} + p_{(n+1|n)} \tilde{f}_{LS(n+1|n)} \tag{4}$$

where $\tilde{f}_{LS(n+1|n)} = \dfrac{y(t_{n+1}) - \vec{h}^\tau_{n+1} \hat{\vec{\alpha}}_{LS(1 \to n)}}{(1 + \vec{h}^\tau_{n+1}(H^\tau_{(1 \to n)} H_{(1 \to n)})^{-1} \vec{h}_{n+1})^{1/2}}$ and $p_{(n+1|n)} = \dfrac{(H^\tau_{(1 \to n)} H_{(1 \to n)})^{-1} \vec{h}_{n+1}}{\sqrt{1 + \vec{h}^\tau_{n+1}(H^\tau_{(1 \to n)} H_{(1 \to n)})^{-1} \vec{h}_{n+1}}}$.

From formula (3), if the process runs properly we can conclude that the recursive LS fitting of the trajectories at time t is equal to

$$\hat{y}_{LS(1 \to l+n)}(t) = \sum_{j=1}^{s} \hat{a}_{j,LS(1 \to l+n)} x_j(t) \tag{5}$$

Correspondingly, the predictor one-step ahead of the process output $y(t_{n+1})$ is $\hat{y}_{LS(1 \to n)}(t_{n+1})$. The error of the one-step forward prediction is equal to

$$\hat{\varepsilon}_{LS(n+1|1 \to n)} = y(t_{n+1}) - \hat{y}_{LS(1 \to n)}(t_{n+1}) \tag{6}$$

Theorem 1. If mean and variance of the dynamic noise $\{\varepsilon(t_i) : i = 1, 2, \cdots\}$ are equal to zero and σ^2 respectively, variance of the error $\hat{\varepsilon}_{LS(n+1|1 \to 1+n)}$ is equal to

$$Var(\hat{\varepsilon}_{LS(n+1|1 \to 1+n)}) = (1 + \vec{h}^\tau_{n+1} J_{(1 \to 1+n)} \vec{h}_{n+1}) \sigma^2 \tag{7}$$

Proof: Substituting equations (3) and (5) into formula (6) and after some mathematical simplifications, we can obtain formula (7).   ∎

2.2 Outlier-Tolerance Improvement of the LS Fitting

The recursive estimators (4) are minimizing-variance unbiased estimators of the fitting coefficients when the process runs properly and export output without faults. So, the recursive LS fitting possesses excellent statistical properties.

It should be pointed out that the recursive LS fitting has the same weakness as the ordinary LS fitting: it can break down in the case where there exist outliers in the running process. In fact, if there exists an outlier at time t_0, magnitude of which is $\lambda(t_0)$, namely,

$$\tilde{y}(t) = \begin{cases} y(t), & t \neq t_0 \\ y(t) + \lambda(t), & t = t_0 \end{cases} \tag{8}$$

the error of the recursive LS predictor one-step ahead can be expressed as

$$\hat{\tilde{\varepsilon}}_{LS(n+1|1 \to 1+n)} = \hat{\varepsilon}_{LS(n+1|1 \to 1+n)} + \begin{cases} 0, & t_0 > t_{n+1} \\ \omega(t_{n+1}, t_s), & t_1 \leq t_0 < t_{n+1} \\ \lambda(t_{i_0}), & t_0 = t_{n+1} \end{cases} \tag{9}$$

where $\omega(t_{n+1}, t_0) = -\vec{h}_{n+1}^{\tau}(H_{(1 \to 1+n)}^{\tau} H_{(1 \to 1+n)})^{-1} \vec{h}_0$.

Expression (9) shows that pulse-type faults or outliers occurring in a running process may result in an evident increased predictor error, the numerical value of which is not equal at different gliding interval. If we view $\hat{\alpha}_{LS(1 \to 1+n)}$ in formulae (4) as a modification to $\hat{\alpha}_{LS(1 \to n)}$ by the LS filtering residual (6) and the predicting error $\hat{\varepsilon}_{LS(n+1|1 \to n)}$, then an outlier having occurred at time t_{n+1} is not only unconventionally larger than the predictor error $\hat{\varepsilon}_{LS(n+1|1 \to n)}$, but also evidently changes the estimators $\hat{\alpha}_{LS(1 \to 1+n)}$ and even breaks down algorithm (4).

In order to overcome the bad influence from the exceptional change brought about by an outlier on the gliding recursive estimators of model coefficients, we set a re-descending ϕ-function as follows

$$\phi_{rd}(x) = \begin{cases} x & |x| < c_1 \\ c_1 sign(x) & c_1 \leq |x| < c_2 \\ \dfrac{c_2 - |x|}{c_2 - c_1} c_1 & c_2 \leq |x| < c_3 \\ 0 & |x| \geq c_3 \end{cases} \tag{10}$$

where (c_1, c_2, c_3) are constants.

Using this kind of ϕ-function, it is able to cut down the bad influence of the abnormal predicting error of the recursive identification algorithms.

By ϕ-function (10), we construct an improved algorithm for formula (4) as following:

$$\hat{\alpha}_{\phi(1 \to n+1)} = \hat{\alpha}_{\phi(1 \to n)} + p_{(n+1|n)} \phi_{rd}(\tilde{f}_{\phi(n+1|n)}) \tag{11}$$

where $\tilde{f}_{\phi(n+1|n)} = \dfrac{y(t_{n+1}) - \vec{h}_{n+1}^{\tau}\hat{\vec{\alpha}}_{\phi(1\to n)}}{(1 + \vec{h}_{n+1}^{\tau}(H_{(1\to n)}^{\tau}H_{(1\to n)})^{-1}\vec{h}_{n+1})^{1/2}}$.

Theorem 2. If a noise series $\{\varepsilon(t), t \in T\}$ of model (2) is stationary and its distributions is symmetrical, whose mean and variance are equal to zero and σ^2 respectively, the estimators $\{\hat{\vec{\alpha}}_{\phi(1\to n)}, i = 1,2,3,\cdots\}$ are unbiased in cases where there are not any outliers occurring before the time t_n and the initial value $\hat{\vec{\alpha}}_{\phi(1\to n_0)}$ of the algorithm (11) is selected as $\hat{\vec{\alpha}}_{LS(1\to n_0)}$.

Proof: Distinctly, $\hat{\vec{\alpha}}_{\phi(1\to n_0)}$ is an unbiased estimator of the vector $\vec{\alpha}$. Using the property that the integral of an odd function on a symmetrical interval is equal to zero, we can also prove that $\hat{\vec{\alpha}}_{\phi(1\to n_0+1)}$ is unbiased. Similarly, it can be proven that the estimators $\{\hat{\vec{\alpha}}_{\phi(1\to n)}, i = 1,2,3,\cdots\}$ are unbiased by means of mathematical induction. ▮

Now, let's expatiate on the rationality of the new algorithm (11). The one-step predicting error $\hat{\varepsilon}_{LS(1+n\|\to n)}$ can be regarded as innovation brought by the measuring data at time t_{1+n}. It is obviously reasonable that the re-descending function ϕ_{rd} in formula (10) is used to take the place of the linear function $\phi(x) = x$ implied in (4), because of the following reasons:

1). when an innovation of sampling data falls into the anticipated bound, we think that this new sampling data is reasonable and should make full use of this accept use all of this innovation;
2). when the innovation of sampling data goes beyond a selected bound only by a small amount, we must confine the bad influence from this sampling data;
3). we must restrict use of information from untrustworthy sampling data;
4). when the innovation distinctly departs from the normal value and is exceptionally large, we may eliminate the bad influence from them.

Based on the explanations stated above, we may find out that the modified recursive algorithms (11) can more reasonably contain the innovation from sampling data $y(t_{1+n})$ to update the identification of parameters than the estimators (4), when there exists a large discrepancy between a sampling data $y(t_{1+n})$ and the predictor $\hat{y}(t_{1+n}) = \vec{h}_{1+n}^{\tau}\hat{\vec{\alpha}}_{\phi(1\to n)}$. In other words, the outlier-tolerant algorithm (11) is able to improve reliability of estimators of parameters by reducing optimality of algorithms. It is a compromise between statistical optimality and outlier-tolerance.

3 Outlier-Tolerant Detection of Outliers

Generally, if there do not exist any outliers at time t_{1+n}, we have pointed out that the prediction error $\hat{\varepsilon}_{LS(n+1\|\to n)}$ obeys the normal distribution $N(0, d_{(1\to n)}\sigma)$ when the process noise $\{\varepsilon(t), t \in T\}$ is white and stationary Gaussian noise. Based on this property, we may use the following detecting statistics to diagnose whether there is an outlier occurring at time t_{n+1} or not:

$$\Re_{LS}(t_{n+1}) = \frac{y(t_{n+1}) - \vec{h}_{n+1}^{\tau}\hat{\vec{\alpha}}_{LS(1 \to n)}}{d_{(1 \to n)}} \tag{12}$$

where $d_{(1 \to n)} = \sqrt{1 + \vec{h}_{1+n}^{\tau}J_{(1 \to n)}\vec{h}_{1+n}}$.

Now, the problem is that the detection statistics can not be used in the case when there exists one or more outliers occurring before time t_{n+1} because the detection statistics (12) is based on the LS algorithms and is hypersensitive to outliers[9] in sampled data. Namely, algorithm (12) can not be used in monitoring multiple faults of a dynamic process.

In order to protect a detection statistics against any bad influence from historical outliers, it is reasonable to substitute the outlier-tolerant estimators for the LS estimators.

In section 2.2, it has been pointed out that the estimators $\hat{\vec{\alpha}}_{\phi(1 \to n)}$ given by formulae (11) have the ability to overcome bad influence from outliers and to guarantee the reliability of estimators. So we replace $\hat{\vec{\alpha}}_{LS(1 \to n)}$ in expression (12) with $\hat{\vec{\alpha}}_{\phi(1 \to n)}$. This is a practical approach without failure for online monitoring dynamic processes in the case when there are multiple faults having occurred before the sampling moment detected.

According to all of the analysis stated above, a series of detecting strategies, which are based on the outlier-tolerant (short as Out-T) recursive estimators, are built as following:

1). Selecting $n_0 > \min\{s, n-1\}$, let's do some detection offline to diagnose whether there exist any outliers before the time t_{n_0} or not with the robust-likelihood ratio detection algorithm given in [9] and correct the outliers by interpolation;

2). $\hat{\vec{\alpha}}_{LS(n_0 - n + 1 \to n_0)}$ is calculated by (3) and set as the initial value of the recursive algorithm formula (11);

3). Using formula (11), a series of gliding calculation is done to obtain $\hat{\vec{\alpha}}_{\phi(i+1 \to i+n)}$;

4). The detection statistics is done as following

$$\Re_{\phi}(t_{n+1}) = \frac{y(t_{n+1}) - \vec{h}_{n+1}^{\tau}\hat{\vec{\alpha}}_{\phi(1 \to n)}}{d_{(1 \to n)}} \tag{13}$$

5). A criterion is checked: if $|\Re_{\phi}(t_{n+1})| \geq c$, there is an outlier occurring at time t_{n+1}; otherwise, the sampling data is normal and the process is running without any outliers, where the constant c is a bound selected properly (its default value is suggested as 3σ).

6). With the process running continuously, step3)~5) are repeated.

4 Outlier-Tolerant Identification of Outliers

Setting $\vec{h}_{n+1}^{\tau}\hat{\vec{\alpha}}_{\phi(1\to n)}$ as a predicting value of $y(t_{n+1})$, a statistics is constructed to determine the magnitude of an outlier:

$$\hat{\lambda}_{\phi}(t_{n+1}) = \hat{\mathcal{E}}_{\phi(n+1\|1\to n)} = \{ y(t_{n+1}) - \vec{h}_{n+1}^{\tau}\hat{\vec{\alpha}}_{\phi(1\to n)} \} \tag{14}$$

Theorem 3. Assuming that the noise process $\{\varepsilon(t), t \in T\}$ is white stationary Gaussian noise, whose mean is zero, the mathematical expectation of statistics $\hat{\lambda}_{\phi}(t_{i+n+1})$ is equal to zero or $\lambda(t_{n+1})$ in the case that the dynamic process runs properly or there exists an outlier, whose magnitude is $\lambda(t_{n+1})$, occurring at time t_{n+1} respectively.

Proof: The result of the theorem can be deduced by theorem 2 and expression (14) obviously. ∎

5 Simulation

The simulation model is selected as the stochastic polynomial

$$y(t) = b_0 + b_1 t + b_2 t^2 + \varepsilon(t), \varepsilon(t) \sim N(0,1) \tag{15}$$

And, setting $b_0 = 100.0, b_1 = 10.0, b_2 = -0.25$, we use the Monte Carlo method and the model (15) to generate 100 sampling data at time set $\{t_i = ih \mid i = 1, \cdots, 100, h = 1s\}$.

By intentionally shifting the sampling data $(-1)^{i+1}100$ at time set $\{t_{51}, \cdots, t_{55}\} \cup \{t_{75}\}$ respectively, we get a new series of output data with multiple relative outliers (outlier patches) and an isolated outlier as in Fig 1.

From Fig 1, we find that the magnitudes of the isolated outlier and the relative outliers are not prominent.

In order to evaluate the behaviors of outlier-tolerant estimators, the sample data in Fig 1 and the residual generating algorithm formula (6) of the recursive LS fitting are used. The residuals of the recursive LS prediction are plotted in Fig 2. At the same time, we use the following generation algorithms of the recursive Out-T prediction residuals:

$$\hat{\mathcal{E}}_2(t_{n+1}) = y(t_{n+1}) - \sum_{i=1}^{s} \hat{a}_{i,LS(1\to n)} \hbar_i(t_{n+1}) \tag{16}$$

and plot the Out-T prediction residuals in Fig 3:

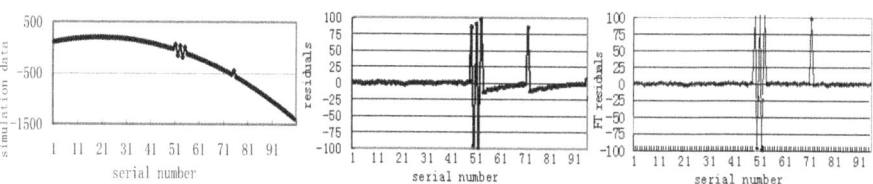

Fig. 1. Simulation data   **Fig. 2.** The LS residuals   **Fig. 3.** The Out-T residuals

Comparing Fig 2 with Fig 3, we are convinced that the recursive LS estimators of model coefficients are influenced badly by outliers and that the recursive Oou-T algorithm (11) has commendable resistance to outliers.

In order to detect and to identify outliers in sampling data series, the LS prediction residuals plot Fig 2 and the Out-T prediction residuals plot Fig 3 are used and two series of different estimators of the outlier magnitudes are given in table 1.

Table 1. The LS estimators and the Oou-T estimators of fault magnitudes

No.	51	52	53	54	55	56	75	76
True Values	100.0	-100.0	100.0	-100.0	100.0	0.0	100.0	0.0
LS Fitting	85.9	-96.7	89.8	-98.5	97.0	-14.4	85.4	-12.1
Out-T Fitting	100.9	-99.6	101.5	-99.9	102.2	-0.4	97.6	-0.7

Table 1 shows that the Out-T estimators $\hat{\lambda}_\phi(t)$ are markedly closer to the true magnitude values of outliers that are designed for simulation than the LS estimating values $\hat{\lambda}_{LS}(t)$ $(i_0 = 51 \sim 55,75)$. So, the detection algorithms given in this paper are reliable in detecting outliers and identifying outlier magnitudes.

6 Conclusion

In practical signal processing and computer controlled engineering, how to prevent breakage coming from outlier patches in sampling data is an open problem. In this paper, a series of recursive outlier-tolerant fitting algorithms are built, which have strong tolerance to outliers as well as outlier patches and can be used to fit reliably the trajectories of a non-stationary sampling process. Using these recursive outlier-tolerant fitting algorithms, a series of practical programs are given to online detect and to diagnose outliers as well as outlier patches in dynamic process. Simulation results show that these new methods are efficient in detecting outlier patches and the estimating magnitudes of outlier patches are approximately equal to true values.

Acknowledgments. This paper is supported by the National Nature Science Fund of China (61074077, 11026224).

References

1. Patton, R.J., et al.: Fault Diagnosis in Dynamic Systems, Theory and Application. Prentice Hall, New York (1989)
2. Isermann, R.: Process Fault Detection Based on Modeling and Estimation Methods—a Survey. Automatica 20(4), 387–404 (1989)
3. Shaolin, H., Guoji, S.: Review for Process Monitoring and Fault-Tolerant Processing (in Chinese). J. of Measurement and Control 18(12), 1–4 (1999)

4. Hu, S., Sun, G.: Detection and Identification for Abrupt Faults in Sensors (in Chinese). Information and Control 28(7), 613–619 (1999)
5. Dose, V., Linden, W.: Outlier tolerant parameter estimation. In: Maximum Entropy and Bayesian Methods. Kluwer Academic, Dordrecht (1999)
6. Chatzis, P., Kosmopoulos, I., et al.: Robust Sequential Data Modeling Using an Outlier Tolerant Hidden Markov Model. IEEE Trans on Pattern Analysis and Machine Intelligence 31(9), 1657–1669 (2009)
7. Gadhok, N., Kinsner, W.: Outlier-robust clustering using independent components. In: Proceedings of the 2008 ACM SIGMOD International Conference on Management of Data, pp. 185–198 (2008)
8. Pesonen, H.: Outlier-robust Bayesian Filter with Integrity Monitoring for GNSS Positioning (2009), http://www.math.tut.fi/posgroup
9. Hu, S., Sun, G.: Changes Detection and Its Applications for Processes (in Chinese). Journal of North China Institute of Technology 19(4), 312–320 (1998)

Cooperative Interactive Cultural Algorithms Based on Dynamic Knowledge Alliance

Yi-nan Guo[1], Shuguo Zhang[1], Jian Cheng[1,2], and Yong Lin[1]

[1] College of Information and Electronic Engineering, China University of Mining
and Technology, Xuzhou, 221116 Jiangsu, China
nanfly@126.com
[2] Department of Automation, Tinghua University, Beijing 100084, China

Abstract. In cooperative interactive genetic algorithms, each user evaluates all individuals in every generation through human-machine interface, which makes users tired. So population size and generation are limited. That means nobody can evaluate all individuals in search space, which leads to the deviation between the users' best-liked individual and the optimal one by the evolution. In order to speed up the convergence, implicit knowledge denoting users' preference is extracted and utilized to induce the evolution. In the paper, users having similar preference are further divided into a group by K-means clustering method so as to share knowledge and exchange information each other. We call the group as knowledge alliance. The users included in a knowledge alliance vary dynamically while their preferences are changed. Taken a fashion evolutionary design system as example, simulation results show that the algorithm speeds up the convergence and decreases the number of individuals evaluated by users. This can effectively alleviate users' fatigue.

Keywords: Cooperative Interactive Culture Algorithms, K-means, Dynamic Knowledge Alliance.

1 Introduction

In interactive genetic algorithms (IGAs),the fitness values of individuals are evaluated by human[1]. The evolution operations of IGAs are usually implemented in a computer node for one user. Because human is easy to feel tired when he does one work for a long time, the generation and population size are limited. So it is difficult to obtain the satisfying solution in limited generation aiming at the optimization problems with large search space. Moreover, there are often more than one users participating in the evolution through human-machine interfaces in different computer nodes so as to obtain the satisfying individuals meeting themselves needs.

In order to improve the performances of the evolution and effectively alleviate users' fatigue, Guo[2] introduced dual structure of cultural algorithms into IGAs. Frequency pattern mining methods are adopted to extract key gene-meaning-unit which reflects users' preferences in the evolution as implicit knowledge. Aiming at multiuser IGAs, many researchers proposed the methods to exchange the evolution information among users. This can improve the diversity of population in each clients and

H. Deng et al. (Eds.): AICI 2011, Part III, LNAI 7004, pp. 204–211, 2011.

the convergence. Based on the satisfying degree of group decision-making and users' preferences, Sun [3] proposed a distributed collaborative interactive genetic algorithm. How to confirm the number of sharing individuals and select them are illustrated. Mitsunori [4] introduced asynchronous collaborative IGA. An elite sample database is built to solve the limits at time and space in parallel IGAs. Tomoyukii [5] gave the idea about collaboration into online shopping navigation system. The satisfying products are obtained automatically in terms of user's current preferences. Based on interactive cultural algorithms (ICAs), Guo [6] further proposed cooperative ICAs. Each user's preference is noticed to other users by adopting IP multicast technology so as to exchange the evolution information in knowledge level. So the effective experiences of other users are used for reference in the co-evolution. In this method, the cost of network communication is increasing along with the increasing number of users. In order to avoid network congestion caused by knowledge sharing among all users, a clustering method for users based on knowledge alliance is proposed. The users with similar preferences are classified into a knowledge alliance. The information is noticed to all user inside the alliance by IP broadcast. Common knowledge reflecting all users' common preferences is exchanged among alliances by tree network. This can effectively decrease the cost for information transfer.

2   Algorithm Description

Multi-user cooperative interactive culture algorithm is similar to the traditional culture algorithms. They are essentially dual-layer evolution model.

IGA is implemented in population space. In each independent computer node, human gives qualitative evaluation for all individuals via human-machine interface. The evolution operations including selection strategy, crossover operator and mutation operator are carried out based on the evaluated fitness values. Some better individuals are selected to belief space as samples by acceptance function in terms of certain rules. Obviously, these samples contain the information about users' personal preference.

In belief space, knowledge reflecting users' preference is extracted from samples by frequency pattern mining in every independent computer node. It is shared with other users. Considering the communication cost of information migration among users, a hierarchical sharing mechanism of knowledge based on knowledge alliance is proposed by adopting construction method of agent alliances in multi-agent system.

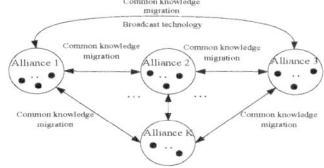

Fig. 1. Dynamic knowledge alliance in belief space

As shown in Fig.1, K-means clustering algorithm is used to partition users to knowledge alliances. Here, there are K alliances. Each user is described by a black dot in the alliance. Users belonging to the same knowledge alliance have similar preferences. The common knowledge is migrated among alliances in the manner of broadcast. When a alliance receives migrated information from other alliances, migrated knowledge will be integrated with its own common knowledge. Then inconsistent information is noticed to all users in the alliance by IP broadcast. This hierarchical information exchange mechanisms can decrease network communication cost and effectively share evolution information among users.

3   Extraction and Utilization of Knowledge in ICAs

In ICAs, user's preferences are extracted from the better individuals as knowledge. The individuals are usually encoded by binary. In existing knowledge extraction methods, one or more bits with large percentage are obtained by statistical methods directly. However, the relationship among the gene-meaning-units cannot be effectively reflected. So an extraction method based on frequency pattern mining is presented. Suppose $[0, f_{max}]$ is the range of individuals' fitness values. Let $E(t)$ be the individual set meeting $f(x_i) \in [0.5f_{max}, f_{max}]$. The algorithm's steps are shown as follows:

Step1: In $E(t)$, each individual is encoded by binary. Suppose there are G gene-meaning-units in an individual. Each gene-meaning-units x_{ij} is converted into non-overlapping real coding x'_{ij}[8] and saved into database Q.

$$x'_{ij} = |\Omega| \times j + 1 + x_{ij}, j = 0,1,2...G \qquad (1)$$

Step2: After the database Q is scanned, the frequent items and their support counts is collected. Then FP-tree is constructed based on the minimum support counts. If FP-tree contains a single path, the frequent patterns corresponding to the path are directly formed. Otherwise, the condition pattern database for each node is generated. The condition FP-tree is recursively obtained to get the frequent patterns.

Step3: Each gene-meaning-units with certain values in obtained frequent patterns is transformed to corresponding gene-meaning-unit value with binary genotype by formula (2). Other uncertained bits are described as "*".

$$x_{ij} = x'_{ij} - |\Omega| \times j - 1, j = 0,1,2...G_q \qquad (2)$$

Here, the converted frequent patterns reflect the gene-meaning-units with largest frequency and maximum correlation in the evolution. They also note the most-liked favorite gene by users, called knowledge of users' preferences. In this paper, frequent patterns are adopted to induce the evolution in next generation.

- If each bit of x_{ij} is 0 or 1, the phenotype of this gene-meaning-unit is directly shown in human-machine interface to be evaluated.
- If $x_{ij} = *...*$ is uncertain, it is "add" with own knowledge. If the uncertain gene-meaning-unit still exists, it is randomly generated by 0 or 1. In order to reserve own

preference, the number of individuals influenced by migrated common knowledge are limited. Suppose knowledge influencing rate is $\gamma \in (0,1)$. Let *pop* is the population size. M' is the number of individuals influenced by knowledge. The constrain for influenced population size is $M' \leq \lfloor \gamma \cdot pop \rfloor$.

4 Construction of Dynamic Knowledge Alliances

Due to human's cognitive is variable, users' preferences may change along with the evolution. So it's difficult to obtain the labeled training data reflecting user fixed preferences. Because K-means clustering method does not dependent on prior knowledge, a classification method for users by this algorithm is given.

4.1 Construction of Alliance Based on K-Means Clustering Method

According to the knowledge extracted from computer nodes, the users having similar preference are collected by using K-means clustering method. A knowledge alliance for the users having common preference is constructed. Suppose $\{FP_1, FP_2, \cdots, FP_N\}$ is users' preferences set. N is the number of users. K users' preferences are randomly selected as initial cluster centers expressed by $C_i (i=1,\cdots,K)$. The similarity of categories between the initial cluster center and jth user's preference is calculated.

$$S_j^i = \frac{1}{G} \sum_{i=1}^{K} \sum_{l=1}^{G} \delta(FP_{jl}, C_{il}) \tag{3}$$

$$\delta(FP_{jl}, C_{il}) = \begin{cases} 1 & if \ FP_{jl} = C_{il} \\ 0 & if \ FP_{jl} \neq C_{il} \end{cases} \tag{4}$$

Here, $\delta(FP_{jl}, C_{il})$ describes the correlation between two frequent patterns. Based on the similarity of categories, user is classified into the category with $\max_i S_j^i$. Thus, N users are divided into K knowledge alliances according to their evolution knowledge. Then the cluster centers in all knowledge alliances denoted by $\bar{C}_i = (\bar{C}_{i1}, \bar{C}_{i2}, \cdots \bar{C}_{iG})$ are adjusted according to the above classification results until they are no longer changed.

$$\bar{C}_{il} = \frac{1}{N_i} \sum_{i=1}^{N_i} C_{il} \tag{5}$$

The number of users in a knowledge alliance is dynamically changed along with the evolution and the variation of users' preferences. After the evaluation by users is finished in each generation, the similarity of categories between user's evolution knowledge and the corresponding cluster center is calculated.

● If the similarity of category is less than a certain threshold, the member of knowledge alliance does not change.

● If the similarity of category exceeds a certain threshold, this user exits from corresponding alliance. The similarity of categories between this user and other cluster centers are computed. The user joins an alliance with the maximum similarity. Then the cluster center of corresponding alliance is modified.

4.2 Knowledge Migration Strategy

In cooperative ICAs, hierarchical knowledge migration strategy is adopted. It contains the user-oriented knowledge migration within the alliance and the alliance-oriented knowledge migration among alliances.

A) The migration mode
After the evolution operations in each generation is completed, knowledge reflecting user's preference is extracted and sent to the server. The classification is done by the server before the evolution in next generation. Because human has own cognition and the degree of fatigue in the evaluation for individuals or the time spending on the evaluation is different, knowledge from different users may be asynchronous. So asynchronous knowledge migration is used in the paper.

In asynchronous knowledge migration strategy, knowledge alliances may be constructed when knowledge from some of users is sent to the servers. But the maximum proportion of users participating in the classification must be ensured. Assume that T_i is the evaluation time for ith user from the 1th generation to the generation sending knowledge to the sever at first time. If more than $0.8N$ users have submitted the knowledge to the sever, knowledge alliances are constructed for the first time. Users are gradually familiar with the system and know which kinds of individuals they like. So the evaluation time is decreasing. The interval for knowledge migration among alliances is defined by average T_i, expressed by τ. Knowledge migration among alliances is done every $i\tau$ generation.

$$\tau = \left\lfloor \frac{1}{N} \sum_{i=1}^{N} T_i \right\rfloor + 1 \tag{6}$$

B) Knowledge fusion method
After an alliance receives common knowledge from other alliances, the knowledge is sent to all users in the alliance in the form of broadcast and used to induce the evolution. Here, the gene-meaning-unit is used as a unit. Migrated common knowledge and self knowledge are fused by "and" operation. Suppose g is the number of the gene-meaning-units with certain values in self knowledge of alliance M_i. g' denotes the gene-meaning-units set with certain values from common knowledge of alliance M_j. Then the effect of common knowledge on alliance M_i is analyzed in two aspects:

• If $g' \supset g$, the self knowledge of the alliance is replaced by common knowledge from M_j to induce the evolution.
• If $g \not\subset g'$ and $g' \cap g \neq \Phi$, the genes with same values are retained. At the genes with different values, M_i is replaced by the corresponding parts of the knowledge from M_j. If $g \not\subset g'$ and $g' \cap g = \Phi$, common knowledge from M_j has a direct impact on the evolution.

c) Communication complexity analysis of the algorithm
In cooperative ICAs, a dual-layer communication structure is formed by the establishment of dynamic knowledge alliance. Compared with CICAs without knowledge alliance, the communication complexity is further analyzed as follows.

● No classification for users: Suppose there are N users participating in the evolution. If users are not classified, the knowledge reflecting users' preferences is notified to other users in the form of broadcast in each generation. Therefore, the communication complexity is $N(N-1)$.

● Classification for users: Suppose there are K alliances formed in the evolution. If users are classified to knowledge alliances, the common knowledge reflecting users' same preference in a alliance is notified to other users in the alliance in the form of broadcast. Two layer communication mode including information exchange within and among alliances is formed. So the communication complexity is $N+K(K-1)$. Obviously, the larger N is, the communication complexity of CICA with knowledge alliances is less. This will make the quantity of exchanged information less so as to effectively avoid network congestion in the communication process.

5   Simulation Results and Their Analysis

In order to validate the rationality of the algorithm, fashion evolutionary design system is taken as examples. The goal of fashion evolutionary design system is to find the satisfying dress for users. A dress is composed of coat and skirt. Each part includes pattern and color, which are described by binary code with nine bits[12]. The same evolution operations and parameters are adopted in each computer node. Roulette selection method combing with elitist strategy are used. Multi-point crossover operator and one-point mutation operator are adopted. The detailed parameters' values are: $f_{max}=100$, $pop=8$, $Pc=0.4$, $Pm=0.01$, $T=200$, $N=10$, $K=3$.

A) Dynamic analysis of knowledge alliance
Ten users are participated in the evolution. The same evolutionary operations are done by everyone in each computer node. The simulation results are shown in Table.1. All users can find their own satisfying solutions. But the evaluation time and the evaluated individuals are different. That means everybody has different cognition.

The knowledge alliance containing certain users varies along with the evolution, as shown in Table.2. Each user participates in the evolution asynchronously. The alliance containing them varies along with the evolution. If the evolution is finished in some computer node, corresponding user will not belong to any alliance.

Table 1. The simulation results

User ID	1	2	3	4	5	6	7	8	9	10
iteration	5	11	12	12	9	6	10	6	8	9
evaluation time	4'58"	9'19"	9'10"	6'52"	5'54"	5'08"	7'33"	6'07"	6'36"	7'55"
evaluated individuals	36	68	76	61	53	45	76	44	58	67
whether the satisfying dress is found	yes	yes	yes	yes	yes	yes	yes	yes	yes	yes

Table 2. The variation of knowledge alliance

times	1	2	3	4
1th alliance	4/5/8	1/5/8	6/9	4
2th alliance	1/2/10	2/3/4/10	3/10	3/10
3 th alliance	4/5/8	6/7/9	2/7/9	2/7

The variation of alliances' cluster centers is shown in Table.3. Along with the evolution, one user may belong to different alliances. So the cluster centers may be changed. It is obvious that the number of certain gene-meaning-unit in cluster centers is increasing. That means the accuracy of common knowledge is increasing. Common knowledge is exchanged in an alliance or among the alliances so as to guide the evolution. This improves the diversity of population and accelerates the convergence.

Table 3. The variation of cluster centers

times	1th cluster center	2th cluster center	3th cluster center
1	**************1001	10111*************	*****10001********
2	01000********1001	10111*****0011****	*****10001********
3	01000*****01111001	10111*****0011****	0010110001********
4	01000*****01111001	10111*****00110111	00101100011010****

B) Comparison of performances among different algorithms
In order to show the important role of knowledge alliance to improve the performances of cooperative ICAs(CICADKA), it is compared with cooperative interactive cultural algorithms without users clustering(CICAs) and traditional interactive genetic algorithm(IGAs). The simulation results are shown in Table.4.

Table 4. Comparison of performances among different algorithms

algorithms	generation	time	the evaluated individuals	satisfaction rate
CICADKAs	8.3	6'57"	58.4	100%
CIGAs	10.4	8'47"	73	100%
IGAs	15.8	9'52"	99.1	70%

CICADKA can effectively decrease the number of individuals evaluated by users and find satisfying solutions in a shorter time and smaller generation. Compared with traditional IGAs, CICADKA not only improves the rate of obtained satisfying individuals, but also accelerated the convergence at the same time. In conclusion, this algorithm is consistent with the principles of alleviating user's fatigue.

6 Conclusions

A multi-user cooperative ICAs with dynamic knowledge alliances is proposed. In each computer node, interactive cultural algorithms based on frequency pattern mining are done. Based on the knowledge given by nodes, users are dynamic classified to many alliances according to their preference by using K-means clustering method. Common knowledge is shared among these alliances. Knowledge is noticed to everyone inside the alliance by broadcast. Take fashion evolutionary design system as example, more than one user participates in the evolution. Simulation results show that the proposed algorithm can alleviate user's fatigue more and speed up the convergence. In a word, cooperative ICAs based on dynamic knowledge alliances is a feasible and effective multi-user interactive evolutionary algorithm.

Acknowledgment. This work was supported by National Natural Science Foundation of China under Grant 60805025, Natural Science Foundation of Jiangsu under Grant BK2010183, the China Postdoctoral Science Foundation Funded Project under Grant 20090460328.

References

1. Takagi, H.: Interactive evolutionary computation: fusion of the capabilities of EC optimization and human evaluation. Proceedings of the IEEE 89(9), 1275–1296 (2001)
2. Guo, Y.-N., Lin, Y.: Interactive genetic algorithms with frequent-pattern mining. In: Proceedings of the 6th International Conference on Natural Computation, pp. 2381–2385 (2010)
3. Sun, X.-Y., Wang, X.-F., Gong, D.-W.: A distributed co-Interactive genetic algorithm and its applications to group decision-making. Information and Control 36(5), 557–561 (2007)
4. Miki, M., Yamamoto, Y., Wake, S.: Global asynchronous distributed interactive genetic algorithm. In: 2006 IEEE International Conference on Systems, Man and Cybernetics, pp. 3481–3485 (2006)
5. Hiroyasu, T., Yokouchi, H.: Extraction of Design Variables using Collaborative Filtering for Interactive Genetic Algorithms. In: IEEE International Conference on Fuzzy Systems, pp. 1579–1584. IEEE, Piscataway (2009)
6. Guo, Y.-N., Lin, Y., Yang, M., Zhang, S.: User's preference aggregation based on parallel interactive genetic algorithms. Applied Mechanics and Materials Journal 34, 1159–1164 (2010)
7. Wang, J.P., Chen, H., Xu, Y., et al.: An architecture of agent-based intelligent control systems. In: Proceedings of the World Congress on Intelligent Control and Automation, pp. 404–407. IEEE, Piscataway (2000)
8. Le, M.N., Ong, Y.S.: A frequent pattern mining algorithm for understanding genetic algorithms. In: International Conference on Natural Computation, pp. 131–139. IEEE, Piscataway (2008)

Group Search Optimizer with Interactive Dynamic Neighborhood

Guohua He⋆, Zhihua Cui, and Jianchao Zeng

Complex System and Computational Intelligence Laboratory
Taiyuan University of Science and Technology
Taiyuan, China
heguohua40@163.com, cuizhihua@gmail.com, zengjianchao@263.net

Abstract. Group search optimizer(GSO) is a new novel optimization algorithm by simulating animal behaviour. It uses the Gbest topology structure, which leads to rapid exchange of information among particles. So,it is easily trapped into a local optima when dealing with multi-modal optimization problems. In this paper,inspiration from the Newman and Watts model,a improved group search optimizer with interactive dynamic neighborhood (IGSO) is proposed.Adopting uniform design and the linear regression method on the parameter selection, four benchmark functions demonstrate the effectiveness of the algorithm.

Keywords: Group search optimizer, Network topology, Uniform design.

1 Introduction

In the past few decades, nature-inspired optimization has been widely used to solve various scientific and engineering problems. Among them, the most successful are Evolutionary Algorithms (EAs) which drew inspiration from evolution by natural selection. Lately, a new global optimization algorithm paradigm, Swam Intelligence (SI), has been proposed. Currently, SI includes two different algorithms. The first one is Ant Colony Optimization (ACO) which was developed based on real ant foraging behavior [1]. Another SI algorithm is Particle Swarm Optimizer (PSO) which inspired by swarm behavior of bird flocking or fish schooling [2].

Recently, Inspired by animal behavior,especially animal searching behavior, a novel swarm intelligence algorithm Group Search Optimizer (GSO) has been proposed [3].GSO is a novel population based stochastic optimization algorithm which was inspired by animal searching behavior and group living theory. The algorithm is based on the Producer-Scrounger model [4], which assumes group members search either for 'finding' (producer) or for 'joining' (scrounger) opportunities. Animal scanning mechanisms (e.g., vision) are incorporated to develop the algorithm.

⋆ Corresponding author.

H. Deng et al. (Eds.): AICI 2011, Part III, LNAI 7004, pp. 212–219, 2011.
© Springer-Verlag Berlin Heidelberg 2011

In these years, some variants has been proposed aiming to increased it's convergence speed and efficiency. Fang et al.[5]proposed a hybrid group search optimizer with metropolis rule to solve Optimization problems.He et al.[6]proposed Interactive Dynamic Neighborhood Differential Evolutionary GSO(IDGSO)for handing high dimension problems. S. He, Q. H. Wu and J. R. Saunders[7] apply the GSO to Articial Neural Network (ANN) training to further investigate its applicability to real-world problems.such as diagnosis of breast cancer.It also has a better convergence rate and generalization performances.

Compared with EAs, GSO has a markedly superior performance in terms of accuracy and convergence speed, especially on high-dimensional multi-modal problems.But it also have some defects, such as the network topology of the information transmission in animal groups, the vast majority of individuals simply to share the current best individual information, the model itself has some limitations, and this affects the performance of the algorithm to some extent. In this paper, Group search optimizer with interactive dynamic neighborhood(IGSO) is proposed to improve the performance of GSO.

The rest of this paper was organized as follows: in section 2,we introduce the concepts of group search optimizer, and the Group search optimizer with interactive dynamic neighborhood is discussed in section 3. The simulation experiments are compared and discussed in section 4.

2   Group Search Optimizer

Basically GSO is a population based optimization algorithm. The population of the GSO algorithm is called a group and each individual in the population is called a member. In an n-dimensional search space, the i_{th} member at the k_{th}searching bout (iteration), has a current position $X_i^k \in R^n$ a head angle $D_i^k(\Phi_i^k) = (d_{i1}^k, ..., d_{in}^k) \in R^n$, and a head direction $\Phi_i^k = (\psi_{i1}^k, ..., \psi_{in}^k) \in R^{n-1}$, which can be calculated from ψ_i^ka Polar to Cartesian coordinates transformation:

$$\begin{cases} d_{i1}^k = \prod_{p=1}^{n-1} \cos(\psi_{ip}^k) \\ d_{ij}^k = \sin(\psi_{i(j-1)}^k) \cdot \prod_{p=i}^{n-1} \cos(\psi_{ip}^k) \\ d_{in}^k = \sin(\psi_{i(n-1)}^k) \end{cases} \tag{1}$$

In the GSO, a group comprises three kinds of members: producers, scroungers and rangers. In the GSO algorithm, there is only one producer at each searching bout and the remaining members are scroungers and rangers. The simplest joining policy, which assumes all scroungers will join the resource found by the producer, is used.

During each search bout, a group member, located in the most promising area, conferring the best fitness value, acts as the producer. It then stops and scans the environment to search resources (optima). In the GSO algorithm, at the k_{th} iteration the producer X_p behaves as follows:

1) The producer will scan at zero degree and then scan laterally by randomly sampling three points in the scanning field[8]: one point at zero degree;one point in the right hand side hypercube;and one point in the left hand side hypercube:

$$
\begin{cases}
X_z = X_p^k + r_1 l_{max} D_p^k(\phi^k) \\
X_r = X_p^k + r_1 l_{max} D_p^k(\phi^k + r_2 \theta_{max}/2) \\
X_l = X_p^k + r_1 l_{max} D_p^k(\phi^k - r_2 \theta_{max}/2)
\end{cases}
\tag{2}
$$

where $r_1 \in R^1$ is a normally distributed random number with mean 0 and standard deviation 1 and $r_2 \in R^{n-1}$ is a random sequence in the range $(0, 1)$.

2) The producer will then find the best point with the best resource (fitness value). If the best point has a better resource than its current position,then it will fly to this point. Otherwise it will stay in its current position and turn its head to a new angle:

$$
\psi^{k+1} = \psi^k + r_2 \alpha_{max}
\tag{3}
$$

Where α_{max} is the maximum turning angle.

3) If the producer cannot find a better area after a iterations, it will turn its head back to zero degree:

$$
\psi^{k+a} = \psi^k
\tag{4}
$$

where a is a constant given by round.

A number of group members are selected as scroungers.The scroungers will keep searching for opportunities to join the resources found by the producer.

$$
X_i^{k+1} = X_i^k + r_3(X_p^k - X_i^k)
\tag{5}
$$

where $R_3 \in R^n$ is a uniform random sequence in the range $(0,1)$.

The remaining are the rangers they random walks searching for randomly distributed resources.

$$
X_i^{k+1} = l_i D_i^k(\phi^{k+1})
\tag{6}
$$

where $l_i = \alpha \cdot r_1 l_{max}$,and $\psi_i^{k+1} = \psi^k + r_2 \alpha_{max}$.

In order to maximize their chances of finding resources, animals restrict their search to a profitable patch.

3   Group Search optimizer with Interactive Dynamic Neighborhood

As the study of complex networks continued to grow in importance and popularity, many other aspects of network structure have attracted attention as well. Specially, Most of the recent works on small world were performed using the Newman and Watts model[9]. The advantages of Newman and Watts model is that it's simplifies the theoretical analysis, and the model would not exist isolated nodes.

Newman and Watts model specific structure as follows: (1) For each particle, generate the order number (1,2,3, ... N),choose k of particles $i - \lceil\frac{k}{2}\rceil, i - \lceil\frac{k}{2}\rceil + 1, ..., i - 1, i + 1, ..., i + \lfloor\frac{k}{2} - 1\rfloor, i + \lfloor\frac{k}{2}\rfloor$ connected directly,while making maximum and minimum number of particles end to end.This leads to ring regular network. (2) Corresponding to each edge of each node, maintain each edge of regular network fixed, than select a smaller probability p to establish long-distance connections outside of it's neighborhood.Such construction process can been see from (a) to (c)in Figure 1.

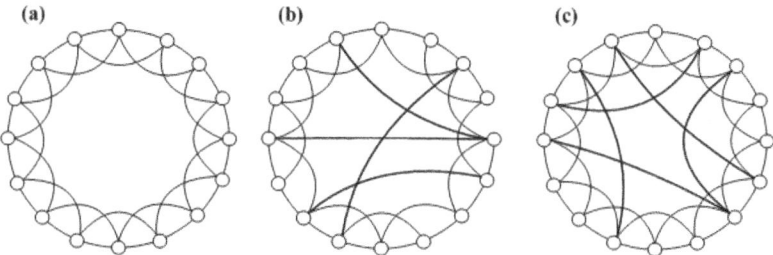

Fig. 1. The evolution of Newman and Watts model

Inspired by the Newman and Watts model, the GSO with interactive dynamic neighborhood(IGSO)is proposed in this article. In the Newman and Watts model, the adjacency relations between network nodes dynamically increasing, which has been introduced into the GSO. In order to make the situation easier to control, we use $p = 1$ to design the algorithm. In the initial, members has less contraction. By controlling the speed of the network evolution, it becomes a global coupled network in the latter. Parameter selection is a key of the algorithm, here we take the uniform design method. Several test functions verify the validity of IGSO.

In IGSO,scroungers update its position according to their best neighborhood location X_e.

$$X_i^{k+1} = X_i^k + r_3(X_e^k - X_i^k) \tag{7}$$

The population of all particles is initialized to a ring neighborhood, each individual only communicate with two individuals. The network update after the generation of m_1,while adding the new edge of m_2,which increases the diversity of the algorithm.

The detail steps of IGSO are listed as follows:

Stept1: Initialized the topology to ring neighborhood; Randomly initialize positions and head angles of all members; Choose the the parameters about m_1 and m_2;Calculate the fitness values of initial members;

Stept2: Choose producer: Calculate the fitness values of initial members;Find the producer of the group;

Stept3: Perform producing: 1) The producer will scan at zero degree and then scan laterally by randomly sampling three points in the scanning field using equations (2).2) Calculate the fitness values of the three points: Find the best point with the best resource (fitness value). If the best point has a better resource than its current position, then it will fly to this point.Otherwise it will stay in its current position and turn its head to a new angle using equation (3).3) If the producer can not find a better area after a iterations, it will turn its head back to zero degree using equation (4);

Stept4: Perform scrounging: Randomly select 80% from the rest members to perform scrounging using equation (5);

Stept5: Perform dispersion: For the rest members, they will be dispersed from their current position to perform ranging using equation (6);

Stept6: Calculate fitness: Calculate the fitness value of current member.If the value achieved our need or exceed the max iteration,than stop,otherwise return to Step2.

4   Simulation Results

4.1   Benchmark Function

This paper selects four Benchmark functions [10]to make experiments, the details of these benchmark functions are showed in Table 1:

Table 1. Test functions

f	function	space
Rosenbrock	$f(x) = \sum_{i=1}^{n-1}[100(x_{i+1} - x_i^2)^2 + (x_i - 1)^2]$	$[-30, 30]^n$
Griewank	$\frac{1}{4000}\sum_{i=1}^{n} x_i^2 - \prod_{i=1}^{n} \cos[\frac{x_i}{\sqrt{i}}] + 1$	$[-600, 600]^n$
Penalized1	$f(x) = \frac{\pi}{n}\{10\sin^2(\pi y_1) + \sum_{i=1}^{n-1}(y_i - 1)^2[1 + 10\sin^2(\pi y_{i+1})]$ $+(y_n - 1)^2\} + \sum_{i=1}^{n} u(x_i, 10, 100, 4)$	$[-50, 50]^n$
Penalized 2	$0.1\{\sin^2(\pi 3x_1) + \sum_{i=1}^{n}(x_i - 1)^2[1 + \sin^2(3\pi x_{i+1})] + (x_n$ $-1)^2[1 + \sin^2(2\pi x_n)]\} + \sum_{i=1}^{n} u(x_i, 5, 100, 4)$	$[-50, 50]^n$

The number of local minima increases exponentially with function dimensions. And n is the dimension of each function in the formulas.All of our test function's best values is zero($f_{min} = 0$).

4.2   Experimental Setting

The key of the algorithm is how to control the evolution rate from the ring to the fully coupled topology. The parameters setting about m_1 and m_2 is the key. If evolution too fast, global search capability can not be given fully, and too slow the algorithm can not effectively converge to the global optimum in the latter. The uniform design is used to choose parameters of m_1 and m_2.

Uniform design[11]proposed by Professor Kaitai Fang and Professor Yuan Wang.it is an experimental design. Its mathematical principle is the same number of distribution theory. The experimental points uniformly scattered in the test range. In order to test least but get most information. Uniform design is a table which has been a designed carefully, each table comes with a use table. Here we selection $U_{10}(10^8)$table,and the results show that the combination of $m_1 = 15$, $m_2 = 80$is the best.

4.3   Algorithm Performance Analysis

We compared the performance of IGSO with two different EAs: 1) Standard Particle Swarm Optimization (SPSO) 2) Standard Group Search Optimizer (SGSO).

The scroungers is 80% of the group. Because the producer requires three function evaluations, the population size of the GSO and IGSO was set to be 48 in order to keep the number of function evaluations as same as other algorithms in a generation.

Fixed Number of Function Evaluations. Table 1 show the comparison results of four benchmark functions under the same evolution generations respectively. And the dimension is 300.Obviiously,the IGSO performance is much better than SPSO and SGSO.

In the fixed number of function evaluations, we evaluate the optimize performance of SPSO, SGSO, IGSO. Although the results may not be close to the optimal result, it is only a point near to an local optimum point, this performance reflect the convergence speed to a certain extent. In this article, the number of fixed-function is 10^6, each function runs 10 times independently. From Table 2 ,we see IGSO in terms of mean Value, standard Deviation and best Value is better than SPSO and SGSO.

Table 2. Comparison Results for Functions

Function	Algorithm	Mean Value	Standard Deviation	Best Value
	SPSO	9.1385e+004	1.0298e+005	7.9584e+004
Rosenbrock	SGSO	2.3401e+003	1.5916e+003	1.3719e+003
	IGSO	1.0457e+003	4.3401e+002	4.9076e+002
	SPSO	1.9884e+000	8.0148e-001	1.0356e+000
Griewank	SGSO	5.7679e-001	2.5799e-001	2.4823e-001
	IGSO	2.6019e-002	1.8912e-002	1.3217e-002
	SPSO	2.9091e+004	3.1212e+004	1.6321e+004
Penalized1	SGSO	1.2981e+003	2.9071e+002	8.9382e+002
	IGSO	1.9809e+001	1.5120e+001	3.0934e+000
	SPSO	1.8608e+005	1.4986e+005	1.3526e+004
Penalized2	SGSO	1.2990e+003	2.5453e+002	9.2539e+002
	IGSO	1.2230e+002	2.0291e+002	4.0519e+000

The Average Iteration Reached the Determined Threshold. This performance indicator is also used for evaluate the evolutionary speed, but unlike the above indicators, the algorithm has been close to the global best position this time. The Rosenbrock function of the threshold is taken as 5E +003, Griewank function of the threshold is taken as 5E-002, a threshold of Penalized1 function is 5E +001 and Penalized2 function threshold is taken as 5E +002. When running 20000 times but not reached our required accuracy, we believe that the algorithm has been trapped into local optimal.In addition, we calculate the proportion, which the number of reaching the preset threshold out of the total number of the provisions of evolution, for testing the reliability of the algorithm.

Table 3 show the performance of different algorithms.Rate is the reaching rate.For all test functions, SPSO has no rate, SGSO on all test functions has some rate but much less than IGSO. The performance of IGSO is the best, especially on Griewank function, Penalized1 function and Penalized1 function, the rate has reached 100%.

Table 3. Reaching rate and mean iteration of Functions

Function	Algorithm	Rate	mean(iteration)
Rosenbrock	SPSO	0	/
	SGSO	88%	19047
	IGSO	88%	16940
Griewank	SPSO	0	/
	SGSO	20%	19886
	IGSO	100%	15604
Penalized1	SPSO	0	/
	SGSO	34%	19746
	IGSO	100%	11306
Penalized2	SPSO	0	/
	SGSO	40%	19971
	IGSO	100%	17323

5   Conclusion

This paper has proposed a new variation of the Group search optimizer called IGSO. The adjacency relations between network nodes dynamically increasing.This modification can improve the information utilizations. It changes particles' behaviors and search space. The simulation results show that IGSO have better performance.

Acknowledgments. This paper are supported by National Natural Science Foundation of China under Grant 61003053, the Key Project of Chinese Ministry of Education under Grant 209021 and Shanxi Science Foundation for Young Scientists under Grant 2009021017-2.

References

1. Dorigo, M., Birattari, M., Stutzle, T.: Ant colony optimization-Artificial ants as a computational intelligence technique. IEEE Computational Intelligence Magazine 1(4), 28 39 (2006)
2. Eberhart, R.C., Kennedy, J.: New optimizer using particle swarm theory. In: Proc.of the 6th International Symposium on Micro Machine and Human Science, pp. 39–43. IEEE, Piscataway (1995)
3. He, S., Wu, Q.H., Saunders, J.R.: Group search optimizer - an optimization algorithm inspired by animal searching behavior. IEEE Transaction on Evolutionary Computation 13(5), 973–990 (2009)
4. Barnard, C.J., Sibly, R.M.: Producers and scroungers: a general model and its application to captive flocks of house sparrows. Animal Behaviour 29, 543–550 (1981)
5. Fang, J.Y., Cui, Z.H., Cai, X.J., Zeng, J.C.: A Hybrid Group Search Optimizer With Metropolis Rule. In: Proceeding of by 2010 International Conference on Modeling. Identification and Control, Okayama,Japan, pp. 556–561 (2010)
6. He, G.H., Cui, Z.H., Tan, Y.: Interactive Dynamic Neighborhood Differential Evolutionary Group Search Optimizer. Journal of Chinese Computer Systems (accepted, 2011)
7. He, S., Wu, Q.H., Saunders, J.R.: Breast Cancer Diagnosis Using An Artificial Neural Network Trained by Group Search Optimizer. Transactions of the Institute of Measurement and Control 31(6), 517–531 (2009)
8. Giraldeau, L.-A., Lefebvre, L.: Exchangeable producer and scrounger roles in a captive flock of feral pigeons-a case for the skill pool effect. Animal Behaviour 34(3), 797–803 (1986)
9. Newman, M.E.J., Watts, D.J.: Renormalization group analysis of the small-world network model. Phys. Lett. A 263, 341–346 (1999)
10. Yao, X., Liu, Y., Lin, G.M.: Evolutionary Programming Made Faster. IEEE Transactions on Evolutionary Computation 3(2), 82–102 (1999)
11. Fang, K.T., Ma, C.X.: Orthogonal and Uniform Design of Experiments. Science Press, Beijing (2005)

Identification of Parameters in Chemical Kinetics Using a Hybrid Algorithm of Artificial Bee Colony Algorithm and Simplex

Guangzhou Chen[1], Jiaquan Wang[2,*], and Ruzhong Li[2]

[1] Department of Environmental Engineering,
Anhui University of Architecture, Hefei 230022, China
[2] School of Resources and Environmental Engineering,
Hefei University of Technology, Hefei 230009, China
{chgzh5,jiaquan wang}@163.com

Abstract. Parameter identification is a key step in establishing kinetic models. Aimed at the above problem, it can be transformed into an optimization problem by constructing objective function that minimizes simulation errors. Two examples of chemical kinetics are analyzed. Among them, the second case is a more complicated nonlinear problem, so using ABC individually can not obtain better results. Then a hybrid algorithm of ABC and simplex is proposed. The method firstly uses ABC to carry out global search so as to obtain better initial point. Secondly, simplex is employed to process local search based on the above initial point. Compared with that of modified genetic algorithm, hierarchical differential evolution, adaptive differential evolution, the results show that the new hybrid algorithm can obtain better optimization precision by combining global searching ability of ABC with strong local searching ability of simplex. So it is an effective optimization method.

Keywords: artificial bee colony algorithm, simplex, parameter identification, chemical kinetics, global optimization.

1 Introduction

Parameter identification is a problem faced widely in establishing mathematical models for many specialties. It can be transformed into an optimization problem by constructing objective function that minimizes simulation errors. In the beginning, some traditional optimization techniques are employed to solve them such as the multivariable regression, the gradient-based optimization method, coordinate transformation, simplex and so on. Because of the multi-dimensional and complex nonlinear characteristics, they are usually easy to trap into local optima. Among them, simplex was proposed by Spendley et al. in 1962. Subsequently, it was improved by Nelder and Mead in 1965[1]. It is a direct search optimization method, and has the directional fast searching ability to the local optimization without the need of gradient

---

* Corresponding author.

H. Deng et al. (Eds.): AICI 2011, Part III, LNAI 7004, pp. 220–227, 2011.

information; however, its global optimization searching ability depends on whether the initial point is located on the nearby of the point or not. So it is limited to use to some degree.

Recently, many swarm intelligence optimization algorithms such as ant colony, particle swarm, fish swarm, bee colony and so on have been put forward unceasingly. Some swarm intelligence algorithms have been applied in the parameter identification from engineering domains. In chemical kinetic models, Yan et al. [2], Xu et al.[3], Shi et al.[4], Hu et al.[5] used chaos genetic algorithm, clonal selection algorithm, hierarchical differential evolution, adaptive differential evolution to estimate kinetic parameters, respectively. Artificial bee colony algorithm (ABC) is a novel swarm intelligence optimization algorithm proposed by Karaboga in 2005 [6].Since proposed, it has been used in function optimization, constrained numerical optimization, training feed-forward neural networks, and good optimization results were obtained [7, 8].Though ABC has strong global search ability, it is also found that it has weak local search ability in practice. Therefore, it is still worth of improving basic ABC algorithm. With regard to the combination of global optimization algorithm and traditional local search method, the combination had been used in some literatures. Han et al. [9] proposed a global optimization algorithm: genetic algorithm-simplex; Chelouah R. et al. [10] combined Genetic Algorithm with Nelder-Mead Algorithm to form a more accurate global optimization; Kuo et al. [11] hybridized algorithm of evolution and simplex method to apply to global optimization; Wang et al.[12] studied the combining effect on the particle swarm optimization with simplex method operator; Atef A. Lasheen et al.[13] used hybrid genetic and Nelder-Mead algorithm for decoupling of MIMO systems.

The above modified algorithms were proved to be effective. To own both the merits of the better local searching ability from the simplex method and the global searching ability from the evolutionary algorithm, a combined algorithm of artificial bee colony and simplex, is tested. This paper is organized as follows. In section 2 we will review the principles and computing steps of ABC. In section 3 we will review the principles and computing steps of simplex. In section 4 we propose a hybrid ABC, followed by the two cases analysis in section 5. The conclusions are given in section 6.

2   Artificial Bee Colony Algorithm

2.1   Terms and Explanations of Algorithm

Artificial bee colony (ABC) algorithm, proposed by Karaboga for optimizing numerical problems, simulates the intelligent foraging behavior of honey bee swarms. In ABC, the colony of artificial bees contains three groups of bees: employed bees, and unemployed bees: onlookers and scouts. In ABC, first half of the colony consists of employed artificial bees and the second half constitutes the artificial onlookers. The honey bee which waits in the dance area and makes decision to choose food source is called an onlooker; the honey bee which goes food source found by oneself is called an employed bee; the honey bee which carries out stochastic search is called a scout bee. The employed bee whose food source has been exhausted becomes a scout bee. The position of a food source represents a possible solution to the optimization problem and the nectar amount of a food source corresponds to the quality (fitness) of the associated solution. The number of the employed bees is equal to the number of food sources, each of which also represents a site, which is exploited at the moment.

2.2 Steps of Algorithm [14]

1) Initialize the population of solutions $x_{ij}, i = 1,..., SN$, $j = 1,... D$, where SN is the number of food sources, D is the dimension of the variables;
2) Compute the fitness values and evaluate the population;
3) Produce new solutions (food source positions) v_{ij} in the neighborhood of x_{ij} for the employed bees, using the formula (1):

$$v_{ij} = x_{ij} + \phi_{ij}(x_{ij} - x_{kj}) \tag{1}$$

where x_k is a randomly selected solution except x_i, ϕ_{ij} is a random number within the range$[-a, a]$, a is usually set to 1, then apply the greedy selection process between v_i and x_i;
4) Calculate the probability values p_i for the solutions x_i by means of their fitness values fit_i, using expression (2):

$$p_i = fit_i / (\sum_{i=1}^{SN} fit_i) \tag{2}$$

where the fitness values might be calculated using the expression (3) for minimization problems:

$$fit_i = \begin{cases} 1/(1+f_i) & if \quad f_i \geq 0 \\ 1 + abs(f_i) & if \quad f_i \prec 0 \end{cases} \tag{3}$$

where f_i is objective function value;
5) Produce new solutions (new positions) v_i for the onlookers from the solutions x_i selected depending on p_i, then apply the greedy selection process between v_i and x_i;
6) Determine the abandoned solution x_i, if exists, and replace it with a new randomly produced solution x_i' for the scout:

$$x'_{ij} = x\min_j + rand(0,1) * (x\max_j - x\min_j) \tag{4}$$

where $x\min_j$ is the lower bound of the parameter j and $x\max_j$ is the upper bound of the parameter j.
7) Memorize the best food source position (solution) achieved so far; if the stopping criteria is satisfied, then stop and output the best solution, otherwise go to step (2) and continue the loop.

3 Simplex Method

It belongs to a class of methods which do not require derivatives and which are often claimed to be robust for problems with discontinuities or where function values are noisy. It solves an unconstrained minimization problem in dimensions by maintaining at each iteration points that define a simplex. At each iteration, this simplex is updated by applying certain transformations to it so that it "rolls downhill" until it finds a minimum.

3.1 Steps of Algorithm [15]

1) Build the initial simplex. Set up the first vertex of initial simplex $x^{(0)}$, then produce the other vertexes by expression (5):

$$x^{(i)} = x^{(0)} + \alpha \cdot d^{(i)}, i = 1,2,...,n \qquad (5)$$

where n is dimensions of variables, α is step factor and $d^{(i)}$ is unit stochastic vector calculated according to expression (6):

$$d^{(i)} = rand\ (n,1) * 2 - 1, d^{(i)} = d^{(i)} / \left\| d^{(i)} \right\|_2 \qquad (6)$$

2) Compare the function values and compute centroid of simplex according to expression (7):

$$x_c = \frac{1}{n} (\sum_{i=0}^{n} x^{(i)} - x_{max}), x^{(i)} \neq x_{max} \qquad (7)$$

3) Reflection computation. Reflection point is obtained by expression (8):

$$x_r = x_c + \rho(x_c - x_{max}) \qquad (8)$$

where ρ is reflection coefficient.

4) Expansion computation. If $f(x_r) < f_{max}$, then the new point x_e is obtained by expression (9):

$$x_e = x_r + \gamma(x_r - x_c) \qquad (9)$$

where γ is expansion coefficient. If $f(x_e) < f(x_r)$, then replace x_{max} with x_e and jump to step (2), or replace x_{max} with x_r and jump to step (2).

5) Contraction computation. If $f(x_r) > f_{max}$, then shrink to a new point by expression (10):

$$x_s = x_{max} + \beta(x_c - x_{max}) \qquad (10)$$

where β is shrink coefficient.

6) Edge shrink computation. New $x^{(i)}$ can be obtained by expression (11):

$$x^{(i)} = x_{min} + 0.5(x^{(i)} - x_{min}), i = 1, 2, ..., n \tag{11}$$

4 Combination of ABC and Simplex

A new hybrid ABC algorithm is proposed combining the global search ability of ABC with the local search ability of simplex. The above two algorithms form consecutive structure. It firstly uses ABC to carry out global search so as to obtain better initial solution. Secondly, simplex method is employed to process local search based on the above initial solution. Therefore, it effectively absorbs the advantages of ABC and simplex method. It not only can overcome the deficiency that ABC has weak local search ability, but also can effectively solve the sensitivity problem of simplex to the initial points of search.

5 Applications of Examples and Analysis

5.1 Case1: Pyrolysis and Dehydrogenation of Benzene

Biphenyl and paraterphenyl are obtained in the following reaction [4]:

$$2C_6H_6 \Leftrightarrow C_{12}H_{10} + H_2 \tag{12}$$

$$2C_6H_6 + 2C_{12}H_{10} \Leftrightarrow 2C_{18}H_{14} + 2H_2 \tag{13}$$

The proposed kinetic model is:

$$dx_1/dt = -r_1 - r_2 \tag{14}$$

$$dx_2/dt = r_1/2 - r_2 \tag{15}$$

$$r_1 = k_1[x_1^2 - x_2(2 - 2x_1 - x_2)/(3K_1)] \tag{16}$$

$$r_2 = k_2[x_1x_2 - (1 - x_1 - 2x_2)(2 - 2x_1 - x_2)/(9K_2)] \tag{17}$$

where x_1 and x_2 are the residual volume of benzene and biphenyl, respectively. k_1 and k_2 are the reaction rate constants that are to be estimated. $K_1 = 0.242$ and $K_2 = 0.428$ are the equilibrium constants. The experimental sample data from the literature are shown in Table 1[4].The initial condition is $t = 0$, $x_1 = 1$ and $x_2 = 0$.

Table 1. Experimental data of pyrolysis and dehydrogenation of benzene

$t \times 10^4$	5.63	11.32	16.07	22.62	34	39.7	45.2	169.7
x_1	0.828	0.704	0.622	0.565	0.499	0.482	0.47	0.443
x_2	0.0737	0.113	0.1322	0.14	0.1468	0.1477	0.1477	0.1476

The objective function is defined as

$$\min \ f = \sum_{j=1}^{n} \sum_{i=1}^{2} (x_{i,j} - x'_{i,j})^2 \tag{18}$$

where n is the sample size, $x_{i,j}$ is the experimental value of x_i in the jth sample while $x'_{i,j}$ is the value obtained by the kinetic model.

The population of bees is set to 20, the total iterative number is 200, the limit value is 50, the scopes of three parameters are all the interval [0, 1000]. In order to prevent influence of random factor, the algorithm is executed in 20 independent runs and the best, average and the worst value of the results are recorded. The optimization results are listed in Table 2 in detail. And results of other algorithms are also shown in Table 2.

Table 2. Objective function values obtained by different algorithms

Algorithms	Best	average	worst
DE [4]	8.372e-4	8.383e-4	8.434e-4
PSO [4]	8.372e-4	8.379e-4	8.390e-4
Hierarchical differential evolution [4]	8.372e-4	8.372e-4	8.372e-4
ABC	8.3717e-4	8.3717e-4	8.3717e-4

Table 2 shows that the best objective function value achieved by four algorithms are the same while ABC obtains better optimization results and outperforms DE and PSO in terms of the average and worst values. Moreover, ABC has the characteristic with few parameters of algorithm that need to be set. The kinetic parameters found by ABC are $k_1 = 358.3246, k_2 = 404.2742$.

5.2 Case2: Supercritical Water Oxidation

Supercritical water oxidation is an effective treatment technology for organic waste in environmental field. The removing rate expression for dichloropheno (2-cp) is as follows:

$$r = A \exp(-E_a / RT)[2CP]^a [O_2]^b [H_2O]^c \tag{19}$$

where r is the removing rate of 2-cp, A is the pre-exponential factor, E_a denotes the apparent activation energy, R is the molar gas constant, a, b and c are the order of reaction of 2-cp, O_2 and H_2O, respectively. After the analysis, the following equations can be obtained [4]:

$$\ln(1-X) = -A \exp(-E_a / RT)[O_2]^b [H_2O]^c \tau \quad \text{if } a = 1 \tag{20}$$

$$[(1-X)^{1-a} - 1] = (a-1)A \exp(-E_a / RT)[2CP]^{a-1}[O_2]^b [H_2O]^c \tau \quad \text{if } a \neq 1 \tag{21}$$

The objective is to identify the five parameters (A, E_a, a, b, c) according to the experimental data provided in literature[16]. This optimization problem is the one with high non-linearity besides possess many local optima. The objective function is defined as:

$$\min \quad f = \sum_{i=1}^{n} (X_i - X_i')^2 \tag{22}$$

where n is the sample size, X_i is the conversion rate of 2-cp in the ith sample data while X_i' is the conversion rate calculated by the kinetic model.

In the experiments, the population of bees is set to 50, the total iterative number is 500, the limit value is 100, the ranges of are [0,200], [30000, 50000],[0,2], [0,2] and [0,2], respectively. In order to prevent influence of random factor, the algorithm is executed in 20 independent runs and the best, average and the worst value of the results are recorded. After many experiments, we find that using ABC individually cannot obtain better results. Therefore, a new hybrid algorithm combined ABC with simplex is proposed. The parameters of simplex are α =1.3, ρ =1, γ =1.2 and β =0.6. The algorithm is executed in 20 independent runs and the best, average and the worst value of the results are recorded. The optimization results are listed in Table 3 in detail. As a comparison, the best results of other some algorithms are 0.2225(CGA) [2], 0.2494(NLR) [2], 0.2177(ADE) [5], 0.2177(HACS) [17].

Table 3. Objective function values obtained by different algorithms

Algorithms	Best	average	worst
DE[4]	0.217685	0.217725	0.218037
PSO[4]	0.217685	0.217819	0.218733
Hierarchical differential evolution [4]	0.217685	0.217685	0.217685
ABC	0.233919	0.292802	0.421080
Hybrid ABC (HABC)	0.217685	0.217685	0.217685

Table 3 shows that the best objective function value achieved by four algorithms (DE, PSO, HDE, HABC) are the same while the average and worst values obtained by hybrid ABC outperforms those of DE and PSO. Moreover, compared with other algorithms, hybrid ABC is also found to be more profitable operating than those reported earlier in the literature.

6 Conclusion

Parameter estimation plays an important role in establishing the models in many specialties. It can be transformed into an optimization problem. To pursuit a highly efficient optimization technique, many new algorithms are used unceasingly. The article applies ABC and a hybrid ABC to solve the two optimization problem under the case that each variable is optimized according to its own reasonable scope. The hybrid ABC firstly uses ABC to carry out global search so as to obtain better initial solution. Secondly, simplex method is employed to process local search based on the above initial solution. The results from two chemical kinetic models show the hybrid ABC has the advantages of strong global search ability of ABC and strong local search ability of simplex, and can obtain better solutions. So it is a promising technique to estimate parameters.

Acknowledgments. We would like to thank Yuan Shi for his guidance in constructing the objective function. Moreover, the work is supposed by the following foundations: Natural Science Foundation of Anhui Province under Grant No.11040606M99, Initial Foundation of University for Doctor and College Natural Science Foundation of Anhui Province under Grant No. KJ2010A060.

References

1. Nelder, J.A., Mead, R.: A Simplex Method for Function Minimization. Computer Journal 4, 308–3134 (1965)
2. Yan, X.F., Chen, D.Z., Hu, S.X.: Estimation of Kinetic Parameters Using Chaos Genetic Algorithms. Journal of Chemical Industry and Engineering (China) 23(8), 810–814 (2002)
3. Xu, Y., Zhang, G.H., Fen, Q.: New Clonal Selection Algorithm in Kinetic Parameter Estimation. Computers and Applied Chemistry 25(10), 1175–1179 (2008)
4. Shi, Y., Zhong, X.: Hierarchical Differential Evolution for Parameter Estimation in Chemical Kinetics. In: Ho, T.-B., Zhou, Z.-H. (eds.) PRICAI 2008. LNCS (LNAI), vol. 5351, pp. 870–879. Springer, Heidelberg (2008)
5. Hu, C.P., Yan, X.F.: A Novel Adaptive Differential Evolution Algorithm with Application to Estimate Kinetic Parameters of Oxidation in Supercritical Water. Engineering Optimization 41(11), 1051–1062 (2009)
6. Karaboga, D.: An Idea Based on Bee Swarm for Numerical Optimization. Technical Report-TR06, Turkey: Erciyes University (2005)
7. Karaboga, D., Basturk, B.: A Powerful and Efficient Algorithm for Numerical Function Optimization: artificial bee colony (abc) algorithm. Journal of Global Optimization 41(39), 459–471 (2007)
8. Karaboga, D., Basturk, B.: On the Performance of Artificial Bee Colony (abc) Algorithm. Applied Soft Computing 8(1), 687–697 (2008)
9. Han, W., Liao, Z.P.: A Global Optimization Algorithm: Genetic Algorithm-Simplex. Earthquake Engineering and Engineering Vibration 21(2), 6–12 (2001)
10. Chelouah, R., Siarry, P.: Genetic and Nelder-Mead Algorithms Hybridized for a More Accurate Global Optimization of Continuous Multiminima Functions. European Journal of Operational Research 148(2), 335–348 (2003)
11. Kuo, H.C., Chang, J.R., Shyu, K.S.: A Hybrid Algorithm of Evolution and Simplex Methods Applied to Global Optimization. Journal of Marine Science and Technology 12(4), 280–289 (2004)
12. Wang, F., Qiu, Y.H.: Empirical Study of Hybrid Particle Swarm Optimizers with the Simplex Method Operator. In: Paprzycki, M., Kwasnicka, H. (eds.) 5th International Conference on Intelligent Systems Design and Applications, pp. 308–313 (2005)
13. Atef, A., Lasheen, A.M., El-Garhy, E.M., Saad, S.M.: Eid: Using Hybrid Genetic and Nelder-Mead Algorithm for Decoupling of MIMO Systems with Application on Two Coupled Distillation Columns Process. International Journal of Mathematics and Computers in Simulation 3(3), 146–157 (2009)
14. Karaboga, D.: Artificial Bee Colony Algorithm. Scholarpedia 5(3), 6915 (2010)
15. Li, W.X.: Engineering Optimization Design and MATLAB Program. Tsinghua University Press, Beijing (2010)
16. Li, R.K., Savage, P.E.: Journal of AICHE 39(1), 178–187 (1993)
17. He, Y.J., Chen, D.Z., Wu, X.H.: Estimation of Kinetic Parameters Using Hybrid Ant Colony System. Journal of Chemical Industry and Engineering 56(3), 487–491 (2005)

Extraction of Breast Cancer Areas
in Mammography Using a Neural Network
Based on Multiple Features

Meigui Chen, Qingxiang Wu[*], Rongtai Cai, Chengmei Ruan, and Lijuan Fan

School of Physics and OptoElectronic Technology, Fujian Normal University
Fuzhou, China
chenmeigui06@163.com, Q.Wu@ulster.ac.uk,
rtcai@fjnu.edu.cn,
lupin_3rd@126.com, fanlijuannihao@163.com

Abstract. Brest cancer is the leading cause of death among women. Early detection and treatment are the keys to reduce breast cancer mortality. Mammography is the most effective method for the early detection at present. In this paper, an approach, which combined multiple feature extraction and a neural network model, is proposed to segment the breast cancer X-ray images. Firstly the visual system inspired model is used to extract the feature information of colors, gray scale, entropy, mean and standard deviation in receptive fields of the input neurons in the network. And then the neural network is trained to segment a breast cancer X-ray image into normal area and cancer area. The experiment results show that the approach is able to extract the cancer area in an X-ray image efficiently. This approach can be applied in automatic diagnosis systems of breast cancer.

Keywords: Neural Network, receptive field, mammography, feature extraction, spicules.

1 Introduction

Breast cancer is one of the most common malignancy tumors among women. According to statistics, there are about 1200,000 women suffered from breast cancer each year in the world [1]. The National Cancer Institute estimates that one out of eight women in the United States will develop breast cancer at some point during her lifetime[2][3]. With the improvement of people's living standard, its incidence is rising year by year, and its development trends younger. Similar to other cancers, complete prevention seems impossible because the causes of this disease still remain unknown. Early detection and treatment are the keys to reduce breast cancer mortality. Medical imaging technologies are the primary method for the detection of breast cancer signs and lesions, and it is convenient and noninvasive. It is suitable for age-appropriate women to census. The common medical imaging technologies [4] for

---

[*] Corresponding author.

H. Deng et al. (Eds.): AICI 2011, Part III, LNAI 7004, pp. 228–235, 2011.

the detection of breast cancer include clinical touch, mammography, near infrared scanning, ultrasound diagnosis, thermal image scanning, computer tomography, magnetic response imaging and so on. Mammography has the best effect for the detection of early asymptomatic secretiveness breast cancer with low cost in all of medical imaging technologies. It's the primary method in the clinical detection of breast cancer, and it's the most effective method in breast cancer census. The latest mammography has already made images and gray levels clear. However, the detection results are influenced by many reasons, for example , the features of lesions are not obvious; the doctors' eyes feel tired; doctor's experiences are different; there are noises in the image and so on [5]. They cause high misdiagnosis rate and the low specificity in the detection of cancer true positive. In order to reduce the misdiagnosis rate and improve the specificity [6], scientists begin to envision cancer detection using computers instead of human, and it is called the computer-aided diagnosis (CAD) [7]. CAD systems have been developed to assist radiologists in detecting signs of early breast cancer [8][9].

The representations of breast cancer X-ray can be divided into direct signs and indirect signs. Direct signs include masses, calcification, breast architectural distortion, density asymmetry, the emergence of new abnormal density and so on. Indirect signs contain skin thickening or retraction, anomalies of nipple and areola, abnormal thickness of blood vessels and so on. For masses, their characteristic mainly display for nodules, group, or irregular shape, gray scale descends from center to peripheral. They are characterized by a pattern of radiating lines known as spicules that emanate from a central mass [10]. At a roughly look, masses are bright spots in images, and the gray value of the central regions is very high. In order to distinguish normal and cancer areas in mammographic images, this paper presents a neural network based on multiple features such as gray scale, entropy, mean, and standard deviation. The neural network is derived from the visual system inspired neural network in [11], but the network has been extended to deal with multiple features. Therefore, the proposed network can identify small differences between normal and cancer areas. The experimental results show that the neural network is able to segment the normal area and the cancer area in an X-ray image of breast cancer and obtain satisfactory results.

The remainder of this paper is organized as follows. In Section 2, the architecture of the neural network is proposed. Section 3 describes the segmentation algorithms based on the neural network. In Section 4, the results achieved using the proposed approach are presented and discussed. Finally, conclusions are presented in Section 5.

2   Architecture of Neural Network Model

Neurological scientists have found that there are different kinds of receptive fields in the visual system [12]. Taking the properties of receptive fields for rods and cones in retina and combining them with entropy, mean and standard deviation, an architecture of neural network, which is shown as Fig.1, is proposed to segment breast cancer areas.

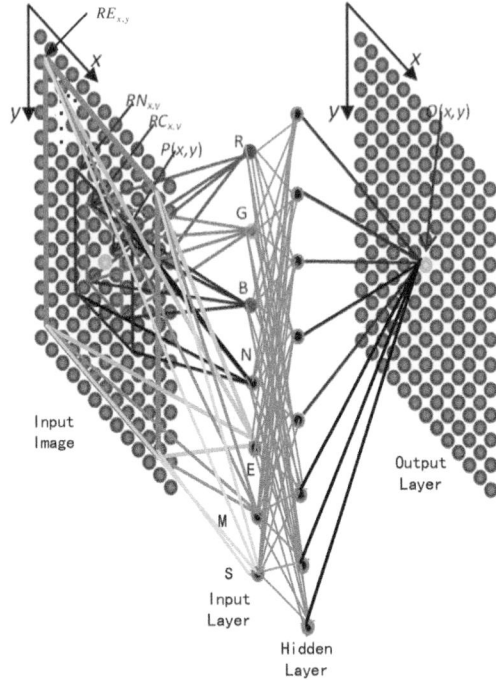

Fig. 1. Architecture of the Neural Network Model

The first layer indicates an input image. Let the dimension of the image be $M{\times}N$. A pixel in the image is labeled with $P(x,y)$, $x=1,2,...,M$, $y=1,2,...,N$. There are three receptive fields centred at $P(x,y)$. They are $RC_{x,y}$, $RN_{x,y}$ and $RE_{x,y}$. The second layer represents the input layer, which includes three types of cones and one type of rod. The cones labeled with R, G and B are corresponding to the receptive field $RC_{x,y}$. They respond to red light, green light and blue light in the receptive field respectively. The rod N is corresponding to the receptive field $RN_{x,y}$. Based on the network in [11], the more input neurons, which include entropy, mean and standard deviation, are extended in the network. The input neurons E、 M and S are corresponding to the receptive field $RE_{x,y}$. The third layer is the hidden layer, which reflects the number of feature objects required to be identified. The neurons in the input layer are fully connected to the layer. The last layer indicates the output layer. The neurons in the hidden layer are linked to neuron $O(x,y)$ in the output layer. The output value of neuron $O(x,y)$ is determined by three receptive fields $RC_{x,y}$, $RN_{x,y}$ and $RE_{x,y}$ which are centred at $P(x,y)$. Therefore, the neural network can be trained to identify breast cancer images by the features of colors, gray scale, entropy, mean and standard deviation in the receptive fields. Entropy is used to extract texture features for making a distinction between cancer area and normal area. Mean is to describe the concentration trend of data in breast cancer images. Considering its low representative for discrete data, standard deviation is added to represent the data discrete degree.

3 Algorithms for Extraction of Breast Cancer X-Ray Images

Let $(R_{x,y}, G_{x,y}, B_{x,y}, N_{x,y}, E_{x,y}, M_{x,y}, S_{x,y})$ indicates an input vector of the neural network and $O(x,y)$ is an output value of the output neuron. Their relationship is represented by the following expression.

$$O(x, y) = NET(R_{x,y}, G_{x,y}, B_{x,y}, N_{x,y}, E_{x,y}, M_{x,y}, S_{x,y}) \tag{1}$$

The output value $O(x,y)$ is a group of classification numbers. It can be adjusted according to requirements. In this paper, it is defined as three numbers $\{0,1,2\}$, '0' represents background in a breast cancer X-ray image. '1' represents normal area. '2' represents cancer area.

Let $r(x',y')$, $g(x',y')$, $b(x',y')$, $n(x',y')$, $e(x',y')$ and $m(x',y')$ represent values of colors R, G, B, gray scale, entropy, mean and standard deviation of pixel $P(x',y')$ in the input image respectively. According to the receptive fields in the neural network, we have

$$R_{x,y} = \frac{1}{A} \sum_{(x',y') \in RC_{x,y}} r(x',y') \tag{2}$$

$$G_{x,y} = \frac{1}{A} \sum_{(x',y') \in RC_{x,y}} g(x',y') \tag{3}$$

$$B_{x,y} = \frac{1}{A} \sum_{(x',y') \in RC_{x,y}} b(x',y') \tag{4}$$

$$N_{x,y} = \frac{1}{B} \sum_{(x',y') \in RN_{x,y}} n(x',y') \tag{5}$$

$$E_{x,y} = \frac{1}{C} \sum_{(x',y') \in RE_{x,y}} e(x',y') \tag{6}$$

$$M_{x,y} = \frac{1}{C} \sum_{(x',y') \in RE_{x,y}} m(x',y') \tag{7}$$

$$S_{x,y} = \sqrt{\frac{1}{C} \sum_{(x',y') \in RE_{x,y}} [n(x',y') - M_{x,y}]^2} \tag{8}$$

where A is the area of the receptive field $RC_{x,y}$ for cone neurons, B is the area of the receptive field $RN_{x,y}$ for rod neurons, C is the area of the receptive field $RE_{x,y}$, $m(x',y')$ are pixels in the matrix of the receptive field $RE_{x,y}$. In this paper, gray scale is obtained using

$$n(x',y') = 0.2989 \times r(x',y') + 0.587 \times g(x',y') + 0.114 \times b(x',y') \tag{9}$$

The entropy is computed by the following expression.

$$e(x',y') = -n(x',y')\log_2 n(x',y')$$

(10)

In order to analyze the efficiency of entropies, mean values and standard deviations in extraction of cancer areas, we have calculated entropies, mean values and standard deviations of 100 images with size 50×50. 50 images are cut from normal area and other 50 images are cut from cancer area. It is found that entropies, mean values and standard deviations in the images of cancer area are much larger than those in the images of normal area, and values in unevenly distributed images are much larger than that in evenly distributed images.

In the experiments, sizes of receptive fields $RC_{x,y}$, $RN_{x,y}$ and $RE_{x,y}$ are set to 3×3, 5×5 and 50×50 respectively . Therefore, $A=9$, $B=25$ and $C=2500$. Also, they can be adjusted to get good results for different cases.

In order to train the neural network, a training data set is sampled from three areas from mammographic images. They are background, normal area and cancer area. While sampling, a classification number for the corresponding area is assigned to each sample in the training set. Therefore, the network trained with the training data set can be used to identify which area the receptive field belongs to. Marks of the three areas are obtained in the output layer. There is a mark map of three areas in the experiments. The numbers {0,1,2} are corresponding to background, normal area and cancer area respectively. The algorithms are proposed based on the features of R, G, B, gray scale, entropy, mean and standard deviation in the three areas. Breast cancer X-ray images are separated in different areas by the multiple features.

4   Experimental Results

The neural network has been simulated in Matlab 7.1. In the experiments, the neuron number in the input layer is set to 7 and the neuron number in the hidden layer is 8. Levenberg-Marquardt optimization is used as training algorithm to train the neural network. Using the approach, calcified parts and other cancer parts of breast cancer images can be identified by the neural network based on the multiple features of R, G, B, gray scale, entropy, mean and standard deviation, and good results can be obtained. The training data set is sampled from the points shown in Fig.2. Each point corresponds to a training sample. The stars represent sample points for background. The vector ($R_{x,y}$, $G_{x,y}$, $B_{x,y}$, $N_{x,y}$, $E_{x,y}$, $M_{x,y}$, $S_{x,y}$) is sampled from a star point (x,y) according to (2)-(8) and the output value of the network is set to '0'. The squares are sample points for normal area. The vector ($R_{x,y}$, $G_{x,y}$, $B_{x,y}$, $N_{x,y}$, $E_{x,y}$, $M_{x,y}$, $S_{x,y}$) is sampled from a square point (x,y) according to (2)-(8) and the output value is set to '1'. The circles indicate the sample points for cancer area. The vector ($R_{x,y}$, $G_{x,y}$, $B_{x,y}$, $N_{x,y}$, $E_{x,y}$, $M_{x,y}$, $S_{x,y}$) is sampled from a circle point (x,y) according to (2)-(8) and the output value is set to '2'. In the experiments, 50 points are sampled from every area and then a training set is obtained.

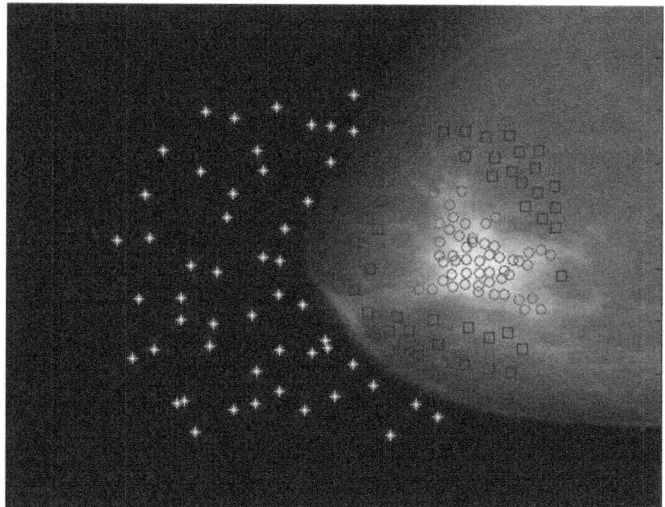

Fig. 2. Sample points

When the training set is used to train the network, changes of errors are shown in Fig.3. It can be found that the network converges very fast during training process from this figure.

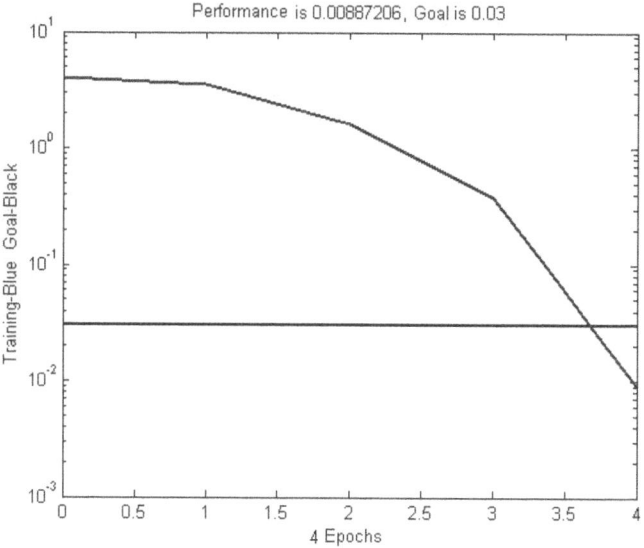

Fig. 3. Changes of errors

Using the algorithms proposed in this paper, the normal area and the cancer area are obtained as shown in Fig.4.

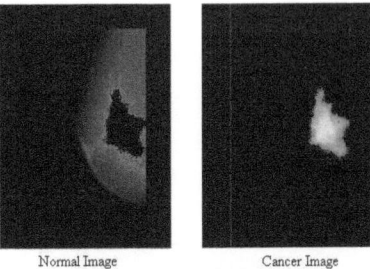

Normal Image   Cancer Image

Fig. 4. Final separated images

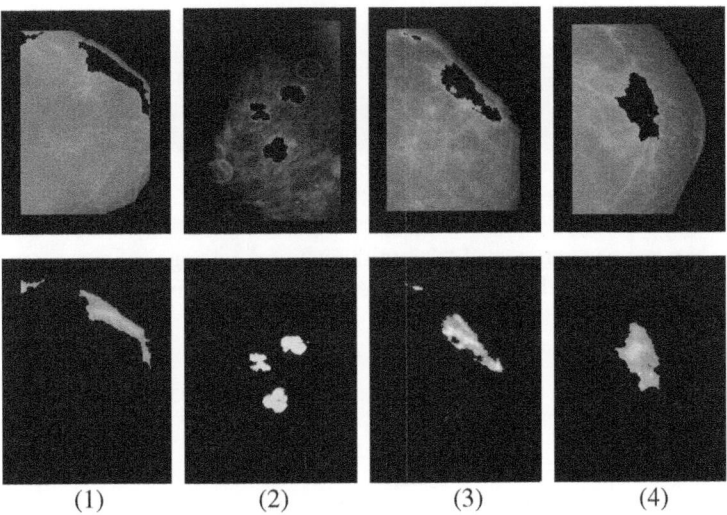

(1)   (2)   (3)   (4)

Fig. 5. Some other results

The proposed approach has been tested using 50 mammographic images taken from the Medical Image Database [13]. Fig.5 shows four examples of the algorithms results. The top figure represents the normal area whereas the bottom figure depicts the cancer area. The above results show that no matter how many cancer areas there is in an image, this approach is able to segment cancer areas and normal areas. These experimental results prove the suitability of this approach to identify both masses and calcifications. This approach can be used to automatic diagnosis systems of breast cancer.

5   Conclusion

Mammography is the most effective method for the early detection at present. The approach presented in this paper is based on the neural network to segment the cancer area in a breast cancer X-ray image. The advantage of using the computer-aided diagnosis is to reduce the misdiagnosis rate and improve the specificity. According to the characteristics of breast cancer X-ray images, the proposed neural network model is able to extract the features of colors, gray scale, entropy, mean and standard deviation in receptive fields. The proposed algorithms can separate a breast cancer image into two areas: normal area and cancer area. The experimental results show that the proposed approach is able to extract the cancer area in an image efficiently.

Acknowledgment. The authors gratefully acknowledge the support from the Natural Science Foundation of Fujian Province, China (Grant No. 2009J05141) and the Science-Technology Project of Education Bureau of Fujian Province, China (Grant No. JA09040).

References

1. Boring, C.C., Squires, T.S., Tong, T.: Cancer Statistics 42, 19–38 (1992)
2. Wun, L.M., Merril, R.M., Feuer, E.J.: Estimating lifetime and age-conditional probabilities of developing cancer. Lifetime Data Anal. 4(2), 169–186 (1998)
3. Houssami, N., Brennan, M., French, J., Fitzgerald, P.: Breast imaging in general practice. Clinical Practice: Breast Imaging in General Practice 34(6), 467–473 (2005)
4. Giger, M.L., Huo, Z., Kupinski, M.A., Vyborny, C.J.: Computer-aided diagnosis in mammography. In: Sonka, M., Fitzpatnck, M. (eds.) Handbook of Medical Imaging, Washington, pp. 915–986 (2000)
5. Giger, M.: Overview of computer-aided diagnosis in breast imaging. In: Proceedings of the First International Workshop on Computer-Aided Diagnosis, Chicago, U.S.A, pp. 167–176 (1998)
6. Nishikawa, R.M.: Current status and future directions of computer-aided diagnosis in mammography. Computerized Med. Imag. Graphics 31, 224–235 (2007)
7. Shi, J., Sahiner, B., Chan, H.P., Ge, J., Hadjiiski, L., Helvie, M.A., Nees, A., Wu, Y.T., Wei, J., Zhou, C., Zhang, Y., Cui, J.: Characterization of mammographic masses based on level set segmentation with new image features and patient information. Med. Phys. 35, 280–290 (2008)
8. Sampat, M.P., Markey, M.K., Bovik, A.C.: Computer-aided detection and diagnosis in mammography. In: Handbook of Image and Video Processing, New York, pp. 1195–1217 (2005)
9. Castellino, R.A.: Computer aided detection(CAD): An overview. Cancer Image 5, 17–19 (2005)
10. Sampat, M.P., Whitman, G.J., Broemeling, M.D., Broemeling, L.D., Heger, N.A., Bovik, A.C., Markey, M.K.: The reliability of measuring physical characteristics of speculated masses on mammography. Br. J. Radio 79, S134–S140 (2006)
11. Wu, Q.X., Huang, X., Cai, J.Y., Wu, Y., Lin, M.Y.: Segmentation of Lerkocytes in Blood Smear Images Using Color Processing Mechanism Inspired by The Visual System. Biomedical Engineering and Informatics, 368–372 (2009)
12. Kandel, E.R., Shwartz, J.H.: Principles of neural science. Edward Amold (Publishers) Ltd. (1981)
13. http://rad.usuhs.edu/medpix/
   parent.php3?mode=tf2&been_here=-1&action=pre&acr_pre=0

Software Dependability Metrics and Analysis Based on AADL Error Model

Xin-ning Liu[*] and Hong-bing Qian[**]

G313, New Main Building, Software Engineering Institute
No. 37, College Road, Haidian District, Beihang University, Beijing, China
cherry523680602@sina.com, qhb@buaa.edu.cn

Abstract. To analyze the software products dependability early in the software life cycle is an important means to assure the final product quality. This paper firstly defines the rules of transforming the AADL error model into expanded Markov chain, and then builds a dependability measurement model based on AADL error model. After discussing how to use the property of Markov chain to measure the software, a method is presented to measure the software dependability as a whole combined with AADL core model. Finally an example is given to explain the use of the measurement method and to analyze the measurement results.

Keywords: AADL error model, dependability metrics, Markov analysis method, probabilistic reasoning.

1 Introduction

The research on software dependability is one of trusted computing branches and it has become an important research issue in recent years. As the complexity of embedded real-time systems increasing, how to improve software quality will be a major challenge in the future. The model-driven development can guarantee the system quality. The system model built early is directly related to the final actual system quality, and the software dependability reflects comprehensive quality attributes of a system. Therefore, to analyze software model dependability at an early stage can find the problems as soon as possible, and it consequently can improve the quality of software.

AADL (Architecture Analysis & Design Language) is a basis of the design and the implementation based on model-driven embedded system, and it supports the early analysis on the architecture and the design of system [1]. A software system model described by standard AADL (called AADL core model) can be extended by the annexes. Error Model Annex (EMA) is one of them. Currently, the research on software quality measurement based on AADL model is mainly by the method of

---

[*] Master. Research area: software test, software quality metrics.
[**] Associate professor. Research area: software quality assurance, software process improvement and measurement, software testing process and test model.

H. Deng et al. (Eds.): AICI 2011, Part III, LNAI 7004, pp. 236–244, 2011.
© Springer-Verlag Berlin Heidelberg 2011

transforming the AADL model into Generalized Stochastic Petri Nets or fault tree, which is used to measure the software reliability [2]. But the dependability is a comprehensive concept, So how to measure the software dependability based on AADL model from a comprehensive perspective still needs to be further studied. Therefore, this paper presents a method of measurement and analysis on software dependability based on AADL error model. First of all, by analyzing the relevant information of the error model, a semi-formal error model is transformed into formal expanded Markov chain. Then a dependability metrics model is built to measure individual component, and AADL core model which helps to measure the software dependability as a whole is introduced. At last, the result is analyzed by a simple method.

2   Transition from Error Model to Expander Markov Chain

The AADL Error Model Annex defines the statement rules and the semantic sets of the components and the connections to build error model. The Error Model Annex consists of two parts: the error model type and the error model implementation. The error model type declares a set of error states, error events and error propagations. The error model implementation declares error transitions between the states, which are triggered by events, and propagations declared in the error model type. Therefore, the transitions of the error states can be understood as stochastic automata. The error model type and error model implementation can all define the Occurrence properties for error events and error propagations. Occurrence properties specify the arrival rate or the occurrence probability of the events and the propagations. For the arrival rate, Occurrence properties specify an index value λ, and its probability density is $1-e^{-\lambda}$; for the Occurrence probability, Occurrence properties specify a decimal value from 0 to 1 [2]. Usually Occurrence properties are also used to indicate the recovery rate from error state to error-free state.

AADL with its extension annexes is a semi-formal language, so it is difficult to measure them. The formal method can describe the semantics more precisely, and it can be better used for the analysis for the model dependability, so this paper uses a method that transforms the error model into formal expanded Markov chain.

Markov chain points out the transitions from one state to another state, and the likelihood value from one state to another state is the transition probability. Through the analysis for EMA above, the error model can also points out the transitions of the states, which are the transitions from one error state to another error state, and the likelihood of the transitions from one error state to another error state can be pointed out by the Occurrence properties [3]. Therefore, the overall rules of the transition between the two models are: the error state in the error model corresponds to the state in the Markov chain, the transition between the error states corresponds to the transition between states in the Markov chain, the Occurrence properties of the transitions between error states correspond to the probabilities of the transitions between states in the Markov chain. In order to embody the information of error model, this paper puts forward an expanded Markov chain.

Definition1. The expanded Markov chain (EMC): EMC=(S, S_0, $\sum$, P, Q), where:

1. S is an error state set of the component; it is a finite set, and S can be expressed as: $\{S_1, S_2, S_3, ... , S_n\}$;
2. S_0 is an initial error state; it is generally error-free state, and $S_0 \in S$;
3. $\sum$ is a set of transitions between error states, in which $\sum_i$ is the ith element of $\sum$, and $\sum_i$ = {TriggerType, TriggerName}, where TriggerType is a type that triggers the transition between the error state, and it consists of two types: error event and error propagation. This paper considers the independent component, so all the types are error events; TriggerName$_i$ is the name of the error event;
4. P is the probability set of the transition between the error state, in which P_i is the ith element of P, and P_i= {Probability, ProbabilityType, ProbabilityDefinition}, where Probability is the ith probability of the transition between the error states, ProbabilityType points that it is a failure rate or recovery rate, ProbabilityDefinition indicates the transition probability, it can be an exponential distribution or a number between 0 and 1;
5. Q is the relationship of the transitions between the error states, that is $S \times \sum \rightarrow S$.

According to the above formal description of expanded Markov chain based on AADL error model, we can get the corresponding relations from AADL error model to expanded Markov chain in Table 1.

Table 1. The corresponding relations from AADL error model to expanded Markov chain

Expanded Markov chain	AADL error model
S	error state
S_0	initial error state
TriggerType	error event
Probability	Occurrence
ProbabilityDefinition	Poisson or fixed
Q	transitions

Table 2. An instance of a component error model

error model independent	**Error Model Implementation**
features	**[independent.general]**
Error_Free: **initial error state**;	**error model implementation**
Erroneous: **error state**;	independent.general
Failed: **error state**;	**transitions**
Temp_Fault: **error event{Occurrence**	Error_Free-[Perm_Fault]-
=> fixed 0.0000125}	>Failed;
Perm_Fault: **error event{Occurrence**	Error_Free-[Temp_Fault]-
=> fixed 0.0000075};	>Erroneous;
Restart: **error event{Occurrence =>**	Failed-[Restart]->Error_Free;
fixed 0.999825};	Erroneous-[Recover]-
Recover: **error event{Occurrence =>**	>Error_Free;
fixed 0.999795};	**end** independent.general;
end independent;	

Table 2 is an instance of a component error model, it can be transformed into expanded Markov chain according to the above transition   rules:

EMC={S,   Error_Free,$\sum$,   P,   Q}, in   which: S={   Error_Free,   Erroneous, Failed}; $\sum$={ $\sum_1$, $\sum_2$, $\sum_3$, $\sum_4$},in which $\sum_1$={error event, Pcrm_Falult},$\sum_2$={error event, Temp_Fault },$\sum_3$={ error event, Restart },$\sum_4$={ error event , Recover }; P={ P_1, P_2, P_3, P_4}, in which P_1={0.0000125, failure rate, fixed },P_2={0.0000175, failure rate, fixed },P_3={0.999825, recovery rate, fixed},P_4={0.999795, recovery rate, fixed}; Q={   Error_Free×$\sum_1$→Failed,Error_Free   ×$\sum_2$→Erroneous,   Failed×$\sum_3$ →Error_Free, Erroneous×$\sum_4$→Error_Free }.

3   Dependability Metrics Based on AADL Error Model

In this section, a software dependability model is firstly built based on AADL error model, then a method is discussed to analyze the individual component dependability by using of the expanded Markov chain which is transformed from error model, and an overall metrics on software dependability attributes with AADL core model is discussed.

3.1   Dependability Attribute Metrics Model Based on AADL Error Model

The software dependability is a complex combination of many quality attributes; now the main research on dependability has five aspects which are reliability, safety, security, maintainability and availability. According to the five quality attributes, we divide them into two categories: direct metrics and indirect metrics. The direct metrics include reliability, safety and availability, and they can be measured by the existing model; the indirect metrics include security and maintainability, and it can be measured indirectly by the factors of reducing the software dependability [6].

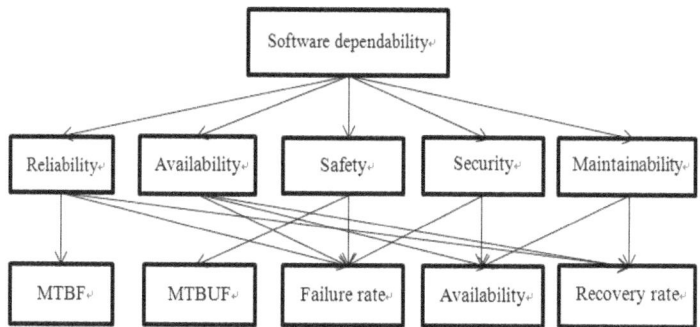

Fig. 1. Metrics model of software dependability based on AADL error model

According to the quality attributes metrics and the factors of reducing the software dependability, this paper gives a metrics model of software dependability based on AADL error model in order to reflect the error model standard. The metrics model is shown in the Fig.1.

3.2 Dependability Attribute Metrics on Component-Level

The dependability of the whole system is closely related to the individual component, so this paper firstly begins with the individual components, and discusses the method of using the properties of Markov chain to measure the individual component.

The state transition probability of Markov chain P_{ij} is $p_{ij}=p_{ij}(1)=P\{x_{m+1}=a_j|x_m=a_i\}$, which is called one-step state transition probability. A matrix which is formed by state transition probability is called state transition probability matrix, and the sum of each row is 1. A matrix which is formed by one step state transition probability is called one-step state transition probability matrix. If the transition probability is not relevant to n, then the chain is homogeneous, that is $p\{x_{n+1}=j|x_n=i\}=p_{ij}=$ constant. The error model meets the condition, so the expanded Markov chain transform from error model is homogeneous. For homogeneous Markov chain, it has the ergodicity as follows:

Lemma1 [4]: The state space of homogenous Markov chain is $S=\{s_1,s_2,\ldots\ldots,s_n\}$, p is one-step transition probability matrix. If there exists an integer m which is for any $a_i,a_j \in S$, there is $p_{ij}(m)>0, i,j=1, 2, \ldots, n$, then this chain has the ergodicity. And there is a limiting distribution $p(n)=(p_1,p_2,\ldots, p_n)$, it is a unique solution of the equation $p(n)P=p(n)$, where $p_i(1 \leq i \leq n)$ meets that conditional probability distribution $p_j>0, \sum_{i=1}^{i=n} p_i=1$.

The limit state of n-step transitions is the steady state of the process that is call steady state. According to Lemma 1, this paper supposes that the row vector of steady state probability state is $p(n)=\{p_1,p_2,p_3\ldots,p_n\}$, and P is one-step state transition probability matrix, p_{ij} is the probability of transition from state i to state j, then the steady state probability can be obtained by using of the following equations:

$$\begin{cases} p(n) = \sum_{i-0}^{i=n} p(n) \, p_{ij} \\ \sum_{i=1}^{i=n} \mathrm{pi} = 1 \end{cases} \tag{1}$$

In the formal description of error model, we can not only get failure rate from error-free state to error state, but also get recovery rate from error state to error-free state, then one-step state transition matrix can be obtained, and according to the Markov analysis method, a failure rate can be obtained after a long running [5]. Here this paper takes the error model in Table 2 as an example. This error model has one initial error-free state and two error states, it can be transformed into three-states Markov chain. The model's one step state probability matrix is as follows:

$$\begin{bmatrix} 0.99998 & 0.0000125 & 0.0000075 \\ 0.999825 & 0.000175 & 0 \\ 0.999795 & 0 & 0.000205 \end{bmatrix}$$

It is supposed that the vector of steady-state probability is $Y(3)=\{y_1,y_2,y_3\}$, where y_1 is normal state probability after a long running of the component, y_2 and y_3 are two error state probabilities after a long running, then $y_2+ y_3$ is the overall failure rate after a long running. By the equations (1), we can get the solution. The steady state vector is Y (3) = {0.9998, 0.000125, 0.0000075}, the steady-state failure rate λ of the component is $y_2+y_3=0. 0.0002$. The MTBF=$1/v \approx 5000$, v is steady-state failure frequency and $v=\frac{\mu}{\mu+\lambda} \times \lambda$ where μ is recovery rate. Then $MTBF=\frac{1}{V}=\frac{\mu+\lambda}{\mu \times \lambda}=\frac{1}{\lambda}+\frac{1}{\mu}$. When $\mu>>\lambda$, $MTBF=\frac{1}{\lambda}$ [7].

3.3 Metrics of Dependability on System-Level

Because the importance is different for each component in the system, the component's effect is different for the system. The metrics which comes from error model only for individual component. To measure the whole system, it is necessary to calculate the importance of each component as a whole system. Because AADL core model describes the system information of each component from the whole, this paper considers two aspects to measure the component importance: the interactions between the components and the mode in the AADL core model.

The interactions between one component and other components are more closely, it indicates that other components have greater dependence on this component, and it shows that this component is more important. From the perspective of the interaction, this paper gives a method to calculate the importance of each component. The number of interactions is expressed with C_i($1 \leq i \leq n$), and it is initialized to be 0. When a component interacts with other components, the number of this component's interaction increases 1. At last the numbers of interactions of each component are C_1, C_2, ...,C_n. The importance of each component is expressed with $Imp1_i$ ($1 \leq i \leq n$), then $Imp1_i= C_i/ (C_1+C_2+......+C_n)$.

The mode in the AADL core model shows the changes of states. One component can declare many modes. In some mode the component is active, to some extend it shows this component is important in this mode. From the perspective of the mode, this paper gives another method to calculate the importance of each component. The number of activities is expressed with $Active_i$ ($1 \leq i \leq n$), and it is initialized to be 0. When a component is active in one mode, the number of this component's activity increases 1. At last the numbers of activities of each component are $Active_1$, $Active_2$, ..., $Active_n$. The importance of each component is expressed with $Imp2_i$ ($1 \leq i \leq n$), then $Imp2_i=Active_i/ (Active_1+ Active_2+......+ Active_n)$.

Now the comprehensive importance of each component is $Simp_i=(Imp1_i+Imp2_i)/2(1 \leq i \leq n$).Through the failure rate and recovery rate which are provided by the component, the metrics of the system can be got.

The failure rate of the system is $\lambda_{sum}=\sum_{i=1}^{i=n} \lambda_i \times Simp_i$, where λ_i is the failure rate of the ith component. The recovery rate of the system is $\mu_{sum}=\sum_{i=1}^{i=n} \mu_i \times Simp_i$, where μ_i is the steady-state recovery rate of the ith component. It can be drew through the property set of AADL core model. The MTBF of the system is $MTBF_{sum}=\sum_{i=1}^{i=n} MTBF_i \times Simp_i$, where $MTBF_i$ is the steady-state MTBF of the ith component. The MTBUF of the system is $MTBUF_{sum}=\sum_{i=1}^{i=n} MTBUF_i \times Simp_i$, where the $MTBUF_i$ is the steady-state MTBUF of the ith component, and $MTBUF_i=MTBT_i/1-\mu_i$. The system availability can be calculated by Markov analysis method. When the Markov chain is homogeneous and the steady state failure rate and recovery rate of the system is λ_{sum} and μ_{sum},

$A(t) = \frac{\mu_{sum}}{\mu_{sum}+\lambda_{sum}} + \frac{\mu_{sum}}{\mu_{sum}+\lambda_{sum}} e^{-\mu_{sum}+\lambda_{sum}t}$. And when $t \to \infty$, the steady state availability of the system is $A = \lim_{t \to \infty} A(t) = \frac{\mu_{sum}}{\mu_{sum}+\lambda_{sum}}$.

According to the dependability metrics model proposed in Section 3.1, we can use the fuzzy comprehensive evaluation method or other methods to evaluate the software dependability combined with the computational method of dependability attribute discussed in this section.

4 Case Study

This section takes the flight control system as an example to analyze and demonstrate the software dependability measurement and analysis method based on AADL error model. The Fig.2 shows flight_mgmt. RS in AADL graphical.

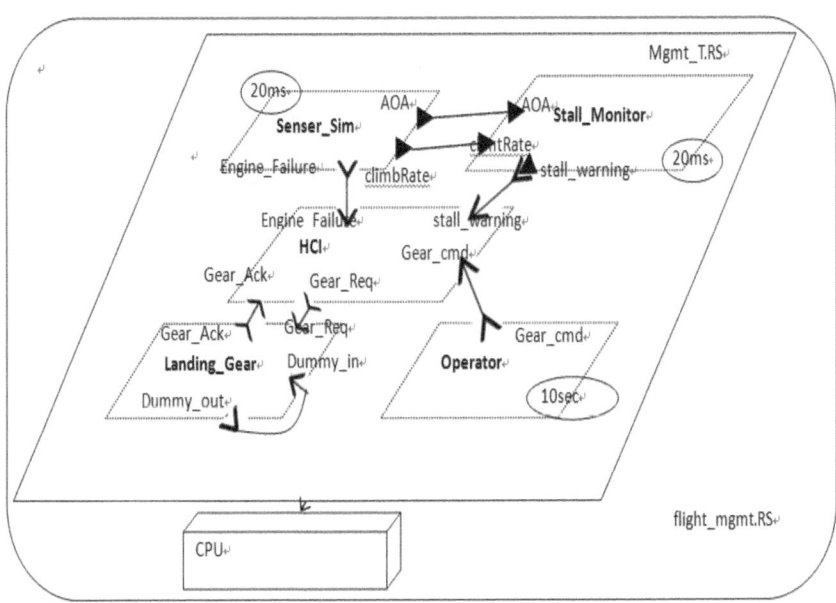

Fig. 2. AADL model for flight_mgmt.RS

This system flight_mgmt.RS is composed of a process called Mgmt_T.RS which has five threads in it, and a processor called CPU binding to it. The five threads in Mgmt_T.RS are Senser_Sim, Stall_Monitor, HCI, Landing_Gear and Operator(this paper uses T1, T2, T3, T4 and T5 to denote each thread).The recovery rate of each thread is defined in each property set of AADL core model, and the values are all 0.9997. The property set of the AADL model is shown in Table 3.

The error model of the system flight_mgmt.RS is shown in Table 2 ,and we have calculated the steady-state failure rate λ and the MTBF in section 3.1. Because the recovery rate of this component is 0.9997, then MTBUF≈16666667. In the same way, the values of other four threads about steady-state failure rate λ, recovery rate μ, MTBF and MTBUF can also be got. The values of them are shown in Table 4.

As shown in Fig.2, this system transmits information by port connection which belongs to the first type of connection in section 3.3. Then the interaction numbers and the importance of each component are calculated ,and the results are shown in Table 5.

Table 3. The property set for flight_magt.RS

property set metric_set **is**
Failure _Rate : **constant aadlreal** => 0.0002;
Recovery_Rate: **constant aadlreal** =>0.9998;
MTBF: **constant aadlinteger** =>3300;
MTBUF: **constant aadlinteger** =>1500000;
Availability : **constant aadlreal** =>0.9997;
end metric _set

Table 4. Metrics values of each thread

λ	Λ	μ	**MTBF**	**MTBUF**
T2	$\lambda_2 \approx 0.000315$	$\mu_2 \approx 0.9997$	$MTBF_2 \approx 3174$	$MTBUF_2 \approx 10580000$
T3	$\lambda_3 \approx 0.000275$	$\mu_3 \approx 0.9997$	$MTBF_3 \approx 3636$	$MTBUF_3 \approx 12120000$
T4	$\lambda_4 \approx 0.000325$	$\mu_4 \approx 0.9997$	$MTBF_4 \approx 3077$	$MTBUF_4 \approx 10256667$
T5	$\lambda_5 \approx 0.000215$	$\mu_5 \approx 0.9997$	$MTBF_5 \approx 4651$	$MTBUF_5 \approx 15503333$

Table 5. The importance degree of each thread

	T1	T2	T3	T4	T5
Interaction number	3	3	5	2	1
Importance degree	$Simp_1 = \frac{3}{14}$	$Simp_2 = \frac{3}{14}$	$Simp_3 = \frac{5}{14}$	$Simp_4 = \frac{2}{14}$	$Simp = \frac{1}{14}$

According to the above, the total failure rate is $\lambda_{sum} = \sum_{i=1}^{i=n} \lambda_i \times Simp_i \approx 0.9997$, the total recovery rate is $\mu_{sum} = \sum_{i=1}^{i=n} \mu_i \times Simp_i \approx 0.9997$, the total MTBF is $MTBF_{sum} = \sum_{i=1}^{i=n} MTBF_i \times Simp_i \approx 382$, the total MTBUF is $MTBUF_{sum} = \sum_{i=1}^{i=n} MTBUF_i \times Simp_i \approx 12739762$, the total availability is $A = \lim_{t \to \infty} A(t) = \frac{\mu_{sum}}{\mu_{sum} + \lambda_{sum}} \approx 0.99973$.

Table 6. The results of analysis

metrics	compare	relationship	result
Failurerate	$\lambda_{sum} > \lambda'$	NR	Don't meet require of the user
Recovery rate	$\mu_{sum} > \mu'$	PR	Meet require of the user
MTBF	$MTBF_{sum} > MTBF'$	PR	Meet require of the user
MTBUF	$MTBUF_{sum} < MTBUF'$	PR	Don't meet require of the user
Availability	$A > A'$	PR	Meet require of the user

The Table 3 shows AADL property set from which we can get the values, they are $\lambda'=0.0002$, $\mu'=0.9998$, MTBF'=3300, MTBUF'=1500000 and A'=0.9997. Compared the calculated metrics values with metrics values which the user needs, the results can be analyzed as shown in Table 6. Here this paper uses NR PR to represent negative relationship and positive relationship. Table 6 shows that the design of AADL core model and error model do not meet the user's requirement on failure rate and MTBUF, and designer can modify these two designs to meet the user's needs so that the developers can develop a system with higher dependability.

5   Conclusion

AADL standard has been widely used in the development of aerospace embedded system, by analyzing AADL error model, the dependability problem can be found early in the software life cycle. So his paper discusses to transform AADL error model into expanded Markov chain, and a method is presented to measure and analyze the software dependability combined with AADL core model.

The measurement method proposed in this paper only uses some main criteria and attributes in the AADL error model. In order to measure the dependability more accurately, more attributes in AADL error model should be considered. Of course, it is not enough to consider AADL error model only, we should add more aspects with AADL core model to measure and analyze the software dependability, and this will be the next job objectives.

Acknowledgement. This work is supported by:

1. One Eleventh Five-Year Project of The General Reserve Department of PLA, one Basic Software Project of COSTIND;
2. Major National Science and Technology Programs of Core Electronics Components, High-end General Chips and Basic Software (CHB) of China under grant NO. 2009ZX01045-005-002;
3. One pre-research fund of The General Reserve Department of PLA.

References

1. An SAE International Group. (R) Architecture Analysis & Design Language (AADL) (January 2009)
2. Rugina, F.P.: A Dependability Modeling with the Architecture Analysis & Design Language(AADL) (2007)
3. Dong, Y.-W., Wang, G., Zhao, H.-B.: A Model-based Testing for AADL Model of Embedded Software. In: The 9th International Conference on Quality Software (QSIc 2009) (2009)
4. Guo, Y.: Probability Theory and Mathematical Statistics. Science Press (2007)
5. Liu, Y.: The Research of Software Reliability Based on Markov Analysis Method. Changchun University of Science and Technology (December 2005)
6. Tan, Z.: Research on Testing and Evaluation Theory of Reliability and Safety for High Dependability Software. University of Electronic Science and Technology of China (September 2005)
7. Software R. Utility Guide of Dependability. BUAA Press (January 1, 2005)

Online Hand Gesture Recognition Using Surface Electromyography Based on Flexible Neural Trees

QingHua Wang[1], YiNa Guo[1], and Ajith Abraham[2]

[1] Taiyuan University of Science and Technology, ShanXi Taiyuan 030024, China
wangqh904@126.com, zulibest@gmail.com
[2] Machine Intelligence Research Labs (MIR Labs), Scientific Network for Innovation and Research Excellence, P.O. Box 2259, Auburn, Washington 98071-2259, USA
ajith.abraham@ieee.org

Abstract. Normal hand gesture recognition methods using surface Electromyography (sEMG) signals require designers to use digital signal processing hardware or ensemble methods as tools to solve real time hand gesture classification. These ways are easy to result in complicated computation models, inconvenience of circuit connection and lower online recognition rate. Therefore it is imperative to have good methods which can avoid the problems mentioned above as more as possible. An online hand gesture recognition model by using Flexible Neural Trees (FNT) and based on sEMG signals is proposed in this paper. The sEMG is easy to record electrical activity of superficial muscles from the skin surface which has applied in many fields of treatment and rehabilitation. The FNT model can be created using the existing or modified tree- structure- based approaches and the parameters are optimized by the PSO algorithm. The results indicate that the model is able to classify six different hand gestures up to 97.46% accuracy in real time.

Keywords: Surface Electromyography (sEMG), Flexible Neural Trees (FNT), Pattern recognition, Particle swarm optimization (PSO).

1 Introduction

A sign language is a language, which uses visually transmitted sign patterns (manual communication, body language and lip patterns) to convey meaning simultaneously combining hand shapes, orientation and movement of the hands, arms or body, and facial expressions to fluidly express a speaker's thoughts. Recently, the sign language as an important interact method of body languages is paid attention by many scientists of all over the world. From the recognition signals, the recognition methods of the sign language are mainly divided into hand gesture signals, visual hand gesture images and surface Electromyography (sEMG) signals. In 2008, Ganesh N. Naik, Dinesh K. Kumar and Sridhar P. Arjunan of RMIT University proposed Multi run Independent Component Analysis (ICA) and sEMG based signal processing system for recognizing hand gestures. This method improved the offline hand gesture recognizing rate to 99% [1]. However, the separated signals of Blind Source Separation (BSS) based on ICA are disorder and not available for online hand gesture

H. Deng et al. (Eds.): AICI 2011, Part III, LNAI 7004, pp. 245–253, 2011.

recognition. In 2007, Mahdi Khezri and Mehran Jahed proposed to use an intelligent approach based on adaptive neuro-fuzzy inference system (ANFIS) integrated with a real-time learning scheme to identify palm and wrist flexion and extension with 96.7% average accuracy[2]. This algorithm is not applied to finger flexion in recent reports nevertheless. It is of great importance to have good methods to explore a more suitable online choice, which can avoid the problems mentioned above as more as possible[3] .

An online hand gesture recognition model by using flexible neural trees (FNT) based on sEMG signals is proposed in this paper. With a view of non-intramuscular and easy to record electrical activity of superficial muscles from the skin surface, the sEMG is adopted in the model. In consideration of avoiding complicated computation, solving inconvenience of circuit connection, providing flexible time-series forecasting and having higher online recognition rate, the FNT model is generated initially as a flexible multi-layer feed-forward neural network. The fine tuning of the parameters encoded in the structure is accomplished using the PSO algorithm. Testing has been conducted using several continuous experiments conducted with five participants. The results indicate that the model is able to recognize six different hand gestures up to 97.46% accuracy in real time.

2   Theory

2.1   Feature Selection of sEMG

SEMG is a complex electrical activity of muscles under the skin surface, which is the integrated results of the skin at the time and space. In order to accurately identify actions, Feature extraction is the key to the whole system. A time domain feature is described in this section. Root Mean Square (RMS) can be done in real-time and electronically and it is simple for implementation. The features are normally used for onset detection, muscle contraction and muscle activity detection.

RMS is modeled as amplitude modulated Gaussian random process whose RMS is related to the constant force and non-fatiguing contraction. It relates to standard deviation, which can be expressed as in

$$\text{RMS} = \sqrt{\frac{1}{N} \sum_{n=1}^{N} x_n^2} \qquad (1)$$

where N denotes the length of the signal and x_n represents the SEMG signal in a segment.

2.2   Flexible Neural Trees

Artificial neural networks (ANNs) have been successfully applied to a number of scientific and engineering fields in recent years, i.e., function approximation, system identification and control, image processing, time series prediction. However, a neural network's performance is highly dependent on its structure. Depending on the problem, it may be appropriate to have more than one hidden layer, feed-forward or feedback connections, or in some cases, direct connections between input and output layer [1] .

Flexible neural tree (FNT) is a new tree model, which similar to the neural network .The flexible neural tree is a fuzzy model which is proposed initially for solving highly structure dependent problem of the artificial neural network (ANN). The model is computed as an irregular flexible multi-layer feed-forward neural network. Based on the pre-defined instruction/operator sets, a flexible neural tree can be created and evolved. FNT model consists 2 types of instruction component which is the function instruction operators F and instruction terminals T. The function instruction operators F is non-leaf node and the instruction terminals T is Input feature. The function instruction operators F and instruction terminals T are described as in

$$S = F \bigcup T = \left\{+_2, +_3, \cdots, +_N\right\} \bigcup \left\{x_1, x_2, \cdots, x_n\right\} \tag{2}$$

Where $+_n$ ($i=2,3,\ldots,N$) denote instructions of non-leaf nodes which taking i arguments and $x_1, x_2,\ldots, x_n$ represent instructions of leaf nodes which taking no other arguments.

It is shown clearly that the output of a non-leaf node $+_n$, which is also called a flexible neuron operator, is calculated as a flexible neuron model with n arguments in Fig. 1.

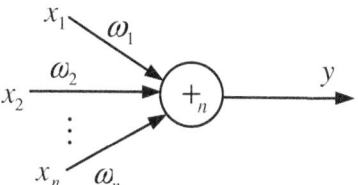

Fig. 1. A flexible neuron operator

In the construction process of FNT, when a non-leaf instruction $+_n$ ($i=2,3,\ldots,N$) is selected, i real values are evolved automatically and used for demonstrating the connection strength between the node $+_i$ and its' children. The output of a flexible neuron $+_n$ can be calculated as in

$$net_n = \sum_{j=1}^{n} \omega_j * x_j \tag{3}$$

Where x_j ($j = 1,2,\cdots,n$) are the inputs to node $+_n$.

Gaussian function, Unipolar sigmoid function, Bipolar sigmoid function, Non-local radial coordinates, Thin- plate s-spline function and General multiquadratics all can be adopted as flexible activation function[4].

In flexible activation function $f(a_i, b_i, x)$, two adjustable parameters a_i and b_i are randomly created for using as flexible activation function parameters.

When flexible activation function is determined, the output of the node $+_n$ is then calculated by

$$out_n = f(a_n, b_n, net_n) \tag{4}$$

A typical flexible neuron operator and a neural tree model are illustrated in Fig. 2. The overall output of flexible neural tree can be computed recursively from left to right by depth-first method.

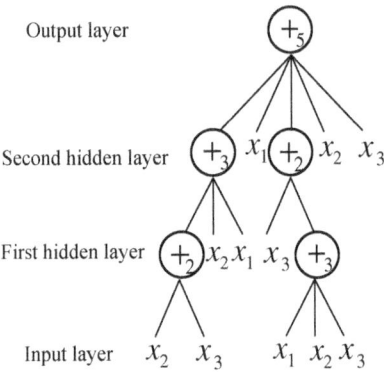

Fig. 2. A typical representation of neural tree with function instruction operators F ={+2,+3,+4,+5} and instruction terminals T = {x1, x2, x3}.

The FNT model can be created and evolved using the existing or modified tree-structure-based approaches which include Genetic Programming (GP), Probabilistic Incremental Program Evolution (PIPE) and Ant Programming (AP). Normally, the fitness function used for the PIPE and SA can be given by mean square error (MSE) or root mean square error (RMSE). the variable parameters of Flexible neural tree model are optimized by evolutionary algorithm , such as particle swarm optimization, genetic algorithms and so on.

3   Methodology

3.1   The sEMG Signals Model

The structure of the sEMG model is depicted in Fig.3, which is composed of sEMG data record part, feature selection part and FNT classification part. sEMG record circuit and sEMG record interface are components of the sEMG data record part. Feature selection part takes the responsibilities for selecting and computing features of sEMG signals. In FNT classification part, the FNT is adopted to train a fuzzy classification model according to the selected sEMG features and the initialization construction. The trained classification model is applied in online test of FNT classification part.

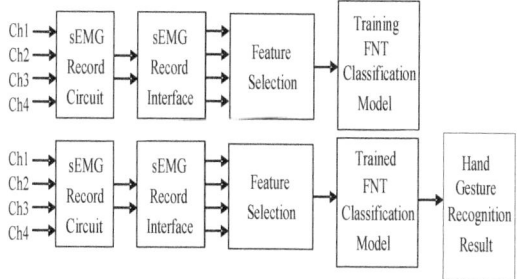

Fig. 3. The structure of online hand gesture recognition model

Five volunteers participated in the experiments. Each participant has tested one kind of flexion for 6 times. Electrodes were placed on the forearm muscles of Brachioradialis, Flexor Carpi Radialis (FCR), Extensor digitorum superficialis (EDS) and Flexor Digitorum Superficialis (FDS). sEMG signals record when the participant maintain specific finger flexions of middle finger flexion, all fingers flexion and so on. The flexions have been performed without any resistance. These flexions are chosen as they are very convenient to and easily reproducible by the participant. The order of the flexions is arbitrary and each flexion is maintained for about 10 secs to record sEMG and the duration of each run of the experiment is about 60 secs.

When hand gestures change alternately, sEMG signals change accordingly. However, transitional signals between two hand gestures are easy to reduce the hand gestures classification rate. In this work, we used a time domain window of 500 (ms) for collecting sEMG signal. For above reason, overlapped length of sEMG signals used 200 (ms) segmented signal (see Fig.4). The rms is applied in each window of the experiments as sEMG feature. The overlapped method solves part effect of transitional signals.

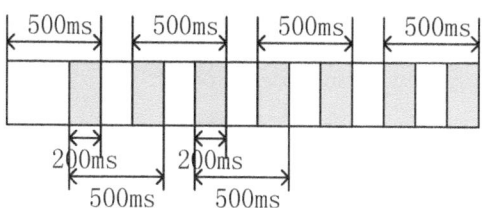

Fig. 4. Segment theory of collection window

3.2   A Flexible Neural Tree Structure

The online hand gesture recognition model is approximated by using the neural tree model with the pre-defined instruction sets. The instructions of root node, hidden nodes and input nodes are selected from three instruction sets.

We have used two instructions in the experiments. The instruction sets are as follows (see Fig.5):

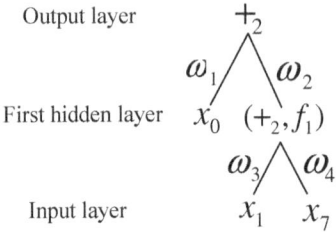

Output layer

First hidden layer

Input layer

Fig. 5. A flexible neural tree with function instruction sets

$$I = \{+_2, x_0, x_1, x_2, x_3, x_4, x_5, x_6, x_7\} \tag{5}$$

For developing the FNT classifier, the following flexible activation function is used:

$$f(a_i, b_i, x) = e^{-((x-a_i)/b_i)^2} \tag{6}$$

The output of the node $+_n$ is then calculated by

$$out_n = f(a_n, b_n, net_n) = e^{-((net_n - a_n)/b_n)^2} \tag{7}$$

The PIPE is selected as a tree-structural based encoding method with specific instruction set for fine tuning the parameters encoded in the structure.

Starting with initial set structures and corresponding parameters, it first tries to improve the structure and then as soon as an improved structure is found. The parameters of the structure are fine tuned. It then goes back to improving the structure again and finds a better structure. The rules' parameters are fine tuned again.

A fitness function arranges FNT to scalar and real-valued fitness values that reflect the FNT performances according to a given task. In experiments, the fitness function used for the PIPE is given by mean square error (MSE).

$$Fit(i) = \frac{\sum_{j=1}^{P} (y_1^j - y_2^j)^2}{P} \tag{8}$$

The loop continues until a satisfactory solution is found or a time limit is reached.

The evolved neural tree model is obtained at generation 20 with function instruction sets $I = \{+_2, x_0, x_1, x_2, x_3, x_4, x_5, x_6, x_7\}$.

3.3 Parameter Optimization with PSO

The FNT model is fixed, and it is the best tree developed during the end of run of the structure search. The parameters of FNT model encoded in the best tree formulate an individual. The parameters mainly include the connection weights (w_1, w_2, w_3, w_4)

between nodes and the flexible activation function parameters (a_i and b_i). In the paper, we optimize the parameters using particle swarm optimization. We randomly generated particles, the dimension of which represents weights and flexible activation function parameters. Updating formula of particles is described as:

$$V_i(t+1) = wV_i(t) + c_1 r_1 \left(P_i(t) - X_i(t) \right) + c_2 r_2 \left(P_g(t) - X_i(t) \right) \tag{9}$$

$$X_i(t+1) = X_i(t) + V_i(t+1) \tag{10}$$

Here, $X_i=(x_{i1}, x_{i2},..., x_{id},..., x_{iD})$ and $V_i=(v_{i1}, v_{i2},..., v_{id},... ,v_{iD})$ represent the position vector and velocity vector of the ith individual respectively, while $P_i=(p_{i1}, p_{i2},..., p_{id},..., p_{iD})$ is the best previous position discovered by the ith individual, $P_g=(p_{g1}, p_{g2},..., p_{gd},..., p_{gD})$ stands for the global best position searched by the whole swarm; the inertia weigh ω is a scaling factor controlling the influence of the old velocity on the new one; c_1 and c_2 are constants known as "cognitive" and "social" coefficients which determine the weight of P_i and P_g respectively; r_1 and r_2 are two random numbers generated by uniformly distribution in the range [0,1] separated.

The online version of the volume will be available in LNCS Online. Members of institutes subscribing to the Lecture Notes in Computer Science series have access to all the pdfs of all the online publications. Non-subscribers can only read as far as the abstracts. If they try to go beyond this point, they are automatically asked, whether they would like to order the pdf, and are given instructions as to how to do so.

Please note that, if your email address is given in your paper, it will also be included in the meta data of the online version.

4 Results

Five volunteers participated in the experiments. Each participant has tested one kind of flexion for 6 times. Four channels of surface EMG signals are used in the experiment. The selected feature is RMS. FNT is applied as classifier in the experiment.

FNT selects proper input variables or time-lags automatically. In addition, the parameters used for experiment is as: Population size is 100; Elitist learning probability is 0.01; Learning rate is 0.01; Fitness constant is 0.000001; Overall mutation probability is 0.4; Mutation rate is 0.4; Prune threshold is 0.999; Maximum random search steps is 2000; Initial connection weights is rand[-1, 1]; Initial parameters a_p, b_p are rand[0,1]; inertia weigh ω is 0.9.

For the experiment, 10 inputs variables are used for constructing a FNT model. The instruction set is $I = \{+_2, x_0, x_1, x_2, x_3, x_4, x_5, x_6, x_7\}$ (see Fig. 5).

The six special hand gestures of the experiment are shown in Table 1. From the results, the model is able to classify six different hand gestures up to 97.46% accuracy in real time.

Table 1. List of classification rates with different hand movements

Hand gesture	Ring finger	Index finger	Wrist	Middle finger	All fingers	Relax
Mean recognition rate	93.72%	92.43%	92.16%	97.28%	97.46%	97.31%

5   Conclusion

A real time hand gesture recognition model by using flexible neural trees (FNT) based on sEMG signals is proposed in this paper. With a view of non-intramuscular and easy to record electrical activity of superficial muscles from the skin surface, the sEMG is adopted in the model. In consideration of avoiding complicated computation, solving inconvenience of circuit connection, providing flexible time-series forecasting and having higher online recognition rate, the FNT model is generated initially as a flexible multi-layer feed-forward neural network and evolved using an evolutionary procedure. In the paper, the parameters of the FNT model are evolved by particle swarm optimization. Testing has been conducted using several continuous experiments conducted with five participants. The results indicate that the model is able to recognize six different hand gestures up to 97.46% accuracy in real time. The work demonstrates that the FNT model with automatically selected input variables has better accuracy (low error) and good generalization ability.

Acknowledgement. This work was supported by the grants of Study Abroad of Shanxi Scholarship Council of China [No. 20101069] and Youth Foundation of Taiyuan University of Science and Technology of China [No. 20103004].

References

1. Chen, Y., Abraham, A.: Flexible Neural Trees: Theoretical Foundations. In: Perspectives and Applications, June 27. Springer, Heidelberg (2009)
2. Lichtenauer, J.F., Hendriks, E.A., Reinders, M.J.T.: Sign Language Recognition by Combining Statistical DTW and Independent Classification. IEEE Transactions on Pattern Analysis and Machine Intelligence 30(11), 2040–2046 (2008)
3. Phinyomark, A., Limsakul, C., Phukpattaranont, P.: A Novel Feature Extraction for Robust EMG Pattern Recognition. Journal of Computing 1(1), 71–80 (2009)
4. Chen, Y., Abraham, A., Yang, B.: Feature selection and classification using flexible neural tree. Neurocomputing 70, 305–313 (2006)
5. Kennedy, J., Eberhart, R.C.: Particle Swarm Optimization. In: Proceeding of 1995 IEEE International Conference on Neural Networks, pp. 1942–1948. IEEE, New York (1995)
6. Khezri, M., Jahed, M.: Real-time intelligent pattern recognition algorithm for surface EMG signals. BioMedical Engineering OnLine (December 2007)
7. Arjunan, S.P., Kumar, D.K., Naik, G.R., Guo, Y., Shimada, H.: A framework towards real time control of virtual robotic hand: Interface based on low-level forearm muscle movements. In: IEEE International Conference on Intelligent Human Computer Interaction, Allahabad, India, January 16-18 (2010)

8. Guo, Y., Li, Y.: Wireless Surface Electromyography Sensor Network Based on Rapid Prototyping. Sensor Letters 9(5) (2011) (accepted September 5, 2010)
9. Dong, Z.S., Guo, Y., Zeng, J.C.: Recurrent Hidden Markov Models Using Particle Swarm Optimization. Int. J. Modelling, Identification and Control (November 2010) (accepted)
10. Guo, Y., Li, Y.: Single Channel Electromyography Blind Recognition System of 3D Hand. Computer Applications and Software (September 2010)
11. Yina, G.: Research of Hand Gesture Identification of sEMG based on SCICA. In: IEEE The 2nd International Conference on Signal Processing Systems (ICSPS 2010), Dalian, China (July 2010) [EI 20104013270588]
12. Naik, G.R., Kumar, D.K., Arjunan, S.: Pattern classification of Myo-Electrical signal during different Maximum Voluntary Contractions: A study using BSS techniques. Measurement Science Review 10(1), 1–6 (2010)
13. Naik, G.R., Kumar, D.K.: Inter-experimental discrepancy in Facial Muscle activity during Vowel utterance. In: Computer Methods in Biomechanics and Biomedical Engineering. Taylor and Francis, Abington (2009) (accepted), SCI Impact factor 1.301
14. Naik, G.R., Kumar, D.K., Jayadeva: Twin SVM for Gesture Classification using the Surface Electromyogram. IEEE Transactions on Information Technology in BioMedicine (November 2009) (accepted). SCI Impact factor 1.94

A Saturation Binary Neural Network for Crossbar Switching Problem

Cui Zhang[1], Li-Qing Zhao[2], and Rong-Long Wang[2]

[1] Department of Autocontrol, Liaoning Institute of Science and Technology,
Benxi, China
bxlkyzhangcui@163.com
[2] Graduate School of Engineering, University of Fukui, Bunkyo 3-9-1,
Fukui-shi, Japan
nkzlq@hotmail.com, wang@u-fukui.ac.jp

Abstract. A saturation binary neural network is proposed to solve the crossbar switching problem. In the proposed algorithm, neurons are updated according to different formula, then neurons enter into saturating state, and as a result, it makes the neural network escape from a local minimum stagnation. The proposed algorithm has been tested on a large number of instances and compared with other algorithms. The experimental results show that the proposed algorithm is superior to its competitors.

Keywords: Saturation binary neuron model, Combinatorial optimization problems, Crossbar switching problem.

1 Introduction

Binary Hopfield networks (Hopfield networks with two-state threshold neurons) (HNNs) have been applied to large amount of difficult combinatorial optimization problems [1]-[3] because of its advantages. The advantages include massive parallelism, convenient hardware implementation of the neural network architecture, and a common approach for solving various optimization problems [4]. One of the combinatorial optimization problems is the real-time control of a crossbar switch (crossbar switch problem (CSP)). The Hopfield neural network architecture has been applied to CSP used for switching high-speed packets at maximum throughput [5]-[7]. However the work by Wilson and Pawley showed that the Hopfield neural networks often failed to converge to valid solutions. When it converged, the obtained solution was often far from the optimal solution. Since their report various modifications have been proposed to improve the convergence of the Hopfield neural networks.

In this paper we propose a saturation binary neuron model and use it to construct a Hopfield-type neural network for efficiently solving the crossbar switching problem. In the proposed saturation binary neuron model, once the neuron is in excitatory state, then its input potential is in positive saturation where the input potential can only be reduced but cannot be increased, and once the neuron is in inhibitory state, then its

H. Deng et al. (Eds.): AICI 2011, Part III, LNAI 7004, pp. 254–261, 2011.
© Springer-Verlag Berlin Heidelberg 2011

input potential is in negative saturation where the input potential can only be increased but cannot be reduced. Using the saturation binary neuron model, a saturation binary neural network is constructed to solve the crossbar switching problem. The simulation results show that the saturation binary neural network can find better solutions than the original Hopfield neural network.

2 Saturation Binary Neural Network

In the proposed algorithm, a novel neuron updating rule is proposed. To avoid the neural network entering a local minimum stagnation, the neuron network is updated according to the state of the neuron. According to different states, the updating rule is different. In this section, the proposed saturation binary neural network is introduced.

In binary neuron model, the updating method of input potential U_i is especially important. In conventional neuron model [8] [9], the input potential U_i is updated from the Eq. 1 or Eq.2 The updating process of the neuron is no matter with the state of the neuron.

$$U_i(t+1) = \frac{dU_i(t)}{dt} \tag{1}$$

$$U_i(t+1) = U_i(t) + \frac{dU_i(t)}{dt} \tag{2}$$

Where $dU_i(t)/dt$ derives from the energy function E based on the gradient descent method:

$$\frac{dU_i(t)}{dt} = -\frac{\partial E(V_1, V_2, ..., V_n)}{\partial V_i} \tag{3}$$

The Hopfield-type binary neural network is usually constructed using the above neuron model. In order to improve the global convergence quality and shorten the convergence time, we propose a new neuron model called saturation binary neuron model (SBNM) which consists of the following important ideas.

(1). Once the neuron is in excitatory state (the output $V_i=1$), then the input potential is assumed to be in positive saturation. In the positive saturation, the input potential U_i can only be reduced but cannot be increased.

For the case of $V_i=1$:

if $dU_i(t)/dt < 0$

$$U_i(t+1) = U_i(t) + \frac{dU_i(t)}{dt} \tag{4}$$

else

$$U_i(t+1) = U_i(t) \tag{5}$$

(2). Once the neuron is in inhibitory state (the output V_i=0), then the input potential is assumed to be in negative saturation. Then the input potential can only be increased but cannot be reduced.

For the case of V_i=0

if $dU_i(t)/dt > 0$

$$U_i(t+1) = U_i(t) + \frac{dU_i(t)}{dt} \tag{6}$$

else

$$U_i(t+1) = U_i(t) \tag{7}$$

Note that the input/output function in the McCulloch-Pitts neuron [8] or hysteresis McCulloch-Pitts neuron [9] can be used to update the output V_i. Using the above neuron model, we construct a Hopfield-type neural network called saturation binary neuron network (SBNN). Comparing to the McCulloch-Pitts neuron [8] and hysteresis McCulloch-Pitts neuron [9], the neuron updating rule is improved in the proposed SBNN. The following procedure describes the synchronous parallel algorithm using the SBNN to solve combinatorial optimization problems. Note that N is the number of neuron, *targ_cost* is the target total cost set by a user as an expected total cost and *t_limit* is maximum number of iteration step allowed by user.

1. Set t=0 and set *targ_cost*, *t_limit*, and other constants.
2. The initial value of U_i for $i=1,...,N$ is randomized.
3. Evaluate the current output $V_i(t)$ for $i=1,...,N$.
4. Check the network, if *targ_cost* is reached, then terminate this procedure.
5. Increment t by 1. if $t > t\_limit$, then terminate this procedure.
6. For $i=1,...,N$
   a. Compute Eq. 3 to obtain $dU_i(t)\big/dt$
   b. Update $U_i(t+1)$, using the proposed saturation binary neuron model(Eq. 4-Eq. 7).
7. Go to the step 3.

3   Crossbar Switching Problem

In the communication systems, crossbar packet switches route from the input to output where a message packet is transmitted from the source to the destination. The randomly incoming packets must be controlled to eliminate conflict at the crossbar switch where the conflict is that two or more packets may simultaneously access to a single output [10]. The goal of crossbar switching problem is to maximize the throughput   of   packets   through   a   crossbar   switch.   In   packet-switched telecommunication networks, switches are located at nodes, routing randomly arriving packets so that they may be transmitted from the source to the destination, the basic switch is the $n \times n$ crossbar switch. It consists of a grid of n input lines by n output lines with a switch at each of the cross. Thus, the crossbar switch can route a packet arriving at any input line to any output line. Multiple packets, however, can arrive simultaneously at different input lines destined for the same output line and cannot be routed to the same output line at the same time without collision. In such a case, one packet is sent, and others must be blocked and queued at each input line for the next transmission time period. These are based on the asynchronous transfer mode (ATM) protocol. Thus, at most one packet can be transmitted from each input line and to each output line. This is a physical constraint of crossbar switches [11].

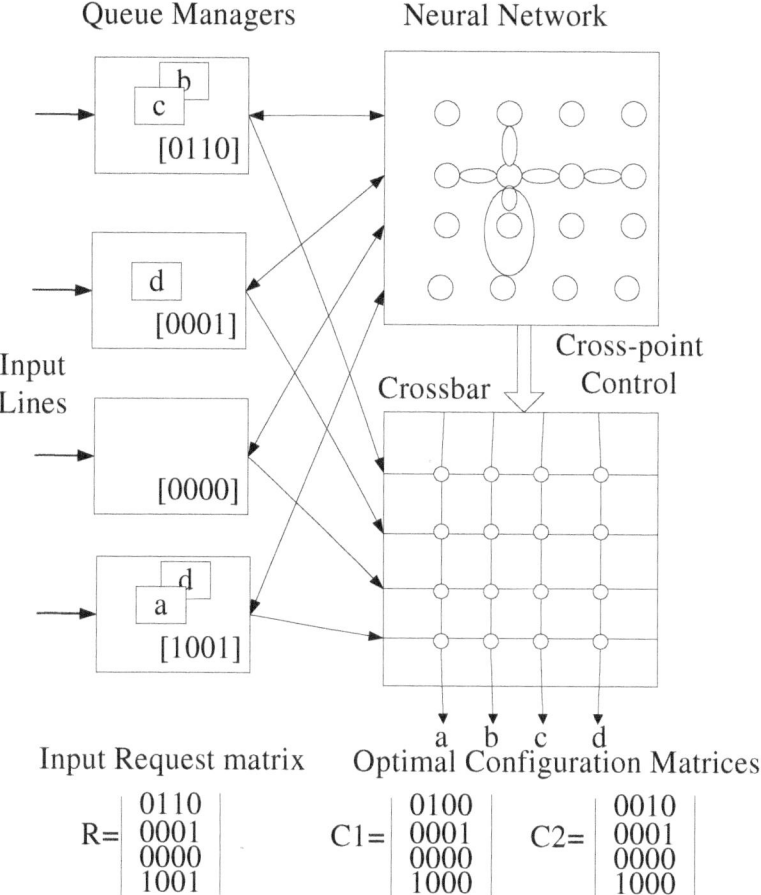

Fig. 1. Schematic architecture of crossbar control with an example of input request matrix and its optimal configuration matrices

To show the request for packet transmission, $n \times n$ crossbar switches can be represented by an $n \times n$ binary request matrix $R=(r_{ij})$. Rows and columns of the matrix R are associated with inputs and outputs, respectively, of the crossbar switch. A matrix element $r_{ij}=1$ indicates that there is a request for switching at least one packet from input line i to output line j of the switch; otherwise $r_{ij}=0$. If we consider the crossbar switch for point-to-point connections, then at most one cross-point may be closed on any row or column of the switch during packed transmission. The state of the switch can be represented by an $n \times n$ binary configuration matrix $C=(c_{ij})$, where $c_{ij}=1$ indicates that input line i is connected to output line j by the "closed" cross-point (ij). $c_{ij}=0$ indicates that cross-point (ij) is "open". For proper operation of the switch, there should be at most one closed cross-point in each row and each column. The throughput of the switch is optimal when the matrix C, which is a subset of the matrix R (i.e., $c_{ij} \leq r_{ij}$ for every (i,j)), contains at most a "1" in each row/column. In other words, we call the throughput maximum if C has a maximum overlap with R, and $\sum_i \sum_j r_{ij} c_{ij}$ is the maximum [12]. Thus, crossbar packet switching is basically a combinatorial optimization problem, which finds the configuration matrix C having a maximum overlap with R. Example of optimal matrices is shown in Fig. 1 for a 4×4 crossbar.

Thus the crossbar switching problem can be mathematically transformed into the following optimization problem:

$$\text{Maximize:} \quad \sum_{i=1}^{n} \sum_{j=1}^{n} c_{ij} \cdot r_{ij} \tag{8}$$

Constraint condition:

$$\sum_{i=1}^{n} \left(\sum_{j=1}^{n} c_{ij} - 1 \right)^2 + \sum_{j=1}^{n} \left(\sum_{i=1}^{n} c_{ij} - 1 \right)^2 = 0 \tag{9}$$

Equation (8) is used to maximize the throughput of packets through a crossbar switch, and equation (9) demonstrated the physical constraints of the crossbar switch.

4   Solving CSP Using SBNN

The crossbar switching problem has been introduced above. The crossbar switch is controlled by a neural network that has one neuron in correspondence to each switch cross-point. Row request vectors from all the inlets are supplied to the neural network, which used them to compute an optimal configuration matrix for the switch. The resulting row configuration vectors are then returned to the corresponding queue manager, while the crossbar switch cross-points selected by the computed configuration matrix are closed. Each queue manager presents to its input line a single packet destined to the output line selected by the row vector returned by the neural network, which thus gets routed through the closed cross-point to its proper output line. The queue manager also updates it row request vector by cleaning the selected column bit, provided that no packets remain queued for that output.

The crossbar switch problem can be solved by constructing an appropriate energy function and minimizing the energy function to zero ($E=0$) using an $n \times n$ two-dimensional Hopfield neural network.

The objective energy function of the crossbar switching is given by:

$$E = \frac{A}{2} \sum_{i=1}^{n} \left(\sum_{k=1}^{n} c_{ik} r_{ik} - 1 \right)^2 + \frac{B}{2} \sum_{j=1}^{n} \left(\sum_{k=1}^{n} c_{kj} r_{kj} - 1 \right)^2 \tag{10}$$

Where A and B are coefficients. We can get the total input (μ_{ij}) of neuron by using the partial derivation term of the energy function. Then the weights and threshold of the neural network are derived as follows:

$$w_{ij,kl} = -A r_{kl} r_{kj} \delta_{ik} - B r_{kl} r_{il} \delta_{lj}$$

$$\delta_{ik} = \begin{cases} 1, (i = k) \\ 0, (i \neq k) \end{cases}$$

$$\delta_{lj} = \begin{cases} 1, (l = j) \\ 0, (l \neq j) \end{cases} \tag{11}$$

5   Simulation Result

Since our architecture is valid for any Hopfield neural networks as illustrated in the previous section, we used the architecture for some randomly generated problems and a large number of real crossbar switch problems.

We now present simulation results of the architecture when applied to real crossbar switching. The parameters A and B were set to A=1.0, B=2.0. The weights and external input currents were all the same as the original Hopfield neural network. In simulations, 100 simulation runs with different randomly generated initial states were performed on each of these instances. To evaluate our results, we compared the results of the original Hopfield neural network [9] with our results. Information of the crossbar switch as well as all the results is shown in Table I. In Table I, the column labeled "optimal" is the global convergence times among 100 simulations and the column labeled "steps" is the average number of iteration steps required for the convergence in the 100 simulations. The simulation results show that the proposed saturation binary neuron network with could almost find optimum solution to most crossbar switch problems within short computation times while the original Hopfield neural network could hardly find any optimum solution to the crossbar switching, especially for large size problems.

Table 1. Simulation result

Crossbar Switches	Hopfield Network		Proposed Algorithm	
	optimal	steps	optimal	steps
4x4	100	3	100	2
6x6	100	4	100	3
8x8	100	5	100	5
10x10	100	14	100	8
20x20	100	41	100	24
30x30	100	91	100	36
50x50	100	120	100	79
80x80	86	440	100	184
100x100	43	479	88	296
200x200	9	745	47	437
300x300	--	--	14	653

6 Conclusion

We have proposed a saturation binary neuron model and use it to construct a Hopfield-type neural network called saturation binary neural network (SBNN). In the proposed algorithm, neurons are updated according to different formula, then neurons enter into saturating state, and as a result, it makes the neural network escape from a local minimum stagnation. The SBNN is used to solve the crossbar switching problem. The simulation results show that SBNN is capable of finding better solutions than other method. Also, it can be seen that the SBNN is problem independent and can be used to solve other combinatorial optimization problems.

References

1. Hopfield, J.J.: Neurons and physical systems with emergent collective computational abilities. Proc. Natl. Acad. Sci. USA 79, 2554–2558 (1982)
2. Smith, K., Palaniswami, M., Krishnamoorthy, M.: Neural techniques for combinatorial optimization with applications. IEEE Trans. Neural Networks 9(6), 1301–1318 (1998)

3. Hopfield, J.J., Tank, D.W.: "'Neural' computation of decisions in optimization problems. Biol. Cybern. 52, 141–152 (1985)
4. Zeng, X.C., Martinez, T.: A newrelaxation procedure in the Hopfield neural networks for solving optimization problems. Neuron Processing Lett. 10, 211–222 (1999)
5. Marrakchi, A., Troudet, T.: A neural nct arbitrator for large crossbar packet switches. IEEE Trans. Circuits Syst. 36(1), 1039–1041 (1989)
6. Troudet, T.P., Walters, S.M.: Neural-network architecture for crossbar switch control. IEEE Trans. Circuits Syst. 38(1), 42–56 (1991)
7. Xia, G., Tang, Z., Li, Y., Wang, J.: A binary Hopfield neural network with hysteresis for large crossbar packet-switches. Neurocomputing 67, 417–425 (2005)
8. McCulloch, W.S., Pitts, W.H.: A logical calculus of ideas immanent in nervous activity. Bull. Math. Biophys 5, 115–133 (1943)
9. Takefuji, Y., Lee, K.C.: An artificial hysteresis binary neuron: A model suppressing the oscillatory behaviors of neural dynamics. Biol. Cybern. 64, 353–356 (1991)
10. Matsuda, S.: Theoretical Limitations of a Hopfield Network for Crossbar Switching. IEEE Transactions on Neural Networks 12(3) (May 2001)
11. Nitnaware, V.N., Limaye, S.S.: Folded architecture of scheduler for area optimization in an on-chip switch fabric. International Journal of Hybrid Information Technology 4(1) (January 2011)
12. Li, Y., Tang, Z., Xia, G., Wang, R.: A Positively Self-Feedbacked Hopfield Neural Network Architecture for Crossbar Switching. IEEE Transactions on Circuits and Systems-I: Regular Papers 52(1) (January 2005)

Financial Data Forecasting by Evolutionary Neural Network Based on Ant Colony Algorithm

Wei Gao

Wuhan Polytechnic University, Hubei, Wuhan 430023, P.R. China
gaow@whpu.edu.cn

Abstract. The financial system is generally a very complicated system. So, it is very hard to be predicted. For example, it is a hard work to forecast the stock market. Here, from analyses the mathematic description of stock market system, a new forecasting method based on new evolutionary neural network is proposed here. In this new evolutionary neural network, the traditional BP algorithm and immune continuous ant colony algorithm proposed by author is combined. In order to verify this new prediction method, the stock market data of Shanghai market in 1996 is used. The results show that, our new method is very good to real practice.

Keywords: Financial data, forecasting, stock market, evolutionary neural network, immune continuous ant colony algorithm.

1 Introduction

Big disturbance, serious non-linearity and blindness of investor all make the stock market prediction very complicated and very hard. So, how to forecast stock market very well is a very interesting work for researchers and security analyzers [1-2].

To forecast stock market, we must acknowledge that, there are some basic laws that can be repeated in stock market. And those laws are hided in history data. From mathematic aspect, those laws are function relationship. Because the neural network can draw its law from very complicated data, and can approximate very complicated function, then the neural network is a very good method to model non-linear dynamic system. So, neural network is a very good method to forecast stock market. Nowadays, there are some researches on this field [3-5], but in those studies, the stock market can not be analyzed from mathematic aspects. So, to do this study better, firstly, the mathematic description of stock market has been founded. And based on this mathematic description, one new method with new evolutionary neural network is proposed. At last, this new method is applied in real stock market of Shanghai.

2 Mathematic Description of Stock Market

For the stock market system is a very complicated dynamic system, it can be described mathematically as follows.

H. Deng et al. (Eds.): AICI 2011, Part III, LNAI 7004, pp. 262–269, 2011.

To a dynamic system, its evolvement can be described by differential equations. Here, we suppose that the stock market can be described by follow p-th order ordinary differential equation.

$$\frac{d^p x}{dx^p} = f(x, x', \cdots, x^{(p-1)}).$$
(1)

To study simply and not lose its typicality, the follow third order ordinary differential equation is used.

$$\frac{d^2 x}{dt^2} = f(x, \frac{dx}{dt})$$
(2)

Supposing the solution of above equation is a time series with step h, $x(j), j = 1 \sim n$, and then the model of system can be made with the numerical solution of above ordinary differential equation.

The solution of differential coefficient at j in above equation is replaced by difference as follows.

$$\frac{d^2 x}{dt^2}\Big|_j = \frac{x(j+1) - 2x(j) + x(j-1)}{h^2} + o(h^2)$$
(3)

$$\frac{dx}{dt}\Big|_j = \frac{x(j) - x(j-1)}{h} + o(h)$$
(4)

So, we can get the follow function.

$$x(j+1) = h^2 f[x(j), \frac{x(j) - x(j-1)}{h}] + 2x(j) - x(j-1) + o(h^3)$$
(5)

The high order minim in above function is retrieved. The above function can be described as follow general function.

$$x(j+1) = F[x(j), x(j-1), h]$$
(6)

The above function is generalized to p-th order, the follow function can be gotten.

$$x(j+1) = F[x(j), x(j-1), \cdots, x(j-p+1), h]$$
(7)

So, we can see that, the dynamic evolvement model of stock market can be described by above function. The main aspect of above function is to confirm the function relationship F.

In traditional method, the F is supposed as a linear function. But to stock market, the F is a very complicated non-linear function. So, the above function is always very complicated and its description cannot be confirmed. In neural network, the information is stored in linkage of network hiddenly, and cannot be described with one function. For the non-linear transferring function applied in neural network, the complicated non-linear problem can be solved very well by neural network. Also, the neural network has the adaptivity for dynamic process. So, the above function F can be approximated very well by neural network.

3   Evolutionary Neural Network for Stock Market Prediction

From above analysis, we can see that, the number of input neuron in neural network can be confirmed by dynamic system model, but the stock market system described by p-th order differential equation is an uncertain system. So, the lingering time step of time series for neural network cannot be gotten. But this is a very important parameter to construct neural network samples.

So, to construct a neural network model for stock market, the construction of neural network is the main problem to be solved. This problem can be solved by bionics algorithm very well [6-8]. Here, as a primary study, the evolutionary neural network which construction is confirmed by bionics algorithm and which weight is confirmed by MBP algorithm is proposed. To make problem simpler and generalization bigger, the three layers neural network is studied. So, here, only the number of input neuron and number of hidden layer neuron are to be confirmed. In MBP algorithm, there are two parameters, iterating step η and inertia parameter α, to be confirmed. These two parameters affected MPB algorithm very seriously. So, these two parameters are all confirmed by evolutionary algorithm. And then, in evolutionary neural network, there are four parameters to be evolved.

To get a kind of good evolutionary neural networks, here the immune continuous ant colony algorithm [9] proposed by author is introduced and one new kind of evolutionary neural network is proposed.

3.1   Immune Continuous Ant Colony Algorithm

For imitation information exchange among ant colony, the ant colony algorithm can solve the complicated combination optimization problem, and its effect is better than that of traditional methods. So according to the information cooperation of ant colony, the continuous optimization method based on principles of ant colony should be feasible.

Based on above thought, some continuous ant colony algorithms have been proposed [10-12]. To improve continuous ant colony algorithm, the mature methods used in evolutionary algorithm and artificial immune system are introduced into continuous ant colony algorithm, and a new immune continuous ant colony algorithm is proposed [9].

3.2 New Evolutionary Neural Network

The flow charts of new evolutionary neural network are as follow Fig. 1 and 2.
The details of new evolutionary neural network are as follows.

(1) The search range of input neuron and hidden layer neuron are given firstly. And also the search ranges of two parameters in MBP algorithm are given. And some evolutionary parameters, such as stop criteria, individual number in one population, the error criteria of algorithm, number of output neuron in neural network, iterating stop criteria and iterating error criteria in MBP algorithm are all given.

It must be pointed out that, to construct the suitable samples, the number of input neuron must be smaller than total number of time series.

(2) One network construction is generated by two random numbers in search range of input neuron and hidden layer neuron. And also, one kind of MBP algorithm is created by two random numbers in search range of parameters η and α. And then, one individual can be generated by the four parameters.

(3) To one individual, its fitness value can be gotten by follow steps.

a. The whole time series of stock market is divided to construct the training samples based on number of input neuron and number of hidden layer neuron. And also, the total number of samples is noted.

b. The whole learning samples are to be divided into two parts. One part is the training samples, which is to get the non-linear mapping network. The other part is the testing samples, which is to test the generalization of network.

c. The initial linking weights of network individual are generated.

d. The iterating step of MBP algorithm is taken as $j = 1$.

e. This network individual is trained by testing samples, and the square error $E(j)$ is computed, and this error is taken as minimum error of the whole training, $\min E = E(j)$. If $\min E$ is smaller than the error criteria of evolutionary algorithm, then the fitness value is $\min E$. And the computing process is changed to step (3).

f. This network individual is trained by training samples. If its training error is smaller than iterating error criteria of MBP algorithm, then the fitness value is also the $\min E$. And the computing process is changed to step (3).

g. The whole linking weights are adjusted by MBP algorithm.

h. $j = j + 1$, and the computing process is changed to step e.

i. If j is lager than iterating stop criteria of MBP algorithm, then the fitness value is also the $\min E$. And the computing process is changed to step (3).

(4) If the evolutionary generation reaches its stop criteria or computing error reaches error criteria of evolutionary algorithm, then the algorithm stop. At this time, the best individual in last generation is the searching result.

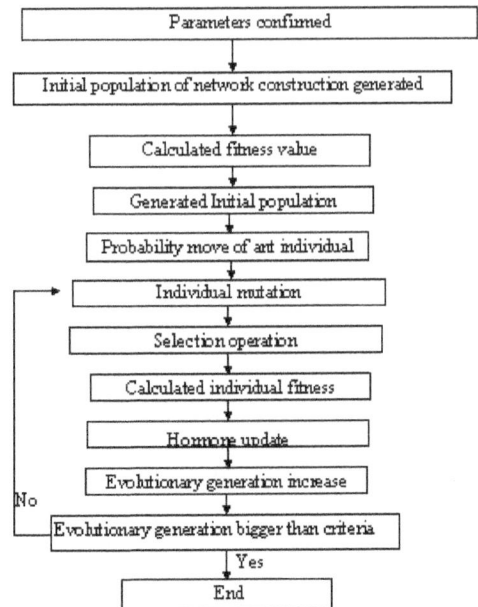

Fig. 1. Flow chart of new evolutionary neural network

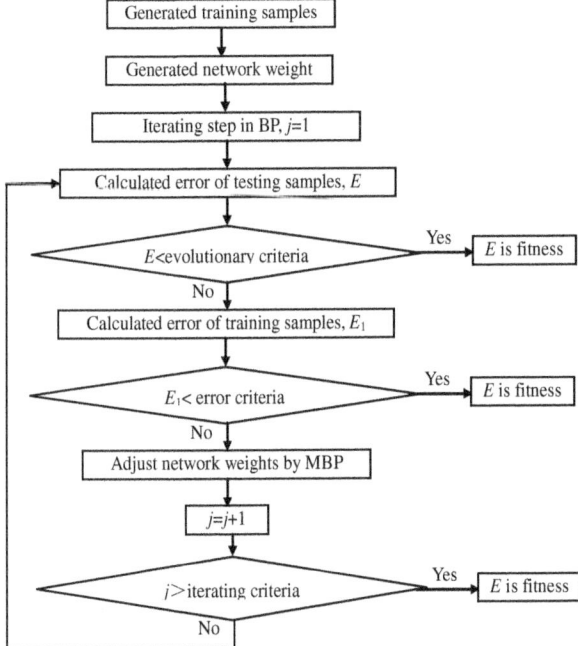

Fig. 2. Flow chart of fitness computation operation

(5) The probability move operation is done to every ant individual.

(6) Every individual in population is mutated. For there are different data types in one individual, the different mutation types are used for each parameter. For numbers of input neuron and hidden layer neuron are integer number, the uniform mutation is used. For parameters η and α are real numbers, the adaptive Cauchi mutation is used. And then the offspring population is generated.

(7) The set of offspring population and parent population is selected by selection operation based on thickness, then the new offspring population is generated.

(8) The fitness value of each individual in offspring population is calculated by the method in step (3).

(9) The hormone update operation is implemented.

(10) The number of evolutionary generation increases 1, then the computing process is changed to step (4).

From the above algorithm, the four parameters, number of input neuron, number of hidden layer neuron, two parameters η and α in MBP algorithm can be confirmed. So, the optimization neural network for stock market forecasting will be gotten.

4 Real Example

To verify the above algorithm, the stock market of Shanghai in 1996.3-1996.6 is used. In this example, the time series of 53 stock index and daily turnover is used, which is showed in follow Fig. 4 and 5.

The stock index data time series and daily turnover data time series are taken into our algorithm. In two time series, the 48 teams data is used for computation, and while 5 teams data is for forecasting. In the 48 teams computation data, 30 teams is training samples, and the other 18 teams is testing samples.

In real practice, in order to get the better results, the rolling model method is used, which principles can be showed in Fig. 3. In this method, as a new serial value is produced, this value is added into time serial and the oldest one is displaced. So, the time serial that is used to construct neural network model is all new serial, and then the timeliness effect can be maintained.

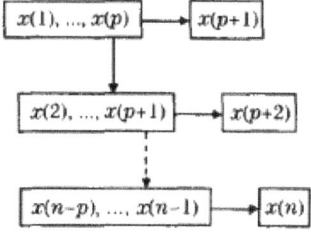

Fig. 3. Principles of rolling model for stock market time serial forecasting.

After computation, we will know that the best neural network construction for stock index forecasting is 7-13-1, and for daily turnover is 9-21-3. With those neural networks, the forecasting results are showed in Fig. 4 and 5.

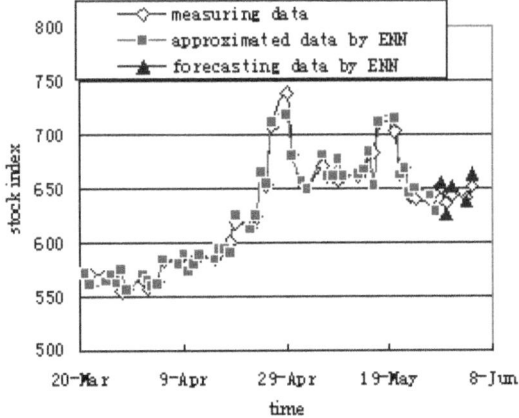

Fig. 4. Stock index data time series

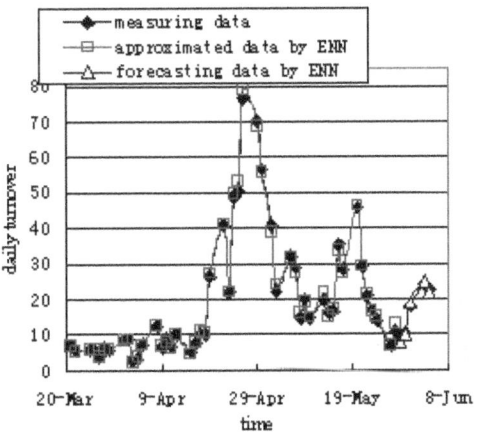

Fig. 5. Daily turnover data time series

From above two figures, we can conclude that, using our evolutionary neural network algorithm for stock market forecasting, not only the approximation is good, but also the forecasting is satisfactory. So, our algorithm is a good method for stock market forecasting.

5   Conclusions

Stock market is a very complicated dynamic system affected by many factors. It has very important theory and real meaning for stock investment and market manage for stock market forecasting. In this paper, the development law of stock market is described mathematically, and one new method for stock market forecasting based on new evolutionary neural network is proposed. At last, this method is verified by real stock market data of Shanghai market in 1996. The results show that, our new algorithm is a very good method for stock market forecasting, and can be used in real practice.

Acknowledgments. The financial supports from The National Natural Science Foundation of China under Grant No. 41072233 and 40872187 are gratefully acknowledged.

References

1. Hao, F., Chen, H.L.: Methods for Economic Forecasting and Decision. Minnan University Press, Guangdong (1991)
2. Chen, M.S.: Stock Market Analysis. Anhui People Press, Hefei (1995)
3. Refenes, A.N., Zapranis, A., Francis, G.: Stock Performance Modeling Using Neural Networks: a Comparative with Regression Model. Neural Network, 375–388 (1994)
4. Chavarnakul, T., Enke, D.: Intelligent technical analysis based equivolume charting for stock trading using neural networks. In: Expert Systems with Applications, pp. 1004–1017 (2008)
5. Hassan, M.R., Nath, B., Kirley, M.: A fusion model of HMM, ANN and GA for stock market forecasting. In: Expert Systems with Applications, pp. 171–180 (2007)
6. Xin, Y., Yong, L.: A New Evolutionary System for Evolving Artificial Neural Networks. IEEE Trans. on NN, 694–713 (1997)
7. Gao, W.: Study on new evolutionary neural network. In: Proc. of ICLMC 2003, pp. 1287–1293. IEEE, New York (2003)
8. Fang, J., Xi, Y.: Neural Network Design Based on Evolutionary Programming. In: Artificial Intelligence in Engineering, pp. 155–161 (1997)
9. Gao, W.: Study on immunized Ant Colony Optimization. In: Proceedings of Third International Conference on Natural Computation, pp. 792–796. IEEE, New York (2007)
10. Dorigo, M., Stutzle, T.: Ant Colony Optimization. MIT Press, Cambridge (2004)
11. Dréo, J., Siarry, P.: Continuous interacting ant colony algorithm based on dense heterarchy. In: Future Generation Computer Systems, pp. 841–856 (2004)
12. Mohit, M., Sachin, B.K., Sidhartha, P., et al.: Ant Colony Approach to Continuous Function Optimization. Ind. Eng. Chem. Res., 3814–3822 (2000)

RVAB: Rational Varied-Depth Search in Siguo Game

ZhengYou Xia and Hui Lu

Department of Computer, Nanjing University of Aeronautics and Astronautic,
Nanjing, China
zhengyou_xia@nuaa.edu.cn

Abstract. Game playing is one of the classic problems of artificial intelligence. The Siguo game is an emerging field of research in the area of game-playing programs. It provides a new test bed for artificial intelligence with imperfect information. To improve search efficiency for Siguo with more branches and the uncertain payoff in the game tree, this paper presents a modified Alpha-Beta Search algorithm, which is called rational varied-depth Alpha-Beta (RVAB). The RVAB The basic ideas of RVAB algorithm is : if player get much information about opponent during playing game, they can do more deep thinking about strategies of game. If player can only get few, very uncertain information about opponent during playing game, they don't think more deep about their strategy because it is worthless for player to speculate the strategies of game under very uncertain. Experiments show that RVAB achieves the goals of the improvability of visited nodes efficiency, although it costs a little more memory.

1 Introduction

Search algorithms play an important role in the field of computer game. The alpha-Beta tress searching algorithm has been in use since 1960's. Fourty years of research has found ways of improving the algoritms'efficicency and variants suuch as NegaScout and PVS are quite popular. In 1979, Stcokman introduced SSS*, which looked like a different approach from Alpha-Beta for searching fixed-depth minimax tree. Many researchers has made numerous simulations to show that on average SSS* evaluate considerably fewer leaf nodes. To make SSS* into practial vesion, some novel framework is presesnted[1][2].Most game-tree search has focused on algorithms that make the same decisions as full-width, fixed-depth Minimax, searching every move to the same depth in the perfect information game. These include Alpha-Beta pruning [3], Aspiration-windows [4], PVS [5], SSS*[6] and MT-SSS*[7], etc. Most these fixed depth or variable depth algorithms often consider the perfect information game. Researches on imperfect information games are often focused on Poker,bridge,and kriegspiel, etc. Smith *et al.*

In this paper, we define a search algorithm as one that searches to variable depth in Siguo military game [8, 9, 10, 11]. We describe an extremely simple search algorithm, which is called reason varied-depth Alpha Beta algorithm (RVAB). In some imperfect information games, payoff of game tree is often uncertain and fuzzy since piece of game is invisible for players. This algorithm includes the two basic ideas: 1) if player

H. Deng et al. (Eds.): AICI 2011, Part III, LNAI 7004, pp. 270–277, 2011.

get much information about opponent during playing game, they can do more deep thinking about strategies of game. If player can only get few, very uncertain information about opponent during playing game, they don't think more deep about their strategy because it is worthless for player to speculate the strategies of game under very uncertain. In other words, when more certain information about payoff of game tree, we can search more deep, in contrast, we search more low. 2) Player often first to think the certain information part about opponent during playing game, in other words, we first search the most certain information node of game tress. We use RVAB algorithm in our Siguo military game system and have achieved good results.

2 Dynamic Threshold

We supposed that there are n pieces of opponent. According to the position of opponent' pieces at the opening phase, we label the n piece with $P=(p_1; p_2; ::::; p_n)$. Let the types of pieces be $T=(t_1; t_2; ::::; t_m)$. Each piece of players must be only one of these types $p_i \in T$. Since player cannot see the type of opponent' piece, player can guess the type distribution of n pieces of opponent. Player can make statistic analysis by collecting the plenty of chess manual. Let $p_i(T) = (p_i(t_1); ::::; p_i(t_m))$, which denotes type probability distribution of ith piece.

$$P_i(T) = (P_i(t_1), P_i(t_2), ..., P_i(t_m)) \quad \text{, where} \sum_{j=1}^{m} P_i(t_j) = 1 \quad (1)$$

We let type possible distribution of seven pieces be the following Table 1. In this table, we suppose there are seven pieces and five types. We use the seven pieces to build game tree (see Fig2). In the Fig2, Max is denoted as player I(e.g., computer System)and Min is denoted as opponent of player I. In this game tree, Pi(i=1,2,..7) is denoted as piece with uncertain type of opponent.

Table 1. Piece information and Type

Piece/Type	t_1	t_2	t_3	t_4	t_5	PieceEntropy$_i$
P_1	0	0	0.9	0	0.1	0.468996
P_2	0.8	0.1	0.1	0	0	0.921928
P_3	0.1	0	0	0.9	0	0.468996
P_4	0.2	0.18	0.22	0.2	0.2	2.319038
P_5	0.3	0.5	0.2	0	0	1.485475
P_6	0.2	0.2	0.2	0.2	0.2	2.321928
P_7	0.19	0.21	0.22	0.18	0.2	2.318316

To analyze the game tree of Fig1, we define entropy of piece, node strategy path and node path entropy as follows.

Definition 1. Entropy value of opponent' piece (*Pi*) on chessboard is defined as

$$PieceEntropy_i = -\sum_{j=1}^{12} P_i(t_j) * \log_2 P_i(t_j) \qquad (2)$$

Where, $P_i(t_j)(1 \le i \le 7, 1 \le j \le 5)$ is denoted as the jth type probability of the ith piece. t_j is type of piece. $PieceEntropy_i$ is entropy of ith piece, which is used to measure uncertain degree.

Definition 2. Strategy Path of node *i* is denoted as the path from the root to the node *i*, which is consisted of Max and Min nodes that are on this path.

Definition 3. Path Entropy of node *i* is total entropy value of piece on the strategy path of the node *i* .

Strategy path of node i is consisted of Max node and Min node. In the Figure 1, we suppose that Max node is computer system, which means that computer system can know information about itself pieces. Since information about pieces is certain, the pieces entropy of Max node is zero. Therefore, path entropy of node i is consisted of entropy of Min nodes. The Path entropy of node i can be described as

$$PathEntroy_i = \sum_{k=root}^{i} PieceEntropy_k \qquad (3)$$

The basic notion about search with threshold in this paper is that system can set the threshold value to control depth of search. If path entropy is more than one threshold value, search action is stopped along this path. Therefore, threshold value setting is key parameters in the game tree search. If value is set too little, some worth node may be omitted during search and depth of game tree is not enough. It will affect the intelligence of computer system. If the value is set too big, depth on very uncertain path is too big, it is not worth and it affect the efficiency of computer system.

In this paper, we give an experience math model to analyze threshold. Before discussion, we make some donations.

T: each player can allow max thinking time each round during play game. Each game has different T.

Ψ : Computer can search number of nodes each second. Ψ can be gotten be experimental computing.

L: average braches of game tree, which also can be gotten by experimental computing.

D: depth of game tree.

PieceEntropy$_i$: entropy of opponent' alive piece

TotalEntropy$_t$: total entropy of opponent alive pieces at t round

N$_t$: is the number of alive pieces of opponent at t round.

If we know the max thinking time T and number of nodes Ψ that is search by computer each second, we can get the max allowable number of visited nodes $T * \psi$.

It is well known that the best efficiency of alpha-beta search algorithm can be arrived $L^{D/2}$. The efficiency of alpha-beta algorithm is affected by node order in the game tree. Therefore, it often cannot arrive the best efficiency. We use $a * L^{D/2}$ to describe efficiency of alpha-beta algorithm, where a is a parameter and is between 0 and 1.

When number of nodes that are visited by computer is equal to number of nodes that alpha-beta visit, it is the best efficiency for one computer intelligent system. Therefore, we can get the following equation

$$T * \psi = a_1 * L^{d/2} \qquad (4)$$

Number of average branch(L) can computed by experimental computing each game. We can get depth that can visit by following equation

$$\ln(T * \psi) = \ln(a_1) + d/2 * \ln(L) \qquad (5)$$

$$\Rightarrow d = \frac{2(\ln(T * \psi) - \ln(a_1))}{\ln(L)} \qquad (6)$$

Since we can know the number of alive nodes of opponent, we can compute total entropy about opponent' alive pieces and average entropy of pieces,

$$TotalEntropy_t = \sum_{i=1}^{N_t} PieceEntropy_i \qquad (7)$$

$$AverageEntrogy_t = \frac{TotalEntropy_t}{N_t} \qquad (8)$$

The game tree is consisted of max node and Min node. We suppose that Max node is machine and it know type of itself piece. Therefore there is not uncertain about itself piece and entropy of Max node is supposed as zero. The entropy of path is consisted of Min node entropy that Min node is opponent's strategy. If the depth of search is D. the path is consisted of D/2 Min node. The above equation computes average entropy of piece. We can get the path entropy of depth D, which is the threshold value we need. The computing equation is as follow.

$$Threshold_t = \frac{D * AverageEntrogy_t}{2}$$

$$= \frac{2 * (\ln(T * \psi) - \ln(\alpha)) * AverageEntropy}{2 * \ln(L)}$$

$$= \beta * \frac{2 * \ln(T * \psi) * AverageEntropy}{2 * \ln(L)}$$

$$\text{where } \beta \in (0,1]. \qquad (9)$$

Where, a parameter is litter than $(T * \psi)$ and we omit it in the above equation, we use new parameter instead of it in the equation 9.

3   Reason Variable Depth Alpha Beta(RVAB)

We use the above notion to alpha-beta search algorithm. Fig 1 shows cutoff process of game tree. A node is the root node. Variable depth alpha-beta begins to search from node A. Alpha cutoff and Beta cutoff is generated, respectively, during process of search. When path entropy is bigger than threshold, cutoff will be happened. In this example, we suppose that threshold is 3.0. The variable depth alpha-beta algorithm will visit node A, B, C, D.E.F.G. G node is leaf node and return payoff 9. node G will

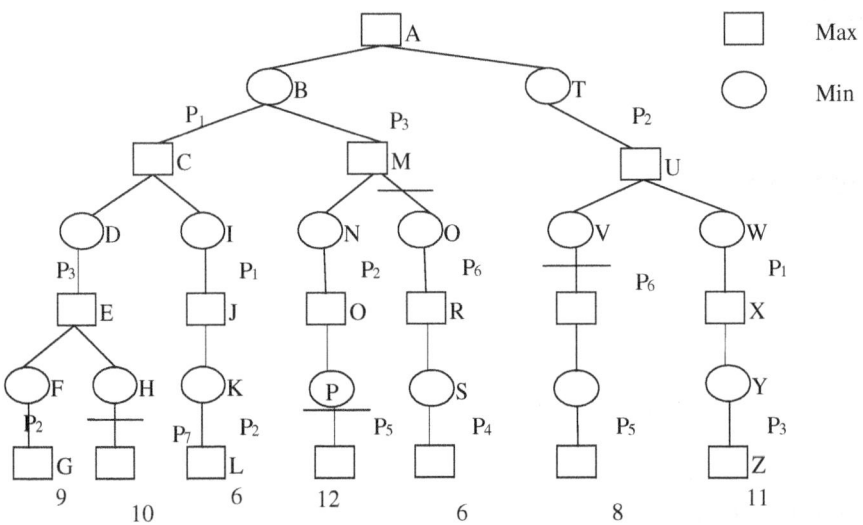

Fig. 1. RABT algorithm in a game tree

return 9 to its parents' node F, similarly, node F will return value to node E. then visit node H and find path entropy is P1+P2+P3=4.272787,which is bigger than Threshold(3.0).Therefore, cutoff is happened and make H node as leaf node. E is Max node and achieves the max payoff among its child node. Therefore payoff of node is 10 and return 10 to node C. then, the algorithm will visit node I, J, K and L. it will return payoff of node L to I by order. Since C is the Max node, and achieve the max payoff from its child nodes and return payoff 10 to node B. then will visit node M,N,Q,P and find the path entropy is bigger than threshold. Cutoff is happened and make node P as leaf node. It will return payoff 12 to M. since B has get payoff 10 previous search. B is min node and will achieve the min payoff. Since M is Max node and will achieve the max payoff from its children nodes. Therefore, payoff that M will return to B is not litter than 12. Therefore, node Q and itself children nodes will all cut off. At this time, B will return 10 to node A and algorithm will visit T,U and V. however path entropy is P2+P6=0.921928+2.343856>3.0. and make V as leaf node. The rest may be deduced by analogy. At last node A return payoff 11. Fig 3 is algorithm code of RABT.

```
Function RVAB(n,Alpha,Beta)
{
        if(n->Flag==Leaf)
        {
                n->PathEntropy=n->NodeEntropy;
                g=eval(n) ;
        }
        else if(n->Flag==MAX)
        {
                g=-∞;
                child=firstchild(n);
                while(g<Beta and child≠⊥)
                {
                        child->PathEntropy=n->PathEntropy;
                        g=max(g, RABT(child, Alpha, Beta)) ;
                        Alpha=max(Alpha, g) ;
                        child=nextbrother(child) ;
                }
        }
        else if(n->Flag=MIN)
        {
                g=+∞;
                child=firstchild(n);
                while(g>Alpha and child≠⊥)
                {
                        child->PathEntropy=n->PathEntropy+child-
>NodeEntropy;
                        if(n->PathEntropy⩾Threshold)
                                n=Flag=leaf;
                        g=min(g, RABT(child, Alpha, Beta)) ;
                        Beta=min(Beta, g) ;
                        child=nextbrother(child) ;
                }
        }
        return g;
```

Fig. 2. RVAB algorithm Code

4   Experiments and Discuss

Using random game tree is the common method to test the efficiency of search algorithm. Since the depth and branch of practical game tree is difficult to control, many researcher use random game tree to test the efficiency of search algorithms. In this paper, we also use random game tree to test our algorithms. We can control depth, branch and node entropy to test the efficiency of search algorithm in the different conditions. Path entropy threshold is computed by equation 9. At each phase of siguo game, ti can compute each piece entropy and can get average entropy of piece. Plenty of experiments is test and B is set 0.9.

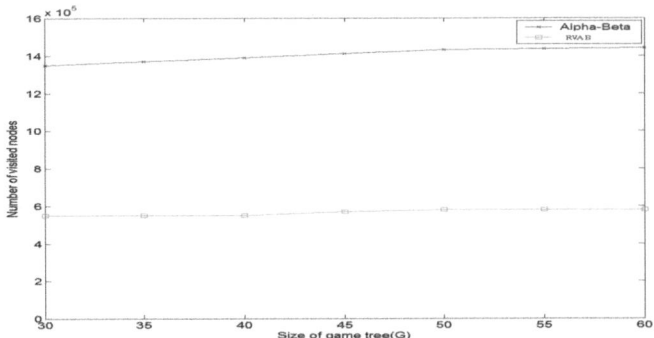

Fig. 3. Visited nodes based on two RVAB and Alpha-Beta algorithms

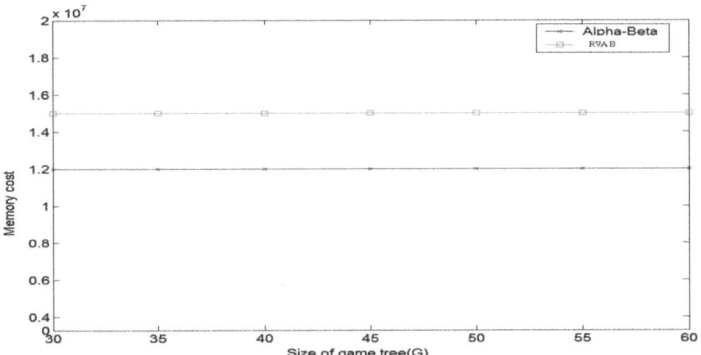

Fig. 4. Memory analysis based on RVAB and Alpha-Beta algorithms

In the Fig 3, alpha-beta, variable depth and RVAB algorithm visit nodes increase with scale of game trees. RVAB algorithm visit the least nodes in these algorithm. the reason is that RVAB order by payoff before research. It make RVAB can search well payoff value and generate many cutoff. Since RVAB made order by payoff and entropy, it will need plenty of memory to store these value. The Fig 4 shows that RABT spend more memory than alpha beta algorithm.

5 Conclusion

In this paper, we present a novel search algorithm called reason variable alpha-beta algorithm in our Siguo game system. The basic ideas of RVAB algorithm is : if player get much information about opponent during playing game, they can do more deep thinking about strategies of game. If player can only get few, very uncertain information about opponent during playing game, they don't think more deep about their strategy because it is worthless for player to speculate the strategies of game under very uncertain. In other words, when more certain information about payoff of game tree, we can search more deep, in contrast, we search more low. We use the

RVAB algorithm in our Siguo military game system and have achieved good results in our system. At opening phase of siguo game, since piece information about opponent is very uncertain and path entropy is high, depth of search is very shallow. When game is enter middle phase and end phase, plenty of information about pieces is achieved during playing game, entropy of piece becomes little, at this time, depth of search becomes.

Acknowledgement. Our work is supported by the ministry of science and technology of the People's Republic of China NO 2009GJE00035 and NUAA foundation founds NS2010111.

References

1. Bud, A.E., Albrecht, D.W., et al.: Playing Invisible Chess with Information-Theoretic Advisors. In: AAAI Spring Symposium G3: Game Theoretic and Decision Theoretic Agents, USA, March 26-28 (2001)
2. Billings, D., Davidson, A., Schaeffer, J., et al.: The challenge of poker. Artificial Intelligence 134, 201–240 (2002)
3. Albrecht, D.W., Zukerman, I., Nicholson, A.E., Bud, A.: Towards a bayesian model for keyhole plan recognition in large domains. In: UM 1997, Italy, June 2-5 (1997)
4. Frank, I., Basin, D.: Search in games with incomplete information: A case study using bridge card play. Artificial intelligent 100, 87–123 (1996)
5. Ginsberg, M.: GIB: steps toward an expert-level bridge playing program. In: Proc. Sixteenth IJCAI, pp. 584–589 (1999)
6. Koller, D., Pfeffer, A.: Generating and solving imperfect information games. In: Proc. Fourteenth IJCAI, pp. 1185–1192 (1995)
7. Korb, K.B., Nicholson, A.E., et al.: Bayesian poker. In: Laskey, K.B., Prade, H. (eds.) Proceedings of the fifteenth Conference on Uncertainty in Artificial Intelligence, pp. 343–350 (1999)
8. Xia, Z.Y., Hu, Y.A., Wang, J., Jiang, Y.C., Qin, X.L.: Analyze and guess type of piece in the computer game intelligent system. In: Wang, L., Jin, Y. (eds.) FSKD 2005. LNCS (LNAI), vol. 3614, pp. 1174–1183. Springer, Heidelberg (2005)
9. Xia, Z., Zhu, Y., Lu, H.: Using the Loopy Belief Propagation in Siguo. ICGA Journal 30(4), 209–220 (2007)
10. Xia, Z., Zhu, Y., Lu, H.: Evaluation Function for Siguo Game Based on Two Attitudes. In: Wang, L., Jiao, L., Shi, G., Li, X., Liu, J. (eds.) FSKD 2006. LNCS (LNAI), vol. 4223, pp. 1322–1331. Springer, Heidelberg (2006)
11. Hui, L., Xia, Z.: AWT: Aspiration with Timer Search Algorithm in Siguo Computers and Games 2008, pp. 264–274 (2008)

Performance Modeling of Engine Based on Artificial Neural Networks[*]

Wenping Wang, Xiaofeng Yin[**], Yongzhong Wang, and Jianjun Yang

Key Laboratory of Automotive Engineering of Sichuan Province,
Xihua University, Jinniu District, 610039 Chengdu, P.R. China
xiaofengyin@vip.sina.com

Abstract. In order to further improve the precision and generalization ability of the neural network based performance model of engine, back propagation neural network (BPNN), radial basis function neural network (RBFNN) and generalized regression neural network (GRNN) have been investigated. The topologies and algorithms of these three different types of neural networks have been designed to meet the same goal of convergence, and a same set of testing data have been used to test the trained neural networks. Comparison of the training and testing errors as well as the generalization ability of these neural networks shows that RBFNN is more suitable for modeling the performance of engine than BPNN and GRNN.

Keywords: performance, model, engine, back propagation neural network, radial basis function, generalized regression neural network.

1 Introduction

In the process of making automotive automatic gear-shifting schedule based on performance constraints, the model of engine performance must be established to estimate engine's output torque and fuel consumption. The precision of engine performance model is very important to implement the optimal match between engine and drive- line [1].

The common method of building the performance model of engine is to identify certain representative data that are obtained through engine stable experiments. There are two main identification methods: the polynomial fitting method and the neural networks method [2]. The polynomial fitting method is easy to use, however, its precision is comparatively low and the ability of generalization is weak. Due to its capabilities of massively parallel processing, high self-learning, and strong

[*] The work reported in this paper was supported in part by National Natural Science Foundation of China (Grant No. 60970072), Scientific Research Fund of Sichuan Provincial Education Department (Grant No. 10ZA100, KYTD201003), Innovation Fund of Postgraduate, Xihua University, and Research Fund of Key Discipline of Vehicle Engineering of Sichuan Province (Grant No. SZD0410-08-0).
[**] Corresponding author.

H. Deng et al. (Eds.): AICI 2011, Part III, LNAI 7004, pp. 278–285, 2011.
© Springer-Verlag Berlin Heidelberg 2011

generaliz- ation, artificial neural networks can approximate any nonlinear functions with whatever precision [3]. Therefore, more and more models of nonlinear systems are built using neural networks.

In this paper, three different types of neural networks including back propagation neural network (BPNN), radial basis function neural network (RBFNN) and generalized regression neural network (GRNN), have been used to identify the model of engine's output torque and fuel consumption, respectively, and the performance of BPNN, RBFNN and GRNN have been compared to find the best one suitable for performance modeling of engine.

2   Neural Network Identification Methods for Engine Performance

Neural network identification structure for engine performance model of engine is shown as Fig. 1. Here, P represents the input of engine, and T represents the output of engine. As shown in formula (1), P comprises throttle position α and engine speed n_e, and T comprises output torque T_e and fuel consumption Q_e.

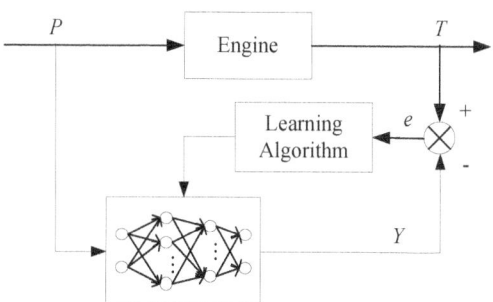

Fig. 1. Identification structure

$$\begin{cases} P=[\alpha,n_e]^T \\ T=[T_e,Q_e]^T . \end{cases} \tag{1}$$

Using the deviation e between the output of engine T and the actual output of network Y as a learning signal, e could be leveled off to zero finally through weights updating by means of certain learning algorithm [4]. The performance model of engine can be identified in such way [5].

2.1   Back Propagation Neural Network (BPNN)

BPNN is a multi-layer feedforward neural network. It has been proved that a BPNN with one hidden layer can approximate any functions [6]. The topology of one-hidden-layer BPNN is shown as Fig. 2, and the transfer function of the hidden layer is a sigmoid function (shown as formula (2)).

$$f(x) = (1 - e^{-2x})/(1 + e^{-2x}).$$ (2)

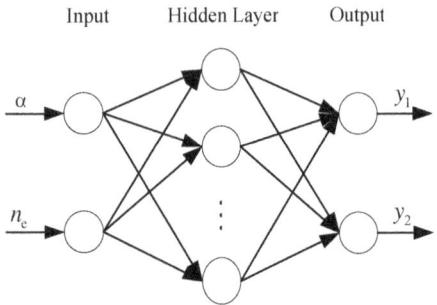

Fig. 2. Topology of one-hidden-layer BPNN

An error back propagation algorithm is used as the learning algorithm in BPNN [6]. And the error function for the output layer is defined as mean square error (MSE).

$$E = \frac{1}{N} \sum_{i=1}^{N} \sum_{j=1}^{L} (t_j^i - y_j^i)^2.$$ (3)

Here, N is the number of data in the training set; L is the number of network outputs. Since the performance model of engine is a MIMO system that has 2 inputs and 2 outputs, in this case L equals to 2.

Generally in error back propagation algorithm, weights are modified in proportion to the negative gradient of the E. But this gradient descent learning algorithm is poor regarding convergence, and easy to fall in local optimal solution. In order to overcome these problems, the Levenberg-Marquardt (LM) learning algorithm is applied to train the network in this paper. LM algorithm [7] can be described as

$$\begin{cases} \omega(k+1) = \omega(k) + \Delta\omega(k+1) \\ \Delta\omega(k+1) = (J^T J + \mu I)^{-1} J^T E. \end{cases}$$ (4)

Here, μ is a nonnegative numerical value; J is the Jacobian matrix of E.

2.2 Radial Basis Function Neural Network (RBFNN)

RBFNN is a class of feedforward neural networks that consists of two layers: a hidden radial basis layer and a linear output layer [3]. The former consists of a number of radial basis neurons each with structure shown as Fig. 3.

The expression of the net input of a hidden neuron is different from that of neurons in other layer. The net input to the transfer function of the hidden neurons is the vector distance between its weight vector W and the input vector P, multiplied by the bias [8]. The transfer function of the hidden neuron is a Gaussian function that can be expressed as formula (5).

$$f(x) = e^{-x^2}.$$
(5)

Input   Radial Basis Neuron

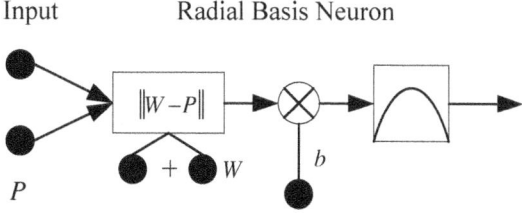

Fig. 3. Structure of radial basis neuron

The learning process of RBFNN can be divided into two phases [4]. The first phase is to obtain the center vector of the Gaussian function that is also the weight vector of the radial basis layer commonly by clustering the input set. The second phase is to get the weight vector of the output layer using the least square method since the output layer is linear.

The only precondition is to make sure that the spread constant SPREAD is large enough, i.e., the active input regions of the radial basis neurons overlap enough so that several radial basis neurons always have fairly large outputs at any given moment. This makes the network function more smoother and results in better generalization for new input vectors occurring between input vectors used in the design [8]. The trial-and–error method is often used to determine it.

2.3   Generalized Regression Neural Network (GRNN)

GRNN is a special kind of RBFNN that has a radial basis layer and a special linear layer. Its structure is same as RBFNN's except the output layer. The difference is that the input of the second layer is the dot product of its weight vector and the output vector of the first layer; all normalized by the sum of the elements of the first layer's output.

The number of neurons in the first layer equals to the size of input/target vectors in P. Specifically, the weight vector of the first layer is set to P^T, and the bias is set to be a column vector with value of 0.8326/SPREAD. The number of neurons in the second layer does also equal to the size of input/target vectors. The weight vector of the second layer is set to T [8].

3   Performance Modeling of Engine

The performance models of engine have been built separately by the aforementioned neural networks using MATLAB Neural Network Toolbox. Regarding each type of neural network, the best model has been found using trial-and-error method through comparing the training precision and the generalization effect.

3.1 Settings of Neural Networks

The topology of BPNN is $2 \times 13 \times 2$: there are 2 inputs corresponding to throttle opening degree and engine speed; the hidden layer has 13 neurons; the output layer has 2 neurons corresponding to the values of torque and fuel consumption. The goal of training accuracy is 0.001.

The topology of RBFNN is $2 \times 9 \times 2$: there are 2 inputs; the hidden layer has 9 neurons; the output layer has 2 neurons. The goal of training accuracy is 0.001. The SPREAD is set to 0.55.

The topology of GRNN is $2 \times 144 \times 2$: there are 2 inputs; the hidden layer has 144 neurons; the output layer has 2 neurons. The SPREAD is 0.09.

3.2 Performance Models of Engine

The performance models including models of torque and fuel consumption of engine described by BPNN, RBFNN and GRNN are shown as Fig. 4, Fig. 5 and Fig. 6 respectively.

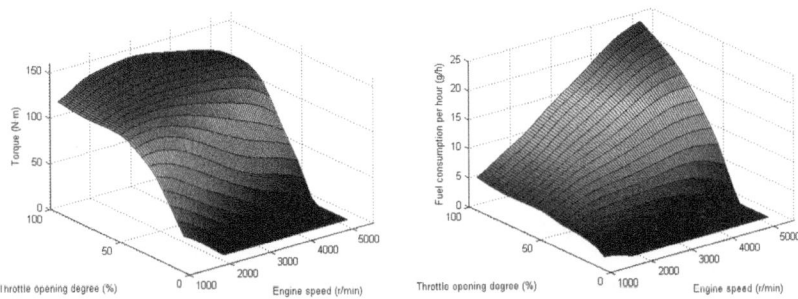

Fig. 4. BPNN-based performance model of engine

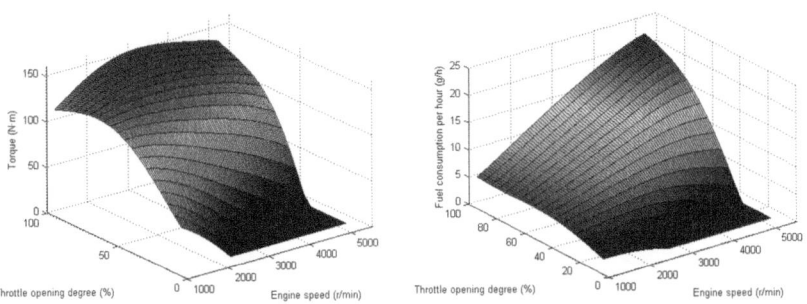

Fig. 5. RBFNN-based performance model of engine

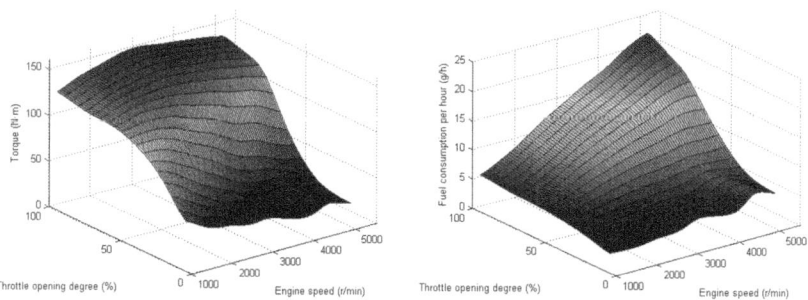

Fig. 6. GRNN-based performance model of engine

After training of these three types of neural networks, 1/4 of the experimental data have been chosen to test the generalization ability for each type of neural network. The absolute and relative errors between network outputs and engine actual outputs have also been calculated during these processes, which are shown as Fig. 7, Fig. 8 and Fig. 9 respectively.

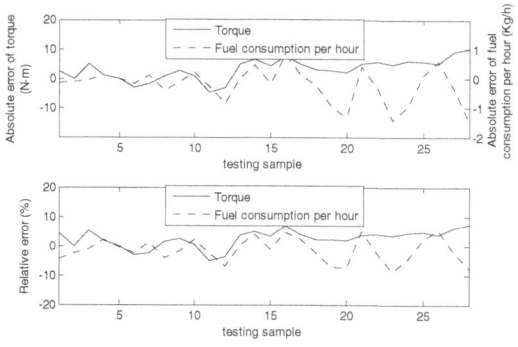

Fig. 7. Test error of BPNN

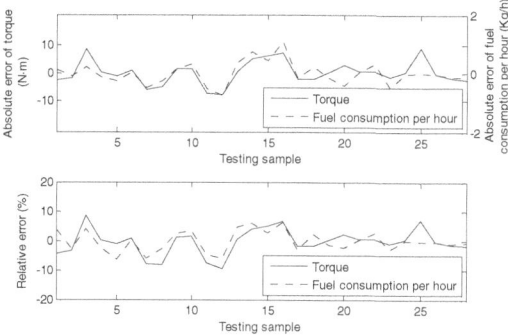

Fig. 8. Test error of RBFNN

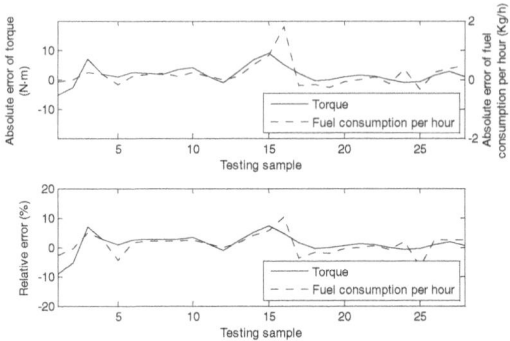

Fig. 9. Test error of GRNN

Once training and testing processes completed, the training time, and MSE in training as well as in testing process can be calculated for each type of neural network, which are listed in Table 1.

Table 1. Performance comparision

Network type	Training time (s)	MSE in training	MSE in testing
BPNN	0.41	0.00087	0.00078
RBFNN	1.05	0.00076	0.00048
GRNN	0.21	0.00095	0.00038

3.3 Comparison Analysis

As shown in Fig. 7, Fig. 8 and Fig. 9, the relative test errors of BPNN, RBFNN and GRNN for torque and fuel consumption are all smaller than 10%, which means all of them satisfy the basic demand of engine performance estimating.

As shown in Table 1, the training precision of RBFNN is higher than those of the other two types of neural networks. The network having the lowest MSE in testing is GRNN, but as shown in Fig.6, there are notable errors in small throttle opening area (under 15%), which means its generalization ability is poorer than the other two.

MSE's in training and testing BPNN are larger than those in training and testing RBFNN (as shown in Table 1), and the actual time used to train BPNN is much more longer than that listed in Table I since the initial weights of BPNN are random that makes it need more loops of training to be converged to the target goal.

4 Conclusion

The performance models of engine have been established by BPNN, RBFNN and GRNN separately. The comparison of precision and generalization ability shows that RBFNN is more suitable for modeling engine performance including torque and fuel consumption. And this provides a practicable way to build a more precise performance model of engine for further development of more reasonable automotive gear-shifting schedules.

References

1. Ge, A.: Theory and Design of Automatic Transmission for Vehicle (in Chinese). Mechanical Industry Press, Beijing (1993)
2. Wu, G., Yang, W., Qin, D.: Key Technique of Dual Clutch Transmission Control System (in Chinese). Chinese Journal of Mechanical Engineering 43(2), 13–21 (2007)
3. Kumar, S.: Neural Networks. Tsinghua University Press, Beijing (2006)
4. Li, G.: Intelligent Control and Application of MATLAB simulation (in Chinese). Publishing House of Electronics Industry, Beijing (2005)
5. Yin, X., Ge, A.: A Dynamic Model of Engine Using Neural Network Description. In: IEEE International Vehicle Electronics Conference, Tottori, Japan, pp. 109–114 (September 2001)
6. Yan, P., Zhang, C.: Artificial Neural Networks and Evolutionary Computing (in Chinese). Tsinghua University Press, Beijing (2005)
7. Hagan, M.T., Menhaj, M.B.: Training feedforward networks with the Marquardt algorithm. IEEE Transactions on Neural Networks, 989–993 (May 1994)
8. Beal, M.H., Hagan, M.T., Demuth, H.B.: Neural Network Toolbox user's guide. MathWorks Inc. (2010)
9. Song, Y., Wang, P.: A Nonlinear Model Recognition Based on RBF Neural Network (in Chinese). Computer Engineering 30(5), 142–143 (2004)

Approximation of Curves Contained on the Surface by Freed-Forward Neural Networks

Zhenghua Zhou and Jianwei Zhao

Department of information and mathematics Sciences
China Jiliang University, Hangzhou, 310018, China
zzhzjw2003@163.com

Abstract. Based on Freed-forward Neural Networks, we develop a new method to approximate curves contained on the given surface; the main contribution is to convert the problems of space curve approximation on surfaces into the plane curve approximation by point projection. The final approximation curve restricted on the surface is achieved via the intersection of surface and cylinder whose directrix is plane approximation curve by freed-forword Neural Networks method, we also give an upper bound estimation about approximation accuracy.The experiment results show that the method achieve good effect compared to traditional methods nusing piecewise function to represent the curve on the surface.

Keywords: Neural networks, Approximation, curve.

1 Introduction

It is a interpolation problem to construct a space (plane)curve by using the sequences of given position points, however, due to noises or error affection, the position data points acquired are not accurate, the corresponding results by rigorous interpolation is not satisfied. It is more reasonable to find approximation curve than the interpolation curve. Curve approximation on surface is a important research content in graphics, Its main process is to use the given position data to construct a curve for approximating the unknown curve on surface, Such algorithms show more and more important effection. For example, in order to design a geometrical pattern, we may sample sequences of data on the surface, then constructing a curve on the model surface as the profile of geometrical pattern to achieve designing of geometrical pattern. In addition, similar problems exist in cutters trajectory design of numerical control process and robot path design.

2 Related Work

In the fields of CAD, computer animation, and so on, many practical problems involve the representation of a curve on surface, recently curve approximation contained on surface attracts more attention. However, so far, only several efforts

H. Deng et al. (Eds.): AICI 2011, Part III, LNAI 7004, pp. 286–292, 2011.

have been made towards developing effective methods for approximation of surface curves. Pobegailo[1] gave an approach for G^1 interpolation on a sphere. Dietz [2] presented G^0 interpolation problem on quadrics. Hartmann [3] developed a method for curvature-continuous G^2 interpolation of an arbitrary sequence of points on a surface with the specified tangent and a geodesic curvature at every point. Other related researches focus on G^1 and C^1 interpolation presented in Refs.[4~5] respectively. In addition, direct approximation such as that with piecewise 4-point Bézier cubic curves or linear curves was also applied to the representation of surface curves in practical applications [6, 7]. In practical application, the given data always contains noises, interpolation is not appropriate. In a certain meaning, approximation is more suitable than interpolation, however, little works involves approximation of curve contained in the specified surfaces.

Due to their ability to approximate complex nonlinear mappings directly from the input sampling data points, neural networks are widely applied in many fields. Neural networks can provide many models for a lot of natural and artificial phenomena that are difficult to handle using other methods. Among many kinds of neural networks, feed-forward neural networks have been widely investigated by a lot of researchers [8-12]. In this paper, motivated by the Cao's work [13], we will approximate curve contained on surface via single-hidden layer feed-forward neural networks by a constructive approach. It's proved that the approximation is simple and fast.

The aim of this paper is to develop methods for smooth approximation of an curve on surfaces with a prescribed points without any tangent or curvature information. With the help of neural network, we convert the problems of space curve approximation on surfaces into the plane curve approximation. We also give the approximation order of the curve approximation on the surface.

The paper is organized as follows. Section 2 describes previous work on curve approximation especially interpolation on surface. Section 3 introduces the necessary mathematical knowledge involved in the presented methods for the approximation of surface curves, problem statements are given in Section 4. Curve approximation issues are discussed in Section 5, section 6 describes numerical aspects and results; conclusions and future work is presented in section 7.

3   Mathematical Preliminary and Problem Statement

Definition 1. Let f be a real-valued function defined on [a,b], define the modulus of continuity of f by $\omega(f,\delta) = \sup_{0<h<\delta} \|f(\cdot+h) - f(\cdot)\|$,Obviously, we have $\lim_{\delta \to 0} \omega(f,\delta) = 0$.

Definition 2. The function f is called Lipschitz α $(0 < \alpha \le 1)$ continuous and is written as $f \in Lip_{C(f)}\alpha$, if there exists a constant $C(f)$ such that $\omega(f,\delta) \le C(f)\delta^\alpha$.

The problem discussed in the paper can be described as follows: given a smooth explicit surface function $z = f(x, y)$ defined on D and point clouds data $\left\{ p_i = (x_i, y_i, z_i) \middle| p_i \in S, i = 0, 1, \cdots, n \right\}$ which sampled from curve $\mathbf{r}(t)$ contained on the surface, the x-coordinate of the data points satisfy $a = x_0 < x_1 < \cdots < x_n = b$, let $\Delta x_i = x_i - x_{i-1}$, $\lambda = \max_i \left\{ \Delta x_i \right\}$, require to construct a smooth curve to approximate original curve contained on the surface, this kind of problem is called curve approximation on the surface, the methods adopted to resolve this problem as follows: first, the space data are projected onto the xoy coordinate plane, according to the projection points $\left\{ \widetilde{p}_i = (x_i, y_i), i = 0, 1, \cdots, n \right\}$,

we construct a approximation curve $y = g(x)$ in the x-o-y coordinate plane based on single-hidden layer feed-forward neural networks, furthermore, a cylinder is established by using the plane curve as directrix, corresponding generatrix is parallel to z-axis. The approximation curve is achieved via the intersection of the cylinder and surface containing the curve $\begin{cases} z = f(x, y) \\ y = g(x) \end{cases}$.

4 Constructing Approximation Curve

4.1 Constructing Approximation Curve Based on Projection Points

Suppose that the data on the surface be represented as:

$\left\{ p_i = (x_i, y_i, z_i) \middle| p_i \in S, i = 0, 1, \cdots, n \right\}$, $(x_0, y_0), (x_1, y_1), \ldots, (x_n, y_n)$ denotes the corresponding projection data on the xoy plane, where $a = x_0 < x_1 < x_2 < \cdots < x_n = b$.we construct a free-forward neural networks curve to approximate the projection points by adopting the method of the reference [13].the process of construction is as follows: define single-hidden layer feed-forward neural networks

$$N_n(x) = c_0 + \sum_{i=1}^{n} c_i \phi(\omega_i \cdot x + \theta) \tag{1}$$

Lemma 1 [13]. Suppose ϕ is a bounded strictly monotone and odd function defined on R, $f \in C[a, b]$ and $n \in N$, Then there exists a feed-forward neural network with one hidden layer $N_n : [a, b] \to R$ defined by

$N_n(x) = c_0 + \sum_{i=1}^{n} c_i \phi(\omega_i x + \theta)$, where c_i, ω_i are defined as below, such that

$$\sup_{x \in [a,b]} \left| N_n(x) - f(x) \right| \le \frac{5}{2}\omega\left(f, \frac{b-a}{n} \right) \tag{2}$$

Here we use, for

$$i = 1, \cdots, n, x_i = a + i\frac{b-a}{n}, x_0 = a, m = \sup_{x \in R} \phi(x),$$

$$c_i = \frac{1}{2m}\left(f(x_i) - f(x_{i-1}) \right), \; c_0 = f(a) - \sum_{i=1}^{n} c_i\phi(\omega_i a + \theta_i), \; \omega_i = \frac{2nd_n}{b-a},$$

$$\theta_i = -\frac{nd_n}{b-a}\left(2a + (2i-1)\frac{b-a}{n} \right), \; d_n = \phi^{-1}\left(m - \frac{m}{2n} \right),$$

where $\omega\left(f, \frac{b-a}{n} \right) = \sup_{0 < h < \frac{b-a}{n}} \left\| f(\cdot + h) - f(\cdot) \right\|.$

Now a cylinder is constructed, its directrix is $y = N_n(x)$, its generatrix is parallel to Z-axis.the approximation curve is achieved via the intersection of cylinder and surface.

Theorem. suppose curve $\mathbf{r}(t) = \left(x(t), y(t), z(t) \right), a \le t \le b$ is contained on the explicit surface $z = f(x, y)$,when the given data satisfy $a = x_0 < x_1 < x_2 < \cdots < x_n = b$,and $\lambda = \max_i \left\{ \Delta x_i \right\} \to 0$, Then, there exists a feed-forward neural network with one hidden layer $N_n : [a,b] \to R$ defined by

$$N_n(x) = c_0 + \sum_{i=1}^{n} c_i\phi(\omega_i x + \theta) \quad \text{,such that the constructing curve}$$

$$\tilde{\mathbf{r}}(x): \begin{cases} x = x \\ y = N_n(x) \\ z = f(x, N_n(x)) \end{cases} \quad \text{can infinitely approximate the original curve of the}$$

surface.

Proof: Suppose the original curve denoted by $r(x)$,its corresponding parameter equation is represented as $\begin{cases} x = x \\ y = \varphi(x) \\ z = f(x, \varphi(x)) \end{cases}$, $a \le x \le b$,the corresponding approximation curve denoted by $\tilde{r}(x)$,its parameter equation is represented as $\begin{cases} x = x \\ y = N_n(x) \\ z = f(x, N_n(x)) \end{cases}$ $a \le x \le b$,from the above Lemma 1,we know that

$\sup\limits_{x\in[a,b]} |N_n(x) - \varphi(x)| \le \dfrac{5}{2}\omega(\varphi, \lambda)$,we use the Euclidean norm $\|\cdot\|_2$ to measure the approximation extent.

$$\left\|\tilde{\mathbf{r}}(x) - \mathbf{r}(x)\right\|_2^2 = (x - x)^2 + \left[N_n(x) - \varphi(x)\right]^2 + \left[f(x, \varphi(x)) - f(x, N_n(x))\right]^2$$
$$= \left[N_n(x) - \varphi(x)\right]^2 + \left[f(x, \varphi(x)) - f(x, N_n(x))\right]^2$$

As $f(x, y)$ is a continuous function on definition domain D ,when $\lambda \to 0$, We have $\omega(\varphi, \lambda) \to 0$,hence $N_n(x) \to \varphi(x)$, $f(x, \varphi(x)) \to f(x, N_n(x))$. $(n \to \infty)$,so $\left\|\tilde{\mathbf{r}}(x) - \mathbf{r}(x)\right\| \to 0$,that is to say $\tilde{\mathbf{r}}(x) \to \mathbf{r}(x)$

Corollary. Suppose curve $\mathbf{r}(t) = (x(t), y(t), z(t)), \alpha \le t \le \beta$ is contained on the smooth explicit surface $z = f(x, y)$, furthermore, $f \in Lip_M(1)$,.Then there exists a feed-forward neural network with one hidden layer $N_n : [a, b] \to R$ defined by

$N_n(x) = c_0 + \sum\limits_{i=1}^n c_i \phi(\omega_i x + \theta)$,   such   that   the   constructing   curve

$\tilde{\mathbf{r}}(x): \begin{cases} x = x \\ y = N_n(x) \\ z = f(x, N_n(x)) \end{cases}$ can infinitely approximate the original curve of the surface, furthermore.

$$\sup\limits_x \left\|\tilde{\mathbf{r}}(x) - \mathbf{r}(x)\right\| \le \sqrt{\left(M + \dfrac{5}{2}\right)\omega(\varphi, \lambda)} \tag{3}$$

5   Experimental Result

We show our theoretical result by using sigmoidal function and suggest the error bound of neural network approximation. All computations were done in Matlab. We choose an curve $r(x)$ as target curve, its corresponding parametric equation is

$$\begin{cases} x = x \\ y = x^2 + \sin(x) \\ z = -x^2 - y^2 \end{cases} , x \in [-3,3], \text{ which contained on surface } S : z = -x^2 - y^2,$$

the corresponding projection curve on the xoy coordinate plane is $y = x^2 + \sin(x)$ .we adopt the neural network of sigmoidal activation function $\phi(x) = \dfrac{2}{\pi} \arctan(x), x \in R$,According to the properties of arctan x ,we can find

$$m = 1, \phi^{-1}(x) = \tan(\frac{\pi}{2} x) \text{ and } d_n = \tan\left(\frac{\pi}{2}(1 - \frac{1}{2n})\right),$$

$$c_i = \frac{1}{2}\left(\left(\frac{-36}{n} + \frac{(2i-1)}{n^2}\right) + \sin\left((6i + -3n)/n\right) - \sin\sin\left((6(i-1) - 3n)/n\right)\right)$$

$$\theta_i = (n - 2i + 1)\tan\left(\frac{\pi}{2}\left(1 - \frac{1}{2n}\right)\right), \quad w_i = \frac{n}{3}\tan\left(\frac{\pi}{2}\left(1 - \frac{1}{2n}\right)\right), 1 \le i \le n.$$

$$c_0 = 9 - \sin(3) - \sum_{i=1}^{n}\frac{1}{2}\left(\left(\frac{-36}{n} + \frac{(2i-1)}{n^2}\right) + \sin\left((6i + -3n)/n\right) - \sin\sin\left((6(i-1) - 3n)/n\right)\right)$$

$$\times \frac{2}{\pi}\arctan\left(-n\tan\left(\frac{\pi}{2}\left(1 - \frac{1}{2n}\right)\right) + (n - 2i + 1)\tan\left(\frac{\pi}{2}\left(1 - \frac{1}{2n}\right)\right)\right)$$

Fig. 1-4 show some figure experimental results.

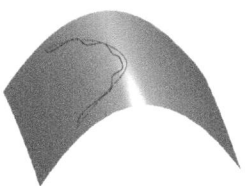

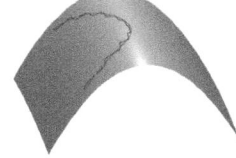

...

Fig. 1. n=5 case   **Fig. 2** n=10 case

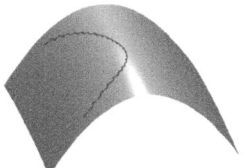

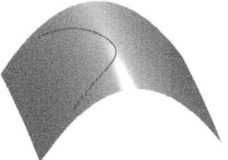

Fig. 3. n=25 case   **Fig. 4.**n=50 case

6 Conclusion

Based on Freed-forward Neural Networks, the paper presents a novel method to approximate curves contained on the given surface, the main progress is to convert the problems of space curve approximation on surfaces into the plane curve approximation by points projection. The resulting approximation curve restricted on the surface is achieved by the intersection of the given surface and cylinder constructed by freed-forward Neural Networks method, we also give an upper bound estimation about approximation accuracy. The experiment result shows that the method adopted in the paper achieves good effect compared to traditional methods which often use piecewise function to represent the curve on the surface.

Acknowledgements. The research of this paper is supported by the National Nature Science Foundation of China (No. 60873130) and the Nature Science Foundation of Zhejiang Province (No. Y6110117).

References

1. Pobegailo, A.: Spherical splines and orientation interpolation. The Visual Computer 11(2), 63–68 (1994)
2. Dietz, R., Hoschek, J., Jüttler, B.: Rational patches on quadric surfaces. Computer Aided Design 27(1), 27–40 (1995)
3. Hartmann, E.: G2 interpolation and blending on surfaces. The Visual Computer 12(4), 181–192 (1996)
4. Zhang, H.: Algorithm of C1 interpolation restricted on smooth surface. Journal of Computer Aided Design and Computer Graphics 9(5), 385–390 (1997) (in Chinese with English abstract)
5. Lin, H., Wang, G.: G1 interpolation curve on smooth surface. In: Zhang, C.M. (ed.) Proc. of CSIAM (China Society of Industrial and Applied Mathematics) Geometric Design & Computing 2002, pp. 50–53. Petroleum University Press, Qindao (2002) (in Chinese with English abstract)
6. Kumar, S., Manocha, D.: Efficient rendering of trimmed NURBS surfaces. Computer Aided Design 27(7), 509–521 (1995)
7. Piegl, L., Tiller, W.: Geometry-Based triangulation of trimmed NURBS surfaces. Computer Aided Design 31(1), 11–18 (1998)
8. Hornik, K., Stinchombe, M., White, H.: Universal approximation of an unknown mapping and its derivatives using multilayer feedforward networks. Neural Networks 3, 551–560 (1990)
9. Jones, L.K.: A simple lemma on greedy approximation in Hilbert space and convergence rates for projection pursuit regression and neural network training. Ann. Stat. 20, 765–772 (1992)
10. Korain, P.: On the complexity of approximating mappings using neural networks. Neural Networks 6, 649–653 (1993)
11. Leshno, M., Lin, V.Y., Pinks, A., Schocken, S.: Multilayer feedforward networks with a nonpolynomial activation function can approximate any function. Neural Networks 6, 861–867 (1993)
12. Li, X.: On simultaneous approximations of by radial basis function neural networks. Appl. Math. Comput. 95, 75–89 (1998)
13. Cao, F.L., Xie, T.F., Xu, Z.B.: The estimate for approximation error of neural networks: A constructive approach. Neurocomputing 71, 626–630 (2008)

Attractors of Discrete Cellular Neural Networks

Run-Nian Ma[1], Gang Wen[1], and Hong Xiao[1,2]

[1] Telecommunication Engineering Institute, Air Force Engineering University
Xi'an, 710077, China
[2] Key Laboratory of advanced Design and Intelligent Computing, Dalian University,
Ministry of Education
Dalian, 116622, China
m314@163.com

Abstract. The dynamic behavior of discrete cellular neural networks (DCNN) with zero threshold value, which is strict, is mainly studied. For the DCNN with zero threshold value and no self-feedback, if a state is a fixed point, then a lot of unstable points are given, and under some conditions these unstable points can converge to the fixed point. In this paper, the properties of k-attractor of the DCNN are mainly studied, and some conditions are obtained under which the k-attractor is a fixed point, and lots of unstable points are attracted to the fixed point. The results obtained here on k-attractor improve the results in the previous references.

Keywords: discrete cellular neural networks, fixed point, k-attractor.

1 Introduction

Recently numerous models of nervous system and brain which are called artificial neural networks have been extensively studied and developed. Dynamic behavior analysis of neural networks has been an important topic in the neural network field since it has great significance for many applications. From both theoretical and applied points of view, the most popular models in the literature are cellular neural networks, which have been extensively studied. The discrete cellular neural network (DCNN) is one of the famous neural networks with a wide range of applications, such as signal processing and pattern [1-2]. These applications heavily depend on the dynamic behavior of the neural networks, and in designing a neural networks, it is usually of very importance to guarantee the asymptotical stability of the corresponding dynamic system. Therefore, the researches on the dynamic behavior are a necessary step for the design of the neural networks and its applications.

The stability of the DCNN means that every trajectory must converge towards an equilibrium (or convergent, or fixed) point, or a limit cycle. Because the stability of the DCNN is the foundation of the network's applications and is the most basic and important problem, the stability analysis of the DCNN has been extensively studied with considerable interest [1-6]. In this paper, some results on stability and k-attractor are presented, too. This paper is organized as follows. Section one is introduction. Section two introduces most of the notations and definitions used in this paper.

H. Deng et al. (Eds.): AICI 2011, Part III, LNAI 7004, pp. 293–299, 2011.

Section three presents some results on stability and k-attractor of the DCNN. Section 4 concludes the paper.

2 Notations and Preliminaries

We assume a DCNN defined on a rectangular or torus $M \times N$ cell grid $S, C(i, j)$ denotes the intersection of row i and column j. $N_r(i, j)$ denotes the r-neighborhood of cell $C(i, j)$:

$$N_r(i, j) = \{C(u, v) : |u - i| \le r, |v - j| \le r\} \tag{1}$$

Let $B = \{-1, 1\}$, $B^{M \times N} = \{-1, 1\}^{M \times N}$, $X(t) \in B^{M \times N}$ denote the state of the DCNN at time t, where $x_{ij}(t)$ is the state of cell $C(i, j)$ at time t. Let us consider the updating equations of the DCNN as follows:

$$x_{ij}(t+1) = \begin{cases} \operatorname{sgn}(\omega_{ij}(t)), & \text{if } C(i, j) \in \Omega(t+1) \subset S, \\ x_{ij}(t), & \text{otherwise.} \end{cases} \tag{2}$$

where $\Omega(t+1)$ is a subset of the cell grid S. The sequence $\Omega(t+1)$, $t = 0, 1, 2, \cdots$, defines the particular updating sequence or updating mode. If each $\Omega(t+1)$ $\forall t$ contains a single cell, then the DCNN is said to be operating in a serial (or asynchronous) mode. If $\Omega(t+1)$ $\forall t$ coincides with the cell grid S, then the DCNN is said to be operating in a parallel (or synchronous) mode. Here the sign function and $\omega_{ij}(t)$ are respectively defined as follows:

$$\operatorname{sgn}(u) = \begin{cases} +1, & \text{if } u \ge 0 \\ -1, & \text{if } u < 0 \end{cases}$$

$$\omega_{ij}(t) = \omega_{ij}((X(t))) = (A * X(t))_{ij}$$

$$= \sum_{C(u,v) \in N_r(i,j)} A(u - i, v - j) x_{uv}(t)$$

$$= \sum_{C(u,v) \in N_r(i,j)} a_{u-i, v-j} x_{uv}(t)$$

$1 \le i \le M, 1 \le j \le N$, where $A \in R^{(2r+1) \times (2r+1)}$ represents the feedback cloning template. The template coefficients for $r = 1$ and $r = 2$ in the following:

$$A = \begin{pmatrix} a_{-1-1} & a_{-10} & a_{-11} \\ a_{0-1} & a_{00} & a_{01} \\ a_{1-1} & a_{10} & a_{11} \end{pmatrix}, \quad A = \begin{pmatrix} a_{-2-2} & a_{-2-1} & a_{-20} & a_{-21} & a_{-22} \\ a_{-1-2} & a_{-1-1} & a_{-10} & a_{-11} & a_{-12} \\ a_{0-2} & a_{0-1} & a_{00} & a_{01} & a_{02} \\ a_{1-2} & a_{1-1} & a_{10} & a_{11} & a_{12} \\ a_{2-2} & a_{2-1} & a_{20} & a_{21} & a_{22} \end{pmatrix}$$

The DCNN (2) is said to be convergent if, there is one time t_0 , such that $x_{ij}(t) = x_{ij}(t_0)$, for every $C(i, j) \in S$, and every $t \geq t_0$. The set of convergent points of the DCNN is defined by the following necessary and sufficient conditions:

$$x_{ij}\omega_{ij} > 0$$

or

$$x_{ij}\omega_{ij} = 0 , \ x_{ij} = 1$$

for all cells $C(i, j)$.

If $\omega_{ij}(X) \neq 0$ for all $X \in B^{M \times N}$, then the DCNN (2) is said to be strict.

Let $H(X,Y)$ denote the Hamming distance between states X and Y , for $X, Y \in B^{M \times N}$. $S_k(X) = \{Y | H(X,Y) = k\}$ is the Hamming sphere of radius k centered at X .

$\delta(X,Y) = \{C(i, j) \in S | x_{ij} \neq y_{ij}\}$ is the set of grid positions in which $x_{ij} \neq y_{ij}$.

$\delta_k^r(X) = \{Y \| \delta(X,Y) \cap N_r(i, j)| \leq k, 1 \leq i \leq M, 1 \leq j \leq N\}$ is the set of states which differ from X at most k grid positions in each r-neighborhood.

A state X^* is a fixed (or convergent) state if and only if, for all cells $C(i, j)$

$$x_{ij}^* = \text{sgn}((A * X^*)_{ij}) = \sum_{C(u,v) \in N_r(i, j)} a_{u-i, v-j} x_{uv}^* \tag{3}$$

We can prove that a state X^* is one convergent point if and only if the following condition (4) satisfies for strict DCNN.

$$x_{ij}^*(A * X^*)_{ij} > 0, \text{ if } (A * X^*)_{ij} \neq 0 \tag{4}$$

The notation $Y \to X$ means that Y is strongly attracted to X , i.e. every orbit starting at Y converges to X in a finite number of steps. The basin of strong attraction of X is defined as $D(X) = \{Y | Y \to X\}$.

The state X is said to be a k-attractor if, for each $Y \in S_k(X)$

$$\text{sgn}((A * Y)_{ij}) = x_{ij} \tag{5}$$

for $1 \leq i \leq M, 1 \leq j \leq N$.

Obviously, if we assume the DCNN (2) is strict, and state X is a k-attractor, then $-X$ is a k-attractor, too. If the DCNN (2) is strict, then the state X is a k-attractor if and only if, for each $Y \in S_k(X)$

$$x_{ij}(A * Y)_{ij} > 0 \tag{6}$$

3 The k-Attractors

The k-attractor is a very important notation. The following conclusions A and B are given in reference [1]. We will give one example to illustrate the conclusions to be wrong and present two correct conclusions.

Conclusion A[1] (theorem 3 in reference [1]). If a k-attractor exists, we must have $k < (2r+1)^2/2$. Especially, if the shape of cell grid is a rectangular, we must have $k < (r+1)^2/2$.

Conclusion B[1] (theorem 4 in reference [1]). Let X be a k-attractor. Then

(1) it is a fixed point
(2) $S_h(X) \subseteq D(X)$, $1 \leq \forall h \leq k$
(3) $\delta_k^r(X) \subseteq D(X)$, $1 \leq \forall h \leq k$.

Example 1. We assume that S is a rectangular or a torus 3×3 cell grid, $r = 1$, $a_{00} = a$, $a_{01} = -1$, $a_{0-1} = -0.5$, other $a_{ij} = 0$, $-1 \leq i, j \leq 1$, and $|a| < 0.5$. We give respectively the connection matrix of the DCNN as follows, according to the rectangular or torus cell grid S.

	11	12	13	21	22	23	31	32	33
11	a	-1	0	0	0	0	0	0	0
12	-0.5	a	-1	0	0	0	0	0	0
13	0	-0.5	a	0	0	0	0	0	0
21	0	0	0	a	-1	0	0	0	0
22	0	0	0	-0.5	a	-1	0	0	0
23	0	0	0	0	-0.5	a	0	0	0
31	0	0	0	0	0	0	a	-1	0
32	0	0	0	0	0	0	-0.5	a	-1
33	0	0	0	0	0	0	0	-0.5	a

Cell grid S is rectangular

	11	12	13	21	22	23	31	32	33
11	a	-1	-0.5	0	0	0	0	0	0
12	-0.5	a	-1	0	0	0	0	0	0
13	-1	-0.5	a	0	0	0	0	0	0
21	0	0	0	a	-1	-0.5	0	0	0
22	0	0	0	-0.5	a	-1	0	0	0
23	0	0	0	-1	-0.5	a	0	0	0
31	0	0	0	0	0	0	a	-1	-0.5
32	0	0	0	0	0	0	-0.5	a	-1
33	0	0	0	0	0	0	-1	-0.5	a

Cell grid S is torus

Whatever the cell grid S is a rectangular or torus, we can easily test that DCNN is strict, and states $e = (x_{11}, x_{12}, x_{13}, x_{21}, x_{22}, x_{23}, x_{31}, x_{32}, x_{33})^T = (1,1,1,1,1,1,1,1,1)^T$ and $-e$ are a 9-attractor. But neither the state e, nor the state $-e$ is a k-attractor ($|k| \le 8$). This illustrates that neither the conclusion A nor the conclusion B holds. Also, it shows that, even if we assume DCNN (2) is strict, and the conditions in conclusions A and B are satisfied, the corresponding results can not be guaranteed.

In the following, in order to study the properties of k-attractor, we define

$$n = \min_{C(i,j) \in S} |N_r(i,j)| \tag{7}$$

Obviously, the value n not only rely on the neighborhood radius r, but also the shape of cell grid S.

We can easily prove that, if cell grid S is torus, and $\min(M, N) \ge 2r+1$, then $n = (2r+1)^2$, if cell grid S is rectangular, and $\min(M, N) \ge r+1$, then $n = (r+1)^2$.

We give the conclusions on properties of k-attractor as follows.

Theorem. Let the DCNN (2) be strict and exist a k-attractor. If

$$k < n \le M \times N/2 \tag{8}$$

then $k < n/2$. Especially, if the cell grid S is torus, and $\min(M, N) \ge 2r+1$, $k < n \le M \times N/2$, then $k < (2r+1)^2/2$. If the cell grid S is rectangular, and $\min(M, N) \ge r+1$, $k < n \le M \times N/2$, then $k < (r+1)^2/2$.

Proof. Reduction to absurdity. Assume state X to be a k-attractor, $n/2 \le k < n$, and $n = |N_r(i,j)|$.

Since $n/2 \le k < n$ and $n = |N_r(i,j)|$, there exists a subset $N'_r(i,j)$ in $N_r(i,j)$ such that $k = |N'_r(i,j)|$, then $|N_r(i,j) - N'_r(i,j)| = n - k \le k$.

We define state $Y \in B^{M \times N}$, where

$$y_{uv} = \begin{cases} -x_{uv}, & \text{if } C(u,v) \in N'_r(i,j) \\ x_{uv}, & \text{otherwise} \end{cases} \tag{9}$$

Because of $|N_r(i,j) - N'_r(i,j)| \le k$, $k < n \le M \times N/2$, then we can take cells subset $S' \subseteq S - N_r(i,j)$ such that $|S'| = k - |N_r(i,j) - N'_r(i,j)| \ge 0$.

Again, we define $Y' \in B^{M \times N}$, where

$$y'_{uv} = \begin{cases} -x_{uv}, & \text{if } C(u,v) \in S' \cup (N_r(i,j) - N'_r(i,j)) \\ x_{uv}, & \text{otherwise} \end{cases} \tag{10}$$

Obviously, from (9) and (10), we know $Y, Y' \in S_k(X)$.

Since DCNN (2) is strict, and X is a k-attractor, from (6), we have

$$x_{ij}(A*Y)_{ij} > 0.$$

By the definition of Y and Y', when $C(u,v) \in N_r(i,j)$, we have $y'_{uv} = -y_{uv}$. Hence

$$x_{ij}(A*Y')_{ij} = -x_{ij}(A*Y)_{ij} < 0.$$

This is in conflict with $Y' \in S_k(X)$.

Especially, if cell grid S is torus, and $\min(M,N) \geq 2r+1$, $k < n \leq M \times N/2$, then, because of $n = (2r+1)^2$, we have $k < (2r+1)^2/2$.

Also, if cell grid S is rectangular, and $\min(M,N) \geq r+1$, $k < n \leq M \times N/2$, then, because of $n = (r+1)^2$, we have $k < (r+1)^2/2$.

Therefore, the theorem holds.

Remarks 1. The condition DCNN to be strict can not get rid of. Otherwise, we may give a rectangular or a torus $M \times N$ cell grid with 0 template, the 0 template means every element in template to be 0. Moreover, we can test that DCNN has only one $M \times N -$ attractor e, and e is an $M \times N$ dimension vector with every element to be 1, which conflicts with the conclusion $k < n/2$ of theorem.

Remarks 2. The condition $k < n$ can not be got rid of. We may use example 1 to shed light on the condition $k < n$ can not be got rid of.

Remarks 3. The condition $n \leq M \times N/2$ can not be thrown off, either. Otherwise, the theorem does not hold by the example 1.

Certainly, we may consider that $n \leq M \times N/2$ holds in general. This is because, if M or N is large enough, the condition $n \leq M \times N/2$ is guaranteed.

We define $m = |N_r(i,j)|$. From the proof of theorem, we can not hardly find that, if, after we replace n by m, the conditions in the theorem hold, the corresponding results in theorem hold, too.

We give an important corollary as follows. See appendix in reference [1], the proof can be found.

Corollary 1. Let X be a k-attractor of strict DCNN (2), and condition (8) holds, then X is an h-attractor for each integer h ($0 \leq \forall h < k$).

By corollary 1, the following corollary 2 is easily proved.

Corollary 2. Let X be a k-attractor of strict DCNN (2), and condition (8) holds, then state X is a convergent point or a fixed point.

4   Conclusions

Some properties of k-attractor of strict DCNN are presented. If the strict DCNN satisfies some conditions, then a k-attractor X must be a fixed point, and the attraction basins of a k-attractor X includes all states which differ from X in at most

k positions per neighborhood. Also, one examples is given to illustrate that the conditions can not be got rid of.

Acknowledgments. The project was supported by the National Natural Science Foundation of Shaanxi province (Grant No.SJ08-ZT13), and partly supported by Key Laboratory of Advanced Design and Intelligent Computing (Dalian University), Ministry of Education (Grant No.ADIC2010002).

References

1. Perfetti, R.: Some properties of the attractors of discrete-time cellular neural networks. International Journal of Circuit And Applications 23(4), 485–499 (1995)
2. Chua, L.O., Yang, L.: Cellular Neural Networks: Theory. IEEE Trans. Circuits and System-I: Fundamental Theory and Applications 35(10), 1257–1272 (1988)
3. Perfetti, R.: On the Convergence of Reciprocal Discrete-Time Cellular Neural Networks. IEEE Trans. Circuits and System-I: Fundamental Theory and Applications 40(4), 286–287 (1993)
4. Harrer, H., Nossek, J.A.: Discrete-Time Cellular Neural Networks. International Journal of Circuit Theory and Applications 20(4), 453–467 (1992)
5. Ma, R., Zhang, Q., Xu, J.: Convergence of discrete-time cellular neural networks. Chinese Journal of Electronics 11(3), 352–356 (2002)
6. Ma, R., Xi, Y.: Attractors and the attraction basins of discrete-time cellular neural networks. Journal of Systems Engineering and Electronics 16(1), 204–208 (2005)

Artificial Neural Networks Based War Scene Classification Using Various Feature Extraction Methods: A Comparative Study

S. Daniel Madan Raja[1,*], A. Shanmugam[2], and G. Srinitya[1]

[1] Department of Information Technology
[2] Department of Electronics and Communication Engineering
Bannari Amman Institute of Technology, Sathyamangalam, Tamilnadu, India- 638401
cross4u@rediff.com, dras@yahoo.co.in, cross4u@gmail.com

Abstract. In this paper we are trying to identify the best feature extraction method for classifying war scene from natural scene using Artificial Neural Networks. Also, we are proposed a new hybrid method for the same. For this purpose two set of image categories are taken viz., opencountry & war tank. By using the proposed hybrid method and other feature extraction methods like haar wavelet, daubechies (db4) wavelet, Zernike moments, Invariant moments, co-occurrence features & statistical moments, features are extracted from the images/scenes. The extracted features are trained and tested with Artificial Neural Networks (ANN) using feed forward back propagation algorithm. The comparative results are proving efficiency of the proposed hybrid feature extraction method (i.e., the combination of GLCM & Statistical moments) in war scene classification problems. It can be concluded that the proposed work significantly and directly contributes to scene classification and its new applications. The complete work is experimented in Matlab 7.6.0 using real world dataset.

Keywords: Scene Classification, Hybrid Features, Feature Extraction, Artificial Neural Networks.

1 Introduction

Scene and object classification are important research topics in robotics and computer vision. Computer Vision generally focuses on extracting what is where by merely looking at it. Many research problems have been studied and reported by the research community in the recent years. The Scene classification refers to classifying the images into semantic categories (e.g. street, bedroom, mountain, or coast) [1], [2], [3]. Scene classification underlies many problems in visual perception such as object recognition and environment navigation. Classification is one of the several primary categories of machine learning problems [4]. For the indoor - outdoor scene retrieval problem, the authors addressed how high-level scene properties can be inferred from

---

* Corresponding author.

H. Deng et al. (Eds.): AICI 2011, Part III, LNAI 7004, pp. 300–309, 2011.
© Springer-Verlag Berlin Heidelberg 2011

classification of low-level image features [5]. Authors propose an automated method based on the boosting algorithm to estimate image orientations [6]. In [7], Bosch et al. present a scene description and segmentation system capable of recognizing natural objects (e.g., sky, trees, grass) under different outdoor conditions. In paper [8], the authors propose a new technique for the classification of indoor and outdoor images based on edge analysis. Analysis of texture [9] requires the identification of proper attributes or features that differentiate the textures of the image. In our previous work [10][11][12], haar wavelet, daubechies (db4) wavelet, Zernike moments, invariant moments and gray level co-occurrence matrices features are used to classify the war scene from natural scene using artificial neural networks and Support Vector Machines.

This paper presents to identify the best feature extraction method for classifying war scene from natural scene using Artificial Neural Networks with feed forward back propagation. The organization of the paper is as follows: Section 2 describes Various Feature Extraction methodologies, Section 3 elaborates on Artificial Neural Networks, Section 4 explains the proposed work, Section 5 deals with implementation using ANN, Section 6 deals with discussion, and finally Section 7 concludes with conclusion.

2   Feature Extraction Methodologies

2.1   Haar and Daubechies (db4) Wavelet

Haar and Daubechies [13] wavelets are a widely used technique for feature extraction, which are single-level one-dimensional wavelet decomposition and gives both an approximation and detailed coefficients. Approximation coefficients which are of size 128x1 for Haar wavelet and 131x1 for Daubechies wavelet are considered as the feature set for our problem domain. Pictorial representation of approximation coefficients and detailed coefficients of the above mentioned wavelets are shown in the Fig. 1. Hence, features F1 to F128 and F1 to F131 are considered as feature sets for Haar and Daubechies wavelets respectively.

2.2   Zernike Moments

Zernike polynomials were first proposed in 1934 by Zernike [14]. Their moment formulation appears to be one of the most popular, outperforming the alternatives (in terms of noise resilience, information redundancy and reconstruction capability). The use of the Zernike moments have been frequently utilized for a number of image processing and computer vision task [15] [16]. The kernel of Zernike moments is a set of orthogonal Zernike polynomials defined over the polar coordinate space inside a unit circle. The image is considered as a single block, feature vector of 36x1 is extracted. Thus features F1 to F36 are considered as a feature set in Zernike Moments.

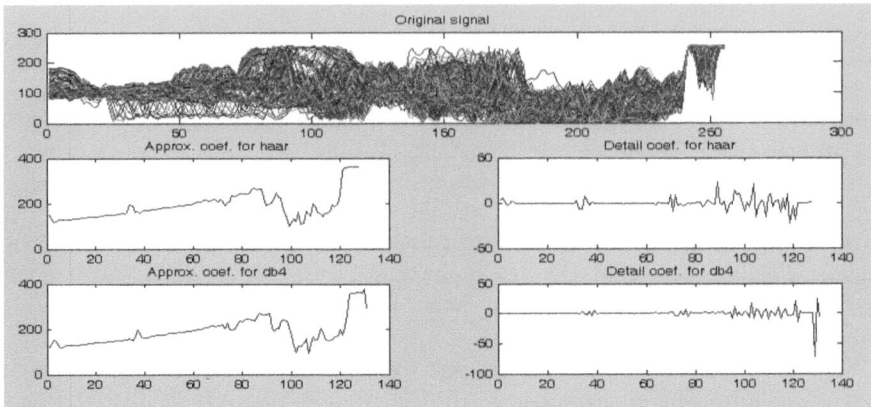

Fig. 1. Original, Approximation and Detailed Coefficients of Haar and Daubechies Wavelets

2.3 Invariant Moments

The Moment invariants are important shape descriptors in computer vision. The set of seven invariant moments ($\phi_1 - \phi_7$) was first proposed by Hu [17] for 2D images which was widely used contour-based shape descriptor. In terms of the normalized central moments, the seven moments are given below:

$$\phi_1 = \eta_{20} + \eta_{02}$$
$$\phi_2 = (\eta_{20} - \eta_{02})^2 + 4\eta_{11}^2$$
$$\phi_3 = (\eta_{30} - 3\eta_{12})^2 + (3\eta_{21} - \eta_{03})^2$$
$$\phi_4 = (\eta_{30} + \eta_{12})^2 + (\eta_{21} + \eta_{03})^2$$
$$\phi_5 = (\eta_{30} - 3\eta_{12})(\eta_{30} + \eta_{12})[(\eta_{30} + \eta_{12})^2 - 3(\eta_{21} + \eta_{03})^2] + (3\eta_{21} - \eta_{03})(\eta_{21} + \eta_{03})[3(\eta_{30} + \eta_{12})^2 - (\eta_{21} + \eta_{03})^2]$$
$$\phi_6 = (\eta_{20} - \eta_{02})[(\eta_{30} + \eta_{12})^2 - (\eta_{21} + \eta_{03})^2] + 4\eta_{11}(\eta_{30} + \eta_{12})(\eta_{21} + \eta_{03})$$
$$\phi_7 = (3\eta_{21} - \eta_{03})(\eta_{30} + \eta_{12})[(\eta_{30} + \eta_{12})^2 - 3(\eta_{21} + \eta_{03})^2] + (3\eta_{12} - \eta_{30})(\eta_{21} + \eta_{03})[3(\eta_{30} + \eta_{12})^2 - (\eta_{21} + \eta_{03})^2]$$

The images are divided into four equal blocks and extracted seven values from each block. Thus, 4x7=28 features are used to represent an input image. Thus features F1 to F28 are considered as a feature set in invariant moments.

2.4 Gray Level Co-occurrence Matrix (GLCM)

The procedure for extracting textural properties of image in the spatial domain was presented by Haralick *et al* [18]. The Gray Level Co-occurrence Matrix (GLCM) method considers the spatial relationship between pixels of different gray levels. The method calculates a GLCM by calculating how often a pixel with a certain intensity i occurs in relation with another pixel j at a certain distance d and orientation θ. For instance, if the value of a pixel is 1 the method looks, for instance, the number of times this pixel has 2 in the right side. Each element (i, j) in the GLCM is the sum of the number of times that the pixel with value i occurred in the specified relationship to a pixel with value j in the raw image.

In this work, we are using eight texture descriptors i.e., energy; inertia; entropy; homogeneity; maxprob; contrast; inverse; correlation. Co-occurrence matrices are calculated for four directions: 0^0, 45^0, 90^0 and 135^0 degrees. Thus features F1 to F32 are considered as a feature set in GLCM.

2.5 Statistical Moments

We compute statistical central moments of image histogram. We compute upto 12 statistical moment of histogram whose components are in vector P. The length of P must equal to 256. The features F1 to F12 are extracted as follows:

> F1 = Mean
> F2 = Variance
> F3 = 3rd Order moment
> $\cdots$
> F12= 12th Order Moment.

2.6 Hybrid Features

In Hybrid 44 feature extraction method, we are considering all the features of Gray Level Co-occurrence Matrix (GLCM) method (i.e. eight texture descriptors are calculated for four directions: 0^0, 45^0, 90^0 and 135^0 degrees) and Statistical Moment features (i.e. 12 statistical moments). So the total feature of Hybrid 44 is 44 (F1 to F44).

In Hybrid 22 feature extraction method, we are considering 16 features from Gray Level Co-occurrence Matrix (GLCM) method (i.e. four texture descriptors are calculated for four directions: 0^0, 45^0, 90^0 and 135^0 degrees) and the first 6 features from Statistical Moment features. So,22 features are considered as a feature set for Hybrid 22(F1 to F22).

3 Artificial Neural Networks

The first neurological network model was introduced by McCulloch and Pitts [19]. The Hebbian rule[20] represents neural learning procedures, which implies that the connection between two neurons is strengthened when both neurons are active at the same time. In [21], Werbos developed a learning procedure called backpropagation of error. Later on, the backpropagation of error learning procedure was separately developed and published by parallel distributed processing group [22], in which weights and biases are adjusted by error-derivative (delta) vectors backpropagated through the network. Backpropagation is commonly applied to feedforward multilayer networks. Sometimes this rule is called the generalized delta rule. Numerous ANN models are constructed; the differences in them might be the functions, the accepted values, the topology, the learning algorithms, etc.

In this work we use feed-forward artificial neural network using backpropagation algorithm. This is the most widely used neural network model, and its design consists of one input layer, at least one hidden layer, and one output layer as shown in "Fig. 2". Each layer is made up of non-linear processing units called neurons, and the connections between neurons in successive layers carry associated weights. Connections are directed and allowed only in the forward direction, e.g. from input to hidden, or from hidden layer to a subsequent hidden or output layer. Back-propagation is a gradient-descent algorithm that minimizes the error between the output of the training input/output pairs and the actual network output.

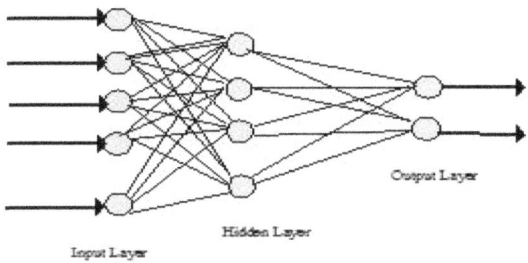

Input Layer   Hidden Layer   Output Layer

Fig. 2. Simple Neural network Structure

Back propagation algorithm is applied for learning the samples, Tan-sigmoid and log-sigmoid functions are applied in hidden layer and output layer respectively, Gradient descent is used for adjusting the weights as training methodology.

4 Proposed Work

In classification, a classifier is trained to identify a type of example or differentiate between examples that fall in separate categories. In the case of computer vision, the examples are representations of photographic images and the task of the classifier is to indicate whether or not a specific object or phenomena of interest is present in the image. In order to successfully accomplish this, the classifier must have sufficient prior knowledge about the appearance of the image/scene. This paper is trying to identify the best combination of feature extraction method and classifier to recognize the scenes of two different categories called 'Opencountry' and 'War tank scene' i.e. War tanks in opencountry. The detailed work flow of the proposed system is shown in "Fig. 3".

The sample images are taken from the Computational Visual Cognition Laboratory (opencountry) [23] and (War Tank scenes) is collected from the sources [24-33] with 200 samples each. Sample scenes are given in "Fig. 4" and "Fig. 5".

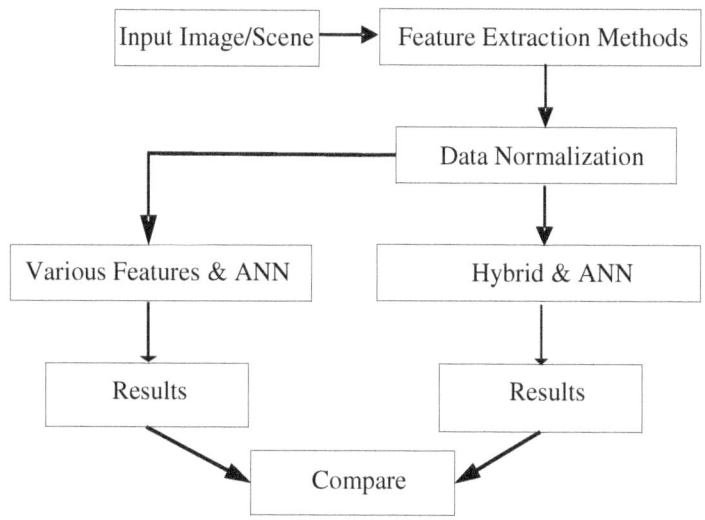

Fig. 3. Detailed Description of Proposed Work

Fig. 4. Sample images of 'Opencountry' category

Fig. 5. Sample images of *'War Tank''* category

Haar wavelets, Daubechies (db4) wavelets, Zernike Moments, Invariant Moments, GLCM Features, Statistical moments, and Hybrid features (which combine GLCM and statistical moments) are used to extract features from the images/scenes. The total numbers of features extracted from the images/scenes using all the mentioned feature extraction methodologies are given in the Table 1.

Table 1. Total number of features extracted

Feature Extraction Methodology	Number of Features
Haar Wavelet(HW)	128
Daubechies(db4)wavelet (DW)	131
Zernike Moments(ZM)	36
Invariant Moments(IM)	28
Gray Level Co-occurrence Matrix (GLCM)	32
Statistical Moments(SM)	12
Hybrid 44(GLCM+SM)	44
Hybrid 22(Reduced feature set of GLCM+SM)	22

Normalization is then applied using Zero-mean normalization method in order to maintain the data within the specified range and also found suitable to improve the performance of the classifier.

5   Implementation Using ANN

Neural classifier is trained and tested with all the extracted features individually to recognize and classify the scenes. In Training phase, 200 samples are used including 100 samples from 'Opencountry' and 100 samples from 'War Tank Scenes'. In testing phase, 200 more samples are used including 100 samples from 'Opencountry' and 100 samples from 'War Tank Scenes'. The neural structure is normalized such that it gives the maximum performance. The detailed results are given in Table 2.

6   Discussion

This paper discusses to identify the best feature extraction method for classifying the war scenes from natural scene using Artificial Neural Networks. The efficiency of the proposed hybrid features is compared with the commonly used feature extraction methodologies like, Haar wavelets, Daubechies wavelets, Zernike Moments, Invariant Moments, GLCM Features and Statistical Moments. The sample images are taken from the Computational Visual Cognition Laboratory [23] and [24-33]. Features are extracted from the scene categories and raw images are taken without any preprocessing steps to make the system robust to real scene environments. The pictorial representation which shows the comparative study of the performances of various feature extraction methods using Artificial Neural Network are shown in "Fig. 6" and "Fig. 7". The proposed Hybrid 44 and Hybrid 22 gives 88% and 88.5% of classification rate which are highest performance among all the features.

Table 2. Performance using Artificial Neural Networks

Feature Extraction	Open Country		War Tank		Classification %	Exec. Time (in Sec)
	TP	TN	TP	TN		
Haar	80	20	71	29	75.5	52.89
Daubechies (db4)	77	23	68	32	72.5	60.49
Zernike	72	28	65	35	68.5	398.61
Invariant	53	47	64	36	58.5	41.32
GLCM	82	18	91	9	86.5	68.84
Statistical Moment	100	0	57	43	78.5	921.9
Hybrid 44	80	20	96	4	88	68.11
Hybrid 22	84	16	93	7	88.5	69.12

TP = True Positive & TN = True Negative.

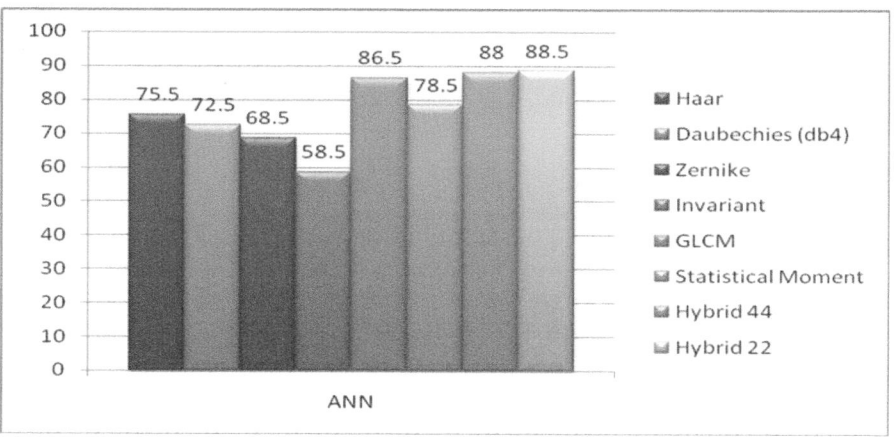

Fig. 6. Performance of Various Feature Extraction Methods

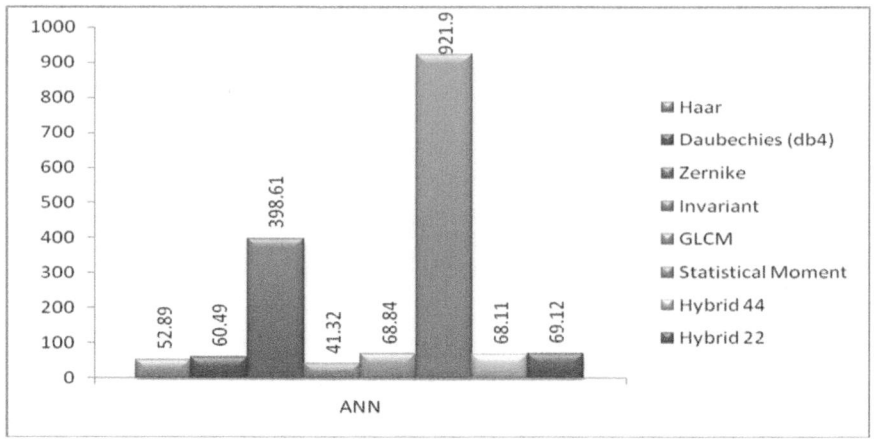

Fig. 7. Execution Time (in Seconds) for Various Feature Extraction Methods

7   Conclusion

This paper concentrates on identifying the best feature extraction method using Artificial Neural Networks in war scene classification problem. The results are proving that Hybrid 44 & Hybrid 22 features based ANN is giving higher classification rate i.e. 88% and 88.5% compared with other feature extraction methods in war scene categorization problems. This work can be further extended to classify war scene categories using various feature extraction methodologies and classifiers. The complete work is implemented using Matlab 7.6.0.

Acknowledgement. The authors are extremely thankful to Computational Visual Cognition Laboratory and websites mentioned in the references [24-33].

References

[1] Gokalp, D., Aksoy, S.: Scene Classification Using Bag-of-Regions Representations. In: IEEE Conference on Computer Vision and Pattern Recognition, CVPR, pp. 1–8 (2007)

[2] Vailaya, A., Figueiredo, A., Jain, A., Zhang, H.: Image classification for content-based indexing. IEEE Transactions on Image Processing 10, 117–129 (2001)

[3] Bosch, A., Zisserman, A., Muñoz, X.: Scene classification using a hybrid enerative/discriminative approach. IEEE Trans. on Pattern Analysis and Machine Intelligence 30(4), 712–727 (2008)

[4] Chella, A., Frixione, M., Gaglio, S.: Understanding dynamic scenes. Artificial Intelligence 123, 89–132 (2000)

[5] Szummer, M., Picard, R.W.: Indoor-Outdoor Image Classification. In: Proceedings of the 1998 International Workshop on Content-Based Access of Image and Video Databases (CAIVD 1998), January 03, p. 42 (1998)

[6] Zhang, L., Li, M., Zhang, H.-J.: Boosting Image Orientation Detection with Indoor vs. Outdoor Classification. In: Proceedings of the Sixth IEEE Workshop on Applications of Computer Vision, December 03-04, p. 95 (2002)

[7] Bosch, A., Munoz, X., Freixenet, J.: Segmentation and description of natural outdoor scenes. Image and Vision computing 25, 727–740 (2007)

[8] Payne, A., Singh, S.: Indoor vs outdoor scene classification in digital photographs. Pattern Recognition 38, 1533–1545 (2005)

[9] Arivazhagan, S., Ganesan, L.: Texture Segmentation Using Wavelet Transform. Pattern Recognition Letters 24(16), 3197–3203 (2003)

[10] Daniel Madan Raja, S., Shanmugam, A.: ANN and SVM Based War Scene Classification using Wavelet Features: A Comparative Study. Journal of Computational Information Systems 7(5), 1402–1411 (2011)

[11] Daniel Madan Raja, S., Shanmugam, A.: Zernike Moments Based War Scene Classification using ANN and SVM: A Comparative Study. Journal of Information and Computational Science 8(2), 212–222 (2011)

[12] Daniel Madan Raja, S., Shanmugam, A.: ANN and SVM based War Scene Classification using Invariant Moments and GLCM Features: A Comparative Study. In: Proceedings of 3rd International Conference on Machine Learning and Computing (ICMLC 2011), February 26-28, vol. 3, pp. 508–512 (2011)

[13] Wang, J.Z., Wiederhold, G., Firschein, O., Wei, S.X.: Content-Based Image Indexing and Searching Using Daubechies' Wavelets. Int. J. on Digital Libraries 1(4), 311–328 (1997)

[14] Zernike, F.: Beugungstheorie des schneidenverfahrens und seiner verbesserten form, derphasenkontrastmethode. Physica 1, 689–704 (1934)

[15] Khotanzad, A., Hong, Y.H.: Invariant Image Recognition by Zernike Moments. IEEE Transactions on Pattern Analysis and Machine Intelligence 12(5), 489–497 (1990)

[16] Teh, C.H., Chin, R.T.: On image analysis by the methods of moments. IEEE Trans. Pattern Anal. Machine Intell. 10, 496–512 (1988)

[17] Hu, M.K.: Visual pattern recognition by moments invariants. IRE Trans. Information Theory 8, 179–187 (1962)

[18] Haralick, R.M., Shanmugam, K., Dinstein, I.: Textural features for image classification. IEEE Transactions on Systems, Man, and Cybernetics 3(6), 610–621 (1973)

[19] McCulloch, W., Pitts, W.: A Logical Calculus of the Ideas Immanent in Nervous Activity. Bulletin of Mathematical Biophysics 5, 115–133 (1943)

[20] Hebb, D.O.: The Organization of Behavior: A Neuropsychological Theory. Wiley, New York (1949)

[21] Werbo, P.J.: Beyond Regression: New Tools for Prediction and Analysis in the Behavioral Sciences. PhD thesis, Harvard University (1974)

[22] Rumelhart, D., Hinton, G., Williams, R.: Learning representations by back-propagating errors. Nature 323, 533–536 (1986)

[23] http://cvcl.mit.edu/database.htm

[24] http://www.archives.gov/research/ww2/photos/

[25] http://www.militaryphotos.net/

[26] http://www.military.com/

[27] http://www.worldwar1.com/pharc.htm

[28] http://www.gwpda.org/

[29] http://www.historyofwar.org/

[30] http://en.wikipedia.org/wiki/Tanks_in_World_War_I

[31] http://en.wikipedia.org/wiki/Tanks_in_the_Cold_War

[32] http://en.wikipedia.org/wiki/Tanks_in_World_War_II

[33] http://en.wikipedia.org/wiki/Tank_classification

Resolve of Multicomponent Mixtures Using Voltammetry and a Hybrid Artificial Neural Network Method

Shouxin Ren and Ling Gao

Department of Chemistry, Inner Mongolia University
Huhhot, Inner Mongolia, China
cersx@mail.imu.edu.cn, lingyuxi@hotmail.com

Abstract. This paper suggests a novel method named DOSC-DF-GRNN, which is based on generalized regression neural network (GRNN) combined with direct orthogonal signal correction (DOSC) and data fusion (DF) to enhance the ability to extract characteristic information and improve the quality of the regression for the simultaneous simultaneous diffrential pulse voltammetric determination of Ni(II), Zn(II) and Co(II). In this case, the relative standard errors of prediction (RSEP) for total elements with DOSC-DF-GRNN, DOSC-GRNN, DF-GRNN, GRNN and PLS were 9.70, 10.8, 11.5, 12.2 and 12.3 %, respectively. Experimental results showed the DOSC-DF-GRNN method was successful for diffrential pulse voltammetric determination even when there were severe overlaps of voltammograms existed and was the best among the five methods.

Keywords: Voltammetry, Artificial neural network, Direct orthogonal signal correction, Data fusion, Generalized regression neural network.

1 Introduction

One of the major difficulties in performing multicomponent analysis using conventional voltammetry is to discriminate overlapped peaks of multi-components with very similar half-wave potentials. The problem of how to resolve overlapped signals is very critical and has not been fully solved yet. Artificial neural networks (ANN) are a form of artificial intelligence that mathematically simulate biological nervous system [1, 2]. Recently, it has been proposed that ANN be used to solve regression problems by acting as non-parametric calibration methods, which have the ability to learn from a set of examples without requiring any knowledge of the model type and generalize this knowledge to new situation [3]. Currently the most widely used ANN is a multilayer feedforward network (MLFN) with back propagation algorithm (BP). However, the BP-MLFN method often has the deficiency of slow convergence, is prone to the existence of many local minima during training, and tends to overfit. Much attention has been paid to solve these problems and to facilitate the training process into the global minimum. Generalized regression neural network (GRNN) [4, 5] is among the most efficient solutions and applied in this paper. The GRNN is a feedforward network based on non–linear regression theory and a kind of normalized radial basis function network. The main drawback of GRNN is that they

H. Deng et al. (Eds.): AICI 2011, Part III, LNAI 7004, pp. 310–317, 2011.
© Springer-Verlag Berlin Heidelberg 2011

suffer seriously from the curse of dimensionality; GRNN cannot ignore irrelevant input and have shown difficulty in handling a large number of input data. In order to enhance the predictive ability of a multivariate calibration models, raw data are often pre-processed to eliminate irrelevant information prior to calibration. In order to avoid removing relevant information for prediction, Wold and his coworkers developed a novel pre-processing technique for raw data called orthogonal signal correction (OSC) [6]. The goal of this algorithm is to remove information in the response matrix D, which is mathematically orthogonal and unrelated to concentration matrix C. Westerhuis and his coworkers introduced an interesting OSC method named direct orthogonal signal correction (DOSC) [7]. DOSC is also applied to remove structured noise that is extraneous to the concentration variables. In order to eliminate noise and irrelevant information, wavelet transform (WT) and wavelet packet transform (WPT) denoising methods were used as a preprocessing step to remove noise and irrelevant information. WT represents relatively recent mathematical developments, and can offer a successful time-frequency signal for enhanced information localization [8-11]. WT and WPT have the ability to provide information in the time and frequency domain, so they can be used to convert data from their original domain into the wavelet domain, where the representation of a signal is sparse and it is easier to remove noise from the signal.

Analytical signals are inherently multiscale, thus, developing multiscale approaches for data analysis and modeling relies on the extraction of various pieces of information from different wavelet scales, which is a challenging task. In fact, integrating the information from different wavelet scales is like processing large amounts of data from several sources by data fusion. In essence, combining different sources of information would lead to better information. While data fusion has been applied in military affairs, robotics, remote sensing, image analysis and computer science, there are very few publication in the literature that address the utilities of data fusion in chemistry [12].

A novel approach named DOSC-DF-GRNN tested here is the combination of GRNN with DOSC and DF to eliminate noise and model linear and non-linear information and is proposed for analyzing overlapping voltammogram. This method combines the techniques of DOSC and data fusion with GRNN regression to enhance the ability to extract characteristic information and improve the quality of regression. Wavelet analysis and ANN are two of the most successful advances in the field of applied mathematics in the last few years. The DOSC-DF-GRNN method is a hybrid technique that combines the best properties of the three methods and dramatically increases the problem-solving capacity. This seems to be the first application of a combined DOSC-DF-GRNN approach to simultaneous diffrential pulse voltammetric determination of Ni(II), Zn(II) and Co(II).

2 Theory

2.1 Generalized Regression Neural Network

The GRNN is a kind of radial basis function network. Each GRNN consists of four layers: the input layer, the pattern layer, the summation layer and the output layer.

The input layer does not process information; it serves only to distribute the input data among the pattern layer. The input and pattern layer are fully connected. Each node on the pattern layer represents a radial basis function. A general Gaussian kernel function is used in the pattern layer:

$$H_i(X) = \exp\left(\frac{-(X - C_i)^T (X - C_i)}{2\sigma^2}\right) \tag{1}$$

where the vector X denote the noisy input data i.e. a current matrix of voltammograms constructed by 9 samples. The vector C_i represents the ith input pattern, that is, a current vector constructed by sample i. The width σ of the Gaussian kernel function is a parameter controlling the smoothness properties of the function and is called smoothing factor σ. Processing for summation layer nodes is very simple. The dot product is performed between the weights W_i and the output signals $H_i(x)$ from the pattern layer nodes in such a way: $\sum_{i=1}^{N} W_i H_i(x)$, where N is the number of training pairs. The $\sum_{i=1}^{N} H_i(x)$ were calculated by a single special node in the summation layer. The summation and pattern layers are fully connected. The weights between pattern and summation layer are just as same as the target vectors t_i. The summation layer consists of two types of nodes termed A and B. The A node computes the summation of each kernel function weighted by the known concentration: $\sum_{i=1}^{N} t_i H_i(x)$; while the B node simply computes the summation of the distance: $\sum_{i=1}^{N} H_i(x)$. The final layer in the GRNN is the output layer consisting of one node for each variable to be investigated. Output layers output predicted concentrations of the three kinds of analytes. In this case, the output layer performs the actual divisions. The output node divides B into A to provide the predicted concentration: $\hat{Y}(x) = \dfrac{\sum_{i=1}^{N} t_i H_i(x)}{\sum_{i=1}^{N} H_i(x)}$. The summation layer always has exactly one more node than the output layer. The standard equation of the GRNN is given by:

$$\hat{Y}(X) = \frac{\sum_{i=1}^{N} t_i \exp\left(\frac{-(X - C_i)^T (X - C_i)}{2\sigma^2}\right)}{\sum_{i=1}^{N} \exp\left(\frac{-(X - C_i)^T (X - C_i)}{2\sigma^2}\right)} \tag{2}$$

2.2 Direct Orthogonal Signal Correction

The DOSC algorithm is based on least squares steps to find components that are orthogonal to matrix C and account for the largest variation of D. This is a single process that does not require iterations. DOSC as a necessary pre-processing method can effectively removes structured noise, which can come from different sources such as baseline, instrument variation and measurement conditions, interfering physical and chemical process and other interferences. The theoretical background of DOSC was described in detail by the authors of this paper [11].

2.3 Wavelet Multiscale and Data Fusion

The basic idea of wavelet analysis is multiresolution, which is known as the simultaneous appearance of a signal on multiple scales. The concept of multiresolution was introduced by Mallat [9], and it provided a powerful framework for understanding wavelet decomposition. Mallat utilized the attractive feature of multiresolution analysis to construct an efficient algorithm named Mallat's Pyramid algorithm for decomposing a signal into its wavelet coefficients and reconstructing the signal from the coefficients. The fast discrete wavelet transform (FDWT) can be implemented by means of the Mallat's pyramid algorithm [9], which is more efficient than computing a full set of inner products. The theoretical background of FDWT was described in detail by the authors of this paper [10]. The multiresolution of WT means an original signal is decomposed into multiple scales. Integrating the information from different wavelet scales is like processing large amounts of data from several sources by data fusion. The technique of data fusion enables integrating the information from different wavelet scales to obtain a GRNN model.

2.4 DOSC-DF-GRNN Algorithm

Details about the DOSC-DF-GRNN algorithm are presented below:

(1) The whole set of voltammagrams obtained from the standard mixture is used to build the experimental data matrix D. Before starting the DOSC-DF-GRNN calculation, mean centering and data standardization are performed.

(2) The DOSC method is one of most promising signal correction tools. With DOSC, the D matrix is corrected by subtracting the structured noise that is orthogonal to the concentration matrix C. The structured noise belongs to system variation unrelated to predictive components. The DOSC method indeed removes redundant information that is not necessary for prediction, and the DOSC-corrected data only contain elements that are important for prediction. Sometimes a second DOSC component needs to be removed from the first DOSC component filtered data by applying the next filtering cycle and so on. The number of DOSC components is the number of times that DOSC is applied to raw matrix D and varies from 1 to 3 in general. In order to obtain the best corrective power of DOSC, the optimal DOSC parameters such as the number of DOSC components and tolerance factor must be selected by trial and error.

(3) The DOSC-corrected data matrix is transformed to the WT domain by Mallat's algorithm. In the wavelet domain, it is easier to perform feature extraction, data

compression, and denoising. Due to its multiscale nature, the original signal is decomposed and separated into a set of multifrequency scales, each of which is treated as a separate source of information. In this paper a scale-dependent threshold method is performed. The thresholding operation is implemented in each scale by HYBRID soft thresholding method. The wavelet coefficients of approximation and detail are reconstructed separately from a different scale denoised block. The reconstructed data in each scale, including the details at all levels, and the approximation at the coarsest level can be treated as separate sources of information. The augmented matrix can be constructed easily due to every blocks keep the same data points as the original spectra data. In essence, this process of data processing is one kind of data fusion technique. The large amount of data from different sources can be easily combined by means of data fusion techniques to obtain a better regression model.

(4) The augmented matrix that resulting from data fusion was used as input data to GRNN. The training of the GRNN model is performed with the augmented current matrix of voltammograms and the concentration matrix as inputs. The concentrations of the predictive components can be calculated based on the trained GRNN model. The optimum kernel width σ parameter is the crucial element in GRNN. In this case, the kernel width σ parameter is selected by trial and error. Currently, there is no theoretical guidance on selecting the optimal values of σ, which depends on problem and data itself.

According to these algorithms, three programs, PGRNN, PDFGRNN and PDOSCDFGRNN were designed to perform relative calculations.

3 Experimental

A training set of 16 samples formed by mixing Ni(II), Zn(II) and Co(II) was designed according to four-level orthogonal array design with the L_{16} (4^5) matrix. Differential pulse voltammograms (DPV) were recorded between -700 mv and -1400 mv at 4.0 mv intervals. The whole set of voltammograms obtained at 16 standard mixtures was used to build up the matrix D. According to the same procedures a D_u matrix for unknown mixtures was built up. The following instrumental parameters were used to record the DPV: scan rate, 10 mV/s; pulse amplitude, 50 mV; sample width, 20 ms; pulse width, 50 ms; pulse period, 200 ms.

4 Results and Discussion

4.1 Wavelet Multiscale Properties

In order to visually inspect the multiscale property of WT, the scales (A_7, D_7, D_6, D_5, D_4, D_3, D_2 and D_1) were converted back to its original domain by Mallat's algorithm to retain the original length of the signal. The reconstructed components (Ra_7, Rd_7, Rd_6, Rd_5, Rd_4, Rd_3, Rd_2 and Rd_1) are shown in Figure 1. These reconstructed components are mutually orthogonal and contribute to the original signal from different scales having different frequencies. From Figure 1, it is fairly obvious that Rd_1, Rd_2 and Rd_3 centered in the high frequency ranges resemble noise and should be eliminated. Ra_7 appears in the lowest frequency ranges,which often contains backgrounds and drifts. Ra_7 also contains the useful information too, so that to eliminate Ra_7 is in danger of losing valuable information. Thus,in this case, the scale (Ra_7) is selected and added the augmentation data matrix. Other scales (Rd_7, Rd_6, Rd_5 Rd_4 and Rd_7) contain pertinent information and should be retained, because analytical signals usuallyare found in the low frequency ranges.

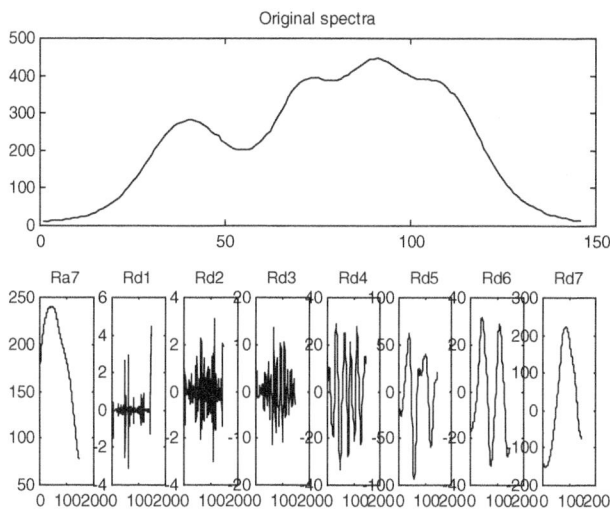

Fig. 1. The original signals and their reconstructed components from different wavelet scales

4.2 DOSC-DF-GRNN

In order to optimize the DOSC-DF-GRNN method, six parameters, i.e., the number of DOSC components, tolerance factor, wavelet functions, decomposition level, and thresholding methods and the width (σ) of GRNN are required to be optimized by trial and error. It is possible to use the absolute and relative standard errors of prediction (SEP and RSEP) of total elements [14] to find the optimum choice of parameters. By optimization as mentioned above, the number of DOSC factor = 1, tolerance factor = 0.001, Db 4, L = 7, HYBRID thresholding and σ=1.6 were selected as optimal parameters. A training set of 9 samples formed by the mixture of Ni(II), Zn(II) and Co(II) was designed based on a three-level orthogonal array design with the $L_9(3^4)$ matrix. The experimental data obtained from the training set were arranged in matrix D, where each column corresponded to the current of different mixtures at a given potential and each row represented the voltammogram obtained at a given mixture.

Using program PDOSCDFGRNN, the concentrations of Ni(II), Zn(II) and Co(II) for a test set were calculated. The experimental results showed that the SEP and RSEP for total elements were 1.439×10^{-5} mol l^{-1} and 9.7 %.

4.3 A Comparison o f PLS, DOSC-DF-GRNN, DF-GRNN, DOSC-GRNN and GRNN

An intensive comparative study was performed between five methods (DOSC-DF-GRNN, DF-GRNN, DOSC-GRNN, GRNN and PLS) with a set of synthetic unknown samples. The SEP and RSEP for the five methods are given in Table 1.

Table 1. SEP and RSEP values for Ni(II), Zn(II) and Co(II) system by the five methods

Method	SEP (10^{-5}molL^{-1})				RSEP (%)			
	Ni(II)	Zn(II)	Co(II)	Total elements	Ni(II)	Zn(II)	Co(II)	Total elements
DOSC-DF-GRNN	1.481	1.498	1.332	1.44	9.98	10.1	8.98	9.70
DOSC-GRNN	1.426	1.826	1.547	1.61	9.61	12.3	10.4	10.8
DF-GRNN	1.937	1.452	1.692	1.71	13.1	9.79	11.4	11.5
GRNN	2.022	1.581	1.776	1.80	13.6	10.7	12.0	12.2
PLS	1.867	1.662	1.953	1.83	12.5	11.2	13.2	12.3

DF-GRNN method combines the idea of data fusion with GRNN. DOSC-GRNN method combines the idea of DOSC with GRNN. Experimental results indicated that DOSC-GRNN method gave better results than that of DF-GRNN method. Hence, in this case DOSC pre-processing method is the most important step in the analysis of multivariate data. DOSC-DF-GRNN is a method that combines the advantages of the three techniques to effectively eliminate noise and unrelated information and to improve the performance of regression. The RSEP values for total elements using DOSC-DF-GRNN, DOSC-GRNN, DF-GRNN, GRNN and PLS were 9.70, 10.8, 11.5, 12.2 and 12.3%, respectively. These results indicate that   DOSC-DF-GRNN has the best performance among the five methods. Thus, it can be concluded that the DOSC-DF-GRNN method is successful at the simultaneous voltammetric determination of overlapping voltammograms.

5 Conclusion

A method named DOSC-DF-GRNN was developed for multicomponent differential voltammetric determination. This approach combines DOSC, DF and GRNN to enhance the ability to eliminate noise and unrelated information and improve the quality of regression method. Experimental results demonstrated that the DOSC-DF-GRNN approach was successful and delivered more satisfying results among the five methods.

Acknowledgment. The authors would like to thank National Natural Science Foundation of China (21067006 and 60762003) and Natural Science Foundation of Inner Mongolia (2009MS 0209) for financial support of this project.

References

1. Marini, F., Magri, A.L., Bucci, R., Magri, A.D.: Use of different artificial neural networks to resolve binary blends of monocultivar Italian olive oils. Anal. Chim. Acta 599(2), 232–240 (2007)
2. Verikas, A., Bacauskien, M.: Using artificial neural networks for process and system modeling. Chemomotr. Intell. Lab. Syst. 67, 187–191 (2003)
3. Choi, S.W., Lee, D., Park, J.H., Lee, I.B.: Nonlinear regression using RBFN with linear submodels. Chemometr, Intell. Lab. Syst. 65, 191–208 (2003)
4. Specht, D.F.: Probabilistic neural networks. Neural Networks 3, 109–118 (1990)
5. Specht, D.F.: A general regression neural network. IEEE Transactions on Neural Network 2(6), 568–576 (1991)
6. Wold, S., Antti, H., Lindgren, F., Ohman, J.: Orthogonal signal correction of near-infrared spectra. Chemometr. Intell. Lab. Syst. 44, 175–185 (1998)
7. Westerhuis, J.A., de Jong, S., Smilde, A.G.: Direct orthogonal signal correction. Chemometr. Intell. Lab. Syst. 56, 13–25 (2001)
8. Daubechies, I.: Orthogonal bases of compactly supported wavelets. Commun. Pure Appl. Math. 41, 909–996 (1988)
9. Mallat, S., Hwang, W.L.: Singularity detection and processing with wavelets. IEEE Trans. Inform. Theory 38(2), 617–643 (1992)
10. Ren, S.X., Gao, L.: Simultaneous quantitative analysis of overlapping spectrophotometric signals using wavelet multiresolution analysis and partial least squares. Talanta 50(6), 1163–1173 (2000)
11. Gao, L., Ren, S.X.: Combining direct orthogonal signal correction and wavelet packet transform with partial least squares to analyze overlapping voltammograms of nitroaniline isomers. Electrochimica Acta 54, 3161–3168 (2009)
12. Ruhm, H.: Sensor fusion and data fusion-mapping and reconstruction. Measurement 40, 145–157 (2007)

Application of Neural Network in Trajectory Planning of the Entry Vehicle for Variable Targets

Bin Zhang, Shilu Chen, and Min Xu

College of Astronautics, Northwestern Polytechnical University, Xi'an, China
zb.my@163.com

Abstract. A method for onboard generation of entry trajectory for variable targets is discussed. Conventional trajectory planning algorithms can only be used for the fixed terminal conditions without considering the variable targets. In case the vehicle needs to alert the entry trajectory due to damage or effectors failure, the entry guidance system must real-time design a feasible entry trajectory according to another feasible landing site from current flight conditions. The conventional approaches must be augmented to provide the real-time redesign capability for variable targets, and the redesign trajectory would also satisfy all path constraints and altered terminal conditions. This paper makes use of the neural network as a major controller to overcome this problem. The redesign trajectory problems and control parameter generations online problems can be transformed into the neural network offline training problem, given the initial conditions and the selected terminal conditions. Numerical simulations with a reusable launch vehicle model for various terminal conditions are presented to demonstrate the capability and effectiveness of the approach.

Keywords: trajectory planning, neural network, entry, variable targets, onboard, real-time.

1 Introduction

An important capability for the next generation entry vehicle is to autonomous return from any initial states, meaning that the guidance system is able to fast design a complete and feasible entry trajectory online from any initial position and velocity without any intervention. This guidance system can provide some benefits unmatched by the current guidance system. It would allow a vehicle can abort any abnormal fly mission during ascent or entry and choice the available landing site from current fly conditions without waiting for the guidance updates from the ground. It would also require significantly less the pre-mission analysis and planning for different missions, reduce dramatically the re-occurring optional costs associated with entry guidance.

Conventional approach for entry mission operation consists of offline reference trajectory design and onboard tracking of the reference trajectory [1]. Before every mission, the reference trajectory would be accomplished on the ground and never be altered, which hasn't apparent satisfactory the requirements of the next generation entry vehicle. Under the supports of the Advanced Guidance and Control (AG&C) Project [2, 3], many advanced guidance technologies have been developed in recent

H. Deng et al. (Eds.): AICI 2011, Part III, LNAI 7004, pp. 318–325, 2011.

years. Gamble *at el* proposed an analytic predictor-corrector algorithm and a numeric predictor-corrector algorithm for the aero-assist flight experiment [4]. Fury *at el* presented an atmospheric guidance for steering the Kistler K-1[5], a fully reusable launch vehicle prior to deployment of the stabilization parachute with numeric predictor-corrector technology. Youssef and Chowdhry described a predictor-corrector guidance algorithm for X-33 [6]. Saraf *at el* designed an acceleration guidance algorithm for entry vehicle [7]. Zimmerman and Dukeman presented an automated method to design entry trajectory with heating constraints [8]. Z Shen and P Lu sought an approach for onboard generation of three dimensional entry trajectories [9].

An ideal algorithm for onboard planning trajectory should satisfy these requirements: guaranteed satisfaction of all inequality constraints, reliability, efficiency, less computational load and precise flight termination. The entry dynamic model is a typical nonlinear multi-input-multi-output (MIMO) system. Numerical predictor-corrector algorithms require repeated integration of the equations of motion, and conventional approaches suffer from the highly constrained nonlinear MIMO system, and don't consider the trajectory redesign capability for variable targets. Hence, new guidance system that enables fully autonomous and adaptive entry guidance should be searched. In this paper, a real-time redesign trajectory algorithm for variable targets based on artificial neural network (ANN) is described. An onboard three-dimensional entry trajectory generation algorithm is used to obtain a set of training space to train the ANN. Numerical simulations show that trained neural network controller can handle the complicated non-linear MIMO system, design an approximate optimal feasible trajectory, and given a set of landing sites, the neural network controller can generate a series of control commands to maneuver the vehicle to reach the desired terminal conditions while imposing all the trajectory constraints.

2 The Entry Dynamics

The following normalized three-dimensional point-mass dynamics of the vehicle over a spherical non-rotating Earth are discussed.

$$\dot{r} = V \sin \gamma \tag{1}$$

$$\dot{\theta} = \frac{V \cos \gamma \sin \psi}{r \cos \phi} \tag{2}$$

$$\dot{\phi} = \frac{V \cos \gamma \cos \psi}{r} \tag{3}$$

$$\dot{V} = -D - \sin \gamma / r^2 \tag{4}$$

$$\dot{\gamma} = (L/V)\cos \sigma + \left(V^2 - \frac{1}{r}\right)\frac{\cos \gamma}{Vr} \tag{5}$$

$$\dot{\psi} = \frac{L\sin\sigma}{V\cos\gamma} + \frac{V}{r}\cos\gamma\sin\psi\tan\phi \tag{6}$$

Where r is the radial distance from the center of the earth to the vehicle, normalized by earth radius R_e. The longitude and latitude are θ and ϕ, respectively. The earth-relative velocity V is normalized by $V_c = \sqrt{g_0 R_e}$. The time is normalized by $\tau = t/\sqrt{R_e/g_0}$. σ is the bank angle which is used by the primary control command. L and D are the dimensionless aerodynamic lift and drag accelerations as follows:

$$L = \rho(V_c V)^2 S_{ref} C_L / (2mg_0) \tag{7}$$

$$D = \rho(V_c V)^2 S_{ref} C_D / (2mg_0) \tag{8}$$

Where S_{ref} is the reference area of the vehicle, ρ is the atmospheric density, m is the mass of the vehicle, C_L and C_D are the lift and drag coefficients, respectively.

3   Entry Trajectory Constraints

A feasible entry trajectory must satisfy path constraints. The typical inequality constraints considered here are:
(1) Heating rate constraint:

$$\sqrt{\rho}(VV_c)^3 \le \dot{Q}_{max} \tag{9}$$

This corresponds to stagnation-point heating rate based on a reference sphere of radius 1m.
(2) Normal load factor constraint:

$$\sqrt{L^2 + D^2} \le n_{max} \tag{10}$$

It is a constraint on the aerodynamic load in the normal direction.
(3) Equilibrium glide constraint:

$$\left[\frac{1}{r} - V^2\right]\left(\frac{1}{r}\right) - L\cos\sigma \le 0 \tag{11}$$

This constraint serves to reduce the phugoid oscillations in altitudes along the entry trajectory.
(4) Dynamic pressure constraint:

$$q \le q_{max} \tag{12}$$

Where q_{max} is maximum allowable dynamic pressure. $\dot{Q}_{max}$, n_{max}, q_{max} are the vehicle-depend parameters which would be enforced strictly.

4 Neural Network

The artificial neural network is a mathematical tool inspired in the brain of animals, which is composed of information-processing neuron similar to the neurons of living creatures. The power of ANN lies in their ability to model the nonlinear or constrained systems when conventional analytical methods fail, which determines the ANN is capable of learning more information and is suitable to work as a surrogate model.

Giving the learning information, the ANN is trained by iterative process which consists of two steps, the first is forward process which is termed "feed-forward" and the second is error correction process which is called "backpropagation". In each process, real inputs are processed in a mathematical model to produce model outputs, the same real inputs are processed in a real world simulation to produce real outputs which are the target for the model, the real and model outputs are compared to produce error feedback which is used to correct the model. There are several training algorithms known, among which the Levenberg-Marquardt backpropagation is one of the most efficient for multilayer networks.

The most usual model of neuron is the feed-forward ANN. In this model the input signals from other artificial neurons are multiplied by the weights that measure the net connections importance, which results in amplification or attenuation. They are added and the result is compared to the bias, creating the activation input for the activation function. The output of the activation function is the output of the node. The synaptic weights resembling the synapse of biological neurons are adjusted according to selected training algorithm. The process is repeated for every set of input parameters until the network performance reaches an acceptable level as measured by parameters such as error, gradient, or number of epochs.

This learning feature of ANN makes the inputs are not included in the training set can generate expected results, the results for these variable inputs is called "generalization" and measures how well the ANN reacts to unforeseen data, and it becomes a criterion for a trained ANN is successful or not.

In the paper, the RBF NN is chosen. The RBF neural net is a simply composed of three layers: an input layer, a hidden layer and an output layer. The connections between each layer are associated to synaptic weights. The output of layer y can be described as:

$$y(x) = \sum_{i=1}^{N_o} w_i \phi(\|x - c_i\|, \sigma_i) + w_0 \tag{13}$$

Where x is input vector to the output nodes, $\phi(\bullet)$ represents transfer function of hidden nodes i, c_i is the center of radial basis function of hidden nodes i, σ_i is the width of the radial basis function, w_i is the connection weight between node i and the node in output layer, N_o is the number of nodes in hidden layer, w_0 is bias.

In the hidden layer, the Gaussian kernel function is described as:

$$\phi\left(\|x - c_i\|, \sigma_i\right) = \exp\left(-\frac{\|x - c_i\|}{\sigma_i^2}\right) \tag{14}$$

It is the most commonly used radial basis function. The closer the input x_p is to be center of the Gaussian function c_i, the larger is the output of the basis function.

5   Training

The center purpose of trajectory onboard planning algorithm is to develop a high-performance controller to generate approximate control commands with respect to the nonlinear system imposed by nonlinear constraints. In order to purpose this goal, a set of training samples would be created to train the weight matrix W.

The next generation reusable launch vehicles (RLV) would be high lift-to-drag ratio entry vehicles. This feature makes the entry trajectory has some obvious characteristics, it consists of three different phases: initial descent phase, quasi-equilibrium glide (QEG) phase, and pre-TAEM (terminal area energy management) phase [9]. The characteristic of initial descent phase is low atmospheric density and the vehicles have not enough control authority to steer the RLV, which is called the "controlled fall" that takes the RLV to the QEG interface where the dynamic pressure can shape the trajectory. The QEG phase is most critical flight phase, the trajectory must observe all of the inequality path constraints, the achieved range would reach the landing site, and the control commands suffer from the highly constrained nonlinear MIMO dynamics system. In the pre-TAEM phase, the trajectory must satisfy all of the equality constrains, meaning that the trajectory would meet the TAEM conditions at the end of this phase.

Determining the real-time trajectory for high nonlinear entry vehicles has been of considerate research interest in past years. Conventional approaches can not alter the entry trajectory, and can not also deal the abort missions which need redesign the new trajectory for feasible new landing sites. Continued efforts have been made to search for adaptive entry guidance methods that enable fully autonomous capability of guidance system to provide precise flight termination. Ref [9] has developed a completely new and efficient onboard algorithm for RLV. It makes novel use of quasi-equilibrium glide phenomenon in lifting entry as a center piece for efficient enforcement of the inequality constraints, and the longitudinal and lateral trajectory profiles planning problem is reduced to one parameter search problem. This approach can generate a complete and feasible 3DOF entry trajectory in about 2 to 3 seconds on a desktop computer. In this text, this approach is used to create the training samples.

A three layer RBF neural network is used to approximate the dynamics model of the entry trajectory discussed above. The network uses the structure of 6 neurons in the input layer, 6 neurons in the hidden layer and one neuron in the output layer. The input to the network is the state variables $\left[r, \phi, \theta, v, \gamma, \psi\right]^T$, and its output is bank angle σ, the angle of attack profile does not change significantly from mission to mission, including the abort missions. This paper uses the nominal angle of attack profile. The

ANN training process is repeated for each selected initial condition and accomplished via Levenberg-Marquardt backpropagation algorithm.

6 Testing

The nominal vehicle model, X-33, is used in this paper. The corresponding aerodynamic parameters can be cited from [6]. The nominal initial entry states are:

$\left[r_0, \theta_0, \phi_0, V_0, \gamma_0 \right] = \left[120km, 208^\circ, 76^\circ, 7650m/s, -0.5^\circ \right]$. The desired

longitudinal terminal states are: $\left[r_0, V_0, \gamma_0 \right] = \left[25km, 1760m/s, -4^\circ \right]$. Random

landing sites are chosen to generate a set of training data.

There are five cases to demonstrate the generalization capability of the well trained neural network. The corresponding longitudes and latitudes for all of the cases are random generated based on the acceptable limit of the vehicle maneuverability. Table 1 shows the TAEM comparative errors for all the cases. The results illuminate that these errors are small and the terminal landing sites generated by ANN can be accepted. Fig.1 shows the altitude history, Fig.2 shows the velocity history. These two figures describe that the trajectories generated by ANN are very close. The three-dimensional trajectories can be shown in Fig.3. All these figures and table reveal that the RBF ANN can successfully design the entry trajectory and the entry vehicle can reach the terminal states with an acceptable error range.

Table 1. TAEM Comparative errors

	Δr_f (km)	ΔV_f (m/s)	$\Delta \theta_f$ (deg)	$\Delta \phi_f$ (deg)
Case1	0.276%	0.285%	0.225%	0.387%
Case2	0.171%	0.313%	0.364%	0.413%
Case3	0.114%	0.152%	0.146%	0.345%
Case4	0.152%	0.396%	0.254%	0.263%
Case5	0.147%	0.354%	0.312%	0.154%

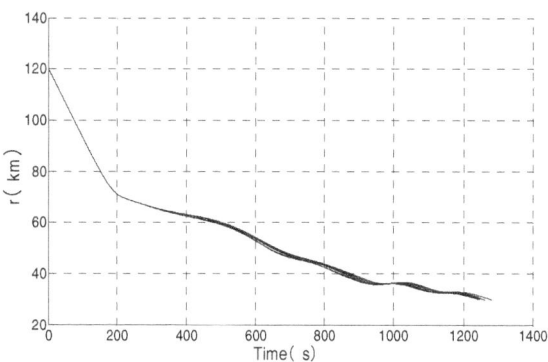

Fig. 1. Trajectories altitudes for different terminal conditions

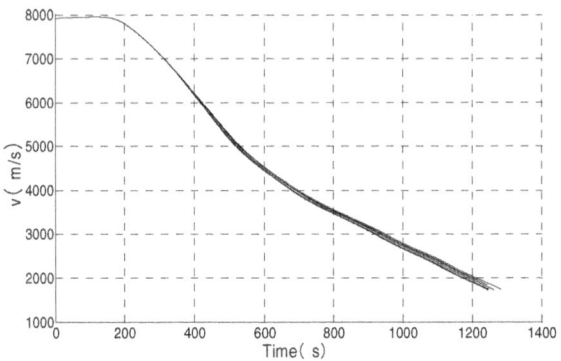

Fig. 2. Trajectories velocities for different terminal conditions

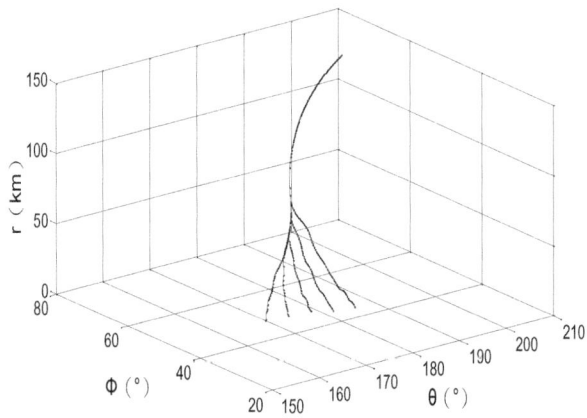

Fig. 3. Three-dimensional trajectories for different terminal conditions

7   Conclusion

In this paper, an artificial neural network trained by the three-dimensional onboard
trajectory generation algorithm is applied to real-time design different entry trajectory
according to different landing sites. Theoretical analysis and simulation results show
that the well trained neural network has good generalization capability, and the each
trajectory generated by neural network is feasible solution with acceptable terminal
states, meaning that a well trained artificial neural network augments the entry
vehicles autonomous redesign trajectory capability and is more suitable for complex
entry dynamics system.

References

1. Harpold, J.C., Graves, C.A.: Shuttle entry guidance. Journal of the Astronautical Sciences 27, 26–29 (1979)
2. Hanson, J.: A plan for advanced guidance and control technology for 2nd generation reusable launch vehicles. In: AIAA Guidance, Navigation, and Control Conference and Exhibit, pp. 1–9. AIAA Press, New York (2002)
3. Hanson, J.: Advanced guidance and control project for resuable launch vehicles. In: AIAA Guidance, Navigation, and Control Conference and Exhibit, pp. 1–10. AIAA Press, New York (2000)
4. Gamble, J.D., Cerimele, C.J., Moore, T.E., Higgins, J.: Atmospheric guidance concepts for an aeroassist flight experiment. Journal of the Astronautical Sciences 36, 45–71 (1988)
5. Fury, D.P.: Adaptive atmospheric entry guidance for the kistler K-1 orbital vehicle. In: AIAA Guidance, Navigation, and Control Conference, pp. 1275–1288. AIAA Press, New York (1999)
6. Youssef, H., Chowdhry, R.S., Lee, H., Rodi, P., Zimmerman, C.: Predictor-corrector entry guidance for reusable launch vehicles. In: AIAA Guidance, Navigation, and Control Conference, pp. 1–8. AIAA Press, New York (2001)
7. Saraf, A., Leavitt, J.A., Chen, D.T., Mease, K.D.: Design and evaluation of an acceleration guidance algorithm for entry. Journal of Spacecraft and Rockets 41, 986–996 (2004)
8. Zimmerman, C., Dukeman, G., Hanson, J.: Automated method to compute orbital reentry trajectories with heating constraints. Journal of Guidance, Control, and Dynamics 26, 523–529 (2003)
9. Shen, Z., Lu, P.: On-board generation of three-Dimensional constrained entry trajectories. Journal of Guidance, Control, and Dynamics 26, 111–121 (2003)

An Optimization Algorithm for WNN Based on Immune Particle Swarm

Fei Wang[1], Jianfang Shi[1], and Jing Yang[1,2]

[1] College of Information Engineering, Taiyuan University of Technology
[2] Information Center, Taiyuan University of Technology
Taiyuan, Shanxi, China
wangfei02@tyut.edu.cn,
shijianfang@tyut.edu.cn, yangjing@tyut.edu.cn

Abstract. Wavelet neural network (WNN) is a combination of wavelet analysis and neural network and has the strong fault tolerance, the strong anti-jamming and the strong adaptive ability. However, WNN is likely to trap local minimum and premature convergence. According to these shortcomings, particle swarm optimization (PSO) algorithm is applied to wavelet neural network (WNN) and has good effect. This paper presents a PSO algorithm based on artificial immune (AI). Through importing antibody diversity keeping mechanism, this algorithm can retain high fitness of particles and ensure the diversity of population. Then, the new algorithm is applied to the training of WNN and the parametric optimization. Through some simulation experiments, this paper concludes that the presented algorithm has stronger convergence and stability than the basic particle swarm optimization algorithm on optimizing WNN, and has the better performance of reducing the number of training and error.

Keywords: PSO algorithm, WNN, artificial immune algorithm.

1 Introduction

Wavelet neural network is developed into a kind of neural network on basis of wavelet transform and artificial neural network. It inherits the localization nature of wavelet transform and self-learning ability of neural network, so it has the good approximation and fault tolerance, better convergence speed and prediction effect. According to these advantages, wavelet neural network is widely used in signal and image processing, seismic exploration, fault diagnosis, data compression, pattern recognition, numerical calculation and control, etc [1-3]. Wavelet neural network used commonly the gradient descent method. However, this method is easy to trap local minimum and slow convergence speed. In recent years, some researchers use particle swarm optimization algorithm to train the parameters of wavelet neural network. Particle swarm optimization algorithm gains optimized neural network through sharing information between the populations. But the improved effect is not obvious. This paper presents a particle swarm optimization algorithm based on artificial immune selection. The algorithm combines the simple realization, global optimization of PSO algorithm and antibodies diversity mechanism of AI algorithm, thus, it can

H. Deng et al. (Eds.): AICI 2011, Part III, LNAI 7004, pp. 326–333, 2011.

avoid PSO algorithm trapping local minimum and slow convergence speed, and improve precision. Finally, through the comparative experiments of two algorithms, this paper indicates the immune PSO (IPSO) algorithm not only reduces the iteration times, but also improves precision.

2   Wavelet Neural Network

WNN replaces Sigmoid function with wavelet function as excitation function of neural network in neurons, and its signal representation is realized by linear superposition of wavelet function [4-5]. The output signal $S(t)$ is approached by wavelet function $h(a,b,t)$, as follows:

$$S(t) = \sum_{k=1}^{K} W_k * h\left(\frac{t-b_k}{a_k}\right) . \tag{2-1}$$

Where $S(t)$ is the estimate of the original signal $F(t)$, W_k is weight coefficient, b_k is translation parameters, a_k is extension parameters, K is the node number of hidden layer. Figure 1 describes structure of WNN.

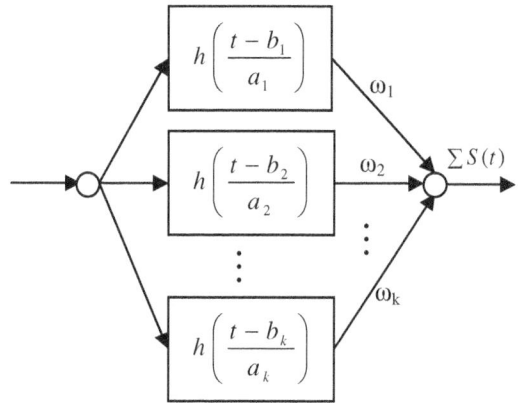

Fig. 1. Structure of WNN

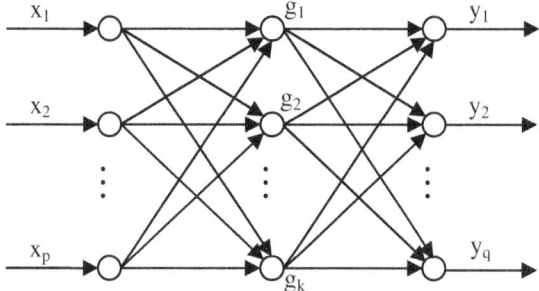

Fig. 2. Tight Structure of WNN

WNN replaces S function of hidden layer with wavelet function in neural network, corresponding to the weight value of input layer to hidden layer and threshold value of hidden layer are replaced with extension parameters and translation parameters of wavelet function. Tight structure is the most widely used. Figure 2 describes the tight structure.

Where $(x_1,\ldots,x_i,\ldots,x_p)^T$ is input sample, $(g_1(x),\ldots,g_j(x),\ldots,g_h(x))^T$ is wavelet function. Output function is as follow:

$$y_i = \sum_{j=1}^{h} C_{ji} g_j(x) \ . \tag{2-2}$$

C_{ji} is weight value. W_k, b_k, a_k can be optimization by mean-square error energy function, the function is as follow:

$$E = \frac{1}{2} \sum_{t=1}^{T} [F(t) - S(t)]^2 \ . \tag{2-3}$$

3   Basic PSO Algorithm

PSO algorithm is an evolution computation and presented by Eberhart and Kennedy in 1995 [6]. It comes from the predatory behavioral research of birds. PSO algorithm is similar to the genetic algorithm. It is an optimization algorithm based on iterations. A group of random solutions search the most optimal value through iterations. PSO algorithm does not have the crossover and mutation used by the genetic algorithm, but particles search the most optimal value by following the most optimal particle in the search space. The principle of PSO algorithm is as follows:

When the optimization problem is solved in basic PSO (bPSO) algorithm, a particle of search space is regarded as a solution of the problem [7-10]. Each particle consists of three parts: the current position x, flight speed v and the fitness of particle, and is expressed as $P(x, v, fitness)$. In iteration process, a particle is updated by updating two extremes. One is the optimal solution of particle itself, called own cognitive ability and expressed as P_{best}; the other is the optimal solution of particle swarm, called social cognitive ability and expressed as G_{best}. Then, they are updated themselves by equation, as follows:

$$v_i(t+1) = \omega \cdot v_i(t) + c_1 \cdot r_1 (P_{besti}(t) - x_i(t)) + c_2 \cdot r_2 (G_{best}(t) - x_i(t)) \tag{3-1}$$

$$x_i(t+1) = x_i(t) + v_i(t+1) \ . \tag{3-2}$$

Where $v_i(t)$ and $x_i(t)$ are velocity vector and position of the particle currently, $P_{besti}(t)$ and $G_{best}(i)$ denote the position of the optimal solutions that is found by a particle itself and the whole particle swarm, ω is a nonnegative inertial factor, c_1 and c_2 are learning parameters, r_1 and r_2 are random number from 0 to 1.

Although bPSO algorithm is widely applied to complex engineering optimized problems and achieves a great success, it also has some faults, for instance, trapping local minimum, the poor local optimized ability and the poor ability of keeping the populational diversity, etc. Thus, this paper improves PSO algorithm based on bPSO algorithm.

4 Artificial Immune Algorithm

The basic function of biological immune system is distinguishing between self and not-self. The immune discrimination is the basic of the various functions of the biological immune system. According to the cloning selection theory of Burnet, the immune cells happen to the gene mutation in the process of the proliferation since the embryonic period, and form the cellular diversity, so the biological immune system is able to distinguish and oppose a great variety of antigen attacks. The immune system has various functions, for instance, pattern recognition, learning and memory, noise tolerance, induction and generalization, distributional detection and the optimization, etc. AI algorithm [11-12] is proposed on the basis of the simulation biological immune system, and the basic idea of AI algorithm comes from biological immune system. Through abstracting, summarizing, processing and inducting the biological immune system, AI algorithm forms a series of steps like clone, mutation and immune selection and so on. The basic working principle of AI algorithm is that after the body suffering the invasion, The **B** cells in the immune system identify antigens by antibodies on the surface. If the antigen is known, immune system searches corresponding antibody from the memory cells library, but if not, the system is stimulated to produce new antibodies by antigens. Because of the stimulation of antigen, in the whole immune process, The **B** cells secrete new antibodies through continuously differentiation and breeding, and finally reach the purpose of eliminating antigens. At the same time, **T** cells play a role of control and adjust. When the antibody concentration reaches a certain value, it can be restrained. Conversely, it can be promoted. Because of this mechanism of **T** cells, the diversity of antibody population is maintained. Some relevant definitions are as follows:

1) Affinity is the degree of closeness between antigen and antibody, as follows:

$$affinity(x_i) = \frac{1}{f+1} \quad . \tag{4-1}$$

Where f is optimal objective function, solutions of the function are antigens, candidate solutions are antibodies (particles).

2) Vaccine is the best estimate of individual genes. This paper considers the average of some best individuals as *vaccine*. This paper assumes $X=(x_1, x_2,..., x_a)^T$ is the best population of antibodies. The definition of vaccine is as follows:

$$vaccine(i) = \frac{1}{a} \sum_{j=1}^{a} x_j \qquad i = 1, 2, \cdots, k \quad . \tag{4-2}$$

3) Antibody density is an important index of antibody diversity, and describes the difference of affinities among antibodies. As follows:

$$density(x_i) = D(L_j) = \frac{Count(j)}{m} \qquad i = 1, 2, \cdots, n, \quad j = 1, 2, \cdots, m \quad . \tag{4-3}$$

Where $Count(j)$ is the number of antibody affinity in every equal interval, L_j is No. j of equal intervals, m is the number of equal interval, n is the number of antibody.

4) In the immune mechanism, some antibodies of high density and low affinity are restrained, conversely, they are promoted. So the probability(P_S) of some antibodies

entering this generation is jointly determined by two probabilities. One is the probability of density(P_d), the other is the probability of affinity(P_f), as follows:

$$P_d(x_i) = 1 - \frac{D(x_i)}{\sum\limits_{i=1}^{n} D(x_i)} \qquad i = 1, 2, \cdots, n \quad . \tag{4-4}$$

$$P_f(x_i) = \frac{fitness(x_i)}{\sum\limits_{i=1}^{n} fitness(x_i)} \qquad i = 1, 2, \cdots, n \quad . \tag{4-5}$$

$$P_s(x_i) = \alpha P_f(x_i) + (1-\alpha) P_d(x_i) \qquad 0 < \alpha, P_f, P_d < 1 \quad . \tag{4-6}$$

Where α is used to adjust the balance of two probability, usually α=0.7.

5   IPSO and Application

This paper presents IPSO algorithm, which is a combination of bPSO and AI. IPSO algorithm introduces the antibody diversity mechanism into bPSO, and improves convergence speed and accuracy. More concretely, put the particle of PSO algorithm as the antibody, the optimal solution as the antigen, the proximity between the antibody and the antigen as the affinity. Finally, it can achieve the optimal process by a series of operations, for instance, the immune memory, the promotion and suppression of antibodies, the immune selection. Theoretically, IPSO has the following features [13]:

1) Inherit learning and information sharing mechanism of bPSO algorithm;
2) The antigen recognition and immune memory strengthen the information sharing among particles. On the one hand, they can ensure the excellent individual into next generation through the survival of the fittest. On the other hand, they can keep the diversity of population and improve the convergence speed through re-initialization;
3) Because of the mechanism that some antibodies of high density and low affinity are restrained, conversely, they are promoted, it can keep better the diversity of population and reduce the probability of trapping local minimum;
4) Vaccination and immunization make excellent individual be inherited and improve the ability of searching optimum solution.

Based on these features, this paper introduces IPSO into WNN, and the procedure is as follows:

1) Select the wavelet function. This paper selects the Morlet function as the wavelet function. The function expression is as follows:

$$h(t) = \cos(1.75 \cdot t)\, e^{-\frac{t^2}{2}} \quad . \tag{5-1}$$

2) Initialize parameters: I is input layer node number, k-hidden layer node number, O is output layer node number, c_1 and c_2 are learning parameters, N is particle swarm (antibody) number, M is immune memory cell number, P_S is probability selected threshold;

3) The position vector of each particle (antibody) is $(a_1,b_1,\omega_1),\ldots, (a_k,b_k,\omega_k)$. The flight velocity of particles N is random number;

4) Equation (2-3) is the optimal objective function. Equation (4-1) calculates fitness. According to the fitness, P_{best} and G_{best} can be found;

5) Put all affinities from big to small and keep some particles (antibodies) from NO.1 to NO.M as immune memory cells and replace the worst M particles;

6) Equation (4-4) calculates P_f, and put some particles that their P_f is greater than P_s into (3-1) and (3-2);

7) Judge whether the result meets the conditions of termination, if met, terminate procedure, and then, output best particles and their corresponding WNN parameters $(a_1,b_1,\omega_1),\ldots, (a_k,b_k,\omega_k)$; otherwise turn (4).

6 Simulation and Analysis

In order to verify the efficiency of IPSO algorithm, this paper makes IPSO approach a piecewise function [14], as follows:

$$f(x) = \begin{cases} -2.186x-1.286 & -1 \le x < -0.2 \\ 4.246x & -0.2 \le x < 0 \\ e^{-0.5x-0.5}\sin[(3x+7)x] & 0 \le x < 1 \end{cases} \quad (6\text{-}1)$$

On interval [-1,1], produce 50 equally distributed random nodes, and set as x_k, $k=1,2,\ldots,50$, and then $y_k=f(x_k)+\varepsilon_k$, where ε_k is noise independent and obey $N(0,0.1)$.

Select Morlet as wavelet function and use it to train WNN. Then, this paper uses IPSO to search optimal solutions, and sets as $I=50$, $O=50$, $N=50$, $M=10$, $c_1=c_2=2$. After 5000 iterative trainings, simulation output is as follows:

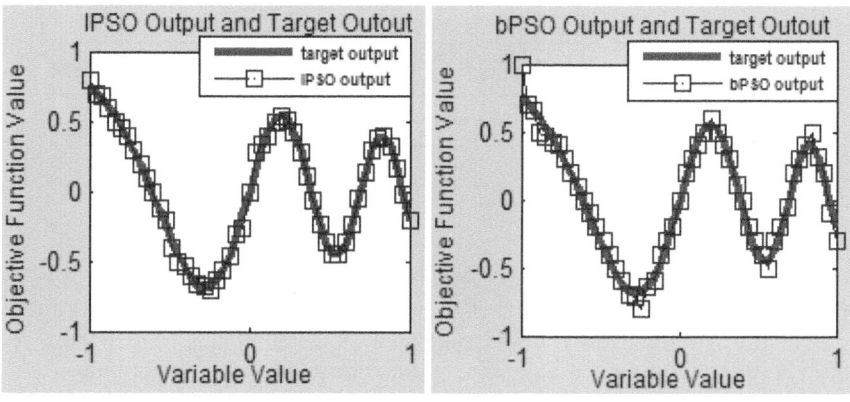

Fig. 3. Simulation Output of IPSO   **Fig. 4.** Simulation Output of bPSO

As can be seen from Figure 3, the IPSO output and the target output are basically consensus, and the error is relatively small. At the same time, this paper uses bPSO to search the optimal solutions under the same conditions. Figure 4 is the bPSO output and the target output. As can be seen from Figure 4, there is a big error between the bPSO output and the target output.

Then, Figure 5 and Figure 6 respectively is the error curves of bPSO algorithm and IPSO algorithm. As can be seen from two figures, two errors are almost identical before 1500 iterations. But after 1500 iterations, the error of IPSO training network is clearly smaller than the error of bPSO training network. Finally, through the same 5000 iterations, the error of IPSO training network is closer to 0.

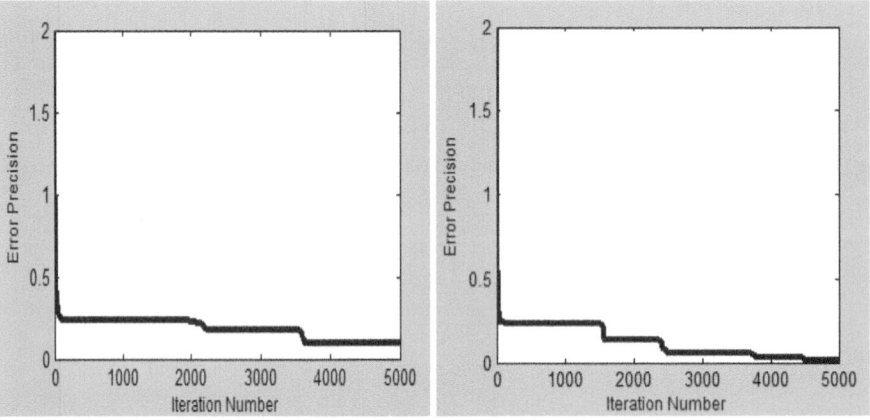

Fig. 5. Error curve of bPSO algorithm   **Fig. 6.** Error curve of IPSO algorithm

A lot of simulation experimental results prove that IPSO algorithm is more suitable for optimizing WNN. The results are table 1.

Table 1. Training error comparison between bPSO algorithm and IPSO algorithm

Times	bPSO Training Error	IPSO Training Error
1	0.1056	0.0612
2	0.0878	0.0347
3	0.0601	0.0136

7   Conclusions

This paper presents the immune particle swarm (IPSO) algorithm for optimizing wavelet neural network (WNN). Density and affinity are added to the IPSO algorithm so as to effectively prevent it from trapping into local minimum. Experimental results illustrate that the presented algorithm is superior to the bPSO algorithm in training WNN. Our future work focuses mainly on the study of target tracking based on WNN based on IPSO.

Acknowledgments. This work is supported by the Natural Science Funded Project in Shanxi Province of China. (Project No. 2009011018-2).

References

1. Jin, Y., Chen, G., Liu, H.: Fault Diagnosis of Analog Circuit Based on Wavelet Neural Network. Chinese Journal of Scientific Instrument 28(9), 1600–1603 (2007)
2. Jin, H., Qu, J.: Study of Target Tracking Based on Wavelet Neural Network. Microcomputer Information 25(8), 129–130 (2009)
3. Li, H., Zhang, A., Shen, Y., Cheng, C.: An Application of Neural Network in Multiple Target Tracking. Chinese Journal of Sensors and Actuators 19(6), 2563–2566 (2006)
4. Shi, J., Zhang, F., Hao, B.: A Method of Image Segment Based on Wavelet Transform and Mathematical Morphology. Journal of Taiyuan University of Technology 40(5), 490–493 (2009)
5. Galvao, R.K.H., Yoneyama, T.: A Competitive Wavelet Network for Signal Clustering [J]. IEEE Transactions on Systems Man and Cybernetics 34(2), 1282–1288 (2004)
6. Kennedy, J., Eberhart, R.C.: Particle Swarm Optimization. In: Proceedings of IEEE International Conference on Neural Networks, vol. 4, pp. 1942–1948 (1995)
7. Ren, Z.-H., Wang, J.: Accelerate Convergence Particle Swarm Optimization Algorithm. Control and Decision 26(2), 201–206 (2011)
8. Liu, Z., Liang, H.: Parameter Setting and Experimental Analysis of The Random Number in Particle Swarm Optimization Algorithm. Control Theory and Applications 27(11), 1489–1496 (2010)
9. Zhang, W., Shi, Y., Zhou, L., Lu, T.: Wavelet Neural Network Classifier Based on Improved PSO Algorithm. Chinese Journal of Scientific Instrument 31(10), 2203–2209 (2010)
10. Xu, X.-P., Qian, F.-C., Liu, D., Wang, F.: A Novel Wavelet Neural Network Based on Improved Particle Swarm Optimization Algorithm. Information and Control 37(4), 418–422 (2008)
11. Dasgupta, D.: Advances in Artificial Immune Systems. IEEE Computational Intelligence Magazine 1(4), 40–49 (2006)
12. Basu, M.: Artificial Immune System for Fixed Head Hydrothermal Power System. Energy 36(1), 606–612 (2011)
13. Afshinmanesh, F., Marandi, A., Rahimi-Kian, A.: A Novel Binary Particle Swarm Optimization Method Using Artificial Immune System. In: EUROCON 2005 – The International Conference on "Computer as a Tool", vol. 1, pp. 217–220 (2005)
14. Yang, D., Li, S., Shen, Y.: Wavelet Neural Network Learning Algorithm Based on Particle Swarm Optimization. Chinese Journal of Engineering Geophysics 4(6), 529–532 (2007)

A Study of Sudden Noise Resistance Based on Four-Layer Feed-Forward Neural Network Blind Equalization Algorithm

Yanqi Kang[1] and Liyi Zhang[2]

[1] College of Mining Engineering, Taiyuan University of Technology,
Taiyuan Shanxi 030024, China
[2] College of Information Engineering, Tianjin University of Commerce, Tianjin 30072, China
tykangyq@126.com

Abstract. In the study of feed-forward neural network blind equalization algorithm, three-layer BP neural network structure is usually adopted .In this paper, iterative formula of four-layer feed forward neural network blind equalization algorithm was deduced by way of adding hidden layers and computer simulations of its properties on sudden noise resistance were done. The experimental results demonstrate that three-layer and four-layer neural network have similar inhibitory action and the fault tolerance to the sudden noise, but four-layer neural network surpasses three-layer in steady-state residual error aspect.

Keywords: Blind Equalization Algorithm, Four-layer Feed-forward Neural Network, Sudden Noise, Steady-state Residual Error.

1 Introduction

Neural network as a discipline involved in neural science, information science, and computer science has been widely applied in pattern recognition, system control, and etc [1].It has been a research hotspot due to its strong ability to learn and its robustness [2]. The multilayer feed forward neural network is currently one of the most widely used ones of all sorts of neural networks [4]. The blind equalization algorithm [3-5] based on the feed-forward neural network usually adopts a three-layer neural network structure, namely from the input layer to the hidden layer to the output layer. The three-layer network structure has a fast convergence speed, but the sudden noise signals greatly influence steady-state residual error and bit error rate and therefore reduce the quality of communication. In this study, four-layer feed forward neural network is applied in blind equalization algorithm, the comparison between its function and that of the three-layer are made by computer simulations. The experimental results show that the four-layer has a better performance.

H. Deng et al. (Eds.): AICI 2011, Part III, LNAI 7004, pp. 334–339, 2011.

2 Blind Equalization Algorithm of Four-Layer Feed Forward Neural Network

2.1 Four-Layer Feed Forward Neural Network Model

Fig. 1 shows a four-layer feed forward neural network structure.

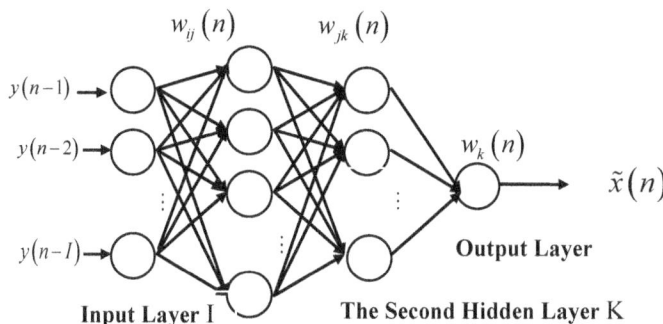

Fig. 1. The topology structure of the four-layer feed forward neural network blind equalizer

In the figure, there is only forward output in neural network, and neurons are connected by weight value [6]. The connection weight value between the input layer and the first hidden layer is $w_{ij}(n)(i = 1,2,\cdots,I; j = 1,2,\cdots,J)$, the connection weight value of the first and second hidden layer is $w_{jk}(n)(k = 1,2,\cdots,K)$, the connection weight value of the second hidden layer and the output layer is $w_K(n)$. "u and v" stands for input and output of Neurons. Their superscripts stand for layer, the subscripts for neurons of the same layer. $y(n-i)$ stands for the input of the neural network, $\tilde{x}(n)$ is output of the neural network. Then the state equation of the feed-forward neural network is as follows:

$$u_i^I(n) = y(n-i) \tag{1}$$

$$v_i^I(n) = u_i^I(n) = y(n-i) \tag{2}$$

$$u_i^J(n) = \sum_{i=1}^{I} w_{ij}(n) v_i^I(n) = \sum_{i=1}^{I} w_{ij}(n) y(n-i) \tag{3}$$

$$v_i^J(n) = f_1\left(u_i^J(n)\right) = f_1\left(\sum_{i=1}^{I} w_{ij}(n) y(n-i)\right) \tag{4}$$

$$v_k^K(n) = f_2\left(u_k^K(n)\right) = f_2\left(\sum_{j=1}^{J} w_{jk}(n)v_j^J(n)\right) \tag{5}$$

$$v_k^K(n) = f_2\left(u_k^K(n)\right) = f_2\left(\sum_{j=1}^{J} w_{jk}(n)v_j^J(n)\right) \tag{6}$$

$$u(n) = \sum_{k=1}^{K} w_k(n)v_k^K(n) \tag{7}$$

$$v(n) = \tilde{x}(n) = f_3\left(u(n)\right) = f_3\left(\sum_{k=1}^{K} w_k(n)v_k^K(n)\right) \tag{8}$$

2.2 The Iterative Form of Four-Layer Feed-Forward Neural Network Blind Equalization Algorithm

The key to solve problems by the use of feed-forward neural network based on blind equalization is to choose a suitable transfer function. Because the transfer function determines the relationship between input and output of the entire network, it also determines the output. The transfer function in this study is [7]

$$f_1(x) = f_2(x) = f_3(x) = f(x) = x + \alpha \sin \pi x \qquad \alpha > 0 \tag{9}$$

According to the traditional constant-modulus (CMA) algorithm and feed-forward neural network training methods, a new cost function is redefined as follows:

$$J(n) = \frac{1}{2}\left[\left|\tilde{x}(n)\right|^2 - R_2\right]^2 \tag{10}$$

In the equation, R_2 is the same to the traditional CMA[8], i.e.

$$R_2 = E\left\{\left|x(n)\right|^4\right\} / E\left\{\left|x(n)\right|^2\right\} \tag{11}$$

In Blind equalization algorithm, the network weight value's iteration formula generally uses the steepest gradient descent method formation, namely

$$\mathbf{w}(n+1) = \mathbf{w}(n) - \eta \frac{\partial J(n)}{\partial \mathbf{w}(n)} \tag{12}$$

$$\frac{\partial J(n)}{\partial \mathbf{w}(n)} = 2\left[\left|\tilde{x}(n)\right|^2 - R_2\right]\frac{\partial \tilde{x}(n)}{\partial \mathbf{w}(n)} \tag{13}$$

In the equation, η is the length of the iteration step.

The four-layer feed-forward neural network contains two hidden layers and two output layers, so its value iteration formula is different from that of three layers'.

(1) Weight Value Iteration Formula of the Output Layer

$w_K(n)$ is the connection weight value between the output layer and the second hidden layer, the weight value iteration formulas are as follows:

$$w_k(n+1) = w_k(n) - 2\eta_1 \left[|\tilde{x}(n)|^2 - R_2 \right] \frac{\partial \tilde{x}(n)}{\partial w_k(n)} \tag{14}$$

$$\frac{\partial \tilde{x}(n)}{\partial w_k(n)} = f'\left(\sum_{k=1}^{K} w_k(n) v_k^K(n) \right) v_k^K(n) \tag{15}$$

$$w_k(n+1) = w_k(n) - 2\eta_1 \left[|\tilde{x}(n)|^2 - R_2 \right] f'\left(\sum_{k=1}^{K} w_k(n) v_k^K(n) \right) v_k^K(n) \tag{16}$$

In the equation, η_1 is the length of the iteration step of the output layer.

(2) Weight Value Iteration Formula of the First and Second Hidden Layer

$w_{jk}(n)$ is the connection value between the first and second hidden layer, the weight value iteration formulas are as follows:

$$w_{jk}(n+1) = w_{jk}(n) - 2\eta_2 \left[|\tilde{x}(n)|^2 - R_2 \right] \frac{\partial \tilde{x}(n)}{\partial w_{jk}(n)} \tag{17}$$

$$\frac{\partial \tilde{x}(n)}{\partial w_{jk}(n)} = f'\left(\sum_{k=1}^{K} w_k(n) v_k^K(n) \right) f'\left(\sum_{j=1}^{J} w_{jk}(n) v_j^J(n) \right) w_k(n) v_j^J(n) \tag{18}$$

$$w_{jk}(n+1) = w_{jk}(n) - 2\eta_2 \left[|\tilde{x}(n)|^2 - R_2 \right]$$
$$\times f'\left(\sum_{k=1}^{K} w_k(n) v_k^K(n) \right) f'\left(\sum_{j=1}^{J} w_{jk}(n) v_j^J(n) \right) w_k(n) v_j^J(n) \tag{19}$$

In the equation, η_2 is the length of the iteration step of the first and second hidden layer.

(3) Weight Value Iteration Formula of Input Layer and the First Hidden Layer

$w_{jk}(n)$ is the connection value between input layer and the first hidden layer, their weight value iteration formulas are as follows:

$$w_{ij}(n+1) = w_{ij}(n) - 2\eta_3 \left[\left| \tilde{x}(n) \right|^2 - R_2 \right] \frac{\partial \tilde{x}(n)}{\partial w_{ij}(n)} \tag{20}$$

$$\frac{\partial \tilde{x}(n)}{\partial w_{ij}(n)} = f'\left(\sum_{k=1}^{K} w_k(n) v_k^K(n) \right) f'\left(\sum_{j=1}^{J} w_{jk}(n) v_j^J(n) \right)$$

$$\times f'\left(\sum_{i=1}^{I} w_{ij}(n) y(n-i) \right) w_k(n) w_{jk}(n) y(n-i) \tag{21}$$

$$w_{ij}(n+1) = w_{ij}(n) - 2\eta_3 \left[\left| \tilde{x}(n) \right|^2 - R_2 \right] f'\left(\sum_{k=1}^{K} w_k(n) v_k^K(n) \right)$$

$$\times f'\left(\sum_{j=1}^{J} w_{jk}(n) v_j^J(n) \right) f'\left(\sum_{i=1}^{I} w_{ij}(n) y(n-i) \right) \tag{22}$$

$$\times w_k(n) w_{jk}(n) y(n-i)$$

In the equation, η_3 is the length of the iteration step of first and second hidden layer.

3   Computer Simulations of Four-Layer Feed-Forward Neural Network Blind Equalization Algorithm

In order to test the validity of the four-layer feed-forward neural network blind equalization algorithm in resistance of sudden noise, signal-to-noise ratio was 20dB at the very beginning of simulation. When iteration became 20,000 times, signal-to-noise ratio reduced to 3dB. When it went through 100 code elements, signal-to-noise ratio came back to the 20dB.

Shown in Fig. 2 (a) and Fig. 2 (b) are the sudden noise resistance convergence curves of typical phone channel and ordinary channel gotten from four-layer feed-forward

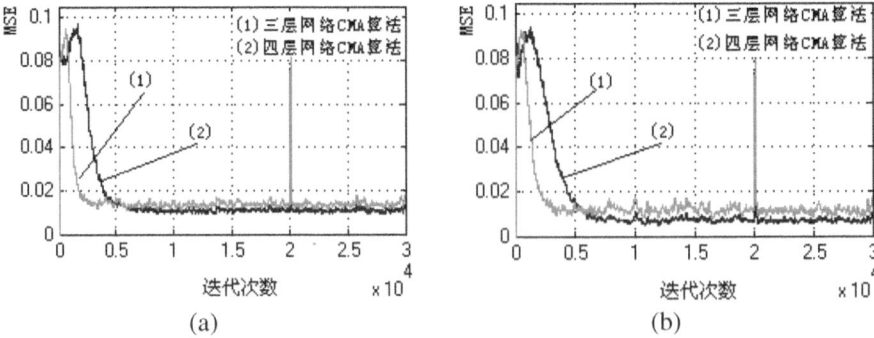

Fig. 2. Sudden noise resistance convergence curves of 8PAM signal in a typical phone channel (a) and ordinary channel (b)

neural network blind equalization algorithm and traditional three-layer feed-forward neural network for 8PAM signal blind equalization algorithm. As can be seen from the graph, the two algorithms all have good inhibition and fault tolerance to sudden noises, but four-layer neural network surpasses three-layer in steady-state residual error aspect while its convergence speed is slower.

4 Conclusions

Due to the defects of the traditional three-layer feed-forward neural network blind equalization algorithm in its influence on the steady-state residual error, this study deduced iterative formula of four-layer feed-forward neural network blind equalization algorithm by way of adding hidden layers and compared the difference by computer simulations between its function in sudden noise resistance and that of three-layer feed-forward neural network blind equalization algorithm. The experimental results demonstrated that three-layer and four-layer neural networks had similar inhibitory action and the fault tolerance to the sudden noise, but four-layer neural network surpassed three-layer network in steady-state residual error aspect while its convergence speed was slower.

References

1. Zhang, L., Sun, Y., Zhang, X., Liu, T., Wang, H.: The Application Research of Fuzzy Neural Network in Blind Equalization Algorithm. In: Seventh International Conference on Electronic Measurement and Instruments, pp. 676–678 (2005)
2. Robust, S.Q.: Training Algorithm of Multilayered Neural Networks for Identification of Nonlinear Dynamic Systems. IEE Control Theory and Applications 145(1), 41–46 (1988)
3. Jiang, X., Zhou, Y., Wang, S., Chen, J.: Multilayer Feedforward Neural Network and Its Application for Switching Converters. Electrical Measurement & Instrumentation (9), 53–58 (2008)
4. Liang, Q.-L., Zhou, Z., Liu, Z.-M.: A New Approach to Global Minimum and Its Applications in Blind Equalization, pp. 2113–2117. IEEE, Los Alamitos (1996)
5. Zhang, L., Lu, R., Wang, H., Sha, D.: A Blind Equalization Algorithm Based on Feed forward Neural Network in PAM System. In: 5th International Symposium on Test and Measurement, pp. 4717–4720 (2003)
6. Weng, Z., Huang, X., Wang, P., Zhang, X.: A Study on Networks Based on Weight-function Neutron. Journal of Fujian Normal University (Natural Science Edition) 26(2), 52–56 (2010)
7. You, C., Hon, D.: Nonlinear Blind Equalization Schemes Using Complex-Valued Multilayer Feed-forward Neural Networks. IEEE Trans. on Neural Networks 8(6), 1442–1455 (1998)
8. Treichter, J.R.: A New Approach to Multi-path Correction of Constant Modulus Signal. IEEE Trans. ASSP 31, 459–471 (1983)

SVM Based MLP Neural Network Algorithm and Application in Intrusion Detection

Yong Hou[1,2] and Xue Feng Zheng[1]

[1] School of Information Engineering, University of Science and Technology Beijing,
Beijing 100083, China
ZXFXUE@263.net
[2] Shan Dong Vocational College of Economics and Business, Wei fang, 261011, China
aspnetcs@163.com

Abstract. This paper proposes a novel learning algorithm- SVM based MLP neural network algorithm (SVMMLP), which based on the Maximal Margin (MM) principle and take into account the idea of support vectors. SVMMLP has time and space complexities O(N) while usual SVM training methods have time complexity $O(N^3)$ and space complexity $O(N^2)$, where N is the training-dataset size. Intrusion detection benchmark datasets – NSL-KDD used in experiments that enable a comparison with other state-of-the-art classifiers. The results provide evidence of the effectiveness of our methods regarding accuracy, AUC, and Balanced Error Rate (BER).

Keywords: MLP neural network, convergence, SVMMLP, intrusion detection.

1 Introduction

Intrusion Detection Systems (IDS) are now mainly employed to secure company networks. Ideally, an IDS has the capacity to detect in real-time all (attempted) intrusions, and to execute work to stop the attack (for example, modifying firewall rules).

We present in this paper a novel classifier SVMMLP, which combine MLP Neural Network and SVM advantage, for intrusion detection.

This paper is organized as follows: Section 2, we briefly describe the MLP neural network model. Section 3 we describe SVMMLP algorithms. Experimental and results are presented in Section 4 and conclusions are in Section 5.

2 MLP Neural Network Model

Typically, a MLP neural network has one sigmoidal hidden layer and one linear output layer, according to the following model:

$$yh = \varphi\left(W_1 \bullet x + b_1\right) \tag{1}$$

$$\hat{y} = W_1 \bullet yh + b_2 \tag{2}$$

H. Deng et al. (Eds.): AICI 2011, Part III, LNAI 7004, pp. 340–345, 2011.
© Springer-Verlag Berlin Heidelberg 2011

where yh is the output vector of the hidden layer, W_1 (l=1, 2) is the synaptic weights matrix of the layer l, b1 is the bias vector of layer 1, x is the input vector, and $\varphi(\bullet)$ is the sigmoid function.

The separating-hyperplane of model (3) is given by

$$W_2 yh^{limit} = 0 \tag{3}$$

Where yh^{limit} is a point belonging to the hyperplane. Considering yh^{proj} as the projection of point yh on the separating hyperplane (3) and d as the distance between the separating hyperplane (3) and yh, yields:

$$yh - yh^{proj} = d \frac{W_2^T}{\|W_2\|} \tag{4}$$

Multiplying both sides of (4) by W_2 yields:

$$W_2 yh - W_2 yh^{proj} = d \frac{W_2 W_2^T}{\|W_2\|} \tag{5}$$

As yh^{proj} belongs to hyperplane (3), substituting (3) and (2) in (5), yields

$$d = \frac{\hat{y}}{\|W_2\|} \tag{6}$$

As the sigmoid activation function bounds the hidden neuron output in the interval [0; 1], the norm of vector yh has its maximum value equal to $\sqrt{n}$, where n is the number of hidden neurons. Taking into account that the norm of $W2/\|W_2\|$ is bounded in the interval [0, 1] we can deduce that

$$-\sqrt{n} \le \frac{W2}{\|W_2\|} yh \le \sqrt{n} \tag{7}$$

I.e. the distance d from (6) is bounded in the interval $\left[-\sqrt{n}, \sqrt{n}\right]$. Therefore, as the target output yi (where i denotes the training example index) assumes the values -1 or 1, we propose the error function

$$J = \|E\|^p \tag{8}$$

Where $\|\bullet\|^p$ is the Lp-norm, $E = [e_1, e_2, \cdots, e_N]$ is the error vector, and e_i is defined in (9).

$$e_i = \left(yi\sqrt{n} - \frac{\hat{y}_i}{\|W_2\|} \right) \tag{9}$$

In order to force the MLP to stretch out the value of d_i (in this work defined as the classification margin of example i) to its limit, creating a hidden output space where the distance between patterns of different classes is as larger as possible.

3 SVMMLP Algorithm

The main idea of SVMMLP is to calculate the functional J focusing especially on the support vectors margins, inspired on the SVM soft-margin training algorithm. The Lp-norm is a trick to avoid the constrained optimization problem usual in the SVM-like approach.

The weights of layer 1 are updated as follows:

$$W_{1,k+1}^{L_n} = W_{1,k}^{L_n} - r_1 \left(\left| \frac{\nabla W_{1,k}^{L_n} - \nabla W_{1,k-1}^{L_n}}{W_{1,k}^{L_n} - W_{1,k-1}^{L_n}} \right| \right)^{-1} \nabla W_{1,k}^{L_n} \tag{10}$$

Where

$$\nabla W_{1,k}^{L_n} = \left. \frac{\partial J}{\partial W_1^{L_n}} \right|_k \tag{11}$$

$$\frac{\partial J}{\partial W_1^{Ln}} = -g \frac{W_2^n}{\|W_2\|} \sum_{i=1}^{N} e_i^{(p-1)} \varphi'\left(v_i^n\right) x_i \tag{12}$$

And

$$E\left(W_{1,k+1}^{L_n}\right) - E\left(W_{1,k}^{L_n}\right) \le \alpha_1 \left\langle \nabla E\left(W_{1,k}^{L_n}\right), \left(W_{1,k+1}^{L_n} - W_{1,k}^{L_n}\right) \right\rangle \tag{13}$$

$$\left\langle \nabla E\left(W_{1,k+1}^{L_n}\right), \left(W_{1,k+1}^{L_n} - W_{1,k}^{L_n}\right) \right\rangle \ge \beta_1 * \left\langle \nabla E\left(W_{1,k}^{L_n}\right), \left(W_{1,k+1}^{L_n} - W_{1,k}^{L_n}\right) \right\rangle \tag{14}$$

The weights of layer 2 are updated as follows:

$$W_{2,k+1} = W_{2,k} - r_2 \left(\left| \frac{\nabla W_{2,k} - \nabla W_{2,k-1}}{W_{2,k} - W_{2,k-1}} \right| \right)^{-1} \nabla W_{2,k} \tag{15}$$

Where

$$\nabla W_{2,k} = \left. \frac{\partial J}{\partial W_2} \right|_k \tag{16}$$

$$\frac{\partial J}{\partial W_2} = -g \sum_{i=1}^{N} e_i^{(p-1)} \left(\frac{yh_i}{\|W_2\|} - \frac{W_2 yh_i W_2^T}{\left(\|W_2\|\right)^3} \right) \tag{17}$$

And

$$E\left(W_{2,k+1}\right) - E\left(W_{2,k}\right) \le \alpha_2 \left\langle \nabla E\left(W_{2,k}\right), \left(W_{2,k+1} - W_{2,k}\right) \right\rangle \tag{18}$$

$$\left\langle \nabla E\left(W_{2,k+1}\right), \left(W_{2,k+1} - W_{2,k}\right) \right\rangle \ge \beta_2 * \left\langle \nabla E\left(W_{2,k}\right), \left(W_{2,k+1} - W_{2,k}\right) \right\rangle \tag{19}$$

The bias of layer 2 is updated as follows:

$$b_{1,k+1}^n = b_{1,k}^n - r_3 \left(\left| \frac{\nabla b_{1,k}^n - \nabla b_{1,k-1}^n}{b_{1,k}^n - b_{1,k-1}^n} \right| \right)^{-1} \nabla b_{1,k}^n \tag{20}$$

Where

$$\nabla b_{1,k}^n = \left. \frac{\partial J}{\partial b_1^n} \right|_k \tag{21}$$

$$\frac{\partial J}{\partial b_1^n} = -g \frac{W_2^n}{\|W_2\|} \sum_{i=1}^{N} e_i^{(p-1)} \varphi'\left(v_i^n\right) \tag{22}$$

And

$$E\left(b_{1,k+1}^n\right) - E\left(b_{1,k}^n\right) \le \alpha_3 \left\langle \nabla E\left(b_{1,k}^n\right), \left(b_{1,k+1}^n - b_{1,k}^n\right) \right\rangle \tag{23}$$

$$\left\langle \nabla E\left(b_{1,k+1}^n\right), \left(b_{1,k+1}^n - b_{1,k}^n\right) \right\rangle \ge \beta_3 * \left\langle \nabla E\left(b_{1,k}^n\right), \left(b_{1,k+1}^n - b_{1,k}^n\right) \right\rangle \tag{24}$$

Where k is the iteration, $W_1^{L_n}$ is the nth row of matrix W1, W_2^n is the nth element of vector W_2, b_1^n is the nth position of vector b_1, $\varphi'(\bullet)$ is the derivative of the sigmoid function, $v_i^n = W_1^{L_n} x_i + b_i^n$ is the activation function of neuron n, and yh_i is the hidden layer output vector in response to example xi.

$$g = \left(\sum_{i=1}^{N} e_i^p\right)^{\left(\frac{1-p}{p}\right)} \tag{25}$$

Where $0 < \alpha_i < \beta_i < 1$, the inequalities (13), (18),(23)ensures that the error function is reduced sufficiently, and the inequalities (14),(19),(24) prevents the steps from being too small.

For each epoch, properly tune learning rate r_i(i=1,2,3),which satisfying the inequalities(13),(14),(18),(19),(23),(24) respectively. the theorem [4] states that if E is bounded below and continuously differentiable, then there always exist learning rate r_i(i=1,2,3), which satisfying the inequalities (13),(14),(18),(19),(23),(24) respectively.

A high level description of this SVMMLP algorithm is given below.

SVMMLP Algorithm
Input: $\{x_{train}\}, \{y_{train}\}$ training dataset

$\{x_{valid}\}, \{y_{valid}\}$: validation dataset (for AUC calculation)

n: number of neurons in the hidden layer

τ : number of iterations between each AUC checking

ξ: stop criterion (maximum number of repetitions of the event AUC$\le$ AUC$_{max.}$

Output: W1; W2; b1; b2: network parameters

1: initiate weights according to Fan-In Weight Randomization algorithm;

2: i$\leftarrow$0; AUCmax $\leftarrow$0; k$\leftarrow$0;

3: while i $\le\xi$ do

4: for epoch = 1: τ do

5: k$\leftarrow$k + 1;

6: update weights by means of (11), (12), (13), (14),(15), and (16);

7: propagate $\{x_{train}\}$ through the formulas (1) and (2) obtaining $\{\hat{y}_{train}\}$;

8: apply $\{\hat{y}_{train}\}$ and $\{y_{train}\}$ in equations (8) and (9) in order to check J_k;

9: properly tune learning rate r_i (i=1, 2, 3), which satisfying the inequalities (13),(14), (18),(19), (23),(24) respectively.

10: end for

11: propagate $\{x_{valid}\}$ through the model (3) obtaining $\{\hat{y}_{valid}\}$;

12: calculate AUC using $\{\hat{y}_{valid}\}$ and $\{y_{valid}\}$;

13: if AUC > AUC_{max} then

14: $AUC_{max} \leftarrow AUC$; $W_1^{stored} \leftarrow W_1$; $W_2^{stored} \leftarrow W_2$; $b_1^{stored} \leftarrow b_1$

15: else

   i←i + 1;

16: end if

17: end while

18: $W_1 \leftarrow W_1^{stored}$; $W_2 \leftarrow W_2^{stored}$; $b_1 \leftarrow b_1^{stored}$

19: adjust threshold (i.e. network parameter b_2) by means of ROC curve information

Notice that, at each Algorithm iteration the non-recursive equations (8)-(25), that demand a number of iterations directly proportional to the total number of training examples N, are calculated. Therefore, the SVMMLP has time complexity O(N). Similarly to other first-order optimization methods, the SVMMLP does not need to store second-order derivatives to compose Jacobian matrix, therefore it has space complexity O(N).

4 Experiments

NSL-KDD is a data set suggested to solve some of the inherent problems of the KDD'99 data set which are mentioned in [1]. We apply the SVMMLP algorithm to NSL-KDD data set for binary testing, which train and classify normal data and 4 kinds of attack (DoS, PROBE, R2L, U2R) data respectively.

In the experiments, the parameters of the SVMMLP method were set as follows: initial learning rate $r_1 = 1e-6$, $r_2 = 1e-8$, $r_3 = 1e-7$, $\tau = 20$, $\gamma = 0.618$, and stop criterion $\xi = 62$. It was tested 5, 7, 10, 12, and 15 neurons in the hidden layer, one neuron in output layer. The architectures and norms were selected based on the better mean accuracy over 20-fold cross-validation.

The results reported in table 1 are averaged over the classification performance through the 620 evaluations.

In the experiments, SVMMLP is the first ranked method compared with the classifier in [10], what gives evidence of the robustness of SVMMLP.

Table 1. Detection result by SVMMLP classifiers

class	Detection rate [%]	Missing alarm rate [%]	False alarm rate [%]	BER [%]	AUC [%]
DoS	99.63	0.5	0.3	2.618	0.998
PROBE	99.07	0.75	1.0		
R2L	92.15	6.33	8.3		
U2R	99.02	30.0	0.4		

5 Conclusion

The experimental results using NSL-KDD applied to intrusion detection benchmarks provide evidence of the effectiveness of those methods regarding accuracy etc though neural models trained by the SVMMLP have been applied without feature selection. SVMMLP deserve special credit due to its high cost-benefit, good results, and model simplicity (a simple MLP model) when compared with the other algorithms [10]. Actually, usual SVM training algorithms have $O(N^3)$ time and $O(N^2)$ space complexities, where N is the training dataset size [8]. The SVMMLP methods have the same time and space complexities of $O(N)$, being a suitable option of MM-based classifier for datasets with large number of features and examples.

References

1. Demuth, H., Beale, M.: Neural Network Toolbox Users Guide: For Use with MATLAB, Version 4.0. The Math Works Inc (2000)
2. Franke, U., Heinrich, S.: Fast obstacle detection for urban traffic situations. IEEE Transactions on Intelligent Transportation Systems 3(3) (September 2002)
3. Guyon, I., Gunn, S., Nikravesh, M., Zadeh, L.: Feature Extraction, Foundations and Applications. Springer, Heidelberg (2006)
4. Boser, B., Guyon, I., Vapnik, V.: A training algorithm for optimal margin classifiers. In: Proceedings of the Fifth Annual Workshop on Computational Learning Theory, pp. 144–152 (1992)
5. Breiman, L.: Random forests. Machine Learning 45(1), 5–32 (2001), URL citeseer. http://nj.nec.com/breiman01random.html
6. Chang, C.-C., Lin, C.-J.: LIBSVM: a library for support vector machines (2001), Software available at http://www.csie.ntu.edu.tw/~cjlin/libsvm
7. Chapelle, O., Vapnik, V., Bousquet, O., Mukherjee, S.: Choosing multiple parameters for support vector machines. Machine Learning 46, 131–159 (2002)
8. Chu, W., Keerthi, S.S., Ong, C.J.: Bayesian trigonometric support vector classifier. Neural Computation 15(9), 2227–2254 (2003)
9. Chung, K.-M., Kao, W.-C., Sun, C.-L., Wang, L.-L., Lin, C.-J.: Radius margin bounds for support vector machines with the RBF kernel. Neural Computation 15, 2643–2681 (2003)
10. Yuan, L.H., Shun, S.R.: The Application of The Improved BP Algorithm in The Intru-sion Detection System. Computer Security 8, 3 (2009)

Training Neural Networks by Rational Weight Functions

Daiyuan Zhang

College of Computer
Nanjing University of Posts and Telecommunications
Nanjing, China 210003
dyzhang@njupt.edu.cn, zhangdaiyuan2011@sina.com

Abstract. A new algorithm using rational weight functions for training neural networks is proposed in this paper. Distinct from the constant weights obtained by traditional learning algorithms (such as BP, RBF algorithms and so on), the new algorithm finds rational weight functions using reciprocal differences with simple network's topology by two layers. The process of how to get the rational weight function networks from the sample interpolation points is given. The results of numerical simulation show that the rational weight functions can find some useful information inherent in the source of data, and the new algorithm has high approximation accuracy, high learning speed and good performance of generalization.

Keywords: neural network, algorithm, weight function, rational weight function, rational interpolation.

1 Introduction

Learning algorithm with weight functions [1] [2] [3] [4] is a new kind of algorithm for training multilayer feed-forward neural networks (MFNNs) developed in recent years. A new form of neural networks (NNs) using rational weight functions is proposed in this paper and is called rational weight function (RWF) algorithm. By using the training samples as interpolating points, we can get the rational weight functions. In the new kind of network model proposed in this paper, the weights are functions instead of the traditional constants. On constructing of weight functions, we choose rational approximate functions as the weight functions, as the reasons of some problems are raised from unknown rational models.

It is well known that multilayer feed-forward neural network is one of the most popular models in neural networks. In some traditional algorithms[5] [6] [7] [8] (such as BP, RBF algorithms) for training the MFNNs, the input layer, hidden layer and output layer are composed of the layered arrangement of neuron nodes, of which the networks' architecture is complex. In one layer, all of its neuron nodes can just receive the signals from that of the previous layer. When gradient descent is used in solving some parameters, there are disadvantages like local minimum, slow convergence speed, non-convergence and difficulty in obtaining the global optimal point, and the weights obtained are constants by which we can not understand any important information inherent in the source of data. Against those disadvantages,

H. Deng et al. (Eds.): AICI 2011, Part III, LNAI 7004, pp. 346–353, 2011.

with simple network topology constituted by input layer and output layer only, the new neural networks with the rational weight functions is proposed in this paper. The trained weights, instead of constants, consist of the rational weight functions defined on the sets of input variables (input patterns). By the weight functions we can understand some important information inherent in the source of data. The rational weight functions can be used to train the neural networks with the problems associated with rational patterns.

Finally, some examples are given, which show that the RWF algorithm is better than BP and RBF algorithms both in calculation accuracy and training speed, and can get some useful information inherent in the source patterns.

2 Architecture of Neural Networks

Neural networks using rational weight functions is a kind of neural networks which is trained by the algorithm of obtaining the rational weight functions. The architecture of Rational Weight Function Neural Networks (RWFNNs) is showed as Figure 1.

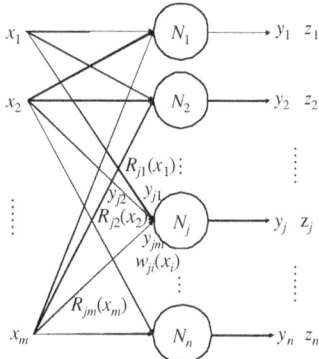

Fig. 1. The architecture of neural network with rational weight functions

Suppose the dimension of the output sample is n, then the output layer has n nodes. The jth (i=1,2,…, n) neuron of output layer is the jth (j=1,2,…, n) output node.

In Figure 1, x_i is the ith input component of an input sample. z_i is the theoretical output value (target value) corresponding to the ith neuron of output layer, y_j is the real output value corresponding to the jth neuron of output layer. $w_{ji}(x_i)$ is the jth theoretical weight function associated with the ith input point (node), $R_{ji}(x_i)$ is the corresponding practical rational weight function, N_j is the processing unit which is used as an adder in this paper.

Note that each of the m inputs is connected to each of the neurons (adders).

The number of neurons is independent on the number of samples, and is equal to $m \times n$, or the number of neurons depends only on the number of input and output nodes (or depends only on the dimension m of input vector and the dimension n of target vector).

For the neural networks as shown in Figure 1, only the weight functions connects to the input layer have to be trained, which means that only one layer weight functions need to be trained.

3   Principles of Neural Networks with Rational Weight Functions

Each circle in Figure 1 represents an adder, which is denoted by N_j, $j=1,2\ldots,n$. The mapping relations between output layer and input layer are

$$y_j = \sum_{i=1}^{m} R_{ji}(x_i)$$

(1)

The one-variable function $R_{ji}(x_i)$ describes the rational weight function between the jth output point (neuron) and the ith input point (variable).

Expression (1) indicates that, distinct from the constant training weights obtained by traditional learning algorithms (such as BP, RBF algorithms and so on), the weights ($R_{ji}(x_i)$) obtained are one-variable functions in this new algorithm.

In the following, we will establish the rational weight functions with simple network topology constituted by two layers (see Figure 1).

Obviously, the target value z_j can be written in a sum of the following m items, i.e.,

$$z_j = \sum_{i=1}^{m} \eta_{ji} z_j$$

(2)

$$\sum_{i=1}^{m} \eta_{ji} = 1$$

(3)

$$0 \le \eta_{ji} \le 1$$

(4)

where j, i indicate the j-th neuron (adder, N_j) and the i-th dimension of input layer respectively, see Fig.1. the coefficients η_{ji} are constants.

Equation (2) indicates that the target value z_j is now divided into m items.

In Figure 1, we assume each input variable x_i has total $N+2$ samples need to be trained. Because $N+2$ samples need to be trained, each input variable (node) x_i has $N+2$ distinct input values. We denote those $N+2$ input samples in the following:

$$x_i = \left(x_{i0}, x_{i1}, \cdots, x_{i(N+1)}\right). x_{i0} < x_{i1} < \cdots < x_{i(N+1)}$$

(5)

As well, the corresponding target vector ($N+2$ dimensional vector) is expressed as follows:

$$z = (z_0, z_1, \cdots, z_{N+1})$$

(6)

Applying expression (5) and (6), we get the corresponding interpolation nodes:

$$IP_i = \left\{(x_{i0}, \eta_i z_0), (x_{i1}, \eta_i z_1), \cdots, (x_{i(N+1)}, \eta_i z_{N+1})\right\} = \left\{x_{ip}, \eta_i z_p\right\}_{p=0}^{N+1} \tag{7}$$

If the index j (see Figure 1) is introduced in (7), we have

$$IP_{ji} = \left\{(x_{i0}, \eta_{ji} z_{j0}), (x_{i1}, \eta_{ji} z_{j1}), \cdots, (x_{i(N+1)}, \eta_{ji} z_{j(N+1)})\right\} = \left\{x_{ip}, \eta_{ji} z_{jp}\right\}_{p=0}^{N+1} \tag{8}$$

Based on (7), we can deduce the approximating weight function $R_{ji}(x_i)$ by interpolation theory. This approximating weight function has the same values as that of theoretical weight function $w_{ji}(x_i)$ at the interpolation nodes described in (7), but it has error outside those interpolation nodes.

For a given set $D_N = \left\{(x_i, y_i) \mid i = 0,1,\cdots,N+1\right\}$, and $y_i = f(x_i)$, $i = 0,1,\cdots,N+1$ $(N = r+1)$, the definition of reciprocal differences is:

$$\varphi(x_i, x_j) = \frac{x_j - x_i}{y_j - y_i}, \quad i \neq j, \ i,j = 0,1,\cdots,N+1$$

$$\varphi(x_i, x_j, x_k) = \frac{x_k - x_j}{\varphi(x_i, x_k) - \varphi(x_i, x_j)}, \quad k > j \tag{9}$$

$$\varphi(x_i, \cdots, x_t, x_u, x_v) = \frac{x_v - x_u}{\varphi(x_i, \cdots, x_t, x_v) - \varphi(x_i, \cdots, x_t, x_u)}, \quad v > u > t \tag{10}$$

Assume $r=l$, let $R_{ll}(x_i) = y_i$ $i = 0,1,\cdots,2l+1$, we have $R_{ll}(x) = P_l(x)/Q_l(x)$, and

$$R_{ll}(x) = \frac{P_l(x)}{Q_l(x)} = y_0 + \frac{P_l(x)}{Q_l(x)} - \frac{P_l(x_0)}{Q_l(x_0)} = y_0 + (x - x_0)\frac{P_{l-1}(x)}{Q_l(x)} = y_0 + \frac{x - x_0}{Q_l(x)/P_{l-1}(x)} \tag{11}$$

In equation (11), let $x = x_i$, we have

$$\frac{Q_l(x_i)}{P_{l-1}(x_i)} = \frac{x_i - x_0}{y_i - y_0} = \varphi(x_0, x_i), \ i = 1,\cdots, 2l+1$$

$$\frac{Q_l(x)}{P_{l-1}(x)} = \varphi(x_0, x_1) + \frac{Q_l(x)}{P_{l-1}(x)} - \frac{Q_l(x_1)}{P_{l-1}(x_1)} = \varphi(x_0, x_1) + \frac{x - x_1}{P_{l-1}(x)/Q_{l-1}(x)} \tag{12}$$

From (12) and (11), we can get the following equation:

$$R_{ll}(x) = y_0 + \cfrac{x - x_0}{\varphi(x_0, x_1) + \cfrac{x - x_1}{P_{l-1}(x)/Q_{l-1}(x)}}$$

In equation (12), let $x = x_i$, we have

$$\frac{P_{l-1}(x_i)}{Q_{l-1}(x_i)} = \frac{x_i - x_1}{\varphi(x_0, x_i) - \varphi(x_0, x_1)}, \ i = 2,3\cdots, 2l+1$$

Repeat the above steps, we can get the following formula:

$$R_{ll}(x) = \varphi(x_0) + \cfrac{x - x_0}{\varphi(x_0, x_1) + \cfrac{x - x_1}{\varphi(x_0, x_1, x_2) + \cdots + \cfrac{x - x_{2l}}{\varphi(x_0, x_1, \cdots, x_{2l+1})}}} \qquad (13)$$

where, $\varphi(x_0) = y_0$.

When $r \neq l$, using a similar derivation process with that mentioned above, the expression of rational function for the interpolation nodes can be described in the following:

$$R_{rl}(x) = \varphi(x_0) + \cfrac{x - x_0}{\varphi(x_0, x_1) + \cfrac{x - x_1}{\varphi(x_0, x_1, x_2) + \cdots + \cfrac{x - x_{r+l}}{\varphi(x_0, x_1, \cdots, x_{r+l+1})}}} \qquad (14)$$

From (7), we can get the following equation:

$$\begin{cases} R_{rl}(x_i) = \varphi(x_{i0}) + \cfrac{x - x_{i0}}{\varphi(x_{i0}, x_{i1}) + \cfrac{x - x_{i1}}{\varphi(x_{i0}, x_{i1}, x_{i2}) + \cdots + \cfrac{x - x_{iN}}{\varphi(x_{i0}, x_{i1}, \cdots, x_{i(N+1)})}}} \\ \varphi(x_{i0}) = \eta_i z_0 \end{cases} \qquad (15)$$

From (8), we have

$$\begin{cases} R_{rl}(x_{ji}) = \varphi(x_{ji0}) + \cfrac{x - x_{ji0}}{\varphi(x_{ji0}, x_{ji1}) + \cfrac{x - x_{ji1}}{\varphi(x_{ji0}, x_{ji1}, x_{ji2}) + \cdots + \cfrac{x - x_{jiN}}{\varphi(x_{ji0}, x_{ji1}, \cdots, x_{ji(N+1)})}}} \\ \varphi(x_{i0}) = \eta_j z_{j0} \end{cases} \qquad (16)$$

Both of x_{ip} and x_{jip} are $N+2$ dimensional vectors. The samples of neural networks are usually divided into training samples and test samples. The training samples can be used to find interpolation functions, and the test samples are usually used for network's generalization.

4 Examples

The training samples for example 1 and example 2 were obtained in the following: the number of $N+2$ input samples was obtained by

$$\begin{cases} z_1 = z_1(x_1) = \cfrac{1}{x_1 + 3} \\ z_2 = z_2(x_2) = \cfrac{e^{x_2}}{x_2 - 3} \end{cases} \qquad (17)$$

where the learning curve in the linearly spaced interval of $t \in [t_{min}, t_{max}] = [0, 2]$ was

$$\begin{cases} x_1 = t \\ x_1 = t \end{cases} \tag{18}$$

$$t = \frac{t_{max} - t_{min}}{(N+2)-1} p = \frac{t_{max} - t_{min}}{N+1} p, \quad p = 0,1,\cdots,N+1 \tag{19}$$

And the output samples were calculated by

$$z = z_1 + z_2 \tag{20}$$

Therefore the network's architecture of the RWF algorithm was 2-1, or there were 2 input nodes and 1 output node.

Example 1: Approximation and Generalization

Let the number of samples be $N+2=100$, $t_{min} = 0$, $t_{max} = 2$ and $\eta_1 = \eta_2 = 0.5$ ($\eta_1 + \eta_2 = 1$).

Figure 2 showed good performance of approximation by RWF algorithm.

In order to show the network's performance of generalization, 200 test samples in the interval of $t \in [0,2]$ were randomly given, the result was showed in Figure 3, which described that the magnitude of the absolute error between the theoretic output values and the network's output values calculated by RWF algorithm was very small.

Example 2: Weight Functions

Let the number of samples be $N+2=20$, the theoretic values of output neuron and the rational weight function between output neuron and the first node were showed in Figure 4 and Figure 5. The trained weights consist of the rational weight functions (see Figure 5) instead of constants defined on the sets of input variables (input patterns). The curve in Figure 5 looks like that in Figure 4, or by the rational weight functions, we can understand some important information inherent in the source of data. The rational weight functions can be used to train the neural networks with the problems associated with rational patterns.

Example 3: Learning Speed

The example of learning speed was given in Figure 6, in which we compared the learning speed of the RWF algorithm with that of the traditional algorithms (such as BP and RBF algorithms).There were 20 to 180 randomly test points (test samples) in the interval of $t \in [0,2]$, the network's architecture of BP algorithm was 2-15-1, and the error performance target value was set to 0.04. The network's architecture and parameters of RBF algorithm were the default values found by Matlab. The result of example 2 was showed in Figure 6.

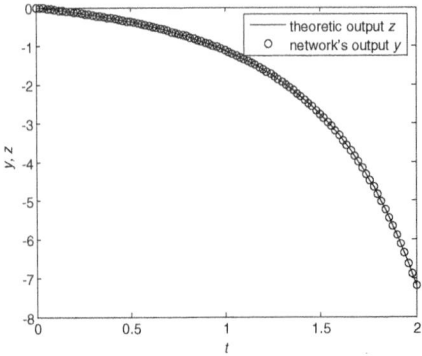

Fig. 2. Values of the theoretic output and the network's output

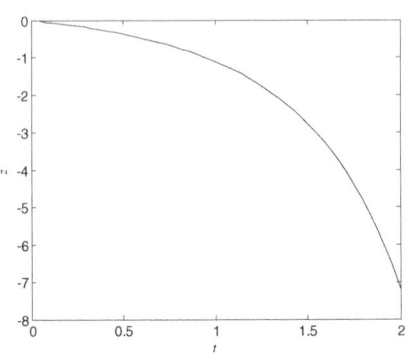

Fig. 4. Theoretic values of output neuron

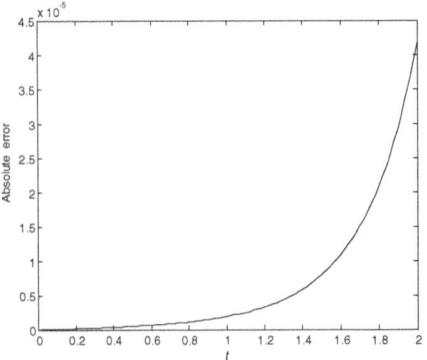

Fig. 3. The error curve of test samples

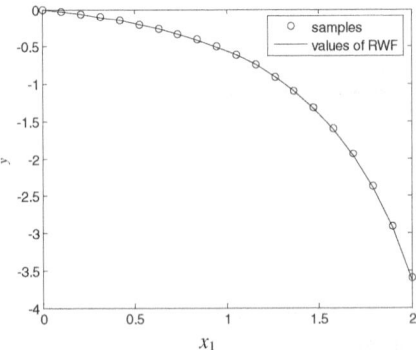

Fig. 5. Rational weight function between output neuron and first node

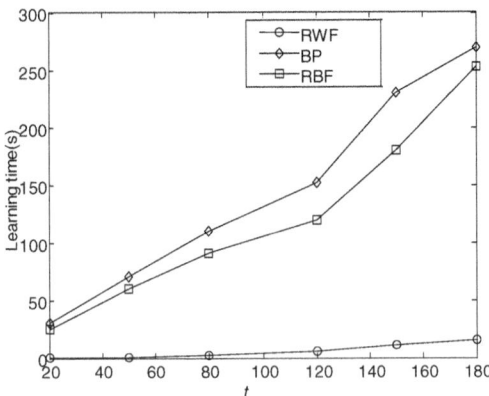

Fig. 6. Learning speed for RWF, BP and RBF algorithms

5   Conclusions

A new RWF algorithm for training multilayer feedforward neural networks is proposed in this paper. By using the training samples as interpolating points, we can find the rational weight functions.

The trained weights of RWF algorithm consist of the rational weight functions defined on the sets of input variables (input patterns), distinct from the constant weights obtained by traditional learning algorithms (such as BP, RBF algorithms).

The RWF algorithm can be used to train the neural networks with the problems associated with rational patterns.

The neural network's architecture is simple, without hidden layer and the number of the rational weight functions is mn (see Figure 1), where m and n are the neural networks' input and output dimension respectively.

The results of numerical simulation show that the rational weight functions can be used to get some useful information, and the RWF algorithm has high approximation accuracy, high learning speed and good performance of generalization.

References

1. Zhang, D.: New theories and methods on neural networks. Tsinghua university press, Beijing (2006) (in Chinese)
2. Zhang, D.: New algorithm for training feedforward neural networks with cubic spline weight functions. Jounal of Systhms Engineering and Electronics 28, 1434–1437 (2006) (in Chinese)
3. Zhang, D.: New algorithm for training neural networks based on generalized Чебышев polynomials. Jounal of Systhms Engineering and Electronics 30, 2274–2279 (2008) (in Chinese)
4. Zhang, D.: Training algorithm for veural networks based on distributed parallel calculation. Jounal of Systhms Engineering and Electronics 32, 386–391 (2010) (in Chinese)
5. Rumelhart, D.E., McClelland, J.L.: Parallel Distributed Processing: Explorations in the Microstructure of Cognition, vol. 1. MIT Press, Cambridge (1986)
6. Hagan, M.T., Demuth, H.B., Beale, M.: Neural Network Design. China Machine Press, Beijing (2002)
7. Ampazis, N., Perantonis, S.J.: Two highly efficient second order algorithms for training feedforward networks. IEEE Transactions on Neural Networks 13, 1064–1073 (2002)
8. Cortes, C., Vapnic, V.: Support Vector Networks. Machine Learning 20, 273–297 (1995)

An Efficient Graph Coloring Algorithm by Merging a Rapid Strategy into a Transiently Chaotic Neural Network with Hysteretic Output Function

Xiuhong Wang[1] and Qingli Qiao[2]

[1] College of Management and Economics, Tianjin University, Tianjin 300072, China
wangxh1965@tju.edu.cn
[2] Department of Biomedical Engineering, Tianjin Medical University, Tianjin 300070, China
Qlqiao@gmail.com

Abstract. In this paper an efficient graph coloring algorithm based on the transiently chaotic neural network (TCNN) is presented. This algorithm apply the TCNN with hysteretic output function instead of logistic output function, this make the model has higher ability of overcoming drawbacks that suffer from the local minimum. Meanwhile, a rapid strategy is merged in this model in order to avoid oscillation and offer a considerable acceleration of converging to the optimal solution. The numerical simulation results demonstrated that the proposed model has higher ability and more rapid speed to search for globally optimal solution of the graph coloring problem than the previous TCNN model with logistic output function and without the rapid strategy.

Keywords: graph coloring problem, hysteretic neural networks, transient chaos, rapid searching strategy.

1 Introduction

The graph coloring problems is one of the classical combinatorial optimization problems having widespread applications in areas such as frequency assignment problems and computer compiler optimization. The graph coloring problem is to color or label the vertices of a graph with the minimum number of colors, such that no two adjacent vertices are the same color. It is more difficult with constraint that the minimum number of colors is required for a given map or graph. In 1976, Appel and Haken [8] solved the four-color problem based on the sequential method whose computation time may be proportional to $O(n^2)$ (where n is the number of regions to be colored) so that it took many hours to solve a large problem.

Solving combinatorial optimization problems has been one of the main motifs for the development of neural networks since Hopfield and Tank [1] proposed their recurrent network to traveling salesman problem (TSP). Takefuji [2] have used a discrete Hopfield-type network to solve the four-coloring map problem. While the classical Hopfield model may be trapped at local minimum and fail to reach global minimum of the objective functions, the transiently chaotic neural network (TCNN) was developed [3]. We have applied a TCNN to solve the four-coloring map problems, which have higher ability of searching for the globally optimal solution

H. Deng et al. (Eds.): AICI 2011, Part III, LNAI 7004, pp. 354–361, 2011.

because of its complicated chaotic dynamics [4]. Recently, non-monotonous output functions have been employed in various neural networks. The neuro-dynamics with a non-monotonous have been reported to possess an advantage of the memory capacity superior to the neural network models with a monotonous output function [5]. We have proposed a transiently chaotic neural network model with a hysteresic output function (HTCNN) to solve the graph coloring problems, which has higher ability of overcoming drawbacks that suffered from the local minimum [6]. In order to simulate continuous dynamics and accomplish fast calculation with parallel digital computers, our previous algorithm is operated in a synchronous and discrete way in which case much iteration is required before converging to optimal solution with small time difference. When time difference is large, however, the system becomes oscillatory and the search fails completely. This will make the speed of converging to the optimal solution slower. In this paper, a rapid searching algorithm is proposed and merged into the HTCNN, which offers a considerable acceleration of converging to the optimal solution when the TCNN is updated in a synchronous discrete manner.

2   TCNN with Hysteretic Output Function for the Graph Coloring Problems

In order to map the four-coloring graph problems to Hopfield network, a $n \times 4$ two-dimensional neural array is needed, where n is the number of regions to be colored, and a single region requires four neurons for the single-color assignment. Seven-region graph are colored by four colors as shown in Fig. 1 (a). If red, yellow, blue and green are represented respectively by 1000, 0100, 0010 and 0001, the neural representation for the problem is given in Fig.1 (b), where a 7×4 neural array is used. Fig. 1 (c) shows the 7×7 adjacency matrix d of the seven-region graph, which gives

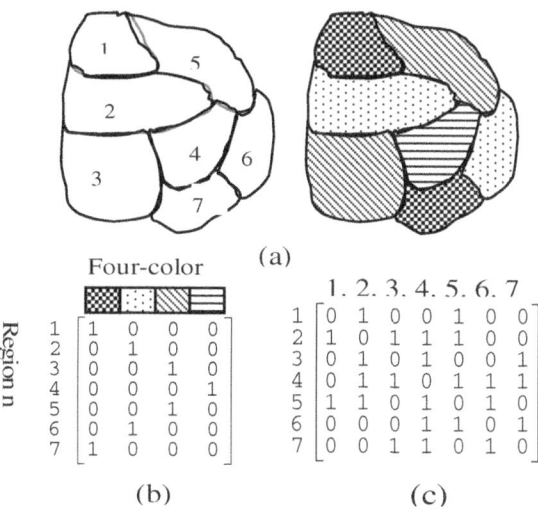

Fig. 1. (a) A 7-region map and four-colored map. (b) Neural representation for the map. (c) An adjacency matrix of the map

the boundary information between regions, where $d_{XY}=1$ if regions X and Y are adjacent to each other, and $d_{XY}=0$ otherwise.

In order to consider in such a way that no two adjacent regions are of the same color, the energy function is given by

$$E = \frac{A}{2}\sum_{X=1}^{n}\sum_{i=1}^{4}\sum_{\substack{j=1 \\ j\neq i}}^{4} v_{Xi}v_{Xj} + \frac{B}{2}(\sum_{X=1}^{n}\sum_{i=1}^{4} v_{Xi} - n)^2 + \frac{C}{2}\sum_{X=1}^{n}\sum_{\substack{Y=1 \\ Y\neq X}}^{n}\sum_{i=1}^{4} d_{XY} v_{Xi}v_{Yi} \quad (1)$$

Where A, B and C are constant, d is the adjacency matrix. V_{Xi} is the output of the ith neuron in the X region. The first term corresponds to the row constraint in the neural array, which forces one region to be colored by only one color. The second term is the global inhibition to enforce the requirement that exactly "n" neurons are "1". The third term describes the boundary violation between regions; If X and Y regions have a common boundary ($d_{XY}=1$), X and Y region should not have the same color i. The minima of energy function E, that is, $E=0$ corresponds to the optimal solution of the four-coloring graph problem.

The connection weighting values $W_{Xi,Yj}$ of the neurons and threshold I_{Xi} of the neural network are

$$W_{Xi,Yj} = -A\delta_{XY}(1-\delta_{ij}) - B - Cd_{XY}\delta_{ji} \quad (2)$$

$$I_{Xi} = nB \quad (3)$$

Where $\delta_{ij}=1$, if $i=j$, otherwise $\delta_{ij}=0$. The dynamic equation of the neurons is

$$\frac{du_{Xi}}{dt} = -\frac{u_{Xi}}{\tau} + \sum_{Y}\sum_{j}W_{XiYj}v_{Yj} + I_{Xi} \quad (4)$$

$$v_{Xi}(t) = \frac{1}{1+e^{-u_{Xi}(t)/\varepsilon}} = f(u_{Xi}) \quad (5)$$

Where τ is the time constant, ε is constant controlling the steepness of the sigmoid curve $f(u_{Xi})$. u_{Xi} is the internal state of neuron Xi.

A transiently chaotic neural network with hysteretic output function (HTCNN) for solving the graph coloring problems is created by introducing transient chaos into the system, and its output function is hysteresis [6]. The continuous dynamics of the HTCNN is

$$\frac{du_{Xi}}{dt} = -\frac{u_{Xi}}{\tau} + \sum_{Y}\sum_{j}W_{XiYj}v_{Yj} + I_{Xi} - z(v_{Xi} - I_0) \quad (6)$$

$$\frac{dz}{dt} = -\beta_0 z \quad (7)$$

Where $z(t)$ is the self-feedback connection weight, β_0 ($0<\beta_0<1$) is damping factor, and I_0 is a positive parameter. A value of z is used such that is strong enough to generate the chaotic dynamics for searching the global minima. It is then gradually decayed according to (7) such that the system becomes convergent to a stable fixed point. The transient chaos improved optimization ability is apparent in solving the graph coloring problems [4].

The output function of above HTCNN is a hysteretic function which is depicted in Fig. 2 and is described as:

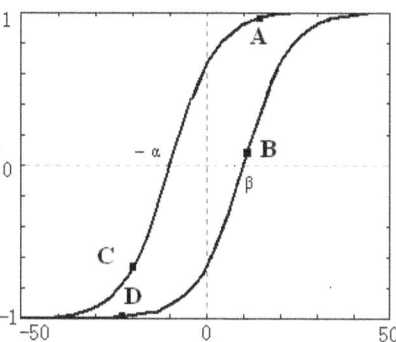

Fig. 2. Hysteretic output function

$$v(u / \dot{u}) = \phi(u - \lambda(\dot{u})) = \tanh(\gamma(\dot{u})(u - \lambda(\dot{u}))) \tag{8}$$

Where $\gamma(\dot{u}) = \begin{cases} \gamma_\alpha, \dot{u} \geq 0 \\ \gamma_\beta, \dot{u} < 0 \end{cases}$, $\lambda(\dot{u}) = \begin{cases} -\alpha, \dot{u} \geq 0 \\ \beta, \dot{u} < 0 \end{cases}$ and $(\gamma_\alpha, \gamma_\beta) > 0$, $\beta > -\alpha$.

HTCNN includes memory because of using hysteretic function as neuron's output function. And due to a change in the direction of the input, a system can pull itself out of a saturated region by jumping from one segment of the hysteretic output function to the other segment. This make the HTCNN has a tendency to overcome local minima. The HTCNN improve the optimization capacity in solving the graph coloring problems [6].

The calculation of the above differential equation must be converted to the difference equation by using the Eular discretization when a digital computer is used. Thus, the difference equation is written in the form:

$$u_{Xi}(t+1) = (1 - \frac{\Delta t}{\tau})u_{Xi}(t) - z(t)(v_{Xi}(t) - I_0) + \Delta t(\sum_Y \sum_j W_{Xi,Yj} v_{Yj}(t) + I_{Xi}) \tag{9}$$

$$z(t+1) = z(t)(1 - \beta) \tag{10}$$

Where let's set $k = (1 - \Delta t / \tau)$, and $\alpha_0 = \Delta t$.

If the time difference $\triangle t$ is small, the search can be carried out successfully, but it requires much iteration before reaching optimal solutions. It is expected that the number of iterations can be reduced by using larger $\triangle t$. When $\triangle t$ is too large, however, the network becomes oscillatory and the searching for the optimal solution fails completely. This has shown that the use of synchronous discrete computation cannot quickly converge to an optimal solution when analog HTCNN is a dopted to the searching. In the following section, we propose an algorithm that overcomes the above dilemma.

3   Merging a Rapid Strategy into HTCNN

Kindo and Kakeya [7] have proposed a geometrical method for analyzing the properties of associative memory model and provided the geometrical outline of the model's dynamics. Based on it, we give a short review of the geometrical explanation on neural dynamics. For simplicity, assume $v=f(u)=sgn(u)$, $I=0$ ($\forall i$ and j), and $z=0$($\forall i$ and j), Then $|v| = \sqrt{N}$ holds, for the state vector v has +1 or −1 as its components. Therefore v is always on the surface of the hypersphere SN-1 with radius $\sqrt{N}$, N is the number of mutually interconnected neurons. The neural dynamics are divided into two phases. In the first phase, the state vector $v(t)$ is transferred to the vector $u(t+1)=(1-\triangle t)u(t)+\triangle tWv(t)$ linearly ($\tau=1$) with the weight matrix W. In the second phase, the vector is quantized to the nearest state vector that requires the least angle rotation. Therefore, from the hyperspherical viewpoint, linear transformation gives the major driving force of dynamics, while nonlinear transformation generates the terminal points of dynamics. That is to say linear transformation is more important than the nonlinear transformation when we discuss non-equilibrium dynamical properties of neural network. This suggests that the eigenspace analysis of the weight matrix gives major information to explain the global feature of the dynamics. Now we apply this approach to analyze the weight matrix of the neural network for solving the graph coloring problems.

As stated above, the good solutions of the graph coloring problems are located in the low energy area of the state space, and the low energy state of the network corresponds to the state that is composed mainly of the eigenvectors with large eigenvalues. Therefore good solutions have large components of eigenvectors with large eigenvalues and almost no components of eigenvector with negative eigenvalues.

While the synchronous discrete dynamics with large $\triangle t$ do not always realize state transition toward the low energy. Fig. 3 is used to illustrate the simple mechanism. Here the nonlinear transformation is neglected for simplicity, and the dynamics given by $u(t+1)=(1-\triangle t)u(t)+\triangle tWv(t)$ are illustrated. When $\triangle t$ is small, the state vector converges to the eigenvector of W with the largest positive eigenvalue, which spans the low energy states. When $\triangle t$ is large, however, the state vector is attracted to the eigenvector of W whose eigenvalue has larger absolute value. This means that the state vector stays in the higher energy states when a negative eigenvalue has larger absolute value than the maximum positive eigenvalue. In this case, $\triangle t$ has to be kept small to ensure convergence to a low energy state though larger $\triangle t$ leads to faster convergence when positive eigenvalues are dominant.

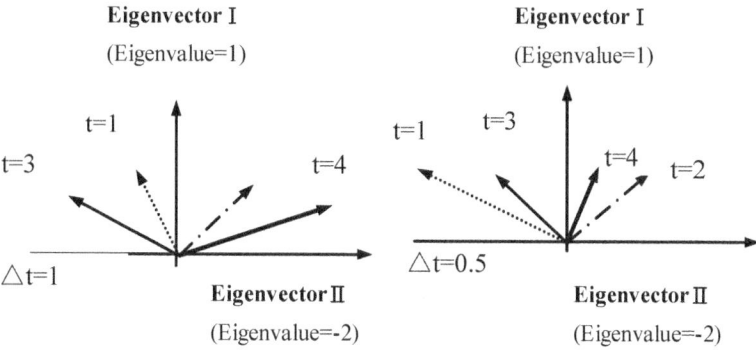

Fig. 3. Convergence of dynamics given by difference equation with small and large time differences $\triangle$t

From this discussion, it is expected that synchronous and discrete state transition with large $\triangle t$ can proceed toward the low energy states if the effect of the minimal eigenvalue is canceled. The component of the eigenvector with the minimal eigenvalue is reduced from the weight matrix W of neural network for the graph coloring problem by calculating

$$\Psi_{XiYj} = W_{XiYj} - \rho\lambda_{\min}e_{Xi}^{(\min)}e_{Yj}^{(\min)} \tag{11}$$

Where $\lambda_{\min}$ is the minimal eigenvalue and $e_{ij}^{(\min)}$ is its normalized eigenvector, ρ is a positive constant, when $\rho=1$, the minimal eigenvalue component is eliminated from W completely. However, because reduction of small eigenvalues increases the firing rate of the network, the network converge to a solution which does not satisfy the constraints. To adjust the firing rate, the threshold should be raised in accordance with the increase of the average weight. Since the threshold is always active while the firing rate of neurons in the feasible solutions is $1/N$, the effect of the threshold is N times larger than that of the neurons. Therefore the threshold is

$$\Phi_{Xi} = I_{Xi} + \frac{1}{N}\rho\lambda_{\min}\sum_{Y,j}e_{Xi}^{(\min)}e_{Yj}^{(\min)} \tag{12}$$

This can keep the firing rate to the proper level.

4 Solving Graph Coloring Problems by Merging the Rapid Strategy into HTCNN

In this section, we solve the graph coloring problem based on the transiently chaotic neural network with hysteretic output function which is merged the above rapid searching strategy (RHTCNN), where, the neuron output function is given by the hysteretic function as follows:

$$v_{Xi} = \begin{cases} 0.5\tanh(\gamma_{Xi}^{\alpha}(u_{Xi}+\alpha_{Xi}))+0.5; \dot{u}_{Xi} \geq 0 \\ 0.5\tanh(\gamma_{Xi}^{\beta}(u_{Xi}-\beta_{Xi}))+0.5; \dot{u}_{Xi} < 0 \end{cases} \quad (13)$$

Where, v_{Xi} and u_{Xi} are output value and internal input value of neuron $X\,i$.

We use RHTCNN to solve the 7-region and 30-region graph four-coloring problems. In the simulation of 7-region graph four-coloring problem, the parameters are chosen as $A=1$, $B=1$, $C=1$, $k=0.985$, $\alpha_0=0.015$, $I_0=0.65$, $\beta_0=0.01$, $z_0=0.08$, $\varepsilon=0.04$, $\gamma_{Xi}^{\alpha} = \gamma_{Xi}^{\beta} = 50$, $\alpha_{Xi} = \beta_{Xi} = 0.02$, The eigenvalue distribution of the weight matrix W is shown in Fig. 4.(a). It has a extremely small eigenvalue –61.4267. Chose $\rho=0.73$ for calculating weight matrix Ψ and threshold Φ, time difference $\triangle t=0.05$, the results with 100 different initial conditions in RHTCNN, HTCNN and TCNN are summarized in Table 1.

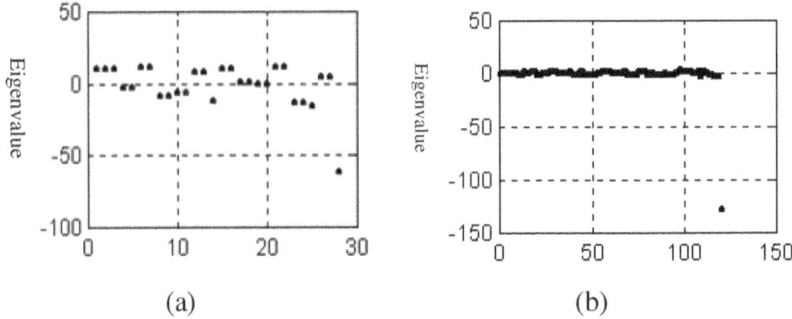

(a)   (b)

Fig. 4. Eigenvalue distribution of weight matrix for 7-region and 30-region map four-coloring problem

Part of Chinese map consists of 30 provinces or cites, so the adjacency matrix is given by 30×30 array, and 30×4 neural array is used. The parameters are chosen as $A=1$, $B=1$, $C=1$, $k=0.998$, $\alpha_0=0.012$, $I_0=0.65$, $\beta_0=0.03$, $z_0=0.1$, $\varepsilon=0.04$, $\gamma_{Xi}^{\alpha} = \gamma_{Xi}^{\beta} = 50$, $\alpha_{Xi} = \beta_{Xi} = 0.02$, The eigenvalue distribution of the weight matrix W is shown in Fig. 4.(b). It has an extremely small eigenvalue –127.4.

Chose $\rho=0.55$ for calculating weight matrix Ψ and threshold Φ, time difference $\triangle t=0.02$. The results with 100 different initial conditions in RHTCNN, HTCNN and TCNN are summarized in Table 2.

Table 1. Results of RHTCNN, HTCNN and TCNN for 7-region graph four-coloring problems

Neural network	RHTCNN	HTCNN	TCNN
minima of E	0.00227	0.0023	0.0056
Average iterations for convergence	106	137	280

Table 2. Results of rhtcnn, HTCNN and TCNN for 30-region graph four-coloring problems

Neural network	RHTCNN	HTCNN	TCNN
minima of E	1.29×10^{-7}	2.4×10^{-7}	0.0509
Average iterations for convergence	198	238	439

5 Conclusion

In this paper, we proposed an efficient graph coloring algorithm by merging a rapid strategy into a transiently chaotic neural network with hysteretic output function. By using hysteretic output function and transiently chaotic dynamics simultaneously, this algorithm has higher ability of searching global optimal solution. Meanwhile, by eliminating the components of the eigenvectors with eminent negative eigenvalues of the weight matrix, a rapid strategy is presented, which can avoid oscillation and converge to the optimal solution quickly and stably. Numerical simulations of 7-region and 30-region graph four-coloring problems show that the proposed algorithm can accelerate the speed of searching for optimal solution of the graph coloring problems under the synchronous discrete computation.

Acknowledgments. This work was partly supported by the National Nature Science Foundation of China (30870649), the National Basic Research Program (also called 973 Program) of China (Grant No. 2005CB724302) and Natural Science Funds of Tianjin (08JCYBJC03300).

References

1. Hopfield, J.J., Tank, D.W.: "Neural" Computation of Decisions in Optimization Problems. Biolog. Cybern. 52, 141–152 (1985)
2. Takefuji, Y., Lee, K.C.: Artificial neural networks for four-coloring map problems and K-colorability problems. IEEE Trans. Neural Networks 38(3), 326–333 (1991)
3. Chen, L., Aihara, K.: Chaotic simulated annealing by a neural network model with transient chaos. Neural Networks 8(6), 915–930 (1995)
4. Wang, X.H., Wang, Z.O., Qiao, Q.L.: Artificial neural network with transient chaos for four-coloring map problems and k-colorability problems. System Engineering–Theory and Practice 22(5), 92–96 (2002)
5. Nakagawa, M.: An Artificial Neuron Model with a Periodic Activation Function. Journal of the Physical Society of Japan 64, 1023 (1995)
6. Wang, X.H., Qiao, Q.L.: Solving Graph Coloring Problems Based on a Chaos Neural Network with Non-monotonous Activation Function. In: Proceedings of Fifth International Conference on Neural Computation, vol. 1, pp. 404–517 (2009)
7. Kindo, T., Kakeya, H.: A geometrical analysis of associative memory. Neural Networks 11, 39–51 (1998)
8. Appel, K., Haken, W.: The solution of the four-color-map problem. Scientific American (10), 108–121 (1977)

Study of Detection Method of Cashmere and Wool Based on Near Infrared Spectroscopy and Elman Neural Network

Fei Guo[1,*], Shuyuan Shang[1], and Ming Qi[2]

[1] School of Information Engineering, Beijing Institute of Fashion Technology,
100029 Beijing, China
[2] Beijing Founder Electronics Co., Ltd, 100085 Beijing, China
feierguo@163.com

Abstract. In order to realize the fast and nondestructive detection, we propose a detection method based on Near Infrared Spectroscopy and Elman Neural Network. Based on the preprocessing Near Infrared Spectroscopy data of cashmere and wool, we analyze the principal components of the data, and build the detection model of cashmere and wool with Elman Neural Network. From the detection application of cashmere and wool, we propose a Variable Structure Hybrid Genetic Elman ANN prediction and modeling method in which an improved hybrid genetic algorithm is used to synchronously and dynamically optimize network structure, weights and self-feedback gains. The experiments based on the data of cashmere and wool from various districts demonstrate that the method combining Near Infrared Spectroscopy, Principal Components Analysis and Variable Structure Hybrid Genetic Elman ANN is a nondestructive detection method for cashmere and wool, and it can rapidly build high-accuracy detection models of cashmere and wool.

Keywords: Near Infrared Spectroscopy, Cashmere, Wool, Principal Components Analysis, Elman Neural Network.

1 Introduction

Cashmere is a very precious animal fiber, with the good reputations of "fiber diamonds". Wool and cashmere are natural protein fibers, and both are very similar on the surface morphology, structure and chemical properties, and the thinner the wool is, the closer it is to the cashmere, the more difficult to identify them[1]. However, since cashmere fiber has characteristics of gloss, fineness of uniform, smooth and soft, it is far more than wool fiber in its economic value. In the field of textiles and garments, cashmere and wool detection has been the research priorities. To guarantee the quality of cashmere products and improve the country position in the international trade of cashmere products, accurate, rapid and nondestructive identification of cashmere and wool is extremely important. At present, cashmere and wool identification methods

---

* Author: Fei Guo, female, lecturer; Research Interests: Artificial Intelligence, Computer Application, Textile Automation.

H. Deng et al. (Eds.): AICI 2011, Part III, LNAI 7004, pp. 362–369, 2011.

mainly are: Morphological Characteristics Analysis, Chemical Method, Computer Image Analysis, Biological Chip [2][3][4]. These methods have the defaults of low accuracy; more relies on experience of testing personnel, high cost, and so influence their uses in practice.

In recent years, as a fast and nondestructive testing technology, Near Infrared Spectroscopy attracts more and more attentions of both domestic and abroad scholars, and has been used in a variety of industries, including agriculture, light industrial, food, medicine, petro-chemical, environmental protection [5][6][7][8], so it has become an important testing technology.

With the development of artificial intelligence technology, Neural Network, because of its good ability of nonlinear mapping, has been widely used in System Identification [9]. Genetic Algorithm [10] has successfully solved the problem of optimization of many complex issues. We applied an improved Hybrid Genetic Algorithm to Elman Neural Network structure, weights and synchronous training of self-feedback gains, so it formed a Variable Structure Hybrid Genetic Elman ANN, and applied it to the cashmere and wool testing based on Near Infrared Spectroscopy and realized fast, nondestructive and accurate identification of cashmere and wool.

2 Variable Structure Genetic Elman Neural Network based on Hybrid Genetic Algorithm

2.1 Elman Neural Network

The Elman Neural Network is a widely used Dynamic Recursive Neural Network, Its structures see Fig.1.

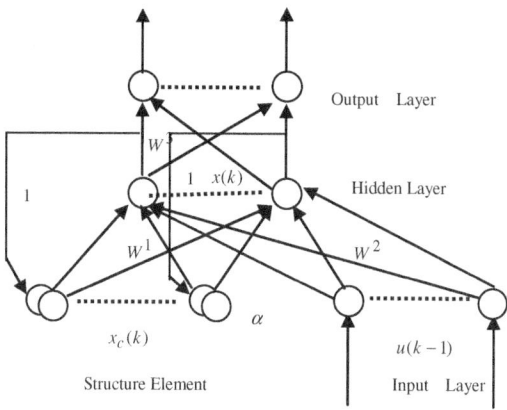

Fig. 1. Structure of Elman ANN

In Fig.1 network external input is $u \in R^r$, output is $y \in R^m$, hidden layer output is $x \in R^n$, structure element output is $x_c \in R^n$。 W^1, W^2, W^3 are connection weights matrixes. The relation of nonlinear input and output for the Elman ANN is:

$$x(k) = f(W^1 x_c(k) + W^2 u(k)) \ . \tag{1}$$

$$x_c(k) = x(k-1) + \alpha x_c(k-1) \ . \tag{2}$$

$$y(k) = g(W^3 x(k)) \ . \tag{3}$$

$f(\cdot), g(\cdot)$ are inspire functions respectively for the hidden layer and output elements. α is self-connect feedback gain factor. Elman ANN based on BP algorithms see reference [11], they have great limitations, such as network structure non-dynamic learning, easy to fall into the local minimum value. We uses an improved Hybrid Genetic Algorithm (HGA) to dynamically study Elman ANN weights, structure and self-feedback gains at the same time, which formed a Variable Structure Genetic Neural Network based on the new hybrid genetic algorithm and overcomes the above defects of Elman Neural Networks.

2.2 Encoding Problem and Structure Adjustment

Because real-coded has no encoding and decoding process, it does not have error problems in the course of encoding and decoding caused by binary encoding, so we use real-coded in the paper.

In order to realize the network structure evolution, it is necessary to add the development and degradation operations of network structure. In the process of evolution we decide whether or not to add the hidden layer neurons and their connection weights in accordance with the development probability p_a, and we decide whether or not to delete some neurons and their connection weights of network structure in accordance with the degradation probability p_b.

2.3 Fitness Function and Choose Operation

Fitness Function is as follows.

$$f_k = \frac{1}{E_k} = \frac{p}{\displaystyle\sum_{i=k-p+1}^{k} \left[y_d(i) - y(i) \right]^2} \ . \tag{4}$$

f_k is the fitness value at the time of k ; p is identification width; y_d, y is expectation output and network output

Fitness is the key to guide the search, in order to avoid "premature" phenomena and ensure the diversity of populations in the species we need to adjust fitness function online. We analyze the advantages and disadvantages of Simulated Annealing Algorithm [12][13] and Genetic Algorithm, and introduce the idea of Simulated Annealing Algorithm into Genetic Algorithm. We adjust fitness online by Simulated Annealing Algorithm according to Eq.(5), and then choose them in the way of roulette.

$$f_i = \frac{e^{f_i/T}}{\sum\limits_{i=1}^{M} e^{f_i/T}} \quad . \tag{5}$$

M is the size of species; f_i is the fitness of the i-th individual; T is coefficient, $T=T_0(0.99^{g-1})$, T_0 is original value; g is genetic algebra.

2.4 Crossover and Variation

Crossover probability p_c and variation probability p_m directly influence the convergence speed of the algorithm, we adopt adaptive algorithm to optimize the crossover probability and variation probability and realize the nonlinear adaptive adjustment for crossover probability and variation probability, the formulas see (6), (7).

$$p_c = \begin{cases} \dfrac{p_{c2}(f'-f_a)}{f_m - f_a} & f' \ge f_a \\ p_{c1} & f' < f_a \end{cases} \quad . \tag{6}$$

$$p_m = \begin{cases} \dfrac{p_{m2}(f_m - f)}{f_m - f_a} & f \ge f_a \\ p_{m1} & f < f_a \end{cases} \quad . \tag{7}$$

f_m is the max value of fitness of the species; f_a is the current average value of fitness; f' is the bigger value of fitness of the two crossover individuals; f is the value of fitness of the variation individual; $p_{c1}, p_{c2}, p_{m1}, p_{m2}$ are all less than 1.

For the individuals whose fitness are higher than the average fitness, p_c and p_m are smaller, so the individuals can been protected to enter the next generation; for the individuals whose fitness are lower than the average fitness, p_c and p_m are bigger, so they are eliminated. By adaptive adjustment of p_c and p_m, better p_c and p_m can be got, so it maintain the diversity of species and guarantee the convergence of algorithm.

2.5 Optimal Solution Store

With roulette the selection operation cannot guarantee the global convergence of the genetic algorithm, so we have to retain the optimal solution of parent generation in the next generation. We replace the worst individual in the current species with the optimal individual of all generations, so far the best individual will not be distroyed by the genetic operations of choice, crossover and mutation.

3 Experiments on NIR Spectrum of Cashmere and Wool

3.1 Spectral Data Gathering and Pre-processing

Within the wavelength scope of 1,100~2,500, cashmere and wool original NIR spectrum is shown in Fig.2 below.

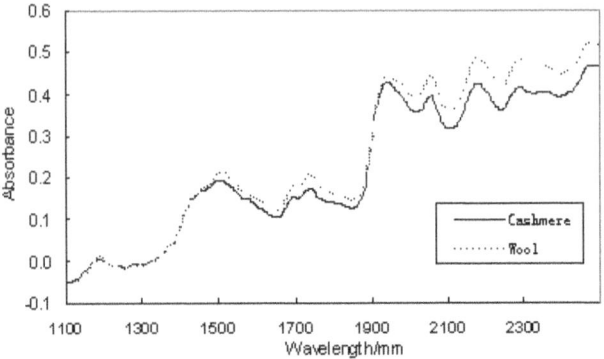

Fig. 2. Original NIR spectrum of cashmere and wool

The original spectrum of cashmere and wool look very similar, it is difficult to directly identify cashmere and wool through the original spectrum. The paper process the original spectra by second derivative to reduce the baseline drift and strengthen spectrum signal[14]. Fig.3 is the spectrogram processed by the second derivative.

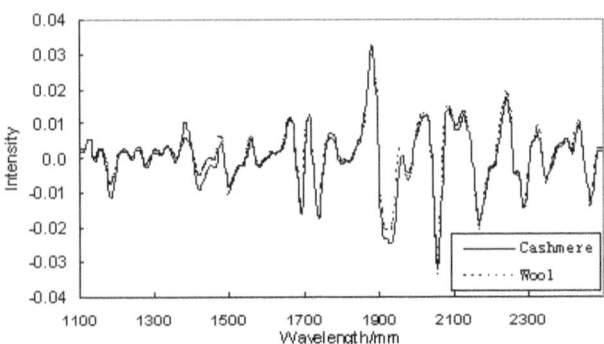

Fig. 3. NIR spectrum of cashmere and wool by second derivative

3.2 Principal Components Analysis

Principal Components Analysis is a data mining technology in multivariate statistical, and its purpose is to reduce dimensions. The basic idea is to combine spectral matrix variables linearly and construct a few comprehensive and unrelated principal components variables, which not only represent as many original variables without losing information as possible, but also better than the original variables[15].

The spectrum matrix $X = [x_1 \quad x_2 \quad ... \quad x_n]$, among them $x_{i=}[x_{1i} \quad x_{2i} \quad ... \quad x_{mi}]^T$ is the ith variable. Spectrum matrix X is the projection matrix of m samples projected to n wavelengths. Projecting X to α_i direction and we get a new variable y_i, then

$$y_i = X\alpha_i \ . \tag{8}$$

α_i is the project direction, y_i is the new variable. Principal Components Analysis aims to find projection direction α_i to make the new variable variance largest in accordance with the direction of projection. The new variable which contains the most information is the principal component. The principal components are arranged in the amount of information contained, and the accumulated contribution rate reflects the representation ability of the former n principal components to the original data and information. In general the top several principal components can express main characteristics of spectrum matrix X, and so they can achieve the purposes of data compression and characteristics variable extraction.

The cashmere and wool spectrums from 1,100~2,500mm have a large amount of data and redundant information. After principal components analysis and calculation on spectral data, the accumulated contribution rate of the former 12 principal components has reached 99.713(see table 1), which demonstrates that the 12 variables well represent the original spectral feature.

Table 1. Reliabilities of principal components

PCs	Reliabilities/%	PCs	Reliabilities/%	PCs	Reliabilities/%
PC1	78.693	PC5	94.82	PC9	98.392
PC2	87.652	PC6	96.153	PC10	98.991
PC3	90.784	PC7	97.053	PC11	99.49
PC4	93.019	PC8	97.764	PC12	99.713

3.3 Cashmere and Wool Detection Model

Fig.4 is the Cashmere and wool detection model based on Variable Structure Genetic Elman ANN. The output of object and ANN are $y_d(k+1)$ and $y(k+1)$. We correct network weights, network structure and self-feedback gain factor using hybrid genetic algorithm based on the difference between the two outputs.

We take the 50 groups of cashmere and 15 groups of wool spectral data as the training sets. The former 12 principal components are the inputs of Variable Structure Genetic Neural Network, and the output is 1(1 for cashmere, 2 for wool), the target

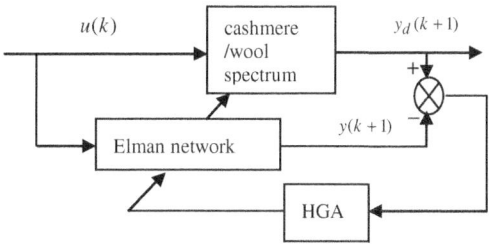

Fig. 4. Identification model based on Variable Structure Genetic Elman ANN

error is 0.002. The parameter are: Species 100; p_{c1}=0.75, p_{c2}=0.6, p_{m1}=0.1; p_a, p_b=0.1; max generation 1500. Fig.5 is the error curve of cashmere and wool detection model, and we can see that the errors has basically reached the objective requirements of convergence after the evolution of about 400 generations.

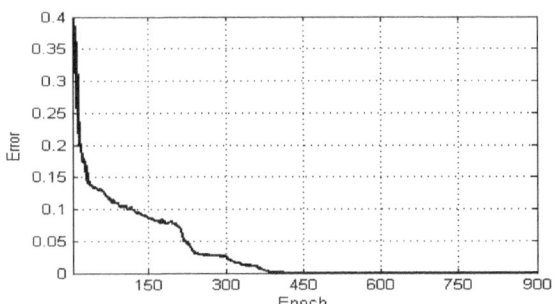

Fig. 5. Curve of error

With the model combining Principal Components Analysis and Variable Structure Genetic Elman ANN we took the qualitative identification on 12 groups of unknown samples, prediction results are all right, shown in table 2 below.

Table 2. Prediction results for unknown samples by Variable Structure Genetic ANN

Samples	Real Values	Prediction Values	Samples	Real Values	Prediction Values
1	1	1	7	2	2
2	1	1	8	2	2
3	1	1.001	9	2	2
4	1	1	10	2	2.002
5	1	1	11	2	1.999
6	1	1.002	12	2	1.998

4 Conclusion

In fiber identification, cashmere and wool identification is recognized as the biggest technology difficulty and they are the most difficult fibers to identify. Many scientists and technologists were committed to cashmere and wool identification studies for a long time, but have not achieved the ideal results. The paper studies on using Near Infrared Spectroscopy with Principal Components Analysis and Elman Neural Network technology to do qualitative identification on cashmere and wool, and has build the Near Infrared Spectroscopy model of cashmere and wool. The qualitative identification on the unknown cashmere and wool has good prediction effects. The experiments demonstrate that the model is accurate and quick for cashmere and wool identification, and meet the actual apply needs to a great extent. It has provided a solid foundation to develop simple, low-cost, nondestructive and rapid testing equipments for cashmere and wool.

Acknowledgments. We thank the Beijing Outstanding Talent Cultivation and Funded Project (Grant No. 2009D005001000003) for financial support.

References

1. Jin, M.-J., Ruan, Y., Shi, D.-L., Liu, Y.-N.: A Review on Identification of Cashmere and Wool Fibers. Shandong Textile Science & Technology, 28–30 (April 2007)
2. Zhang, X.-L., Chi, H.-T., Zhang, J.-H., Liu, Q.: Research progress in the detection technique of cashmere and wool. Wool Textile Journal, 56–59 (March 2009)
3. He, L.-Z., Chen, L.-P., Wang, X.-M.: Detection methods of distinguishing cashmere and wool fibers. Progress in Textile Science & Technology, 64–65 (February 2008)
4. Sheng, G.-Z., Li, L.: Study on distinguishing problem of cashmere fiber. Wool Textile Journal, 52–55 (December 2007)
5. McCaig, T.N.: Extending the use of visible/near-infrared reflectance spectrophotometers to measure color of food and agricultural products. Food Research International, 731–736 (August 2002)
6. Qi, Li., Ng, B., et al.: Near -Infrared Spectroscopic Assay of Principal Milk Constituents. Food Science, 121–124 (June 2002)
7. Wei, H.-J., Xing, D., He, B.-H., et al.: Canceration and Thermal Coagulation of Human Liver Induced Changes in the Absorption and Scattering Properties of Liver-Tissue at NearInfrared in vitro. Spectroscopy and Spectral Analysis, 868–872 (May 2007)
8. Qian, P., Sun, G.-Q., et al.: A Novel Fuzzy Neural Network Method for Diesel Quantitative Analysis with Near Infrared Spectroscopy. Spectroscopy and Spectral Analysis, 2851–2854 (December 2008)
9. Cong, S., Gao, X.P.: Recurrent neural networks and their application in system identification. Systems Engineering and Electronics, 194–197 (February 2003)
10. Zhang, L., Chai, Y.: Actuality and developmental trend for genetic algorithms. Information and Control, 53–58 (June 2001)
11. Yan, P., Zhang, C.: Artificial Neural Networks and Evolutionary Computing. Tsinghua University Press, Beijing (2005)
12. Sun, L., Zhang, Q., Chen, X., et al.: Thermal contour model of work roll in plate mills by simulated annealing algorithm. Journal of University of Science and Technology, 313–317 (March 2002)
13. Zhang, L., Li, R., Qin, Z., et al.: Elman network using simulated annealing algorithm and its application in thermal process modeling. In: Proceedings of the CSEE, vol. 25, pp. 90–94 (November 2005)
14. Wu, G.-F., Zhu, D.-S., He, Y.: Identification of Fine Wool and Cashmere by Using Vis/NIR Spectroscopy Technology. In: Spectroscopy and Spectral Analysis, pp. 1260–1263 (June 2008)
15. Lu, W.: Modern Near Infrared Spectroscopy Analytical Technology(Second Edition). China Petrochemical Press (2007)

Research on Edge Detection Algorithm of Rotary Kiln Infrared Color Image

Jie-sheng Wang[1,2] and Yong Zhang[2]

[1] Hubei Province Key Laboratory of Systems Science in Metallurgical Process, Wuhan University of Science and Technology, Wuhan 430081, China
wang_jiesheng@126.com
[2] School of Electronic and Information Engineering, Liaoning University of Science & Technology, Anshan 114044, China
zy9091@163.com

Abstract. Shuffled frog leaping algorithm (SFLA) is a meta-heuristic optimization method that mimics the memetic evolution of a group of frogs in nature seeking for food, which has been very successful in a wide variety of optimization problems. A hybrid optimization method is proposed for self-tuning pulse coupled neural network (PCNN) parameters, a biologically inspired spiking neural network, based on SFLA and was used to detect rotary kiln infrared image edges automatically and successfully. The effective of the proposed method is verified by simulation results, that is to say, the quality of the rotary kiln grayscale image edge detection is much better and parameters are set automatically.

Keywords: Pulse-Coupled Neural Network, Shuffled Frog Leaping Algorithm, Edge Detection, Rotary Kiln Infrared Image.

1 Introduction

Edge detection is a terminology in image processing and computer vision, particularly in the areas of feature detection and feature extraction, to refer to algorithms which aim at identifying points in a digital image at which the image brightness changes sharply or more formally has discontinuities [1]. There are many ways to perform edge detection. However, the majority of different methods may be grouped into two categories: gradient and Laplacian. Recently, pulse coupled neural network (PCNN) originally presented to explain the synchronous burst of the neurons in the cat visual cortex by Eckhorn has been widely used in many digital image processing research fields, such as segmentation, edge extraction, texture extraction, object identification, object isolation, motion processing, noise suppression and image fusion effectively [2-3]. However, up to now the parameters of the PCNN model (such as amplified coefficient of creep age integrator, damply time constant and weighted coefficient) are always adjusted and confirmed manually for different images, which impede PCNN's application in image processing.

According to the maximal entropy of segmented binary image of PCNN output, iterative times is determined automatically [4]. However, the coupling coefficient,

H. Deng et al. (Eds.): AICI 2011, Part III, LNAI 7004, pp. 370–377, 2011.

threshold value and damply coefficient is determined by trial and error. Reference [5] put forward a new method of improved PCNN image segmentation based on the criterion of minimum cross-entropy in order to determine the cyclic iterative times and also select the best threshold automatically. An automated PCNN system based on genetic algorithm was proposed in the image segmentation field [6]. A self-tuning optimized method for PCNN parameters based on PSO algorithm is proposed to be used to detect gray image edges [7]. However, the genetic algorithm has too many parameters to be set in advance and the local search ability of PSO algorithm is not strong.

In this paper, a new hybrid optimization method is proposed for self-tuning PCNN parameters based on SFLA was used to detect rotary kiln infrared image edges automatically and successfully. Simulation results show the effectiveness of the proposed method. The rest of the paper is organized as follows. In next section, the improved standard model of PCNN is introduced in short. Section 3 describes self-tuning method of PCNN parameters based on SFLA. Section 4 gives simulation results and contrasts with other approaches, and discusses the performance of our method. Conclusions are summarized in the end.

2 Improved Standard Model of PCNN

PCNN is a novel biological neural network developed by Elkhorn et al in 1990 and based on the experimental observations of synchronous pulse bursts in cat and monkey visual cortex [2]. The pulse coupled neuron (PCN) structure of such PCNN is exhibited in Fig.1 [7].

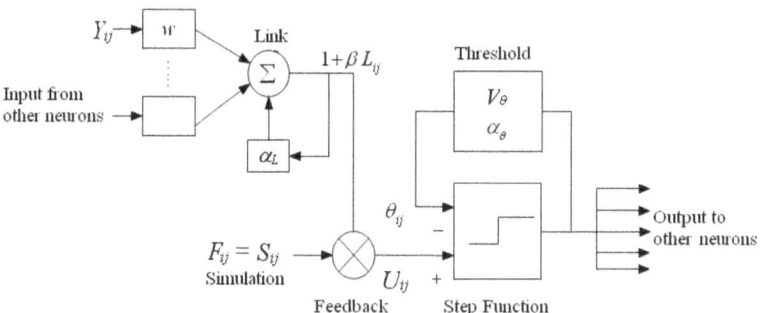

Fig. 1. Schematic representation of a PCNN processing element

The improved standard model of pulse coupled neural network [6] adopted in the paper is illustrated as follows:

$$F_{ij}[n] = S_{ij} \ . \tag{1}$$

$$L_{ij}[n] = \sum w_{ijkl} Y_{kl}[n-1] \ . \tag{2}$$

$$U_{ij}[n] = F_{ij}[n](1 + \beta L_{ij}[n]) \ . \tag{3}$$

$$Y_{ij}[n] = 1 \quad if \quad U_{ij}[n] > \theta_{ij}[n] \quad or \quad 0 \quad otherwise \; . \tag{4}$$

$$\theta_{ij}[n] = \exp(-\alpha_\theta)\theta_{ij}[n-1] + V_\theta Y_{ij}[n-1] \; . \tag{5}$$

Where n is the number of iteration and feeding input F_{ij} is simplified with the input impulse signal S_{ij}, the gray scale of pixel corresponding to neurons. L_{ij} is the link input. U_{ij} is the internal activity of corresponding neurons and decided by the feedback input F_{ij} and the link input L_{ij}, which means the state of the neuron is affected by the state of its neighborhood. Y_{ij} is the output and θ_{ij} is the dynamic threshold of the neurons. The weight matrix w_{ij} is the local interconnection. The output of neurons is only 1 or 0 based on the formula 4. When the internal activity U_{ij} is larger then the temporal dynamic threshold θ_{ij}, the neuron output is "1" or "pulsing", otherwise, it is "0" or "not pulsing". The threshold θ_{ij} corresponding to each neuron is exponential damping according to formula 5 and damping coefficient is α_θ. Interaction value between current pixel and around pixels can be adjusted by connective coefficient β.

For a two-dimensional image of $M \times N$, the PCNN can have $M \times N$ input neurons, each corresponding to a pixel in the image and taking its grayscale as the external stimulus. Neurons pulsing at the same time (which is called synchronous pulsing) have the same external stimulus, and neurons pulsing at different times (which are called asynchronous pulsing) have different external stimuli. This leads to a binary segmentation of the processed image. Apparently, the effectiveness of PCNN segmentation also relies on the parameters used in the network, such as w, β, α_θ and V_θ. The selections and adjustments of these parameters often make proper image segmentation unreliable. The local interconnection weight matrix w is easily to be set the reciprocal of distance square between pixels at nine tenths occasions. The other three parameters are adjusted in the solution space by means of SFLA.

3   Self-tuning of PCNN Parameters Based on Shuffled Frog Leaping Algorithm

3.1   Shuffled Frog Leaping Algorithm

The SFLA is a meta-heuristic optimization method that mimics the memetic evolution of a group of frogs when seeking for the location that has the maximum amount of available food[8]. It is based on evolution of memes carried by the interactive individuals, and a global exchange of information among themselves [9]. Since its inception, SFLA has found several applications in a wide variety of practical optimization problems like the water distribution network design [8], scheduling problem [10-11] and clustering problem [12].

The SFLA is described in details as follows [13]. First, an initial population of N frogs $P = \{X_1, X_2, \cdots, X_N\}$ is created randomly. For S-dimensional problems (S variables), the position of a frog i in the search space is represented as $X_i = [x_{i1}, x_{i2}, \cdots, x_{iS}]$. After the initial population is created, the individuals are sorted in a descending order according to their fitness. Then, the entire population is divided into m memeplexes, each containing n frogs (i.e. $N = m \times n$), in such a way that the first frog belongs to the first memeplex, the second frog goes to the second memeplexe, the mth frog goes to the mth memeplexe, and the $(m+1)^{th}$ frog goes back to the first memeplex, etc. Let M^k is the set of frogs in the kth memeplex; this dividing process can be described by the following expression:

$$M^k = \{X_{k+m(l-1)} \in P \mid 1 \le l \le n\}, (1 \le k \le m) . \tag{6}$$

In the each memeplex, the frogs with the best fitness and worst fitness are identified as X_b and X_w. The frog with the global best fitness in the population is identified as X_s. Then the local searching is carried out in each memeplex, that is to say the worst frog X_w leaps towards to the best frog X_b according to the original frog leaping rules described as follows.

$$D = r \cdot (X_b - X_w) . \tag{7}$$

$$X_w' = X_w + D, (\|D\| \le D_{\max}) . \tag{8}$$

Where r is a random number between 0 and 1 and $D_{\max}$ is the maximum allowed change of frog's position in one jump. If the new frog X_w' is better the original frog X_w, it replaces the worst frog. Otherwise, X_b is replaced by X_g and the local search is carried out again according to the formula (7-8). If no improvement is got in this case, the worst frog is deleted and a new frog is randomly generated to replace the worst frog X_w. The local search continues for a predefined number of memetic evolutionary steps $L_{\max}$ within each memeplex, and then the whole population is mixed together in the shuffling process. The local evolution and global shuffling continue until convergence iteration number $G_{\max}$ is arrived.

3.2 Coding and Fitness Function

In practice, the optimization of three parameters of the simplified PCNN model is multi-dimension function optimization problem. The SFLA adopts the real-number coding method and parameters are coded as ($\beta, V_\theta, \alpha_\theta$). The fitness function the system adopts as performance criterion is the entropy function proposed in reference 4 and is represented as follows:

$$F(p) = -P_1 * \log_2 P_1 - P_0 * \log_2 P_0 . \tag{9}$$

Where P_1 and P_0 represents the probability of "1" or "0" for the pixel in the output image Y[n].

3.3 Algorithm Procedure

The arithmetic procedure for optimizing PCNN model parameters by means of the SFLA to detect rotary kiln infrared image is given as follows:

Step 1: Initialize the objective function and the SFLA algorithm parameters: The parameters include the frog population size N, the searching space dimension S, the number of memeplex n, the maximum allowed change of frog's position D_{max}, the local searching number L_{max} and the global hybrid iteration number G_{max}.

Step 2: Frog population creation. Randomly initial the population of N frogs $P = \{X_1(t), \cdots, X_k(t) \cdots, X_N(t)\}$ $(k = 1, \cdots, N)$. Set the iteration counter $t = 0$. Then calculate the fitness (entropy of rotary kiln infrared image) $F_k(t) = F(X_k(t))$ based on formula (9) by means of decoding the frog individual solution vector $X_k(t)$ into the standard PCNN model (formula 1-5). Then the frogs are sorted in a descending order according to their fitness. The outcome is stored with the style $U_k(t) = \{X_k(t), F_k(t)\}$. The global best frog in the frog population is identified as $X_g(t) = U_1(t)$.

Step 3: Memeplex creation. The U is divided into the m memeplex $M^1(t), \cdots, M^j(t), \cdots, M^m(t)(j = 1, \cdots, m)$ according to the formula (6). Each memeplex includes n frogs. The frogs with the best fitness and worst fitness in the memeplex are identified as $X_b^j(t)$ and $X_w^j(t)$.

Step 4: Memeplex evolution. The worst frog $X_w^j(t)$ in the memeplex $M^j(t)$ is carried out the local search based on the frog leaping rules described in the formula (7-8). Then calculate the fitness (entropy of rotary kiln infrared image) based on formula (9) by means of decoding the frog individual solution vector into the standard PCNN model (formula 1-5). If the new frog is better the original frog, then the $X_w^j(t)$ is substituted. Otherwise, $X_b^j(t)$ is substituted by $X_g(t)$ to carry out the local search again. If no improvement is got, a new frog is created randomly to substitute the $X_w^j(t)$. The local search is gone on the L_{max} iteration to obtain the improved memeplex $M^1(t)', M^2(t)', \cdots, M^m(t)'$.

Step 5: Memeplex shuffled. The frogs in the iterated memeplex $M^1(t)', M^2(t)', \cdots, M^m(t)'$ is mixed together in the shuffling process and identified as $U(t+1) = \{M^1(t)', M^2(t)', \cdots, M^m(t)'\}$. Then the frogs in the $U(t+1)$ are sorted in a descending order according to their fitness. The new global best frog in the population is identified as $X_g(t+1) = U_1(t+1)$.

Step 6: Test the algorithm termination conditon. $t = t+1$, if $t < G_{max}$, go to then step 3. Otherwise output the best frog.

4 Simulation Results

Rotary kiln pellets sintering is the most widely used agglomeration process for iron ores and is a very important chain of iron making. The paper adopts the SFLA to optimize the parameters of PCNN model to detect the rotary kiln infrared image edges. The parameters of the SFLA are: the frog population size N is 50. The searching space dimension S is 3. The number of memeplex n is 10. The maximum allowed change of frog's position D_{max} is 0.02. The local searching number L_{max} is 5. The global hybrid iteration number G_{max} is 100.

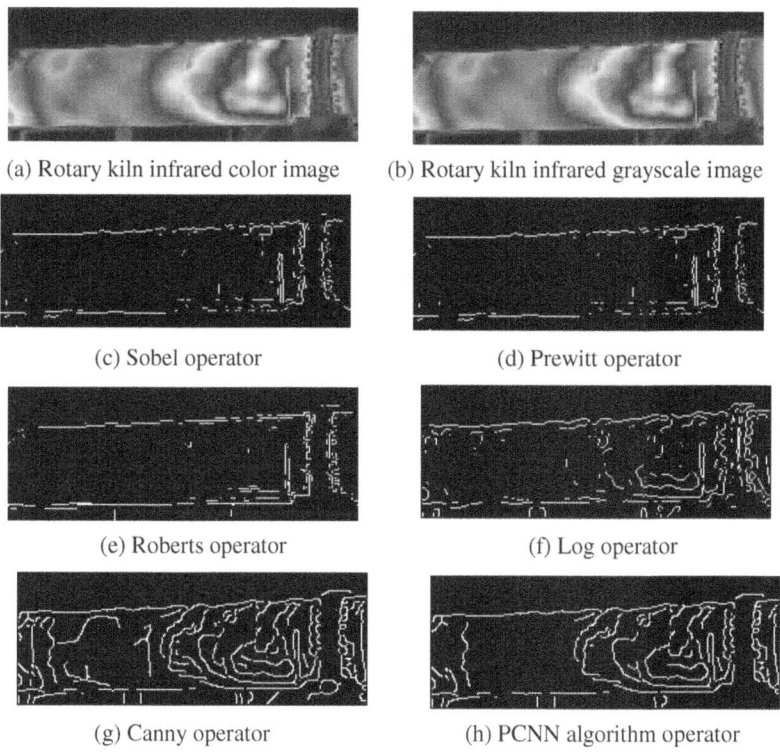

(a) Rotary kiln infrared color image   (b) Rotary kiln infrared grayscale image

(c) Sobel operator   (d) Prewitt operator

(e) Roberts operator   (f) Log operator

(g) Canny operator   (h) PCNN algorithm operator

Fig. 2. Edge detection results of rotary kiln infrared image

In order to validity the proposed method, the paper carries through the simulation tests to detect the edges of rotary kiln infrared image on the platform of MATLAB 7.0. The simulation results are illustrated in Fig.2. Fig.2 (a) and Fig.2 (b) is original rotary kiln infrared color image and the grayscale image, respectively. Fig.2 (c, d, e, f and g) is the edge detection results by means of Sobel operator, Prewitt operator, Roberts operator, Log operator and Canny operator. Fig. 2(h) is edge detection result by means of the proposed method. It is obvious that the detection result by the SFLA is finer and has better effect at the more blurry edge zones.

5   Conclusions

Pulse coupled neural network (PCNN) is a hot research in the intelligent field and has been widely used in denoising, segmentation, edge detection, object identification, and feature extraction effectively. The selection of PCNN model parameters is vital important to the performance. To solve this problem, based on the model of pulse coupled neural network, this paper brings forward a shuffled frog leaping algorithm in the rotary kiln infrared color image edge detection. The SFLA simple in concept, few in parameters, easy in implementation, and does not require any derivative information. The experiment results show the good effect of the proposed method.

Acknowledgments. This work is supported by the Hubei Province Key Laboratory of Systems Science in Metallurgical Process (Wuhan University of Science and Technology), China (Grant No. B201002) and the Program for the Innovative Research Team of Education Bureau of Liaoning Province, China (Grant No. 2008T091).

References

1. Ziou, D., Tabbone, S.A.: Multi-scale Edge Detector. Pattern Recognition 26, 1305–1314 (1993)
2. Johnson, J.L., Padgett, M.L.: PCNN Models and Applications. IEEE Trans. on Neural Networks 10, 480–498 (1999)
3. Kuntimad, G., Ranganath, H.S.: Perfect Image Segmentation Using Pulse Coupled Neural Networks. IEEE Trans. on Neural Networks 10, 591–598 (1999)
4. Ma, Y.D., Dai, R.L., Li, L.: Automated Image Segmentation Using Pulse Coupled Neural Networks and Images Entropy. Journal of China Institute of Communications 23, 46–51 (2002)
5. Liu, Q., Ma, Y.D., Qian, Z.B.: Automated Image Segmentation Using Improved PCNN Model Based on Cross-entropy. Journal of Image and Graphics 10, 579–584 (2005)
6. Ma, Y.D., Qi, C.L.: Study of Automated PCNN System Based on Genetic Algorithm. Journal of System Simulation 18, 722–725 (2006)
7. Wang, J.S., Cong, F.W.: Grayscale Image Edge Detection Based on Pulse-coupled Neural Network and Particle Swarm Optimization. In: 20th Chinese Control and Decision Conference, pp. 2492–2495. IEEE Press, New York (2008)
8. Eusuff, M.M., Lansey, K.E.: Optimization of Water Distribution Network Design Using the Shuffled Frog Leaping Algorithm. Journal of Water Resources Planning and Management 129, 210–225 (2003)

9. Elbeltagi, E., Hezagy, T., Grierson, D.: Comparison Among Five Evolutionary-based Optimization Algorithms. Advanced Engineering Informatics 19, 43–53 (2005)
10. Rahimi-Vahed, A., Mirzaei, A.H.: A Hybrid Multi-objective Shuffled Frog-leaping Algorithm for a Mixed-model Assembly Line Sequencing Problem. Computers and Industrial Engineering 53, 642–666 (2007)
11. Rahimi-Vahed, A., Dangchi, M., Rafiei, H.: A Novel Hybrid Multi-objective Shuffled Frog-leaping Algorithm for a Bi-criteria Permutation Flow Shop Scheduling Problem. International Journal of Advanced Manufacturing Technology 41, 1227–1239 (2009)
12. Amiri, B., Fathian, M., Maroosi, A.: Application of Shuffled Frog-leaping Algorithm on Clustering. International Journal of Advanced Manufacturing Technology 45, 199–209 (2009)

LVQ Neural Network Based Classification Decision Approach to Mechanism Type in Conceptual Design

Jiande Wu

School of Mechanical Engineering & Automation,
North University of China, Taiyuan 030051, China
wjdgjy@163.com

Abstract. A decision approach to mechanism type selection is presented, which employs LVQ neural network as classifier and decision-maker to recognize a satisfactory mechanism from a range of mechanisms achieving a required kinematic function. Through learning from correct samples extracted from different mechanisms, expert knowledge is acquired and expressed in the form of weight matrix by LVQ network. When selecting mechanism type, through digitizing the design requirements, converting into a characteristic factor set, and fed into the trained LVQ network, a satisfactory mechanism can be automatically recognized from a range of mechanisms with the same kinematic function. Under this approach, the problem of knowledge acquisition and expression can be effectively solved, and the rationality of the decision can be improved at some extent. It is verified this approach is feasible to perform mechanism type selection and possesses a better characteristic of pattern classification compared with BP neural network.

Keywords: Mechanism type selection, LVQ neural network, Knowledge acquisition, Mechanical design.

1 Introduction

An approach of function decomposition is generally adopted in conceptual design of mechanical system [1]. The first step is to acquire the general-function of mechanical product. Then using function decomposition, a complicated design problem regarding general-function can be divided into many simple design problems regarding function units. For each function unit, a sequence of function carriers are searched using design catalogue [2]. The following step is to select one satisfactory mechanism in above function carriers, which is called a problem of mechanism type selection. Commonly used approach to this problem is implemented by designers according to their domain experience, which will undoubtedly result in the limitations and blindness of the decision result if domain experience is poor.

Neural network has proven to be an effective and powerful tool to implement mechanism type selection in conceptual design since it possesses the features of non-linearity, self-organization, and fault-tolerance. BP and ART neural network are two popular networks for this purpose [3]. However, the decision performance of BP is affected by its network structure (e.g., the number of layer and node of hidden layer)

H. Deng et al. (Eds.): AICI 2011, Part III, LNAI 7004, pp. 378–384, 2011.

at a large extent, and its node function has a heavy impact on its learning rate and quality. ART network is also affected by its network structure, moreover, similarity discriminant function, standardization and denoising preprocessing function of F1 layer needs to be constructed, which also affects the performance of this network.

Compared with these two networks, LVQ network possesses simpler network structure, faster learning rate, more reliable classification, and better fault tolerance. Thus LVQ neural network is employed as classifier to recognize a satisfactory mechanism from a range of mechanisms through learning and accumulating the domain expertise. The reasoning process of evaluation and decision can be automaticlly implemented and the process of conceptual design can be simplified at some extent.

The remainder of this paper is presented as follows. First, we present the basic process and principle of mechanism type selection based on ANN. Then we propose fuzzy quantization method of the characteristic factor value. Next this LVQ neural network based decision model is illustrated in detail, including the structure of neural network, training and testing, etc. Finally concluding remarks are given.

2 Technical Preliminaries

2.1 Problem Statement

Mechanism type selection can be viewed as a decision problem regarding satisfactory mechanism type on the basis of considering multi-factors synthetically. That means, a decision problem involves six elements, viz. [V, U, W, P, D, R]. V represents the decision set, viz. $V = \{V_1, V_2, ..., V_m\}$, which is a set of m types of mechanisms for decision. U represents a characteristic factor set, viz. $U = \{U_1, U_2, ..., U_n\}$, which is a set of n types of characteristic factors to be considered, where n equals 5 and U_1, U_2, U_3, U_4, and U_5 respectively stand for Working performance, Kinetic performance, Economy, Maneuverability, and Structural compactness. W represents the weight set, viz. $W = \{W_1, W_2, ..., W_n\}$, which shows the importance of each characteristic factor. U and W constitute an evaluation index system. P is called a pre-processor used to transform each evaluation index into the allowable input value for the decision model. D represents the decision model for mechanism type selection, and R represents the decision result [4].

2.2 Decision Principle

The problem of mechanism type selection can be regarded as a pattern classification and recognition problem, viz. classifying different patterns by extracting their typical features and recognizing the result pattern through matching the known design conditions [5]. Here, the characteristic factor set in Table 1 actually represents the optimum application conditions for each mechanism, called the typical characteristic factor set U*. When selecting mechanism type, each performance index determined by design requirements can be fuzzily quantified and constitute a characteristic factor set U, then a type of mechanism is selected according to the above typical characteristic factor set U*, which is the fittest mechanism for characteristic factor set U. The decision can be implemented based on the closeness degree between U* and U by valuators, which is an experiential selection mode in nature. Whereas LVQ neural network has the advantages in classification and decision over BP or ART, it acts as a Classifier and decision-maker for selecting mechanism type through modeling the nonlinear relations between input and output data. When an optimum mechanism is required to be selected from a series of mechanisms achieving a certain function, the typical characteristic factor set U* for each mechanism is regarded as the training sample to train the neural network first, then the required factor set U derived from design requirements is fed into the trained network, finally through the decision a suited mechanism type is exported. This process is facilitated by the way in which the model acts as a knowledge base and reasoning engine for decision. The decision process incorporates the evaluation and ranking process and to some extent it simplifies the process of conceptual design.

2.3 Decision Process

A neural network based decision model is applied to implement mechanism type selection. The decision process is shown in Fig. 1.

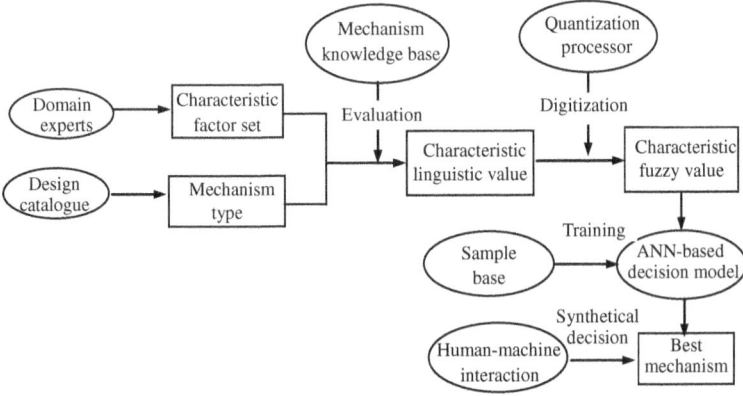

Fig. 1. Process of mechanism type selection

3   Feature Digitization and Extraction for Typical Mechanism

It is obvious that the input values of neural network are numerical data. However, the expressive meanings of above–mentioned characteristic factors of mechanisms are fuzzy in nature, which are usually expressed in a linguistic mode according to the valuator's experience. As a result, it is required to convert this linguistic expression into numerical data. Fuzzy set theory is proved to be an effective tool in implementing a comparative precise quantization for characteristic factor [6]. Through building the membership function for each factor and calculating the corresponding membership degree, a quantitative measurement can be obtained. For example, for the characteristic factor of structural compactness, the number of kinematic pairs, can be used as an independent variable of the membership function, viz. x, the maximum and the minimum membership degrees for the mechanism are respectively 1 and 0, and a membership function in the form of a descending half-trapezoid is obtained.

Using this membership function, the membership degree for the mechanisms with different numbers of kinematic pairs can be calculated. For those characteristic factors, which cannot be easily measured by constructing linear membership function, a fuzzy statistical method or duality contrast ranking method can be used to implement the quantization process. Under this disposal, semantic expression values of characteristic factors are digitized and features of different mechanisms are extracted. Table 1 gives the characteristic factor values of four types of typical mechanisms used to convert continuous rotation into intermittent rotation in a kinematic scheme design of a certain machine tool, viz.Geneva mechanism(V_1),Imperfect gear device(V_2), Cam intermittent mechanism(V_3), and Internal epicycle intermittent mechanism(V_4) [7].

Table 1. Characteristic values and classification values of typical mechanisms

Drive type	Characteristic value					Classification value			
	U_1	U_2	U_3	U_4	U_5	1	2	3	4
V_1	0.95	0.25	0.95	0.65	0.65	1	0	0	0
V_2	0.90	0.20	0.15	0.72	0.60	0	1	0	0
V_3	0.85	0.95	0.15	0.70	0.65	0	0	1	0
V_4	1.00	0.70	0.10	0.68	0.80	0	0	0	1

4 LVQ Neural Network Based Decision Model

4.1 The Structure of Network Model

Learning Vector Quantization (LVQ) is a learning algorithm that combines competitive learning with supervision [8]. It was originally suggested by Kohonen. A LVQ network is a two-layer neural network, including a competitive layer and a linear layer. The competitive layer is the core layer that performs classification through learning. Each neuron in the competitive layer of the LVQ network learns to recognize a prototype vector, which allows it to classify a region of the input space. In using LVQ networks, we directly calculate the distances between the input vectors and the prototype vectors to achieve classification. If two input vectors are close to each other, they belong to a same class. A basic LVQ network is shown in Fig.2. In this figure, R is the number of element of input vector, S is the number of neuron, P is the input vector, W is the weight matrix, and A is the output vector. The competitive layer performs classification of input vectors, and the linear layer converts the classification information into the desired class defined by user and output them automatically. Therefore, the neuron whose weight vector is closest to the input vector will output 1, and the other neurons will output 0.The input vector contains R nodes for R input features, the competitive layer contains equal numbers of nodes for each class, and in the output layer, each output node represents a particular class. It is obvious that the input vectors can be classified into N classes if the LVQ network possesses N neurons. In the decision model, for the reason that there are 5 characteristic factors serving as input values, the number of nodes for the competitive layer is 5 and the number of nodes for the linear layer equals the number of mechanisms in the decision set, in which each mechanism corresponds to an output node and different nodes represent different mechanism types. For the decision model constructed by the data of Table 1, it is obvious that the number of nodes for the linear layer is 4 and its output classification is also given in Table 1.

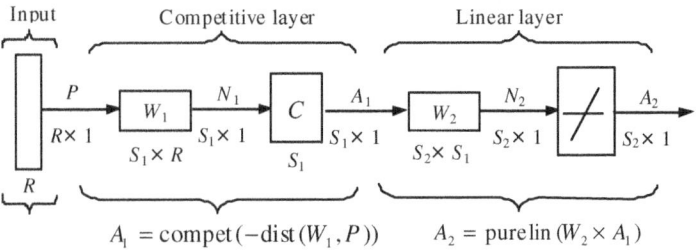

Fig. 2. Structure of LVQ neural network

4.2 Learning and Simulation

Since LVQ performs learning with supervision, correct training samples are required to be provided for neural network's training. The quality of samples has a critical influence on the performance of network. Once the training process terminates, the classification surface is fixed and the corresponding decision system is formed. In this decision model, training samples are typical characteristic factor sets of various mechanisms in decision set. Here, characteristic factor values of 4 types of mechanisms in Table 1 employed as input data, and the corresponding classification results in Table 1 employed as output data, constitute four pairs of training samples from 1 to 4, as shown in Table 2, which can be fed into the network to train it. Neural network toolbox of Matlab 6.5 affords facilities for this learning and training process. First, the LVQ network is constructed by a "newlvq" function provided by neural network toolbox of Matlab 6.5. Then a training function called "train" is applied to implement the training to get the weight matrix. The network is convergent at last after 150 epochs of iteration. Thus it can be employed a decisionmaker to select an appropriate mechanism from a group of mechanisms.

In order to know the performance of this network, a testing process is required to implement after the LVQ have been trained. Here, a "sim" function is used to implement simulation. The character factor values for mechanism can be obtained first according to the concrete design requirements, which is expressed with linguistic mode. Then through fuzzy quantization, the corresponding characteristic factor values are obtained, which can be used as input vectors of this trained network. In Table 2, the vectors from 1 to 4 are fed into the network to implement simulation, and correct decision results are given. The rest of the samples are testing samples derived from other design problems, in which the input values of the 5th and 6th samples are close to the values of a certain mechanism respectively and the correct decision result is given, moreover, the values of the 7th and 8th samples are between the values of two types of mechanisms, which is a difficult decision problem, and where a certain mechanism is selected using this model. The above simulation result shows LVQ classifier has the advantage of better fault torlance and stability over other neural networks.

Table 2. Recognition results of the LVQ network

Sample	Input					Output				Expected result	Decision result
	U_1	U_2	U_3	U_4	U_5	V_1	V_2	V_3	V_4		
1	0.95	0.25	0.95	0.65	0.65	1	0	0	0	V_1	V_1
2	0.90	0.20	0.15	0.72	0.60	0	1	0	0	V_2	V_2
3	0.85	0.95	0.15	0.70	0.65	0	0	1	0	V_3	V_3
4	1.00	0.70	0.10	0.68	0.80	0	0	0	1	V_4	V_4
5	1.00	0.30	0.95	0.50	0.50	1	0	0	0	V_1	V_1
6	0.90	0.35	0.25	0.70	0.50	0	1	0	0	V_2	V_2
7	0.85	0.60	0.65	0.60	0.60	1	0	0	0	V_1 or V_3	V_1
8	0.85	0.20	0.95	0.80	0.50	0	1	0	0	V_1 or V_2	V_2

5   Conclusion

In this paper, an approach to mechanism type selection is proposed according to the nonlinear mapping and clustering characteristic of LVQ neural network. This approach employs neural network as a tool to implement the reasoning process of evaluation and decision-making, in which the process of conceptual design can be simplified at some extent, the problem of the expression and accumulation for expert knowledge can be effectively solved, and the rationality of the decision can be improved. It is concluded that the LVQ network based decision model developed is appropriate to be used for selecting mechanism type at the early design stage.

Acknowledgments. This research was supported by the Youth Science Foundation of Shanxi Province of China under contract number 2007021028.

References

1. Cao, D.X., Tan, R.H., Yuan, C.Y.: Conceptual Design for Mechanical Product Based on function Decomposition. Chinese J. of Mechanical Engineering 37, 13–17 (2001)
2. Feng, P.E., Xu, G.R.: Feature Modeling Based on Design Catalogues for Search of Principle Solutions. Chinese J. of Mechanical Engineering 34, 79–86 (1998)
3. Liu, K.: Compared Research on Classified Decision and Presentation of Mechanical Design between BP net-work and ART Network. Machine Design 15, 14–17 (1998)
4. Bo, R.F.: A New Approach to Mechanism Type Selection by Using Back-Propagation Neural Networks. In: the 2010 International Conference on Artificial Intelligence and Computational Intelligence, pp. 205–209. IEEE Computer Society, Piscataway (2010)

5. Sun, J., Kalenchuk, D.K.: Design Candidate Identification Using Neural Network based Fuzzy Reasoning. Robotics and Computer-Integrated Manufacturing 16, 382–396 (2000)
6. Wang, J.: Ranking Engineering Design Concepts Using a Fuzzy Outranking Preference Model. Fuzzy Sets and Systems 119, 161–170 (2001)
7. Bo, R.F.: An Approach to Mechanism Type Selection Using LVQ Neural Network. Machine Design & Research 25, 18–21 (2009)
8. Dong, C.H.: Neural network and its application. National Defence Industry Press, Beijing (2005)

Research of Bayesian Networks Application to Transformer Fault Diagnosis

Qin Li[1,2], Zhibin Li[1], Qi Zhang[1], and Liusu Zeng[3]

[1] School of Electric Power and Automation Engineering,
Shanghai University of Electric Power, Shanghai, China
liqin@shiep.edu.cn
[2] CIMS Research Centre, Tongji University, Shanghai, China
[3] School of Electric Information and Electrical Engineering,
Shanghai Jiaotong University, Shanghai, China

Abstract. The power transformer as the key equipment in electrical power systems, its operation reliability directly influences security of electrical power systems. Three-ratio method based on the Dissolved Gases Analysis is most widely used for transformer fault diagnosis currently. Considering the incomplete encoding and the over absolute faults classification zone of three-ratio method, this paper proposes no-code ratio method and Bayesian Network to diagnose the faults of transformer. The Bayesian Network diagnostic model is built by Bayesian Network Tool in MATLAB, and the simulation result shows the validity of this method.

Keywords: power transformer, fault diagnosis, Bayesian Network, no-code ratio.

1 Introduction

With complicated structure, high cost and wide distribution, power transformer is one of the key electrical equipments in power systems. The transformer works to convert voltage and transmit power, so its safe operation directly influences the stability and security of the entire power system. The faults diagnosis of transformer is very difficult due to its complicated structure and uncertain factors of faults, and three-ratio method (IEC standard) based on Dissolved Gases Analysis (DGA) is most convenient and effective method for transformer faults diagnosis currently in China [1]. However, this method has some drawbacks found in practical application, such as incomplete encoding, too absolute coding border, and so on. In order to overcome these drawbacks, some intelligent methods like artificial neural networks [2], wavelet analysis [3], gray clustering [4], Petri networks [5], are introduced into the transformer fault diagnosis and achieve better results.

The analysis of faults generation mechanism shows there is no definite function relationship between transformer faults and gas content in oil and it is difficult to speculate the distribution of gas content. In addition, the accuracy and quantity of data acquisition in field is very limit, thus prior knowledge is needed. Bayesian Network

H. Deng et al. (Eds.): AICI 2011, Part III, LNAI 7004, pp. 385–391, 2011.

(BN) may be used to model a system that works with uncertainty, which can be caused by an imperfect or incomplete understanding of the problem [1], with its recent development of Bayesian Network inference theorem, many people are trying to apply it into practice. This paper proposes no-code ratio method and Bayesian Network to diagnose the faults of transformer, and builds Bayesian Network diagnostic model by Bayesian Network Tool (BNT) in MATLAB.

2 Bayesian Network

Bayesian Network is valid knowledge representation and probabilistic reasoning model for uncertain knowledge and which is a popular graphical tools for decision analysis [6].

The Bayesian Network of a variable set $X=\{x1, x2, \cdots, xn\}$ consists of two parts.

- Network structure S, representing the conditional dependence of variables in X.
- Local probability distribution P: Associated with each variable.

The combination of these two parts defines the joint probability distribution of X. Represented in a graphical form, as shown in Fig. 1, Bayesian Network is a directed acyclic graph, where each node corresponding with each variable in X, no arc connected between two nodes shows they are conditional independence. For any given network structure S, the joint probability distribution of X is represented in Eq.1.

$$p(x) = \prod_{i=1}^{n} p(x_i|Pa_i) \tag{1}$$

Where Pa_i is the father nodes set of x_i, the item p in the product, is the local probability, this can bring about the following benefits.

- The capacity of the joint distribution table can be exponentially decreased by the local probability distribution, because the interaction relationship between the variables is sparse in a multivariate Bayesian Network.
- There are many Bayesian inference algorithms for local distribution table.
- It helps to build knowledge engineering model by separating quantitative representation and qualitative representation of Bayesian Network.

Different from the general knowledge-based system, Bayesian Network deals with uncertain knowledge with powerful mathematical tool and interprets it in a simple and intuitive way. In addition, Bayesian Network combines graphical representation method and numerical representation method, which is different from the general probability analysis tools too.

Since Bayesian Network $BN=<S,P>$ is composed by two parts, the network topology S and the set of local probability distribution P, so the learning of Bayesian Networks can be divided into two steps.

- Structural learning, that is directed acyclic graph learning.
- Parameter learning, that is the learning of local conditional probability distribution of each variable in the network.

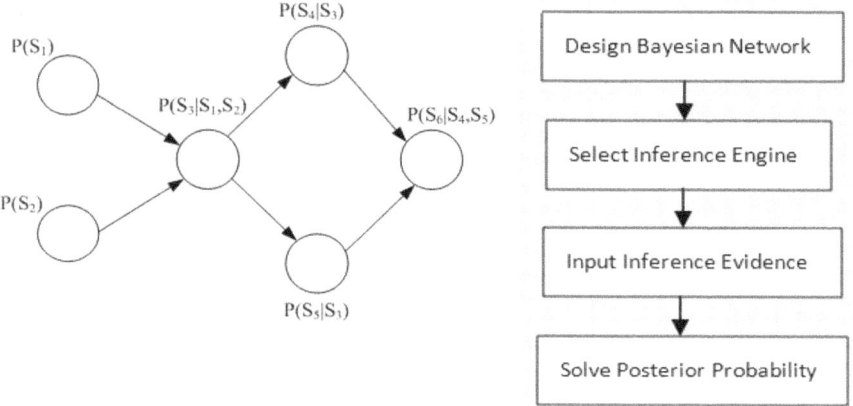

Fig. 1. Bayesian Network
Fig. 2. Inference procedures

3   Introduction of Bayesian Network Toolbox

BNT is software package for Bayesian Network learning based on MATLAB, and developed by Kevin P. Murphy, which provides many underlying basic functions library for Bayesian learning, and supports multiple types of nodes (probability distribution), exact inference & approximate inference, parameter learning & structural learning, static model & dynamic model. BNT software package is free, source code open and easy to be expanded.

BNT offers the following two parameter learning methods.

- For complete data, there are Maximum likelihood estimation (*learn params()*) and Bayesian Network method (*bayes update params ()*).
- For incomplete data, if network topology is known, Expectation Maximization (EM) is used to calculate parameters, if network topology is unknown, SEM (Structural EM) (*learn struct EM()*) can be used.

In order to improve calculating speed and effective application of various inference algorithm, BNT adopts engine mechanism, and different engine completes the transformation, refinement and solving of model by different algorithms. Fig. 2 shows the inference procedures.

4   Transformer Fault Diagnosis Based on No-code Ratio Method and Bayesian Network

4.1   Determination of Attribute Variables, Fault Types, and the Training Sample Set

In order to construct a faults diagnosis Bayesian Network with correct and expansible decision-making, we must firstly collect enough samples for learning. The faults of transformer are diverse; the symptoms of one fault for transformers of different models and different voltage levels are different. When the transformer fault happens, it is usually caused by excessive level of a certain gas or several certain gases, and when it is caused by excessive level of several certain gases, maybe only one or a few are dominant for the fault. Through transformer fault occurrences collecting in Chinese cities more than ten years and analysis of simulated faults chromatographic data from other nations, Chinese power workers no-code ratio method to analyze and diagnose transformer faults. The ratios for this method are CH4/H2, C2H2/C2H4, C2H4/C2H6, C2H2/total(%) , H2/total(%) , C2H4/total(%), CH4/total(%), C2H6/total(%), (CH4+C2H4)/total(%), where total means total hydrocarbon. This method determines one fault directly by the ratio itself, no ratio coding. Comparing with the traditional three-ratio method, no-code ratio method saves the procedures of coding first and then querying the faults type by code, thus simplifies the analytical decision methods and improves the operability. However, no-code ratio method is not suitable for excessive level of pure hydrogen, H2, C2H2, and total hydrocarbons (total) as three characteristic gases are added to the attribute set to overcome the drawback. Thus the faults due to excessive level of some single gas and due to excessive rate of some gas in the total hydrocarbons or in the total gas are both considered. Table 1 shows the selection of the attribute set, and Table 2 shows the fault types according to IEC standards and DL/T 722-2000 guidelines.

Table 1. Attribute set

No.	Attribute	No.	Attribute
M1	H_2	M7	C_2H_2/total (%)
M2	C_2H_2	M8	H_2/total (%)
M3	total	M9	C_2H_4/total (%)
M4	CH_4/H_2	M10	CH_4/total (%)
M5	C_2H_2/C_2H_4	M11	C_2H_6/total (%)
M6	C_2H_4/C_2H_6	M12	$(CH_4+C_2H_4)$ /total (%)

The number of samples employed in this paper are 302, 176 of which are training samples and 126 are testing samples, as shown in Table 4.

Table 2. Fault types

Fault types	Fault description	Fault types	Fault description
C	Normal	PD	Partial discharge(PD)
T1	Low temperature and overheat(LO)	D1	Low energy discharge(LD)
T2	Medium temperature and overheat(MO)	D2	High energy discharge(HD)
T3	High temperature and overheat(HO)		

Table 3. Discretization of fault types

Attribute No.	Code Rules			
	0	1	2	3
M1	[0,1]	[10,130]	[130,180]	[180,∞]
M2	0	[0,1]	[1,5]	[5,∞]
M3	[0,20]	[20,140]	[140,200]	[200,∞]
M4	[0,0.1]	[0.1,1]	[1,∞]	–
M5	[0,0.1]	[0.1,3]	[3,∞]	–
M6	[0,1]	[1,3]	[3,∞]	–
M7~M12	[0,15]	[15,50]	[50,80]	[80,∞]

Table 4. Samples allocation

Samples type	Normal C	LO T1	MO T2	HO T3	PD PD	LD D1	HD D2	TOTAL
Training samples	25	18	27	28	25	25	28	176
Testing samples	19	13	17	20	18	19	20	126
total	44	31	44	48	43	44	48	302

4.2 Bayesian Network Modeling for Transformer Fault Diagnosis by BNT

The Bayesian Network is firstly determined and defined it in MATLAB according to Fig. 2. Secondly, parameter learning is executed and the conditional probability (CPT) of each variable in the Bayesian Network is calculated. Finally, the testing samples are input and inferred. The attribute values in Table 1 are discretized by Table 3 as input of the Bayesian Network. The network output is fault type, which is $[1\ 0\ 0\ 0\ 0\ 0\ 0]^T$ when the transformer state is normal. If there is some certain fault happened, the output of C is 0, and the output of that certain fault is 1, other outputs of faults are all 0. For example, if the $T1$ fault happens, the output of the Bayesian Network is $[0\ 1\ 0\ 0\ 0\ 0\ 0]^T$.

4.3 Fault Testing and Analysis of Application Example

Four groups of transformer DGA faults diagnosis data recognized by maintenance are selected for testing, as shown in Table 5. And these four groups of data are not included in the training samples of Bayesian Network model. The diagnostic results of Bayesian Network in Table 6 shows the diagnostic results completely match the practical fault types, and the transformer faults diagnosis system designed in this paper is valid and effective.

In order to verify the validity of the method presented in this paper, 126 samples are analyzed, and the results are compared with those of three-ratio method, as shown in Table 7.

Table 5. Example faults

μL/L

No.	equipment	H_2	CH_4	C_2H_6	C_2H_4	C_2H_2	Diagnosis result	Check result
1	220kv main transformer	980	570	37	480	54	Arc discharge	Inter-turn short-circuited and burn
2	110kv main transformer	73	520	140	1230	7	High temperature and overheat	Core pallets and core short-circuited and melting point
3	110kv main transformer	259	863	393	994	6	Medium temperature and overheat	Low-pressure casing, conducting rod and screw nut overheat, and obvious overheat signs
4	110kv main transformer	80	20	6	20	62	Spark discharge	Bare conductive wires discharge to casing conducting pipe

Table 6. Output of Bayesian Network faults diagnosis model

No.	Output	Faults
1	0 0 0 0 0 0 1	Arc discharge D2
2	0 0 0 1 0 0 0	HO T3
3	0 0 1 0 0 0 0	MO T2
4	0 0 0 1 0 0 0	Spark discharge D1

Table 7. Comparison of two methods

	Three-ratio method	No-code ratio and Bayesian Network model
Testing samples	126	126
Correct diagnosis	96	117
Wrong diagnosis	19	7
Unable to diagnose	11	2
Correct rate (%)	76.2%	92.8%

The comparison results in Table 7 illustrates that the combination of no-code ratio and Bayesian Network can be used for transformer faults diagnosis, and which has higher correct diagnosis rate than the popular used three-ratio method.

5 Conclusions

This paper combines no-code ratio method and Bayesian Network to build Bayesian Network faults diagnosis model by BNT in MATLAB, which no only overcomes drawbacks of three-ratio method such as implement code, over absolute coding border, but also well utilize the causal reasoning of Bayesian Network to achieve probabilistic reasoning, thus the transformer faults can be quickly determined. Examples illustrates this combined method is valid and feasible, and can be used for uncertainty reasoning. The diagnostic results show the effectiveness of the method.

Acknowledgements. This work is sponsored by National Natural Science Foundation of China (No. 61040013) and Shanghai Science and Technology Commission Key Program (No. 10250502000).

References

1. China Electricity Council: GB / T 7252-2001 transformer oil dissolved gas analysis and determination guidelines. Chinese Standard Press, Beijing (2001)
2. Xiaoxia, W., Tao, W.: Power Transformer Fault Diagnosis Based on Neural Network Evolved by Particle Swarm Optimizaion. High Voltage Engineering 34(11), 2362–2367 (2008)
3. Weigen, C., Chong, P., Yuxin, Y., Youyuan, W., Caixin, S.: Fault diagnostic method for power transformer based on improved wavelet neural network algorithm. Chinese Journal of Scientific Instrument 29(7), 1490–1493 (2008)
4. Jian, L., Caixin, S., Weigen, C., Guoqing, C., Xuemei, C.: Study on Fault Diagnosis of Insulation of Oil-immersed Transformer Based on Grey Cluster Theory. Transactions of China Electrotechnical Soceity 17(4), 80–83 (2002)
5. Jianyuan, W., Yanchao, J.: Application of fuzzy Petri nets knowledge representation in electric power transformer fault diagnosis. Proceedings of the Csee 23(1), 121–125 (2003)
6. Friedman, N., Geiger, D., Goldszmidt, M.: Bayesian Network classifiers. Machine Learning 29(3), 131–163 (1997)

A Noise-Robust Speech Recognition System Based on Wavelet Neural Network[*]

Yiping Wang and Zhefeng Zhao

College of Information Engineering, Taiyuan University of Technology,
030024 Taiyuan, China
ping6998@163.com

Abstract. Aiming at the problem that the performance of speech recognition system will drop severely in noisy environments, this paper proposed a recognition system that has excellent anti-noise performance. The feature parameters of front-end are ZCPA (Zero-Crossings with Peak-Amplitudes) feature and the recognition network of back-end is wavelet neural network. Mexican Hat wavelet was used to replace the Sigmoid or Gaussian basis function of feed-forward neural network. The network structure was three layers. Training network weights, determining the position and scale factor of wavelet function were processed respectively. And the information of training samples was made full use of when estimating the position factor. Hence, the network could converge rapidly and it also avoided the problem of wavelet "dimension disaster". A 50 isolated-word person-independent speech recognition system using BP network or wavelet neural network as recognition network was simulated under different SNRs in this experiment. The experimental results showed that recognition rates using wavelet neural network are higher than using BP network.

Keywords: speech recognition, wavelet neural network, ZCPA feature, mexican hat wavelet.

1 Introduction

Wavelet neural network[1] with a lot of excellent performance is a new feed-forward neural network based on wavelet analysis theory. This paper presented the structure and design method of wavelet network, it also analyzed advantage of this network for speech recognition. Traditional features such as LPC, MFCC have got excellent recognition results under clean environment, but their performance will deteriorate severely in noisy condition. This paper introduced a new anti-noise speech feature parameter named ZCPA and combined with wavelet neural network, a 50 words person-independent speech recognition system can be built. The experiment results showed it has excellent performance with this system in both clean and noisy environments.

[*] This work was partially funded by Shanxi Province Foundation for Returnees(2009-31), International Scientific and Technological Cooperation Projects in Shanxi Province(2008-081026).

H. Deng et al. (Eds.): AICI 2011, Part III, LNAI 7004, pp. 392–397, 2011.

2 Presentation of ZCPA Feature

ZCPA feature[2] represents the signal frequency characteristics via speech signal zero-crossings rate. Signals of different frequency have different zero-crossings rate, and the characteristics of frequency can be reflected by extracting the intervals between adjacent zero-crossings of signals. Fig.1 illustrates the principle of ZCPA system. This system consists of band-pass filters, zero-crossing point detectors, peak value detectors, nonlinear compression and frequency receivers. The band-pass filters are composed of 16 FIR filters, which are used to simulate the cochlear base membrane. While the others simulate the movement of audio nerve fiber in the cochlear, so such features have strong anti-noise performance. The intensity information is obtained from the peak value detector and then compressed nonlinearly. The frequency receiver compounds the frequency and peak value information. Finally, the information through 16 filters is combined to form the whole output with the name of ZCPA feature.

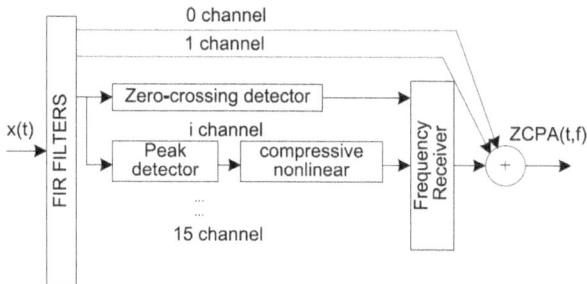

Fig. 1. ZCPA system diagram

3 Constructing Wavelet Neural Network Model for Recognition System

3.1 Network Topology

The diversity and complexity of constructing a wavelet function determine that of constructing a wavelet network. The network structure can vary with different applications, and it is not fixed structure. Present studies about network constructing rules include continuous wavelet transform, orthogonal wavelet transform, wavelet frame and wavelet basis fitting etc. The system in this paper constructs the network according to the wavelet basis fitting. It is known to us that a signal function $\hat{f}(t)$ can be fitted via linear combination of selected wavelet basis [3] :

$$\cdot \; \hat{f}(t) = \sum_{k=1}^{K} \omega_k \phi\left(\frac{t-b_k}{a_k}\right) \tag{1}$$

Where, b_k is position factor, a_k is scale factor and k is the number of basis function. The network topology can refer to Fig. 2:

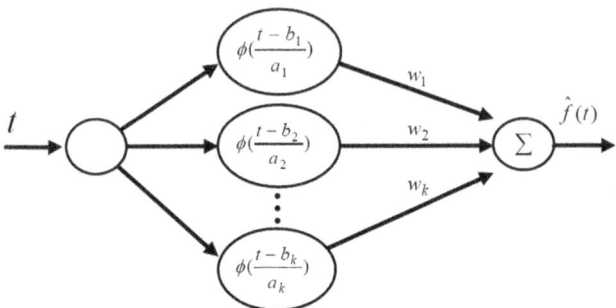

Fig. 2. Wavelet network topology with single input and single output

In Fig.2, a_k and b_k are variable, only w_k acts as the weight between the hidden and output layer, and $\phi\left(\dfrac{t-b_k}{a_k}\right)$ can be regarded as the output value of input nodes. The network structure is similar to the traditional forward multilayer perceptron, and the key difference exists in hidden layer function.

The system in this paper presented a three-layer neural network with multi- input and multi-output. The inputs are the feature parameters of every word, and their dimension is 1024, so the number of input nodes is 1024. The number of hidden nodes depends on words number recognized. Here, 10 nodes correspond to 10 words and 50 nodes correspond to 50 words. It is a direct connection with no weight between input layer and hidden layer, the same as that between hidden layer and output layer, except that they have weights. The number of output layer nodes equals to the classification number of words. So this system has the same nodes in hidden and output layer. The form of the basis function of every hidden node is uniform, while the scale and position parameters vary with nodes. Strictly speaking, this network is not based on the wavelet mathematical analysis theory, in fact, it is used to approximate function in wavelet combination of certain form. In this system, it is used for word recognition.

3.2 Selecting Basis Function

As for selecting method of wavelet basis function, there are no uniform rules in theories. Generally speaking, it can be determined by experiential and practical applications, and also can refer to the experience of wavelet analysis. In the experiments, several different wavelets have been tested. Finally, Mexican Hat[4] wavelet is selected.

3.3 Determining the Parameters of Network

Parameter of hidden nodes the parameters to be determined are number of hidden nodes, scale factor, position factor and connection weights between all hidden and output nodes. Estimation of the number of hidden nodes also has no uniform rules in theory.Because both scale and position parameters can be set as continuous values, infinite number of wavelet functions $\phi_{a, b}$ can be obtained and they are uncorrelated, so the wavelet coefficients are redundant seriously. We can select part of wavelet functions according to practical application, so the created wavelet has less hidden nodes and can also get good generalization ability. In this paper, the hidden nodes number equals to the output layer number, (i.e. the word classification number) . Otherwise, a bias which has fixed value of 1 should be added to hidden layer. This bias factor also should be connected to all the output nodes in order to estimate weights.

Calculating scale factor and position factor Several methods can be used to estimate the parameters of wavelet network, such as BP network training method and orthogonal least square method which optimizes these parameters simultaneously . The network topology of this paper makes it possible that the training of scale and position can be separated from the weights training. One common method of estimating a_k and b_k is clustering. But clustering algorithm just assigns the given vectors into several finite classes according to certain distortion measure. However, this method does not take full advantage of the information of training samples. The clustering algorithm of K-Means has been used in this experiment to estimate the parameter b_k , but the recognition results are not satisfying. Because the given training samples have involved the corresponding classification information of every training feature, these information can be used to estimate the position parameter b_k . The hidden exciting function of wavelet network is a local function, and it has strong approximation ability to the function with large difference in localness. The same as the features with large difference, they can be classified properly. In recognition network, we hope the output of all training samples corresponding to a certain word after they get through the hidden node which is determined by its position factor can get the biggest value. In other words, the more adjacent to position factor b_k , the bigger the output of the kth node will be. Hence, for all the training samples corresponding to a certain word, their centroid can be calculated to be a position factor. Once a position factor has been estimated, there will be a scale factor corresponding to it. There are usually two methods to calculate scale factor and position factor:

- **Method 1.** $a_k = \sqrt{\frac{1}{K} \sum_{k=1}^{K} \|x_k - a_k\|^2}$, where x_k is feature vector, a_k and x_k have the

  same dimension.

- **Method 2.** experiential formula $b_k = \sqrt{\frac{1}{1+\sqrt{2}} \sum_{k=1}^{K} \|x_k - a_k\|^2}$ proposed by Stokbro is also

  available. Where x_k , a_k can refer to Method 1. In this experiment, the first method was adopted.

Training network weights LMS method was adopted to train the weights between hidden and output layer in this paper. Supposed ϕ_k as the output of hidden nodes. The basis function from hidden to output layer can be written as

$$\hat{f}(t) = \sum_{k=1}^{K} \phi_k c_k \tag{2}$$

and it can be denoted in form of matrix as $Y = W\Phi$. Here, Y is the output matrix of output layer, W is the weight matrix to be figured out, and Φ is the output matrix of hidden layer. The aim of LMS method is to minimize the mean square error between desired and real output of network, that is to say $\|Y - W\Phi\|^2$ is least. According to the differential method, matrix W can be obtained from the formula

$$W = (\Phi^T\Phi)^{-1}\Phi^T Y \tag{3}$$

Hence, compared with BP network: firstly, the LMS method can avoid training the network iteratively, it is to say that it can avoid the network spending a longer training time to reach a certain precision. Secondly, it can avoid too much hidden nodes. Lastly, the local minimal problem that is result from the random initial value can be avoided. Training weights by LMS method only has one matrix multiplication, so it needs less training time. And by adding the hidden nodes it can meet the practical requirement. The additional nodes will have little effect on the training time. In this system, the number of input nodes is 1024, generally speaking, wavelet network with high dimension will lead to a "dimension disaster" , which means with the increasing of dimension of input and number of training samples, the converge rate of network will descend severely. In this paper, Training network weights, determining the position and scale factor of wavelet function are processed respectively, so it will avoid the "dimension disaster" effectively due to high dimensional wavelet network.

4 Process of System Implementation and Results

An isolated person-independent recognition system has been implemented in C++ in this experiment. Speech data of 50 words with the pronunciation of 16 persons were used in the experiments. For each word, each person will speak 3 times. Speech data of 9 persons were used to train the system, and the other speech data of 7 persons were used in recognition. One speech sequence of each word for one person was a training file, so there were 1035 files to train the network, and 1050 test files were for recognition. As for the feature extraction, the sampling rate of speech signals was 11.025kHz, and frame length was 10ms, so there were 110 samples for one frame. And the frame shift was 5ms. 1024dimensional speech features were obtained after the ZCPA feature was processed via time and amplitude normalization. These 1024-dimensional features were the inputs of the wavelet network, so the number of input nodes is 1024. After this experiment, a BP network speech recognition system has also been implemented, the files for training and recognition were the same as the wavelet network totally. Tab. 1 is the comparing results of recognition performance.

Table 1. Recognition rate of 50 words based on zcpa feature(%)

SNR(dB)	15	20	25	30	clean
Wavelet network	89.71	91.71	93.43	93.33	94.29
BP network	59.81	68.57	71.24	72.76	73.43

From the table, we can see that the recognition rate of the system constructed by ZCPA feature and wavelet neural network is high in clean condition, and even in noisy environment (in this experiment Gaussian white noise was added in the data), the recognition rate descends little. So we can make a conclusion that the system has a very good anti-noise performance. And compared with BP network, training speed of the system is very fast.

5 Conclusion

Wavelet network uses wavelet function as the exciting function of neuron, and it integrates the advantage of neural network and wavelet decomposition in function approximation. And because of the localized characteristics of wavelet basis function, when given a certain number of samples, the wavelet network will have stronger discrimination ability and need less training time than other ordinary neural network. Applying wavelet neural network to anti-noise speech recognition is very promising.

References

1. Yong, X., Aina, Q.: Noise robust speech recognition based on improved hidden markov model and wavelet neural network. Computer Engineering and Applications 46, 162–164 (2010)
2. Zhang, X., Li, H.: A passwords recognition system based on zcpa feature parameter. Electronic Technology 7, 27–29 (2010)
3. Hou, X.: Noise-robust speech recognition based on wavelet network and RBF network. Computer Engineering and Applications 45, 150–152 (2009)
4. Steven, G., Pan, A., Seddeik, Y.M.: A feature based technique for face recognition using mexican hat wavelets. In: PACRIM, pp. 792–797 (2009)

Drop Fingerprint Recognition Based on Feature Extraction and Probabilistic Neural Networks

Qing Song and Jie Li

Automation School, Beijing University of Posts and Telecommunications,
Xitucheng Road #10, Haidian District,
100876 Beijing, China
songqing512@126.com, 26436884@qq.com

Abstract. Liquid test methods included the authenticity of identification and pattern recognition. Because of the limitation, the authenticity of identification is less useful than pattern recognition. In drop fingerprint pattern recognition, the drop fingerprint data and the eigenvalues of fingerprint are both objects for study. The drop fingerprint feature extraction by waveform analysis can grasp the main features of the liquid, and reduce the amount of data to be processed, greatly improve the recognition efficiency. With the advantage in classification, the Probabilistic Neural Networks provide a good method to the drop fingerprint classification and recognition. By MATLAB simulation, a Probabilistic Neural Networks is established, 8 eigenvalues are set as the pattern stand for a liquid. In the experiment, the rate of correct recognition reach 97.5%.

Keywords: drop fingerprint, pattern recognition, Probabilistic Neural Networks, MATLAB simulation.

1 Introduction

In recent years, Fiber-Capacitive Drop analysis technology developed rapidly, drop fingerprint identification methods are more and more, for example:

Graphics-based fingerprint recognition, the principle for this method is comparing the drop fingerprint graphics between the control group and the test group, if the difference between the graphs within the threshold, the result returns true, otherwise false.

Eigenvector-based fingerprint recognition, the principle for this method is comparing the eigenvectors between the control group and the test group. When the Euclidean distance between the eigenvectors beyond a certain value, the result returns false.

Eigenvalue-based fingerprint recognition, the principle for this method is comparing the eigenvalues between the control group and the test group[1].

The methods described before can only test the liquid is true or false, they can not realize the pattern recognition in drop analysis. In drop fingerprint recognition, different kinds of liquid have different fingerprint. Their eigenvalues are different. The kind of the liquid can be recognized by the eigenvalues.

H. Deng et al. (Eds.): AICI 2011, Part III, LNAI 7004, pp. 398–403, 2011.
© Springer-Verlag Berlin Heidelberg 2011

2 Drop Fingerprint Feature Extraction by Waveform Analysis

Drop fingerprint feature extraction methods include waveform analysis method, the relevant comparison method, data compression method, polynomial regression method and other methods. The feature extraction method used in this paper is waveform analysis."Waveform analysis" means look the drop fingerprint as a waveform which includes peaks and hollows, characterized by calculating the parameters of the waveform peak and hollow characteristics, which quantitatively express the graphical drop fingerprint characteristics. By waveform analysis method, 8 eigenvalues can be obtained, as Fig.1 shows.

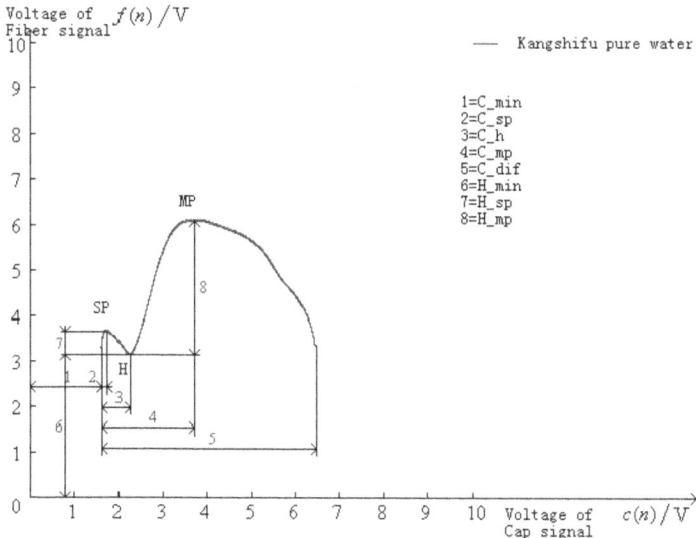

Fig. 1. The waveform feature of Kangshifu pure water

- **The minimum capacitance (C_min/V):** The minimum capacitance signal in droplet growth. Because the capacitance signal increases linearly with the droplet growth, the minimum capacitance signal appears when the drop volume was minimum, which means at the time of residual droplet.
- **The secondary peak capacitance increment (C_sp/V):** The capacitance increment between the minimum capacitance and the secondary peak capacitance. The parameters actually reflect the time to reach the secondary peak of the equivalent droplet size, that is when the fiber signal reaches the secondary peak value.
- **The hollow capacitance increment (C_h/V):** Fiber signal increased from the residual droplets gradually, after it reaches the second peak, it gradually decreased to reach the minimum value at some time, means it reaches the hollow. The increment of the capacitance at this time relative to the initial minimum capacitance, denoted hollow capacitance increment.

- **The main peak capacitance increment (C_mp/V):** Fiber signal is increased from the hollow, this time it reaches the maximum in the entire process of droplet growth. At this time, the capacitance reflects the drop volume increment of main peak.
- **The capacitance increment of the droplet (C_dif/V):** It is the increment of the capacitance in the entire process of droplet growth. It reflects the volume of one drop.
- **The minimum fiber signal (H_min/V):** It is the minimum fiber signal in the entire process of droplet growth. It appears at the point of the hollow.
- **The secondary peak height (H_sp/V):** The increment of the fiber signal from hollow the secondary peak.
- **The main peak height (H_mp/V):** The increment of the fiber signal from the hollow to the main peak. This is also the difference of the minimum fiber signal to the maximum fiber signal in the entire process of droplet growth.

Experimental results show that these eigenvalues can effectively express a liquid.

3   Drop Fingerprint Pattern Recognition

The pattern recognition of drop fingerprint is very important for liquid identification. The method for pattern recognition effects the results of the liquid analysis.

3.1   Neural Networks Used in Drop Fingerprint

Neural networks is widely used in pattern recognition. Master Jing Liu realized drop fingerprint pattern recognition with BP neural network[2]. BP can achieve high accuracy pattern recognition, but its learning rate is very low. Probabilistic neural networks can solve this problem efficiently.

Probabilistic neural networks was created by doctor Specht in 1988[3]. It is a variation of Radial Basis Function Networks. Except input layer, PNN has a two-layer network. The first layer has radial basis neurons. The second layer has competition neurons[4]. Its structure is very simple, as Fig.2. "R" equals the number of input vectors. "Q" equals the number of the input samples. "K" equals the category of the input samples. And in this structure:

```
a1=radbas(||IW1,1-p||b1);
a2=compet(LW2,1-a1);
```

The training for this network is very quickly. It is used widely especially in pattern classification. In pattern classification, it has the advantage of using linear learning algorithms to do the work once only the non-linear learning algorithm can do, while the precision can be as high as the non-linear learning algorithm.

3.2   MATLAB Simulation

In MATLAB Neural Network Toolbox, *newpnn* was a function to establish a Probabilistic neural network. It creates a two-layer network. The first layer has radial

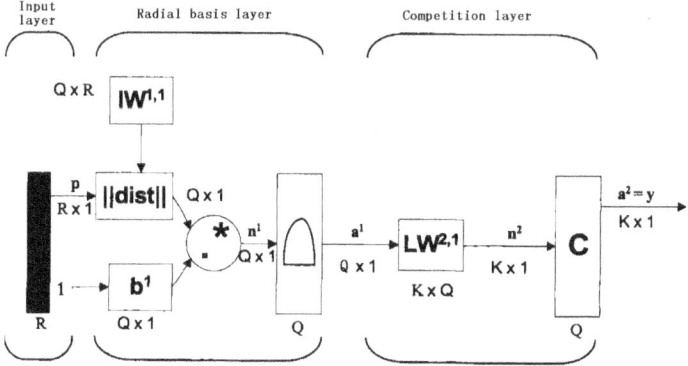

Fig. 2. Structure of Probabilistic Neural Networks

basis neurons, and its input was the product of weighted inputs and the corresponding threshold, the weighted inputs is the distance of the input vector and weight vector. Then calculates it with *radbas()* and get the outputs. The second layer has compete neurons. It compete the input with all kinds of weight vectors. The output of the network is a vector associate with the probability. By calculate with function *compet()*, it gets an output with 1 and 0s, 1 stand for the kind which the greatest probability, 0 stand for other kinds[5].

The format of PNN function is like this:

```
Net=newpnn(P,T,spread);
```

P is the input of the network for training, it is a Q* R-dimensional vector. Because the inputs are the 8 eigenvalues of the waveform, the R is 8. And Q equals to the quantity of the training samples. Target vector T is a sparse matrix that figures the relationship between the training samples and patterns. Take T(2,1)=1 for example, it means the first training sample is classified to pattern 2. The spread is the expansion coefficient for the radial basis. If spread is near zero, the network acts as a nearest neighbor classifier. As spread becomes larger, the designed network takes into account several nearby design vectors.

After the probabilistic neural network is established, do the performance testing for this network is very important. The resulting network can then be simulated and its output vectors converted to class indices. Use the function like this:

```
Y=sim(net,p);
Yc=vec2ind(Y);
```

P is input of the network for recognition. It is a vector with the 8 eigenvalues of drop fingerprint. By calculated with the function dist, the output of the first layer represents the similarity of input sample and training samples. Then the output vector multiply with the threshold vector, after calculated with function *radbas*, it get the results which training sample is most like the input sample. And corresponding element of the neuron output vector is 1, while the other elements are 0. According to the target vector T, there is only one element of each row is 1 as a representing of the corresponding pattern. With the competition in second layer, the network output a result. The result is the kind of the drop fingerprint.

Through the experiment, 11 kinds of liquid drop was test. And every kinds of liquid obtain 40 drop fingerprints. After doing feature extraction, 440 samples are obtained. To test the PNN networks performance. Two groups of experiments are performed. Every group includes 3 experiments. In the first group, the number of training samples of every kind of liquid is 10. And the second group is 20. The values of spread are 0.1, 0.5, 0.9. After these 6 networks are established, all the 440 samples are simulated in these networks. The results showed in Table 1.

Table 1. Recognition results of the samples (%)

The value of spread	The number of training samples	
	10	20
0.1	32.5	68.4
0.5	57.3	84.8
0.9	64.8	97.5

The theory of PNN point out that the smaller value of spread is the more accurate classification result is. But it is not conducive to drop fingerprint recognition. Considering about the characteristic dispersion of drop fingerprint, the value of spread should be set a little larger so that the network has ability for generalization. When increasing the number of training samples, we can see that correct recognition rate increased significantly. Especially when the number of samples is 20 and the value of spread is 0.9, the correct recognition reaches to 97.5%. If the number of training samples become larger, the result for recognition will be better.

4 Conclusion

Probabilistic neural network is a new type of neural network. It is particularly suitable to be used in pattern classification and recognition. With the help of drop fingerprint feature extraction method, probabilistic neural network is applied in the drop fingerprint classification and recognition, and obtain good recognition results. It provides a practical and efficient way to drop fingerprint recognition.

Acknowledgments. The project is supported by the Natural Science Foundation of China （NSFC） and the Fundamental Research Funds for the Central Universities (FRFCU).

References

1. Qing, S.: A Study on the Liquid Identification Method based on the Drop Analysis Technology and the Liquid Drop Fingerprint (2005)
2. Jing, L., Qing, S., Di, W., Jiayong, H., Chunsong, Z.: The Application Of BP Neural Network In Liqud Identification. In: 2010 International Conference on Computer Application and System Modeling (ICCASM 2010), Taiyuan, China (2010)

3. Specht, D.F.: Probabilistic neural networks for classification mapping, or associative memory. In: Proceedings of IEEE International Conference on Neural Networks, pp. 525–532 (1988)
4. Changhong, D.: MATLAB Neural Network and Application, pp. 121–129. National Defence Industry Press (2005)
5. Wasserman, P.D.: Advanced Methods in Neural Computing, pp. 35–55. Van Nostrand Reinhold, New York (1993)

Bibliometric Analysis of Particle Swarm Optimization (PSO) Research 2000-2010

Brahim Hamadicharef

Tiara, 1 Kim Seng Walk, Singapore 239403
bhamadicharef@hotmail.com

Abstract. In the last decade, Particle Swarm Optimization (PSO) has grown in popularity as one important method for optimization, compared to recent Differential Evolution (DE) and Harmony Search (HS). In this paper a bibliometric study is presented, carried out on the PSO research literature from 2000 to 2010. The Thomson Reuters Web of Science (WoS) was used to collect publication records and analyzed to identify authorship, co-authorship, top journals, profile the distribution of citations and references. The study also includes the use keyword co-occurrence frequency from the articles' title, to help getting insights into PSO research trends and fields of applications.

Keywords: Particle Swarm Optimization, bibliometric study, citations.

1 Introduction

Since its introduction in 1995 by J. Kennedy and R. Eberhart [1], Particle Swarm Optimization (PSO) has enjoyed a large popularity compared to other recent methods, from the pioneering Genetic Algorithm (GA) [2], such as as Differential Evolution (DE)[3] or Harmony Search (HS)[4].

The aim of this study was to create an accurate bibliometric picture of the current state of PSO research from its research literature, identifying the most eminent researchers, their collaborations, their country of origin, citation and reference distribution patterns, and finally study keywords related to this research field to get insights into applications, hot topics and trends in PSO research.

The remainder of the paper is organized as follows. In Section 2 we detail the analysis methodology. In Section 3 we present the results from the bibliometric study. Finally in Section 4, we conclude the paper.

2 Methodology

The Web of Science (WoS) online interface (Thomson Reuters) was used to retrieve records (with full abstract and references) of articles on PSO. For each year, one file with all the entries is saved in text format. The records are subsequently processed using MATLAB scripts. The query, use for the year 2009 for e.g., was of the form *Topic=(particle* swarm optimization) AND Year Published=(2009) AND Language=(English) Timespan=All Years. Databases=SCI-EXPANDED, SSCI,*

H. Deng et al. (Eds.): AICI 2011, Part III, LNAI 7004, pp. 404–411, 2011.

A\&HCI, CPCI-S, CPCI-SSH. The procedure is similar as the one used in previous bibliometric studies[5][6]

3   Results

3.1   Growth

The growth of the PSO research literature from 2000 to2010 is shown in Figure 1. Its characteristic was fitted with a power-law curve with the following $N = a \times x^b$, with a = 3.7472 and b = 3.1939 ($R^2 = 0.9921$).

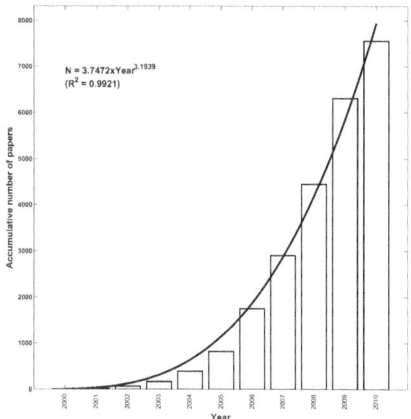

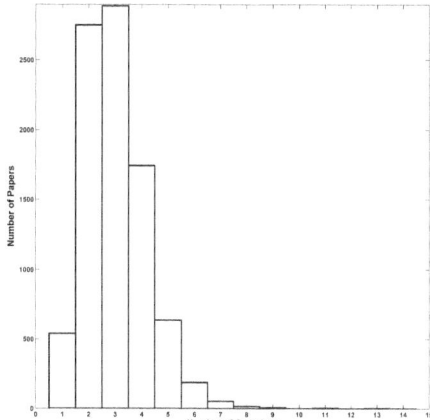

Fig. 1. Growth of the PSO research literature

Fig. 2. Authorship distributions

3.2   Authorship

As shown in Figure 2 the majority co-authors is around1 to 5, with a peak at 2 to 3. In Figure 3, a more detailed picture is shown with the number of co-authors versus number of papers on a yearly basis. We can see an increasing number of papers in the recent years (e.g. in 2010 shown using a star symbol). The most eminent researchers are listed in Table 1, ranked using harmonic counting [7] which provides a more objective measure than the number of publications or geometric counting, to avoid potential bias [8].

3.3   Citations

A loglog scatter plot shows the number of papers versus the number of citations in Figure 4. It has a typical fat tail characteristic. This distribution is robustly fitted with a power-law curve (shown as a line due to the log-log scale axis).

The paper with the highest number of citations was by M. Clerc about *The particle swarm - explosion, stability, and convergence in a multidimensional complex space* [9], with 1191 citations.

Table 1. PSO researchers ranked by harmonic counting

Rank	Name	NP	Harmonic	Arithmetic
1	LIU, Y	147	53.259	92.726
2	WANG, Y	169	52.458	98.267
3	WANG, J	142	51.732	90.193
4	WANG, X	136	46.602	84.883
5	CHEN, Y	122	46.129	80.433
6	WANG, L	136	45.229	81.767
7	LI, Y	125	41.215	75.317
8	ZHANG, X	119	41.157	83.417
9	LI, X	106	38.595	66.302
10	ZHANG, Y	128	38.512	71.483
11	ZHANG, J	117	34.393	62.535
12	SUN, J	102	32.305	61.144
13	LIU, H	82	31.720	52.883
14	VENAYAGAMOORTHY, G	100	31.686	51.533
15	COELHO, L	52	29.807	42.750
16	LIU, J	84	28.449	52.433
17	XU, W	105	27.142	48.410
18	LI, L	79	25.871	48.967
19	LI, J	75	24.693	43.200
20	LIU, X	70	24.558	45.167

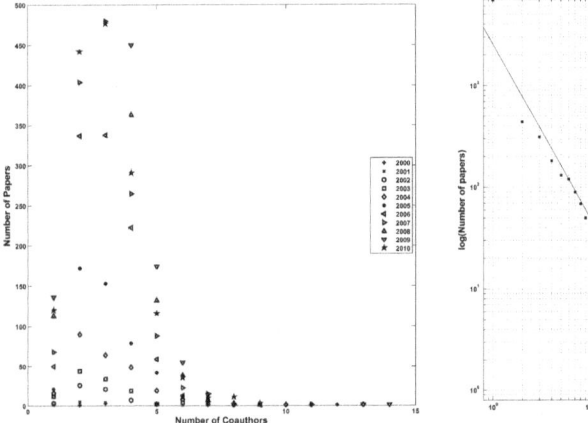

Fig. 3. Yearly authorship distribution

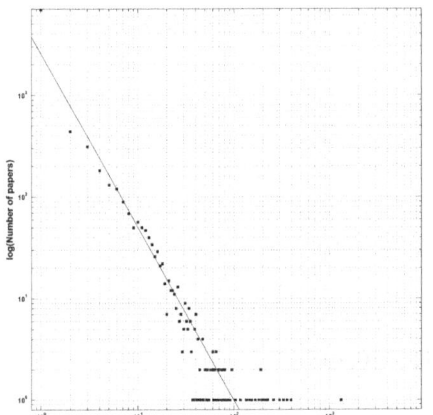

Fig. 4. Citations distribution

3.4 References

Citation counts are related to the number references citing other articles, thus it is important to assess such aspect over the years. The distribution of the number of references is shown in Figure 5. From 2000 to 2010, the yearly average number of references per article grew from 18.33 to 31.47(median 19.77 to 26.05). Articles with large number of references are often reviews like the one on an exploration of the literature on the use of 'swarm intelligence-based techniques' for public service problems [10](with 165 references)or the survey on algorithms simulating bee swarm intelligence [11](with 161 references).

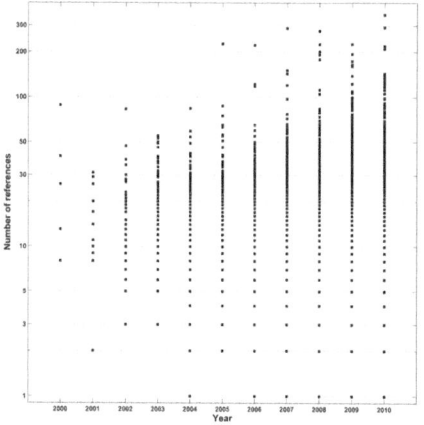

Fig. 5. Distribution of the references

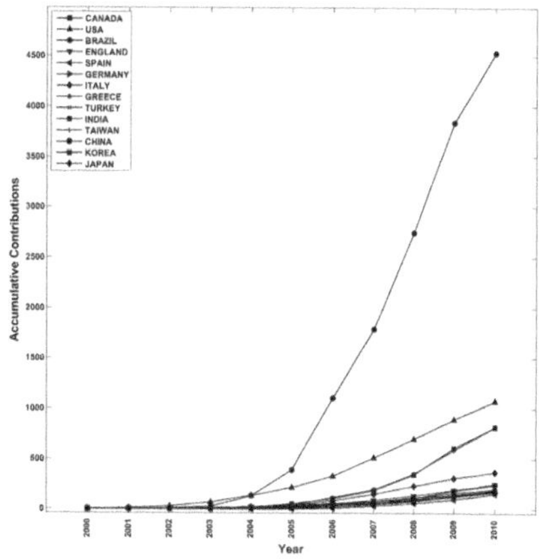

Fig. 6. Countries of origin

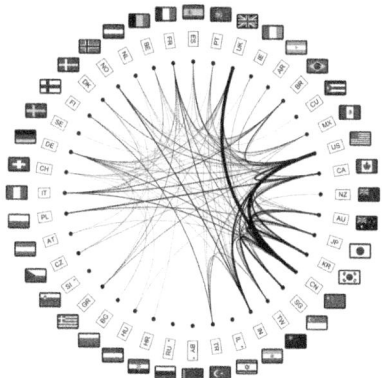

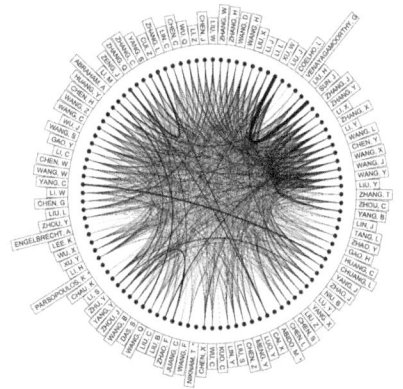

Fig. 7. Countries collaboration network

Fig. 8. Researchers' collaboration network

3.5   Countries of Origin

There are in total 65 countries contributing to the PSOliterature and include China (632, 25.92%), Taiwan (267,10.95%), India (239, 9.80%), USA (224, 9.19%), Iran (182,7.47%), Turkey (74, 3.04%), Japan (71, 2.91%), Brazil (63,2.58%), Italy (55, 2.26%), U.K. (54, 2.21%), Greece (49,2.01%), Korea (48, 1.97%), Spain (45, 1.85%), Canada (36,1.48%), Egypt (32, 1.31%), Singapore (26, 1.07%), South Africa (26), Malaysia (25, 1.03%), Australia (23, 0.94%),Thailand (22, 0.90%), Germany (19, 0.78%), France (17,0.70%), etc. As shown in Figure 6, China is the most publishing country, followed by a group with Taiwan, USA and India.

Table 2. PSO core journals

Rank	Name of the journal	NP	%	IF	EF	PF	Publisher
1	Expert Systems with Applications	137	1.55%	**2.908**	0.00987	12	Elsevier
2	Dynamics of continuous discrete and impulsive systems-series	93	1.05%	-	-	-	DCDIS
3	IEEE CEC 2008	92	1.04%	-	-	-	IEEE
4	IEEE CEC 2007	80	0.90%	-	-	-	IEEE
5	IEEE WCICA 2006	76	0.86%	-	-	-	IEEE
6	IEEE CEC 2010	75	0.85%	-	-	-	IEEE
7	IEEE WCICA 2008	71	0.80%	-	-	-	IEEE
8	IEEE CEC 2008	64	0.72%	-	-	-	IEEE
9	IEEE ICNC 2007	61	0.69%	-	-	-	IEEE
10	IEEE NaBIC 2009	58	0.66%	-	-	-	IEEE
11	IEEE Transactions on Power Systems	57	0.64%	1.938	0.01922	4	IEEE
12	Applied Mathematics and Computation	56	0.63%	1.124	0.04288	24	Elsevier
13	Applied Soft Computing	56	0.63%	**2.415**	0.00373	6	Elsevier
14	IEEE Transactions on Antennas and Propagation	56	0.63%	**2.011**	0.03665	12	IEEE
15	Electric Power Systems Research	53	0.60%	1.259	0.00735	6	Elsevier
16	IEEE CEC 2006	52	0.59%	-	-	-	IEEE
17	Energy Conversion and Management	51	0.58%	1.944	0.01933	12	Elsevier
18	International Journal of Advanced Manufacturing Technology	51	0.58%	1.128	0.01263	24	Springer
19	IEEE CEC 2009	50	0.57%	-	-	-	IEEE
20	IEEE CCDC 2008	42	0.48%	-	-	-	IEEE
21	International Journal of Innovative Computing Information and Control	42	0.48%	**2.932**	0.00435	12	Kyushu Tokai Univ.
22	IEEE SIS 2008	41	0.46%	-	-	-	IEEE
23	Engineering Applications of Artificial Intelligence	40	0.45%	1.444	0.00436	8	Elsevier
24	IEEE Transactions on Evolutionary Computation	40	0.45%	**4.589**	0.00860	6	IEEE
25	International Journal of Electrical Power and Energy Systems	39	0.44%	1.613	0.00362	10	Elsevier
26	Progress In Electromagnetics Research (PIER)	39	0.44%	**3.763**	0.00839	11	EMW Publishing
27	IEEE Transactions on Magnetics	37	0.42%	1.061	0.03472		IEEE
28	IEEE ICIS 2009	36	0.41%	-	-	-	IEEE
29	International Review of Electrical Engineering (IREE)	35	0.40%	0.570	0.00031		Praise Worthy Prize
30	IEEE CCDC 2009	34	0.38%	-	-	-	IEEE

3.6 International Collaborations

Affiliation fields of the PSO researchers were used to extract the country's international collaboration. The results are summarized in a form of a network graph as shown in Figure 7. We can observe that the majority of international collaborations occur between China and USA, and UK with China. In Figure 8, the international collaboration is shown at researchers' level (100 top researchers publishing in PSO)(See PSO researchers ranking in the Supplementary Data at www.tech.plymouth.ac.uk/spmc/brahim/Biblio-PSO).

3.7 Journals Keywords

A list all top 40 core journals publishing research in PSO is given in Table 2. The list includes a broad scope of journal disciplines with computing, mathematics, and engineering (optics, energy, etc.). The journals with the highest Impact Factor (IF) [13][14] include *IEEE Transactions on Industrial Electronics* (IF: 4.678), followed by *IEEE Transactions on Evolutionary Computation* (IF: 4.589), *Progress in Electromagnetics Research* (PIER) (IF: 3.763), followed by *Chaos Solitons and Fractals* (IF: 3.315), *Information Sciences* (IF: 3.291) and *IEEE Transactions on Systems, Man, and Cybernetics, Part B: Cybernetics* (IF: 3.007).

(a) 2009

(b) 2010

(c) All

Fig. 9. TagCloud [12] of PSO literature

3.8 Keywords

We use the tool WORDLE [12] to create TagClouds from the keywords extracted from the articles' titles. In Figure 9, the most recent years are shown. A close look at the keywords can provide insights into research trends within PSO research and help to identify specific small research topic of interest.

4 Conclusions

Since its introduction in 1995, PSO has enjoyed a great deal of popularity over the recent years in the research community. In this paper a scientometric study on the PSO research literature (2000-2010) was presented. Publication records were collected using the online Web of Knowledge (Thomson Reuters ISI), to carry out a bibliometric analysis, identifying distribution of authorship, co-authorship, citations and references, as well as top journals publishing PSO research. Frequency of keywords from the articles' title was used to create TagClouds and get insights into research trends and fields of applications. Comparative bibliometric studies with other conventional and recent optimization methods will be carried out. This current study will help investigate PSO-based framework for research in Brain-Computer Interface (BCI)[15].

References

1. Kennedy, J., Eberhart, R.: Particle Swarm Optimization. In: Proceedings of the IEEE International Conference on Neural Networks (ICNN 1995), Perth, Australia, November 27-December 1, pp. 1942–1948 (1995)
2. Goldberg, D.E.: Genetic Algorithms in Search, Optimization and Machine Learning. Addison-Wesley, Reading (1989)
3. Storn, R.: System Design by Constraint Adaptation and Differential Evolution. IEEE Transactions on Evolutionary Computation 3(1), 22–34 (1999)
4. Geem, Z.W., Kim, J.H., Loganathan, G.V.: A New Heuristic Optimization Algorithm: Harmony Search. Simulation 76(2), 60–68 (2001)
5. Hamadicharef, B.: Brain-Computer Interface (BCI) Literature - A Bibliometric Study. In: Proceedings of the 10th International Conference on Information Science, Signal Processing and their applications (ISSPA 2010), Kuala Lumpur, Malaysia, May 10-13, pp. 626–629 (2010)
6. Hamadicharef, B.: Scientometric Study of the Journal NeuroImage 1992-2009. In: Proceedings of the 2010 International Conference on Web Information Systems and Mining (WISM 2010), Nanjing, China, October 23-24, pp. 201–204 (2010)
7. Hagen, N.T.: Harmonic publication and citation counting: sharing authorship credit equitably - not equally, geometrically or arithmetically. Scientometrics 84(3), 785–793 (2010)
8. Kwok, L.S.: The White Bull effect: abusive coauthorship and publication parasitism. Journal of Medical Ethics 31, 554–556 (2005)
9. Clerc, M., Kennedy, J.: The particle swarm – explosion, stability, and convergence in a multidimensional complexspace. IEEE Transactions on Evolutionary Computation 6(1), 58–73 (2002)

10. Dereli, T., Seckiner, S.U., Das, G.S., Gokcen, H., Aydin, M.E.: An exploration of the literature on the use of 'swarm intelligence-based techniques' for public service problems. European Journal of Industrial Engineering 3(4), 379–423 (2009)
11. Karaboga, D., Akay, B.: A survey: algorithms simulating bee swarm intelligence. Artificial Intelligence Review 31(1), 61–85 (2009)
12. Viegas, F.B., Wattenberg, M., Feinberg, J.: Participatory Visualization with Wordle. IEEE Transactions on Visualization and Computer Graphics 15(6), 1137–1144 (2009)
13. Garfield, E.: Citation indexes to science: a new dimension in documentation through association of ideas. Science 122(3159), 108–111 (1955)
14. Garfield, E.: The history and meaning of the journal impact factor. JAMA 295(1), 90–93 (2006)
15. Hamadicharef, B., Zhang, H., Guan, C., Wang, C., Phua, K.S., Tee, K.P., Ang, K.K.: Learning EEG–based Spectral-Spatial Patterns for Attention Level Measurement. In: Proceedings of the 2009 IEEE International Symposium on Circuits and Systems (ISCAS 2009), Taipei, Taiwan, May 24-27, pp. 1465–1468 (2009)

A Modified Quantum-Inspired Particle Swarm Optimization Algorithm

Ling Wang, Mingde Zhang, Qun Niu, and Jun Yao

Shanghai Key Laboratory of Power Station Automation Technology,
School of Mechatronics and Automation, Shanghai University,
200072, Shanghai, China
wangling@shu.edu.cn

Abstract. This paper presents a modified quantum-inspired particle swarm optimization algorithm (MQPSO) which uses particle swarm optimization algorithm to update quantum coding. The introduction of quantum coding can improve the diversity of algorithm, but may mislead the global search simultaneously. To remedy this drawback, a novel repair operator is developed to improve the search accuracy and efficiency of algorithm. The performance of MQPSO is evaluated and compared with quantum-inspired evolutionary algorithm (QEA), QEA with NOT gate (QEAN) and quantum swarm evolutionary algorithm (QSE) on 0-1knapsack problem and multidimensional knapsack problem. The experimental results demonstrate that the presented repair operator can effectively improve the global search ability of algorithm and MQPSO outperforms QEA, QEAN and QSE on all test benchmark problems in terms of search accuracy and convergence speed.

Keywords: PSO, quantum angle, knapsack problem, quantum-inspired evolutionary algorithm, repair operator.

1 Introduction

In the early 1980s, Benioff firstly proposed the concept of quantum computing [1], which has attracted wide attention and soon become the hot topic of research due to its unique computational performance. On one side, more and more quantum algorithms, such as grove database search algorithm and shor quantum factoring algorithm, were proposed. On the other side, researchers have been introducing the idea and concept of quantum computing to the traditional algorithms to achieve better optimization performance with the classical computer.

In 2000, Han and Kim [2] firstly proposed a novel genetic quantum algorithm. Based on this work, Han and Kim further modified the framework of algorithm and proposed the quantum-inspired evolutionary algorithm (QEA) and developed the quantum NOT gate and $H \in gate$ to improve the optimization ability of QEA [3, 4].

Now QEAs have been successfully applied to tackle various optimization problems in science and engineering such as multi-dimensional knapsack problems, flow shop scheduling and travelling salesman problem. Recently Zhang presented a good survey on QEA and its applications, and more details can be found in [5].

H. Deng et al. (Eds.): AICI 2011, Part III, LNAI 7004, pp. 412–419, 2011.

Encouraged by the success of QEA, the hybrid algorithms are widely researched. Niu et al. [6] combined the immune algorithm with QEA and developed a quantum-inspired immune algorithm to solve the hybrid flow shop problems, in which the crossover operator and mutation operator were used with rotation gate to guide the searching of algorithm. Wang et al. brought QEA into the ant colony optimization and proposed a quantum ant colony optimization algorithm (QACO) to solve numerical optimization [7] and feature selection [8] where the qubit and a modified quantum rotation gate were adopted to represent and update the pheromone respectively.

Particle swarm optimization (PSO) algorithm is another well-known powerful optimization tool due to its ease for implementation and the excellent global optimization ability. Thus, researchers tried to hybridize PSO with QEA to enhance the search ability of algorithm. Wang et al. [9] presented a novel quantum swarm evolutionary algorithm which used the PSO updating formula to determine the quantum rotation angle of QEA. Later, Huang et al. [10], Pan et al. [11] and Xiao [12] developed several hybrid algorithms based on PSO and QEA. However, the uncertainty of qubit may mislead the quantum angle search for PSO and greatly spoils the optimization performance in hybrid quantum PSOs. Thus, a modified quantum-inspired particle swarm optimization algorithm (MQPSO) is proposed in this paper and a new repair operator is developed to remedy this drawback.

The remainder part of paper is organized as follows. Section 2 introduced the proposed MQPSO algorithm, and the encoding strategy, updating operators and the whole process are described in details. In section 3, MQPSO is tested and evaluated on a set of 0-1 knapsack problems and multi-dimensional knapsack problems. The comparison results with QEA, QEA including quantum NOT gate (QEAN) [13] and quantum swarm evolutionary algorithm are also given in this section. Finally, concluding remarks follow in Section 4.

2   Modified Quantum Particle Swarm Optimization Algorithm

2.1   Initialization

QEA adopts the qubit as its encoding strategy which can be defined as Eq. (1)

$$|\psi\rangle = \alpha|0\rangle + \beta|1\rangle \qquad (1)$$

where α and β are the probability amplitudes of the corresponding states. However, the quantum encoding also can be expressed with the form of quantum angle θ, which is described as Eq. (2)

$$x = \begin{bmatrix} \cos\theta_1 \ldots \cos\theta_i \ldots \cos\theta_m \\ \sin\theta_1 \ldots \sin\theta_i \ldots \sin\theta_m \end{bmatrix} \qquad (2)$$

where m is the dimension of the individual, i.e., the string length of the qubit chromosome; $\alpha_i = \cos\theta_i, \beta_i = \sin\theta_i$ and $\sin^2\theta_i + \cos^2\theta_i = 1$. For simplicity, the quantum angle is directly adopted in MQPSO as encoding strategy. Then the population of MQPSO with n individuals and m dimensions can be represented as Eq. (3)

$$Q = \begin{bmatrix} \theta_{11}, \theta_{12}, \theta_{13}, ..., \theta_{1m} \\ \theta_{21}, \theta_{22}, \theta_{23}, ..., \theta_{2m} \\ ... \\ \theta_{i1}, \theta_{i2}, \theta_{i3}, ..., \theta_{im} \\ ... \\ \theta_{n1}, \theta_{n2}, \theta_{n3}, ..., \theta_{nm} \end{bmatrix} \tag{3}$$

Here Q is initialized with a random angle between $[0, \pi / 2]$.

2.2 Quantum Observing Operator

To obtain the traditional solutions to solve the optimization problem, a modified quantum observing operator is adopted to observe the current quantum angle and generate binary-coded individual as Eq. (4) which is used to calculate the fitness of each individual according to the predefined fitness function.

$$x_{ij} = \begin{cases} 0 & \text{if } rand < \cos^2 \theta_{ij} \\ 1 & else \end{cases} \tag{4}$$

2.3 Updating of the Quantum Angle

To find the optimal solution, the quantum angle need be updated which lead the population to perform a biased search based on the guidance from the current optimization information. In MQPSO, the classical PSO algorithm is used to tune the quantum angle as Eq. (5-6)

$$v_{ij}^{t+1} = \omega \cdot v_{ij}^t + c_1 \cdot rand \cdot \left(\theta_{ij}^t (pbest) - \theta_{ij}^t \right) + c_2 \cdot rand \cdot \left(\theta_i^t (gbest) - \theta_{ij}^t \right) \tag{5}$$

$$\theta_{ij}^{t+1} = \theta_{ij}^t + v_{ij}^{t+1} \tag{6}$$

where θ_{ij}^t is the current quantum angle; $\theta_{ij}^t (pbest)$ and $\theta_{ij}^t (gbest)$ are the current individual best and global best; ω is the inertia weight; $rand$ is a random number between [0, 1]; c_1 and c_2 are the learning factors.

As mentioned above, the quantum angle coding can be converted to the traditional qubit, and thus quantum angle can help the algorithm keep the diversity better. But it may mislead the search direction of algorithm. For instance, the $\cos^2 \theta_{ij}$ is 0.2 which means that the corresponding binary value is "0" with probability of 0.2 and "1" with probability of 0.8 respectively. If the generated bit is "0" and this solution is the new global optimal solution, the quantum angle of this dimension in the whole population will be rotated to its value. Thus, the bit "1" will be generated with more probability while the real best bit value is "0", which would greatly reduce the effectiveness and even spoil the optimization ability of algorithm. To make up for it, a new repair operator is presented to fix the $\theta_{ij}^t\left(pbest\right)$ and $\theta_i^t\left(gbest\right)$ as Eq. (7).

$$
\begin{cases}
\theta_{ij}^t\left(pbest\right)=\pi/2-\theta_{ij}^t\left(pbest\right) & if \begin{cases}\left(\theta_{ij}^t\left(pbest\right)>\pi/4\right)\ and\ \left(x_{ij}^t\left(pbest\right)==0\right)\\ \left(\theta_{ij}^t\left(pbest\right)<\pi/4\right)\ and\ \left(x_{ij}^t\left(pbest\right)==1\right)\end{cases}\\[3ex]
\theta_i^t\left(gbest\right)=\pi/2-\theta_i^t\left(gbest\right) & if \begin{cases}\left(\theta_i^t\left(gbest\right)>\pi/4\right)\ and\ \left(x_i^t\left(gbest\right)==0\right)\\ \left(\theta_i^t\left(gbest\right)<\pi/4\right)\ and\ \left(x_i^t\left(gbest\right)==1\right)\end{cases}
\end{cases}
\tag{7}
$$

In summary, the procedure of MQPSO can be described as follows:

Step1: Set the parameters of MQPSO and initialize the population;
Step2: Generate the binary solutions by observing the quantum angle;
Step3: Calculate the fitness values based on the binary solutions and update the global best binary solution and the individual best binary solution;
Step4: remedy and update the global quantum angle and the individual quantum angle with the repair operator;
Step5: rotate the quantum angle with PSO updating strategy as Eq. (5-6).
Step6: go to Steps 2 till the termination criterions are satisfied.

3   Experiments and Results

MQPSO was tested on the 0-1knapsack problems and multidimensional knapsack problems (MKP). For comparisons, QEA[3], QEAN [13]and a novel quantum swarm evolutionary algorithm (QSE) [14]were also used to solve these benchmark problems. The suggested parameters of these 3 algorithms are adopted and listed in the Table 1.

3.1   0-1 Knapsack Problem

The 0-1knapsack problem can be described as selecting a subset from a given set of items so that the profit $f\left(x\right)$ is maximized as Eq. (8)

$$
f\left(x\right)=\sum_{i=1}^m p_i x_i
$$
$$
subject\ to\ \ \sum_{i=1}^m w_i x_i \le C
\tag{8}
$$

where m is the number of the items; C is the capacity of the knapsack; P_i and w_i are the profit and weight of the ith item, respectively. Three knapsack problems with 250, 500, 1000 items are considered in this paper. The population size of all algorithms is 20 and each algorithm independently ran 50 times on each 0-1 knapsack problem with 1000 maximum generation. The optimization results of all algorithms on these three problems, i.e., the optimal value and the mean value are displayed in Table 2.

Table 1. The Parameter setting of algorithm

MQPSO	$\omega = 0.8$,	QSE	$\omega = 0.7298$,
	$c_1 = c_2 = 2$		$c_1 = 1.42, c_2 = 1.57$
QEA	quantum rotation angle refer to [3]	QEAN	quantum rotation angle refer to [13],quantum NOT gate with probability 0.05

Table 2. The Results of QEA, QEAN, QSE and MQPSO on 0-1 knapsack problems

ï	250ï		500ï		1000ï	
	optimal	mean	optimal	mean	optimal	mean
QEA	981.11	967.60	1961.80	1944.08	3879.43	3856.35
QEAN	1003.49	985.41	2003.93	1965.47	3933.79	3873.51
QSE	1005.53	979.45	1995.93	1964.95	3917.54	3882.70
MQPSO	1053.61	1004.52	2098.18	2007.03	4076.20	3949.39

According to the table 2, it is obvious that the proposed MQPSO algorithm outperforms QSE, QEAN and QEA in terms of convergence speed and search accuracy, and the advantage of MQPSO is more evident on the large-scale problems. In additional, we can find that the idea of using PSO to tune the quantum angle is valid as the basic QSE algorithm has better performance than QEA, but the optimization ability of QSE is not ideal and the results is inferior to the QEAN due to the probability of misleading discussed in section 2.3. Compared with QSE, MQPSO with the developed repair operator can effectively guide the algorithm to perform global search and achieve the best optimization ability.

3.2 Multidimensional Knapsack Problem

Multidimensional Knapsack Problem (MKP) is a generalization of the 0-1 knapsack problem and a resource allocation problem, which supposes that we have m resources and n objects, each resource $i \in I$ has a budget M_i, and each object $j \in J$ has a profit p_j and consumes w_{ij} of resource i. The problem is to maximize the profit within a limited budget formulated as Eq. (9-10) [15].

$$\text{Maximize } f(x) = \sum_{j=1}^{n} p_j x_j \tag{9}$$

$$\text{subject to } \sum_{j=1}^{n} w_{ij} x_j \le M_i \quad i = 1, \cdots, m, \ x_j \in \{0,1\}, \ j = 1, \cdots, n \tag{10}$$

$$\text{with} \quad p_j > 0, w_{ij} \ge 0, M_i \ge 0.$$

where $x = (x_1, x_2, ..., x_j, ..., x_n)$ is a binary vector; $x_j = 1$ represents the j-th resource is consumed w_{ij} while $x_j = 0$ means that the corresponding resource is rejected.

To evaluate and compare the optimization ability fairly and clearly, this paper employs the penalty function to adjust the fitness of the illegal individuals as Eq. (11) [16].

$$F(x) = f(x) - \sum_{i=1}^{m} \Phi_i \tag{11}$$

where Φ_i is the penalty function; m is the number of constrains and $F(x)$ is the penalized fitness value when a resource exceed its budget. The population size of all algorithms, i.e., MQPSO, QSE, QEAN and QEA is 40 and each algorithm independently ran 50 times on Pet*, Weing* and Pb* cases with 3000 maximum generation. The optimization results are shown in Table 3 where the success rate (SR %), the mean best fitness value (Mean), the best fitness variance (Var) and the mean generation number (G) are given.

Table 3. The Results of MQPSO, QSE, QEAN and QEA on MKP

	SR%	Mean	Var	G	SR%	Mean	Var	G
		Pet3				Pet4		
MQPSO	100	4015.0	0	48	99	6119.9	1.00	409
QSE	93	4014.3	2.56	469	67	6108.9	22.86	1541
QEAN	90	4014.0	3.01	349	30	6105.3	23.02	2144
QEA	77	4010.8	11.62	726	33	6099.4	25.13	2033
		Pet5				Pet6		
MQPSO	70	12395.6	8.44	1654	6	10566.18	32.38	2935
QSE	17	12350.5	56.03	2724	0	10469.75	74.19	3000
QEAN	54	12360.0	97.78	1484	0	10512.56	76.51	3000
QEA	4	12317.2	70.43	2884	0	10447.53	89.41	3000
		Weing1				Weing2		
MQPSO	98	141271.98	50.31	858	84	130857.4	58.95	1253
QSE	27	140721.34	704.52	2540	33	129663.3	2158.57	2379
QEAN	69	141084.35	298.13	1151	60	130437.8	1358.52	1379
QEA	26	140474.9	864.07	2281	37	129847.6	1759.51	1933
		Pb1				Pb2		
MQPSO	25	3067.36	21.49	2518	18	3155.67	27.92	2708
QSE	8	3048.11	27.39	2843	3	3096.73	47.71	2962
QEAN	14	3055.11	26.75	2634	9	3131.83	39.05	2765
QEA	6	3025.60	36.02	2835	1	3073.93	55.53	2971
		Pb4				Pb5		
MQPSO	34	93024.39	1778.75	2368	49	2124.18	18.62	1886
QSE	7	91663.82	2010.08	2858	24	2108.93	22.01	2583
QEAN	13	92059.79	1575.19	2659	6	2092.01	22.86	2840
QEA	7	90956.15	2415.54	2800	5	2079.04	25.82	2852
		Pb6				Pb7		
MQPSO	7	732.70	31.99	2899	5	1015	12.48	2931
QSE	1	651.08	72.24	2995	0	968.04	36.38	3000
QEAN	1	619.82	74.38	2972	2	1008.39	21.61	2949
QEA	9	721.43	43.97	2784	0	984.94	28.63	3000

From table 3, it is fair to claim that MQPSO has the best performance on all benchmarks and achieves the faster convergence speed and higher accuracy compared with QSE, QEAN and QEA. QSE has a similar performance with QEA, but the convergence speed of QSE is slowest because the misleading of the wrong optimization information. Compared to QEA, QEAN displays a better global search ability as the quantum NOT gate is introduced to help algorithm escape from the local optima. However, the probability of executing quantum NOT gate should be chosen carefully and its value is problem dependent, which can be proved on Pb6 where QEAN is poorer than QEA.

4 Conclusion

In this paper, a modified quantum-inspired PSO algorithm is proposed. Based on the analysis on the drawback of the traditional hybrid quantum PSO algorithm, a novel repair operator is developed which can remedy the wrong optimization information and guide algorithm to perform the correct search. The optimization ability of MQPSO is evaluated and compared with QEA, QEAN and QSE on 0-1knapsack problem and multidimensional knapsack problem. The experimental results demonstrate that the presented repair operator can greatly improve the global search ability and MQPSO outperforms QEA, QEAN and QSE on all test benchmark problems in terms of search accuracy and convergence speed.

Acknowledgement. This work is supported by Research Fund for the Doctoral Program of Higher Education of China (20103108120008), ChenGuang Plan (2008CG48),National Natural Science Foundation of China (Grant No. 60804052), the Projects of Shanghai Science and Technology Community (10ZR1411800 & 08160512100), Mechatronics Engineering Innovation Group project from Shanghai Education Commission, Shanghai University "11th Five-Year Plan" 211 Construction Project.

References

1. Benioff, P.: The computer as a physical system: A microscopic quantum mechanical Hamiltonian model of computers as represented by Turing machines. Journal of Statistical Physics 22, 563–591 (1980)
2. Han, K.H., Kim, J.H.: Genetic quantum algorithm and its application to combinatorial optimization problem. In: IEEE Conference on Evolutionary Computation, vol. 2, pp. 1354–1360. IEEE press, Los Alamitos (2000)
3. Han, K.H., Kim, J.H.: Quantum-inspired evolutionary algorithm for a class of combinatorial optimization. IEEE Trans. Evol. Comput. 6, 580–593 (2002)
4. Han, K.H., Kim, J.H.: Quantum-inspired evolutionary algorithms with a new termination criterion, $H \in$ gate, and two-phase scheme. IEEE Trans. Evol. Comput. 8(2), 156–169 (2004)
5. Zhang, G.X.: Quantum-inspired evolutionary algorithms: a survey and empirical study. Journal of Heuristics, 1–49 (2010)

6. Niu, Q., Zhou, T.J., Ma, S.W.: A Quantum-Inspired Immune Algorithm for Hybrid Flow Shop with Makespan Criterion. Journal of Universal Computer Science 15(4), 765–785 (2009)
7. Wang, L., Niu, Q., Fei, M.: A novel quantum ant colony optimization algorithm. In: Li, K., Fei, M., Irwin, G.W., Ma, S. (eds.) LSMS 2007. LNCS, vol. 4688, pp. 277–286. Springer, Heidelberg (2007)
8. Wang, L., Niu, Q., Fei, M.R.: A novel quantum ant colony optimization algorithm and its application to fault diagnosis. Transactions of the Institute of Measurement and Control 33(3), 313–329 (2008)
9. Wang, Y., Feng, X.-Y., Huang, Y.-X., Zhou, W.-G., Liang, Y.-C., Zhou, C.-G.: A novel quantum swarm evolutionary algorithm for solving 0-1 knapsack problem. In: Wang, L., Chen, K., S. Ong, Y. (eds.) ICNC 2005. LNCS, vol. 3611, pp. 698–704. Springer, Heidelberg (2005)
10. Huang, Y.R., Tang, C.L., Wang, S.: Quantum-Inspired Swarm Evolution Algorithm. In: Conference on Computational Intelligence and Security Workshops, pp. 15–19 (2007)
11. Pan, G.F., Xia, K.W., Shi, J.: An Improved LS-SVM Based on Quantum PSO Algorithm and Its Application. In: Conference on Natural Computation, vol. 2, pp. 606–610 (2007)
12. Xiao, J.: Improved Quantum Evolutionary Algorithm Combined with Chaos and Its Application. In: Yu, W., He, H., Zhang, N. (eds.) ISNN 2009. LNCS, vol. 5553, pp. 704–713. Springer, Heidelberg (2009)
13. Wang, L., Tang, F., Wu, H.: Hybrid genetic algorithm based on quantum computing for numerical optimization and parameter estimation. Applied Mathematics and Computation 171(2), 1141–1156 (2005)
14. Wang, Y., Feng, X.Y., Huang, Y.X., Pu, D.B., Zhou, W.G., Liang, Y.C., Zhou, C.G.: A novel quantum swarm evolutionary algorithm and its applications. Neurocomputing 70(4-6), 633–640 (2007)
15. Kong, M., Tian, P., Kao, Y.: A new ant colony optimization algorithm for the multidimensional Knapsack problem. Computers & Operations Research 35(8), 2672–2683 (2008)
16. Wang, L., Wang, X.T., Fei, M.R.: A Novel Quantum-Inspired Pseudorandom Proportional Evolutionary Algorithm for the Multidimensional Knapsack. In: 2009 World Summit on Genetic and Evolutionary Computation, ShangHai, pp. 546–552 (2009)

DHMM Speech Recognition Algorithm Based on Immune Particle Swarm Vector Quantization

Aiping Ning[1,2], Xueying Zhang[1], and Wei Duan[1]

[1] College of Information Engineering, Taiyuan University of Technology, Taiyuan, China
tyzhangxy@163.com, dw861123@163.com
[2] College of Electronics and Information Engineering,
Taiyuan University of Science and Technology, Taiyuan, China
aiping_ning@126.com

Abstract. This article presents a novel Immune Particle Swarm Optimization (IPSO), which combines the artificial immune system methods like immunologic memory, immunologic selection and vaccination together, by making reference to the self adjusting mechanism derived from biological immune system. IPSO as a method of Vector Quantization applied to the Discrete Hidden Markov Model (DHMM) and proposes IPSO-DHMM speech recognition algorithm. Each particle represents a codebook in the algorithm. The experiments using IPSO vector quantization algorithm get optimal codebook. Finally it enters the DHMM speech recognition system to train and recognize. The experimental results show that the IPSO-DHMM speech recognition system has faster convergence, higher recognition ratio and better robustness than the PSO-DHMM algorithm.

Keywords: IPSO, DHMM, speech recognition, vector quantization.

1 Introduction

As one of the statistical models of speech signals, HMM has been widely applied to the field of speech recognition [1]. The DHMM isolated word speech recognition system involves with vector quantization technology and the key of vector quantization is codebook designing. LBG algorithm was proposed in the 1980s, which has been widely adopted as one of the best codebook designing methods, but it is very sensitive to the initial codebook and is easy to fall into local convergence [2]. Due to its fast convergence rate, simple operation, less parameters, parallel processing ability and other advantages, the PSO has been widely used to solve different kinds of complex optimization problem. Reference [3] proposes applying PSO to image vector quantization and it puts forward a vector quantization codebook designing method based on PSO. But the basic PSO learning mechanism is not strongly connected with vector quantization, thus it caused the unsatisfactory performance. Reference [4~5] proposed some improved PSO algorithm for vector quantization.

In the recent years, inspired by biological immune system and its function, people started to research artificial immune algorithm and have successfully applied it to clustering, anomaly detection, function optimization and other engineering problems

H. Deng et al. (Eds.): AICI 2011, Part III, LNAI 7004, pp. 420–427, 2011.

[6]. This article references the self adjusting mechanism of immune system and integrates the artificial immune system methods like immunologic memory, immunologic selection and vaccination into PSO. It presents a new IPSO. Every particle of the algorithm is an antibody. They helped the algorithm obtain a strong global convergence and improved the diversity of particle swarm. It combines IPSO and LBG together and presents IPSO vector quantization codebook design method. This article applies the method to DHMM speech recognition and proposes IPSO-DHMM speech recognition algorithm. The results show that the IPSO-DHMM speech recognition system has a higher recognition ratio.

2   IPSO Algorithm

PSO is an evolutionary approach introduced by [7]. This algorithm constitutes a metaphoric scheme of bird flocking and fish schooling. In the PSO algorithm, each particle represents a possible solution to the task at hand, and the particle swarm starts with the random initialization of a population of individuals in the space. All particles have fitness values. The particles fly through the D-dimensional problem space by learning from the best experiences of all the particles.

2.1   PSO Algorithm

A particle status on the search space is characterized by two factors: its position and velocity. The position vector and the velocity vector of the particle i in D-dimensional space can be indicated as $\mathbf{x}_i = (x_{i1}, x_{i2}, \cdots, x_{iD})$ and $\mathbf{v}_i = (v_{i1}, v_{i2}, \cdots, v_{iD})$ respectively. The best position encountered by each particle is called pbest ($\mathbf{p}_i = (p_{i1}, p_{i2}, \cdots, p_{iD})$). The best position among all particles found so far at time t is called gbest ($\mathbf{p}_g = (p_{g1}, p_{g2}, \cdots, p_{gD})$).At each iteration t, the position $x_{id}(t)$ and the velocity $v_{id}(t)$ are updated for next iteration $t+1$ by the following equations.

$$v_{id}(t+1) = wv_{id}(t) + c_1r_1(p_{id}(t) - x_{id}(t)) + c_2r_2(p_{gd}(t) - x_{id}(t)) \tag{1}$$

$$x_{id}(t+1) = x_{id}(t) + v_{id}(t+1) \tag{2}$$

Where w is inertia weight; c_1 and c_2 are acceleration Constant; r_1 and r_2 are uniformly distributed random number between 0 and 1.

The value of $v_{ij}(t)$ can be clamped to the range $[v_{min}, v_{max}]$ to control excessive roaming of particles outside the search space. The best position of each particle is updated using equation (3) and the global best position found by using equation (4).

$$p_{id}(t+1) = \begin{cases} x_{id}(t+1) & if\ f(x_{id}(t+1)) < f(p_{id}(t)) \\ p_{id}(t) & otherwise \end{cases} \tag{3}$$

$$p_{gd}(t+1) = \arg\min_{i \in \{1,2,\cdots,N\}} f(p_{id}(t+1)) \tag{4}$$

Where $f(\cdot)$ denotes fitness function.

2.2 IPSO Algorithm

This article treats each particle as an antibody. By using immunologic memory, immunologic selection, vaccination and other processing mechanisms in PSO, it proposes IPSO algorithm.

Immunologic Memory: Immunologic memory means immune system treats the antibody produced by antigens as memory cells and stores them. When it encounters antigens again, immune system will activate memory cells to generate a lot of antibodies to eliminate them. In the article, the best particle P_g generated by iteration was stored as memory cells. When the fitness of some particles can't meet the requirement, they will be replaced by memory cells. Immunologic memory can speed up the search by using immunologic memory function.

Immune Regulation: During the process of particle swarm updating, we always want to store those particles with higher fitness. But when the density of the particle is too high, it can't guarantee the diversity of particles and it is easy to fall into local optimum situation. So the article uses the regulation mechanism of immune system, that is, the higher the antibody particle's density, the greater the inhibitory effect that the system imposes, thus reduces the probability of being chosen; on the contrast, the lower the antibody particle's density, the greater the promoting effect that the system provides, thus increases the probability of being chosen. This regulation mechanism ensures the diversity of particles.

Using equation (5) calculates the density of particle i .

$$D(x_i) = \frac{1}{\sum\limits_{j=1}^{N+M} |f(x_i) - f(x_j)|}, i = 1, 2, \cdots, N+M \tag{5}$$

The probability selection formula of particle density can be derived from formula (5):

$$P(x_i) = \frac{\frac{1}{D(x_i)}}{\sum\limits_{i=1}^{N+M} \frac{1}{D(x_i)}} = \frac{\sum\limits_{j=1}^{N+M} |f(x_i) - f(x_j)|}{\sum\limits_{i=1}^{N+M} \sum\limits_{j=1}^{N+M} |f(x_i) - f(x_j)|}, i = 1, 2, \cdots, N+M \tag{6}$$

Where $f(x_i), i = 1, 2, \cdots N+M$ is the fitness of particle i. We can know from formula (6) that the more the particles similar to particle i, the smaller the probability of particle i being chosen and vice versa.

Vaccination

Vaccination is an important aspect of applying immunologic memory function to medical application. This paper uses this idea in PSO. By using vaccine extracting, vaccination and immunologic selection to complete the search process, which improves the performance of the algorithm and inhibits the degradation. Vaccination means partly change the antibody genes in accordance with the vaccine. If the adaptive degree is not better than before, we'll keep the antibody before vaccination; while if it is better than before, we'll keep the antibody after vaccination.

Generally, vaccine production is according to problem analyzing and feature information. But sometimes the problem to be solved has no prior information, so we can't get the proper vaccine. This paper selects the best particle P_g derived from the particle swarm updating process as vaccine. Vaccination makes those best particles to be inherited, improves search ability and avoids degradation.

The steps of IPSO

The procedures of IPSO algorithm can be illustrated as follows:

Step1: Initialize swarm, randomly generate N particles, spatial dimension is D, Initialize a population of particles with random velocities and positions in the problem space.

Step2: Calculate the fitness of each particle, according to the equations (3) and (4) updating P_i and P_g, store P_g as immunologic memory particle;

Step3: Update the velocities and the positions of particles using the equations (1) and (2);

Step4: Randomly generate M particles to form new particle swarm;

Step5: Calculate density select probability of $N+M$ particles according to formula (6) and choose N particles with higher probability into the next generation;

Step6: Vaccination: Randomly select a gene segment using P_g as vaccine and randomly take a certain number of particles according to a certain percentage. Replace the corresponding part of these particles with the vaccine gene segment;

Step7: Calculate the fitness of those replaced particles, if it is not better than their parents, cancel vaccination; if it is, keep these particles and form new particle swarm;

Step8: If it reaches the maximum iterative number, stop the process; if not, turn to step2.

3   DHMM Speech Recognition System

HMM speech recognition system needs to do preprocessing, feature extracting, vector quantizing, HMM model training and recognizing. HMM speech recognition system is shown in Figure 1.

The procedures of DHMM speech recognition algorithm based on IPSO vector quantization:

Signal preprocessing: Signal sampling, anti-aliasing filtering and other special processing.

Speech signal feature extracting: This article adopts zero-crossing rate and peak altitude method (ZCPA), which is 1024 dimensions speech feature vector.

Speech signal feature vector quantizing: After feature extracting, the data rate of feature vector sequence will be very high and it will affect the following processing. Therefore, coding method must be employed to compress data. Isolated word speech recognition system adopts DHMM, so the feature vector should be quantized. Vector

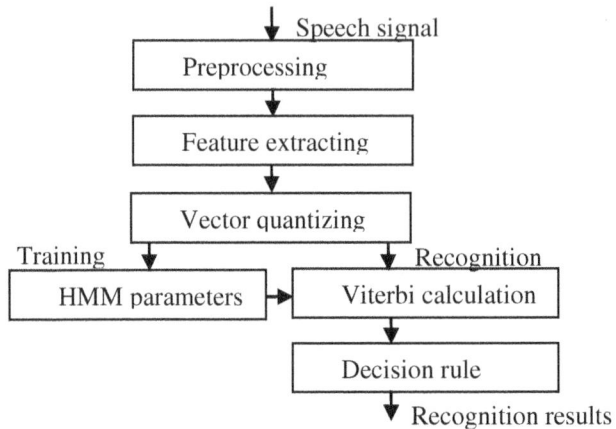

Fig. 1. Speech recognition system based on DHMM

quantization needs to generate codebook first. This article uses IPSO vector quantization to generate codebook. Every word's 1024 dimension feature vector will be quantized. Then these words are replaced by code-vector labels and become input signals of the next step. The specific process:

1) Swarm initialization. Pick out D vectors from the training vector set of speech database randomly to serve as a codebook, repeat N times to get N particles. Initialize particles velocity v_{ij} and position x_{ij} .

2) IPSO optimizes initial codebook. Carry out step 2 to step 7 of Immune Particle Swarm Optimization.

3) In accordance with the nearest-neighbor rule, reassure the cluster partition of each particle or each codebook and calculate the new cluster center to form new codebook.

4) If it reaches the maximum iterative number, stop the process; if not, turn to step2.

HMM model training: The code-vector label of word feature is the input sequence of HMM. The HMM is from left to right and no leaping, each word has 5 status. It adopts the classic Baum-Welch algorithm as training method, every word was trained into a set of model parameters ultimately.

Recognizing result decision: Use Viterbi algorithm to calculate the matching probability of each word and the model parameters are formed by the former step. The model with the biggest probability is the recognizing result.

4   Experiment Methods and Results

4.1   Experimental Setup

This article adopts C++ language to realize IPSO vector quantization HMM isolated word speech recognition system based on ZCPA speech feature.

Experimental data: Experimental data come from 16 persons, they read 10 words, 20 words, 30 words, and 50words under different Gaussian white noise (include 15dB、20dB、25dB、30dB and none) to form a speech database, each person read each word 3 times. 9 persons' voices were used as training database, other 7 persons' voice were used as recognizing database

Parameters Setting: The sampling rate of speech signal is 11.025 kHz. The parameters setting of IPSO algorithm: swarm size $N = 20$; new particles $M = 5$; particle dimension $D = 512$; maximum iterative number $t_{max} = 10$; acceleration Constant $c_1 = c_2 = 1.8$; inertia weight W is updated using formula (7),

$$W = W_{max} - t \times \frac{W_{max} - W_{min}}{t_{max}} \tag{7}$$

W_{max} is the maximum value of inertia factor, value 1.0, W_{min} is the minimum value of inertia factor, value 0.4, t is iteration number, t_{max} is the maximum iteration number; fitness function f is calculated by the following equation,

$$f(i) = \sum_{j=1}^{J} \sum_{x \in \theta_j} \sqrt{(\mathbf{x} - \mathbf{c}_j)^2} \quad i = 1, 2, \cdots N \tag{8}$$

Where $\mathbf{c}_j$ is clustering center jth, θ_j is the data set belonged to clustering center jth, clustering category number J. A smaller $f(i)$ indicates the codebook performance is better. We use 27 samples to train each word of the HMM model training.

Recognizing result is judged by the ratio of correctly recognized words and all the testing words.

4.2 Experimental Results and Analysis

Table 1 shows the recognition results in the experiment of speech recognition using IPSO-DHMM algorithm and PSO-DHMM algorithm on various SNR and various vocabulary cases.

We can see from the table 1 that DHMM speech recognition system based on the IPSO codebook design algorithm is better than that of the PSO in terms of recognition rate under different vocabulary size and different SNR. The IPSO has jumped out of the local optimum and improved the system performance. The recognition rates of the IPSO-DHMM are stable; the data distribution is more concentrated while the data distribution of PSO-DHMM is scattered. This shows that the IPSO-DHMM speech recognition system has a better robustness. But the increasing rate of recognition ratio are almost same under different SNR and the recognition ratio is best in no noise indicates, which shows that the anti-noise performance of the system need to be improved.

Table 1. The Comparision of Recognition Results Based on IPSO-DHMM and PSO-DHMM (%)

Vocabulary size	SNR(dB) Vector Quantization	15	20	25	30	Clean	Average recognition rate
10	PSO	85.7	85.3	85.7	87.6	91.4	87.2
	IPSO	86.7	86.9	87.3	88.7	92.1	88.3
20	PSO	77.2	77.9	81.2	86.4	86.2	81.8
	IPSO	78.6	81.2	83.4	87.5	88.7	83.9
30	PSO	80.2	80.5	84.8	82.9	84.3	82.6
	IPSO	82.1	82.9	87.1	84.9	87.5	84.9
40	PSO	83.3	76.9	77.9	81.2	82.2	80.3
	IPSO	86.2	79.6	81.0	84.2	84.6	83.1
50	PSO	72.6	76.2	81.1	79.0	81.8	78.2
	IPSO	75.1	78.5	82.4	83.0	84.1	80.6
Average recognition rate	PSO	79.8	79.4	82.2	83.4	85.2	--
	IPSO	81.7	81.8	84.2	85.7	87.4	--

5   Conclusion

This paper proposes IPSO algorithm which combines the PSO global optimization ability and the immunologic information processing mechanism of immune system together. This algorithm is easy to realize, improves the ability of getting rid of the local-peak point of PSO and improves the convergence speed and accuracy of the algorithm evolutionary process and ensures the diversity of the particle swarm. IPSO is used to codebook design of vector quantization in the paper and proposes DHMM speech recognition algorithm based on IPSO vector quantization. Experimental results show that the IPSO-DHMM speech recognition system has higher recognition ratio than the PSO-DHMM speech recognition system, which objectively proves the effectiveness of the IPSO.

Acknowledgment. The project is sponsored by Taiyuan University of Science and Technology Research Foundation for Young Scholars（20093013）.

References

1. Vicente-Pena, J., Díaz-de-María, F., Bastiaan Kleijn, W.: The synergy between bounded-distance HMM and spectral subtraction for robust speech recognition. Speech Communication 52, 123–133 (2010)

2. Lib, I., Lin, T.-S., Liao, L.: Codebook Design for Vector Quantization with Most Dispersed Codewords in Initialization. Journal of Chinese Computer Systems 30, 780–783 (2009)
3. Chen, Q., Yang, J., Gou, J.: Image Compression Method Using Improved PSO Vector Quantization. In: Pro. of the International Conference on Advances in Natural Computation, Changsha, China, pp. 490–495 (2005)
4. Li, X.-J., Xu, L.-P., Yang, L.: An Improved Particle Swarm Optimization Algorithm for Vector Quantization. Patter Recognition and Artificial Inteligence 21, 285–289 (2008)
5. Ji, Z., Liao, H.-L., Xu, W.-H.: A Strategy of Particle-pair for Vector Quantization in Image Coding. Chinese Journal of Electronics 35, 1916–1920 (2007)
6. Hart, E., Timmis, J.: Application areas of AIS: The past, the present and the future. Applied Soft Computing 8, 191–201 (2008)
7. Kennedy, J., Eberhart, R.C., Shi, Y.: Swarm Intelligence. Morgan Kaufman Publisher, San Francisco (2001)

Intelligent Tuning Method in Designing of Two-Degree-of-Freedom PID Regulator Parameters

Hai-wen Wang[1,2], Jing-gang Zhang[2], Yue-wei Dai[1], and Jun-hai Qu[3]

[1] Automation School, Nanjing University of Science & Technology, Nanjing 210094
wheaven@126.com
[2] Automation Department, Taiyuan University of Science & Technology, Taiyuan, 030024
[3] China North Industries Group 207 Research Institute, Taiyuan, 030006

Abstract. This paper puts forward a kind of new design method for two degree of freedom (2DOF) PID regulator. Based on sensitivity function, the parameters of two degree of freedom PID regulator are adaptively adjustable using particle swarm optimization(PSO) algorithm, the comparisons of simulation results with the improved GA were given, very good dynamic response performance of both command tracking and disturbance rejection characteristics can be achieved simultaneously, the optimal 2-DOF PID regulator has good robustness, the simulation verified the effectiveness of the PSO algorithm.

Keywords: Two-degree-of-freedom PID regulator, Particle swarm algorithm, Optimization design.

1 Introduction

In many applications, control objectives include both disturbance attenuation and reference tracking. It is well-known that these objectives can be handled independently by the use of so-called two-degrees-of-freedom (2DOF) controller configurations. The idea is to use the feedback component of the regulator to attenuate unmeasured disturbances and the feed-forward part of the controller to obtain the desired response to measured command signals. The 2DOF controller overcomes the shortages existed in the conventional PID regulator. Yet same as the conventional PID regulator, it is relative difficulty in tuning the parameters of 2DOF PID regulator.Generally, the coefficients of 2DOF are determined by experience, and there is a lack of systematic tuning method. So some researchers in recent years use intelligent optimal algorithms in designing of 2DOF regulators[1-7], genetic algorithm (GA)has been successfully used in the optimization design of parameters for 2DOF PID regulators[1-6], the Genetic Algorithm, the Evolutionary Programming, the Genetic Programming and the Evolutionary Strategies. These strategies turn out to be powerful tools, to solve optimization problems, but the main disadvantage of GA is that it usually needs a great number of objective function evaluations to be effective, in problems where the calculation of the objective function is very time consuming, they may become impracticable. In paper [7], modifications of mind evolutionary computation (MEC) was applied to optimize the

H. Deng et al. (Eds.): AICI 2011, Part III, LNAI 7004, pp. 428–435, 2011.

parameters of 2-DOF PID regulator, and simulations prove that the 2-DOF PID regulator optimized by the modified MEC has better performance than GA algorithm. these methods have been achieved very good dynamic response performances for both the command tracking and disturbance rejection simultaneously , however , these methods use the time-domain as the objective function without considering the robustness of the system.

Particle Swarm Optimization (PSO) which is a new robust stochastic evolutionary computation algorithm based on the movement and intelligence of swarms, It is similar in some ways to GA, but requires less computational bookkeeping and generally fewer coding lines [8]. Recently, this new stochastic evolutionary computation technique has been successfully applied to artificial neural network [9], assignment problem [10], electromagnetics[11] size and shape optimization [12], power system [13], chemical process and so on.

2 Particle Swarm Optimization

Particle swarm optimization is a rather new technique introduced by Kennedy and Eberhart in1995. PSO is developed through simulation of bird flocking in multi-dimensional space. PSO is a flexible, robust population based stochastic search/optimization algorithm with non-differential objective functions, unlike traditional optimization method. PSO is less susceptible to getting trapped on local optimization unlike GA, SA, etc. The main idea is to interpret each particle as a solution to the problem being investigated and to let these particles explore the search space. In the standard particle swarm optimizer ,each particle i has a position (xi) in the search space, a velocity vector(vi), the position (pi) and the fitness of the best point encountered by the particle, and index (g) of the best particle in the swarm. The particle's position represent the current solution to the numerical problem. The particle's next position($x_i^/$) determined by the velocity vector:

$$x_i^{\,/} = x_i + v_i \qquad (1)$$

The velocity vector is updated according to the current velocity, the particle's own best position, and the overall best position in the swarm:

$$v_i^{\,/} = \omega v_i + c_1 rand\,()(p_i - x_i) + c_2 Rand\,()(p_g - x_i) \qquad (2)$$

where ω is the inertia weight, pg is the position of the best particle in the swarm .c1 and c2 are positive constant and rand() and Rand() are uniformly distributed random number in [0,1]. The inertia weight is used to balance the global and local search ability. A large inertia weight facilities a global search while a small search facilities a local search. By changing the inertia weight dynamically, the search ability is dynamically adjusted. Since the search process of the PSO is non-linear and very complicated; it is hard to mathematically model the search process to dynamically adjust the inertia weight. Instead of a fixed inertia weight, a linearly decreasing inertia weight is deployed. By linearly decreasing inertia weight from a relatively large value to a small value through the course of the PSO run, PSO tends to have more global search ability at the beginning of the run while having more local search ability near the end of the run. ω in this paper is from 1.1 to 0.3.

3 Design for 2-DOF PID Based on PSO

3.1 2-DOF PID Regulator

In this section we will concentrate on the set point filter type 2-DOF controller which is simple and displayed in Fig. 1. where $G_P(s)$ is the plant, $F(s)$ is the set-point filter, r 、 y and d is the input, output, and the disturbance signal of the control system respectively, K_P, T_I and T_D is the three parameters of the PID controller, α, β and γ is the 2-DOF parameters, With different values of α, β and γ, this structure can various 2-DOF PID.

From the Fig. 1, we compute the transfer functions from the reference and the disturbance to the output, we obtain:

$$Y(s) = \frac{C(s)G_P(s)F(s)}{1+(C(s)+C_b(s))G_P(s)}R(s) + \frac{G_P(s)}{1+(C(s)+C_b(s))G_P(s)}L \quad (3)$$

$$C(s) = K_P(1+\frac{1}{T_I s}) \quad (4)$$

$$C_b(s) = K_P\frac{T_D s}{1+\eta T_D s} \quad (5)$$

$$F(s) = \frac{1+\alpha T_I s}{1+T_I s} + \frac{T_I s}{1+T_I s}(\frac{-\beta}{1+T_I s} + \frac{\gamma T_D s}{1+\eta T_D s}) \quad (6)$$

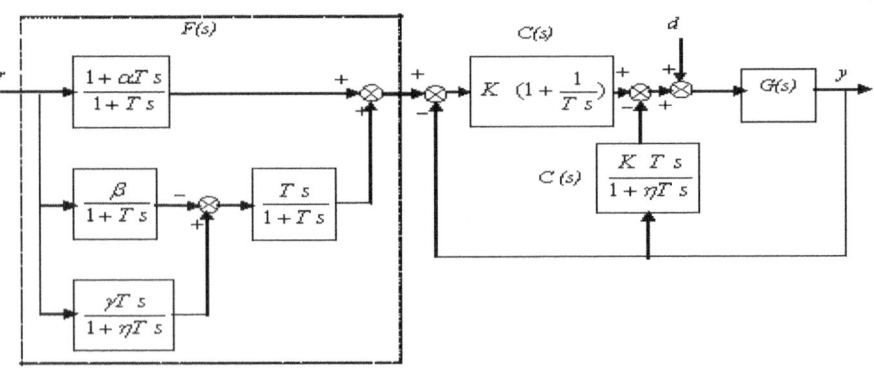

Fig. 1. Set-point Filter Type 2DOF PID Controller

The disturbance rejection algorithm of the the set point filter type 2-DOF controller is described as::

$$C(s) + C_b(s) = K_P (1 + \frac{1}{T_I s} + \frac{T_D s}{1 + \eta T_D s}) \tag{7}$$

From Eq. (7), the best disturbance rejection characteristic can be achieved by regulating K_p, T_i, T_D.

The command tracking algorithm of the the set point filter type 2-DOF controller is described as::

$$F(s)C(s) = K_P \left[\alpha + (\frac{1}{T_I s} - \frac{\beta}{1 + T_I s}) + \frac{\gamma T_D s}{1 + \eta T_D s} \right] \tag{8}$$

By regulating $\alpha 、 \beta 、 \gamma$, the best command tracking characteristic can be achieved.

3.2 2-DOF Regulator Based on PSO

As it has been mentioned, there is the need to include some robustness considerations into the previous designs. One of the features of the presented auto-tuning procedure is its simplicity as the designer just needs to specify the desired outer loop time constants ratio. In order to maintain the same approach, the inclusion of robustness considerations should not include additional requirements or complexities into the tuning procedure. This aim will be accomplished by using the maximum sensitivity as a robustness measure; that is given by

$$M_s = \max_\omega |S(j\omega)| = \max_\omega \frac{1}{|1 + C_v(j\omega)P(j\omega)|} \tag{9}$$

and recommended values for M_s are typically within the range 1.2–2.0; and by obtaining the required minimum values for the desired outer loop time constants ratio that guarantee a minimum robustness level. The use of the maximum sensitivity as a robustness measure, has the advantage that lower bounds to the gain and phase margins can be assured according to

$$A_m > \frac{M_s}{M_s - 1} \tag{10}$$

$$\phi_m > 2 \sin^{-1} (\frac{1}{2 M_s}) \tag{11}$$

As different controllers (PI_2 and PID_2) are used in the inner and outer loop, a different analysis is conducted in each case. However, the final result reads exactly the same way: obtaining a minimum value for the desired time constants ratio in terms of the specified robustness level. The inner loop deserves special attention as producing a closed-loop transfer function of a FOPDT form is also required. Due to this fact, a desired value for the robustness level of the inner loop is fixed to $M_{s2}=1.6$ and the closed-loop time constant for the inner loop is determined as the fastest one that, at the same time, guarantees that value of M_s and guarantees a FOPDT response. Note that by doing it this way the tuning of the overall cascade control system will be finally performed by just specifying one single parameter: the desired robustness level for the outer loop.

The well-known roubust stability is a very general requirement in analysing and designing a control system. Because the physical parameters will change with the working enviornment and time, these uncertainties make the performance of the system without meeting the request and even cause unstability. Therefore, in designing a system, the fast and precise robust control characteristics are of critical importance. The maximum sensitivity of the closed-loop system(Ms) is adopted to evaluate the robustness of the system [6-8], the open-loop transfer function and the sensitivity of the closed-loop system in this paper are

$$L(s) = [C(s) + C_h(s)]G_P(s) \tag{12}$$

$$S(s) = \frac{1}{1 + L(s)} \tag{13}$$

the maximum of (10) in the frequency domain is:

$$M_s = \max_{\omega} |S(j\omega)| \tag{14}$$

The relations between M_s, GM and PM :

$$GM \geq 20 \log(\frac{M_s}{M_s - 1}) \tag{15}$$

$$PM \geq 2 \arcsin(\frac{1}{2M_s}) \tag{16}$$

From the analysis above, we can obtain the optimal model of system as follows:

$$\min J \tag{17}$$
$$1.2 \leq M_s \leq 2.0$$

Step1: The parameters required for the PSO are the following: maximum number of iteration cycles=50, population(n_p)=30,c_1=2, c_2=2, J is given by Eq.(9),weight is updated by the following Eq(10):

$$\omega(iter) = \omega_{max} - (\frac{\omega_{max} - \omega_{min}}{N_m}) * iter \tag{18}$$

Step2: Initialization

Generate randomly initial velocities, positions of all particles, set individual best position, the global best position.

Step3: Velocity updating

Using the global best position and individual best position, the velocity output of any component of jth(j=1,2,..., n_p) particle is updated according to Eq.(2).

Step4: Position updating

Based on the updated velocities, each particle updated its position according to Eq.(1).

Step5: Individual best position updating

Each particle among n_p particles is evaluated as J_i(iter) according to the updated position. If the current J is better, then update individual best position.

Step6: Global best position updating

Search for minimum J_{min}(iter) among all J_j*(iter), j=1,2,...n_p, if J_{min}(iter) is better among n_p particles, then, update global best position.

Step7: Stopping criteria:

If the number of iterations reaches maximum iterations N_m, then stop, or else go to Step3.

4 Simulation and Discussions on the Results

For the 2DOF PID control system shown in Fig·1, choose

$$G_p(s) = \frac{2.194}{(80s + 1)^2}$$

step input $r(t) = 1(t)$, disturbance input $d(t) = -1(t - 1000)$.

The parameters of 2DOF PID controller are tuned by PSO algorithm, The following parameters have been selected for the PSO algorithm: population size=50; generations=30; acceleration constant c_1=2 and c_2=2; inertia weight factor ω is set by Eq.(3), where ωmax=1.1 and ωmin=0.3; the evaluation function f is given by Eq.(14). The tuning results for parameters of 2DOF PID regulator with the PSO algorithm are: $K_P = 2$, $T_I = 115.9241$, $T_D = 1.9786$; $\alpha = 0.7520$, $\beta = 0.0698$, $\gamma = 1.1709$; At the same time, The tuning results in Ref.[7] with the improved GA are: $K_P = 0.5499$, $T_I = 116.2884$, $T_D = 0.0274$; $\alpha = 0.9614$, $\beta = 0.8998$, $\gamma = 1.1175$;

The comparisons of simulation results with the basic PSO and the improved GA are shown in Fig.2 and Fig.3.

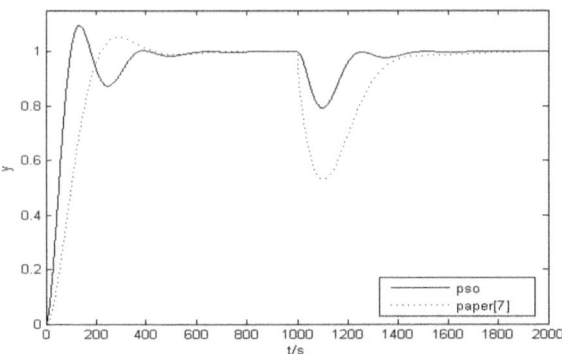

Fig. 2. Output responses of nominal system

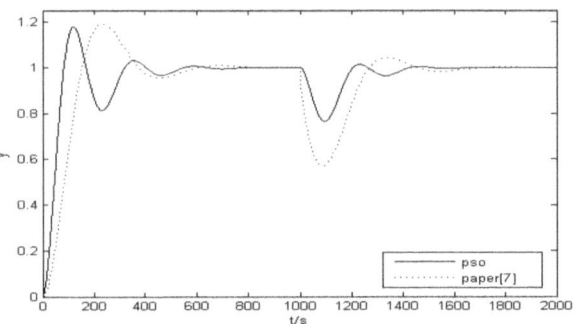

Fig. 3. Output responses of system with parameter variation

5   Conclusions

For the shortage of conventional 2-DOF regulator , a new optimization algorithm, the PSO, is presented to be used in the optimization design of parameters for 2DOF PID regulator, and simulation results show that very good dynamic response performance of both the command tracking and disturbance rejection characteristics can be achieved simultaneously with this method used in the optimization design of parameters for 2DOF PID regulator.

References

1. Xu, H., Xu, M.: Two-degree-of-freedom PID Regulator Design Using an Improved Genetic Algorithm. Journal of System Simulation 10(2), 59–64 (1998)
2. Wang, Q., Ma, L.: Design for 2-DOF PID Controller Based on Hybrid Genetic Algorithm and Its Application. Control and Decision 16(2), 195–199 (2001)
3. Li, P., Wen, L.: Optimal Design for 2-DOF PID Controller. Chinese Journal of Scientific Instrument 24(4), 399–403 (2003)

4. Xu, H.Z., Jin, L.: Design of Three-Axis Flight Simulator Controller Based on Genetic Algorithm. In: Proc. 5th WCICA, Hangzhou, P.R. China, pp. 5430–5434 (2004)
5. Yang, Y., Liu, D.: Optimal Design for 2-DOF PID Controller Based on Fuzzy Genetic Algorithms. Chinese Journal of Scientific Instrument 27(8), 868–872 (2006)
6. Kazuaki, I., Makoto, I.: Optimal Design of Robust Vibration Suppression Controller Using Genetic Algorithms. IEEE Trans. on Industrial Electronics. 51(5), 947–953 (2004)
7. Guo, P., Han, P.: Modifications of Mind Evolutionary Computation and Application in 2-DOF PID Controller. In: Proc. of 5th WCICA, Hangzhou, P.R. China, pp. 2268–2270 (2004)
8. Boeringer, D.W., Werner, D.H.: Particle Swarm Optimization Versus Genetic Algorithms for Phased Array Synthesis. IEEE Transaction on Antennas and Propagation 52(3) (2004)
9. Eberhart, R.C., Shi, Y.: Evolving artificial neural networks. In: Proc. Int. Conf. Neural Networks and Brain, Beijing, P.R.C (1998)
10. Salman, A., Ahmad, I., Al-Madani, S.: Particle swarm optimization for task assignment problem. Microprocessors and Microsystems 26, 363–371 (2002)
11. Robinson, J., Rahmat-Samii, Y.: Particle Swarm Optimization in Electormagnetics. IEEE Transactions on Antennas and Propagation 52(2) (2004)
12. Fourie, P.C., Groenwold, A.A.: The particle swarm optimization algorithm in size and shape optimization. Struct. Multidisc Optim. 23, 259–267 (2002)
13. Abido, M.A.: Optimal Design of Power–System Stabilizers Using Particle Swarm Optimization. IEEE Transactions on Energy Conversion 17(3) (2002)

A Simple Way for Parameter Selection of Standard Particle Swarm Optimization

Wei Zhang, Ying Jin, Xin Li, and Xin Zhang

College of Chemistry and Chemical Engineering,
Taiyuan University of Technology,
Taiyuan 030024, P.R. China
zhangwei01@tyut.edu.cn

Abstract. A simple way is proposed to estimate the non-negative real parameter tuple $\{\omega, c1, c2\}$ of standard Particle Swarm Optimization algorithm using control theory. The distribution of complex characteristic roots on the convergence region of particles is studied by means of linear discrete-time system analysis method. It is pointed out that the critical factors affecting the modulus value and the phase angle of the complex characteristic roots are the maximum overshoot and angular frequency of damped oscillation. The way shows that the product of the maximum overshoot and the angular frequency of damped oscillation approximately equaling to 1 is the promising guideline for parameter selection in PSO when the angular frequency in the range of $(0.65\pi, 0.35\pi)$. Based on this, widely used benchmark problems are employed in series experiments using a stochastic approximation technique, and the results are well back above deduction.

Keywords: particle swarm optimization, statistical experiments, parameter selection.

1 Introduction

Particle swarm optimization (PSO) has been shown to be an efficient, robust and simple optimization algorithm for finding optimal regions of complex search spaces through the interaction of individuals in a population of particles. Accelerating convergence rate and avoiding local minima or prematurely are two main aspects in PSO. Clerc and Kennedy [1] mathematically analyzed the stochastic behavior of the PSO algorithm in stagnation. Trelea [2] analyzed the dynamic behavior and the convergence of the simplified PSO algorithm using standard results from the discrete-time dynamic system theory, and provided a parameter set ($\omega = 0.6$, $c_1 = c_2 = 1.7$) in the algorithm convergence domain. M. Jiang et al. [3] studied the stochastic convergence property of the standard PSO algorithm, and gave a sufficient condition to ensure the stochastic convergence of the particle swarm system. And then, according to the analysis result, a set of suggested parameters ($\omega = 0.715$, $c_1 = c_2 = 1.7$) was given in another literature [4]. J. L. Fern´andez Mart´ınez et al. proved the same stability regions under stagnation and with a moving center of attraction. They also

H. Deng et al. (Eds.): AICI 2011, Part III, LNAI 7004, pp. 436–443, 2011.
© Springer-Verlag Berlin Heidelberg 2011

pointed out that properties of the second-order moments variance and covariance served to propose some promising parameter sets and proposed a good parameter region of inertia value and acceleration coefficients [5]. Above reports provide insights into how particle swarm system works based on mathematical analyses. Besides, the oscillation properties also have important influence on optimization process, while its analysis in optimization process based on control theory was seldom reported by far.

The rest of the paper is organized as follows. Section 2 surveys the standard PSO in the z-plane according to the control theory. A simple principle to find the best parameter values in particle swarm optimization based is presented in Section 3. Section 4 presents the experimental results using seven benchmark functions. Finally, Section 5 concludes the paper.

2 Analysis of Particle Swarm Optimization

2.1 The Difference Equations of Standard PSO Algorithm

PSO uses a set of particles, representing potential solutions to solve the optimization problem. The particles move around in a multidimensional search space with a position x^t_{id} and a velocity v^t_{id}, where $i=1,2,\ldots,N$ represents the index of the particle, t is the time step, and $d =1,2,\ldots,D$ is the dimensionality of the search space. For each generation, the particle compares its current position with the goal (global best/personal best) position and adjusts its velocity towards the goal with the help of the explicit memory of the best position ever found both globally and individually. Then the updating of velocity and particle position can be obtained by using the two following equations

$$v_{id}^{t+1} = \omega \times v_{id}^t + c_1 \times r1_{id}^t \times \left(p_{id}^t - x_{id}^t \right) + c_2 \times r2_{id}^t \times \left(p_{gd}^t - x_{id}^t \right) \tag{1}$$

$$x_{id}^{t+1} = x_{id}^t + v_{id}^{t+1} \tag{2}$$

where c_1 and c_2 are positive constants, defined as acceleration coefficients; ω is the inertia weight introduced to accelerate the convergence speed of PSO algorithm; $r1^t_{id}$ and $r2^t_{id}$ are two random functions in the range of [0,1]; p^t_{id} is the best previous position of x^t_{id}; p^t_{gd} is the position of the best particle among the entire population.

During stagnation, each particle behaves independently and each dimension is treated independently too. So updated equations are rewritten as

$$v_{t+1} = \omega v_t + c_1 r_{1,t} \left(p_i - x_t \right) + c_2 r_{2,t} \left(p_g - x_t \right) \tag{3}$$

$$x_{t+1} = x_t + v_{t+1} \tag{4}$$

By substituting Eq. (3) into Eq. (4), the following non-homogeneous recurrence relation is obtained:

$$x_{t+1} + \left(c_1 r_{1,t} + c_2 r_{2,t} - 1 - \omega \right) x_t + \omega x_{t-1} - c_1 r_{1,t} p_i - c_2 r_{2,t} p_g = 0 \tag{5}$$

Applying the expectation operator to both sides of the Eq. (5), obtaining

$$Ex_{t+2} + \left(\frac{c_1 + c_2}{2} - 1 - \omega \right) Ex_{t+1} + \omega Ex_t - \frac{c_1 P_i - c_2 P_g}{2} = 0 \tag{6}$$

According to the z–transform of the second-order difference Eq. (6), the expectation of $x(z)$ is

$$Ex(z) = \frac{z^2 x_0 + z x_1 + \left(\frac{c_1 + c_2}{2} - \omega - 1 \right) z x_0 + \frac{c_1 P_i + c_2 P_g}{2} \frac{z}{z-1}}{z^2 + \left(\frac{c_1 + c_2}{2} - \omega - 1 \right) z + \omega} \tag{7}$$

and the corresponding characteristic equation is

$$z^2 + \left(\frac{c_1 + c_2}{2} - \omega - 1 \right) z + \omega = 0 \tag{8}$$

Let $c = c_1 = c_2$, the solutions of the corresponding characteristic equation give the eigenvalues

$$z_{1,2} = \frac{1 + \omega - c \pm \sqrt{\Delta}}{2} \tag{9}$$

where

$$\Delta = (c - \omega - 1)^2 - 4\omega \tag{10}$$

The positions of eigenvalues in the z-plane affect the dynamic characteristic of Ex_k, and it can be discussed in two cases, both eigenvalues are real ones or complex ones.

2.2 Dynamic Characteristic Analysis of Complex Eigenvalues

According to the time-domain analysis of linear systems, the complex eigenvalues can be expressed as

$$z_{1,2} = e^{(-\sigma \pm j\omega_d)T} = \left| z_{1,2} \right| e^{\pm j\omega_d T} \tag{11}$$

and the model of the complex eigenvalues is

$$\left| z_{1,2} \right| = e^{-\sigma} = e^{-\xi \omega_n} \tag{12}$$

where $\sigma = \xi \omega_n$ is attenuation coefficient, $\omega_d = \omega_n \sqrt{1 - \xi^2}$ is angular frequency of damped oscillation, ω_n is natural frequency, $\xi (0 < \xi < 1)$ is damping ratio in control.

From inverse z-transform, the transient component of the complex eigenvalues can be derived as:

$$Ex(nT) = -\frac{1}{\sqrt{1-\xi^2}} e^{-\xi\omega_n nT} \sin(\omega_d nT + \beta)$$ (13)

where $\beta = \arccos\xi$, T is sampling period.
    The maximum overshoot

$$M = e^{-\pi\xi/\sqrt{1-\xi^2}} \times 100\%$$ (14)

denotes the maximum peak value of the response. It is decided by system's damping degree, and the greater the value of ξ is, the smaller the maximum overshoot will be.

    The characteristics of Eqs.(12),(13) and (14) can be summarized as follows:
    (1) The complex eigenvalues locate inside the unit circle in the z-plane when $|z_{1,2}| < 1$ and then the dynamic response $Ex(nT)$ is a periodic pulse sequence with damping process. The smaller the value of $|z_{1,2}|$ is, the closer the complex eigenvalues to the origin of the z-plane, and then it will cause the inevitable result of rapid convergence. The convergence rate becomes slower when the value of $|z_{1,2}|$ approaches to 1 and continuous oscillation will occur when $|z_{1,2}| = 1$.
    (2) The dynamic characteristic of $Ex(nT)$ decided by the complex eigenvalues is sinusoidal oscillation with the angular frequency ω_d. The fact that the value of ω_d is too small to favor the system overcoming premature convergence and a much greater one causes the system oscillate seriously and even incapable convergence in limited optimization period.
    (3) The maximum overshoot is only a function of the damping ratio ξ as shown in Eq.(14).The greater the maximum overshoot is, the bigger the oscillation amplitude will be. The value of M is too great to favor the system fast stabilization, and too small to favor the system optimization.

The relationships between the distribution of complex eigenvalues and their corresponding dynamic responses are shown in Fig.1.

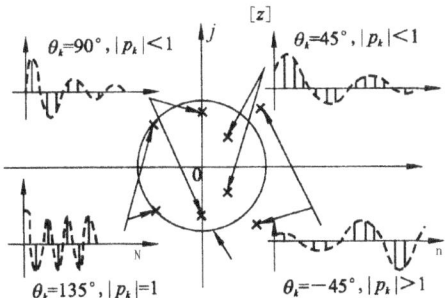

Fig. 1. The distribution of complex characteristic roots and their corresponding dynamic responses

According to the analysis results above, it can be concluded that the maximum overshoot M and the angular frequency of the damped oscillation ω_d affect the optimization behavior mainly. When the value of ω_d is heightened, the maximum overshoot M should be reduced. Conversely when the value of ω_d is decreased, the maximum overshoot M should be increased.

3   A New Simple Parameter Selection Guideline

Based on the theoretical analysis results obtained above and corresponding experimental results, the new   guidelines for parameter selection are proposed as following and detailed discussion are made to show the validity of the new guidelines in [6].

$$M \times \omega_d = 1 \qquad \omega_d \in (0.65\pi, 0.35\pi) \tag{15}$$

According to Eq.(15), PSO algorithm will search the solution space thoroughly, and find the optima with higher probability. The way to get the certain values of ω and c from the relationship of M and ω_d in Eq.(15) is shown as following.

As discussed above, the eigenvalues can be easily obtained from Eqs. (9) and (10) when $\Delta < 0$. The solving formula is

$$z_{1,2} = \frac{1+\omega-c \pm j\sqrt{4\omega-(c-\omega-1)^2}}{2} \tag{16}$$

Let the sampling period $T = 1s$, and from Eqs. (16) and (12) the model of eigenvalues can be expressed as

$$\left| z_{1,2} \right| = \left| \frac{1+\omega-c \pm j\sqrt{4\omega-(c-\omega-1)^2}}{2} \right| = \sqrt{\omega} = e^{-\xi\omega_n} \tag{17}$$

The angular frequency of the damped oscillation in the z-plane is

$$\omega_d = \left(180° + \arctan\frac{\sqrt{4\omega-(c-\omega-1)^2}}{1+\omega-c} \right) \times \frac{\pi}{180} \text{(rad)} = \omega_n\sqrt{1-\xi^2} \tag{18}$$

The solving process can be summarized as following.

(1) Choosing the value of ω_d arbitrarily, such as 0.65π, 0.6π, 0.55π, 0.5π, 0.45π, 0.4π, 0.35π listed in table 1.
(2) Getting the corresponding maximum overshoot M according to Eq.(15).
(3) Then the damping ratio ξ can be calculated from Eq.(14).
(4) The corresponding values of ω and c can be calculated respectively according to Eqs. (18) and (17) finally.

The detailed data are listed in table 1 .

Table 1. Data according to the simple parameter selection guidelines

ω_d	ω	c	$M \times \omega_d$
$\pm 0.65\pi$	0.398	1.971	1
$\pm 0.60\pi$	0.469	1.892	1
$\pm 0.55\pi$	0.551	1.783	1
$\pm 0.50\pi$	0.640	1.640	1
$\pm 0.45\pi$	0.736	1.468	1
$\pm 0.40\pi$	0.836	1.271	1
$\pm 0.35\pi$	0.821	0.998	1
0.456π [1]	0.729	1.494	1
0.521π [2]	0.600	1.700	1
0.473π [4]	0.715	1.700	1

4 Optimization Strategies and Experiment Results

4.1 Test Conditions

The detailed information of three benchmark functions are summarized in Table 2. A fully connected topology (all particles being neighbors) was used in all cases. For each function, the population sizes were set to 30. Defined the maximum velocity according to equation $v_{max}=x_{max}$. The optimization process will stop when the error goal is reached or the numbers of iterations reach 5000.

Table 2. Typical test functions

Name	Formula	Dim.	Range	Error goal
Rastrigin	$f(x)=\sum_{i=1}^{n}\left(x_i^2 - 10\cos(2\pi x_i)+10\right)$	30	$[-5.12,5.12]^n$	10^2
Griewank	$f(x)=\frac{1}{4000}\sum_{i=1}^{n}x_i^2 - \prod_{i=1}^{n}\cos\left(\frac{x_i}{\sqrt{i}}\right)+1$	30	$[-600,600]^n$	10^{-1}
Schaffer's f6	$f(x)=0.5+\dfrac{\left(\sin\sqrt{x_1^2+x_2^2}\right)^2 - 0.5}{\left(1+0.001\left(x_1^2+x_2^2\right)\right)^2}$	2	$[-100,100]^2$	10^{-5}

4.2 Experimental Results

New simple guidelines for parameter selection in PSO are proposed based on the dynamics characteristic analyses of the eigenvalues in the z-plane according to the control theory. To further explain their validity, experimental comparisons between research results in literatures such as [1, 2, 4] and the new simple guidelines are carried out as following. For each setting, 20 runs are performed. During each run, the operation terminates when the fitness score drops below the cutoff error and it is assumed that the global minimum of the function is reached, henceforth; the score is set to 0. The experimental results are listed as follows:

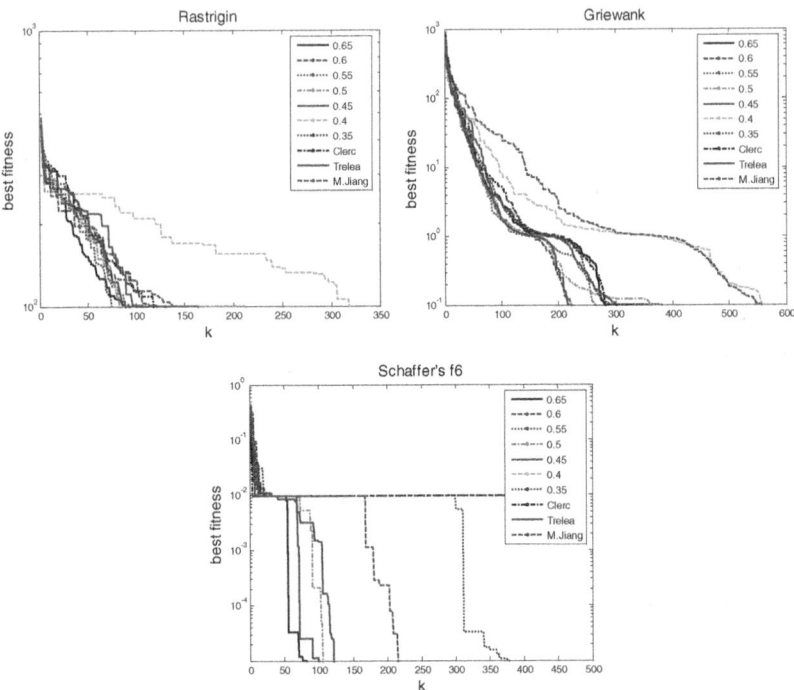

Fig. 2. Iterative comparison with functions of Rastrigin, Griewank and Schaffer's f6

Table 3. Statistical results from 20 runs of the functions

		0.65	0.6	0.55	0.5	0.45	0.4	0.35	0.456 [1]	0.521 [2]	0.473 [4]
Rastrigin function	Suc.	1	1	1	1	1	1	1	1	1	1
	Max.	177	141	151	166	215 •	587	267	343	171	162
	Min.	80	69	64	57	88	159	71	101	67	166
	Mean	115	98	107	102	127	279	122	162	99	178
	St.D	23.5	21.4	21.4	26.4	28.0	103	45.5	62.5	24.8	35.1
Griewank function	Suc.	1	1	0.85	0.95	1	1	0.65	1	0.90	1
	Max.	424	374	339	457	557	724	639	497	337	593
	Min.	243	227	239	225	273	466	216	274	209	423
	Mean	309	289	279	309	328	564	402	356	276	514
	St.D	42.8	39.7	36.5	63.7	64.1	66.8	133	57.4	36.4	50.7
Schaffer's f6 function	Suc.	0.60	0.45	0.60	0.45	0.85	0.75	0.70	0.30	0.55	0.70
	Max.	431	358	440	295	526	554	480	491	460	271
	Min.	4	53	7	9	4	5	5	5	68	5
	Mean	116	184	198	134	145	179	139	200	169	119
	St.D	104	119	133	86	129	182	131	182	140	98

The statistical comparison between the new simple guidelines and research results in literatures are reported in tables 3. Iterative comparisons among new simple way mentioned in this paper and other parameter selection strategies with three functions are showed in Fig.2. The statistics in the tables indicate that the parameters in accordance with the simple way show good performance in speed and reliability. But when ω_d take 0.45π and 0.35π, the values of average and variance are larger in some cases and hence can't avoid getting trapped into local optimum.

5 Conclusion

This paper has presented a simple guideline for parameter selection of standard PSO using control theory. The simple guideline is that the product of the maximum overshoot and the angular frequency of damped oscillation approximately equaling to 1 is the promising guideline for parameter selection in PSO when the angular frequency in the range of $(0.65\pi, 0.35\pi)$. The statistical results well back the superiority of the new simple guidelines in terms of time, iterations and convergence.

References

1. Clerc, M., Kennedy, J.: The particle swarm: explosion, stability, and convergence in a multidimensional complex space. IEEE Transactions on Evolutionary Computation 6(1), 58–73 (2002)
2. Trelea, I.C.: The particle swarm optimization algorithm: convergence analysis and parameter selection. Information Processing Letters 85, 317–325 (2003)
3. Jiang, M., Luo, Y.P., Yang, S.Y.: Stochastic convergence analysis and parameter selection of the standard particle swarm optimization algorithm. Information Processing Letters 102, 8–16 (2007)
4. Jiang, M., Luo, Y.P., Yang, S.Y.: Particle Swarm Optimization-Stochastic Trajectory Analysis and Parameter Selection (2007), Retrieved from
   http://www.i-techonline.com
5. Fernández Martínez, J.L., García Gonzalo, E.: The Generalized PSO: A New Door to PSO Evolution. Journal of Artificial Evolution and Applications, Article ID: 861275, 15 pages (2008), doi:10.1155/2008/861275
6. Zhang, W., Li, H., Zhao, Q., Wang, H.: Guidelines for Parameter Selection in Particle Swarm Optimization According to Control Theory. In: 2009 Fifth International Conference on Natural Computation (ICNC 2009), Tianjin, China, vol. 3, pp. 520–524 (2009)

Blind Source Separation Algorithm Based on PSO and Algebraic Equations of Order Two

Lei Chen[1], Liyi Zhang[1,*], Yanju Guo[2], and Ting Liu[1]

[1] School of Information Engineering, Tianjin University of Commerce,
Tianjin 300134, China
zhangliyi@tjcu.edu.cn
[2] School of Information Engineering, Hebei University of Technology,
Tianjin 300401, China
article.com.cn@126.com

Abstract. A novel blind source separation algorithm based on particle swarm optimization algorithm and algebraic equations of order two was proposed. Particle swarm optimization algorithm was used for solving the objective function based on algebraic equations of order two and the separation matrix for blind separation was achieved. The calculated amount of the algorithm proposed is very low comparing with some blind separation algorithm based on high order cumulant. Simulation result for speech signal blind separation proves the validity of the algorithm proposed.

Keywords: blind source separation, particle swarm optimization, algebraic equations of order two, covariance matrix.

1 Introduction

Blind source separation technology is one important branch of blind signal processing. It has been widely used in fields of speech, image, communication and biomedicine [1-4]. Intelligence optimization algorithm has received more and more recognition in recent years. It has obtained excellent effect for resolution of the complex realistic problem. There will be better development prospect for using intelligence optimization algorithm in resolution of the blind source separation problem.

The selection of objective function and the optimization for objective function are two important things in blind source separation algorithm. Once the objective function has been chosen, a certain intelligence optimization algorithm can be used for optimizing it. In this paper, PSO algorithm is used for optimizing the objective function based on algebraic equations of order two and a new blind source separation algorithm can be got. Because the blind source separation algorithm is based on covariance matrix, the calculated amount of the algorithm proposed is very low comparing with some blind separation algorithm based on high order cumulant.

---

* Corresponding author.

H. Deng et al. (Eds.): AICI 2011, Part III, LNAI 7004, pp. 444–450, 2011.

2 Model of Linear Mixed Blind Source Separation

In blind signal separation problems, the observed signals come from the output of a group of sensors, each of them is the mixture of a group of source signals. Namely, there is an independent signal vector $s(t) = [s_1(t), s_2(t), \cdots, s_N(t)]^T$ comes from N source signals. Under normal circumstances, source signals are instantaneous linear mixed and $N = K$.

$$x(t) = As(t) \tag{1}$$

A is an $N \times N$ constant matrix. $x(t) = [x_1(t), x_2(t), \cdots, x_N(t)]^T$ is the observation signals. The purpose for blind signal separation is to get the estimate $y(t)$ of source signal $s(t)$.

$$y(t) = Wx(t) \tag{2}$$

Where W is the separation matrix.

In linear nonsingular blind signal separation problems, separated signal can be the amplification or reduce of the source signal. The arrangement of the separated signal may be different from source signal. Therefore, the number of the separation matrix is infinite.

According to [5], the separation matrix W can be transformed to the form as follows

$$W = \begin{bmatrix} 1 & w_{12} & \cdots & w_{1N} \\ w_{21} & 1 & \cdots & w_{2N} \\ \vdots & \vdots & 1 & \vdots \\ w_{N1} & w_{N2} & \cdots & 1 \end{bmatrix} \tag{3}$$

Now, the number of the separation matrix has been finite.

3 Blind Separation Principle Based on Algebraic Equations of Order Two

In the process of solving linear mixed blind signal separation problems, source signals are generally assumed as independent stationary signal. The first-order derivative of the source signal is $s'(t) = [s_1'(t), s_2'(t), \cdots, s_N'(t)]^T$. Then the first-order derivative of the observation signal is $x'(t) = [x_1'(t), x_2'(t), \cdots, x_N'(t)]^T$. According to [6], when the component in $s(t)$ is irrelevant, their derivative signal is also irrelevant.

$$x'(t) = As'(t) \tag{4}$$

A blind source separation method based on solving algebraic equations of order two was proposed in [5], we will briefly introduce it as follows.

The covariance matrix of source signal and observation signal can be express as follows

$$C_s = E((s(t) - m_s)(s(t) - m_s)^T) \tag{5}$$

$$C_x = E((x(t) - m_x)(x(t) - m_x)^T) \tag{6}$$

Where $m_s = E(s(t))$ is the mean value of source signal and $m_x = E(x(t))$ is the mean value of observation signal. The covariance matrix of derivative signal for source signal and observation signal can be express as follows

$$C_{s'} = E((s'(t) - m_{s'})(s'(t) - m_{s'})^T) \tag{7}$$

$$C_{x'} = E((x'(t) - m_{x'})(x'(t) - m_{x'})^T) \tag{8}$$

Matrix $WC_x W^T$ and matrix $WC_x W^T$ are diagonal matrix because that component in source signal is independent and component in derivative signal is irrelevant.

$$WC_x W^T = \Lambda_1 \tag{9}$$

$$WC_x W^T = \Lambda_2 \tag{10}$$

i.e.

$$\begin{vmatrix} 1 & w_{12} & \cdots & w_{1N} \\ w_{21} & 1 & \cdots & w_{2N} \\ \vdots & \vdots & & \vdots \\ w_{N1} & w_{N2} & \cdots & 1 \end{vmatrix} \times \begin{vmatrix} c'_{11} & c'_{12} & \cdots & c'_{1N} \\ c'_{21} & c'_{22} & \cdots & c'_{2N} \\ \vdots & \vdots & & \vdots \\ c'_{N1} & c'_{N2} & \cdots & c'_{NN} \end{vmatrix}$$

$$\times \begin{vmatrix} 1 & w_{21} & \cdots & w_{N1} \\ w_{12} & 1 & \cdots & w_{N2} \\ \vdots & \vdots & & \vdots \\ w_{1N} & w_{2N} & \cdots & 1 \end{vmatrix} = \begin{vmatrix} \sigma'_1 & 0 & \cdots & 0 \\ 0 & \sigma'_2 & \cdots & 0 \\ \vdots & \vdots & & \vdots \\ 0 & 0 & \cdots & \sigma'_N \end{vmatrix} \tag{11}$$

$$\begin{vmatrix} 1 & w_{12} & \cdots & w_{1N} \\ w_{21} & 1 & \cdots & w_{2N} \\ \vdots & \vdots & & \vdots \\ w_{N1} & w_{N2} & \cdots & 1 \end{vmatrix} \times \begin{vmatrix} c''_{11} & c''_{12} & \cdots & c''_{1N} \\ c''_{21} & c''_{22} & \cdots & c''_{2N} \\ \vdots & \vdots & & \vdots \\ c''_{N1} & c''_{N2} & \cdots & c''_{NN} \end{vmatrix}$$

$$\times \begin{vmatrix} 1 & w_{21} & \cdots & w_{N1} \\ w_{12} & 1 & \cdots & w_{N2} \\ \vdots & \vdots & & \vdots \\ w_{1N} & w_{2N} & \cdots & 1 \end{vmatrix} = \begin{vmatrix} \sigma''_1 & 0 & \cdots & 0 \\ 0 & \sigma''_2 & \cdots & 0 \\ \vdots & \vdots & & \vdots \\ 0 & 0 & \cdots & \sigma''_N \end{vmatrix} \tag{12}$$

Algebraic equations about w_{ij} can be got because the element in non-diagonal in equation (11) and (12) are all zero.

$$\begin{cases} \sum_{k=1}^{N}\sum_{l=1}^{N} w_{ik} w_{jl} c'_{kl} = 0 \\ \sum_{k=1}^{N}\sum_{l=1}^{N} w_{ik} w_{jl} c''_{kl} = 0 \end{cases} \tag{13}$$

where $i \neq j$, $i, j = 1,2,\cdots,N$ and $j > i$. Separation matrix W can be obtained by solving algebraic equations of order two (13). In [5], algebraic equations of order two (13) was resolved by using diagonalization method.

4 Blind Source Separation Algorithm Based on PSO and Algebraic Equations of Order Two

In this paper, we will use particle swarm optimization algorithm to solve the algebraic equations of order two (13) and the separation matrix W can be obtained.

4.1 PSO Algorithm

Particle Swarm Optimization (PSO) algorithm is one kind of swarm intelligence optimization method proposed in 1995[7]. The optimization concept of PSO comes from feeding process of bird and the optimization property of PSO algorithm is good.

The basic concept for PSO algorithm can be described according to [8]. There are M particles in D dimensional optimization space. The velocity of i th particle is $v_i = (v_{i1}, v_{i2}, \cdots, v_{iD})$ and the position of i th particle is $x_i = (x_{i1}, x_{i2}, \cdots, x_{iD})$. Let $p_i = (p_{i1}, p_{i2}, \cdots, p_{iD})$ be the individual optimal position of i th particle and let $p_g = (p_{g1}, p_{g2}, \cdots, p_{gD})$ be the global optimal position for all particles. Particle condition update function can be described as follows

$$v_{id}(t+1) = w \cdot v_{id}(t) + c_1 r_1 [p_{id} - x_{id}(t)] + c_2 r_2 [p_{gd} - x_{id}(t)] \tag{14}$$

$$x_{id}(t+1) = x_{id}(t) + v_{id}(t+1) \tag{15}$$

Where $i = 1,2,\cdots,M$, $d = 1,2,\cdots,D$. t is the evolution generation for particle swarm, w is inertia weight, c_1 and c_2 are positive learning factor chosen from 0 to 4. r_1 and r_2 is random number respectively chosen from 0 to 1.

4.2 Solve Algebraic Equations of Order Two Using PSO

The parameter coding and setting of initial swarm should be done before using PSO algorithm to solve the algebraic equations. When the number of source signal and observation signal are all N, the objective function can be defined as follows

$$J(W) = \sum_{i \neq j} \left| w_i C_x w_j^T \right| + \sum_{i \neq j} \left| w_i C_{x'} w_j^T \right| \tag{16}$$

Where w_i is i th row of matrix W and w_j is j th row of matrix W. The number of unknown element need to be identified in W is $N^2 - N$, then the dimension of each particle is $N^2 - N$.

After the particle coding and the objective function are determined, we can use PSO algorithm to optimize the objective function. And then, the elements of non-diagonal in separation matrix W which makes objective function to obtain minimum value can be got and the separation matrix W can be got according to (3).

The concrete step of the blind source separation algorithm based on PSO and algebraic equations of order two can be express as follows

(1) Whiten the mixed signal $x(t)$.

(2) Set the particle dimension and particle coding according to the number of source signal.

(3) Generate a certain number of particles randomly and initialize position for each particle.

(4) Calculate the objective function value of each particle according to (16).

(5) Compare particle's current objective function value with its own optimal value. Set the current position of this particle as p_i if its current objective function value is superior to its own optimal value and set the current position as p_g if its current objective function is superior to the global optimal value.

(6) Update each particle's current position according to (14) and (15).

(7) Go to step (8) if meet the end condition, otherwise, return to step (4).

(8) W can be got according to (3).

(9) Separated signal $y(t)$ can be got according to (2).

4.3 Simulation

For verifying the validity of the separation algorithm proposed, two speech signal are mixed by mixture matrix A.

$$A = \begin{bmatrix} 0.887344 & 0.181664 \\ 0.725364 & 0.550729 \end{bmatrix} \tag{17}$$

The mixed signals are separated by the blind source separation algorithm we proposed. The source signal, mixed signal and separation result are respectively shown in figure1, figure2 and figure3. The parameter of PSO in the blind source separation algorithm proposed is set as follows: swarm scale $M = 30$, particle dimension $D = 2$, $c_1 = c_2 = 2$, inertia weight descend from 0.8 to 0.3 linearly and the max iteration number is 100.

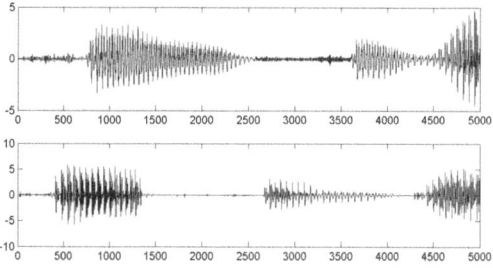

Fig. 1. Source signal

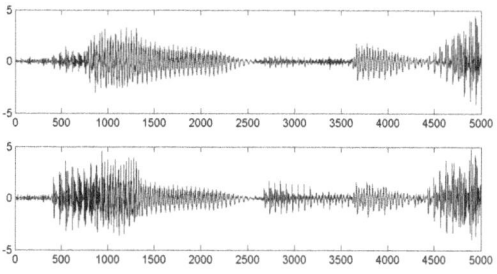

Fig. 2. Mixed signal

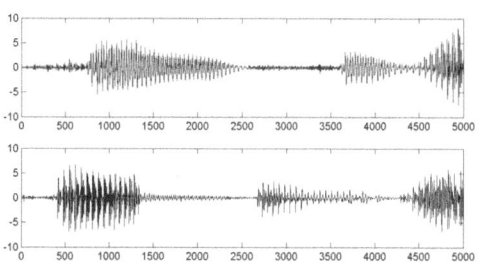

Fig. 3. Separated signal

We can see that the blind source separation algorithm based on PSO and algebraic equations of order two proposed can separated out the source signal from mixed signal by surveying figure3. The calculated amount is low and the elapsed time is short for the separation algorithm proposed because that simply second-order cumulant is used in the separation algorithm.

5   Conclusion

A blind source separation algorithm based on PSO and algebraic equations of order two is proposed. For solving the blind source separation problem, the objective function based on algebraic equations of order two is researched and PSO algorithm is used for optimizing it. Simulation result for speech signal separation shows the validity of the separation algorithm.

Acknowledgments. The author would like to thank Shujun Teng of Tianjin University of Commerce for his helpful comment on the algebraic equations principle.

References

1. Kocinski, J.: Speech Intelligibility Improvement Using Convolutive Blind Source Separation Assisted by Denoising Algorithms. Speech Communication 50, 29–37 (2008)
2. Ozgen, M.T., Kuruoglu, E.E., Herranz, D.: Astrophysical Image Separation by Blind Time–Frequency Source Separation Methods. Digital Signal Processing 19, 360–369 (2009)
3. Jallon, P., Chevreuil, A., Loubaton, P.: Separation of Digital Communication Mixtures with the CMA: Case of Unknown Symbol Rates. Signal Processing 90, 2633–2647 (2010)
4. Langers, D.R.M.: Blind Source Separation of fMRI Data by Means of Factor Analytic Transformations. NeuroImage 47, 77–87 (2009)
5. Xiao, M., Xie, S.L.: Number of the separation matrixes in the linear nonsingular mixture of blind signals. Journal of South China University of Technology 32(10), 41–45 (2004)
6. Barrere, J., Chabriel, G.: A Compact Sensor Array for Blind Separation of Sources. IEEE Transactions on Circuits and Systems I: Fundamental Theory and Applications 49, 565–574 (2002)
7. Kennedy, J., Eberhart, R.: Particle Swarm Optimization. In: IEEE International Conference on Neural Networks, pp. 1942–1948. IEEE Press, New York (1995)
8. Shi, Y., Eberhart, R.: A Modified Particle Swarm Optimizer. In: IEEE World Congress on Computational Intelligence, pp. 69–73. IEEE Press, New York (1998)

Human Action Recognition Based on Random Spectral Regression

GuangFeng Lin[1], Hong Zhu[2], YinDi Fan[3], and CaiXia Fan[1]

[1] Information Science Department, Xi'an University of Technology, Xi'an, China
lgf78103@ xaut.edu.cn, fcx_1981@yahoo.com.cn
[2] Electronic Information Engineering Department,
Xi'an University of Technology, Xi'an, China
zhuhong@ xaut.edu.cn
[3] Shaanxi College of Communication Technology, Xi'an, China
nezimi5584@126.com

Abstract. For solving the uncertain parameter selection, the highly spatio-temporal complexity and the difficulty of effectively extracting feature in manifold learning algorithm processing higher-dimension of human action sequence, human action recognition algorithm based on random spectral regression (RSPR) is presented. The algorithm has three steps. Firstly, according to uniform distribution of human action data in the manifold and the classification labels of human action, the weight matrix is built. This method overcomes the neighborhood parameter selection of the manifold learning algorithm. Secondly, by spectral regression, the spatial manifold based on frame is approximated, and the manifold mapping of unlabeled sample is obtained. At last, the feature of the temporal series is extracted in the spatial manifold based on frame, and then in Gaussian process classification the feature of human action is classified. The experiment has three parts. When RSPR tests the recognition of human action by leave-one-out crossvalidation in Weizmann database, the recognition rate reach 93.2%; comparing RSPR with locality preserving projection (LPP) and neighborhood preserving embedding (NPE), through extracting the statistical feature of temporal sequences RSPR shows better performance; in the test of walk action influenced RSPR displays better adaptability.

Keywords: random spectral regression, manifold learning, locality preserving projection, neighborhood preserving embedding, human action recognition.

1 Introduction

In machine and computer vision research, human action recognition can be applied in many fields, such as video surveillance, human-computer interaction and robot vision. In human action recognition the first problem is feature description, which include two broad categories [1]: the global representation (contour or silhouette [2],grid-based representations[3] and space-time volumes[4]) and the local representation (space-time interesting point detector[5], local descriptors[6], local grid-based

H. Deng et al. (Eds.): AICI 2011, Part III, LNAI 7004, pp. 451–461, 2011.
© Springer-Verlag Berlin Heidelberg 2011

representation[7] and correlations between local descriptors[8]). The above representations mostly involve spatial, temporal features and spatio-temporal features, but no matter what kind of features forming feature vector, the dimensions of which are very large. Now there are many methods of linear dimensionality reduction (principal component analysis, singular value decomposition, independent component analysis and linear discriminant analysis) and nonlinear dimensionality reduction (nonlinear subspace method of kernel mapping, manifold learning) [9]. During the process of the research it is recognized that the non-linear manifold is the perception of the foundation, because highly dimensional information typically exists in a non-linear low-dimensional manifold and to a large extent cognitive processes understands things through the nonlinear low-dimensional manifold [10]. In [11] by local preserving projection the manifold of human action sequence is analyzed, in [12] the manifolds distinguishing feature of the transform is learned, in [13] in spatio-temporal data the manifold discriminant of human action is well identified. However, there are three questions, firstly the traditional manifold building graphic models, using $\varepsilon-\text{ball}$ nearest neighbor or K-nearest neighbor of Euclidean distance constructing neighborhood to calculate the weights, the selection of parameter ε or K greatly affects on the efficiency of the algorithm, moreover the samples of European distance nearest neighbor often do not belong to the same class [14]; secondly in the traditional manifold of human action frames the dimensions of the sample are greater than the number of samples, which involves a possible dense matrix, and increases the complexity of the algorithm [9]; thirdly, the time series of human action have strongly associated, between the different human action frames under some conditions (run and skip) have the greater similarity, whereas the low-dimensional manifold only extracts the local structural feature, and could not obtain the optimal classification feature. For the above three questions random spectral regression algorithm is presented to extract the low-dimensional manifold of human action space, then the time series features of space manifold is obtained, lastly the Gaussian process classifier for classification of human action is used. In the article the study object is the whole human silhouette sequences, and the study mainly focuses on the manifold description of the feature and the classification efficiency of the manifold methods.

This article has five sections. In section 1 the main work associated with this article is narrated; in section 2 the manifold learning algorithm based on RSPR on human actions frame is proposed; in section 3 the time series features are extracted, and Gaussian processes classifier is established; in section 4 the contrast experiment is carried out among LPP, NPE and RSPR; in section 5 the conclusion is obtained.

2   Related Research

Classic manifold learning algorithm is divided into two types, which is global and local. Multidimensional Scaling (MDS) [15] is the global method of the linear dimensionality reduction, in which the structural features are measured by Euclidean distance matrix, but do not represent the nonlinear relationship of the manifold between samples. In Isometric mapping (ISOMAP) [16] the structural feature is measured by geodesic distance, however, the cost of the algorithm is large because of estimating the shortest path on the global neighborhood graph, moreover the noise and empty of the sample influence the efficiency of the algorithm greatly. Locally Linear Embedding (LLE) [17] is the local algorithm of the non-linear dimensionality reduction, which gets neighborhood graph by the linear reconstruction of the sample, then obtains the global linear construction by the local fitting, but the question is the parameter effects the reconstruction and the non-neighborhood data mapping. The learning method of the manifold can find the geometry features of the manifold, and then reflect the nature of the potential contact data. The actual application has two aspects that are neighborhood selection and extension of algorithm generalization. To a certain extent Linear Extension of Graph Embedding (LGE) [18] has solved the extension of algorithm generalization, moreover derived different linear dimensionality reduction algorithms from the different weight matrices selection, such as Locality Preserving Projection (LPP) [19] and Neighborhood Preserving Embedding (NPE) [20]. However neighborhood selection question is not solved all along.

In the ordinary construction of the graphic, $\varepsilon-\text{bal}$ neighbors or K nearest neighbors is used for local neighborhood, between which the weight is obtained by binary number, Gaussian kernel and L2 reconstruction. In [21] L1 reconstruction of the sample data is put forward, and the reconstruction parameter is regarded as the weight of the construction graphic. L1 method has the broader locality than $\varepsilon-\text{ball}$ neighbor or K-nearest neighbor, but its cost is large when reconstructing data in the whole sample.

Spectral regression [22] is the regularization method of the subspace learning, and effectively avoids computational complexity increase, which is produced by the dense matrix decomposition. In face database the efficiency of algorithm is proved, which extends the application scope of the manifold learning algorithm.

To analyze time series data, in [23] one-dimensional sequence the features of the data is described, and forms 13 eigenvector, which is clustered, then the higher accuracy of the clustering is obtained. In [24] human action sequences data is described by the feature, in human action database the better recognition rate is obtained by Gaussian process classifier.

3   Manifold Learning Algorithm Based on Random Spectral Regression

Establishing neighborhood graph of human actions frame is to preserve and extract the frame structure of human action spatial information, which includes the intra-class and inter-class features of human silhouette, and the sequence feature can describe the main discrimination feature of human action, although it might not be the optimal discrimination feature, the method may reduce the spatial dimension of the frame. The article studies the main content that is how to use the random graph to extract the classification information of the manifold structure, and in the spectral regression framework how to obtain the valid feature description and reduce the dimensions of human action frame.

The current manifold learning on face recognition application is more, but on the classification of human action sequence is fewer, and applies only to the dimension reduction of data, does not go into the nature of the data sets. Between human action sequence and face images three differences exist:

(a) Face feature can be clearly represented by the description of the single image, while human actions require the multiple-frame images to describe clearly.

(b) Between face images, the temporal correlation of the data is not strong, from the view of the data distribution that face image is independent, so the independent feature is similar obviously in the same class, and the independent feature is different widely in the different class. Human action images have the strong temporal correlation, from the view of the data distribution human action frames is not independent, so the correlative feature is similar obviously in the different frame of the same class, and the correlative feature is different widely in the different frame of the different class.

(c) The feature extraction of face data only considers the spatial dimension reduction, while the feature extraction of human action data must take account of the spatial and temporal dimension reduction.

Since there are the differences, when building data sets graph the manifold learning should apply the more suitable method for human action recognition. The approximation of the manifold will reflect the nature of the data set.

Human action data is $X_{l \times n} = \{ x_i^c | i \in R \ \ and \ \ 0 < c < m \}$, x_i^c is the ith frame image in the c class action, have m class human action and l frame images, n is each frame image generating the dimension of row vector. Thru the manifold learning the data of the dimension reduction is $Y_{l \times d}$, $d(\ d << n \ )$ is the reductive dimensions. In the actual observation, video image data and neighbors image of its frame sequences is the most correlative image, moreover the correlation reflects the structure of the video image frame, and each image frame of the similar semantics is such. The structural feature distribution of the data frame regarded as the uniform distribution, the structure relation can be viewed as the manifold approximation of the pair data, and when mapping to the low-dimensional space the structure information is preserved.

Building the undirected graphs of human action image frame, the most factors of the inherent manifold structure character considered are multiple frame, strong temporal correlation, spatio-temporal character and priori classification label of data sample. Specific rules are depending on the data manifolds uniform distribution, the pseudo-random sequence of the uniform distribution may show the differences of the frame feature and the uniform distribution of the manifold between the single image sequences of the intra-class, at the same time reflects the strong temporal correlation. In the multiple image sequences of the intra-class, the same pseudo-random sequence represents the manifold of the same action. Between the multiple image sequences of the different class, the different pseudo-random sequence shows the difference of the inter-class. In comparison with the tradition method, the random spectral regression does not need Euclidean distance information of sample when constructing graph, the neighborhood parameter selection and the weight computation. However, the constructing graph depends on two-type natural information of the data, which are the uniform distribution character of the data manifold and the classification label of the data. Fig. 1 shows LPP and RSPR manifold distribution of human action by kernel density estimator. Because the estimator involves all kinds of the action, the character of the distribution presents the similar normal distribution, but one thing may assure manifold distribution of human action is similar in the different methods, moreover RSPR manifold distribution of human action has smaller variance in Fig. 1, which shows the better manifold approximation.

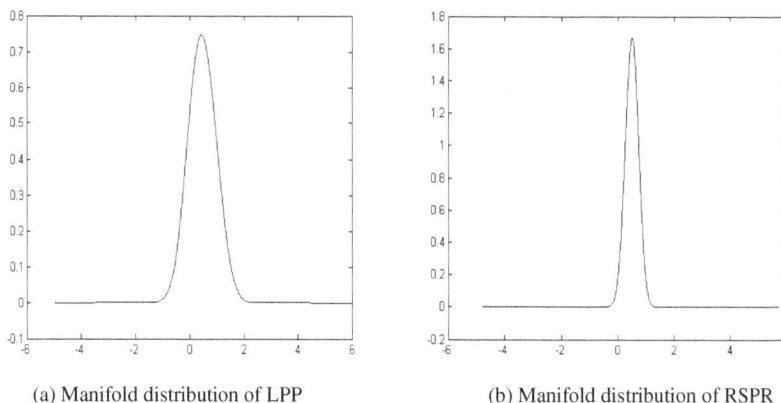

(a) Manifold distribution of LPP   (b) Manifold distribution of RSPR

Fig. 1. Manifold distribution of human action by kernel density estimator

Through the prior knowledge to get m sample class, the pseudo-random square matrix $A_{m \times m}$ of the uniform distribution is generated by subtraction with borrow [24], and then $B_{l \times m}$ is obtained from $A_{m \times m}$ according to the sample label information. In the same class each row of B matches with each row of A. Using Gram-Schmidt orthogonalization orthogonal matrix Q is obtained by QR decomposition of B, but matrix Q isn't square matrix, which isn't good for the manifold approximation and the linear extension, so the weight matrix W is constructed by formula (1).

$$W = QQ^T \tag{1}$$

When constructing the weights matrix W of the graph, which is combined with spectral regression theory, the mapping matrix a of the linear extension can be solved. $y = [y_1,..., y_m]$ is the mapping of the data from the graph. If the mapping of the adjacent node i and j is away from, they will be punished. Minimizing (2) assures the mapping y_i and y_j of the adjacent node i and j is adjacent.

$$\sum_{i,j}(y_i - y_j)^2 W_{ij} \tag{2}$$

From the above (2) formula (3) is derived.

$$y^* = \arg\max_{y^T Dy=I} y^T W y = \arg\max \frac{y^T W y}{y^T D y} \tag{3}$$

In formula (3) $D_{ii} = \sum_j W_{ij}$. Formula (3) deduces formula (4) in Least Square Method. The optimal $y*$ can be obtained by decomposition (4).

$$Wy = \lambda Dy \qquad (4)$$

The linear extension of y is $y = X^T a$, which is imputed formula (3) to obtain formula (5).

$$XWX^T a = \lambda XDX^T a \qquad (5)$$

Because XWX^T is often dense, Cai [18] proposes the regularization method of solving $a*$ which is the optimal fitting for equation (6) in Least Square Method.

$$a^* = \arg\min_a (\sum_i (a^T x_i - y_i)^2 + h\|a\|^2) \qquad (6)$$

When h closes zero, $a*$ has the stable solution.

4　Gaussian Process Classification Based on the Feature of Temporal Series

The d dimension data of human action is obtained by the manifold learning of RSPR, each dimension point sequence is Y_l^d, which is the dth point sequence of the lth action sequence. Y'^d_l is the adjusted data of Y_l^d, and then the statistical features of the temporal series for Y_l^d and Y'^d_l is chosen: trend, seasonality, serial correlation, non-linearity, skewness, kurtosis, self-similarity, chaotic and periodicity [22]. These features form the action feature vector U_{dx13} for each action sequence.

The dimensions reduction data set of human action is $U = \{u_{lable}, u_{unlable}\}$, the classification label is V. U and V exists the implicit function $f(u)\sim GP(M,K)$, which defines the mapping of U and V. GP is Gaussian process [25], and $M(u)$ is mean function, $K(u,u')$ is the covariance function. In the article the radial basis function is defined as formula (7).

$$K(u,u') = \sigma \exp[-\frac{1}{2}(\frac{u-u'}{s})^2] \qquad (7)$$

Input pair is u and u', σ is the variance of input data, s is the length of input data. In Laplace approximation algorithm the maximum posteriori probability $p(f/U,v)$ and the corresponding f is solved. Gaussian process binary classifier firstly computes the corresponding $p(f^*/U,v,u^*)$ of the implicit function f^*, u^* is the test data set.

$$p(f^* | U, v, u^*) = \int p(f^* | U, u^*, f) p(f | U, v) df \qquad (8)$$

In formula (8) $p(f \mid U, v) = p(v \mid f) p(f \mid U) p(v \mid U)$ is the posteriori probability of the implicit function. $p(f^* \mid U, u^*, f)$ is the posteriori probability of the predict data, thru formula (9) the classification label probability of the test data is computed.

$$p(v^* = +1 \mid U, v, u^*) = \int \Phi(f^*) p(f^* \mid U, v, u^*) df^* \qquad (9)$$

In formula (9) $\Phi(f^*)$ is the cumulative Gaussian function, which assures the probability of the classification label within [0, 1].

The multi-class of human action recognition may make the label of one class sample be +1 and the label of other class sample be -1 to construct the classifier. Although the method is not optimal, it is still efficient.

5   Experiment

In the experiment human action database derives from Weizmann action database [26], which has 113 low resolution video sequences(180×140 pixel, 25 frame/second), and includes two parts: one part has 93 video sequences of 10 class action (bend, jack, jump, pjump, run, side, skip, walk, wave1, wave2) which is completed by 9 experimenter, another part is 20 video sequences of 1 class action (walk), which is influenced by several factors: visual angle, occlusion, clothing, accompanying item. Because of the effect of the shadow, color and other noise, the difference exists between the nature silhouette and the extracted silhouette.

The experiment is designed in three parts. Firstly the recognition method based on RSPR is tested. Secondly the performance of RSPR, LPP and NPE is contrasted. At last the robustness of the algorithm is tested.

5.1   Performance Test Based on RSPR

In the performance test of RSPR, in the first part 93 video sequences is used, which have 5687 frames. In these sequences some action are not reduplicate in time series (for instance bend), others are reduplicate (for instance run and walk). In the experiment the overlap action sequence is not segmented, because the redundancy data is eliminated by the statistical features extracted. Video sequences is divided into 10 separated packet, each separated packet has 10 different actions, in these packet there are tow packets belong to the different action of the same person. Classifier is constructed by 9 separated packet learning and 1 separated packet testing. Loop using these data constructs the classifier. Table 1 shows the confusion matrix of the recognition in 10 actions.

In table 1 the result of the experiment shows between pjump and side action the confusion is more, between run and skip action the confusion is such, the observation is the similar state. Finally the average recognition rate reaches 93.2%.

5.2 Contrast and Analysis

In the experiment between RSPR, LPP and NPE the contrast of the performance has three points, which include the time cost of the manifold learning, the error rate of human action recognition and the average time cost. The experimental device is a computer, which has AMD64 bits, 2.3GHz CPU and 2G memory. In LPP and NPE test of the whole data the memory overflows owing to the computation and decomposition dense matrix, so only using one separated packet for the manifold learning explains the above points.

Table 2 shows the time cost of the manifold learning, the error rate of human action recognition and the average time cost in three methods.

Table 1. The confusion matrix of the recognition in 10 actions

	Bend	Jack	Jump	Pjump	Run	Side	Skip	Walk	Wave1	Wave2
Bend	**96%**	2%						2%		
Jack	2%	**98%**								
Jump			**98%**		1%		1%			
Pjump				**90%**		8%			2%	
Run			2%		**88%**		8%	2%		
Side				6%		**92%**				2%
Skip			2%		10%		**88%**			
Walk				2%	2%			**96%**		
Wave1				4%					**92%**	4%
Wave2						2%			4%	**94%**

Table 2. The comparison of three method

method	LPP	NPE	RSPR
Learning time	17.21s	40.87s	5.13s
Average error rate	70%	64%	61%
Average recognition time	2.109s	1.910s	1.904s

According to the experiment results, the analysis has three aspects:

1) From the view of the algorithm theory, LPP makes up the basic framework of the manifold learning extension, by Euclidean distance measuring the local neighborhood and heat kernel function computing the weight matrix, in the low dimension space the minimal optimization question is constructed, and the mapping is obtained from the high dimension data to the low dimension data. The difference of NPE lies in L2 reconstruction in high dimension data and using the reconstructed coefficient as the weight matrix. The characteristic of RSPR is the use of the manifold distribution of high dimension data to product the random distribution matrix, and generate the weights matrix combining with the labels of the known data, which obviates the parameter selection of local neighborhood.

2) From the view of the algorithm time complexity, the Time Complexity of the weight matrix computation by LPP is O (n^2×m); the Time Complexity of the weight matrix computation by NPE is O (n^2×m^2); the Time Complexity of the weight matrix computation by RSPR is O (m).

3) From the view of the algorithm space efficiency, in the experiment of LPP and NPE, the Space Complexity is produced by the dense matrix decomposition, which occupies the enormous memory. When the number of the sample exceeds 800, in the computer the exception of the memory overflowing arises, however, the number of the sample is at least 5000 for the learning action pattern. Therefore, the above contrast experiment is carried out in one separated packet, which includes 701 samples, although the error rate of the recognition is high, the performance of RSPR is better than LPP and NPE.

5.3 Algorithm Robust Test

The images of walk action for robust test in Weizmann action data, walk action for robust test includes 20 sequences, and top 10 sequences are walk action with the view angle change, which is obtained from zero degrees to 90 degrees. The angle is defined the angle of camera imaging plane and walk orientation. The rest 10 sequences respectively are walk with bag, walk with briefcase, kneesup walk, limp, arms straight walk, occluded foot walk, walk, fixed block walk, walk with skirt and walk with dog. The table 3 shows the recognition result of the sequence.

In table 3, the result shows RSPR has certain adaptability for the influence of the view angle, but angle of view changes more than 45 degrees does not correctly recognize the action class. In the greater deformation walk (walk with bag, kneesup walk and arms straight walk) or occluded and confused walk (walk with dog) the recognition is incorrect, while under the rest condition the recognition is correct.

Table 3. The recognition results of the robust test

Name	Recognition conclusion	Name	Recognition conclusion
robust_00	Walk	robust_bag	Jack
robust_09	Walk	robust_briefcase	Walk
robust_18	Walk	robust_kneesup	Side
robust_27	Walk	robust_limp	Walk
robust_36	Walk	robust_moonwalk	Jack
robust_45	Walk	robust_nofeet	Walk
robust_54	Side	robust_normwalk	Walk
robust_63	Jack	robust_pole	Walk
robust_72	Side	robust_skirt	Walk
robust_81	Side	robust_dog	Skip

6 Conclusions

In the article, human action recognition algorithm based on RSPR is presented, which solves the parameter selection of the manifold learning, and reduces the time and space complexity combining with spectral regression, puts forward the feasible method to extract the manifold of the large scale video data, and then the discrimination feature of human action is extracted by using the statistic feature of the mapped data, finally in the experiment the feasibility and efficiency of the algorithm is proved. In the next research the manifold distribution of local feature will be studied, and further human action is analyzed and discriminated.

Acknowledgment. The authors would like to thank the anonymous reviewers for their insightful comments, which have helped to improve the quality of this paper. Scientific Research Program Funded by Shaanxi Provincial Education Department (Program No.2010JK718) supported this research.

References

[1] Poppe, R.: A survey on vision-based human action recognition. Image and Vision Computing 28, 976–990 (2010)
[2] Bobick, A.F., Davis, J.W.: The recognition of human movement using temporal templates. IEEE Trans. Pattern Analysis and Machine Intelligence 23, 257–267 (2001)
[3] Kellokumpu, V., Zhao, G., Pietikainen, M.: Human activity recognition using a dynamic texture based method. In: Proceedings of the British Machine Vision Conference (BMVC 2008), Leeds, United Kingdom, pp. 885–894 (2008)
[4] Gorelick, L., Blank, M., Shechtman, E., Irani, M., Basri, R.: Actions as space–time shapes. IEEE Trans. Pattern Analysis and Machine Intelligence 29, 2247–2253 (2007)
[5] Willems, G., Tuytelaars, T., Van Gool, L.: An efficient dense and scale-invariant spatio-temporal interest point detector. In: Forsyth, D., Torr, P., Zisserman, A. (eds.) ECCV 2008, Part II. LNCS, vol. 5303, pp. 650–663. Springer, Heidelberg (2008)
[6] Wang, H., Ullah, M.M., Klaser, A., Laptev, I., Schmid, C.: Evaluation of local spatio-temporal features for action recognition. In: Proceedings of the British Machine Vision Conference (BMVC 2009), London, United Kingdom (2009)
[7] Zhao, Z., Elgammal, A.: Human activity recognition from frame's spatiotemporal representation. In: Proceedings of the International Conference on Pattern Recognition (ICPR 2008), Tampa, FL, pp. 1–4 (2008)
[8] Farhadi, A., Tabrizi, M.K.: Learning to recognize activities from the wrong view point. In: Forsyth, D., Torr, P., Zisserman, A. (eds.) ECCV 2008, Part I. LNCS, vol. 5302, pp. 154–166. Springer, Heidelberg (2008)
[9] Li, Y.: Researehon Methods of Subspace Feature Extraction Based on Manifold Learning in Face Recognition. Central South University (2009)
[10] Seung, H.S., Lee, D.D.: The manifold ways of perception. Science 290, 2268–2269 (2000)
[11] Wang, L., Suter, D.: Visual learning and recognition of sequential data manifolds with applications to human movement analysis. In: Computer Vision and Image Understanding (CVIU), vol. 110, pp. 153–172 (2008)

[12] Poppe, R., Poel, M.: Discriminative human action recognition using pairwise CSP classifiers. In: Proceedings of the International Conference on Automatic Face and Gesture Recognition (FGR 2008), Amsterdam, The Netherlands, pp. 1–6 (2008)

[13] Jia, K., Yeung, D.-Y.: Human action recognition using local spatio-temporal discriminant embedding. In: Proceedings of the Conference on Computer Vision and Pattern Recognition (CVPR 2008), Anchorage, AK, pp. 1–8 (2008)

[14] Yan, S., Wang, H.: Semi-supervised learning by sparse representation. In: SIAM International Conference on Data Mining (SDM 2009), Sparks, Nevada, USA, pp. 792–801 (2009)

[15] Cox, T.F., Cox, M.A.: Multidimensional scaling, pp. 24–139. Chapman & Hall, London (2001)

[16] Tenenbaum, J.B., De Silva, V., Langford, J.C.: A global geometric framework for nonlinear dimensionality reduction. Science 290, 2319–2323 (2000)

[17] Roweis, S.T., Saul, L.K.: Nonlinear dimensionality reduction by locally linear embedding. Science 290, 2323–2326 (2000)

[18] Deng, C., He, X.F., Han, J.W.: Spectral regression for efficient regularized subspace learning. In: IEEE International Conference on Computer Vision, Rio de Janeiro, Brazil, pp. 214–221 (2007)

[19] He, X.F., Niyogi, P.: Locality preserving projections. In: Proc. Of Advances in Neural Information Processing System, Vancouver, Canada (2003)

[20] He, X.F., Deng, C., Yan, S.C., et al.: Neighborhood preserving embedding. In: Proc. of 10th IEEE International Conference on Computer Vision, Beijing, China, pp. 1208–1213 (2005)

[21] Cheng, B., Yang, J., Yan, S., Huang, T.S.: Learning With L1-Graph for Image Analysis. IEEE Transactions on Image Processing 19, 858–866 (2010)

[22] Wang, X., Smith, K.A., Hyndman, R.J.: Characteristic-based clustering for time series data. Data Mining and Knowledge Discovery 13, 335–364 (2006)

[23] Zhou, H., Wang, L., Suter, D.: Human action recognition by feature-reduced Gaussian process classification. Pattern Recognition Letters 30, 1059–1066 (2009)

[24] Pi, X.: A Soft of Pseudorandom Number Sequences With Extremely Long Period. Journal of Unmerical Methods and Computer Applications 4, 286–292 (2001)

[25] Rasmussen, C.E., Williams, C.K.I.: Gaussian Processes for Machine Learning. The MIT Press, Cambridge (2006)

[26] http://www.wisdom.weizmann.ac.il/~vision/
SpaceTimeActions.html

Wheeled Mobile Robot Control Based on SVM and Nonlinear Control Laws[*]

Yong Feng[1,2], Huibin Cao[2], and Yuxiang Sun[2]

[1] Department of Automation, University of Science and Technology of China
Hefei, Anhui, 230026, China
fengyong@mail.ust.edu.cn
[2] Institute of Intelligent Machine, Chinese Academy of Science
Hefei, Anhui, 230031, China
hbcao@iim.ac.cn, sunyuxiang636@sohu.com

Abstract. Wheeled mobile robot control method based on SVM algorithm and nonlinear control laws is discussed in this paper. The control system includes two parts: nonlinear controller and SVM controller. Nonlinear controller's primary role is to obtain the desired velocity which can make the kinematics stable, SVM controller's primary role is to optimize the control parameters through on-line learning and track the desired velocity. The control method proposed in this paper is independent of the control object model, and has good generalization capability. Simulations illustrate quality and efficiency of this method.

Keywords: wheeled mobile robot, SVM, nonlinear control, tracking control.

1 Introduction

Wheeled mobile robot (WMR) can drive automatically by motion controller and surroundings sensors. In the motion control, WMR should be capable of performing trajectory tracking and stabilization. However, WMR is a nonholonomic dynamic system with intrinsic nonlinearty, and commonly with unmodeled disturbance and unstructured, unmodeled dynamics [1]. Conventionally, this control design relies on engineers to analyze the WMR system so as to synthesize the appropriate controller. But usually difficulties arise from absence of accurate model. Fuzzy control design may skip building the model but needs domain expert to construct the fuzzy rules. Neural networks offer exciting advantages such as adaptive learning, fault tolerance and generalization. In [2] and [3] an artificial neural network-based controller was developed by combining the feedback velocity control technique and torque controller. But the controller structure and the neural network-learning algorithm are very complicated and preparing appropriate training samples usually needs an existing controller. In this paper, we proposed a novel control method based on support vector

[*] This paper is partially supported by National Nature Science Foundation project China (Grant #60910005).

H. Deng et al. (Eds.): AICI 2011, Part III, LNAI 7004, pp. 462–471, 2011.

machine (SVM) and nonlinear laws. We first construct the nonlinear controller using direct Lyapunov method to stabilize the system, but its dynamic performance is bad, then we construct a SVM controller to optimize the control parameters to ensure the well dynamic performance using online samples.

This paper is organized as follows. In section 2 we will present the dynamic model of wheeled mobile robot. In section 3 we will describe a Lyapunov based nonlinear control method for asymptotic stability of kinematic equations. In section 4 we will describe SVM controller to optimize the control parameters. In section 5 we describe the structure of the control system. The simulation results are presented in section 6 and the conclusions are given in the last section.

2   Mobile Robot Dynamic Model

In this paper, we consider the two wheeled differential drive mobile robot (Fig. 1). Two independent analogous DC motors are the actuators of left and right wheels, while one or two free wheel casters are used to keep the robot stable. Point C is the center of axis of driving wheels, and θ is the orientation angle of robot in the inertial frame.

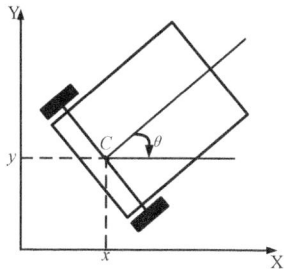

Fig. 1. Coordination of Differential Drive Mobile Robot

Pose vector of robot is defined as $q = [x, y, \theta]^T$, x and y are the coordination of point C. Neglecting the centripetal force, coriolis torque and gravity torque, the dynamic equation is given by

$$
\begin{bmatrix} m & 0 & 0 \\ 0 & m & 0 \\ 0 & 0 & I \end{bmatrix} \begin{bmatrix} \ddot{x} \\ \ddot{y} \\ \ddot{\theta} \end{bmatrix} = \frac{1}{R} \begin{bmatrix} \cos\theta & \cos\theta \\ \sin\theta & \sin\theta \\ L & -L \end{bmatrix} \begin{bmatrix} \tau_1 \\ \tau_2 \end{bmatrix} + \begin{bmatrix} \sin\theta \\ -\cos\theta \\ 0 \end{bmatrix} \lambda
\tag{1}
$$

Where τ_1 and τ_2 are input torques of left and right wheels respectively, m and I are the mass and inertia of robot, R is the radius of the wheel, L is the distance of rear wheels, λ is the Lagrange multipliers of constrained forces [4].

The nonholonomic constraint equation is written as

$$
\dot{x}\sin\theta - \dot{y}\cos\theta = 0
\tag{2}
$$

Assuming $\tau_l = (\tau_1 + \tau_2)/R$ and $\tau_a = L(\tau_1 - \tau_2)/R$, then the dynamic equation can be transformed to

$$\begin{cases} \ddot{x} = \tau_l \cos\theta/m + \lambda\sin\theta/m \\ \ddot{y} = \tau_l \sin\theta/m - \lambda\cos\theta/m \\ \ddot{\theta} = \tau_a/I \end{cases} \tag{3}$$

Where τ_l and τ_a are linear force and angular torque respectively.

Assuming v and w are the linear velocity and angular velocity of robot, the following transformation is obtained:

$$\dot{q} = g(q)\begin{bmatrix} v \\ w \end{bmatrix} \tag{4}$$

Where $g(q) = \begin{bmatrix} \cos\theta & 0 \\ \sin\theta & 0 \\ 0 & 1 \end{bmatrix}$

Then the differential equation can be written as:

$$\ddot{q} = \dot{g}(q)\begin{bmatrix} v \\ w \end{bmatrix} + g(q)\begin{bmatrix} \dot{v} \\ \dot{w} \end{bmatrix} \tag{5}$$

Therefore

$$\begin{cases} \ddot{x} = -v\dot{\theta}\sin\theta + \dot{v}\cos\theta \\ \ddot{y} = v\dot{\theta}\cos\theta + \dot{v}\sin\theta \\ \ddot{\theta} = \dot{w} \end{cases} \tag{6}$$

Comparing Equation (3) and Equation (6), we can obtain

$$\begin{cases} \lambda\sin\theta/m + \tau_l\cos\theta/m = -v\dot{\theta}\sin\theta + \dot{v}\cos\theta \\ -\lambda\cos\theta/m + \tau_l\sin\theta/m = v\dot{\theta}\cos\theta + \dot{v}\sin\theta \\ \tau_a/I = \dot{w} \end{cases} \tag{7}$$

Multiplying the first part of Equation (7) by $\cos\theta$ and the second part by $\sin\theta$ and adding the result the following is obtained

$$\dot{v} = \tau_l/m, \quad \dot{w} = \tau_a/I \tag{8}$$

According to Equation (4), we can obtain:

$$\begin{cases} \dot{x} = v\cos\theta \\ \dot{y} = v\sin\theta \\ \dot{\theta} = w \end{cases} \tag{9}$$

Equation (8) and (9) are the equations of dynamic model and kinematic model equations.

3 Nonlinear Control Model

We can use nonlinear kinematic controller to stabilize the configuration variables. Tracking control of mobile robot is simply reduced to regularization problem of error variables in kinematic model. A path planner defines the reference trajectory as a time variant pose vector: $q_r = (x_r \ y_r \ \theta_r)^T$. This trajectory should satisfy not only the kinematic equations but also the nonholonomic constraint [5]:

$$\dot{x}_r = v_r \cos\theta_r, \quad \dot{y}_r = v_r \sin\theta_r, \quad \dot{\theta}_r = w_r, \quad \dot{x}_r \sin\theta_r = \dot{y}_r \cos\theta_r \tag{10}$$

The error dynamics is written independent of the inertial coordinate frame by Kanayama transformation [6]:

$$\begin{bmatrix} x_e \\ y_e \\ \theta_e \end{bmatrix} = \begin{bmatrix} \cos\theta & \sin\theta & 0 \\ -\sin\theta & \cos\theta & 0 \\ 0 & 0 & 1 \end{bmatrix} \begin{bmatrix} x_r - x \\ y_r - y \\ \theta_r - \theta \end{bmatrix} \tag{11}$$

(x_e, y_e, θ_e) are the error variables in mobile coordinate system which is attached to the robot. Differentiating left hand side of Equation (11), (10) and (2) the error dynamics is written in the new coordinate system:

$$\begin{bmatrix} \dot{x}_e \\ \dot{y}_e \\ \dot{\theta}_e \end{bmatrix} = \begin{bmatrix} v_r \cos\theta_e \\ v_r \sin\theta_e \\ w_r \end{bmatrix} + \begin{bmatrix} -1 & y_e \\ 0 & -x_e \\ 0 & -1 \end{bmatrix} \begin{bmatrix} v \\ w \end{bmatrix} \tag{12}$$

Where $(v, w)^T$ is the control vector of the kinematic model.

We construct control vector using direct Lyapunov method. The constructive Lyapunov function is:

$$V = \frac{1}{2}\left(x_e^2 + y_e^2\right) + \left(1 - \cos\theta_e\right) \tag{13}$$

Time derivative of Equation (13) becomes:

$$\begin{aligned} \dot{V} &= v_r x_e \cos\theta_e - v_d x_e + v_r \sin\theta_e y_e + w_r \sin\theta_e - w_d \sin\theta_e \\ &= (v_r \cos\theta_e - v_d)x_e + \sin\theta_e(v_r y_e + w_r - w_d) \end{aligned} \tag{14}$$

Assuming v_d and w_d are the desired velocities to make the kinematics stable, they are chosen as follow to make $\dot{V}$ negative definite:

$$\begin{cases} v_d = v_r \cos\theta_e + k_x x_e \\ w_d = w_r + v_r y_e + k_\theta \sin\theta_e \end{cases} \tag{15}$$

Where k_x and k_θ are positive reals.

Substituting Equation (15) in Equation (14):

$$\dot{V} = -k_x x_e^2 - v_r k_\theta \sin^2 \theta_e \tag{16}$$

It's clear that $\dot{V}$ is only negative semi definite.

Using LaSalle principle, convergence of x_e, y_e and θ_e to zeros is guaranteed, so the closed loop system is globally asymptotically stable.

Control laws designed according Lyapunov principle can make the robot stabilization, but the dynamic performance is bad, and the robot can not track the path accurately under noisy environment. In order to optimize the dynamic performance of the robot, SVM algorithm is used to design another controller based nonlinear controller.

4 SVM Controller

Originally, SVM was developed for classification problems. It was then extended to regression estimation problems [7]. For regression problem, the basic idea is to map the data to a higher dimensional feature space, via a nonlinear mapping, and then to do the linear regression in this space [8]. Therefore given a training set of training samples $\{x_i, y_i\}_{i=1}^{N} \subset R^n \times R$, we introduce a nonlinear mapping $\varphi(\cdot): R^n \to R^h$, which maps the training samples to a new data set. In ε-insensitive support vector regression the goal is to estimate the following function:

$$\hat{f}(x) = w^T \varphi(x) + b \tag{17}$$

Where $w \in R^{n_h}$ is weight vector, $b \in R$ is threshold. $\hat{f}(x)$ can estimate input x which is not in training set, and give the output y.

Estimation problem can be described as the following optimization problem:

$$\min_{w,b,\xi^*,\xi} J_\varepsilon(w,\xi^*,\xi) = \frac{1}{2} w^T w + \gamma \left\{ \sum_{i=1}^{N} \xi_i^* + \sum_{i=1}^{N} \xi_i \right\}$$

$$s.t. \begin{cases} y_i - w^T \varphi(x_i) - b \le \varepsilon + \xi_i^* & i = 1,...,N \\ -y_i + w^T \varphi(x_i) + b \le \varepsilon + \xi_i & i = 1,...,N \\ \xi_i^* \ge 0 & i = 1,...,N \\ \xi_i \ge 0 & i = 1,...,N \end{cases} \tag{18}$$

Where ξ_i and ξ_i^* are slack variables and γ is a positive real constant. One obtains $w = \sum_{i=1}^{N} (\alpha_i^* - \alpha_i) \varphi(x_i)$ where α_i and α_i^* are the Lagrange multipliers related to the first and second set of constraints. The data points corresponding to non-zero values for $(\alpha_i^* - \alpha_i)$ are called support vectors.

Finally, one obtains the following model in the dual space

$$\hat{f}(x) = \sum_{i=1}^{N} (\alpha_i^* - \alpha_i) K(x_i, x) \tag{19}$$

Where the kernel function K corresponds to

$$K(x_i, x) = \varphi(x_i)^T \varphi(x) \tag{20}$$

One has several possibilities for the choice of this kernel function, including linear, polynomial, splines, RBF.

To the ε-insensitive loss function

$$J_{\varepsilon,p}(w, \xi^*, \xi) = \frac{1}{2} w^T w + \gamma \left\{ \sum_{i=1}^{N} (\xi_i^*)^p + \sum_{i=1}^{N} (\xi_i)^p \right\} \tag{21}$$

Where $p=1$ corresponds to Eq. (21), we employ a least squares version of the support vector method for function estimation (LS-SVM), it corresponds to $p=2$ and the following form of ride regression:

$$\min_{w,b,\xi} J_{LS}(w, b, \xi) = \frac{1}{2} w^T w + \gamma \frac{1}{2} \sum_{i=1}^{N} \xi_i^2$$
$$s.t. \quad y_i = w^T \varphi(x_i) + b + \xi_i \tag{22}$$

One defines the Lagrangian

$$J_{LS}(w, b, \xi; \alpha) = J_{LS}(w, b, \xi) - \sum_{i=1}^{N} \alpha_i (w^T \varphi(x_i) + b + \xi_i - y_i) \tag{23}$$

Where α_i are Lagrange multipliers, it can be positive or negative due to equality constrains as follows from the Kuhn-Tucker conditions. The conditions for optimality

$$\begin{cases} \partial J_{LS} / \partial w = 0 \rightarrow w = \sum_{i=1}^{N} \alpha_i \varphi(x_i) \\ \partial J_{LS} / \partial b = 0 \rightarrow w = \sum_{i=1}^{N} \alpha_i = 0 \\ \partial J_{LS} / \partial \xi_i = 0 \rightarrow \alpha_i = \gamma \xi_i & i = 1,...,N \\ \partial J_{LS} / \partial \alpha_i = 0 \rightarrow w^T \varphi(x_i) + b + \xi_i - y_i = 0 & i = 1,...,N \end{cases} \tag{24}$$

Equation (24) can be written as the solution to the following set of linear equations after elimination of w and ξ_i.

$$\begin{bmatrix} 0 & \vec{1}^T \\ \vec{1} & \Omega+\gamma^{-1}I \end{bmatrix} \begin{bmatrix} x \\ \alpha \end{bmatrix} = \begin{bmatrix} 0 \\ y \end{bmatrix} \tag{25}$$

With $x=[x_1,...,x_N]$, $y=[y_1,...,y_N]$, $\vec{1}=[1,...,1]$, $\alpha=[\alpha_1,...,\alpha_N]$, $\Omega_{ij}=K(x_i,x_j)=\varphi(x_i)^T\varphi(x_j)$.

LS-SVM can be used in many applications in identification and control theory such as in the context of prediction error algorithms [9]. In this paper, we use LS-SVM because of the equality constraints in the problem formulation.

Considering Eq. (8) and tracking error, the following control laws are used to prepare tracking of v_d and w_d:

$$\begin{cases} \tau_l = m\dot{v}_d + k_{le}v_e + k_{ld}\dot{v}_e \\ \tau_a = I\dot{w}_d + k_{ae}w_e + k_{ad}\dot{w}_e \end{cases} \tag{26}$$

Where k_{le}, k_{ld}, k_{ae} and k_{ad} are the weights of v_e, $\dot{v}_e$, w_e and $\dot{w}_e$, they are unknown control parameters which will be estimated by LS-SVM.

In order to have a proper performance of SVM, we need to select as many samples as possible for training, however the dimension of SVM will greatly increase in the process of on-line training. Based on the aim of designing a controller which depends on current state of the nonlinear dynamic system, the training data collected earlier might not suit for real-time system, the large data set might lead to time consuming calculation. Therefore, sliding time window is constructed by N with sample time interval, then sample data is collected orderly from current to past. Moreover, a new data sample is collected while the oldest data being dropped. We assume that the nearest data can more properly describe the feature of the system than the oldest data.

For any given continuous real function $f(x)$ on compact set, for a large enough length of slide time window N combined with properly selected sampling time interval and any given $\varepsilon>0$, there exists an SVM approximation function $\hat{f}(x)$ formed by (19) such that $\sup_{t\in[T,T-N+1]}\left|f(x)-\hat{f}(x)\right|\le\varepsilon$, where T denotes the current time[10].

5   Structure of Control System

The structure of the control system is shown in Fig.2. The control system includes two controllers: nonlinear controller and SVM controller. Nonlinear controller's primary role is to obtain the desired velocity v_d and w_d which can make the Kinematics stable, its inputs are the dynamic errors of reference position and actual position. SVM controller's primary role is to track the desired velocity, its inputs are $(\dot{v}_d,\dot{w}_d)$, (v_e,w_e) and $(\dot{v}_e,\dot{w}_e)$, its output are τ_l and τ_a (force and angular torque respectively).

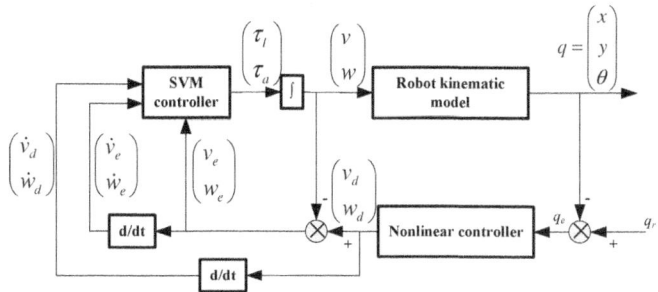

Fig. 2. Block diagram of Control System

6 Simulation

In order to validate the effectiveness of proposed method, simulations were carried out when the robot was disturbed by noise. The structure parameters of the robot are: m=8kg, $I = 2\text{kg} \cdot \text{m}^2$, R=20cm, and L=0.2m; the weights k_x and k_θ of the errors of the nonlinear controller are 0.4 and 0.2; the kernel function is RBF; the initial pose vector $(x, y, \theta)^T$ is $(0,0,0)^T$; the length of sliding time window is two seconds; the sampling frequency of pose position is 500Hz. When the reference track is line, sinusoid and circle, the results of simulation are showed in Fig. 3 to Fig. 5.

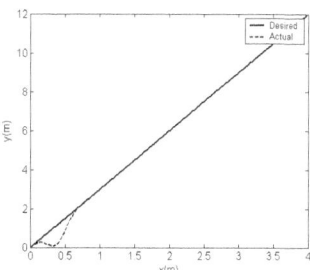

Fig. 3. Tracking of line

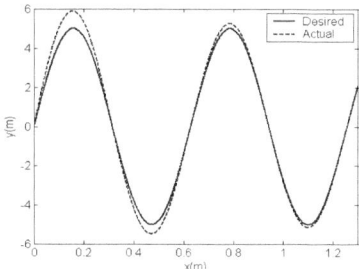

Fig. 4. Tracking of sinusoid

Error of tracking in the beginning is large because the parameters of SVM controller are not adaptive to the environment and the robot, then the error begin to decrease rapidly. The error will converge to zero if the time is long enough.

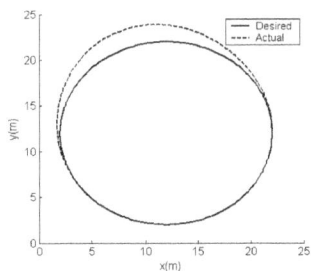

Fig. 5. Tracking of circle

7   Conclusion

In this paper, a novel control method was proposed for tracking of mobile robot. The controller includes two consecutive parts, one is nonlinear kinematic controller to obtain the desired velocity which can make the system stable and the other is the SVM controller to provide tracking of desired linear velocity and angular velocity. The main characteristic of the proposed controller is its robustness of performance against the environment disturbed by noise. Simulation results demonstrate that the system is able to track reference signals satisfactorily.

References

[1] Chen, Q., Ozguner, U., Redmill, K.: Ohio state university at the 2004 DARPA grand challenge: Developing a completely autonomous vehicle. IEEE Intelligent System 19(5), 8–11 (2004)
[2] Das, T., Kar, I.N., Chaudhury, S.: Simple neuron-based adaptive controller for a nonholonomic mobile robot including actuator dynamics. Neurocomputing 69(16-18), 2140–2151 (2006)
[3] Fierro, R., Lewis, F.L.: Control of a nonholonomic mobile robot using neural networks. IEEE Trans. Neural Networks 9(4), 589–600 (1998)
[4] Bloch, A.M., Reyhanoglu, M., McClamroch, N.H.: Control and stabilization of nonholonomic dynamic system. IEEE Transactions on Automatic Control 37(11), 1746–1757 (1992)
[5] Gholipour, A., Dehghan, S.M., Nili, M., Ahmadabadi: Lyapunov based tracking control of nonholonomic mobile robot. In: Proc. of 10th Iranian Conference on Electrical Engineering, pp. 262–269 (2002)
[6] Kanayama, Y., Kimura, Y., Miyazaki, F., Noguchi, T.: A stable tracking control scheme for an autonomous mobile robot. In: Proc. 1990 IEEE Int. Conf. Rob. Autom., pp. 384–389 (1990)
[7] Vapnik, V.: An overview of statistical learning theory. IEEE Trans. on Neural Networks 10(5), 988–999 (1999)

[8] Vapnik, V., Golowich, S.: Support vector method for function approximation, regression estimation, and signal processing. In: Advances in Neural Information Processing Systems, pp. 281–287 (1997)

[9] Suykens, J.A.K., Vandewalle, J., De Moor, B.: Optimal control by least squares support vector machines. Neural Networks 14(1), 23–35 (2001)

[10] Li, Z., Kang, Y.: Dyanmic coupling switching control incorporating Support Vector Machine wheeled mobile manipulators with hybrid joints. Automatic 46(5), 832–842 (2010)

Image Recognition by Affine Tchebichef Moment Invariants

Qian Liu, Hongqing Zhu, and Qian Li

Department of Electronics and Communications Engineering
East China University of Science and Technology
Shanghai 200237, China
hqzhu@ecust.edu.cn

Abstract. Tchebichef moments are successfully used in the field of image analysis because of their polynomial properties of discrete and orthogonal. In this paper, two new affine invariant sets are introduced for object recognition using discrete orthogonal Tchebichef moments. The current study constructs affine Tchebichef invariants by normalization method. Firstly, image is normalized to a standard form using Tchebichef moments as normalization constraints. Then, the affine invariants can be obtained at the standard form. The experimental results are presented to illustrate the performance of the invariants for affine deformed images.

Keywords: Discrete orthogonal moments, affine transform, moment invariants, Tchebichef moments, pattern recognition.

1 Introduction

Moments invariants were firstly introduced by Hu [1], who proposed a method of deriving moment invariants from algebraic methods. He used geometric moments to generate a set of invariants. However, geometric moments are not derived from a family of orthogonal functions, and are sensitive to noise, especially for higher order moments [2]. Thus, Hu's moment invariants have limit applications. Many literatures have presented novel approaches of applying sequential orthogonal moments to construct moment invariants, such as Zernike moment [3], pseudo-Zernike [4], and Legendre moment [5]. But the accuracy of recognition descends due to the discrete approximation of the continuous integrals [6]. Mukundan proposed the discrete orthogonal Tchebichef moments [7]. The use of discrete orthogonal Tchebichef polynomials as basis function for image moments eliminates the discrete approximation associated with the continuous moments. Our previous work [8] proposed a new approach to derive the translation and scale invariants of Tchebichef moments based on the corresponding polynomials. However the descriptors are only invariant with respect to translation and scale of the pattern. In fact, objects may have other deformation, such as elongation, we still expect them to stay in the same category. The moment invariants proposed in refs. [3-5, 8] do not work well under

H. Deng et al. (Eds.): AICI 2011, Part III, LNAI 7004, pp. 472–480, 2011.
© Springer-Verlag Berlin Heidelberg 2011

similar transformation. Moment invariants under affine transformation come up consequently to cope with this problem. Reiss [9] and Flusser and Suk [10] independently introduced affine moment invariants and proved their applicability in recognition tasks. These affine moment descriptors are expressed in terms of the central moments of the image data, and are widely used in many applications such as image analysis; pattern recognition and contour shape estimate [11-14]. Rothe et al [15] first proposed the concept of affine normalization. In their work, two different affine decompositions were used. The first called XSR consists of shearing, anisotropic scaling and rotation. The second is the XYS and consists of two shearings and anisotropic scaling. The normalization methods have then been further improved by other researchers [16]. Recently, Zhang et. al [17] proposed affine Legendre moment invariants for watermark detection. The affine moment invariant using continuous orthogonal Legendre moments [17], Zernike moments [14] have been already obtained, no affine moment invariants take the discrete Tchebichef moments into consideration until now. Motivated by their methods [17~18], this paper presents two sets of discrete orthogonal Tchebichef moment invariants using XYS and XSR decomposition. To obtain the proposed affine moment invariants, the study applies the normalization method which is done via decomposition the affine transformation into three successive steps. Then, the normalization is achieved by imposing normalization constraints on some chosen function parameters. The experiment results demonstrate the proposed invariants are effective.

2   Tchebichef Polynomials and Tchebichef Moments

The discrete Tchebichef polynomials are defined as [7]

$$t_n(x) = (1-N)_n \; {}_3F_2(-n,-x,1+n;1,1-N;1) \quad n,x = 0,1,2,...,N-1 \tag{1}$$

where $(a)_k$ is the Pochhammer symbol given by

$$(a)_k = a(a+1)(a+2)...(a+k-1), \; k \geq 1 \text{ and } (a)_0 = 1 \tag{2}$$

and ${}_3F_2(\cdot)$ is the hypergeometric function

$$_3F_2(a_1,a_2,a_3;b_1,b_2;c) = \sum_{k=0}^{\infty} \frac{(a_1)_k(a_2)_k(a_3)_k}{(b_1)_k(b_2)_k} \frac{c^k}{k!} \tag{3}$$

with the above definitions, Eq.(1) can be rewritten simply as

$$t_n(x) = n! \sum_{k=0}^{n} (-1)^{n-k} \binom{N-1-k}{n-k}\binom{n+k}{n}\binom{x}{k} \tag{4}$$

The discrete Tchebichef polynomials satisfy the following orthogonal property in discrete domain

$$\sum_{x=0}^{N-1} t_n(x)t_m(x) = \rho(n,N)\delta_{nm} \tag{5}$$

where δ_{nm} is the Kronecker symbol and the squared-norm $\rho(n,N)$ given by

$$\rho(n,N) = (2n)! \binom{N+n}{2n+1} \tag{6}$$

The scaled discrete Tchebichef polynomials are defined as

$$\tilde{t}_p(x) = \sum_{k=0}^{p} c_{p,k}^{N} x^k \tag{7}$$

where

$$c_{p,k}^{N} = \sum_{r=k}^{p} S_1(r,k) \frac{(-1)^{p+r}(p+r)!(N-r-1)!}{\sqrt{\rho(p,N)}(p-r)!(r!)^2(N-p-1)!} \tag{8}$$

From (7), one can deduce

$$x^p = \sum_{k=0}^{p} d_{p,k}^{N} \tilde{t}_k(x) \tag{9}$$

where $d_{p,k}^{N}$ ($0 \le k \le p \le N\text{-}1$) is the inverse matrix of the lower triangular matrix $c_{p,k}^{N}$ [18], which can be written as:

$$d_{p,k}^{N} = \sum_{m=k}^{p} S_2(p,m) \frac{\sqrt{\rho(p,N)}(2k+1)(m!)^2(N-k-1)!}{(m+k+1)!(m-k)!(N-m-1)!} \tag{10}$$

here $S_1(i,j)$ and $S_2(i,j)$ are the first kind and the second kind of Stiriling numbers[19], respectively.

The discrete Tchebichef moments can be denoted as

$$T_{pq} = \sum_{x=0}^{N-1}\sum_{y=0}^{N-1} \tilde{t}_p(x)\tilde{t}_q(y)f(x,y) \tag{11}$$

3   Affine Tchebichef Moments Invariants

The geometric deformations of the pattern can be simplified to affine transformations:

$$\begin{pmatrix} X \\ Y \end{pmatrix} = \begin{pmatrix} a_{11} & a_{12} \\ a_{21} & a_{22} \end{pmatrix} \begin{pmatrix} x \\ y \end{pmatrix} + \begin{pmatrix} x_0 \\ y_0 \end{pmatrix} \tag{12}$$

where (x, y) and (X, Y) are coordinates in the image plane before and after the transformations, respectively, and (x_0, y_0) is the image centroid coordinates given by [18].

$$x_0 = \frac{c_{00}^N T_{10} - c_{10}^N T_{00}}{c_{11}^N T_{00}}, \quad y_0 = \frac{c_{00}^N T_{01} - c_{10}^N T_{00}}{c_{11}^N T_{00}} \tag{13}$$

Translation invariance can be achieved by locating the origin of the coordinate system to the center of the object. Thus (x_0, y_0) can be ignored and only take the matrix A into consideration. Form above, Zhang et al [18] defined the two-dimensional $(p+q)$ order Tchebichef moments of the transformed image $g(X, Y)$ as follows:

$$T_{pq}^{(g)} = A \sum_{x=0}^{N-1} \sum_{y=0}^{N-1} \tilde{t}_p(a_{11}x + a_{12}y)\tilde{t}_q(a_{21}x + a_{22}y)f(x, y) \quad A = |a_{11}a_{22} - a_{12}a_{21}| \tag{14}$$

For simplicity, the above equation can be rewritten as

$$T_{pq}^{(g)} = A \sum_{m=0}^{p} \sum_{n=0}^{q} \sum_{s=0}^{m} \sum_{t=0}^{n} \sum_{i=0}^{s+t} \sum_{j=0}^{m+n-s-t} \binom{m}{s}\binom{n}{t}(a_{11})^s (a_{12})^{m-s} (a_{21})^t (a_{22})^{n-t} c_{p,m}^N c_{q,n}^N d_{s+t,i}^N d_{m+n-s-t,j}^N T_{ij}^{(f)} \tag{15}$$

In the following subsection, we will use the normalization method to obtain the affine Tchebichef moment invariants. This study adopts two kinds' decomposition known as XYS and XSR decomposition to reduce the complexity of matrix A, and discusses constraints imposed in each step of XYS and XSR decomposition procedure.

3.1 XYS Decomposition

Using this decomposition method, the transform matrix A can be separated into an x-shearing, a y-shearing and anisotropic scaling matrix, respectively.

$$\begin{pmatrix} a_{11} & a_{12} \\ a_{21} & a_{22} \end{pmatrix} = \begin{pmatrix} \alpha_0 & 0 \\ 0 & \delta_0 \end{pmatrix}\begin{pmatrix} 1 & 0 \\ \gamma_0 & 1 \end{pmatrix}\begin{pmatrix} 1 & \beta_0 \\ 0 & 1 \end{pmatrix} \tag{16}$$

where the coefficients $\alpha_0, \delta_0, \gamma_0$ and β_0 are real numbers.

Depend on this decomposition, we can derive a set of Tchebichef moment invariants I_{pq}^{xsh}, I_{pq}^{ysh} and I_{pq}^{as} through the following theorem, and these invariants are invariant to x-shearing, y-shearing and anisotropic scaling, respectively.

Theorem 1. Suppose f be an origin image and g is its x-shearing transformed version such as $g(x, y) = f(x + \beta_0 y, y)$. Then the following $I_{pq}^{xsh(f)}$ are invariant to x-shearing.

$$I_{pq}^{xsh(f)} = \sum_{m=0}^{p} \sum_{n=0}^{q} \sum_{s=0}^{m} \sum_{i=0}^{s} \sum_{j=0}^{m+n-s} \binom{m}{s} \beta^{m-s} c_{p,m}^N c_{q,n}^N d_{s,i}^N d_{m+n-s,j}^N T_{ij}^{(f)} \tag{17}$$

where β_f is the parameter associated with the origin image f, and the relationship of the origin image parameter and the transformed is $\beta_f = \beta_g + \beta_0$. The parameter β_f can be obtained using method in [15]. Setting $I_{30} = 0$ in (17), one has

$$(c_{33}d_{30}T_{00}+c_{33}d_{31}T_{01}+c_{33}d_{32}T_{02}+T_{03})\times\beta^3+[(c_{32}+3c_{33}c_{00}d_{10})(d_{20}T_{00}+d_{21}T_{01}+d_{22}T_{02})$$
$$+3c_{33}c_{00}d_{11}(d_{20}T_{10}+d_{21}T_{11}+d_{22}T_{12})]\times\beta^2+[(c_{31}+2c_{32}c_{00}d_{10}+3c_{33}c_{00}d_{20})\times(d_{10}T_{00}+d_{11}T_{01})$$
$$+(2c_{32}c_{00}d_{11}+3c_{33}c_{00}d_{21})(d_{10}T_{10}+d_{11}T_{11})+3c_{33}c_{00}d_{22}(d_{10}T_{20}+d_{11}T_{21})]\times\beta$$
$$+[(c_{30}d_{00}+c_{31}d_{10}+c_{32}d_{20}+c_{33}d_{30})T_{00}+(c_{31}d_{11}+c_{32}d_{21}+c_{33}d_{31})T_{10}+(c_{32}d_{22}+c_{33}d_{32})T_{20}+T_{30}]=0 \tag{18}$$

Theorem 2. Suppose f be an origin image and g is its y-shearing transformed version such as $g(x, y) = f(x, \gamma_0 x + y)$. Then the following $I_{pq}^{ysh(f)}$ are invariant to y-shearing.

$$I_{pq}^{ysh(f)} = \sum_{m=0}^{p}\sum_{n=0}^{q}\sum_{t=0}^{n}\sum_{i=0}^{m+t}\sum_{j=0}^{n-t}\binom{n}{t}\gamma^t c_{p,m}^N c_{q,n}^N d_{m+t,i}^N d_{n-t,j}^N T_{ij}^{(f)} \tag{19}$$

where γ_f is the parameter associated with the origin image f, and the relationship of the origin image parameter and the transformed is $\gamma_f = \gamma_g + \gamma_0$. Under this composition, the constraint $I_{11} = 0$ used to calculate the γ_f. One can have

$$\gamma = -\frac{(c_{10}c_{10}d_{00}d_{00}+2c_{10}c_{11}d_{00}d_{10}+c_{11}c_{11}d_{10}d_{10})T_{00}+(c_{10}d_{00}+c_{11}d_{10})(T_{01}+T_{10})+T_{11}}{(c_{10}c_{11}d_{00}d_{10}+c_{11}c_{11}d_{20}d_{00})T_{00}+(c_{10}d_{00}+c_{11}c_{11}d_{21}d_{00})T_{10}+c_{11}c_{11}d_{22}d_{00}T_{20}} \tag{20}$$

Theorem 3. Suppose f be an origin image and g is its scaling transformed version such as $g(x, y) = f(\alpha_0 x, \delta_0 y)$. Then the following $I_{pq}^{as(f)}$ are invariant to anisotropic scaling

$$I_{pq}^{as(f)} = \sum_{m=0}^{p}\sum_{n=0}^{q}\sum_{i=0}^{m}\sum_{j=0}^{n}\alpha_f^{m+1}\delta_f^{n+1}c_{p,m}^N c_{q,n}^N d_{m,i}^N d_{n,j}^N T_{ij}^{(f)} \tag{21}$$

where α_f and δ_f are two parameters associated with the origin image f, such that $\alpha_f = \alpha_0\alpha_g$ and $\delta_f = \delta_0\delta_g$. From above equations, one can receive the invariants, but the problem is how to get the parameters. One way for estimating these parameters is using the constraints $I_{20} = I_{02} = 1$ in (21) to computer parameters α_f and δ_f, such as

$$\begin{cases} (c_{22}d_{20}T_{00}+c_{22}d_{21}T_{10}+T_{20})\alpha^3\delta+(c_{21}d_{10}T_{00}+c_{21}d_{11}T_{10})\alpha^2\delta+c_{20}d_{00}T_{00}\alpha\delta=1 \\ (c_{22}d_{20}T_{00}+c_{22}d_{21}T_{01}+T_{02})\alpha\delta^3+(c_{21}d_{10}T_{00}+c_{21}d_{11}T_{01})\alpha\delta^2+c_{20}d_{00}T_{00}\alpha\delta=1 \end{cases} \tag{22}$$

3.2 XSR Decomposition

This is another widely used affine decomposition method. Under this decomposition, the matrix A can be written as an x-shearing, an anisotropic scaling and a rotation matrix.

$$\begin{pmatrix} a_{11} & a_{12} \\ a_{21} & a_{22} \end{pmatrix} = \begin{pmatrix} \cos\theta & \sin\theta \\ -\sin\theta & \cos\theta \end{pmatrix}\begin{pmatrix} \alpha_0 & 0 \\ 0 & \delta_0 \end{pmatrix}\begin{pmatrix} 1 & \beta_0 \\ 0 & 1 \end{pmatrix} \tag{23}$$

where the coefficients $\alpha_0, \delta_0, \beta_0$ and θ are real numbers.

Using this decomposition, one can derive a set of Tchebichef moment invariants I_{pq}^{xsh}, I_{pq}^{as} and I_{pq}^{rt} through the following theorems, and these invariants are invariant to x-shearing, y-shearing and anisotropic scaling respectively.

Theorem 4. Suppose f be an origin image and g is its x-shearing transformed version such as $g(x, y) = f(x + \beta_0 y, y)$. Then the following $I_{pq}^{xsh(f)}$ is invariant to x-shearing

$$I_{pq}^{xsh(f)} = \sum_{m=0}^{p}\sum_{n=0}^{q}\sum_{s=0}^{m}\sum_{i=0}^{s}\sum_{j=0}^{m+n-s}\binom{m}{s}\beta^{m-s}c_{p,m}^{N}c_{q,n}^{N}d_{s,i}^{N}d_{m+n-s,j}^{N}T_{ij}^{(f)} \tag{24}$$

where β_f is the parameter associated with the origin image f. It can be obtained using the constraint $I_{11}=0$ in (24).

$$\beta = -\frac{(c_{10}c_{10}d_{00}d_{00} + 2c_{10}c_{11}d_{00}d_{10} + c_{11}c_{11}d_{10}d_{10})T_{00} + (c_{10}d_{00} + c_{11}d_{10})(T_{01}+T_{10})+T_{11}}{(c_{10}c_{11}d_{00}d_{10} + c_{11}c_{11}d_{20}d_{00})T_{00} + (c_{10}d_{00} + c_{11}c_{11}d_{21}d_{00})T_{01} + c_{11}c_{11}d_{22}d_{00}T_{02}} \tag{25}$$

The relationship of the origin image parameter and the transformed is $\beta_f = \beta_g + \beta_0$.

Theorem 5. Suppose f be an origin image and g is its scaling transformed version such as $g(x, y) = f(\alpha_0 x, \delta_0 y)$. Then the following $I_{pq}^{as(f)}$ is invariant to anisotropic scaling

$$I_{pq}^{as(f)} = \sum_{m=0}^{p}\sum_{n=0}^{q}\sum_{i=0}^{m}\sum_{j=0}^{n}\alpha_f^{m+1}\delta_f^{n+1}c_{p,m}^{N}c_{q,n}^{N}d_{m,i}^{N}d_{n,j}^{N}T_{ij}^{(f)} \tag{26}$$

where α_f and δ_f are two parameters associated with the origin image f, such that $\alpha_f = \alpha_0 \alpha_g$ and $\delta_f = \delta_0 \delta_g$. Setting $I_{20} = I_{02} = 1$ in (26), one has

$$\begin{cases}(c_{22}d_{20}T_{00} + c_{22}d_{21}T_{10} + T_{20})\alpha^3\delta + (c_{21}d_{10}T_{00} + c_{21}d_{11}T_{10})\alpha^2\delta + c_{20}d_{00}T_{00}\alpha\delta = 1 \\ (c_{22}d_{20}T_{00} + c_{22}d_{21}T_{01} + T_{02})\alpha\delta^3 + (c_{21}d_{10}T_{00} + c_{21}d_{11}T_{01})\alpha\delta^2 + c_{20}d_{00}T_{00}\alpha\delta = 1\end{cases} \tag{27}$$

Theorem 6. Suppose f be an origin image and g is its rotation transformed version such as $g(x, y) = f(\cos\theta x + \sin\theta y, -\sin\theta x + \cos\theta y)$. Then the following $I_{pq}^{rt(f)}$ is invariant to rotation transform.

$$I_{pq}^{rt(f)} = \sum_{m=0}^{p}\sum_{n=0}^{q}\sum_{s=0}^{m}\sum_{t=0}^{n}\sum_{i=0}^{s+t}\sum_{i=0}^{m+n-s-t}\binom{m}{s}\binom{n}{t}(-1)^t(\cos\theta)^{n+s-t}(\sin\theta)^{m+t-s}$$
$$\times c_{p,m}^{N}c_{q,n}^{N}d_{s+t,i}^{N}d_{m+n-s-t,j}^{N}T_{ij}^{(f)} \tag{28}$$

where θ is the parameter associated with the origin image f. Setting $I_{30}+I_{12} = 0$ in (28), the parameter θ can be calculated using the following expression.

$$\theta = \frac{1}{2}\arctan(\frac{uT_{11} - vT_{00}}{T_{20} - T_{02}}), u = \frac{2c_{22}^{N}c_{00}^{N}}{(c_{11}^{N})^2}, v = \frac{2c_{22}^{N}(c_{10}^{N})^2}{c_{00}^{N}(c_{11}^{N})^2} \tag{29}$$

Equation (28) is affine invariant to image geometric deformation.
Theorems 1~6 proof is similar to ref.[17] and is omitted here.

Table 1. Invariants values for image butterfly ($N = 120$)

	(p, q)								
XYS	(1, 0)	-0.2389	-0.2389	-0.2389	-0.2389	-0.2389	-0.2389	-0.2389	-0.2389
	(1, 1)	0.3019	0.3019	0.3019	0.3019	0.3020	0.3021	0.3019	0.3019
	(1, 2)	0.5406	0.5406	0.5406	0.5406	0.5407	0.5408	0.5406	0.5406
	(0, 3)	0.1440	0.1440	0.1440	0.1440	0.1438	0.1437	0.1440	0.1440
	(3, 1)	0.6842	0.6842	0.6842	0.6842	0.6842	0.6842	0.6842	0.6842
	(3, 2)	0.9217	0.9217	0.9217	0.9217	0.9219	0.9222	0.9217	0.9217
XSR	(1, 0)	-0.2389	-0.2389	-0.2389	-0.2389	-0.2389	-0.2389	-0.2389	-0.2389
	(1, 1)	0.3020	0.3020	0.3020	0.3020	0.3021	0.3021	0.3020	0.3020
	(1, 2)	0.5412	0.5408	0.5412	0.5408	0.5411	0.5409	0.5408	0.5408
	(0, 3)	0.1449	0.1431	0.1449	0.1431	0.1446	0.1431	0.1431	0.1431
	(3, 1)	0.6845	0.6854	0.6845	0.6854	0.6844	0.6849	0.6854	0.6854
	(3, 2)	0.9236	0.9241	0.9236	0.9241	0.9235	0.9237	0.9241	0.9241

Table 2. Invariants values for number "0" ($N = 30$)

	(p, q)								
XYS	(1, 0)	-0.1899	-0.1899	-0.1899	-0.1899	-0.1899	-0.1895	-0.1913	-0.1906
	(1, 1)	0.3253	0.3252	0.3253	0.3252	0.3252	0.3259	0.3230	0.3241
	(1, 2)	0.5135	0.5134	0.5135	0.5134	0.5134	0.5142	0.5107	0.5121
	(0, 3)	0.0733	0.0734	0.0733	0.0734	0.0734	0.0717	0.0792	0.0763
	(3, 1)	0.5840	0.5841	0.5840	0.5840	0.5841	0.5840	0.5842	0.5841
	(3, 2)	0.7629	0.7627	0.7628	0.7627	0.7627	0.7658	0.7521	0.7574
XSR	(1, 0)	-0.1899	-0.1899	-0.1899	-0.1899	-0.1899	-0.1895	-0.1913	-0.1906
	(1, 1)	0.3261	0.3260	0.3261	0.3261	0.3260	0.3264	0.3247	0.3254
	(1, 2)	0.5172	0.5147	0.5147	0.5172	0.5147	0.5151	0.5134	0.5179
	(0, 3)	0.0799	0.0666	0.0667	0.0801	0.0666	0.0670	0.0653	0.0866
	(3, 1)	0.5860	0.5927	0.5926	0.5860	0.5927	0.5900	0.6021	0.5871
	(3, 2)	0.7771	0.7814	0.7813	0.7772	0.7814	0.7786	0.7907	0.7797

4 Experimental Results

In this section, three test images with different size, as shown in the first row of Tables 1~3, are used to illustrate the invariance properties of the proposed affine invariants to various geometric transformations. These images are shifted up, down, translation, scale, and rotation. Tables 1, illustrates the proposed six invariants with different order p, q for each image according to XYS and XSR decomposition, respectively. The experiment is performed on another image which is a number "0" and with the size of 30×30. Table 2 is the results of affine Tchebichef moment according to XYS and XSR decomposition. Similarly, Table 3 shows another result of the character "q" with 80×80 pixels. From these Tables, one can found both XYS and XSR decomposition preserve invariance for all affine transformation. Experimental results also illustrate that there are more errors exist in scaling invariants, and errors will be increase while the moment order $(p+q)$ increasing. On the other hand, the experimental results also indicate that the XYS decomposition is better than XSR decomposition.

Table 3. Invariants values for letter "q" ($N = 80$)

	(p, q)	6	q	ɑ	6	q	ᖯ	b	ơ
	(1, 0)	-0.2308	-0.2308	-0.2308	-0.2308	-0.2309	-0.2312	-0.2308	-0.2310
	(1, 1)	0.3057	0.3057	0.3057	0.3057	0.3056	0.3051	0.3058	0.3054
XYS	(1, 2)	0.5360	0.5360	0.5360	0.5360	0.5358	0.5352	0.5361	0.5356
	(0, 3)	0.1324	0.1324	0.1324	0.1324	0.1327	0.1340	0.1322	0.1333
	(3, 1)	0.6675	0.6675	0.6675	0.6675	0.6675	0.6676	0.6675	0.6676
	(3, 2)	0.8950	0.8950	0.8950	0.8950	0.8944	0.8921	0.8953	0.8934
	(1, 0)	-0.2308	-0.2308	-0.2308	-0.2308	-0.2309	-0.2312	-0.2308	-0.2310
	(1, 1)	0.3060	0.3060	0.3060	0.3060	0.3059	0.3056	0.3060	0.3058
XSR	(1, 2)	0.5372	0.5372	0.5372	0.5364	0.5373	0.5360	0.5372	0.5362
	(0, 3)	0.1344	0.1344	0.1345	0.1303	0.1352	0.1299	0.1341	0.1301
	(3, 1)	0.6681	0.6681	0.6682	0.6702	0.6683	0.6729	0.6681	0.6717
	(3, 2)	0.8994	0.8993	0.8994	0.9006	0.8996	0.9033	0.8992	0.9021

5 Conclusions

Considering the orthogonal and discrete characteristics of Tchebichef moments, this study presented two image normalization methods that can give affine Tchebichef moment invariants which were invariant with respect to affine deformation. The numerical experiments were performed with symmetric as well as asymmetric images. The results demonstrated the invariance properties and discriminative capabilities of the proposed descriptors.

Acknowledgments. This work has been supported by National Natural Science Foundation of China under Grant No. 60975004.

References

1. Hu, M.K.: Visual pattern recognition by moment invariants. IRE Trans. Inf. Theory 8, 179–187 (1962)
2. Li, B.: High-order moment computation of gray-level images. IEEE Trans. Image Process. 4, 502–505 (1995)
3. Chong, C.-W., Raveendran, P., Mukundan, R.: Translation invariants of Zernike moments. Pattern Recognit. 36, 1765–1773 (2003)
4. Chong, C.-W., Raveendran, P., Mukundan, R.: The scale invariants of pseudo-Zernike moments. Pattern Anal. 6, 176–184 (2003)
5. Chong, C.-W., Raveendran, P., Mukundan, R.: Translation and scale invariants of Legendre moments. Pattern Recognit. 37, 119–129 (2004)
6. Mukundan, R.: Some computational aspects of discrete orthonormal moments. IEEE Trans. Image Process. 13, 1055–1059 (2004)
7. Mukundan, R., Ong, S.H., Lee, P.A.: Image analysis by Tchebichef moments. IEEE Trans. Image Process. 10, 1357–1364 (2001)
8. Zhu, H., Shu, H., Xia, T.: Translation and scale invariants of Tchebichef moments. Pattern Recognit. 40, 2530–2542 (2007)
9. Reiss, T.H.: The revised fundamental theorem of moment invariants. IEEE Trans. Pattern Anal. Mach. Intell. 13, 830–834 (1991)
10. Flusser, J., Suk, T.: Pattern recognition by affine moment invariants. Pattern Recognit. 26, 167–174 (1993)
11. Papakostas, G.A., Karakasis, E.G., Koulouriotis, D.E.: Novel moment invariants for improved classification performance in computer vision applications. Pattern Recognit. 43, 58–68 (2010)
12. Lin, H., Si, J., Abousleman, G.P.: Orthogonal rotation-invariant moments for digital image processing. IEEE Trans. Image Process. 17, 272–282 (2008)
13. Chen, Z., Sun, S.-K.: A Zernike moment phase-based descriptor for local image representation and matching. IEEE Trans. Image Process. 19, 205–219 (2010)
14. Chen, B., Shu, H., Zhang, H., Coatrieux, G., Luo, L., Coatrieux, J.L.: Combined invariants to similarity transformation and to blur using orthogonal Zernike moments. IEEE Trans. Image Process. 20, 345–360 (2011)
15. Rothe, I., Süsse, H., Voss, K.: The method of normalization to determine invariants. IEEE Trans. Pattern Anal. Mach. Intell. 1, 366–376 (1996)
16. Zhang, Y., Wen, C., Zhang, Y., Soh, Y.C.: On the choice of consisitent canonical from during moment normalization. Pattern Recognit. Lett. 24, 3205–3215 (2003)
17. Zhang, H., Shu, H., Coatrieux, G.: Affine Legendre moment invariants for image watermarking robust to geometric distortions. IEEE Trans. Image Process. 19, 1–9 (2010)
18. Zhang, H., Dai, X., Sun, P., Zhu, H., Shu, H.: Symmetric image recogintion by Tchebichef moment invariants. In: Proc. 2011 IEEE 17th Int. Conf., Image Process., pp. 2273–2276 (2010)
19. Branson, D.: Stirling number representations. Discrete Mathematics 306, 478–494 (2006)

Analysis of Conditional Independence Relationship and Applications Based on Layer Sorting in Bayesian Networks

Guofu Xin, Youlong Yang, and Xia Liu

Department of Mathematics, Xidian University, Xi'an, 710071, China
ylyang@mail.xidian.edu.cn

Abstract. Bayesian networks are a probabilistic representation for uncertain relationships, which has proven to be useful for modeling real world problems. Causal Independence and stochastic Independence are two important notations to characterize the flow of information on Bayesian network. They correspond to unidirectional separation and directional separation in Bayesian network structure respectively. In this paper, we focus on the relationship between directional separation and unidirectional separation. By using the layer sorting structure of Bayesian networks, the condition demanded to be satisfied to ensure d-separation and ud-separation hold is given. At the same time, we show that it is easy to find d-separation and ud-separation sets to identify direct causal effect quickly.

Keywords: Directional separation, unidirectional separation, Bayesian network layer sorting.

1 Introduction

Bayesian networks also called Belief Networks or Causal Networks, are a powerful tool for modeling decision-making under uncertainty (see [1-5]). They have been successfully applied to different fields, such as, Machine learning, Prediction and Bioinformatics (see [1, 7-9]). Bayesian networks excel in knowledge representation and reasoning under uncertainty notion of causality suggests an unidirectional separation as graphical representation of causal conditional independence structures. There has been lots of research on theory and application about causal effects in Bayesian networks, for example [4, 6, 10-15]. Pearl's [3] notion of causality suggests a unidirectional separation as graphical representation of causal conditional independence structures. Causal independence allows for defining a measure to characterize the strength of a causal effect of causal networks which is called information flow by Nihay Ay and Daniel Ploani [4]. The cause contribution of A to B imposing S is zero, then we say there is no information flow between A and B after intervening S. The notion of causal effects is based on the possibility to intervene in causal models. An intervention is an action taken to force a variable into a certain state, without reference to its own current state, or the states of any of the other variables. Direct causal effect $A \rightarrow B$ is the post-interventional probability

H. Deng et al. (Eds.): AICI 2011, Part III, LNAI 7004, pp. 481–488, 2011.

distribution of B which is defined via mechanisms rather than observations. The interventional formalism (see [3]) provided an appropriate framework for the cause mechanisms in the given system. Causal effects can be identified or post-interventional probability distributions can be calculated by interventional formalism if all variables can be observed. There are three popular figure criteria, front-door, back-door and instrumental variables criteria for causal effects. Pearl's notion [3] of identify causal effect demands to meet front-door criteria or back-door criteria if there are some unobserved variables. Zhao and Zheng [10] have discussed and compared identifiability criteria for causal effects in Gaussian causal models. They have obtained that complete data method is better than front-door, back-door criteria and back-door criteria is better than instrumental variables criteria. These results can offer guidance for choosing better identifiability criterion in practice. Hei and Manabu [11] present an extended set of graphical criteria for the identification of direct causal effects in linear Structural Equation Models (SEMs), they introduce a new set of graphical criteria which uses descendants of either the cause variable or the effect variable as "path-specific" instrumental variables" for the identification of the direct causal effect as long as certain conditions are satisfied.

Directional separation (d-separation for short) is a relation among three disjoint sets of nodes in a directed acyclic graph which is defined in [12]. Two subsets of nodes, X and Y, are said to be d-separated by Z if all chains between the nodes in X and the nodes in Y are blocked by Z. While this condition is characterized by its consistency with stochastic independence structures. Pearl's well known d-separation criterion in a directed acyclic graph is a path separation criterion that can be used to efficiently identify all valid conditional independence relationships in the Markov model determined by the graph. A joint distribution represented by a Bayesian network must satisfy the Markov conditions of the structure: each variable must be independent of its non-descendants given its parents. Unidirectional separation (ud-separation for short) which is defined in [4] is used to judge causal conditional independence. Let A, B, S be three disjoint subsets of nodes. We say that B is ud-separated from A by S if all directed paths from A to B go through S. There exists a directed path from A to B that does not meet S if the information flow between A and B is a positive number after intervene S. A necessary and sufficient condition of ud-separation is given in [4]. What is the relationship between d-separation and ud-separation? How to find the d-separation and ud-separation sets quickly?

The purpose of this paper focus on the relationship between d-separation and ud-separation in directed acyclic graphs. By using layer sorting structure of a Bayesian network, d-separation and ud-separation sets are found quickly to identify direct causal effects.

This paper is organized as follows. In section 2, we introduce background knowledge. In section 3, a new definition which is called layer sorting is introduced, and we discuss a special kind of Bayesian networks, and in this case, both d-separation and ud-separation hold when it satisfy certain condition. In section 4, we introduce two applications about layer sorting.

2   The Basic Concepts and Relation Works

In this section, we introduce some notions and discuss previous relevant works on which our results is based. At the same time, we introduce present relevant background knowledge. We assume that the readers have some basic familiarity with graph theory and Bayesian networks.

A Bayesian network is consist of (1) structure: a directed acyclic graph or a DAG for short, $G = (V, E)$; (2) parameters: represent a joint distribution P over variables. We use higher-case Roman letters for sets of nodes, and lower-case Roman letters for singleton node.

We consider a finite set $V \neq \phi$ of nodes and a set $E \in V \times V$ among these nodes. Such a directed graph $G = (V, E)$, if $\langle v_i, v_j \rangle \in E$, it means that it is a directed edge from v_i to v_j, we note $v_i \rightarrow v_j$. If two nodes v_i and v_j, either $v_i \rightarrow v_j$ or $v_j \rightarrow v_i$, we call v_i and v_j are adjacent, we note $v_i - v_j$. An ordered sequence $\pi = (v_1, v_2, \cdots v_n)$ in a DAG $G = (V, E)$ is called a path from v_1 to v_n, if v_i and v_{i+1} are adjacent for all $i = 1, 2, \cdots n-1$. An ordered sequence $\pi = (v_1, v_2, \cdots v_n)$ in a DAG $G = (V, E)$ is called a directed path from v_1 to v_n, if $v_i \rightarrow v_{i+1}$ for all $i = 1, 2, \cdots n-1$. If $v_1 = v_n$, directed path $\pi = (v_1, v_2, \cdots v_n)$ is called a directed cycle. A directed graph with no directed cycles is called a directed acyclic graph.

Let $G = (V, E)$ be a DAG, and x, y, z be three different nodes in G. If $x \rightarrow z \rightarrow y \in G$, we call z is a serial connection node. If $x \leftarrow z \rightarrow y \in G$, we call z is a diverging connection node. If $x \rightarrow z \leftarrow y \in G$, we call z is a collider node. A path $\pi = (v_1, v_2, \cdots v_n)$ is called a compound active path given conditioning set Z in DAG G, if each node v_i in the path has one of the two following properties: (1) v_i is not a collider and v_i is not in Z ; or (2) v_i is a collider and either v_i or a descendant of v_i in G is in Z. D-separation has been identified as the graphical separation property that is consistent with stochastic conditional independence. It is defined as follows. A path $\pi = (v_1, v_2, \cdots v_n)$ is blocked by a set S, if there is a node $v_j (1 < j < n)$ of the path such that: either $v_j \in S$ and v_j is not a collider, or v_j and all its descendants are not in S, and v_j is a collider. Sets A and B are d-separated given a set S in $G = (V, E)$, if every simple active path between a node in A and a node in B is blocked given conditioning set S. Let $(B \perp_d A | S)_G$ denote that A is d-separated from B given S in G. Sets A and B are ud-separated given a set S in $G = (V, E)$, if every directed path from A to B is blocked given conditioning set S. And let $(B \perp_{ud} A | S)_G$ denote that B is unidirectional separated from A given a set S in G.

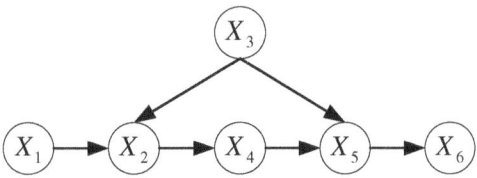

Fig. 1. A directed acyclic graph

For example, we have a set of six nodes $V = \{X_1, X_2, X_3, X_{46}, X_5, X_6\}$, and a set of six edges among these nodes:

$$E = \{\langle X_1, X_2 \rangle, \langle X_3, X_2 \rangle, \langle X_2, X_4 \rangle, \langle X_3, X_5 \rangle, \langle X_4, X_5 \rangle, \langle X_5, X_6 \rangle\},$$

which is shown in Figure 1. The path $X_1 \to X_2 \to X_4 \to X_5 \to X_6$ is direct path. Let $A_1 = \{X_6, X_3\}$, $B_1 = \{X_1\}$ and $S_1 = \{X_4\}$. Then sets A_1 and B_1 are ud-separated by S_1. Let $A_2 = \{X_6\}$, $B_2 = \{X_1\}$, $S_2 = \{X_5\}$. One has that A_2 is d-separated from B_2 given S_2.

3   Main Results and Proof

In this section, we take two parts to discuss the relationship between d-separation and ud-separation.

There is a simple active path between node x and node y given conditioning set Z in G if and only if there is a compound active path between node x and node y given conditioning set Z in G. This implies that simple and compound active paths are interchangeable with respect to the definition of d-separation. Firstly, let us see the following lemma 3.1.

Lemma 3.1. Let $G = (V, E)$ be a DAG, and A, B and S are three disjoint subsets of V, then $(B \perp_d A \mid S)_G$ is the sufficient condition for $(B \perp_{ud} A \mid S)_G$.

Proof. we assume sets A and B are d-separated by S. Let $l = (v_1, v_2, \cdots v_n)$ be an any directed path from the set A to the set B, then l is blocked by S. Each node $v_j (j = 1, 2 \cdots n)$ in l is a serial connection node, according to the definition of d-separation, there must be exist one node $v_j (1 < j < n)$ in S. Therefore each directed path between sets A and B goes through S, then B is d-separated from A given S.   □

We can see this from Figure 1. Suppose $A = \{X_6, X_3\}$, $B = \{X_1\}$, $S = \{X_4\}$, then B is ud-separated from A given S, but B is not d-separated from A given S.

From lemma 3.1, we know that d-separation is the sufficient condition for ud-separation. In order to discuss the condition that both d-separation and ud-separation hold, we introduce the definition of layer sorting.

Let $G = (V, E)$ be a DAG, F_0 be the set of nodes that has no parents nodes. According to $F_{m+1} = \{v \in V \setminus (F_0, F_1, \cdots F_m) : pa(v) \cup (F_0 \cup F_1 \cup \cdots \cup F_m) \neq \phi\}$ where $m = 0, 1, 2 \cdots$, we get next layers. Since V is a finite set, for some m, we have $F_{m+1} = \phi$. Therefore, the layers after F_{m+1} are also empty. Assume $K = \max\{m, F_m \neq \phi\}$, we have the disjoint union $V = F_0 \cup F_1 \cup \cdots \cup F_K$. The corresponding map that $l \to \{0, 1 \cdots K\}$ assigns to each $v \in V$ its layer number $l(v)$ where $0 \leq l(v) \leq K$.

Suppose $A = \{X_1, X_3\}, B = \{X_6\}, S = \{X_5\}$, obviously B is d-separated from A given S and it also is ud-separated A given S.

Theorem 3.1. Suppose $G = (V, E)$ be a DAG, and its layer structure $V = F_0 \cup F_1 \cup \cdots \cup F_K$.

For any non-negative integers a, s, b, then F_b are F_a ud-separated by F_s if $0 \leq a < s < b \leq K$.

Proof. We consider a directed path $\pi = (v_1, v_2, \cdots v_n)$ from F_a to F_b. The corresponding layer numbers are $l(v_1), \cdots l(v_n)$, and $l(v_1) = a$, $l(v_n) = b$. If $l(v_{i+1}) > l(v_i)$, we have $l(v_{i+1}) = l(v_i) + 1$. It implies that there must be one node $l(v_i) = s(a < i < b)$. Therefore, any directed path $\pi = (v_1, v_2, \cdots v_n)$ from F_a to F_b goes through F_s. That is $(F_b \perp_{ud} F_a | F_s)_G$ holds.   □

Theorem 3.2. Suppose $G = (V, E)$ be a DAG, and its layer structure

$$V = F_0 \cup F_1 \cup \cdots \cup F_K.$$

If the parents of F_m are included in $F_0 \cup F_1 \cup \cdots \cup F_m$, for three non-negative integers a, s, b, if $0 \leq a < s < b \leq K$, F_b and F_a are ud-separated and d-separated by F_s.

Proof. Firstly, we prove that $\langle F_a \perp_d F_b | F_s \rangle_G$ holds. Let $l = (v_1, v_2, \cdots v_i, \cdots v_j, \cdots v_k, \cdots v_q)$ be a simple active path from F_a to F_b. There exist one nodes of F_s at least is not a collider in path l. Assume $p = \{v_i \in l\} \cap F_s$ where the path l goes through F_s. If one node in p is not a collider, then the conclusion that $(F_a \perp_d F_b | F_s)_G$ is right. Otherwise, all nodes in p are colliders in the path l. We consider v_k, since $v_k \in p$, then $v_{k+1} \notin F_s$. Then the subpath $l' = (v_{k+1}, v_{k+2}, \cdots v_q)$ of l is a simple active path from F_{s-1} to F_b. According to lemma 3.2, there exists one node in l' goes through F_s. This is contradictory to the definition on p. Therefore $(F_a \perp_d F_b | F_s)_G$ holds.

Because all directed paths from F_a to F_b go through F_s, according to theorem 3.1, $(F_b \perp_{ud} F_a \mid F_s)_G$ holds.   □

In that special kind of Bayesian networks, there is one node on each active path from F_a to F_b which is not a collider in conditioning set F_s.

Let $G = (V, E)$ be a DAG. Further let A, B and S are three disjoint subsets of V. If $(A \perp_d B \mid S)_G$ and $(B \perp_{ud} A \mid S)_G$ hold simultaneously, any active path l from A to B must meet one of the following two conditions.

Either l is a directed path in itself, then l must go through S, or l is not a directed path in itself, (1) l does not go through S, there must be a collider node in l and its descendents are not in S, (2) l goes through S, let $(s_1, s_2, \cdots s_k)$ be the nodes that l goes through S, if $k = 1$, node s_1 is not a collider node in S. If $k \geq 2$, there is a node $s_i (1 \leq i \leq k)$ which is not a collider in l.

Because an active path may be also a directed path in itself, and may be a directed path is a sub-path of an active path. In order to discuss the condition demanded to be satisfied to ensure d-separation and ud-separation hold simultaneously, we discuss it in two special cases, any other cases seems to be these two cases.

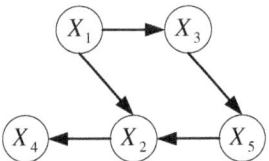

Fig. 2. Two special cases to judge d-separation and ud-separation

Case1: Let $A_1 = \{X_1\}, B_1 = \{X_5\}, S_1 = \{X_3\}$ in Figure 2. Then $(B_1 \perp_d A_1 \mid S_1)_G$ and $(B_1 \perp_{ud} A_1 \mid S_1)_G$ hold simultaneously. Namely, each directed path from A_1 to B_1 goes through S_1. If one has a active paths from A_1 to B_1 which not go through S_1, there is a collider node in these active paths and its descendents are not in S_1.

Case 2: Assume $A_2 = \{X_1\}, S_2 = \{X_2, X_3\}, B_2 = \{X_4, X_5\}$ in Figure 2. Then B_2 is ud-separated from A_2 by S_2 in G. However B_2 is not d-separated from A_2 by S_2 because nodes X_1 and X_5 are not independence given X_2 in path $X_1 \rightarrow X_2 \leftarrow X_5$. In the case, if there is an active path from A_2 to B_2 which has only a collider node in S_2, the case is not right.

4   Applications and Discussion

In this section, we discuss two applications of layer sorting. One is that we can get a Bayesian network's topological sequence using layer sorting. The other is we can get d-separation and ud-separation sets to indentify the direct causal effects.

Assume we give a causal graph G as is shown in Figure 3 and its layer structure is shown in Figure 4.

From Figure 4, one has $F_0 = \{A, B\}, F_1 = \{C, D, E\}, F_2 = \{F, H\}, F_3 = \{G\}$. Firstly, we choose one node from F_0 and delete it until F_0 is empty. Secondly, we select one node that has not parents from $V \setminus F_0$ and delete it. Do like this until all nodes are opted. The topological sequence of causal graph G is

$$(A, B, C, D, E, F, G, H).$$

Let F and H be two different nodes in G. We want to judge whether the causal effect of F on H is identifiable. Using layer sorting, we obtain its layer structure which is shown in Figure 4. From Figure 4, we have F and H are in the same layer. We know the d-separation set is consist of C and D. We use this example to show that we can get the d-separation and ud-separation sets easily using layer sorting for some special kind of Bayesian Networks.

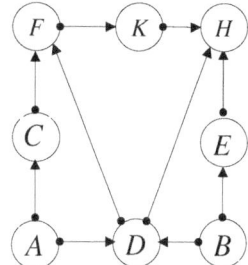
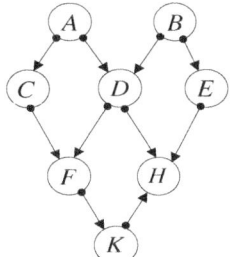

Fig. 3. A causal graph G **Fig. 4.** The layer structure of G

The relationship between d-separated and ud-separated is discussed in this paper, we obtain that d-separated is sufficient condition for ud-separated. By using the layer sorting structure of Bayesian networks, the condition demanded to be satisfied to ensure d-separation and ud-separation hold is given. D-separation and ud-separation play a very important role in the indentify of direct causal effects. In the next time, we will use layer sorting together with d-separation and ud-separation's nature to indentify the direct causal effects.

References

1. Friedman, N.: Inferring Cellular Networks Using Probabilistic Graphical Models. Science 303(5659), 799–805
2. Neapolitan, R.E.: Learning Bayesian Networks. Prentice-Hall, Englewood Cliffs (2003)
3. Pearl, J.: Causality: Models, Reasoning and Inference. Cambridge University Press, Cambridge (2000)
4. Ay, N., Polani, D.: Information Flows in Causal Networks. Advances in Complex Systems 11(1), 17–41 (2008)

5. Chickering, D.M., Meek, C.: On the incompatibility of faithfulness and monotone DAG faithfulness. Artificial Intelligence 170(8), 653–666 (2006)
6. Lauritzen, S.L.: Graphical Models for Causal Inference. Royal Economics Society Summer School, Oxford, Lecture Notes (2000)
7. You-long, Y., Yan, W.: VC dimension and inner product space induced by Bayesian networks. International Journal of Approximate Reasoning 50(7), 1036–1045 (2009)
8. Slezak, D.: Degrees of conditional dependence: a framework for approximate Bayesian networks and examples related to the rough set-based feature selection. Information Sciences 179(3), 197–209 (2009)
9. Yang, Y., Wu, Y.: Inner Product Space and Concept Classes Induced by Bayesian Networks. Acta Application Mathematicae 106(3), 337–348 (2009)
10. Zhao, H., Zheng, Z.-G.: Comparing Identifiability Criteria for Causal Effects in Gaussian Causal Models. Acta Mathematica Scientia 28A(5), 808–817 (2008)
11. Chan, H., Kuroki, M.: Using Descendants as Instrumental Variables for the Identification of Direct Causal Effects in Linear SEMs. In: International Conference on Artificial Intelligence and Statistics (AISTATS), Chia Laguna Resort, Sardinia, Italy (2010)
12. Levitz, M., Perlman, M.D., Madigan, D.: Separation and completeness properties for AMP chain graph Markov Models. The Annals of Statistics 29(6), 1751–1784 (2001)
13. Tian, J., Pearl, J.: On the testable implications of cause models with hidden variables. In: Proceedings of the Eighteenth Annual Conference on Uncertainty in Artificial Intelligence (UAI 2002), pp. 519–527 (2002)
14. Geng, Z., He, Y.-B., Wang, X.-L.: Relationship of causal effects in a causal chain and related inference. Science in China 47A, 730–740 (2004)
15. Tian, J., Pearl, J.: On the identification of cause effects, Technical report 475290-L, Tech. Rep. Cognitive Systems Laboratory, University of California at Los Angeles (2003)

Face Recognition Based on Real AdaBoost and Kalman Forecast

Chao Yan[1], Yuanqing Wang[1], and Zhaoyang Zhang[2]

[1] Stereo Imaging Laboratory, NanJing University, Nan Jing, China
yanchao3756@sina.com, yqwang@shu.nju.cn
[2] Advanced Display Laboratory, Shanghai University, Shanghai, China
zhangzhaoyang@shu.edu.cn

Abstract. In this paper, a novel face recognition method based on Real Ada-Boost algorithm and Kalman Forecast is implemented. Real AdaBoost algorithm can obtain great accuracy with machine learning. Meanwhile, Kalman Forecast is introduced to track human faces detected, making face detection more efficient. We tested our new method with many video sequences. The detection accuracy is 98. 57%, and the average processing time on a windows XP, PIV 2.4GHz PC was less than 20 ms for each 640*480-pixel image. So the proposed face recognition method is real-time.

Keywords: Real AdaBoost, Feature Calculation, Integral Image, Kalman Forecast.

1 Introduction

Face recognition means to obtain the location, size and position of all faces in an image [1]. This technology is used extensively, such as Teleconference, Security Check System, human-computer interaction and so on. Accuracy and speed are two standards of evaluating a face recognition algorithm. For accuracy, face recognition is a complicated and delicate process, face rotation, large-scale head motion and illumination variation will all make influence on the final effect of face recognition. For speed, more and more application of face recognition ask for higher speed than 30fps to fulfill the real-time requirement.

Owing to the importance of itself, face recognition has been recently bringing up a few excellent algorithms. Such as: Template Matching [2], Frame-to-frame Difference [3] , Support Vector Machine SVMs[4].The face recognition systems based on these algorithms behave pretty well in accuracy and recognition speed.

In 2001, Viola combined Discrete AdaBoost algorithm with waterfall structure, making a face recognition system. Then, Schapire improved the output of weak classifier to be continuous and obtained a face recognition system, which was based on Real AdaBoost algorithm and waterfall structure. This kind of face recognition system is one of the systems the accuracy of which are most high, meanwhile, the recognition speed of the system is almost much faster than any other face recognition system.

H. Deng et al. (Eds.): AICI 2011, Part III, LNAI 7004, pp. 489–496, 2011.

Even if the face recognition based on Real AdaBoost algorithm and waterfall structure has those advantages that have been mentioned, face detection for multiple users consumes considerable time. To solve this problem, Kalman Forecast is employed to predict face locations in current frame according to faces detected in the last frame. With Kalman tracking and marking faces detected, the whole detection process is quicker a lot.

The contribution of this paper includes: (1) Real AdaBoost algorithm has continuous output confidence-rate, so it could get classification border more accurately, making the accuracy of face recognition much higher. (2) To optimize recognition speed, Kalman Forecast is utilized to predict face locations, saving the whole detection time. This is very significant for multiple faces detection in real time. (3) We design active infrared illumination, and collect all images in the same illumination condition, so the effect caused by illumination variation is eliminated.

2   Real AdaBoost Algorithm

As implied by the name, boosting algorithm could switch weak classifiers to strong classifiers by integrating and machine learning. AdaBoost algorithm is one kind of Boosting algorithm, which could be adaptive. AdaBoost algorithm is able to adaptively adjust the weight of training samples, and selects the best weak classifiers, then integrates them to become a strong classifier, in which the different weak classifiers vote respectively.

2.1   Feature Calculation and Integral Image

Given limited information, the recognition based on features could code the condition of special areas, and the recognition based on features is much faster than the recognition based on pixels. So AdaBoost algorithm is an algorithm that is based on features. Haar features are used in our AdaBoost algorithm. Haar features are brought up by Paul Viola, which are a kind of simple rectangle features. The value of Haar feature is defined the sum of gray scale value of the black (white) pixels subtracts the sum of gray scale value of the white (black) pixels.

 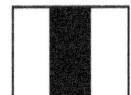 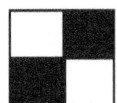  

Fig. 1. Basic Haar feature

These five kinds of basic Haar features in Fig.1are used in our face detection phase, and they behave great for front faces and leaning faces less than 30 degree. Nevertheless, large degree face leaning will cause failure to our face detection. So some kinds of Haar features have been taking into our consideration in order that the large leaning faces could also be detected in our face detection phase. Some of these

Haar features are shown in Fig.2, and the classifiers with these Haar features are now during the process of machine learning.

Fig. 2. Some of improved Haar features

These Haar features could be placed in any size and on any position of images; every placing form could be called a feature. So the same recognition sub-window will have a lot of features. For example, a 24*24-pixel image has more than 160000 Haar features. So if we calculate their feature values directly, it will cost considerable time. So integral image should be used in calculating feature values. Value of every point of integral image is the sum of gray scale values of the point's top-left pixels. For example, the value of point A(x,y) in integral image is:

$$I(x,y) = \sum_{\substack{x' \le x \\ y' \le y}} i(x',y')$$

i(x',y') is gray scale value of point (x',y') in the formula. Besides, we define the sum of gray scale values of point (x,y) and its top points as b(x,y):

$$b(x,y) = \sum_{y' \le y} i(x,y')$$

And we define $b(x,0) = 0, I(0,y) = 0$.

As a result, we could calculate I(x,y) as follows:

$$I(x,\ y) = I(x-1,\ y) + b(x,\ y)$$
$$b(x,\ y) = b(x,\ y-1) + i(x,\ y)$$

With integral image, we could calculate feature values much faster. As is shown in Fig.3, the sum of gray scale values of area 1 could be got only with the values of points A,B,C,D.

$$I_1 = I_A + I_D - I_B - I_C$$

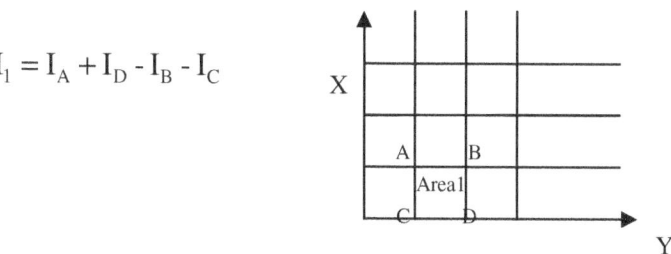

Fig. 3. Integral image

The calculating of rectangle Haar feature values, with integral image, is only related to the values of four rectangle's endpoints and the calculating is only concerning adding and subtracting. Therefore, integral image improves the speed of face recognition largely[5].

2.2 Introduction of Real AdaBoost Algorithm

(1) Given the set of training samples S={(x1,y1),(x2,y2),...... (xn,yn)}, weak classifier space H. In the set, x∈X is a sample vector; y=±1 is class label; n is the number of samples. The initialized sample weight is Dt(i)=1/n,i=1,2,......,n.

(2) For t=1,2,......,T(T is the number of features which are aimed to get.):
①Apply the following steps to every weak classifier in H:
1) Divide the sample space X to x1, x2, x3, ..., xn;
2) With the weight of training samples Dt, calculating:

$$W_k^i = P(x_i \in X_j, y_i = k)$$
$$= \sum_{\substack{x_i \in x \\ y_i = k}} D_t(i), \quad k = \pm 1$$

3) Under the division, set the output of weak classifier as:

$$\forall x \in X_j, h(x) = \frac{1}{2}\ln(\frac{W_{+1}^j + \varepsilon}{W_{-1}^j + \varepsilon}), \quad j = 1,2,......, m.$$

e is a tiny positive number.
4) Calculating the initialization factor:

$$Z = 2\sum_j \sqrt{W_{+1}^j W_{-1}^j}$$

② Select ht in weak classifier space to minimize Z:

$$Z_t = \min_{h \in H} Z,$$
$$h_t = \operatorname{argmin}_{h \in H} Z,$$

③ Update the weight of training samples:

$$D_{t+1}(i) = D_t(i)\frac{\exp[-y_i h_t(x_i)]}{Z_t\%}$$

Zt is the initialization factor, to make Dt+1 a probability distribution.
(3) The final strong classifier is:

$$H(x) = sign[\sum_{t=1}^{T} h_t(x) - b]$$

b is threshold which is set manually, usually 0. Similarly, we define the confidence rate of H is:

$$conf_H(x) = |\sum_t h_t(x) - b|$$

3 Kalman Forecast

Simulating the motion situation of the "ready-for-detect" target in front of CCD camera, we suppose the motion of the target both in x and y axles are even-speed straight motion which is bothered by a random acceleration α[6]. α is a random variable, $a(t) \sim N(0, \sigma_\omega^2)$ .And the motion state vector of the "ready-for-detect" target is supposed as follows:

$$X(k)=[XMO(k),YMO(k),Vx(k),Vy(k)]T,$$

where XMO(k) and YMO(k) are the abscissa and ordinate of the "ready-to-detect" target; Vx(k) and Vy(k) are the speeds of the "ready-to-detect" target in x and y axles. The measure matrix is Y(k):

$$Y(k) =[XME(k),YME(k)]T,$$

where XME(k) and YME(k) are the measure abscissa and measure ordinate of the "ready-to-detect" target. So Kalman anticipation algorithm includes two models:
Motion state vector model:

$$X(k+1)=A(k)X(k)+W(k),$$

where A(k) is state transition matrix and W(k) donates system perturbation.
Measure vector model:

$$Y(k) =C(k)X(k)+M(k),$$

where C(k) is the state transition matrix from current to current measurement and M(k) represents measurement uncertainty. Because the motion of the target is supposed to be even-speed straight motion and Y(k) only involves position, these two models could be also described with the following two matrixes:

$$\begin{bmatrix} X_{MO}(k+1) \\ Y_{MO}(k+1) \\ Vx(k+1) \\ Vy(k+1) \end{bmatrix} = \begin{bmatrix} 1,0,t,0 \\ 0,1,0,t \\ 0,0,1,0 \\ 0,0,0,1 \end{bmatrix} \begin{bmatrix} X_{MO}(k) \\ Y_{MO}(k) \\ Vx(k) \\ Vy(k) \end{bmatrix} + W(k)$$

and

$$\begin{bmatrix} X_{ME}(k) \\ Y_{ME}(k) \end{bmatrix} = \begin{bmatrix} 1,0,0,0 \\ 0,1,0,0 \end{bmatrix} \begin{bmatrix} X_{MO}(k) \\ Y_{MO}(k) \\ Vx(k) \\ Vy(k) \end{bmatrix} + M(k)$$

where t is the time interval between adjacent images; the state transition process noise covariance σ_ω^2 equals 1; M(k) is normally distributed as p(M)~N(0,R), and R represents measurement noise covariance.

4   Active Illumination

The illumination condition influences the effect of face recognition to a great extent because that face recognition is based on the calculating of gray on faces. And in the process of practical face recognition, the illumination condition always changes. Shiny illumination, dark illumination and shadow will all make the accuracy of face recognition descend to a great extent. Up to present, illumination variation is still one of the bottlenecks of the practical face recognition system[7]. So we need to compensate the illumination. Many solutions have been brought up for the illumination compensation, such as SFS method[8], lateral marking of face organs[9], and two-dimensional Gabor strengthening edge outline[10]. Some of these methods are directed against special images, and others have complicated calculating process, so they all have limitation respectively in the practical application.

With the research of infrared illumination condition, we discover that, in infrared illumination condition, the distribution of gray is much more even than that in natural light condition. So against variation of natural light, the variation of infrared illumination influences the effect of face recognition in a much smaller degree. And the active infrared illumination this paper brings up is a kind of illumination compensation based on hardware, which could make sure every image collected is in the same illumination condition. So the active infrared illumination not only compensates illumination condition greatly, but also extends the sphere of illumination compensation.

We use some hardware to supply infrared illumination and capture images, which contains the array of infrared LED, monitor, video capture card, video transmission line and PC. Array of infrared LED is responsible for providing infrared illumination in stable intensity; monitor is responsible for capturing images and video transmission line is responsible for transmitting the images to video capture card which is installed in PC. Then, with some relative program, PC will deal with the images.

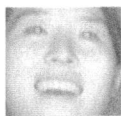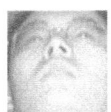

(a)   Examples of face samples(including front faces, a little degree leaning faces, faces with glasses, faces with facial expression and so on)

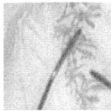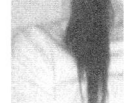

(a)   Examples of non-face samples

Fig. 4. Examples of samples

Fig. 5. Face recognition in practical video sequence (the black frames in the images are face area)

5 Experiment and Conclusion

In our experiment, we train a waterfall face recognition system which has eight layers [11]. Because in practical application, non-face samples are much more than face samples, we decide that the ratio of face number and non-face number is 1:13. The number of face samples in our experiment is 6000, and the number of non-face samples is 78000. Besides, to solve the problem that the non-face samples, which have more abundant texture, are much easier to be classified wrongly, we make sure the non-face samples which have abundant texture are of a certain proportion when we do our best to make non-face samples discrete. Some samples we use in our experiment are shown in Fig.4. Wrong-recognition rate of our face recognition system is less than two percent in our experiment. The practical face recognition in video sequence is shown in Fig.5. There is no miss-recognition of faces in our experiment, and rare wrong-recognition of non-faces.

In this paper, a novel face recognition method based on Real AdaBoost and Kalman Forecast has been brought up. Real AdaBoost algorithm has continuous confidence-rate, so it could raise the face recognition accuracy; with tracking human faces detected, Kalman Forecast can speed up the whole face recognition process; active illumination could provide infrared illumination in stable intensity, and basically eliminate the influence of illumination variation on face recognition. With the experiment, we prove that the new recognition method has great accuracy and it is real-time. At the same time, it is robust for illumination variation, a little degree leaning of human face and variation of facial expression. So the application of this novel face recognition based on Real AdaBoost and Kalman Forecast will have a pretty good future.

Acknowledgement. This research activity has been partially funded by Chinese National Natural Science Fund Commission, the Scientific Research Foundation of Graduate School of NanJing University and Research and Innovation Project for College Graduates of JiangSu Province.

References

1. Liang, L.: A Survey of Human Face Recognition. Chinese Journal of Computer 5, 449–458 (2002)
2. Zhangjie, Yang, X., Zhao, M.: Eyes detection based on Hough transform. Compute Engineering and Application 27, 43–44 (2005)
3. Yano, K., Lshihara, K., Btakikawa, M.: Detection of eye blinking from video camera with dynamic ROI fixation. IEEE International Conference on Systems, Man, and Cybernetics 6, 335–339 (1999)
4. Kumar, V.P., Poggio, T.: Learning based approach to real time tracking and analysis of faces (1999),
   http://cbcl.mit.Edu/cbcl/publications/ai·publications
5. Zhao, N.: Face Recognition Based on AdaBoost. Bachelor Thesis. Peking University (2005)

6. Yan, C., Wang, Y., Zhang, Z.: A Novel Real-Time Eye Detection in Human-Computer Interaction. In: 2010 Second International Conference on E-Learning, E-Business, Enterprise Information Systems, and E-Government (EEEE 2010), December 11, vol. 1, pp. 57–62.

7. Zheng, Q.: Facial illumination compensation based on composite transformation (February 2008)

8. Tsengyc, Chenyy, Panhk: A secure data hiding scheme forbinmy images. IEEE Transactions on Communications 50(8), 1227–1231 (2002)

9. Fridich, J., Goljan, M., Hogea, D.: Steganalysis of JPEG images: Breaking the F5 algorithm. In: Petitcolas, F.A.P. (ed.) IH 2002. LNCS, vol. 2578, pp. 310–323. Springer, Heidelberg (2003)

10. Fridich, J., Goljan, M., Du, R.: Recognition LSB steganography in color and gray-scale images. Magazine of IEEE Multimedia: Special Issue on Security 8(4), 22–28 (2001)

11. Viola, P., Jones, M.: Rapid Object Recognition using a Boosted Cascade of Simple Features. In: Proceeding of IEEE Conference on Computer Vision and Pattern Recognition, Kauai Hawaii, USA, pp. 905–910 (2001)

A Complete Gradient Clustering Algorithm

Piotr Kulczycki[1,2] and Małgorzata Charytanowicz[1,3]

[1] Systems Research Institute, Polish Academy of Sciences,
Center for Stochastic Data Analysis Methods,
Newelska 6, PL-01-447 Warsaw, Poland
{kulczycki,mchmat}@ibspan.waw.pl
[2] Cracow University of Technology, Department of Automatic
Control and Information Technology, Cracow, Poland
[3] Catholic University of Lublin,
Institute of Mathematics and Computer Science,
Lublin, Poland

Abstract. A gradient clustering algorithm, based on the nonparametric methodology of statistical kernel estimators, expanded to its complete form, enabling implementation without particular knowledge of the theoretical aspects or laborious research, is presented here. The possibilities of calculating tentative optimal parameter values, and then – based on illustrative interpretation – their potential changes, result in the proposed Complete Gradient Clustering Algorithm possessing many original and valuable, from an applicational point of view, properties. Above all the number of clusters is not arbitrarily imposed but fitted to a real data structure. It is also possible to increase the scale of the number (still avoiding arbitrary assumptions), as well as the proportion of clusters in areas of dense and sparse situation of data elements. The method is universal in character and can be applied to a wide range of practical problems, in particular from the bioinformatics, management and engineering fields.

Keywords: Data analysis and mining, clustering, nonparametric statistical methods, kernel estimators, numerical algorithms.

1 Introduction

Consider the m-elements set of n-dimensional vectors:

$$x_1, x_2, \ldots, x_m \in \mathsf{R}^n \ . \tag{1}$$

Generally, the task of clustering relies upon the division of the above set of data into subsets (clusters), each containing elements similar to one another, yet significantly differing from elements of other subsets. Such a general definition results in the mathematical apparatus not having a natural methodology, the existence becomes obvious of an excessive number of heuristic iterative procedures, each of them characterized by different advantages and disadvantages, as well as certain properties which may be of benefit in some problems and of no profit in others.

H. Deng et al. (Eds.): AICI 2011, Part III, LNAI 7004, pp. 497–504, 2011.

In the now classic paper [2] Fukunaga and Hostetler formulated a natural idea of clustering, making use of notable possibilities entering into widespread use of statistical kernel estimators at that time, today the main method of nonparametric estimation. The basis of the above concept is treating data set (1) as a random sample obtained from an n-dimensional random variable, calculating the kernel estimator of the density of its distribution, and making the clear assumption that particular clusters correspond to modes (local maxima) of the estimator. The presented method was formulated as a general idea only, leaving the details to the painstaking analysis of the user.

The aim of this publication is to present the Gradient Clustering Algorithm based on Fukunaga's and Hostetler's concept in its complete form, suitable for direct use without requiring users to have a deeper statistical knowledge or conduct laborious research. All parameters appearing here can be effectively calculated using convenient numerical procedures based on optimizing criteria. Moreover, making use of a near-intuitive interpretation of the concept of the gradient algorithm itself, as well as its theoretical base – kernel estimators, an analysis of the significance of particular parameters will be given, and the effects achieved through their possible change with respect to the above mentioned optimal values, depending on conditions of the problem in question and user preferences.

The main feature of the algorithm under research is that it does not demand strict assumptions regarding the desired number of clusters, which allows the number obtained to be better suited to a real data structure. In the paper, the parameter directly responsible for the number of clusters will be indicated. At a preliminary stage its value can be calculated effectively using optimizing criteria. It will also be shown how possible changes to this value influence the increase or decrease in the number of clusters, although without defining their exact number. Moreover, the next parameter is indicated, the value of which will influence the proportion between the number of clusters in dense and sparse areas of data set elements. Here also its value can be assumed based on optimizing reasons, or possibly submitted to modifications with the goal of increasing the number of clusters in dense areas of data set elements while simultaneously reducing or even eliminating them from sparse regions, or vice-versa. This possibility is particularly worth underlining as practically non-existent in other clustering procedures. Moreover, the appropriate relation between the two above mentioned parameters allows for a reduction, or even elimination of clusters in sparse areas, without influencing the number of clusters in dense areas of data set elements.

The broader description of the method presented here is available in the paper [4].

2   Statistical Kernel Estimators

Let the n-dimensional random variable X be given, with a distribution characterized by the density f. Its kernel estimator $\hat{f} : \mathbb{R}^n \to [0, \infty)$, calculated using experimentally obtained values for the m-element random sample (1), in its basic form is defined as

$$\hat{f}(x) = \frac{1}{mh^n} \sum_{i=1}^{m} K\left(\frac{x - x_i}{h}\right), \tag{2}$$

where $m \in N \setminus \{0\}$, the coefficient $h > 0$ is called a smoothing parameter, while the measurable function $K : R^n \rightarrow [0, \infty)$ of unit integral $\int_{R^n} K(x) \, dx = 1$, symmetrical with respect to zero and having a weak global maximum in this place, takes the name of a kernel. The choice of form of the kernel K and the calculation of the smoothing parameter h is made most often with the criterion of the mean integrated square error.

Thus, the choice of the kernel form has – from a statistical point of view – no practical meaning and thanks to this, it becomes possible to take into account primarily properties of the estimator obtained and/or aspects of calculations, advantageous from the point of view of the applicational problem under investigation (for broader discussion see [3 – Section 3.1.3], [8 – Sections 2.7 and 4.5]).

The fixing of the smoothing parameter h has significant meaning for quality of estimation. Too small a value causes a large number of local extremes of the estimator $\hat{f}$ to appear, which is contrary to the actual properties of real populations. On the other hand, too big values of the parameter h result in overflattening of this estimator, hiding specific properties of the distribution under investigation. In practice, the value of the smoothing parameter h can be calculated with confirmed algorithms available in literature. In the multidimensional case the most common and universal cross-validation method is proposed [3 – Section 3.1.5], [7 – Section 3.4.3], however in the one-dimensional case the convenient plug-in method [3 – Section 3.1.5], [8 – Section 3.6.1] can be recommended.

For the basic definition of kernel estimator (2), the influence of the smoothing parameter on particular kernels is the same. Advantageous results are obtained thanks to the individualization of this effect, achieved through so-called modification of the smoothing parameter [3 – Section 3.1.6], [7 – Section 5.3.1]. It relies on mapping the positive modifying parameters $s_1, s_2, \ldots, s_m$ on particular kernels, described as

$$s_i = \left(\frac{\hat{f}_*(x_i)}{\bar{s}} \right)^{-c}, \tag{3}$$

where $c \in [0, \infty)$, $\hat{f}_*$ denotes the kernel estimator without modification, $\bar{s}$ is the geometrical mean of the numbers $\hat{f}_*(x_1)$, $\hat{f}_*(x_2)$, ... , $\hat{f}_*(x_m)$, and finally, defining the kernel estimator with modification of the smoothing parameter in the following form:

$$\hat{f}(x) = \frac{1}{mh^n} \sum_{i=1}^{m} \frac{1}{s_i^n} K \left(\frac{x - x_i}{h s_i} \right). \tag{4}$$

Thanks to the above procedure, the areas in which the kernel estimator assumes small values (e.g. in the range of "tails"), are additionally flattened, and the areas connected with large values – peaked, which allows to better reveal individual properties of a distribution. The parameter c stands for the intensity of the modification procedure. Based on indications for the criterion of the integrated mean square error, the value

$$c = 0.5 \qquad\qquad (5)$$

can be suggested.

Practical applications may also use some other additional procedures, generally improving the quality of the estimator, and others – optional – possibly fitting the model to an existing reality. For the first group one should recommend a linear transformation [3 – Section 3.1.4], [7 – Section 4.2.1], while for the second, the boundaries of a support [3 – Section 3.1.8], [7 – Section 2.10].

Detailed information regarding kernel estimators can be found in the monographs [3], [7], [8].

3 Complete Gradient Clustering Algorithm

Consider – as in the Introduction – the m-elements set of n-dimensional vectors (1). This will be treated as a random sample obtained from the n-dimensional random variable X , with distribution having the density f . Using the methodology described in Section 2, the kernel estimator $\hat{f}$ can be created. Take the natural assumption that particular clusters are related to its modes, or local maxima of the function $\hat{f}$, and mapping onto them elements of set (1) is realized by transposing those elements in the gradient $\nabla\hat{f}$ direction, with the appropriate fixed step.

The above is carried out iteratively with the Gradient Clustering Algorithm, based on the classic Newtonian procedure, defined as

$$x_j^0 = x_j \quad \text{for} \quad j = 1, 2, ..., m \qquad\qquad (6)$$

$$x_j^{k+1} = x_j^k + b\frac{\nabla\hat{f}(x_j^k)}{\hat{f}(x_j^k)} \quad \text{for} \quad j = 1, 2, ..., m \ \text{ and } \ k = 0, 1, ..., k^* , \qquad (7)$$

where $b > 0$ and $k^* \in N \setminus \{0\}$. In practice it is recommended that $b = h^2/(n+2)$.

In order to refine the above concept to the state of a complete algorithm, the following aspects need to be formulated and analyzed in detail:

1. formula of the kernel estimator $\hat{f}$;

2. setting a stop condition (and consequently the number of steps k^*);
3. definition of a procedure for creating clusters and assigning to them particular elements of set (1), after the last, k^* -th step;
4. analysis of influence of the values of parameters on results obtained.

The above tasks are the subjects of the following sections.

3.1 Formula of the Kernel Estimator

For the needs of further parts of the concept presented here, the kernel estimator $\hat{f}$ is assumed in a form with modification of smoothing parameter of standard intensity (5).

The kernel K is recommended in the most universal normal form [3 – Section 3.1.3], [8 – Sections 2.7 and 4.5] due to its differentiability in the whole domain, convenience for analytical considerations connected with gradient, and assuming positive values, which in every case guards against division by zero in formula (7).

3.2 Setting a Stop Condition

It is assumed that algorithm (6)-(7) should be finished, if after the consecutive k-th step the following condition is fulfilled

$$\left| D_k - D_{k-1} \right| \le a D_0 \ , \tag{8}$$

where $a > 0$ and

$$D_0 = \sum_{i=1}^{m-1} \sum_{j=i+1}^{m} d(x_i , x_j) \tag{9}$$

$$D_{k-1} = \sum_{i=1}^{m-1} \sum_{j=i+1}^{m} d(x_i^{k-1} , x_j^{k-1}) \ , \qquad D_k = \sum_{i=1}^{m-1} \sum_{j=i+1}^{m} d(x_i^{k} , x_j^{k}) \ , \tag{10}$$

while d means Euclidean metric in R^n. Therefore, D_0 and D_{k-1}, D_k denote sums of distances between particular elements of set (1) before starting the algorithm and after the $(k-1)$-th and k-th step, respectively. Primarily it is recommended that $a = 0.001$; the potential decrease of this value does not significantly influence the obtained results, although increases require individual verification of their correctness.

Finally, if after the k-th step condition (8) is fulfilled, then

$$k^* = k \tag{11}$$

and consequently this step is treated as the last one.

3.3 Procedure for Creating Clusters and Assigning Particular Elements to Them

At this stage the following set is investigated

$$x_1^{k^*} , \ x_2^{k^*} , ..., x_m^{k^*} \ , \tag{12}$$

consisting of the elements of set (1) after the k^*-th step of algorithm (6)-(7). Following this, the set of mutual distances of the above elements

$$\left\{ d(x_i^{k^*} , x_j^{k^*}) \right\}_{\substack{i=1, 2, ..., m-1 \\ j=i+1, i+2, ..., m}} \tag{13}$$

should be defined. Taking the above set as a sample of a one-dimensional random variable, the auxiliary kernel estimator $\hat{f}_d$ of mutual distances of the elements of set

(12) ought to be calculated. Regarding the methodology of kernel estimators presented in Section 2, normal kernel is once again proposed, as is the use of the procedure of smoothing parameter modification with standard value of parameter (5), and additionally left-sided boundary of a support to the interval $[0, \infty)$.

The next task is to find – with suitable precision – the "first" (i.e. for the smallest value of an argument) a local minimum of the function $\hat{f}_d$ belonging to the interval $(0, D)$, where $D = \max\limits_{\substack{i=1,2,...,m-1 \\ j=i+1,i+2,...,m}} d(x_i, x_j)$. For this purpose one should treat set (13) as a random sample, calculate its standard deviation σ_d, and next take in sequence the values x from the set

$$\{ 0, \; 0.01 \cdot \sigma_d, \; 0.02 \cdot \sigma_d, \; ... \; , \; [\text{int}(100 \cdot D) - 1] \cdot 0.01 \cdot \sigma_d \} , \tag{14}$$

where $\text{int}(100 \cdot D)$ denotes an integral part of the number $100 \cdot D$, until the finding of the first (the smallest) of them which fulfils the condition

$$\hat{f}_d(x - 0.01\sigma_d) > \hat{f}_d(x) \quad \text{and} \quad \hat{f}_d(x) \le \hat{f}_d(x + 0.01\sigma_d) . \tag{15}$$

Such calculated value [1] will be denoted hereinafter as x_d, and it can be interpreted as half the distance between „centers" of potential clusters lying closest together.

Finally, the clusters will be created. To this aim one should:

1. take the element of set (12) and initially create a one-element cluster containing it;
2. find an element of set (12) different from the one in the cluster, closer than x_d; if there is such an element, then it should be added to the cluster; in the other case – proceed to point 4;
3. find an element of set (12) different from elements in the cluster, closer than x_d to at least one of them; if there is such an element, then it should be added to the cluster and point 3 repeated;
4. add the obtained cluster to a "list of clusters" and remove from set (12) elements of this cluster; if this so-reduced set (12) is not empty, return to point 1; in the other case – finish the algorithm.

3.4 Analysis of Influence of the Values of Parameters on Results Obtained

It is worth repeating that the presented clustering algorithm did not require a preliminary, often arbitrary in practice, assumption concerning number of clusters – their size depending solely on the internal structure of data, given as set (1). In the application of the Complete Gradient Clustering Algorithm in the presented above basic form, the values of the parameters used are effectively calculated taking optimizing reasons into account. However, optionally – if the researcher makes the decision – by an appropriate change in values of kernel estimator parameters it is

---

[1] If such a value does not exist, then one should recognize the existence of one cluster and finish the procedure.

possible to influence the size of number of clusters, and also the proportion of their appearance in dense areas in relation to sparse regions of elements in this set.

As mentioned in Section 2, too small a value of the smoothing parameter h results in the appearance of too many local extremes of the kernel estimator, while too great a value causes its excessive smoothing. In this situation lowering the value of the parameter h in respect to that obtained by procedures based on the criterion of the mean integrated square error creates as a consequence an increase in the number of clusters. At the same time, an increase in the smoothing parameter value results in fewer clusters. It should be underlined that in both cases, despite having an influence on size of cluster number, their exact number will still depend solely on the internal structure of data. Based on research carried out one can recommend a change in the value of the smoothing parameter of between -25% and $+50\%$. Outside of this range, results obtained require individual verification.

Next, as mentioned in Section 2, the intensity of modification of the smoothing parameter is implied by the value of the parameter c, given as standard by formula (5). Its increase smoothes the kernel estimator in areas where elements of set (1) are sparse, and also sharpens it in dense areas – in consequence, if the value of the parameter c is raised, then the number of clusters in sparse areas of data decreases, while at the same time increasing in dense regions. Inverse effects can be seen in the case of lowering this parameter value. Based on research carried out one can recommend the value of the parameter c to be between 0 (meaning no modification) and 1.5. An increase greater than 1.5 requires individual verification of the validity of results obtained. Particularly it is recommended that $c = 1$.

Practice, however, often prevents changes to the clusters in dense areas of data – the most important from an applicational point of view – while at the same time requiring a reduction or even elimination of clusters in sparse regions, as they frequently pertain to atypical elements (outliers). Putting the above considerations together, one can propose an increase of both the standard scale of the smoothing parameter modification (5) and the value of the smoothing parameter h calculated on the criterion of the mean integrated square error, to the value h^* defined by the formula

$$h^* = \left(\frac{3}{2}\right)^{c-0.5} h \ . \tag{16}$$

The joint action of both these factors results in a twofold smoothing of the function $\hat{f}$ in the regions where the elements of set (1) are sparse. Meanwhile these factors more or less compensate for each other in dense areas, thereby having practically no influence on the detection of these clusters. Based on research carried out one can recommend a change in the value of the parameter c from 0.5 to 1.0. Increasing it to above 1.0 demands individual verification of the validity of results obtained. Particularly it is recommended that $c = 0.75$.

More details of the method presented above, with illustrative examples, can be found in the paper [4].

4 Final Comments

The algorithm described in this paper was comprehensively tested both for random statistical data as well as generally available benchmarks. It was also compared with other well-known clustering methods, k-means and hierarchical procedures. It is difficult to confirm here the absolute supremacy of any one of them – to a large degree the advantage stemmed from the conditions and requirements formulated with regard to the problem under consideration, although the Complete Gradient Clustering Algorithm allowed for greater possibilities of adjustment to the real structure of data, and consequently the obtained results were more justifiable to a natural human point of view. A very important feature for practitioners was the possibility of firstly functioning using standard parameters values, and the option of changing them afterwards – according to individual needs – by the modification of two of them with easy and illustrative interpretations. These properties were actively used in three projects from the domains of bioinformatics (categorization of grains for seed production [1]), management (marketing support strategy for mobile phone operator [5]) and engineering (synthesis of fuzzy PID controller [6]).

References

1. Charytanowicz, M., Niewczas, J., Kulczycki, P., Kowalski, P.A., Lukasik, S., Zak, S.: Gradient Clustering Algorithm for Features Analysis of X-Ray Images. In: Pietka, E., Kawa, J. (eds.) Information Technologies in Biomedicine, vol. 2, pp. 15–24. Springer, Berlin (2010)
2. Fukunaga, K., Hostetler, L.D.: The estimation of the gradient of a density function, with applications in Pattern Recognition. IEEE Transactions on Information Theory 21, 32–40 (1975)
3. Kulczycki, P.: Estymatory jadrowe w analizie systemowej. WNT, Warsaw (2005)
4. Kulczycki, P., Charytanowicz, M.: A Complete Gradient Clustering Algorithm Formed with Kernel Estimators. International Journal of Applied Mathematics and Computer Science 20, 123–134 (2010)
5. Kulczycki, P., Daniel, K.: Metoda wspomagania strategii marketingowej operatora telefonii komorkowej. Przeglad Statystyczny 56, 116–134 (2009)
6. Lukasik, S., Kowalski, P.A., Charytanowicz, M., Kulczycki, P.: Fuzzy Models Synthesis with Kernel-Density Based Clustering Algorithm. In: Ma, J., Yin, Y., Yu, J., Zhou, S. (eds.) Fifth International Conference on Fuzzy Systems and Knowledge Discovery, vol. 3, pp. 449–453. IEEE Computer Society, Los Alamitos (2008)
7. Silverman, B.W.: Density Estimation for Statistics and Data Analysis. Chapman and Hall, London (1986)
8. Wand, M.P., Jones, M.C.: Kernel Smoothing. Chapman and Hall, London (1994)

Dimensionality Reduction with Category Information Fusion and Non-negative Matrix Factorization for Text Categorization

Wenbin Zheng[1,2], Yuntao Qian[1,*], and Hong Tang[3,4]

[1] College of Computer Science and Technology, Zhejiang University, Hangzhou, China
[2] College of Information Engineering, China Jiliang University, Hangzhou, China
[3] School of Aeronautics and Astronautics, Zhejiang University, Hangzhou, China
[4] College of Metrological Technology & Engineering, China Jiliang University, Hangzhou, China

Abstract. Dimensionality reduction can efficiently improve computing performance of classifiers in text categorization, and non-negative matrix factorization could map the high dimensional term space into a low dimensional semantic subspace easily. Meanwhile, the non-negative of the basis vectors could provide a meaningful explanation for the semantic subspace. However, it usually could not achieve a satisfied classification performance because it is sensitive to the noise, data missing and outlier as a linear reconstruction method. This paper proposes a novel approach in which the train text and its category information are fused and a transformation matrix that maps the term space into a semantic subspace is obtained by a basis orthogonality non-negative matrix factorization and truncation. Finally, the dimensionality can be reduced aggressively with these transformations. Experimental results show that the proposed approach remains a good classification performance in a very low dimensional case.

Keywords: Text Categorization, Dimensionality reduction, Non-negative Matrix Factorization, Category Fusion.

1 Introduction

Text categorization (TC) is a task of automatically assigning predefined categories to a given text document based on its content [1]. Generally, the classical text representation method based on machine learning techniques is the vector space model (VSM) [2] in which the high dimensionality of the input feature space is a major difficulty of TC [3].

The latent semantic indexing (LSI) [4] and the topic model [5] are commonly used dimensionality reduction methods which can map a term space into a latent semantic subspace; however, it is difficult to explain the physic meaning because the negative value is permitted in its basis vectors.

---

* Corresponding author.

H. Deng et al. (Eds.): AICI 2011, Part III, LNAI 7004, pp. 505–512, 2011.
© Springer-Verlag Berlin Heidelberg 2011

Non-negative matrix factorization (NMF) is a matrix factorization method with a non-negative constrain [6], which can map the term space to the semantic subspace for TC [7]. Mathematically, a terms-by-documents matrix X can be decomposed as $X_{m \times n} \approx W_{m \times r} \times H_{r \times n}$, where m and n are the number of the terms and documents respectively, and r is a positive integer, W is called basis matrix and H is called coefficient matrix. Because each column vector of W is constituted with some non-negative values of all terms, it can be regarded as the latent semantic basis vector, and all these basis vectors span a semantic subspace with dimensionality r. When $r \ll \min\{m, n\}$, the dimensionality of the semantic subspace is far less than the dimensionality of the original term space. However, as a linear reconstructed method, it usually could not achieve a satisfied classification performance in that subspace because it is sensitive to the noise, data missing and outlier which will affect the discriminative ability of basis vectors.

This paper proposes a novel method to reduce the dimensionality aggressively by fusing category information and with basis orthogonality non-negative matrix factorization and truncation.

We give a category coding schema and fusing the weighting of training documents with their category coding into an extended matrix. Therefore the extended dimension generated by the category information can decrease the impact of the noise, data missing and outlier. After that, a NMF iteration algorithm is designed in which the basis vectors are driven to orthogonality to enhance the stability of factorization. Furthermore, a transformation matrix mapping the term space to the semantic subspace is obtained via the matrix factorization and truncation. Then a document can be represented as a point in the low dimensional semantic subspace, and TC is implemented in this subspace.

The rest of this paper is organized as follows: Section 2 reviews the related work briefly. Section 3 explains the proposed method in detail. Experimental results and analysis are shown in Section 4. Finally, we give our conclusions in Section 5.

2   Related Works

Some works have used NMF to reduce the dimensionality: Hoyer adds an explicitly constrain to control the sparseness of basis and coefficient matrices, but the sparseness does not necessarily contribute to the classification performance [8]. Guillamet et al. integrate the class information into NMF by assigning large weight values to the minority classes [9], but it is hard to suit the multi-label situation of TC (i.e. a document might belong to multiple categories in the same time). Liu, Yuan et al. utilize the NMF to reduce the dimensionality of the micro-array data but it limits the number of instances [10]. Silva and Ribeiro use NMF to extract the semantic features for TC [7], however it does not take into account the information of the category.

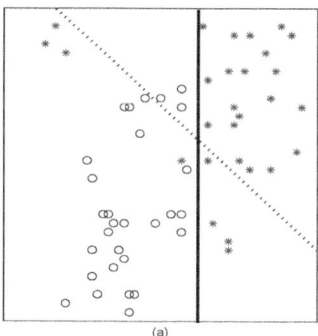 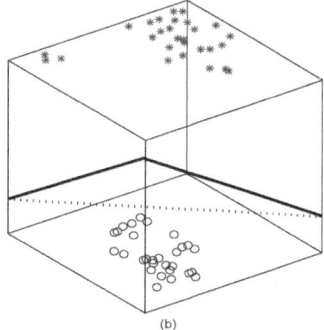

Fig. 1. Panel (a) shows there is no dimensionality extended, the solid line represents an ideally classification bound and the dash line represents the classification bound affected by three outlier points. Panel (b) shows another case of the dimensionality extended. The linear separability increases by adding some new dimension generated by category information.

3   Dimensionality Reduction Method

3.1   Category Information Fusion

Because the NMF is a linear reconstructed method, its goal is to obtain the optimal representative feature rather than the optimal classification feature. So the noise, missing data and outliers existing in the high dimensionality space also exist in the low-dimensional subspace generated by NMF. As panel (a) of Figure 1 shows, these points will affect the establishment of the correct classification boundary. Therefore, we wish to utilize category information as the extended dimensionality and fuse them into training data. So the linear separability of data increases in the new dimensionality extended space illustrated in panel (b) of Figure 1.

The category information fusion can be implemented with three stages: document weighting, category information coding, and fusion. The document weighting is presented as follows:

Given a document $d = (t_1, t_2, \cdots, t_m)$, where m is the number of dimensionality in the feature space. The $tfidf$ value [2] for each term is defined as:

$$tfidf(t_i, d) = tf(t_i, d) \times idf(t_i), \tag{1}$$

where $tf(t_i, d)$ denotes the number of times that t_i occurred in d, and $idf(t_i)$ is the inverse document frequency which is defined: $idf(t_i) = \log(n/df(t_i))$, where n is the number of documents in training set, and $df(t_i)$ denotes the number of documents in training set in which t_i occurs at least once. Then a document can be represented as a vector:

$$d = (w_1, w_2, \cdots, w_m)^T, \tag{2}$$

where w_i is evaluated as: $w_i = tfidf(t_i, d)/\sqrt{\sum\limits_{j}^{m} tfidf(t_j, d)^2}$.

In order to represent the category information uniformly for multi-label or uni-label corpus, we extend the category coding scheme $1-of-K$ [11] to $k-of-K$, i.e. define the class vector corresponding to the document d as follows

$$c = (b_1, \cdots, b_i, \cdots, b_k)^T, \tag{3}$$

where k is the number of category in dataset, and b_i is equal to 1 or 0 depending on whether the related document belongs to the corresponding categories. For example, assuming there are four categories ($k = 4$), a document $d = (w_1, w_2, \cdots, w_m)^T$ belongs to the first and the forth categories, then the related class vector is $c = (1, 0, 0, 1)^T$. Then we fuse d and c into a new extended vector x:

$$x = \begin{bmatrix} d \\ \lambda \times c \end{bmatrix}, \tag{4}$$

where λ is a parameter used to control the tradeoff between train text d and its corresponding category information c. Finally, all train documents are fused into an extended matrix X, represented as

$$X = \begin{bmatrix} D \\ \lambda \times C \end{bmatrix}, \tag{5}$$

where D is the weighting matrix of all train documents, C is the class matrix related to D, and each column of X is an extended vector obtained by Eq. (4). Then X will be decomposed with the orthogonal NMF given below.

3.2   Orthogonal NMF

Given the extended matrix X, let

$$X_{m \times n} \approx W_{m \times r} \times H_{r \times n}. \tag{6}$$

Because of the uniqueness problems of scaling and permutation of NMF, we wish the basis matrix W tends to the orthogonal normalization, i.e. $W^T W - I = O$, where I is the unit matrix and O is the corresponding zero matrix. We consider it as a constrain term with parameter W, and add it into the loss function which can be constructed as follows

$$L(W, H) = ||X - WH||_F^2 + \alpha ||W^T W - I||_F^2, \\ s.t. W, H \geq 0 \tag{7}$$

where α is used to balance the tradeoff between the approximation error and the orthogonal constraint. Same with [12], the multiplicative update algorithm is:

$$W_{i,j} \leftarrow W_{i,j} \frac{(WH^T + 2\alpha W)_{i,j}}{(WHH^T + 2\alpha WW^T W)_{i,j}}, \quad H_{i,j} \leftarrow H_{i,j} \frac{(W^T X)_{i,j}}{(W^T WH)_{i,j}}. \tag{8}$$

3.3   Dimensionality Reduction and TC

Assuming the matrix X (in Eq. (5)) is decomposed (with Eq. (8)) as follows

$$X = \begin{bmatrix} D_{m \times n} \\ \lambda \times C_{k \times n} \end{bmatrix} \approx W_{(m+k) \times r} \times H_{r \times n}, \tag{9}$$

let

$$W_{(m+k) \times r} = \begin{bmatrix} S_{m \times r} \\ L_{k \times r} \end{bmatrix}, \tag{10}$$

where S is obtained by truncating W. Then

$$\begin{bmatrix} D_{m \times n} \\ \lambda \times C_{k \times n} \end{bmatrix} \approx \begin{bmatrix} S_{m \times r} \times H_{r \times n} \\ L_{k \times r} \times H_{r \times n} \end{bmatrix}. \tag{11}$$

So $D_{m \times n} \approx S_{m \times r} \times H_{r \times n}$, where S can be regarded as a matrix formed with the semantic vectors. Defining

$$P = (S_{m \times r})^{\dagger}, \tag{12}$$

then

$$\hat{D}_{r \times n} \approx P \times D_{m \times n}, \tag{13}$$

where P can be regarded as the transformation matrix which maps documents from the term space into a semantic subspace spanned by S, and $\hat{D}$ can be regarded as the projected vector set in the semantic subspace.

Using Eq.(13), the train and test data all can be mapped from the term space to a semantic subspace. In the new semantic subspace, dimensionality could be reduced aggressively, and some classical classification algorithms can be applied. For example using the support vector machine (SVM) algorithm, a pseudo code for TC is given by algorithm 1.

4   Experiments

4.1   Dataset

Two popular TC benchmarks are tested in our experiments: Reuters-21578 and 20-newsgroups. The Reuters-21578 dataset[1] is a standard multi-label TC benchmark and contains 135 categories. In our experiments, we use a subset of the data collection which includes the 10 most frequent categories among the 135 topics and we call it Reuters-top10. We divide it into the train and test set with the standard 'ModApte' version. The pre-processed including: removing the stop words; switching upper case to lower case; stemming[2]); removing the low frequency words (less than three).

The 20-Newsgroups dataset[3] contains approximately 20,000 articles evenly divided among 20 usenet newsgroups. We also remove the low frequency words (less than three) in the data set.

---

[1] Available at http://www.daviddlewis.com/resources/testcollections/
[2] Available at http://tartarus.org/~martin/PorterStemmer/
[3] Available at http://people.csail.mit.edu/jrennie/20Newsgroups/

Algorithm 1. TC implementation

Input: the training and testing set and the setting of parameters
Output: the label of testing set
Learning stage:
 1: **for** each document d in training set **do**
 2:    evaluating the weighting of d with Eq. (2)
 3:    evaluating the extended vector x with Eq. (4)
 4: **end for**
 5: evaluating the extended matrix X with Eq. (5)
 6: factoring X into the form of Eq.(9) with Eq. (8)
 7: evaluating the transformation matrix P using Eq.(10) and Eq. (12)
 8: evaluating the projection of training set in the semantic subspace with Eq.(13)
 9: Learning SVM mode in the semantic subspace
Classification stage:
10: **for** each document d' in testing set **do**
11:    evaluating the weighting of d' with Eq. (2)
12:    evaluating $\hat{d}'$ with Eq. (13)
13:    classifying the document d' with SVM classifier in the semantic subspace
14: **end for**

4.2 Evaluation Measures

In the tests, we adapt the macroaveraged F_1 [1] as the performance measure which is defined as

$$\text{macroaveraged } F_1 = (\sum_{i}^{k} F_{1i})/k, \tag{14}$$

where k is the number of categories, F_{1i} denotes the F_1 value of the ith category.

4.3 Results and Analysis

To verify the performance of the proposed approach (denoting it as CONMF for convention), we compare it with the information grain (IG) (one of the most successful feature selection methods [13]), the ordinary NMF method [7] (denotes it as NMF), and LSI [14]. The classifier is implemented with SVMlight[4] and its default parameters are adapted. We set $\alpha = 0.5$ (Eq. (7)) and $\lambda = 1$ (Eq. (5)). The dimensionality reduction level is from about 1% to 0.1%. For each test dimensionality, we repeat the experimentation ten times and take their means as the result.

    The results are shown in Figure 2. From this figures, we can see that the performance of IG is very awful when the dimensionality is reduced aggressively, it is because that case might induce all zero value of feature vectors using feature selection method, which makes the classification failure.

---

[4] Available at http://svmlight.joachims.org/

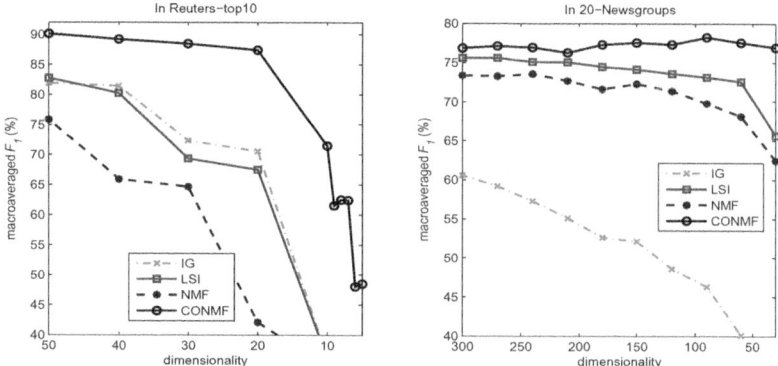

Fig. 2. Performances in Reuters-top10 and 20-newsgroups

According to the ordinary NMF method, although it has a more reasonable physical interpretation than LSI, it does not presents a good classification performance because its objective function is non-convex and it is difficult to obtain the optimal solution. Moreover, it is sensitive to the noise, data missing and outlier which will affect the establishment of the correct classification boundary.

Despite the results that the performance of IG or LSI or ordinary NMF descends drastically in the very low dimensional situation, our CONMF method obtains relatively stable performance in that case.

These figures also reveal a phenomenon that the relationship between the dimensionality of semantic subspace (or the number of semantic concepts) and the TC performance is not a linear function. In other words, the performance does not necessarily increase when the dimensionality of the semantic subspace increases and vice versa, which imply that there might exist an optimized number of semantic concepts in a specific text corpus.

5   Conclusions

This paper proposes a novel approach to reduce dimensionality aggressively. By utilizing category information as the extended dimensions, the impact of the noise, data missing and outlier could be decreased. Furthermore, with basis orthogonality non-negative matrix factorization and truncation, the data in the high dimensional term space could be mapped into a low dimensional semantic subspace. Experimental results show that the proposed approach remains a good classification performance in the very low dimensional case.

The proposed method is simply and effective, and its factorization form as well as its non-negative constrain could provide a more reasonable physical interpretation than LSI. Meanwhile, it reflects the concept about "parts form the whole" in human mind. Furthermore, the form of word-semantic-category is consistent with the cognitive process when people read articles.

For the future researches, we would like to study the dimensionality problem of the semantic subspace to enhance the stability of factorization, and try to incorporate cognitive information into the non-negative matrix factorization to improve the classification performance.

Acknowledgment. This work was supported by the Natural Science Foundation of Zhejiang Province (Grant No. Y6110147) and was supported in part by the Natural Science Foundation of Zhejiang Province (Grant No. Y1110450).

References

1. Sebastiani, F.: Machine learning in automated text categorization. ACM Computing Surveys 34(1), 1–47 (2002)
2. Salton, G., Buckley, C.: Term-weighting approaches in automatic text retrieval. Information Processing & Management 24(5), 513–523 (1988)
3. Zheng, W., Qian, Y.: Aggressive dimensionality reduction with reinforcement local feature selection for text categorization. In: Wang, F.L., Deng, H., Gao, Y., Lei, J. (eds.) AICI 2010. LNCS, vol. 6319, pp. 365–372. Springer, Heidelberg (2010)
4. Landauer, T., Foltz, P., Laham, D.: An introduction to latent semantic analysis. Discourse Processes 25(2), 259–284 (1998)
5. Zhou, S., Li, K., Liu, Y.: Text categorization based on topic model. In: Wang, G., Li, T., Grzymala-Busse, J.W., Miao, D., Skowron, A., Yao, Y. (eds.) RSKT 2008. LNCS (LNAI), vol. 5009, pp. 572–579. Springer, Heidelberg (2008)
6. Lee, D.D., Seung, H.S.: Learning the parts of objects by non-negative matrix factorization. Nature 401(6755), 788–791 (1999)
7. Silva, C., Ribeiro, B.: Knowledge extraction with non-negative matrix factorization for text classification. In: Corchado, E., Yin, H. (eds.) IDEAL 2009. LNCS, vol. 5788, pp. 300–308. Springer, Heidelberg (2009)
8. Hoyer, P.O.: Non-negative matrix factorization with sparseness constraints. Journal of Machine Learning Research 5, 1457–1469 (2004)
9. Guillamet, D., Vitri, J., Schiele, B.: Introducing a weighted non-negative matrix factorization for image classification. Pattern Recognition Letters 24(14), 2447–2454 (2003)
10. Liu, W., Yuan, K., Ye, D.: Reducing microarray data via nonnegative matrix factorization for visualization and clustering analysis. Journal of Biomedical Informatics 41(4), 602–606 (2008)
11. Bishop, C.M.: SpringerLink: Pattern recognition and machine learning, vol. 4. Springer, New York (2006)
12. Zheng, W., Zhang, H., Qian, Y.: Fast text categorization based on collaborative work in the semantic and class spaces. In: To Appear in the International Conference on Machine Learning and Cybernetics (2011)
13. Yang, Y., Pedersen, J.O.: A comparative study on feature selection in text categorization. In: Proceedings of the Fourteenth International Conference on Machine Learning, pp. 412–420, Citeseer. Morgan Kaufmann Publishers Inc, San Francisco (1997)
14. Zhang, W., Yoshida, T., Tang, X.J.: A comparative study of tf*idf, lsi and multi-words for text classification. Expert Systems with Applications 38(3), 2758–2765 (2011)

Uncorrelated Neighborhood Preserving Projections for Face Recognition

Guoqiang Wang and Xiang Gao

Department of Computer and Information Engineering,
Luoyang Institute of Science and Technology,
471023 Luoyang, Henan P.R. China
{wgq2211,gx}@163.com

Abstract. Feature extraction is a crucial step for face recognition. In this paper, based on Neighborhood Preserving Projections (NPP), a novel feature extraction method called Uncorrelated Neighborhood Preserving Projections (UNPP) is proposed for face recognition. The improvement of UNPP method over NPP method benefits mostly from two aspects: One aspect is that UNPP preserves the within-class neighboring geometry by taking into account the class label information; the other aspect is that the extracted features via UNPP are statistically uncorrelated with minimum redundancy. Experimental results on the publicly available ORL face database show that the proposed UNPP approach provides a better representation of the data and achieves much higher recognition accuracy.

Keywords: Feature extraction, Manifold learning, Neighborhood Preserving Projections, Uncorrelated constraint, Face recognition.

1 Introduction

The facial feature extraction is an important step of face recognition. The capability of facial feature extraction directly influences the performance of face recognition. In the past two decades, many feature extraction methods have been proposed, in which the most well-known ones are Principle Component Analysis (PCA) [1, 2] and Linear Discriminant Analysis (LDA) [3]. Affected by many complex factors such as expression illumination and pose, the face images likely reside on a nonlinear face manifold [5, 6, 7]. However, both PCA and LDA effectively discover only the global linear structure.

Recently, learning a compact manifold (subspace) that can preserve local structure of face images has attracted much attention. Locally Linear Embedding (LLE) [4, 5], ISOMAP [6], Laplacian Eigenmap [7] and Local Tangent Space Alignment (LTSA) [8] are the most popular manifold learning methods. But, these methods are defined only on the training set. They cannot be used for online dimensionality reduction of the testing set. So they cannot be used for face recognition directly. Linearization, kernalization, and tensorization are some often used techniques to deal with the problem [9]. Pang et al. proposed a new method, named Neighborhood Preserving

H. Deng et al. (Eds.): AICI 2011, Part III, LNAI 7004, pp. 513–520, 2011.

Projections (NPP) [10, 11], which is a linear approximation of LLE and has the locality-preserving characteristic of manifold learning. Although NPP is successful in many domains, it nevertheless suffers from limitations. Firstly, it deemphasizes discriminant information that is very important for recognition task. Secondly, the basis vectors obtained by NPP are statistically correlated, and so the extracted features contain redundancy, which may distort the distribution of the features and even dramatically degrade recognition performance [14].

In this paper, a novel feature extraction method called uncorrelated neighborhood preserving projections (UNPP) is proposed for face recognition. Based on NPP, UNPP utilizes the class labels information to preserve within-class geometric structure and achieves good discriminant ability. On the other hand, the method obtains statistically uncorrelated features within minimum redundancy by putting a simple uncorrelated constraint on the computation of the basis vectors.

The rest of the paper is organized as following: In section 2, the NPP algorithms are briefly reviewed; Section 3 describes Uncorrelated Neighborhood Preserving Projections (UNPP); Experiments and results are presented in Section 4; Conclusions are given in Section 5.

2 A Brief Review of NPP

Consider a set of sample images $X = [x_1, x_2, \cdots, x_N] \in R^{D \times N}$, and each sample x_i belongs to one of the C classes. The generic problem of linear dimensionality reduction is to find the transformation matrix P to map high-dimensional data X to new data $Y = [y_1, y_2, \cdots, y_N]$ in d dimensional space $(d << D)$, such that y_i represents x_i, where $y_i = P^T x_i$.

NPP is a linear approximation of the original nonlinear LLE [9]. NPP aims to find the optimal transformation matrix P that can preserve the locality manifold structure of the data X by minimizing the following cost function:

$$J_1(A) = \sum_{i=1}^{N} \left\| y_i - \sum_{j=1}^{N} y_j W_{ij} \right\|^2 = \left\| Y(I - W) \right\|^2$$
$$= tr\{ Y(I - W)(I - W)^T Y^T \} \qquad (1)$$
$$= tr\{ (P^T X)(I - W)(I - W)^T (P^T X)^T \}$$
$$= tr\{ P^T XMX^T P \}$$

with the constraint $(1/N)YY^T = (1/N)P^T XX^T P = I$.

where $M = (I - W)^T (I - W)$, I is an identity matrix. The basic idea behind NPP is that the same weights W_{ij} that reconstruct the ith point x_i in D dimensional space should also reconstruct its embedded counterpart y_i in d dimensional space, the weight matrix W can be computed by minimizing the reconstruction error:

$$\varepsilon(W) = \sum_{i=1}^{N} \left\| x_i - \sum_{j=1}^{K} W_{ij} x_j \right\|^2 \tag{2}$$

where $\sum_j W_{ij} = 1$, and $W_{ij} = 0$ if x_j is not one of the K nearest neighbors of x_i.

This minimization problem can converted to solving a generalized eigenvalue problem as follows:

$$XMX^T P = \lambda XX^T P \tag{3}$$

Let the column vectors $p_0, p_1, \cdots, p_{d-1}$ be the solutions of Eq.(3), ordered according to their eigenvalues $\lambda_0 \le \lambda_1 \le \cdots \le \lambda_{d-1}$, and $P = [p_0, p_1, \cdots, p_{d-1}]$. Thus, the embedding is as follows: $x_i \rightarrow y_i = P^T x_i$.

For more detailed information about NPP, please refer to [10, 11].

3 Uncorrelated Neighborhood Preserving Projections

NPP is an unsupervised feature extraction method. As mentioned above, discrminant information is important for recognition problem. In this section, a novel feature extraction method named uncorrelated neighborhood preserving projections (UNPP) is proposed. UNPP not only preserves the locality structure like NPP, but also utilizes the discriminant information. In addition, a simple uncorrelated constraint is considered.

So the objective function of UNPP is defined as follows:

$$\begin{cases} \min \sum_{i=1}^{N} \left\| y_i - \sum_{j=1}^{N} W_{ij} y_j \right\|^2 \\ s.t.\ E[(y_i - E(y_i))(y_j - E(y_j))] = 0 \ \ (i \ne j) \end{cases} \tag{4}$$

where W is the weight matrix. Since class labels are available, each data points is reconstructed by the linear combination of other points which belong to the same class. In other words, the weights W_{ij} is computed by minimizing Eq.(2) with constraints $\sum_{j=1}^{N} W_{ij} = 1$, and $W_{ij} = 0$ if x_i and x_j are from different classes. It means that the within-class geometric relation is emphasized. As a result, the weight matrix W not only reflects local geometry relation but also carries discriminative information. Note that in UNPP, one does not need to set the parameter K, the number of nearest neighbors.

We can simplify the objective function as follows:

$$
\sum_{i=1}^{N} \left\| y_i - \sum_{j=1}^{N} W_{ij} y_j \right\|^2
$$
$$
= \left\| Y(I - W) \right\|^2
$$
$$
= tr\{ Y(I - W)(I - W)^T Y^T \}
$$
$$
= tr\{ P^T X(I - W)(I - W)^T X^T P \}
$$
$$
= tr\{ P^T XMX^T P \}
$$
(5)

where $X = [x_1, x_2, \cdots, x_N]$, $M = (I - W)(I - W)^T$.

$$
E[(y_i - E(y_i))(y_j - E(y_j))]
$$
$$
= p_i^T S_T p_j
$$
$$
= 0
$$
(6)

where p_i and p_j are two different columns of the matrix P, S_T is the total scatter matrix defined as in the LDA.

To simplify the computation, p_i should be normalized. Without loss of generalization, p_i should satisfy the following equation:

$$
p_i^T S_T p_i = 1
$$
(7)

Then, from Eq.(6) and Eq.(7), we can get $P^T S_T P = I$, where I is an identity matrix.

So far, the objective function can be rewritten as:

$$
\min_{P^T S_T P = I} tr(P^T XMX^T P)
$$
(8)

Using Lagrange multiplier, let:

$$
L(P, \lambda) = P^T XMX^T P - \lambda(P^T S_T P - I)
$$

Then

$$
\frac{\partial L(P, \lambda)}{\partial P} = XMX^T P - \lambda S_T P = 0
$$

Thus, the constrained minimization problem can be converted to the following generalized eigenvalue problem:

$$XMX^T P = \lambda S_T P \qquad (9)$$

In fact, S_T can be written as:

$$S_T = \frac{1}{N}\left[\sum_{i=1}^{N}(x_i - \mu)(x_i - \mu)^T\right] \qquad (10)$$
$$= XGX^T$$

where μ is the mean of X, $\mu = \dfrac{1}{N}\sum_{i=1}^{N} x_i$, $G = I - \dfrac{1}{N}ee^T$.

Finally, we can get the following generalized eigenvalue problem:

$$XMX^T P = \lambda XGX^T P \qquad (11)$$

Let $P = [p_1, p_2, \cdots, p_d]$, $p_i(i = 1, 2, \cdots, d)$ are the d eigenvectors corresponding to the d smallest eigenvalues of Eq.(11).

So the embedding is as follows:

$$X \rightarrow Y = P^T X \qquad (12)$$

4 Experiment Results

To demonstrate the effectiveness of our method, experiments were done on the ORL face database. The ORL face database contains 40 different subjects, and each subject has ten different images. The images include variation in face expression (smile or not, open/closed eyes) and pose. Fig.1 illustrates one sample subject of the ORL database along with variations in facial expression and pose.

We compare the proposed UNPP method to well-known related feature extraction algorithms, which are PCA [2], LDA [3], NPP [11] and LPP[12, 13].

For all algorithms expect PCA, the first step is PCA projection. In the following experiments, we project samples to the PCA subspace with N-1 dimension for NPP [11], LPP [12, 13].and UNPP. For LDA [3], we retain $N - C$ dimensions in the PCA step.

In this experiment, the training set and the testing set are selected randomly for each subject on database. The number of training samples per subject, n, increases from 4 to 6 on ORL face database. In each round, the training samples are selected randomly and the remaining samples are used for testing. This procedure is repeated 10 times by randomly choosing different training and testing sets. Finally, a nearest neighbor classifier is employed for classification.

Fig. 1. Sample face images from the ORL database

Fig.2 gives comparison of the recognition rates of five algorithms (PCA, LDA, NPP, LPP and UNPP) under different reduced dimensions. Table 1 contains comparative analysis of the obtained maximal average recognition rate and the corresponding standard deviations and the reduced dimensions for five algorithms on the ORL database. Experimental results show the performance of the UNPP algorithm outperforms other algorithms. It demonstrates that the performance is improved because UNPP algorithm takes into account the class label information to preserve within-class geometric structure and the extracted features are uncorrelated. Due to the two aspects, UNPP achieves better performance.

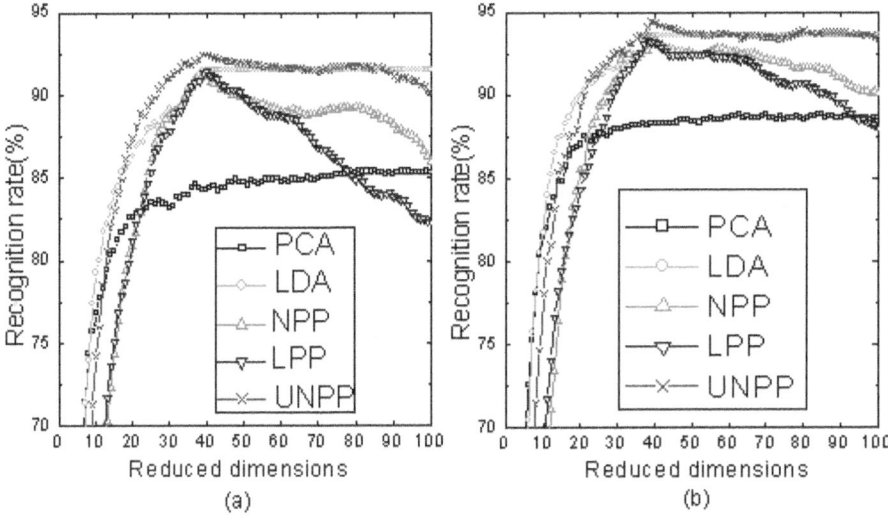

Fig. 2. Recognition rate vs. dimensionality reduction on ORL face database. (a) Four samples for training. (b) Five samples for training. (c) Six samples for training.

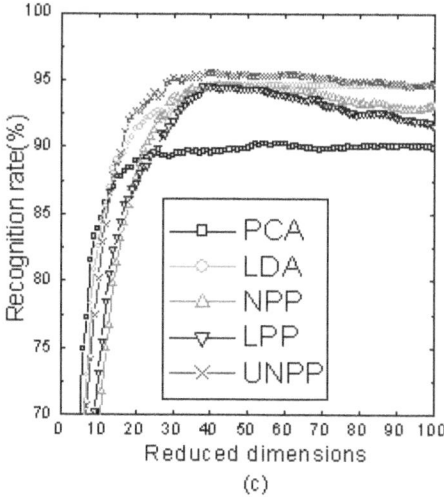

Fig. 2. (*continued*)

Table 1. Recognition accuracy (%) comparison on ORL face database

Method	4Train	5Train	6Train
PCA	$85.87 \pm 2.12\,(159)$	$89.35 \pm 1.60\,(199)$	$90.62 \pm 2.04\,(239)$
LDA	$91.54 \pm 2.52\,(39)$	$93.60 \pm 1.54\,(39)$	$94.62 \pm 2.15\,(39)$
NPP	$91.33 \pm 2.14\,(39)$	$93.60 \pm 1.08\,(39)$	$94.68 \pm 2.17\,(42)$
LPP	$91.41 \pm 2.15\,(40)$	$93.35 \pm 0.88\,(38)$	$94.62 \pm 1.91\,(39)$
UNPP	$\mathbf{92.42 \pm 1.74\,(39)}$	$\mathbf{94.45 \pm 2.05\,(39)}$	$\mathbf{95.56 \pm 1.87\,(39)}$

5   Conclusions and Future Work

A new feature extraction algorithm called Uncorrelated Neighborhood Preserving Projections (UNPP) is proposed for face recognition. UNPP takes both class label information and structure of manifold into account, thus it can preserve the within-class neighborhood geometry structure. In order to further improve recognition rate, an uncorrelated constraint is imposed to make the extracted features statistically uncorrelated. Experimental results on face databases show UNPP has more discriminative power than PCA, LDA, NPP, and LPP. But UNPP algorithm is still linear. In future work, we will extend UNPP to nonlinear form by kernel trick.

Acknowledgments. This work is supported by Foundation of He'nan Educational Committee (number 2010A520028).

References

1. Jolliffe, I.T.: Principal Component Analysis. Springer, New York (1986)
2. Turk, M., Pentland, A.: Eigenfaces for Recognition. Journal of Cognitive Neuroscience 3(1), 71–86 (1991)
3. Belhumeur, P.N., Hespanha, J.P., Kriegman, D.J.: Eigenfaces vs. Fisherfaces: Recognition Using Class Specific Linear Projection. IEEE Trans. Pattern Analysis and Machine Intelligence 19(7), 711–720 (1997)
4. Saul, L., Roweis, S.: Think Globally, Fit Locally: Unsupervised Learning of Low Dimensional Manifolds. Journal of Machine Learning Research 4, 119–155 (2003)
5. Roweis, S., Saul, L.: Nonlinear Dimensionality Reduction by Locally Linear Embedding. Science 290, 2323–2326 (2000)
6. Tenenbaum, J.B., de Silva, V., Langford, J.C.: A Global Geometric Framework for Nonlinear Dimensionality Reduction. Science 290, 2319–2323 (2000)
7. Belkin, M., Niyogi, P.: Laplacian Eigenmaps and Spectral Techniques for Embedding and Clustering. In: Advances in Neural Information Processing Systems 14, Vancouver, British Columbia, Canada (2002)
8. Zhang, Z., Zha, H.: Principle Manifolds and Nonlinear Dimensionality Reduction via Tangent Space Alignment. SIAM J. Sci. Computer 26(1), 313–338 (2004)
9. Yan, S., Xu, D., Zhang, B., Zhang, H.J.: Graph Embedding: a General Framework for dimensionality Reduction. IEEE Trans. Pattern Anal. Machine Intell. 29(1), 40–51 (2007)
10. Pang, Y., Zhang, L., Liu, Z., Yu, N., Li, H.: Neighborhood Preserving Projections (NPP): A Novel Linear Dimension Reduction Method. In: Huang, D.-S., Zhang, X.-P., Huang, G.-B. (eds.) ICIC 2005. LNCS, vol. 3644, pp. 117–125. Springer, Heidelberg (2005)
11. Pang, Y., Yu, N., Li, H., Zhang, R., Liu, Z.: Face Recognition Using Neighborhood Preserving Projections. In: Ho, Y.-S., Kim, H.-J. (eds.) PCM 2005. LNCS, vol. 3768, pp. 854–864. Springer, Heidelberg (2005)
12. He, X., Niyogi, P.: Locality Preserving Projections. In: Proc. Advances in Neural Informaion Processing System Conf. (2003)
13. He, X., Yan, S., Hu, Y., Niyogi, P., Zhang, H.J.: Face Recognition Using Laplacianfaces. IEEE Trans. Pattern Analysis and Machine Intelligence 27(3) (2005)
14. Sun, S.Y., Zhao, H.T., Yang, H.J.: Discriminant Uncorrelated Locality Preserving Projection. In: Proc. of International Conference on Image and Signal Processing, pp. 1849–4852 (2010)

Extracting Hyponymy Patterns in Tibetan Language to Enrich Minority Languages Knowledge Base

Lirong Qiu[1,2], Yu Weng[1,2], Xiaobing Zhao[1,2], and Xiaoyu Qiu[3]

[1] Information technology school, Minzu University of China, 100081 Beijing, China
lirongqqq@163.com, mr.wengyu@gmail.com
[2] Minority Languages Branch, National Language Resource and Monitoring Research Center
[3] Institute of network and education technology, Shandong University of Traditional Chinese Medicine, Jinan, 250355

Abstract. Semantic ontology is a formal, explicit specification of a shared conceptualization. The construction of semantic ontology knowledge base is the vital process in language processing, which is applied in information retrieval, information extraction and automatic translation. Hyponymy pattern is a basic semantic relationship between concepts, which is used to concepts acquisition to enrich ontology automatically. In this paper, the construction idea of multilingual ontology with unified criteria and interface are introduced, and hyponymy pattern is represented as a pair of a meaning frame defining the necessary information extraction in Tibetan language. The research of hyponymy relationship pattern can assist concept enrichment in ontology, which can reduce the cost during the ontology engineering process.

Keywords: knowledge base, semantic ontology, concepts acquisition, hyponymy relation.

1 Introduction

In early 90s of the 20th century, a lot of international symposia on ontology were held by the computer industry, ontology then became the hot topic of many artificial intelligence research groups, which include such branches as knowledge engineering, natural language processing and knowledge representation. The main reason for this trend is that, through ontology, the communication between people and people, people and machine, machine and machine can be built on the basis of shared knowledge [1].

China is a unified, multi-national country, with 56 nationalities in all. All these minorities have a total of 27 scripts of their own in current use, which are all computer-readable. In China, there are six languages to be commonly used, Chinese, Tibetan, Uygur, Mongolian, Kazak and Korean. For those languages, there are huge differences in gammar, pronunciation, spelling, vocabulary, which is increased the difficulty of interoperability between those languages with regard to information retrieval, information extraction and automatic translation.

However, use those languages also occurs some common features, and hold the common regularity to be complied. The common feature is the semantic meaning,

H. Deng et al. (Eds.): AICI 2011, Part III, LNAI 7004, pp. 521–528, 2011.

which is specified when issue the word in the sentence. Those languages have some semantic properties in common, and the differences are shaped because of grammar, spelling etc.

Semantic ontology is a formal, explicit specification of a shared conceptualization [2]. The construction of semantic ontology knowledge base is the vital process in language processing, which is applied in information retrieval, information extraction and automatic translation.

The concept itself defined in the dictionary is not ambiguous; it can be associated with the real-world entity or object uniquely and accurately. However, in sentence processing, the concept of a word is closely related to the sentence. Let's take the word "Trojan horse" for an example; it can be interpreted into at least three meanings in these three sentences below:

(1) Trojan horse is a kind of toy.
(2) Trojan horse is a kind of sports equipment.
(3) Trojan horse is a kind of computer virus.

Therefore, the so-called ambiguity of concept is caused by polysemy, namely, a concept word with two or more different meanings. As in the case of Tibetan language, it can be translated into Chinese in different ways based on its context:

སློབ་ཕྲུག་རྣམས་ཚང་མ་སྐྱང་བཞིན་འདུག

(1) Students are learning Yin Ming Xue.

སྐྱེ་བོ་ཆེད་མ་ནི་ཤཀྱ་ཐུབ་པ་ལྟ་བུའོ

(2) The standard of saint like Shijiamoni

Furthermore, for Tibetan language, there exists a large number of foreign words and transliterated words. For example, the Chinese word "Chengdu" has different translations in the Tibetan language, such as ཁྲེའུ and ཟིང་དུ.

The inherent fuzziness and ambiguity of semantics in language has made the work of machine analysis even more difficult. Word (binary data for the computer) is only a medium of semantics, and semantics is the core and critical part of communication.

For those people who got some knowledge, it is not hard to understand the specific meaning conveyed in the sentence based on the context. For example, if the word "Trojan horse" appeared in a text together with "computer" or "program", then it can be concluded based on common sense that "Trojan horse" here should mean the computer virus most likely.

The acquisition of hyponymy is a basic and vital problem in knowledge acquisition both from a computational linguistic perspective and from a theoretical linguistic one. Hyponymy is useful for the automatic creation or enrichment of an ontology, for tasks such as document indexing, information retrieval, question answering. On the other hand, these hyponymy patterns can be used in papers concerned with this semantic relation [3].

Given all that, the construction of semantic ontology knowledge base is the vital process in language processing, which is applied in information retrieval, information extraction and automatic translation. Hyponymy pattern is a basic semantic relationship between concepts, which is used to concepts acquisition in ontology automatically. In this paper, the construction idea of multi-language ontology with unified criteria and interface are introduced, and hyponymy pattern is represented as a pair of a meaning frame defining the necessary information extraction in Tibetan language. The research of hyponymy relationship pattern can assist concept enrichment in ontology, which can reduce the cost during the ontology engineering process.

2   Multilingual Knowledge Base

Semantic ontology is a formal, explicit specification of a shared conceptualization. To build ontology knowledge base for those minority languages is vital in language processing.

The minority language ontology knowledge base is fruitful for the information processing progress. Building multilingual ontology base is effective in relieving the condition of lack of language materials.

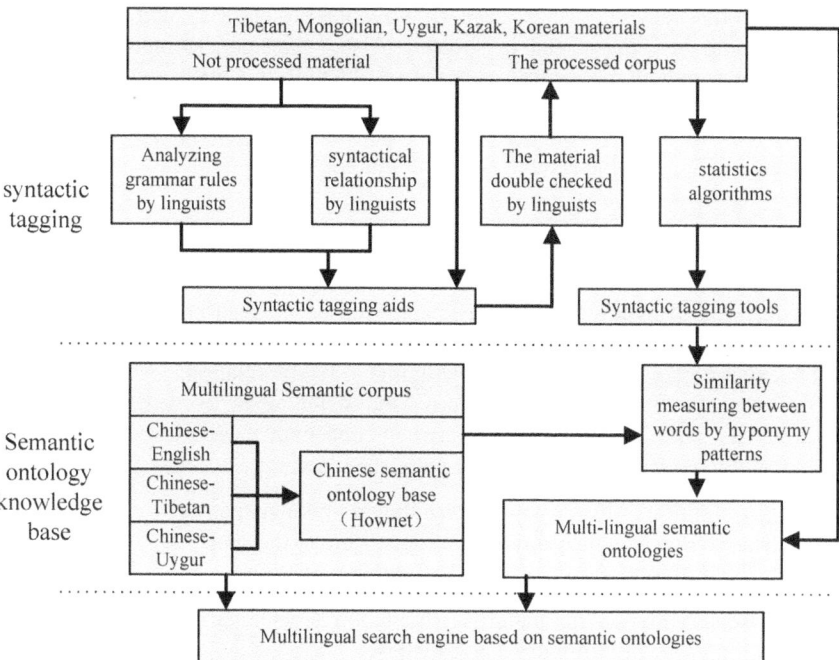

Fig. 1. The methodology of multilingual knowledge base construction

The methodology of multilingual knowledge base construction is shown in fig.1. Firstly, five minority languages materials which are not processed will be analyzed by linguists and will be syntactic tagged. The processed corpus will be double checked by linguists with the help of syntactic tagging tools. Secondly, the multilingual semantic ontologies will be built manually. During the creation of multilingual semantic ontology, the hyponymy pattern is represented as a pair of a meaning frame defining the necessary information, which can used to calculate the similarity between words.

The purpose of multilingual knowledge base construction is to produce a combination of dictionary and thesaurus that is more intuitively usable, to support automatic text analysis and artificial intelligence applications, and to realize great advantages in interoperability and invocation among multilingual languages.

Learning from the construction of HowNet, which is an ontology knowledge base in Chinese, the ontology structure of multilingual knowledge base is identified includes three parts:

(1) The basic properties, such as semantic code, the hyponymy relation, and the information of the word.

(2) The concept properties, such as using the core words to illustrate the meaning and collocation.

(3) The common grammar properties, such as subject, verb, object.

A semantic search engine is developed as a demonstration prototype system of multilingual ontology knowledge base. By now, the prototype system can be searched by words both in Chinese and in Tibetan. Also, when people input a keyword in Tibetan, the search engine can provide the results both in Chinese and in Tibetan, as long as the searching results are semantic related.

As far as we concerned, there hasn't been any research in minority languages processing of China on the level of semantic ontology.

3   Extracting Hyponymy Patterns in Tibetan Language

The acquisition of hyponymy is a basic and vital problem in knowledge acquisition, which is useful for the automatic creation or enrichment of ontologies and also can be used in extracting concepts concerned with this semantic relation.

The hypernym/hyponym relationships among the noun or verb synsets can be interpreted as specialization relations between conceptual categories.

There are three factors in hyponymy pattern extracting:

(1) The definition of hyponymy pattern in certain language;
(2) The selection of hyponymy pattern according to the sentence;
(3) The algorithm to test the selected hyponymy relation.

In this section, the hyponymy patterns extracted in Tibetan language are introduced as an illustration of the multilingual ontology base.

3.1   Hyponymy Pattern Definition

We consulted the hyponymy definition of WordNet and gave the related definitions as follows:

Definition 1: Given a concept C_1 and C_2, the synonym set of C_1 is $\{C_1, C_1', \ldots\}$ and the synonym set of C_2 is $\{C_2, C_2', \ldots\}$. If the semantic meaning of C_1 was consumed by C_2, then C_1 and C_2 are the hyponymy relationship, in which C_1 is a hyponym of C_2, C_2 is called a hypernym of C_1, noted by $hr(C_1, C_2)$.

Definition 2: The hyponymy pattern space Ψ can be defined as a quad (G, P, A, HR).

G is the corpus, which are sentences in Tibetan language $G=\{s_1, s_2, \ldots, s_n\}$.

P is the hyponymic relations set $P=\{p_1, p_2, \ldots, p_n\}$ which is defined by human people and will be given in the next sub-section.

A is the algorithm set, which comprises the pattern learning algorithm.

HR is the hyponymy concepts set $HR=\{hr_1, hr_2, \ldots, hr_n\}$, which can be learned by algorithms automatically.

3.2   The Hyponymy Patterns

Despite the significant amount of work done on acquiring hyponymy pattern automatically or semi-automatically recent years, we propose the hyponymic relation by human.

The reasons of getting hyponymy patterns in Tibetan manually are listed below: (1) Comparing with English or Chinese, not many available and frequently updated websites in minority languages can be downloaded. (2) As most minority languages, the information acquisition researchers face a great many of difficulties in dealing with being lack of text resource. (3) Further, the lack of the available minority languages electronic dictionaries and other useful ontologies acts as a brake to progress.

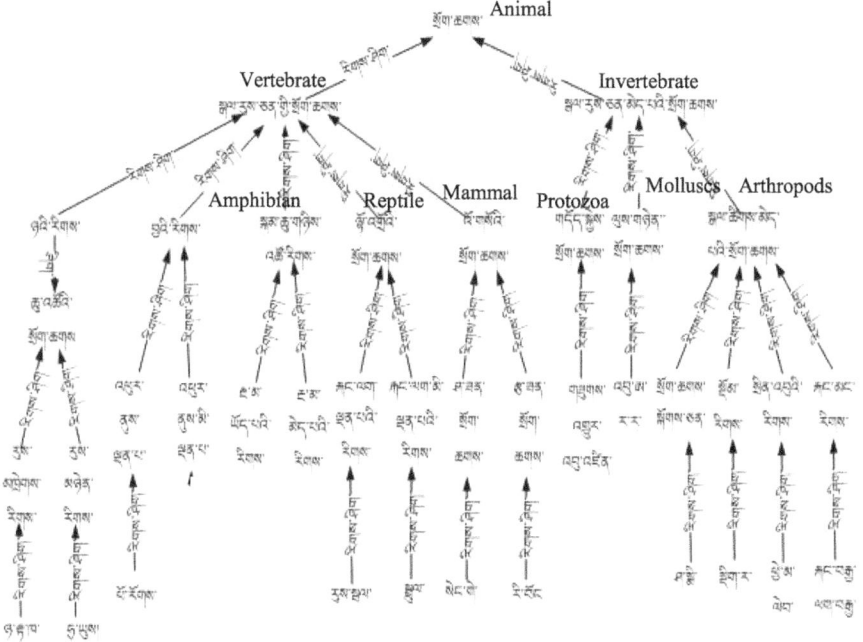

Fig. 2. The illustration of hyponymy concepts in Tibetan Language

The five hyponymy patterns in Tibetan language are defined as follows:

(1) One to one pattern
<?C1> 【ནི་】 <?C2> 【ཞིག་(ལིག་/ཅིག་) ཡིན།】

(2) More to one pattern
<?C1> 【དང་】 <?C2>. 【 】 . <?Cm>. 【ལ་སོགས་པའི་】 .<?Cm+1>་

(3) One to more pattern
<?C1>. 【ནི་】 <?C2>. 【ནིག་/ཞིག་/ཅིག་ ཡིན་ལ་】 .<?C3> 【ནིག་ (ཞིག་/ཅིག་) ཀྱང་ཡིན།】

(4) More to more pattern
<?C1>. 【དང་】.<?C2>. 【ནི་】.<?C3>. 【ནིག་(ཞིག་/ཅིག་ ཡིན་ལ་】 <?C4> 【ནིག་(ཞིག་/ཅིག་)ཀྱང་ཡིན།】་

(5) Multiple level pattern
<?C1>. 【ནི་】 .<?C2>. 【ནང་ཙམ་】 .<?C3> 【ནིག་/ཞིག་/ཅིག་ ཡིན།】

Figure 2 shows the illustration of hyponymy concepts in Tibetan Language, which is extracted from the texts.

3.3 Extracting Hyponymy Patterns

Given the hyponymy pattern set P={p_1, p_2, ..., p_m}, and corpus G, there are sentence set S={s_1, s_2, ..., s_n} in G and pattern p_1, p_2, ..., p_k ($p_i \in$ P, i=1, 2, ... k). Then given $\forall$ s∈ S and $\forall$ $p_i \in$ P, if sentence s matches and p_i according to the pattern match algorithm, that can be noted by (s, {p_1, p_2, ..., p_k }). If there are no pattern matches s, that can be noted (s, Ø).

For example, there is a sentence in the corpus:

གོས་སྣམ་ནང་ལ་སྟོད་ཐུང་དང་གོས་ཐུང་ སྦུ་བ་ལ་སོགས་པའི་ གྱོན་ཆས་མང་པོ་འདུག།

There are some clothes in the wardrobe, such as jackets, trousers, gowns.
Pattern p can be defined as follows:
```
Defpattern hyponymy relation(one to more pattern)
{ Fundamental pattern :
```
<?C1> 【དང་】 <?C2>. 【 】 . <?Cm>. 【ལ་སོགས་པའི་】 .<?Cm+1>
```
The Hyponyms are <?C1>, <?C2> and <?Cm>
The hypernym are <?Cm+1>
}
```
The pattern match outcome is :

གོས་སྣམ་ནང་ལ་སྟོད་ཐུང་ /དང་/གོས་ཐུང་/ /སྦུ་བ་/ལ་སོགས་པའི་ /གྱོན་ཆས་ /མང་པོ་འདུག།

Wardrobe /jackets /、 /trousers /、 /gowns/ clothes

Hyponyms: <?C1> = གོས་སྣམ་ནང་ལ་སྟོད་ཐུང་དང་གོས་ཐུང་

(There are some jackets, trousers in wardrobe)

Hyponyms: <?C2> = སྦུ་བ་ *(gowns)*

Hypernyms: <?C3> = གྱོན་ཆས་ *(clothes)*

The candidate hyponymy relation:

hr(Śྐྱ*རུང*དང*གོས*རུང* , Ŕྱོན*ཆས*) hr(*jackets\trousers, clothes*)

hr(ཕྱུ*པ*, Ŕྱོǹ*ཆས*) hr(*gowns, clothes*)

The correct hyponymy relation:

hr(Śྐྱ*རུང*, Ŕ྾ǹ*ཆས*) hr(*jackets, clothes*)

hr(གོས*རུང*, Ŕྱǹ*ཆས*) hr(*trousers,clothes*)

hr(ཕྱུ*པ*, Ŕྱǹ*ཆས*) hr(*gowns, clothes*)

4 Related Work

As far as we know, there hasn't been any research in minority languages processing on the level of semantic ontology.

Mr. Dong Zhendong, the creator of HowNet, has ever put it [4] that "natural language processing system will eventually need a more powerful knowledge base for support." The core of semantics is knowledge, and semantic ontology is a displayed formal specification of the shared conceptual model, which used to describe (specific areas) knowledge.

With its long history and splendid culture, the Tibetan language has long been the focus of many scholars and researchers both at home and abroad. Coincident with the development of digitalization, the information processing research in Tibetan has also gained rapid progress, covering such aspects as characters, words, phrases, sentences and chapters. The stage of sentence processing has also been addressed ambitiously, with such problems in the basic theoretical research as syntactic knowledge, semantic knowledge and pragmatic knowledge to be solved urgently [5].

Hyponymy is useful for the automatic creation or enrichment of ontologies, there are some research results in English and Chinese.

One of the first studies of hyponymy acquisition was done by Hearst [6]. Hearst proposed a method for retrieving concept relations from text by using predefined lexico-syntactic patterns. Other researchers developed other ways to obtain hyponymy, such as Brent proposes a method of syntactic information from text corpora by using verb sub-categorization frame recognition technique in [7]. Lei Liu proposes a method of extracting hyponymic relations from Chinese free text and using concept space to verify hyponymy in building a hyponymy lexicon in paper [8].

5 Conclusion and Future Work

China is a unified, multi-national country, with 56 nationalities in all. All these minorities have a total of 27 scripts of their own in current use, which are all computer-readable. Semantic ontology is a formal, explicit specification of a shared conceptualization. To build ontology knowledge base for those minority languages is vital in language processing, which can be applied in information retrieval, information extraction and automatic translation. Automatic acquisition and verification of hyponymy relations is a fundamental problem in knowledge acquisition.

In this paper, the construction idea of multilingual ontology with unified criteria and interface are introduced, and hyponymy pattern is represented as a pair of a meaning frame defining the necessary information extraction in Tibetan language. The research of hyponymy relationship pattern can assist concept enrichment in ontology, which can reduce the cost during the ontology engineering process.

The work of this paper is a part of our ongoing research work, which aims to provide an open reusable ontology knowledge base for further minority languages processing progress. Various experiments and applications have been conducting in our current research. Future work includes how to acquire and verify hyponymic relations from Tibetan free text, how to obtain sentences patterns automatically and how to verify the hyponymic relations with self features and context features.

Acknowledgments. Our work is supported by National 985 project "Development of science and technology innovation platform of information technology application in the minority national regions", the key projects in the National Science and Technology Pillar Program "Tibetan language and Uighur language monitoring technology project"(No.2009BAH41B04) and the "Science Fund for Youths" project of Minzu University of China(No. 1112KYQN39).

References

1. Neches, R., Fikes, R.E., Cruber, T.R., et al.: Enabling Technology for Knowledge Sharing. AI Magazine 12(3), 36–56 (1991)
2. Agirre, E., Ansa, O., Hovy, E., Martinez, D.: Enriching very large ontologies using the WWW. In: ECAI 2000 (2000)
3. Mititelu, V.B.: Hyponymy patterns. In: Sojka, P., Horák, A., Kopeček, I., Pala, K. (eds.) TSD 2008. LNCS (LNAI), vol. 5246, pp. 37–44. Springer, Heidelberg (2008)
4. HowNet, http://www.keenage.com/
5. Jiang, D., Long, C.: Research of characters in Tibetan language – character, sound, code, sorting, graph, and rules of Latin interoperability. Social Sciences Academic Press, Beijing (2010)
6. Hearst, M.A.: Automatic acquisition of hyponyms from large text corpora. In: Proceedings of the 14th International Conference on Computational Linguistics, Nantes, France, pp. 539–545 (1992)
7. Brent, M.R.: Automatic acquisition of subcategorization frames from untagged, free-text corpora. In: Proceedings of the 29th Annual Meeting of the Association for Computational Linguistics (1991)
8. Liu, L., Zhang, S., Diao, L.H., Yan, S.Y., Cao, C.G.: Using Concept Space to Verify Hyponymy in Building a Hyponymy Lexicon. In: Deng, H., Wang, L., Wang, F.L., Lei, J. (eds.) AICI 2009. LNCS, vol. 5855, pp. 479–486. Springer, Heidelberg (2009)

Kernel Based Visual Tracking with Reasoning about Adaptive Distribution Image

Risheng Han

College of Mathematics, Physics and Information Engineering, Jiaxing University,
Jiaxing, Zhejiang, China
mailtohrs@163.com

Abstract. A template updating reasoning engine which can deal with fundamental constraints on the spatial-temporal continuity of target's motion is proposed. By analyzing target's continuously adaptive distributions image, a voting method can estimate the tracking window's scale. In updating phase, by making further computation of likelihood of target model and candidate model, both the model and scale can be automatically updated in time. The tracking ability of KBT can be improved.

Keywords: Mean Shift, Adaptive Distribution, Template Updating.

1 Introduction

The template updating problem of KBT (Kernel based visual tracking) includes two aspects: target scale update and target model update. It is reported that when target's scale exceeds the size of tracking window, the tracker outputs poor localization [1,2]. For solving the scale updating problem of KBT, the technique of "tracking through scale space" is proposed in [3]. The method uses Lindeberg's theory to select the best scale of tracking window. In [4], based on the analysis of similarity of object kernel-histogram in different scales, an automatic bandwidth selection method is proposed based on backward tracking and object centroid registration. In [5] and [6], the dimensionality of the measurement space can be increased by using multiple kernels. By analyzing the local statistical characteristics around each data point, the kernel bandwidth can be estimated [7,8]. In [9], the target model can be updated according to the distributions of the target intensity and the local standard deviation measures. In [10], the mean shift algorithm is modified to deal with dynamically changing color probability distributions derived from video frame sequences. The modified algorithm is called the Continuously Adaptive Mean Shift (CAMSHIFT) algorithm.

In this paper, the template updating algorithm can be regarded as a reasoning engine that deals with updating operation and fundamental constraints on the spatial-temporal continuity of target's motion. Based on voting reasoning about the target's adaptive distributions image and target's motion, the proposed algorithm can update the tracking window's scale and target model more stably.

H. Deng et al. (Eds.): AICI 2011, Part III, LNAI 7004, pp. 529–536, 2011.
© Springer-Verlag Berlin Heidelberg 2011

2 Image Probability Distribution

2.1 Kernel Based Visual Tracking

In KBT, a kernel based histogram of object region is often used to represent the tracking template called target model. It can be denoted as follows:

$$\vec{q} = [q_u]_{u=1,...,m}, \text{ and } q_u = \frac{1}{C_h} \sum_{i=1}^{n} Kernel(X_i - c^0) \cdot \delta(b(X_i), u) \tag{1}$$

Where, $\{X_i\}_{i=1,..n}$ are the pixel locations of the target, *Kernel* is a spatially weighting function centered at c^0, and three popular forms of *Kernel.* $(\cdot)$ are: Epanechnikov kernel, Uniform Kernel and Normal Kernel. The $\delta(\cdot)$ is the Kronecker delta function, $b(X_i)$ is a binning function that maps the color of $\{X_i\}_{i=1,..n}$ into a histogram bin u with $u=\{1...,m\}$, and C_h is a normalization term which makes $\sum_{u=1}^{m} q_u = 1$. The initial center of the target is denoted as c^0.

Similarly, the tracking features called "candidate model" can be denoted as follows:

$$\vec{p}(c^k) = [p_u]_{u=1,...,m}, \tag{2}$$

where, $p_u = \frac{1}{C_h} \sum_{i=1}^{n} Kernel(X_i - c^k) \cdot \delta(b(X_i), u)$, and the center of candidate region in sequent frame k is denoted as c^k.

Originally, *KBT* is derived from second order Taylor expansion of Bhattacharyya coefficient, which is defined as follows.

$$B(\vec{p}(c^k), \vec{q}) = \sum_{u=1}^{m} \sqrt{p_u(c^k) \cdot q_u} \tag{3}$$

The Bhattacharyya coefficient is a popular likelihood between two vectors. And the kernel based method realizes target model tracking through maximizing Bhattacharyya coefficient, like the following equation (4)

$$\Delta c^* = \arg \max_{\Delta c^k} B(\vec{q}, \vec{p}(c^k + \Delta c^k)) \tag{4}$$

The *KBT* algorithm outputs the Δc^*, which determines the displacement of object, the Δc^* is also called "mean shift" vector, which can be computed using following formulas iteratively.

$$\Delta c^k = \frac{\sum_{i=1}^{n} Kernel(X_i - c^k) \cdot w(X_i) \cdot (X_i - c^k)}{\sum_{i=1}^{n} Kernel(X_i - c^k) \cdot w(X_i)} \tag{5}$$

$$\text{Where, } w(X_i) = \sqrt{\frac{q_u}{p_u(c^k)}} \tag{6}$$

For finding the proper Δc^* in (4), an iterated computation is needed by computing the $w(X_i)$ using (6) and deriving Δc^k using (5).

2.2 Image's Continuously Adaptive Distribution

In order to create the target's probability distribution image, an initial histogram is computed using equation (1). And then the histogram bins are scaled between the minimum and maximum probability image intensities as follows:

$$\hat{q} = [\hat{q}_u]_{u=1...m} \text{ and } \hat{q}_u = \min\left(\frac{255}{\max(\vec{q})} q_u, 255\right)_{u=1...m} \tag{7}$$

According to (7), the histogram bin q_u are rescaled from $[0, \max(\vec{q})]$ to the new range $[0, 255]$, where pixels with the highest probability of being in the sample histogram will map as visible in the probability distribution image.

In this paper, the mean value of pixels' intensity within the tracking window is used as indicator when the target's scale changes. The indicator is computed within tracking window as follows:

$$TR^k = RECT(x_c^k, y_c^k, s_x^k, s_y^k) \tag{8}$$

$$Cm^k = \frac{\sum_{i=1}^{n} TR^k(x_i, y_i)}{s_x^k \times s_y^k} \tag{9}$$

Where, TR is the tracking window region. $\langle x_c^k, y_c^k \rangle$ is the center of the tracking window ; (s_x^k, s_y^k) is the scale of tracking window in both horizontal and vertical directions respectively.

By analyzing the indicator's variety, the proposed algorithm can decide whether the tracking window's scale should be changed. Based on probability distribution image, window's scale does not change, the mean value become larger if target scale expands. On contrary, the mean value become smaller when target scale shrink.

2.3 Zeroth Moment of Probability Distribution Image

In CAMSHIFT, the scale of tracking window is determined by zeroth moments. After Histogram Back-Projection, given $I(x, y)$ is the intensity of the probability distribution image at (x,y) within the tracking window. The zeroth moment is computed as follows:

$$M_{00} = \sum_x \sum_y I(x, y) \tag{10}$$

And the tracking window's scale in can be determined as follows:

$$s_x = \alpha \cdot \sqrt{M_{00}} \tag{11}$$

$$s_y = \beta \cdot s_x^k \tag{12}$$

Where, α is the scale proportion of tracking window to target. Because the size of the search window is rounded up to the current or next greatest odd number, in practice, the tracking window is set larger than the target. In this paper, $\alpha =1.15$.

β is the proportion of s_y to s_x. According to the indicator's variety, the scale updating can be implemented.

3   Tracking with Reasoning about Adaptive Distribution Image

3.1 Procedure of the Proposed Algorithm

When tracking starts, target region denoted as TR^{k-1}, and corresponding target model is denoted as $\vec{q}^{k-1}$. The target's template and information is completely included in TR^{k-1} and $\vec{q}^{k-1}$. After KBT is executed, the tracking window is moved to candidate region which is denoted as CR^k. Similar to TR^k, CR^k is defined as follows:

$$CR^k = RECT(x_c^k, y_c^k, s_x^k, s_y^k) \tag{13}$$

In candidate region, corresponding feature is called candidate model which is denoted as $\vec{p}^k$. Based on CR^k and $\vec{p}^k$, probability distribution image can be created in the region. And then the CAMSHIFT can be executed to get the target's new scale information (s_x, s_y). In the end, CR^k, $\vec{p}^k$, $\vec{q}^{k-1}$ and (s_x^{k-1}, s_y^{k-1}) are input into the template updating algorithm.

3.2 Scale Updating Criteria

In this paper, the update algorithm can be regarded as a reasoning engine that deals with updating operation and fundamental constraints on the spatial-temporal continuity of target's motion. Let us give the template updating algorithm in detail. For realizing the scale update reasoning, two voting functions are defined as follows:

$$Vote_1(Cm^{k-1}, Cm^k) = \begin{cases} 1, (Cm^{k-1} < Cm^k) \\ 0, (Cm^{k-1} == Cm^k) \\ -1, (Cm^{k-1} > Cm^k) \end{cases} \quad (14)$$

Where, Cm^{k-1} and Cm^k are mean values which are computed in *No.k-1* frame and *NO.k* frame respectively.

$$Vote_2(S, S^{k-1}) = \begin{cases} 1, (S^{k-1} < S) \\ 0, (S^{k-1} == S) \\ -1, (S^{k-1} > S) \end{cases} \quad (15)$$

Where, $S = (s_x, s_y)$ tracking window's scale which is computed according to (11) and (12);

$S^{k-1} = (s_x^{k-1}, s_y^{k-1})$ is tracking window's scale in *No.k-1* frame. Based on voting functions, tracking window's scale updating criteria can be defined as follows:

$$\left\{ \sum_{i=1}^{2} Vote_i(\cdot, \cdot) = 2 \right\} \rightarrow \left\{ S^k = S^{k-1} + \partial \right\} \quad (16)$$

$$\left\{ \sum_{i=1}^{2} Vote_i(\cdot, \cdot) == -2 \right\} \rightarrow \left\{ S^k = S^{k-1} - \partial \right\} \quad (17)$$

$$\left\{ \left\| \sum_{i=1}^{2} Vote_i(\cdot, \cdot) \right\| < 2 \right\} \rightarrow \left\{ S^k = S^{k-1} \right\} \quad (18)$$

Where, the parameter ∂ can be regarded as spatial-temporal constraint of on scale change. Typically, $\partial = 2$.

3.3 The Proposed Algorithm

After initial stage, the tracking starts from the *No.k* (*k=2*) frame as follows:

Input: the target's center position $\left\langle x_c^{k-1}, y_c^{k-1} \right\rangle$, scale :$(S_x^{k-1}, S_y^{k-1})$ and Cm^{k-1} in the previous frame.

Step1:   Determine Tracking Region: $TR^{k-1} = RECT(x_c^{k-1}, y_c^{k-1}, S_x^{k-1}, S_y^{k-1})$;

Step2: Compute mean-shift vector $\Delta c^k = (\Delta x^k, \Delta y^k)$ using (5) and (6);

Update candidate

region: $CR^k = RECT(x_c^{k-1} + \Delta x^k, y_c^{k-1} + \Delta y^k, S_x^{k-1}, S_y^{k-1})$;

Extract new Candidate model $\vec{p}^k$ using (2) in CR^k .

Step3: Transform CR^k by Histogram-Projection according to (7) and $\vec{p}^k$;

Step4: Compute mean value: Cm^k according to (9) in and (13);

Step5: Compute the M_{00} using (10) iteratively until CAMSHIFT converges.

Step6: Compute tracking window scale (S_x, S_y) using (11) and (12).

Step7: Update tracing window scale according to (16), (17) and (18).

Step8: According to (3), compute $B(\vec{q}^{k-1}, \vec{p}^k)$ with new scale: (S_x, S_y) ;

Step9: Update target model as follows:

If $B(\vec{q}^{k-1}, \vec{p}^{k-1}) < B(\vec{q}^{k-1}, \vec{p}^k)$

$$\vec{q}^k = B(\vec{q}^{k-1}, \vec{p}^k) * \vec{p}^k + (1 - B(\vec{q}^{k-1}, \vec{p}^k) * \vec{q}^{k-1}$$

Else

$$\left\langle x_c^k, y_c^k \right\rangle ;$$

End.

Output: $\left\langle x_c^k, y_c^k \right\rangle$, (S_x^{k-1}, S_y^{k-1}), $\vec{q}^k$, and Cm^k .

In the algorithm, the tracking window's scale can be determined using zeroth moment and mean value. And the target model and scale can be updated separately.

4   Experimental Results

Because of the clutter background, both KBT and CAMSHIFT can not fit the target's varying scale in Fig.1(a)-(c) .

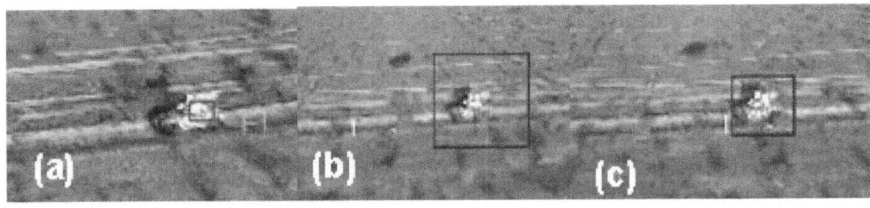

Fig. 1. Tracking Results Comparison of KBT, CAMSHIFT and the proposed algorithm

The tracking results of the proposed algorithm are shown in the Fig.1.(c), the tracking window's scale can be properly updated and the target can be discriminated from clutter background .Tracking region's mean values which are produced by the proposed algorithm, KBT and CAMSHIFT respectively are shown in Fig.2.

In Fig.2, if target scale expands, and tracking window's scale does not change, the mean value will become larger; On contrary, the mean value become smaller when target scale shrink. So the mean value of pixels' intensity within the tracking window can be used as indicator. Based on the proposed reasoning update method, the proposed algorithm can output more stable mean values than KBT and CAMSHIFT.

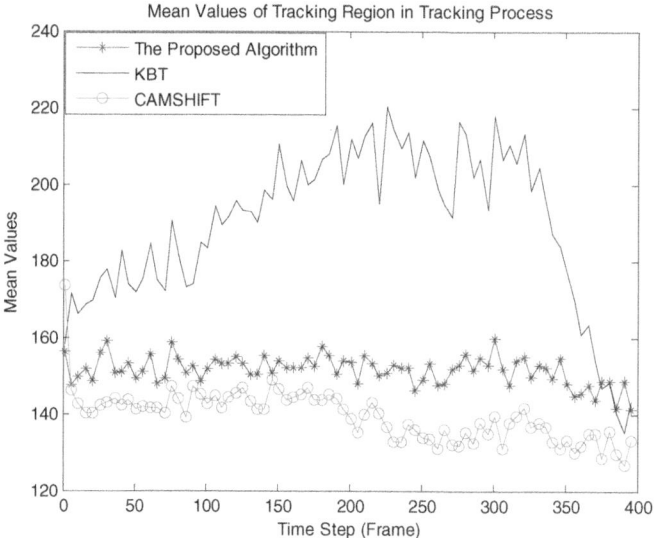

Fig. 2. Tracking window's mean values in tracking process

In Fig.3, variety of tacking window's scale is shown.

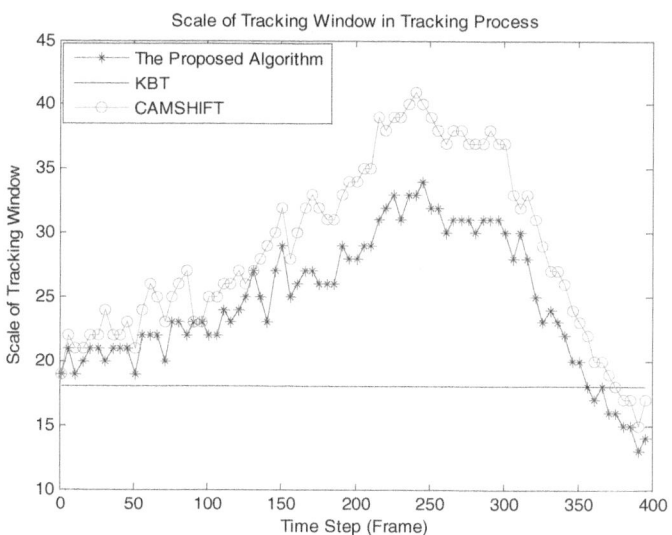

Fig. 3. Tracking window's scale values in tracking process

Although, the CAMSHIT always gets a too big tracking window, it can estimate the changing trend of tracking window's scale properly. The proposed voting method can estimate the tracking window's scale.

5   Conclusion and Discussion

In this paper, there are three major contributions. Firstly, a template updating reasoning engine which can deal with fundamental constraints on the spatial-temporal continuity of target's motion is proposed. Secondly, by analyzing target's continuously adaptive distributions image, a voting method can estimate the tracking window scale. Thirdly, based on voting reasoning about the target's adaptive distributions image and target's motion, the proposed algorithm can update both the tracking window's scale and target model more stably. Further extensions and improvements could be made by combining more efficient similarity measures.

Acknowledgments. This work was supported by Zhejiang Provincial Natural Science Foundation of China (Y1090649).

References

1. Comaniciu, D., Ramesh, V., Meer, P.: Kernel-based object tracking. IEEE Transactions on Pattern Analysis and Machine Intelligence 25, 564–577 (2003)
2. Peng, N., Yang, J., Liu, Z.: Performance analysis for tracking of variable scale objects using mean-shift algorithm. Optical Engineering 44, 7 (2005)
3. Collins, R.: Mean-shift blob tracking through scale space. In: Proc. IEEE Conf. on Computer Vision and Pattern Recognition, pp. 234–240 (2003)
4. Yang, J., Peng, N.: Mean-Shift Object Tracking with Automatic Selection of Kernel-Bandwidth. Journal of Software 16(9), 1542–1550 (2005)
5. Hager, G.D., Dewan, M., Stewart, C.V.: Multiple Kernel Tracking with SSD. In: Proc. IEEE Conf. Computer Vision and Pattern Recognition, vol. 1, pp. 790–797 (2004)
6. Fan, Z., Yang, M., Wu, Y.: Multiple collaborative kernel tracking. IEEE Transactions on Pattern Analysis and Machine Intelligence 29, 1268–1273 (2007)
7. Comaniciu, D.: An algorithm for data-driven bandwidth selection. IEEE Trans. Pattern Anal. Mach. Intell. 25(2), 281–288 (2003)
8. Han, R., Jing, Z., Li, Y.: Kernel Based Visual Tracking with Scale Invariant Features. Chinese Optics Letters 3, 168 (2008)
9. Alper, Y., Khurram, S., Mubarak, S.: Target tracking in airborne forward looking infrared imagery. Image and Vision Computing 21, 623–635 (2003)
10. Bradski, G.R.: Computer vision face tracking as a component of a perceptual user interface. In: Workshop on Applications of Computer Vision, pp. 214–219 (1998)

A Novel Community Structure Detection Algorithm for Complex Networks Analysis Based on Coulomb's Law

Jun Feng, Zhihua Zhang, Zhengxu Zhao, Zhiwei Gao, and Lijia Liu

School of Information Science and Technology,
Shijiazhuang Tiedao University, Shijiazhuang, 050043, P.R. China
fengjun@stdu.edu.cn

Abstract. With the in-depth study of the physical meaning and mathematical characteristics of complex network, community structure is found as a common property for many networks. How to detect community structure is focused recently. In this paper, Coulomb's Law in physics is introduced to the community structure detecting in complex network. According to the law, we present a mathematical model of the community force, and take it as detecting evidence. The detection algorithm based on Coulomb's Law is proposed. Then we mainly study the relation among different engineering software information and establish the Engineering Software Format Network (ESFN). And in the experiment we apply the novel detection algorithm to this network compared with classical Girvan-Newman algorithm. With the high consistent rate, the Coulomb's Law-based algorithm has lower computation complexity than the classical algorithm. The experimental results show that the novel algorithm is effective and promising.

Keywords: Community Structure, Coulomb's Law, Complex Networks, Engineering Software Format Network, Girvan-Newman algorithm.

1 Introduction

The community structure is a universal phenomenon in complex networks and shows the common character of much individuality. The communities are subsets of nodes within which node-node connections are dense, but between which connections are sparser. It is very important for understanding the topology, comprehending the function, finding the hidden rules, analyzing the character and forecasting the action of the network to study and proclaim the community structure. The ability to detect community structure in a network could clearly have practical applications. Communities in a social network might represent real social groupings, perhaps by interest or background. Communities in a citation network might represent related papers on a single topic. Communities in a metabolic network might represent cycles and other functional groupings. Communities on the web might represent pages on related topics [1].

At present some community structure detection algorithms were proposed, which can be divided as graph partition methods in computer science and hierarchical clustering methods in sociology. The representative algorithms are Girvan-Newman

H. Deng et al. (Eds.): AICI 2011, Part III, LNAI 7004, pp. 537–544, 2011.

algorithm [1], Kernighan-Lin algorithm [2], spectral algorithm [3], and so forth [4, 5]. Each algorithm has its own advantages and disadvantages. Some algorithms require the number of communities in advance; otherwise they cannot cluster correctly. Some algorithms with high complexity need large amounts of computation.

We were enlightened by Coulomb's Law in physics. The basic idea is that the node is analogized as charge in vacuum, the link between two nodes as interaction force and the community as static electrization object with some charges. In this paper, we propose force mathematical models including force model between two network communities, and force between the node and the community. A network community structure detection algorithm based on Coulomb's Law is presented.

In this paper, we mainly study the relation among different engineering software information and establish the Engineering Software Format Network (ESFN). In order to solve the incompatible problem during the long-term preservation and reliable call of the engineering information, engineering software format conversion could be considered. During the previous work, we analyzed the unweighted and weighted ESFN from some static index and found that the ESFN has smaller shortest path length and larger clustering coefficient and it corresponds to the small-world effect. In this paper, we analyze the community structure of weighted ESFN based on two community structure detection algorithms.

This paper is organized as follows. In section 2 we will give the force mathematical model based on Coulomb's Law. In section 3 we will present the novel network community structure detection algorithm based on Coulomb's Law. In section 4 we will describe ESFN and give the data representation, followed by the experimental results and analysis in section 5. The conclusions are given in section 6.

2   Force Mathematical Model

2.1   Description of Coulomb's Law

Coulomb's Law in physics is described as follows.

The interaction force value between two static charges q_1 and q_2 in vacuum is directly proportional to charged quantities Q_1 and Q_2, and inversely proportional to the square of the distance r between two charges. The force direction is along their linkage. The formula is given as

$$F = K \frac{Q_1 Q_2}{r^2}.$$ (1)

Here K is a constant.

When Coulomb's Law is applied to network community structure detection, the direction problem of the interaction force is not considered and the attraction relation is default.

2.2   Force Model between Two Network Communities

The charged quantities Q_1 and Q_2 are analogized to the node numbers of two different communities. The distance r between two charges corresponds to the distance between two communities. Therefore, the force model between two network communities is defined as

$$F_c = K \frac{NodeNum_1 \times NodeNum_2}{r^2}.$$

(2)

Where F_c represents the attraction force between communities, $NodeNum_1$ and $NodeNum_2$ corresponds to the node numbers of Community 1 and Community 2 respectively. Here K is given a simple constant, such as value 1. The distance r between two communities is formulated as

$$r = \frac{sumw_1 \times sumw_2}{(sumsharedw)^2}.$$

(3)

Where $sumw_1$ and $sumw_2$ correspond to the sum of all the edge weight of Community 1 and Community 2 respectively, and $sumsharedw$ represents the sum of the shared edge weight of the two communities. If $sumsharedw$ is large, then it shows the communities connection is close together and so the distance r is small.

2.3   Force between the Node and the Community

The force between a single node and the community is used to determine which community the node belongs to. For the single node, $NodeNum_1$ is 1 and $sumw_1$ is 1. Therefore, the force between node and community is defined as

$$F_c = \frac{1 \times NodeNum_2}{\left(\dfrac{1 \times sumw_2}{(sumsharedw)^2}\right)^2} = \frac{NodeNum_2}{\left(\dfrac{sumw_2}{(sumsharedw)^2}\right)^2}.$$

(4)

Where $NodeNum_2$ is the node numbers in the community, $sumw_2$ is the sum of all the edge weight of the community and $sumsharedw$ is the sum of all the weight of the edge between the community and the node.

3   A Network Community Structure Detection Algorithm Based on Coulomb's Law

3.1   Community Initialization

Before community partition, it is necessary to select some suitable representative nodes to initialize the community. In this paper, we select the representative node according to the authority, i.e. search for the maximum strength node within the local area. The strength s_i of the node i is calculated as the formula (5).

$$s_i = \sum_{j \in N_i} w_{ij}.$$

(5)

Where N_i is the neighbor node set of the node i, and w_{ij} represents the edge weight between the node i and j. The strength s_i involves not only the neighbor node numbers, but also the weight between the node i and its neighbor.

The method for determining the representative nodes and initializing the communities is as follow:

Step1 Calculate the node strengths for all the nodes.

Step2 Compare the strength s_i of the node i with its neighbors and choose the node j as the representative node because the strength of this node is maximum within the local area.

Step3 Add these nodes which connect the representative node to this community.

Step4 Repeat from step1 until all the nodes is considered.

3.2 Community Structure Detection Algorithm

The community structure detection algorithm based on Coulomb's Law is proposed as follows:

Step1 Select the suitable representative nodes and use them to identify the initial network community structure.

Step2 If two representative nodes are neighbor relation, then the corresponding communities are combined and the larger strength node is selected as the representative node of the new community.

Step3 Investigate the node which is still not added to any communities but connected to some communities, calculate the forces between the single node and the communities as formula (4), and then add this node to the community with the maximum force.

Step4 Repeat Step3 until each node which connects some communities is considered.

Step5 The nodes which do not connect any community are isolated nodes.

The community detecting procedure based on the above algorithm is illustrated as Fig. 1. The circles with the dash lines represent the communities partition, the black dots represent the initial representative nodes, the red triangles represent the nodes which connect to the representative ones directly and are added to the community at the second batch, the blue squares represent the nodes which connect to the community but not to the representative ones directly and are added to the community at the third batch, and the pink diamonds represent the isolated nodes which do not connect to any community.

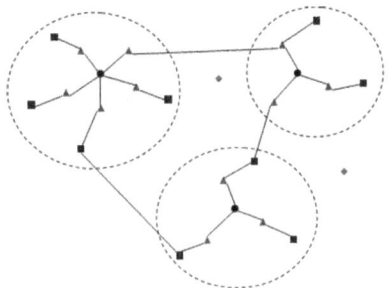

Fig. 1. Diagram of community detecting procedure

4 ESFN Description and Data Representation

There exist inter-linked networks in the elements collections of the grade-level and distributed engineering information. The saved information may not be compatible with its using system. In order to solve this problem, engineering software format conversion could be considered. Therefore, Engineering Software Format Network (ESFN) is established.

In this paper, some commonly used engineering software is studied. From a variety of software, we select 22 software as follows to establish an ESFN: 3ds max8.0, AutoCAD2007, CAXA2007, MATLAB R2008a, SolidWorks2007, UG4.0, Pro/E4.0, I-deas12, VR-Platform4, Virtools4, CATIA, CorelDraw12, Flash9.0, Nero7, Photoshop10, Microsoft Access2003, Geomagic, ACDSee3.1, et al. Then we collect the formats that can be read or written by them. The network takes these formats as its nodes, thus we can establish an ESFN with 470 nodes, which is a directed network. With Photoshop as an example, the data format *.bmp can be converted to *.tif, so in the network, there exists a directed edge from the node bmp to the node tif. The weight on edges is on behalf of the interaction strength between nodes. We adopt the strategy of the similarity weight. That is assigning the number of the software that could complete the conversion between the formats as the weight to the edges connecting the nodes. For instance, there is five software that could converse the format *.igs to *.step, that is CAXA2007, SolidWorks2007, Pro/E4.0, I-deas12 and CATIA. So the weight on the directed edge from the node igs to step is 5. The larger the weight, the closer the relationship between the two nodes, that is the stronger the convertibility between the nodes. At last, an actual weighted ESFN with 470 nodes and 12313 arcs is established. Fig. 2 is a schematic diagram of a part of the weighted ESFN.

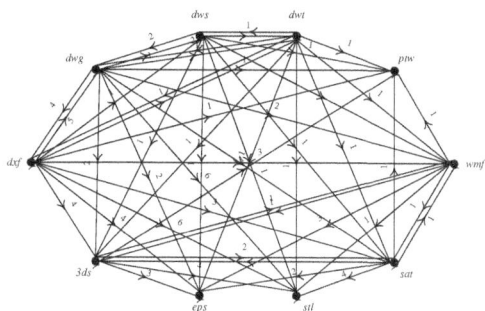

Fig. 2. The schematic diagram of a part of the weighted ESFN

The standard mathematical representation of the network is provided by the adjacency matrix A of elements a_{ij}. For a weighted graph, we construct the weighted adjacency matrix W in which the elements w_{ij} are computed as the sum of ways from *i* to *j*. The elements w_{ij} are null in the case of there being not existing conversion from *i* to *j*, and by definition the diagonal elements are set to zero. According to the assumption, the weighted matrix is asymmetric and the network is described as a directed graph. The weighted graph provides a richer description because it considers both the topology and the quantitative information in the network.

5   Experimental Results and Analysis

In our experiments, we run two algorithms for detecting the community structure of ESFN. As a classical Algorithm, Girvan-Newman Algorithm is used for comparing with the Coulomb's Law-based one.

5.1 Girvan-Newman Algorithm

Girvan and Newman [1] presented a method for detecting the communities, built around the idea of using centrality indices to find community boundaries. The algorithm works by using information about edge betweenness to detect community peripheries. The betweenness centrality of a node *i* is defined as the number of shortest paths between pairs of other nodes that run through *i*. If a network contains communities that are only loosely connected by a few intergroup edges, then all shortest paths between different communities must go along one of these few edges. Thus, the edges connecting communities will have high edge betweenness. By removing these edges, we separate groups from one another and so reveal the underlying community structure of the graph.

In order to measure the network community, Newman [4] define a modularity measure by

$$Q = \sum_i (e_{ii} - a_i^2) = Tre - \| e^2 \| \cdot \tag{6}$$

Where $\|x\|$ indicates the sum of the elements of the matrix X. This quantity measures the fraction of the edges in the network that connect nodes of the same type (i.e., within-community edges) minus the expected value of the same quantity in a network with the same community divisions but random connections between the nodes. In practice, values for such networks typically fall in the range from about 0.3 to 0.7.

We can obtain 8 communities for the above ESFN by using Girvan-Newman algorithm at the maximum modularity measure $Q=0.335$.

5.2 Experimental Results of Community Structure Detection Algorithm Based on Coulomb's Law

We can obtain 8 communities for the above ESFN by using the novel detection algorithm. Part of the experimental result is shown in Table 1. Each data format is given a number label. For example, number 1 represents the data format *.3ds.

Table 1. The Communities obtained by the novel algorithm based on Coulomb's law

No.	Size	Part of the members of the community
1	3	6,10,23
2	156	(part) 1,3,4,5,7,8,9,11,12,13,14,15,16,17,18,19,20,21,22,24,25,27,28,29,30, 31,32,34,36,38,39,41,42,43,44,46,48,49,50,51,53,57,58,59,60,61,62,63,68,69
3	103	(part) 2,26,35,37,40,47,52,54,55,56,64,65,66,67,74,75,76,77,78,82,84,86,96, 124,125,126,127,227,162,165,169,170,171, 172,173,174,175,176,177,178
4	30	317,442,443,444,445,446,447,448,449,450,451,452,453,454,455,456,457, 458,459,460,461,462,463, 464,465,466, 467,468,469,470
5	66	(part) 33,129,167,185,200,220,278,279,280,281,282,283,284,285,286,287, 288,289,290,291,292,293,294, 295,296,297,298,299,300,301,302,303,304
6	21	250,252,256,257,258,259,260,261,262,263,264,265,266,267,268,269,270, 271,272,273,277
7	86	(part) 70,79,80,81,83,120,131,188,204,228,235,237,238,246,253,255,339, 340,341,342,343,344,345,346,347,348,349,350,351,352,353,354,355,356
8	5	45,206,275,423,426

5.3 Experimental Results Analysis

The experimental results based on two algorithms show that the number of the communities is consistent, i.e. there are 8 communities detected. From comparison analysis, we can find that there are 439 nodes which are in the same community. For example, the nodes numbered 6, 10, and 23 are all in the same Community 1 by using any algorithm. The consistent rate about two algorithms is 93.4%, i.e. the proportion of 439 nodes to 470 nodes. While the high consistent rate is obtained, the novel Coulomb's Law-based detection algorithm has lower computation complexity compared with Girvan-Newman algorithm, because it is not necessary for the novel detection algorithm to analyze the link length and other details. The time complexity of the novel algorithm is $O(n^2)$ and the one of Girvan-Newman Algorithm is $O(n^3)$. Therefore, the experimental results show that the novel Coulomb's Law-based community structure detection algorithm is effective and promising.

6 Conclusion

In this paper, we proposed a novel Coulomb's Law-based community structure detection algorithm for complex networks analysis. Then, we established an engineering software format network and applied two algorithms (i.e. Coulomb's Law-based algorithm and Girvan-Newman algorithm) to detect the community structure of the weighted ESFN. The experimental results show the high consistent rate of these two algorithms. And the novel algorithm is superior in low time complexity. In the future, we will apply the novel community detecting algorithm in other networks, such as citation network, metabolic network, and web page network.

Acknowledgement. This work is supported by the National Natural Science Foundation of China (No.60873208) and the Hebei Province Science & Technology Research and Development Plan Key Program (No. 10213516D).

References

1. Girvan, M., Newman, M.E.J.: Community Structure in Social and Biological Networks. Proceedings of the National Academy of Sciences 99, 271–350 (2002)
2. Kernighan, B.W., Lin, S.: A Efficient Heuristic Procedure for Partitioning Graphs. Bell System Technical Journal 49, 921–307 (1970)
3. Pothen, A., Simon, H., Liou, K.P.: Partitioning Sparse Matrices with Eigenvectors of Graphs. SIAM J. Matrix Anal. Appl. 11, 430 (1990)
4. Newman, M.E.J., Girvan, M.: Finding and Evaluating Community Structure in Networks. Phys. Rev. E 69, 96–113 (2004)
5. Blondel, V.D., Guillaume, J., Lambiotte, R.: Etienne Lefebvre: Fast Unfolding of Communities in Large Networks. Journal of Statistical Mechanics: Theory and Experiment 10, 10008–10019 (2008)

Dynamic Texture Modeling Applied on Computer Vision Based Fire Recognition

Yang Zhao, Jianhui Zhao[*], Erqian Dong, Bingyu Chen, Jun Chen,
Zhiyong Yuan, and Dengyi Zhang

Computer School, Wuhan University, Wuhan, Hubei, 430072, P.R. China
jianhuizhao@whu.edu.cn

Abstract. In computer vision based fire detection systems, the fire sensing algorithm usually consists of two main parts: fire pixel classification, and analysis of the candidate regions. Purpose of the first step is to find a set of pixels which may be fire, and the second step is used to make decisions whether fire exists in the region. The algorithm proposed in this paper works on the second step. Different with the traditional methods using color or shape information, candidate fire regions in video are taken as dynamic textures in our approach, and dynamic texture modeling is adopted for fire testing. That is, for a candidate region, we build dynamic texture models, e.g. LDS, NLDS, and our proposed MRALDS, then parameters of the models are employed to determine the presence or absence of fire using our proposed recognition framework. Performance of our method has been tested with 68 videos including 32 fire videos and 36 non-fire videos. The experimental results are quite encouraging in terms of correctly classifying the videos.

Keywords: Fire detection, LDS model, NLDS model, dynamic texture model, multi-resolution analysis.

1 Introduction

In general, the existing computer vision based fire detection systems employ two major stages: fire pixel classification, and then analysis of the candidate regions. There are a lot of algorithms for fire pixel classification, but the algorithms to analyze the candidate regions and make the final determination are relatively few.

Many fire detection methods directly used raw RGB color information to classify the pixels, such as method proposed in [1]. Toreyin et al. [2] applied a mixture of Gaussian models in RGB space for pixel classification, while the mixture model is obtained from a set of training pixels. Based on the classified pixels, candidate fire regions are obtained but need further determination, e.g. filtering the segmented fire like areas of red soil or red buildings. In Reference [3,4,5], motion information of the candidate regions are analyzed, and Markov field modeling method is adopted to represent the fire flicker process. After segmentation with CIE L*a*b* color model, Celik [6] presented a fire detection method using shape based motion information, i.e. taking the

---

[*] Corresponding author.

H. Deng et al. (Eds.): AICI 2011, Part III, LNAI 7004, pp. 545–553, 2011.
© Springer-Verlag Berlin Heidelberg 2011

number of fire pixels to describe the variation of region area. Although analysis of the segmented regions helps filter some fake objects having fire like color, there are still certain objects similar with fire in both color and shape, and even motion property of them, such as flying red flag, dancing red cloth, shaking red flowers, or waving red leaves. For these cases, dynamic texture analysis has to be considered.

In this paper, we work on the novel analysis method based on dynamic texture, which views the burning fire as dynamic texture procedure, and it provides proofs for us to classify fire from other objects. The method can be simply described as: for a candidate region full of possible fire pixels, we build dynamic texture models for it, and then the parameters of the models are obtained and applied in making final decisions. There are several existing models for dynamic textures. The most often used model is Derotto's Linear Dynamic System (LDS) model [7,8,9]. As an improvement for LDS, Non-linear Dynamic System (NLDS) model was proposed by Lu [10]. To describe the dynamic texture of fire better, in this paper we propose the Multi-resolution Analysis Linear Dynamic System (MRALDS) model. Some dynamic objects have similar color and shape with fire, but their motion patterns may be different from fire, and the parameters of dynamic texture models can help capture the difference. Through comparing the calculated parameters, it is possible to separate fire from other objects and thus reduce the false alarm rate.

Our paper is organized as follows. Section 2 presents the essentials of LDS model and NLDS model, and the dynamic texture based recognition algorithms using them. Section 3 describes the proposed MRALDS model and the related dynamic texture recognition algorithm based on it. Section 4 provides the fire recognition framework with dynamic texture analysis. Section 5 displays the experimental results. Then the conclusion is given in Section 6.

2 Dynamic Texture Models and Recognition Algorithm

2.1 LDS Model and NLDS Model

LDS model is an improved model based on Szummer's STAR model [11]. Assume that $y(t) \in R^N$ is one N-dimensional frame data in the dynamic texture at a certain time t, $x(t) \in R^M$ is the M-dimensional state vector at time t $(M \ll N)$. The LDS's model equation can be expressed:

$$\begin{cases} x(t+1) = Ax(t) + v(t) \\ \quad y(t) = Cx(t) + w(t) \end{cases} \tag{1}$$

In the above formula, the time-invariant matrix A and matrix C are state transition matrix and system output matrix respectively, $v(t) \sim N(0,Q)$ and $w(t) \sim N(0,R)$ are both independent identically distribution noises, while $x(t)$ can be considered as the PCA decomposition result of $y(t)$.

NLDS model is an improved model for LDS. NLDS makes use of Kernel PCA algorithm to reduce dimension of the original image data. Kernel PCA is a non-linear dimension reduction algorithm. The mathematical definition of NLDS is:

$$\begin{cases} x(t+1) = Ax(t) + Bv(t) \\ y(t) = C(x(t)) + w(t) \end{cases} \tag{2}$$

The mapping from the original data space $\{y_i \mid i = 1 \cdots n\}$ to $\{x_i \mid i = 1 \cdots n\}$ is non-linear, which is denoted by the non-linear function $C()$. Similar with LDS model, $v(t)$ and $w(t)$ are both independent identically distribution white noises, while $x(t)$ is the dimension reduction result of $y(t)$ through Kernel PCA algorithm.

2.2 LDS and NLDS Based Dynamic Texture Recognition

LDS model originated from automatic control theory, and can be applied in both dynamic texture synthesis and dynamic texture recognition, e.g. Saisan et al. [12] proposed a dynamic texture classification algorithm based on system recognition theory. Martin distance is adopted to represent the similarity between two dynamic textures. The two dynamic textures are more similar if the martin distance between them is smaller.

Let $M_1(A_1, C_1)$ and $M_2(A_2, C_2)$ represent two LDS models, and the extended observing matrix for LDS model M_i is denoted by:

$$O_\infty(M_i) = [C_i^T \ A_i^T C_i^T \ \cdots (A_i^T)^n C_i^T] \tag{3}$$

where matrix $O_\infty(M_i)$ has infinite dimensions, and we can only approximately calculate it. In our experiments, $O_\infty(M_i)$ is approximately represented with $O_{100}(M_i)$.

Then we can compute matrix X according to the following formula:

$$X = \begin{pmatrix} 0 & O_{100}(M_1)^T O_{100}(M_2) \\ O_{100}(M_2)^T O_{100}(M_1) & 0 \end{pmatrix} \tag{4}$$

where

$$O_{100}(M_1)^T O_{100}(M_2) = \sum_{i=0}^{n} (A_1^i)^T C_1^T C_2 A_2^i \tag{5}$$

We obtain the first m eigen-values of the matrix X in descending ordered eigen vector. The m eigen-values are denoted as $\lambda_i (i = 1, 2, \cdots m)$, Martin distance can finally be calculated by:

$$d = (-2) \sum_{i=1}^{m} \log \lambda_i \tag{6}$$

Different with LDS, the model parameter C in NLDS do not have explicit expressions. Therefore, A_i can be directly calculated from the result of KPCA, but $C_1^T C_2$ in Formula (5) can not be computed directly. In this case, "kernel strategy" [13,14] is employed to solve the problem [15], i.e. the data of original image is used to compute $C_1^T C_2$. Although $C_1^T C_2$ can be obtained in this way, certain calculation errors may be brought, especially for the dynamic textures with much noise. And the reason is obvious: PCA or KPCA analyze and only use the principal components of original data, which is less sensitive to the noise.

3   Dynamic Texture Model with Multi-resolution Analysis

3.1   MRALDS Model

The traditional LDS method builds models from the image data space. Obviously, we can first do some transforms on the image data and then build models from the new data space, e.g. the LDS model built in the frequency-domain space which is transformed from the original pixel space. Therefore, the transformed dynamic texture signal may include the information of different scales and directions. In our method, multi-resolution analysis methods are used to decompose the original image texture data into multiple sub-bands with different details, and then the decomposed results are used to build LDS models respectively. The LDS model based on multi-resolution analysis is denoted as MRALDS model. The mathematic definition of MARLDS is:

$$
\begin{cases}
\{y_1(t), y_2(t), \cdots y_S(t)\} = MRA(I(t)) \\
\quad x_i(t+1) = A_i x_i(t) + B_i v(t) \\
\quad\quad y_i(t) = C_i x_i(t) + w(t)
\end{cases}
\tag{7}
$$

where $I(t)$ represents the t-th fame of the original video clip, $y_i(t)$ represents the transformed results after multi-resolution analysis on $I(t)$, and the total number of the decomposed sub-bands is S. The other parameters and variables are similar with the formula of LDS.

There are some kinds of multi-resolution analysis methods for image processing. We choose three of them which are often used: laplacian pyramid decomposition, wavelet decomposition, and steerable pyramid decomposition. Fig.1 shows the results of these three decomposition methods on one fire image, and all the obtained sub-bands are considered simultaneously in pattern classification.

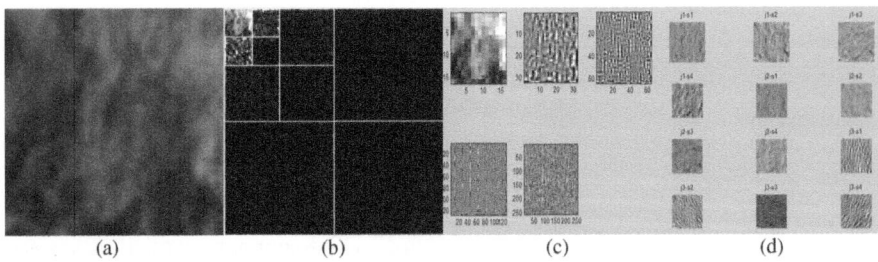

| (a) | (b) | (c) | (d) |

Fig. 1. Multi-resolution analysis on fire image, (a) the original fire image; (b) results of wavelet decomposition; (c) results of laplacian pyramid decomposition; (d) results of steerable pyramid decomposition.

3.2 Dynamic Texture Recognition with MRALDS

MRALDS builds LDS model at each scale and direction, so the models can generate several groups of parameters. But the martin distance is defined for two LDS models. Thus we need to find a new way to calculate the martin distance of two MRALDS models. First we calculate the martin distance of two LDS models which are at the same scale and the same direction in two corresponding MRALDS models. Imagine $M_1, M_2, \cdots M_S$ are S NLDS models that are built form dynamic texture D1 based on multi-resolution analysis method, correspondingly $M'_1, M'_2, \cdots M'_S$ are S NLDS models that are generated from dynamic texture D2 with multi-resolution analysis method. Suppose the weights of S NLDS models on martin distance are $w_1, w_2, \cdots w_S$. Thus the MRALDS martin distance of dynamic texture D1 and dynamic texture D2 can be calculated with the following formula:

$$Martin(D_1, D_2) = \sum_{i=1}^{S} w_i * Martin(M_i, M'_i) \tag{8}$$

It can be found that MRALDS martin distance is the weighted-sum of LDS martin distances of all decomposed sub-bands. Of course, choosing the best set of weights is a very difficult problem.

Just like MARLDS, we can use the NLDS model based on multi-resolution analysis, and denote it as the MRANLDS model. Obviously, MRANLDS definition and application on dynamic texture recognition are both in the same way as those of MARLDS.

4   Fire Recognition Framework with Dynamic Texture Analysis

When dynamic texture analysis is used on dynamic texture based classification, the recognition algorithm can make use of the calculated martin distances from two dynamic texture models. Here the pattern recognition framework is presented for fire recognition based on dynamic texture models.

First a standard sample database is built with fire videos and test videos. There are N fire videos in the database and they are denoted as $\{Ts_1, Ts_2, \cdots, Ts_N\}$, M test videos and they are denoted as $\{Te_1, Te_2, \cdots, Te_M\}$. Martin distance between Te_i and Ts_j is denoted as $MDis(Te_i, Ts_j)$. For a given test sample, we have two kinds of methods to judge whether the test sample is fire sample, i.e. average distance method and minimum distance method.

Average distance method makes use of the average martin distance between the given test sample Te_i and all of the fire samples in the standard sample database. Each test sample has an average martin distance and we denote the average martin distance of Te_i as $Mean\_MDS(Te_i)$, $Mean\_MDS(Te_i)$ can be calculated as:

$$Mean\_MDS(Te_i) = \frac{1}{N} \sum_{j=1}^{N} MDis(Te_i, Ts_j) \tag{9}$$

Then we set a threshold Th_1 to judge whether the test video is a fire video, and the judge formula is:

$$\begin{cases} Mean\_MDS(Te_i) <= Th_1, \ Te_i \ is \ fire \ video \\ Mean\_MDS(Te_i) > Th_1, \ Te_i \ is \ not \ fire \ video \end{cases} \tag{10}$$

The minimum distance method makes use of the minimum martin distance between the given test sample Te_i and all of the fire samples in the standard database. Each test sample has a minimum martin distance and the minimum martin distance of Te_i is denoted as $Min\_MDS(Te_i)$, $Min\_MDS(Te_i)$ can be calculated as:

$$Min\_MDS(Te_i) = \min\{MDis(Te_i, Ts_j)\}(j = 1, 2, ...N) \tag{11}$$

Then we set a threshold Th_2 to decide the test sample and the judge formula is:

$$\begin{cases} Min\_MDS(Te_i) <= Th_2, \ Te_i \ is \ fire \ video \\ Min\_MDS(Te_i) > Th_2, \ Te_i \ is \ not \ fire \ video \end{cases} \tag{12}$$

The choice of Th_1 and Th_2 depends on experiments and experience, and the setting of them will affect the final result of pattern classification.

Obviously, the presented pattern recognition framework can work on any kind of dynamic texture model, including LDS, NLDS, MARLDS, MARNLDS, etc.

5   Experimental Results

In our experiment, we choose 5 fire videos as standard fire samples, and use other 32 fire videos and 36 non-fire videos as test samples, as shown in Fig.2. For each of the 32 fire videos, we select one window from the fire region and build dynamic texture models on the window, i.e. make sure that the window is full of fire. To test our algorithm effectively, the 36 non-fire videos are all similar with fire, including flying red flag, shaking red flowers, and waving red leaves.

Fig. 2. Some test samples, fire videos in the first row and non-fire videos in the second row

Three parameters are utilized to evaluate the classification performance, and they are: error number, false number and recognition rate. Error number (EN) is defined as the number of test samples which are non-fire videos but classified as fire videos. False number (FN) is defined as the number of test samples which are fire videos but classified as non-fire videos. Recognition rate (RR) is defined as the value of the number of correctly recognized samples divided by the number of total test samples.

We tested the dynamic texture based recognition algorithm with LDS model and NLDS model respectively. For each kind of model, we have compared the recognition performances based on both average distance method (ADM) and minimum distance method (MDM). As shown in Table 1, performance of LDS is much better than that of NLDS, while there is no obvious difference between ADM and MDM.

As mentioned in Section 2, LDS use the result of PCA to compute the parameters, and less sensitive to the noise; while NLDS also use the original data besides KPCA result, thus sensitive to the noise. All the test samples in our database are captured real videos including fire, flag, flowers, leaves, etc. They are not ideal videos with dynamic texture property that can be mathematically described, and have much noise. Therefore, it is reasonable that LDS performs better than NLDS. Based on the same reason, we only need to test MRALDS, the LDS dynamic texture model with multi-resolution analysis.

Table 1. Results of dynamic texture recognition algorithm based on LDS model and NLDS model

Methods	LDS			NLDS		
	EN	FN	RR	EN	FN	RR
ADM	0	5	92.65%	5	9	79.41%
MDM	0	5	92.65%	5	9	79.41%

For experiments with MRALDS model, the aforementioned three decomposition methods are tested, including laplacian pyramid, wavelet, and steerable pyramid. From the experimental results, it can be found that fire recognition algorithm using MRALDS model has the best performance, which proves that multi-resolution analysis method can describe the textures better.

Table 2. Results of dynamic texture recognition algorithm based on MRALDS model

Methods	LP			Wavelet			SteerPyr		
	EN	FN	RR	EN	FN	RR	EN	FN	RR
ADM	0	4	94.12%	0	4	94.12%	3	1	94.12%
MDM	0	4	94.12%	0	5	92.65%	0	5	92.65%

6 Conclusion

Different with the traditional approaches, we tried the fire recognition method based on dynamic texture analysis. The models including LDS, NLDS, MARLDS and MARNLDS are built to represent dynamic texture of the videos, then the parameters of the models are extracted, computed, and used for pattern classification. In fire recognition framework, both average distance method and minimum distance method are applied on martin distance between different models, and final results are determined basically with the help of predefined threshold value.

The proposed dynamic texture models and fire recognition framework are tested with experiments on a lot of samples including fire videos and non-fire videos. The experimental results illustrate the ability of dynamic texture analysis to recognize fire from fire like moving objects. Within all the models, MARLDS has the best performance, since it is less sensitive to the noise, while can describe the information of different scales and directions with multi-resoultion analysis using decomposition methods.

Acknowledgement. This work was supported by Hubei Provincial Natural Science Foundation of China, National Basic Research Program of China (973 Program, No. 2011CB707904), Research Foundation (No. AISTC2008_16) from State Key Laboratory of Aerospace Information Security and Trusted Computing Ministry of Education, Fundamental Research Funds for the Central Universities, and 985 Project of Cognitive and Neural Information Science, Wuhan University (No. 904273258).

References

1. Chen, T., Wu, P., Chiou, Y.: An Early Fire-Detection Method Based on Image Processing. In: IEEE 2004 International Conference on Image Processing, vol. 3, pp. 1707–1710 (2004)
2. Toreyin, B.U., Dedeoglu, Y.: Flame Detection in Video Using Hidden Markov Models. In: IEEE 2005 International Conference on Image Processing, vol. 4, pp. 1230–1233 (2005)
3. Brand, M., Oliver, N.: Coupled hmm for complex action recognition. In: Proceedings of Conference on Computer Vision and Pattern Recognition, pp. 213–244 (1997)
4. Toreyin, B.U., Dedeoglu, Y., Cetin, A.E.: Computer Vision Based Method for Real-Time Fire and Flame Detection. Pattern Recognition Letters 27, 49–58 (2006)
5. Byoung, C.K., Cheong, K.H., Nam, J.Y.: Fire detection based on vision sensor and support vector machine. Fire Safety Journal 44, 322–329 (2009)
6. Celik, T.: Fast and Efficient Method for Fire Detection Using Image Processing. ETRI Journal 32, 881–890 (2010)
7. Doretto, G., Chiuso, A., Soatto, S., Wu, T.N.: Dynamic Textures. International Journal of Computer Vision 51, 91–109 (2003)
8. Black, M.G.: Explaining optical flow events with parameterized spatio-temporal models. In: Proceedings of Conference on Computer Vision and Pattern Recognition, vol. 1, pp. 326–332 (1999)
9. Martin, R.: A metric for arma processes. IEEE Transactions on Signal Processing 48, 1164–1167 (2000)
10. Lu, Y., Chen, G.M.: Improved dynamic texture synthesis algorithm based on kernel PCA. Computer Engineering and Design 29, 3687–3689 (2008)

11. Szummer, M., Picard, R.W.: Temporal texture modeling. In: IEEE International Conference on Image Processing, vol. 3, pp. 823–826 (1996)
12. Saisan, P., Derotto, G.: Dynamic Texture Recognition. In: Proceedings of the 2001 IEEE Computer Society Conference on Computer Vision and Pattern Recognition, pp. 58–63 (2001)
13. Scholkopf, B., Smola, A., Muller, K.R.: Nonlinear component analysis as a kernel eigen-value problem. Neural Computation 10, 1299–1319 (1998)
14. Torre, F.: Robust principal component analysis for computer vision. In: Proceedings of IEEE International Conference on Computer Vision, vol. 1, pp. 362–369 (2001)
15. Kwok, J.T., Tsang, I.W.: The pre-image problem in kernel method. IEEE Transactions on Neural Network 15, 1517–1525 (2004)

Adaptively Weighted Subpattern-Based Isometric Projection for Face Recognition

Lai Wei[1,*], Weiming Zeng[1], and Feife Xu[2]

[1] Department of Computer Science, Shanghai Maritime University,
Haigang Avenue 1550, Shanghai, China
{weilai,wmzeng}@shmtu.edu.cn
[2] Department of Computer Science, Shanghai University of Electric Power,
Pingliang Road 2103, Shanghai, China
xufeifei1983@hotmail.com

Abstract. In this paper, we propose an adaptively weighted subpattern-based isometric projection (Aw-spIsoP) algorithm for face recognition. Unlike IsoP (isometric projection) based on a whole image pattern, the proposed Aw-spIsoP method operates on sub-patterns partitioned from an original whole face image and separately extracts corresponding local sub-features from them. Moreover, the adjacency graph used in the algorithm is constructed based on path-based distance optimized neighborhoods of the sub-patterns and the contribution of each sub-pattern is adaptively computed in order to enhance the robustness to facial pose, expression and illumination variations. Experimental results on three bench mark face databases (ORL, YALE and PIE) show that Aw-spIsoP can overcome the shortcomings of the existed subpattern-based methods and achieve the promising recognition accuracy.

Keywords: face recognition, subpattern, path-based distance, isometric projection.

1 Introduction

Face recognition has been among the most active research topics in pattern recognition, computer vision and machine learning communities[1,2,3]. One of the most successful and well-studied techniques are the appearance-based methods[4,5,6]. Two of the most representative subspace techniques for face recognition are principal component analysis (PCA)[4] and fisher linear discriminant analysis (LDA)[5]. PCA is designed to reduce the dimension of the data by projecting the original data onto a linear subspace spanned by the leading eigenvectors of the data's covariance matrix. LDA searches for a low-dimensional subspace in which the data samples from the same class will assemble and the data samples with different class labels will lie apart.

Recently, a few new subspace techniques including locality preserving projection (LPP)[7], isometric projetion (IsoP)[8] and non-negative matrix factorization (NMF)[9], have attracted many researchers' attention. LPP is a manifold

---

* Corresponding author.

H. Deng et al. (Eds.): AICI 2011, Part III, LNAI 7004, pp. 554–561, 2011.
© Springer-Verlag Berlin Heidelberg 2011

learning based method which is effective in maintaining the locality of the face image data sets. Unlike LPP, IsoP aims to preserve the global manifold structure of the original data set. NMF is designed to capture part-based structures inherent in the face images space. The non-negative constraints of NMF do not allow negative elements either in the basis vectors or weighted vectors.

Subpattern-based algorithm[10,11,12] have also been proposed for face recognition. In the subpattern-based algorithms, face images are firstly divided into several small sub-images, and then the subpattern features are extracted by applying a given dimensionality reduction algorithm to all sub-image blocks. At last, faces are classified by comparing and combining the corresponding local features. A popular subpattern based technique is subpattern PCA (SpPCA)[13]. Besides PCA, some other techniques are also used for subpattern-based face recognition. Zhu proposed a subpattern non-negative matrix factorization (SpNMF)[14] algorithm. Wang et al. proposed an adaptively weighted subpattern-based LPP (Aw-spLPP) algorithm[11] and extended spLPP to a structure-preserved local matching approach (spLMA)[12].

In this paper, we propose an adaptively weighted subpattern-based isometric projection (Aw-spIsoP) algorithm for face recognition. In the proposed algorithm, the whole face images are also firstly partitioned into a set of equal-size sub-patterns in a non-overlapping way. Then IsoP algorithm is implemented on each of subpattern sets. Different from the traditional IsoP algorithm which uses Euclidean distance to find the k nearest neighbors for constructing the adjacent graph, we use path-based distance to determine the neighbors for each sample. In succession, the contribution of each sub-pattern to recognition is adaptively computed using path-based distance and class information. Finally, subpattern-based features are compared and combined for face recognition. Experimental results on the bench mark face databases show that the Aw-spIsoP algorithm achieves the promising recognition accuracy.

2   Review of Isometric Projection

Let $\mathbf{X} = [\mathbf{x}_1, \mathbf{x}_2, ..., \mathbf{x}_n] \in \mathbb{R}^{D \times n}$ be the data matrix, $d_{\mathcal{M}}$ be the geodesic distance measure on the data manifold $\mathcal{M}$ and d_e the standard Euclidean distance measure in $\mathbb{R}^d$. Isometric Projection aims to find a embedding function f such that Euclidean distances in $\mathbb{R}^d$ can provide a good approximation to the geodesic distances on $\mathcal{M}$. That is,

$$f = \arg\min_f \sum_{i,j} \Big(d_{\mathcal{M}}(\mathbf{x}_i - \mathbf{x}_j) - d_e\big(f(\mathbf{x}_i) - f(\mathbf{x}_j)\big) \Big)^2 \qquad (1)$$

The geodesic distances $d_{\mathcal{M}}(i, j)$ between all pairs of points on the manifold $\mathcal{M}$ can be estimated by computing their shortest path distances $d_{\mathcal{G}}(i, j)$ on the adjacency graph G modeling the local geometry of the data set. The graph usually is constructed by KNN (k-nearest-neighbors) or $\epsilon - ball$ method.

Let D be the distance matrix such that D_{ij} is the distance between $\mathbf{x}_i$ and $\mathbf{x}_j$. Define matrix $S_{ij} = D_{ij}^2$ and $H = I - \frac{1}{m}\mathbf{e}\mathbf{e}^T$, where I is the identity matrix and

$\mathbf{e}$ is the vector of all ones. It can be shown that $\tau(D) = -HSH/2$ is the inner product matrix. Let D_Y denote the Euclidean distance matrix in the reduced subspace, and $\tau(D_Y)$ be the corresponding inner product matrix. Thus, the objective function (1) becomes minimizing the following:

$$\|\tau(D_G) - \tau(D_Y)\|_{L^2} \tag{2}$$

where $\| \cdot \|$ is the L^2 matrix norm.

Consider a linear function $Y = (\mathbf{y}_1, ..., \mathbf{y}_n) \in \mathbb{R}^{d \times n} = \mathbf{w}^T X$, d is the dimensions of embedding subspace. Then $\tau(D_Y) = Y^T Y = X^T \mathbf{w} \mathbf{w}^T X$. According to function (2), the optimal projection is given by solving the following minimization problem:

$$\mathbf{w}^* = \min_{\mathbf{w}} \|\tau(D_G) - X^T \mathbf{w} \mathbf{w}^T X\| \tag{3}$$

To avoid degenerate solutions, an additional constrain $\mathbf{w}^T X X^T \mathbf{w} = 1$ should be imposed on the above problem. With simple algebric formulation, the optimization problem can be expressed as follows:

$$\arg \max_{\mathbf{w}^T X X^T \mathbf{w} = 1} \mathbf{w}^T X \tau(D_G) X^T \mathbf{w} \tag{4}$$

3   Adaptively Weighted Isometric Projection

The proposed algorithm consists of three main steps: (1) partition face images into sub-patterns, (2) apply IsoP to local feature extraction and compute the contribution of each subpattern (3) classify an unknown face image.

3.1   Face Image Partition

In subpattern-based face recognition methods, a face image can be partitioned into a set of equally or unequally sized sub-images. Without loss of generality, equally sized partition is adopted in our approach as in many other approaches(such as Aw-spPCA, Aw-spLPP, spNMF and spLMA)[11,12,13,14].

Let $\mathbf{X} = [\mathbf{x}_1, \mathbf{x}_2, ..., \mathbf{x}_n]$ denote n face images belonging to n_p persons, and the size of each image is $H_1 \times H_2$. We first partition each face image into C equally sized sub-images in a non-overlapping way, and further concatenate them into corresponding column vectors with dimensionality of $H_1 \times H_2/C$. Afterwards, the sub-pattern vectors at the same position of all face images are collected to form a specific subpattern set. Therefore, we can get C separate subpattern sets totally. The procedure of image partition is illustrated in Figure 1.

3.2   Subpattern-Based IsoP and Contributions Computation

A.Subpattern-based IsoP. In the traditional IsoP algorithm, Euclidean distance is used to find the k nearest neighbors of each sample. In this paper, we will

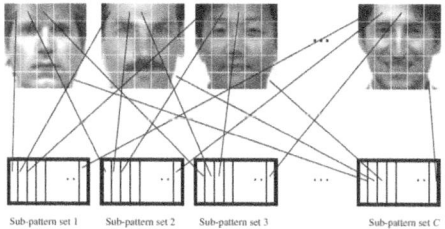

Fig. 1. The construction of sub-image sets[13]

use path-based distance[15,16] to build the neighborhood graph for Aw-spIsoP. We briefly introduce the definition of path-based distance as follows.

Let $G = (V, V \times V)$ be the complete Euclidean graph of all data points. And P_{ij} denote the set of all paths from vertex i to vertex j through the graph. The path-based distance $d_p(v_i, v_j)$ can be defined as follows:

$$d_p(v_i, v_j) = \min_{\mathbf{p} \in P_{ij}} \{ \max_{1 \le h \le |\mathbf{p}|} d_e(v_h, v_{h+1}) \} \tag{5}$$

Then for each subpattern set $S_m(m = 1, 2, \cdots, C)$, its low-dimensional features can be extracted by IsoP with path-based distance. Let $Z_m = [\mathbf{z}_{m1}, \mathbf{z}_{m2}, \cdots, \mathbf{z}_{mn}]$ denote n column vectors in S_m. According to the description in Section 2, the projection matrix $\mathbf{W}_m$ of S_m can be composed of the eigenvectors corresponding to its largest d eigenvalues of the following generalized eigenvalue problems:

$$Z_m \tau (D_{mG}) Z_m^T \mathbf{w}_{mj} = \lambda Z_m Z_m^T \mathbf{w}_{mj} \tag{6}$$

where $j = 1, 2, \cdots, d$. $\mathbf{W}_m = [\mathbf{w}_{m1}, \mathbf{w}_{m2}, \cdots, \mathbf{w}_{md}]^T$. Then the low-dimensional embedding of $\mathbf{z}_{m1}$ can be achieved as $\mathbf{y}_{m1} = \mathbf{W}_m^T \mathbf{z}_{m1}$.

Contributions computation. In our method, the contribution of each subpattern to recognition is computed through the label information of one subpattern and its k nearest neighbors chosen by path-based distance.

Suppose $\mathbf{z}_{mi}$ is the mth subpattern of the ith image $\mathbf{x}_i$. Then the weight of the mth sub-pattern can be obtained as

$$E_m = \frac{1}{n} \sum_{i=1}^{n} \frac{\sum_j exp(d_p(\mathbf{z}_{mi}, \mathbf{z}_{mj})/t)}{\sum_l exp(d_p(\mathbf{z}_{mi}, \mathbf{z}_{ml})/t)} \tag{7}$$

where $j, l \in \mathcal{N}(\mathbf{z}_{mi})$, $\mathcal{N}(\mathbf{z}_{mi})$ is the neighborhood of $\mathbf{z}_{mi}$. t is a positive parameter(in the following experiments, t is empirically set as the mean of the all pairwise distance of the data points). $\mathbf{x}_j$, $\mathbf{x}_i$ should be the face images of same person. Obviously, we have $0 \le E_m \le 1$.

3.3   Face Recognition

For the sake of classifying an unknown face image, the unknown face image x^* should be firstly divided into C sub-images in the same way previously applied to the training images. Then, each unknown subpattern's features are extracted by using the corresponding projection matrix $\mathbf{W}_i(i = 1, 2, \cdots, C)$. The class label of each sub-pattern is determined by a nearest neighbor classifier using Euclidean distance. Since one classification result for the unknown sample is generated independently in each subpattern, there will be total C results from C sub-patterns. To combine C classification results from all sub-patterns of this face image, a weighted voting method is used. Let the probability of the unknown image x^* belonging to the cth class be

$$p_c = \sum_{i=1}^{C} E_i q_i^c \tag{8}$$

where
$$q_i^c = \begin{cases} 1, \text{ if the } i\text{th sub-pattern belongs to } c\text{th class}; \\ 0, \text{ otherwise}. \end{cases} \tag{9}$$

The final classification result is

$$L(\mathbf{x}^*) = \arg\max_c(p_c) \tag{10}$$

4   Experiments

In this section, the performance of the proposed algorithm (Aw-spIsoP) will be explored systematically on three standard face databases(ORL, YALE and PIE). The information of each data set is briefly introduced as follows.

ORL[1] database contains 10 different images of each of 40 distinct subjects. For some subjects, the images were taken at diffrent times, varying the lighting, facial expressions. YALE[2] database contains 165 grayscale images of 15 individuals. There are 11 images per subject, one per different facial expression or configuration. The CMU PIE[3] face database contains 68 subjects with 41,368 face images as a whole. The face images were captured by 13 synchronized cameras and 21 flashes, under varying pose, illumination, and expression. We only use a subset containing 5 near frontal poses (C05, C07, C09, C27, C29) and all the images under different illuminations and expressions. In our experiments, all the face images are resized to 64×64. The sample images of these three data sets are shown in Figure 3.

Recognition accuracy is used to evaluate the algorithm's performance. For comparisons, the seven different algorithms that we evaluated are Aw-SpPCA,

---

[1] http://www.uk.research.att.com/facedatabase.html
[2] http://cvc.yale.edu/projects/yalefaces/yalefaces.html
[3] http://www.ri.cmu.edu/projects/project_418.html

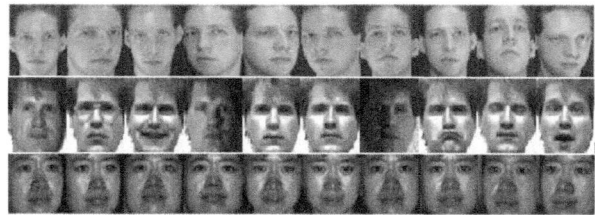

Fig. 2. The sample images of different face datasets. The images in the first, second and third rows are sample images of ORL database, YALE database and CMU PIE database respectively.

Aw-spLPP(the kernel width is empirically set as the mean of all pairwise distance of the data points), spNMF, IsoP, PCA, supervised LPP (SLPP, namely the affinity graph is constructed using label information of the training samples) and NMF. We first randomly select a certain number of face images from each person for each data set. Those selected images will be used as training samples and the remaining images will be used for testing. To control the balance of computation cost and recognition accuracy, the size of sub-image is set to 16×8 for subpattern-based algorithms. The experiments are conducted over 10 times independent runs.

A. Experimental results using ORL dataset. The recognition results on ORL dataset versus subspace dimensions are shown in Figure 4. Figure 4(a) and 4(b) show the performance of different algorithms with 4 and 5 training samples respectively. In these experiments, the neighbor parameters in Aw-spIsop, IsoP and Aw-spLPP are set as 4.

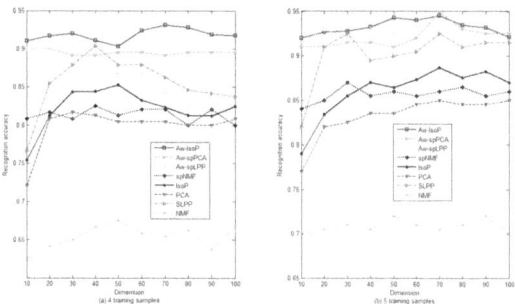

Fig. 3. Performance comparisons of different algorithms on ORL database

B. Experimental results using YALE dataset. The recognition results on YALE dataset versus subspace dimensions are shown in Figure 5. Figure 5(a) and 5(b) show the performance of different algorithms with 5 and 6 training samples

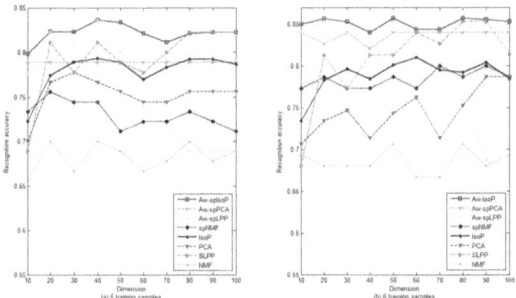

Fig. 4. Performance comparisons of different algorithms on YALE database

respectively. The neighbor parameters in Aw-IsoP, Isop and Aw-spLPP are set as 5.

C. Experimental results using PIE dataset. We randomly select 6 images for each individual on each pose (C05, C07, C09, C27, C29) to build up a new data set (denotes as S-PIE) used in the following experiments. Hence, there are 30 images for each individual in S-PIE. The performance of different algorithms with 10 and 15 training samples are evaluated. The experimental results are shown in Figure 6. The neighbor parameters in Aw-IsoP, Isop and Aw-spLPP are set as 8.

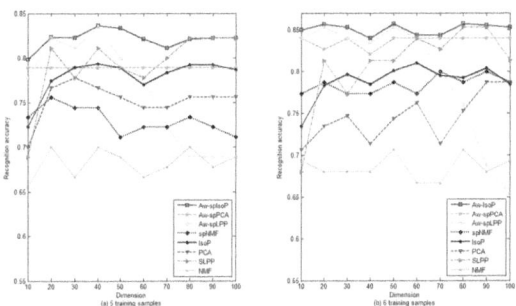

Fig. 5. Performance comparisons of different algorithms on S-PIE database

5   Conclusion

In this paper, we propose a new subpattern-based face recognition algorithm, called adaptively weighted subpattern-based isometric projection (Aw-spIsop). Aw-spIsoP uses path-based distance to construct the adjacency graph and computes the contribution of each subpattern adaptively with class information and path-based distance. We perform experiments on three face image databases

(ORL ,YALE and PIE). The experimental results indicate that our proposed approach is effective.

References

1. Pantic, M., Rothkrantz, L.: Automatic analysis of facial expressions: the state of art. IEEE Transactions on Pattern Analysis and Machine Intelligence 22(12), 1424–1445 (2000)
2. Fasel, B., Luettin, J.: Automatic facial expression analysis: a survey. Pattern Recognition 36, 259–275 (2003)
3. Tan, X., Chen, S., Zhou, Z., Zhang, F.: Face recognition from a single image per person: A survey. Pattern Recognition 39, 1725–1745 (2006)
4. Turk, M., Pentland, A.: Face recognition using eigenfaces. In: Proceedings of the IEEE Conference on Computer Vision and Pattern Recognition, pp. 586–591 (1991)
5. Belhumeur, P., Hespanha, J., Kriegman, D.: Eigenfaces vs. fisherfaces: recognition using class specific linear projection. IEEE Transactions on Pattern Analysis and Machine Intelligence 19(7), 711–720 (1997)
6. Levin, A., Shashua, A.: Principal Component Analysis over Continuous Subspaces and Intersection of Half-Spaces. In: Heyden, A., Sparr, G., Nielsen, M., Johansen, P. (eds.) ECCV 2002. LNCS, vol. 2352, pp. 635–650. Springer, Heidelberg (2002)
7. He, X., Yan, S., Hu, T., Niyogi, P., Zhang, H.: Face recognition using Laplacianfaces. IEEE Transactions on Pattern Analysis and Machine Intelligence 27(3), 328–340 (2005)
8. Cai, D., He, X., Han, J.: Isometric Projection. In: Proc. 22nd Conference on Artifical Intelligence (AAAI), Vancouver, Canada (July 2007)
9. Lee, D., Seung, H.: Algorithms for non-negative matrix factorization. In: Advances in Neural Information Process, pp. 556–562 (2000)
10. Zou, J., Ji, Q., Nagy, G.: A comparative study of local matching approach for face recognition. IEEE Trans. Image Process 16(10), 2617–2628 (2007)
11. Wang, J., Zhang, B., Wang, S., Qi, M., Kong, J.: An adaptively weighted subpattern locality preserving projection for face recognition. Journal of Network and Computer Applications 33, 323–332 (2010)
12. Wang, J., Zhang, B., Wang, S., Qi, M., Kong, J.: A structure-preserved local matching approach for face recognition. Pattern Recognition Letters 32, 494–504 (2011)
13. Chen, S., Zhu, Y.: Subpattern-based principle component analysis. Pattern Recognition 37, 1081–1083 (2005)
14. Zhu, Y.: Sub-pattern non-negative matrix factorization based on random subspace for face recognition. In: International Conference on Wavelet Analysis and Pattern Recognition, pp. 1356–1360 (2007)
15. Fischer, B., Buhmann, J.: Path-based clustering for grouping of smooth curves and texture segmentation. IEEE Trans. Pattern Analysis and Machine Intelligence 25(4), 513–518 (2003)
16. Wen, G., Jiang, L., Shadbolt, N.: Using Graph Algebra to Optimize Neighborhood for Isometric Mapping, In:Veloso MM,ed. In: Veloso, M.M. (ed.) Proc.of the 20th Int'l Joint Conf. on Artificial Intelligence (IJCAI 2007), pp. 2398–2403 (2007)

An Improvement to Matrix-Based LDA

Chongyang Zhang and Jingyu Yang

Nanjing University of Science and Technology, Nanjing, China
zcy603@163.com

Abstract. The matrix-based LDA method is attracting increasing attention. Compared with classic LDA, this method can overcome the small sample size (SSS) problem. However, previous literatures neglect the fact that there are two available matrix-based LDA algorithms and usually use only one of the two algorithms to perform the experiment. By experimental analysis, this work point out the combination of the two available matrix-based LDA algorithms can obtain a better performance.

Keywords: feature extraction, LDA, biometric images.

1 Introduction

In the field of face recognition, one of the hottest branches of biometrics, Fisher discriminant analysis (FDA) has attracted much attention [1-8]. It has also been used in a variety of pattern recognition and computer vision problems. In the past years, a number of FDA methods such as Foley-Sammon linear discriminant analysis, Fisherfaces, uncorrelated linear discriminant analysis and 2DLDA have been proposed [9-17]. Besides these linear discriminant analysis methods, kernel discriminant analysis has also been developed as the nonlinear version of FDA [18-25].

Recently, the matrix-based LDA method is attracting increasing attention. Compared with classic LDA, this method can overcome the small sample size (SSS) problem. It also seems that in the matrix-based LDA method, the between-class scatter matrix and the within-class scatter matrix can be evaluated more accurately than the scatter matrices in the classic FDA owing to the lower dimension. However, previous literatures neglect the fact that there are two available matrix-based LDA algorithms and usually use only one of the two algorithms to perform the experiment.

We note that different discriminant analysis methods have different motivations. For example, Foley-Sammon linear discriminant analysis aims at generating orthogonal discriminant vectors, whereas uncorrelated linear discriminant analysis aims at obtaining uncorrelated feature components. Differing from both of Foley-Sammon linear discriminant analysis uncorrelated Foley-Sammon linear discriminant analysis, Xu et al. [9] proposed a discriminant analysis method that inherits the advantages of both uncorrelated linear discriminant analysis and Foley-Sammon linear discriminant analysis. It is also noticeable that kernel discriminant analysis has a better capability of capturing the complex features of samples.

H. Deng et al. (Eds.): AICI 2011, Part III, LNAI 7004, pp. 562–568, 2011.

Motivated by the reference [26], we formally present two available matrix-based LDA algorithms and propose to combine them for face recognition. The experimental results show that the combination algorithm can obtain a better performance.

The other parts of this paper are organized as follows: In Section 2 we describe two available matrix-based LDA algorithms. In Section 3 we present our scheme that combines the two available matrix-based LDA algorithms for face recognition. In Section 4 we show the experimental results and in Section 5 we provide a short conclusion.

2 Two Available Matrix-Based LDA Algorithms

In this section we will formally describe two available matrix-based LDA algorithms, respectively.

2.1 The First Matrix-Based LDA Algorithm

Suppose that there are L classes. Let A^i_j represent the j th training sample of the i th class and N_i denote the number of the training samples of the i th class. Let A^i denote the mean of the i th class and $\overline{A}$ denote the mean of all the training samples. For simplicity, we assume that each sample is a m by n matrix. The first matrix-based LDA algorithm defines S_b and S_t as follows:

$$S_b = \frac{1}{L}\sum_{i=1}^{L} N_i (A^i - \overline{A})(A^i - \overline{A})^T \tag{1}$$

$$S_t = \frac{1}{L}\sum_{i=1}^{L} \sum_{j=1}^{N_i} (A^i_j - A^i)(A^i_j - A^i)^T . \tag{2}$$

S_b and S_t are the so-called between-class and within-class scatter matrices, respectively. A^i_j stands for the j th training sample of the i th class. The first matrix-based LDA algorithm is based on the following eigen-equation:

$$S_b w = \lambda S_t w , \tag{3}$$

Suppose that the eigenvalues of Equation (3) is $\lambda_1 \geq \lambda_2 ... \geq \lambda_m$ and the corresponding eigenvectors are $w_1, w_2, ..., w_m$, respectively. The first matrix-based LDA algorithm takes the first d eigenvectors, $w_1, w_2, ..., w_d$ as discriminant vectors and exploits the following equation to transform a sample A into a d by n matrix.

$$B = W^T A , \tag{4}$$

where $W = [w_1...w_d]$. B is referred to as the feature extraction result, of A, obtained using the first matrix-based LDA algorithm.

2.2 The Second Matrix-Based LDA Algorithm

The second matrix-based LDA algorithm defines the between-class and within-class scatter matrices as follows:

$$S_b' = \frac{1}{L}\sum_{i=1}^{L} N_i (A^i - \overline{A})^T (A^i - \overline{A}) \tag{5}$$

$$S_t' = \frac{1}{L}\sum_{i=1}^{L}\sum_{j=1}^{N_i} (A_j^i - A^i)^T (A_j^i - A^i). \tag{6}$$

The eigen-equation of this algorithm is as follows:

$$S_b' w' = \lambda S_t' w', \tag{7}$$

Suppose that the eigenvalues of Equation (7) is $\lambda_1' \geq \lambda_2' ... \geq \lambda_n'$ and the corresponding eigenvectors are $w_1', w_2',..., w_m'$. The second matrix-based LDA algorithm takes the first d eigenvectors, $w_1', w_2',..., w_d'$ as discriminant vectors and exploits the following equation to transform a sample A into an m by d matrix.

$$B' = AW', \tag{8}$$

where $W' = [w_1'...w_d']$. B' is referred to as the feature extraction result, of A, obtained using the second matrix-based LDA algorithm.

3   The Scheme to Combine the First and Second Matrix-Based LDA Algorithms

The scheme that combines the two available matrix-based LDA algorithms for face recognition is based a matching score level fusion strategy and works as follows: it first divides all of the samples into two parts, the training set and test set. Then it exploits the samples in the training set to produce the eigen-equation and to compute the discriminant vectors and perform feature extraction, which will be implemented for the first and second matrix-based LDA algorithms, respectively. Suppose that for a test sample A, the feature extraction results obtained using the first and second matrix-based LDA algorithms are B and B' respectively. Then our scheme calculates the distances between B and the feature extraction results, of all the training samples, obtained using the first matrix-based LDA algorithm and denotes these distances by $dist1_j^i$. Specifically, $dist1_j^i$ stands for the distance between B and the feature extraction result of the j th training sample of the i th class. Our scheme denotes the distances between $B^{'}$ and the feature extraction results, of all the training samples, obtained using the second matrix-based LDA algorithm by $dist2^i_j$.

Our scheme then calculates $dist^i_j = u_1 * dist1^i_j + u_2 * dist2^i_j$. u_1, u_2 are the weighting coefficients. It is clear that our scheme considers $dist^i_j$ as the distance between the test sample and the j th training sample of the i th class. Our scheme identifies the training sample that has the minimum distance with the test sample and assumes that the test sample is from the same class as the identified training sample. It is clear that our scheme uses a matching score level fusion strategy and treats the distance as the matching score. As a larger distance means a low similarity, our scheme indeed classifies the test sample into the class of the training sample that has the maximum matching score. This is different from the conventional matching score level fusion strategy.

4   Experiments

The ORL face database contains a set of face images taken between April 1992 and April 1994 at the lab. The database was used in the context of a face recognition project carried out in collaboration with the Speech, Vision and Robotics Group of the Cambridge University Engineering Department [27]. There are ten different images of each of 40 distinct subjects. For some subjects, the images were taken at different times, varying the lighting, facial expressions (open / closed eyes, smiling / not smiling) and facial details (glasses / no glasses). All the images were taken against a dark homogeneous background with the subjects in an upright, frontal position (with tolerance for some side movement) [27]. The files are in PGM format, and can conveniently be viewed on UNIX (TM) systems using the 'xv' program. The size of each image is 92x112 pixels, with 256 grey levels per pixel. The images are organised in 40 directories (one for each subject), which have names of the form sX, where X indicates the subject number (between 1 and 40). In each of these directories, there are ten different images of that subject [27]. Figure 1 shows some face images from the ORL database.

In order to implement the algorithm computationally efficient, we first resized each face image into 46x56 pixels using the downsampling algorithm proposed in [28]. We respectively took the first five and four samples of each subject as training samples and used the other samples as test samples. Figures 2 and 3 show the rates of the classification errors obtained using our scheme, the first and second matrix-based LDA algorithms. In these two figures, the horizontal ordinate shows the number of the discriminant vectors used for feature extraction. The vertical ordinate shows the rate of the classification errors. In the experiment on Figure 2, weighting coefficients u_1, u_2 were set to 0.5 and 0.5, respectively. In the experiment on Figure 3, u_1, u_2 were set to 0.4 and 0.6, respectively. We see that our scheme, the first and second matrix-based LDA algorithms all obtain their lowest rates of classification errors when using a small number of discriminant vectors. Moreover, the lowest rate of classification errors of our scheme is less than those of the first and second matrix-based LDA algorithms. For example, when the first five samples of each subject were used as training samples and the other samples were used as test samples, the lowest rate of classification errors of our scheme is 8.5%, whereas mples and the other samples were used as test samples, the lowest rates of classification errors of the first and second matrix-based LDA algorithms are 14.5% and 11%, respectively. The experimental results also show that the two available matrix-based LDA algorithms have a clear difference in classification performance.

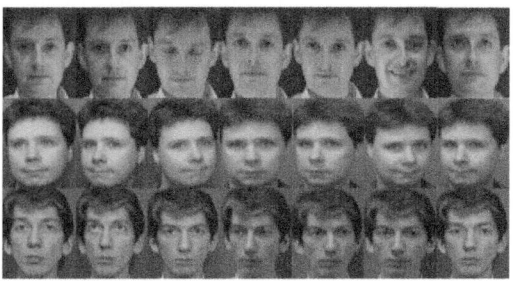

Fig. 1. Some face images from the ORL database. The images in the first, second and third rows are face images of three different subjects, respectively.

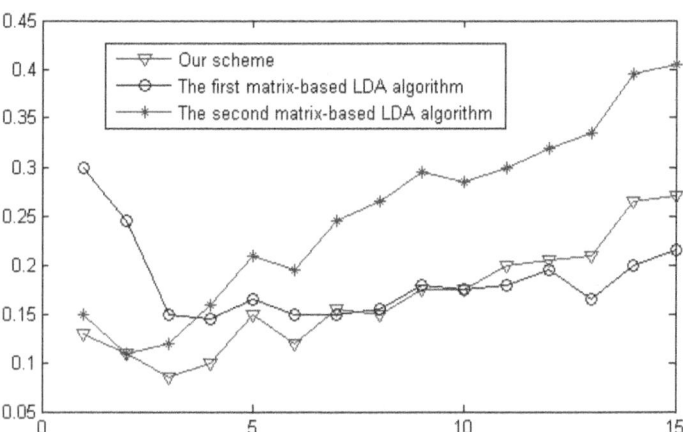

Fig. 2. The rate of the classification errors obtained using our scheme, the first and second matrix-based LDA algorithms. The horizontal ordinate shows the number of the discriminant vectors used for feature extraction. The vertical ordinate shows the rate of the classification errors. The first five samples per subject were used as training samples and the other samples were used as test samples.

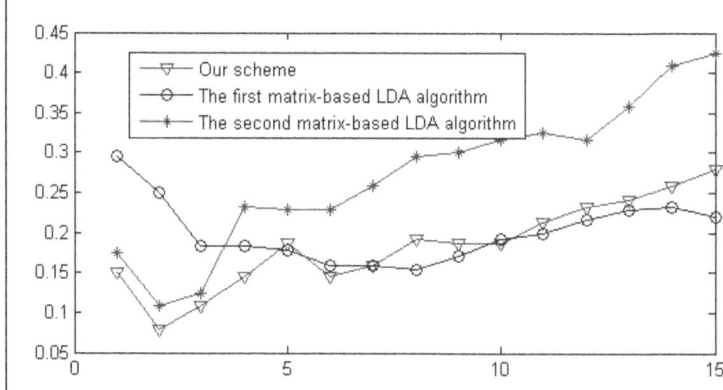

Fig. 3. The rate of the classification errors obtained using our scheme, the first and second matrix-based LDA algorithms. The horizontal ordinate shows the number of the discriminant vectors used for feature extraction. The vertical ordinate shows the rate of the classification errors. The first four samples per subject were used as training samples and the other samples were used as test samples.

5 Conclusion

Compared with classic LDA, the matrix-based LDA method can overcome the small sample size (SSS) problem. However, previous literatures neglect the fact that there are two available matrix-based LDA algorithms and usually use only one of the two algorithms to perform the experiment. By experimental analysis, this work point out the two available matrix-based LDA algorithms might have a difference in performance and the combination of them can obtain a better performance.

References

1. Turk, M., Pentland, A.: Eigenfaces for Recognition. Journal of Cognitive Neurosicence 3(1), 71–86 (1991)
2. Turk, M., Pentland, A.: Face Recognition Using Eigenfaces. In: Proc. IEEE Conf. On Computer Vision and Pattern Recognition, pp. 586–591 (1991)
3. Beymer, D., Poggio, T.: Face recognition from one example view. In: Proceedings of the International Conference on Computer Vision, pp. 500–507 (1995)
4. Xu, Y., Yao, L., Zhang, D.: Improving the Interest Operator for Face Recognition. Expert System With Applications 36(6), 9719–9728 (2009)
5. Bowyer, K.W., Kyong, C., Flynn, P.: A survey of approaches and challenges in 3D and multi-modal 3D+2D face recognition. Comput. Vision Image Understanding 101(1), 1–15 (2006)
6. Xu, Y., Feng, G., Zhao, Y.: One improvement to two-dimensional locality preserving projection method for use with face recognition. Neurocomputing 73, 245–249 (2009)
7. Zhang, D., Song, F., Xu, Y., Liang, Z.: Advanced pattern recognition technologies with applications to biometrics. Medical Information Science Reference, IGI Global (2009)

8. Xu, Y., Zhong, A., Yang, Zhang, D.: LPP solution schemes for use with face recognition. Pattern Recognition, doi:10.1016/j.patcog.2010.06.016

9. Xu, Y., Yang, J.-Y., Jin, Z.: A novel method for Fisher discriminant Analysis. Pattern Recognition 37(2), 381–384 (2004)

10. Yu, H., Yang, J.: A direct LDA algorithm for high-dimensional data—with application to face recognition. Pattern Recognition 34(10), 2067–2070 (2001)

11. Chen, S., Zhu, Y., Zhang, D., Yang, J.-Y.: Feature extraction approaches based on matrix pattern: MatPCA and MatFLDA. Pattern Recognition Letters 26(8), 1157–1167 (2005)

12. Xu, Y., Zhang, D.: Represent and fuse bimodal biometric images at the feature level: complex-matrix-based fusion scheme. Optical Engineering 49(3) (2010), doi:10.1117/1.3359514

13. Belhumeur, P.N., Hespanha, J.P., Kriengman, D.J.: Eigenfaces vs. Fisherfaces: recognition using class specific linear projection. IEEE Trans. Pattern Anal. Machine Intell. 19(7), 711–720 (1997)

14. Foley, D.H., Sammon Jr., J.W.: An optimal set of discriminant vectors. IEEE Trans. Comput. 24(3), 281–289 (1975)

15. Phillips, P.J., Moon, H., Rizvi, S.A., Rauss, P.J.: The FERET evaluation methodology for face-recognition algorithms. IEEE Transactions on Pattern Analysis and Machine Intelligence 22(10), 1090–1104 (2000)

16. Jing, X.-Y., Zhang, D., Jin, Z.: Improvements on the uncorrelated optimal discriminant vectors. Pattern Recognition 36(8), 1921–1923 (2003)

17. Xu, Y., Yang, J.-Y., Jin, Z.: A novel method for Fisher discriminant Analysis. Pattern Recognition 37(2), 381–384 (2004)

18. Scholkopf, B., Smola, A.: Learning With Kernels. MIT Ppress, Cambridge (2002)

19. Scholkopf, B., Smola, A., Muller, K.R.: Nonlinear Component Analysis as a Kernel Eigenvalue Problem. Neural Computation 10(5), 1299–1319 (1998)

20. Xu, Y., Yang, J.-Y., Yang, J.: A reformative kernel Fisher discriminant analysis. Pattern Recognition 37(6), 1299–1302 (2004)

21. Mika, S., Rätsch, G., Weston, J., Schölkopf, B., Müller, K.-R.: Fisher discriminant analysis with kernels. In: Neural Networks for Signal Processing IX, pp. 41–48. IEEE, New York (1999)

22. Muller, K.-R., Mika, S., Rätsch, G., Tsuda, K., Schölkopf, B.: An introduction to kernel-based learning algorithms. IEEE Trans. Neural Network 12(1), 181–201 (2001)

23. Steve, B., Kian, L.: Nonlinear Fisher discriminant analysis using a minimum squared error cost function and the orthogonal least squares algorithm. Neural Networks 15(1), 263–270 (2002)

24. Cristianini, N., Shawe-Taylor, J.: Kernel Methods for Pattern Analysis. Cambridge Univ. Press, New York (2004), [2]

25. Scholkopf, B., Mika, S., Burges, C., Knirsch, P., Muller, K.R., Ratsch, G., Smola, A.: Input Space versus Feature Space in Kernel-Based Methods. IEEE Trans. on Neural Networks 10(5), 1000–1017 (1999)

26. Xu, Y., Zhang, D., Yang, J., Yang, J.-Y.: An approach for directly extracting features from matrix data and its application in face recognition. Neurocomputing 71(10-12), 1857–1865 (2008)

27. http://www.cl.cam.ac.uk/research/dtg/attarchive/facedatabase.html

28. Xu, Y., Jin, Z.: Down-sampling face images and low-resolution face recognition. In: The Third International Conference on Innovative Computing, Information and Control, Dalian, China, June 18-20, pp. 392–395 (2008)

Weighted Principal Component Analysis

Zizhu Fan, Ergen Liu, and Baogen Xu

School of Basic Science, East China Jiaotong University, Nanchang, Jiangxi 330013, China
zzfan3@yahoo.com.cn

Abstract. In this paper, we proposed a weighted PCA (WPCA) method. This method first uses the distances between the test sample and each training sample to calculate the 'weighted' covariance matrix. It then exploits the obtained covariance matrix to perform feature extraction. The experimental results show that the proposed method can obtain a high accuracy than conventional PCA. WPCA has the underlying theoretical foundation: through the 'weighted' covariance matrix, WPCA takes emphasis on the training samples that are very close to the test sample and reduce the influence of the other training samples. As a result, it is likely that the test sample is easier to be classified into the same class as the training samples that are very close to it. The experimental results show the feasibility and effectiveness of WPCA.

Keywords: principal component analysis (PCA), face recognition, eigenvectors, dimensionality reduction.

1 Introduction

Face recognition is one of the most attracting pattern classification and computer vision applications [1-9]. As we know, principal component analysis (PCA) has been widely used in the field of face recognition [12, 8]. This method is indeed a classical linear feature extraction method. When this method transforms samples into a lower-dimensional space, it is able to capture the data components that most vary. PCA is also a method that adopts orthogonal projection axes to transform vector data into uncorrelated components. Actually, PCA can be also applied in data compression.

People have also extended conventional PCA into other versions of PCA. For example, people have proposed modular PCA [10, 11], two-dimensional PCA [12, 13, 14], sparse kernel principal component analysis [15] and curvelet based PCA [16]. These methods have different justifications and advantages. For instance, two-dimensional PCA can overcome the problem of inaccurate evaluation of the covariance matrix that conventional PCA usually encounters and has a low computational cost. Kernel principal component analysis can do well in extracting the information of the samples with a complex distribution. It has been also shown that modular PCA can obtain higher face recognition accuracy than conventional PCA. It achieves by partitioning each face image into a number of blocks and by applying PCA to each block. Moreover, it is noticeable that Xu. et al. has proposed the very promising matrix-based complex principal component analysis (MCPCA) method. MCPCA has achieved very good performance in bimodal biometrics [17]. This

H. Deng et al. (Eds.): AICI 2011, Part III, LNAI 7004, pp. 569–574, 2011.

method first denotes two biometrics traits of one subject by a complex matrix and then applies the PCA procedure to the complex matrix.

It should be pointed out that when conventional PCA is used in feature extraction of a test sample, it treats all the training samples in the same way. Actually, in the pattern recognition problems, it seems that the training samples that are far from the test sample probably have little influence on the test sample, whereas the training samples that are very close to the test sample probably have very great influence. Inspired by this, we proposed a weighted PCA (WPCA) method with this paper. This method first depends on the distances between the test sample and each training sample to calculate the 'weighted' covariance matrix. This method then exploits the obtained covariance matrix to perform feature extraction. The experimental results show that the proposed method can obtain a higher accuracy than conventional PCA. WPCA has the following underlying theoretical foundation: through the 'weighted' covariance matrix, WPCA takes emphasis on the training samples that are very close to the test sample and reduces the influence of the other training samples. As a result, it is likely that the test sample is easier to be classified into the same class as the training samples that are very close to it.

The remainder of the paper is organized as follows: Sections 2 and 3 present conventional PCA and WPCA, respectively. Section 4 shows the experimental results. Section 4 presents the summary of the paper.

2   Conventional PCA

The conventional PCA aims at obtaining an optimal projection through which the projected data have the maximal variance. Suppose that there are N training samples (or n-dimensional vectors) $x_i \in R^n$ ($i = 1,2,...,N$) and m is the mean of the total training samples. The covariance matrix of the training data set is defined by

$$C = \frac{1}{N}\sum_{i=1}^{N}(x_i - m)(x_i - m)^T = \frac{1}{N}XX^T,\tag{1}$$

where $X = [x_1 - m, x_2 - m,..., x_N - m]$. If the dimension of the covariance matrix C is so larger (usually $n>>N$) that the eigen-decomposition of C is very difficult even infeasible, we need to define a new matrix $D = \frac{1}{N}X^TX$. It is easy to prove that two matrices C and D have the same non-zero eigenvalues denoting as λ_i ($i =1,2,...,r$). We denote the normalized eigenvectors of the matrix D by v_i ($i =1,2,...,r$). The normalized eigenvectors of the covariance matrix C should be

$$u_i = \frac{1}{\sqrt{\lambda_i}}Xv_i \quad (i =1,2,...,r).\tag{2}$$

Conventional PCA transforms the arbitrary sample x into the r-dimensional space using $f = x^T U$ and $U = [u_1...u_r]$. f is called feature extraction result, of sample x, obtained using PCA.

3 WPCA

WPCA implements a 'weighted' PCA procedure for each of all the test samples, respectively. Let y be the test sample and $x_1...x_N$ still denote the training samples. WPCA calculates the 'weighted' covariance matrix using

$$C_w = \frac{1}{N} \sum_{i=1}^{N} x_i' x_i'^T , \qquad (3)$$

where $x_i' = w_i x_i$, $w_i = \exp(-\dfrac{max\_dist - dist(x_i, y)}{\mu})$. $dist(x_i, y)$ stands for the distance between x_i and y. max_dist represents the maximum value of the distance between $x_1,...,x_N$ and y. μ is a positive constant. w_i is called weight coefficient. C_w is the so-called weighted variance matrix. It is clear that the smaller $dist(x_i, y)$, the larger w_i. In other words, if a training sample is close to the test sample, then it has a large weight coefficient and has great influence on the variance matrix. Actually, WPCA uses this way to generate different variance matrices for the test samples. As a result, the projection axes generated from the variance matrix will be very suitable for extracting features of the test sample.

WPCA takes the eigenvectors corresponding to the first r largest eigenvalues of C_w as projection axes and exploits these projection axes to transforms the sample into a r-dimensional space. In other words, for a test sample, if the eigenvectors corresponding to the first r largest eigenvalues of the weighted variance matrix are $u_1'...u_r'$ ($u_1'...u_r'$ can be calculated using a procedure similar to the procedure to compute $u_1...u_r$), respectively, then the feature extraction result of the arbitrary sample x is $f' = x^T U'$, where $U' = [u_1'...u_r']$. f' is called feature extraction result, of sample x, obtained using WPCA. It should be pointed out that the 'weighted' PCA procedure must be implemented one time for each of the test samples.

WPCA has the following motivation: by using the weighed coefficient, it aims to take emphasis on the training samples that are very close to the test sample and to reduce the influence of the other training samples. As a result, it is likely that the test sample is easier to be classified into the same class as the training samples that are very close to it.

4 Experiments

We used the ORL face database to conduct experiments. This database contains a set of face images taken between April 1992 and April 1994 at the lab [18]. The database was used in the context of a face recognition project carried out in collaboration with the Speech, Vision and Robotics Group of the Cambridge University Engineering Department. There are ten different images of each of 40 distinct subjects. For some subjects, the images were taken at different times, varying the lighting, facial expressions (open / closed eyes, smiling / not smiling) and facial details (glasses / no glasses). All the images were taken against a dark homogeneous background with the subjects in an upright, frontal position (with tolerance for some side movement) [18]. Figure 1 shows some face images from this database.

We randomly selected five samples of each subject as training samples and took the remaining samples as test samples. We generated 100 sets of training samples and the corresponding sets of test samples in this way and used all the sets to conduct experiments. Each image was converted into a column vector in advance. Every column vector was also normalized to a unit vector. μ was set to 10. We used the neighbor nearest classifier and the feature extraction result of every training and test sample to perform classification. That is, when classifying the test sample, we first calculate the distance between the feature extraction results of the test sample and every training sample. We then classify the test sample into the same class as the training sample whose feature extraction result is the most nearest to that of the test sample. Figure 2 shows the experimental results of conventional PCA and WPCA. The horizontal coordinate shows that the number of projection axes varies from 50 to 100. The horizontal coordinate shows the mean of the classification right rates of 100 sets of test samples. We see that WPCA obtains a higher classification right rate than conventional PCA.

We also used the Yale face database to conduct experiments. The Yale Face Database contains 165 grayscale images in GIF format of 15 individuals. There are 11 images per subject, one per different facial expression or configuration: center-light, with/no glasses, happy, left-light, with/no glasses, normal, right-light, sad, sleepy, surprised, and wink [19]. We resized each image into a 40×50 image. Each image

Fig. 1. Some face images in the ORL face database

was also converted into a unit column vector in advance and μ was set to 10. We randomly selected five samples of each subject as training samples and took the remaining samples as test samples. We generated 50 sets of training samples and the corresponding sets of test samples in this way and used all the sets to conduct experiments. Table 1 shows the experimental result. We see again that WPCA obtains a higher classification right rate than conventional PCA.

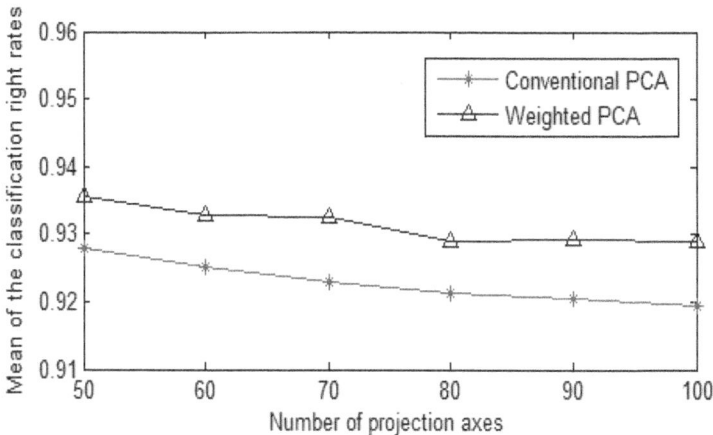

Fig. 2. Means of the classification right rates of weighted PCA and conventional PCA on 100 sets of test samples of the ORL face database

Table 1. The means of the classification right rates of weighted PCA and conventional PCA on the Yale face database

Number of projection axes	50	60	70
Conventional PCA	95.85%	95.94%	95.94%
Weighted PCA	96.38%	96.87%	96.59%

5 Conclusions

By setting different weight coefficients for different training samples, WPCA enables the training samples that are close to the test sample to have great influence on the covariance matrix of the test sample, whereas makes the training samples that are far from the test sample to have little influence. As a result, different training samples also have the similar influence to the feature extraction of the test sample. As a result, the projection axes generated from the variance matrix   will be very suitable for extracting features of the test sample.

Acknowledgements. This work was supported by the National Natural Science Foundation of China (Grant No. 61071179, 11061014, 60803090, 61001037 and 61065003) and Jiangxi Provincial Natural Science Foundation of China (Grant No. 2010GQS0027).

References

1. Turk, M.A., Pentland, A.P.: Face Recognition Using Eigenfaces. In: IEEE Conf. on Computer Vision and Pattern Recognition, pp. 586–591 (1991)
2. Diamantaras, K.I., Kung, S.Y.: Principal Component Neural Networks: Theory and Applications. John Wiley & Sons, Inc., Chichester (1996)
3. Hadid, A., Pietikäinen, M.: Manifold learning for video-to-video face recognition. In: COST 2101/2102 Conference 2009, pp. 9–16 (2009)
4. Xu, Y., Zhong, A., Yang, J., Zhang, D.: LPP solution schemes for use with face recognition. Pattern Recognition 43(12), 4165–4176 (2010)
5. Xu, Y., Yang, J.-Y., Lu, J., Yu, D.: An efficient renovation on kernel Fisher discriminant analysis and face recognition experiments. Pattern Recognition 37(10), 2091–2094 (2004)
6. Phillips, P.J., Grother, P., Micheals, R.J., et al.: Face recognition vendortest 2002: evaluation report. Face Recognition Vendor Test 2002 Results (2003)
7. Zhao, W., Nandhakumar, N.: Linear discriminant analysis of MPF for face recognition. In: Proc. Int. Conf. Pattern Recognition, pp. 185–188 (1998)
8. Turk, M., Pentland, A.: Eigenfaces for recognition. J. Cognitive Neurosci. 3(1), 71–86 (1991)
9. Graham, D.B., Allinson, N.M.: Characterizing virtual eigensignatures for general purpose face recognition. In: Face Recognition: From Theory to Applications. NATO ASI Series F, Computer and Systems Sciences, vol. 163, pp. 446–456 (1998)
10. Pentland, A., Moghaddam, B., Starner, T.: View-Based and Modular Eigenspaces for face recognition. In: Proceedings of 1994 IEEE Computer Society Conference on Computer Vision and Pattern Recognition, pp. 84–91 (1994)
11. Gottumukkal, R., Asari, V.K.: An improved face recognition technique based on modular PCA approach. PRL 25(4), 429–436 (2004)
12. Xu, Y., Zhang, D., Yang, J., Yang, J.-Y.: An approach for directly extracting features from matrix data and its application in face recognition. Neurocomputing 71(10-12), 1857–1865 (2008)
13. Xu, L., Wang, Y., Sun, C.: Face recognition based on two dimension double PCA and affinity propagation. In: ICNC, vol. 5, pp. 43–47 (2009)
14. Yang, J., Zhang, D., Frangi, A.F., Yang, J.-Y.: Two-dimensional PCA: A new approach to appearance-based face representation and recognition. IEEE Trans. Pattern Anal. Mach. Intell. 26(1), 131–137 (2004)
15. Tipping, M.E.: Sparse Kernel Principal Component Analysis. In: Leen, T.K., Dietterich, T.G., Tresp, V. (eds.) NIPS 2000: Neural Information Processing Systems, pp. 633–639. MIT Press, Cambridge (2000)
16. Mandal, T., Wu, Q.M.J.: Face recognition using curvelet based PCA. In: 19th International Conference on Pattern Recognition, ICPR 2008 (2008)
17. Xu, Y., Zhang, D., Yang, J.-Y.: A feature extraction method for use with bimodal biometrics. Pattern Recognition 43, 1106–1115 (2010)
18. http://www.cl.cam.ac.uk/research/dtg/attarchive/facedatabase.html
19. http://www.abc-directory.com/site/956163

Pattern Recognition of Hand Gesture Based on LVQ Neutral Network

Xiuping Zheng, Yina Guo, and Huaxia Wang

Taiyuan University of Science and Technology,
College of Electronic Information and Engineering, 030024 Taiyuan Shanxi, China
zhengxiuping9898@163.com, zulibest@gmail.com,
feiren8486@sina.com

Abstract. Pattern recognition of hand gesture is currently research hot spot. It is important for rehabilitation training, human-computer interaction, prosthetic control and sports science research etc. The brachioradialis, extensor digitorum communis, flexor carpi ulnaris muscle and flexor carpi radialis muscle as signal acquisition points; this paper captures four channel sEMG signals. Aiming at the sEMG signals of hand gesture, this paper uses the eigenvalue processed by RMS and MOV as training data samples, which is regarded as the input of LVQ neural network. Through training and learning samples, the better training result is got. The results of the study indicate that the LVQ neural network can effectively identify three action modes, all fingers, relax and middle, by adopting the four channel sEMG signals. The simple algorithm, small calculation and more than 89 percent recognition rate shows that it is a very good method of pattern recognition.

Keywords: LVQ, sEMG, neural network, pattern recognition.

1 Introduction

The hand gesture research mainly includes finger freedom, bend degrees, power, and morphology information, and so on[1] .This information is important for rehabilitation training, human-computer interaction, prosthetic control and sports science research etc. The surface electromyography signals (sEMG) are electrical signals when muscle contracts, and it is an important method to Noninvasive testing muscle activity. When hands act, sEMG signals have the apparent response in The brachioradialis, extensor digitorum communis, flexor carpi ulnaris muscle and flexor carpi radialis muscle response. This paper selects The brachioradialis, extensor digitorum communis, flexor carpi ulnaris muscle and flexor carpi radialis muscle as signal acquisition points, while capturing sEMG signal, then extracts eigenvalue by RMS and MOV as the input of LVQ neural network. After repeated training the neural network can effectively recognize three movements and the recognition rate has reached more than 89%.

Neural network is used to static gestures identification early [2].Then improved algorithms is applied to time-varying delays and parametric uncertainties [3]. And derive stability conditions for dynamic neural networks with different time-scales[4].

H. Deng et al. (Eds.): AICI 2011, Part III, LNAI 7004, pp. 575–580, 2011.

Based on neural network of pattern recognition, as one of sEMG signal processing, is be concerned [5-8].

In the paper, the LVQ neural network is researched. The advantages of LVQ neural network [9] is calculated directly the distance between input vector and competition layers and to achieve pattern recognition. Don't need to input vector normalization and positive change in concevt. It is simple.

2   Methods of Implementation

2.1 sEMG Signal and Eigenvalue Extraction Based on RMS and MOV

The brachioradialis, extensor digitorum communis, flexor carpi ulnaris muscle and flexor carpi radialis muscle as signal acquisition points, this paper captures four channel sEMG signal. Keeping four groups silver cup electrodes, the sEMG signals are obtained. It has two electrodes of every group. The ground electrode is posted on a suitable electrically inactive area on the selected Volunteers. Acquisition signals are shown in figure 1.

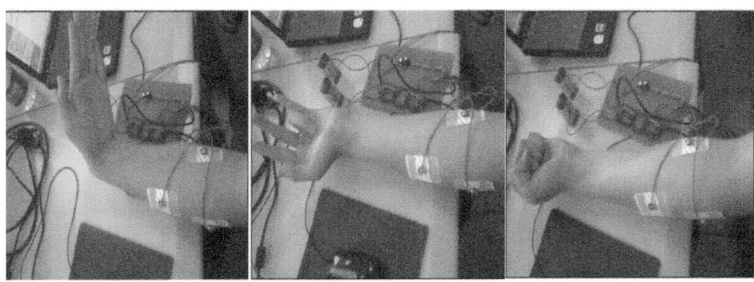

Fig. 1. Signals of sEMG collecting

The main part has four IC(integrated circuit) and instrumentation amplifiers (INA 128, Texas Instruments). There are two additional components to impact high-pass filtering about IC. In the circuit ground, the IC is controlled by two 9-V batteries joint in series, with the central common terminal. The magnification is 400. There were four sEMG signals collected, and then processed the signals by RMS and MOV. As training data sample, the RMS and MOV eigenvalues were classified by trained LVQ neural network. Then the hand gestures could be recognized.

At present the typical eigenvalue extraction method mainly has time domain method, the frequency domain method, a frequency domain method and nonlinear dynamics analysis, etc. The time domain method applied to muscle signal analysis, easy to extract and simple. In the time dimension, the root mean square (RMS) is used commonly. It reflects sEMG signal amplitude variation features, muscle load factors, muscle itself physiological and the inner relation of biochemical process. Therefore, it is often used for in real-time, no damaged reflecting muscle activity state, and has good real-time quality [10].

$$X_{RMS} = \sqrt{\frac{1}{N} \sum_{n=1}^{N} x_n^2(t)} \qquad (1)$$

Moving average (MOV) is the average of the signal in a period of time, which is used speculate type. The advantage of moving average method is simple, easy to do, and to a certain extent eliminate some accidental element influence by N.

$$X_{MOV} = \frac{1}{N} \sum_{n=1}^{N} x_n(t) \qquad (2)$$

In this paper, we selected four muscles to acquisition signal. Then 4 -channel signal is processed by RMS and MOV. As LVQ neural network's input, these signals are for pattern recognition.

2.2   The LVQ Neural Network Parameter Selection

Learning Vector Quantization (LVQ) neural network is the learning algorithm training competition layer in the teacher state. When correlation among indices is high, the changing is nonlinear, or data is incomplete, it still can achieve more satisfied classification results, so the application in pattern recognition and optimize field is wide.

A LVQ neural network belongs to the basic competitive neural network, includes input layer, hidden layer and output layer. The input layer has L neurons. Input vector is $X_l = [x_1^l, x_2^l, x_3^l, \cdots, x_N^l]$. The hidden layer has M neurons. The structure of LVQ neural network is shown in figure 2. Network connection weight is $\{w_{ij}\}$.

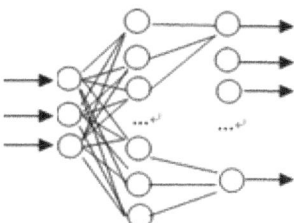

Fig. 2. The structure of LVQ neural network

The neural network learning needs to have a group of network behavior of examples to training. In this paper, extracting features of the 4 sEMG signals respectively by RMS and MOV, which results is as the input features of LVQ neural network.

The sEMG signals after processing by the RMS and MOV is shown Fig.3 and Fig.4.

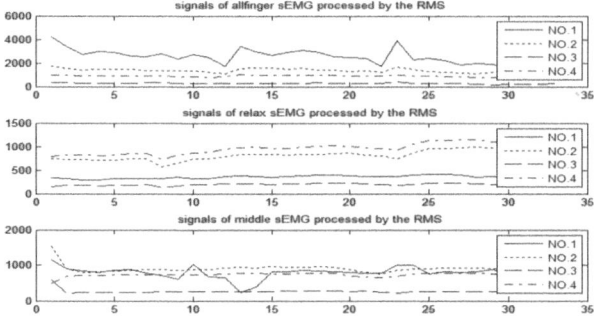

Fig. 3. Signals of sEMG processed by the RMS

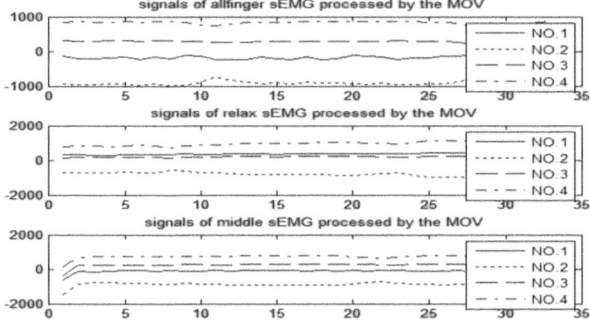

Fig. 4. Signals of sEMG processed by the MOV

To establish LVQ neural network:

```
net=newlvq(minmax(P),10,[0.33 0.33 0.34]);
```

P is 2×n matrix which is the input vector of the training samples, first row is after processing data of the RMS, the second row is the data after MOV processing, which is the feature vector of LVQ neural network.

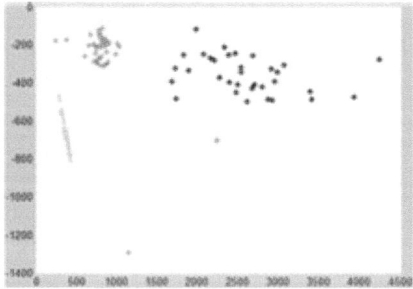

Fig. 5. P, the input vector of the training samples

10 represent the number of neurons network. [0.33 0.33 0.34] shows that input samples belong to category 1 data of 33%, belong to category 2 accounted for 33%, belongs to the category 3 of 34%.

To train the LVQ neural network:

```
net=train(net,P,T);
```

After many tests, performance (Mean Squared Error) can reach 0.01, even 0. Train results are ideal.

This paper use 4 sEMG signals respectively for training, establish 4 LVQ neural networks for comprehensive classification and test network performance.

This results is one of the classification results, selected thirty test points, correct classification result is

y=[1 1 1 1 1 2 2 2 2 2 3 3 3 3 3 1 1 1 1 1 2 2 2 2 2 3 3 3 3 3]

The classification results by LVQ neural network:

yc=[1 2 1 1 1 2 2 2 2 2 3 3 3 3 3 1 1 1 1 1 2 2 2 3 2 3 3 2 3 3], classification and recognition rate for 90% this time.

After many tests, identify three action mode are classified effectively, recognition rate all reached 89% above.

3   Conclusion

The brachioradialis, extensor digitorum communis, flexor carpi ulnaris muscle and flexor carpi radialis muscle as signal acquisition points, this paper captures four channel sEMG signals at the same time. Processing by RMS and MOV, as the input signals for LVQ neural network, establish LVQ neural network for pattern recognition after training for many times.

RMS is often used for real-time, no damaged reflecting muscle activity state, and has good real-time quality. And MOV reduces a certain extent eliminate some accidental element influence by N. The two as the characteristic value educed the computation time and complexity. The sEMG signals feature is apparent. RMS and MOV algorithm is simple and easy to achieve.

After many tests, the three finger gestures of all finger, relax and middle are classified. Recognition rate all reached 89 percent above. The LVQ neural network is very good pattern recognition tools which can effectively classified, have very good promotion value and practical value should further research, for real-time signal pattern recognition.

Acknowledgment. Funding for this work was provided by the grants of Study Abroad of Shanxi Scholarship Council of China [No. 20101069] and Youth Foundation of Taiyuan University of Science and Technology of China [No. 20103004].

References

1. Vigouroux, L., Quaine, F., Labarre-Vila, A., et al.: Using EMG Data to Constrain Optimization Procedure Improves Finger Tendon Tension Estimations During Static Fingertip Force Production. Journal of Biomechanics 40(13), 2846–2856 (2007)
2. Murakami, K., Ta Guchi, H.: Gesture recognition using recurrent neural network. In: Proc. of the CHI 1991, pp. 237–241. ACM Press, New York (1991)
3. Chen, Y., Wang, H., Xue, A.: Passivity analysis of stochastic time-delay neural networks. Nonlinear Dyn. 61, 71–82 (2010)
4. Yu, W., Li, X.: Passivity Analysis of Dynamic Neural Networks. Neural Processing Letters 25, 143–155 (2007)
5. Li, Y., Chen, X., Zhang, X., Yang, J.: Hand Gesture SEMG Signal Recognition Based on ART2 Neutral Network. Journal of University Of Science And Technology of China 40(8), 829–834 (2010)
6. Yang, A., Chang, D.: Hand Gesture Recognition System Based on Neural Network and Hidden Markov Model. Electronic Measurement Technology 33(4), 60–64 (2010)
7. Luo, Z.-Z., Xiong, J., Liu, Z.-H.: Pattern Recognition of Hand Motions Based on WPT and LVQ. Pattern Recognition and Artificial Intelligence 23(5), 695–700 (2010)
8. Hou, W.-S., Ma, L., Wu, X.-Y., Zheng, X.-L., Peng, C.-L.: Motion Identification of Finger Based on Auto – regressive Model and Learning - vector - quantization Neural Network. Chinese Journal of Ergonomics 15(3), 18–21 (2009)
9. Fecit technology product research and development center: Neural Network and MatLab7 Application. Publishing House of Electronics Industry, Beijing (2005)
10. Wu, D., Sun, X., Zhang, Z.-C., Du, Z.-J.: Feature Collection and Analysis of Surface Electromyography Signals. Journal of Clinical Rehabilitative Tissue Engineering Research 14(43), 8073–8076 (2010)

Estimating the Fundamental Matrix Using Second-Order Cone Programming

Min Yang

College of Automation,
Nanjing University of Posts and Telecommunications
Nanjing, China
yangm@njupt.edu.cn

Abstract. Computing the fundamental matrix is the first step of many computer vision applications including camera calibration, image rectification and structure from motion. A new method for the estimation of the fundamental matrix from point correspondences is presented. The minimization of the geometric error is performed based L- infinity norm minimization framework. A single global minimum exists and it may be found by SOCP (Second-Order Cone Programming), which is a standard technique in convex optimization. In a SOCP a linear function is minimized over the intersection of an affine set and the product of second-order (quadratic) cones. Several efficient primal-dual interior-point methods for SOCP have been developed. Experiments on real images show that this method provides a more accurate estimate of the fundamental matrix and superior to previous approaches, and the method is no need for normalization of the image coordinates.

Keywords: Fundamental matrix, L-infinity norm minimization, Second-Order Cone Programming, Optimal algorithms, Multiview geometry.

1 Introduction

The epipolar geometry is the intrinsic projective geometry between two views. It is independent of scene structure, and only depends on the cameras' internal parameters and relative pose. The fundamental matrix F encapsulates this intrinsic geometry. It is a 3×3 matrix of rank 2. Computing the fundamental matrix from point correspondences is the first step of many vision applications including camera calibration, image rectification, structure from motion, and new view generation[9].

The classic eight-point algorithm is a widely used linear approach to estimating the fundamental matrix, usually in the 'normalized' form recommended by Hartley in [7]. Linear methods are quick, easy to code and usually provide good estimates in the absence of outliers and they are often used to initialize iterative methods that are more accurate. Iterative methods minimize some symmetric distance, such as the distance between points and epipolar lines (as defined by a candidate fundamental matrix). Chojnacki et al. [8] proposed a iterative methods based on an approximate maximum likelihood estimate which can be applied to estimate the fundamental matrix. Such

H. Deng et al. (Eds.): AICI 2011, Part III, LNAI 7004, pp. 581–586, 2011.

method is called Constrained Fundamental Numerical Scheme (CFNS), and the method is based on Newton–Raphson minimization technique.

Recently, there has been interest in solving geometric vision problems such as triangulation and camera resectioning using L_∞ minimization[2][3][4]. One key advantage of using the L_∞ norm rather than the L_2 norm is that the L_∞ cost function has a single minimum unlike the commonly used L_2 cost function which typically has multiple local minima. In all these cases, a single global minimum exists and it may be found by SOCP (Second-Order Cone Programming). The SOCP problem is easily solvable using commonly available SeDuMi software[5].

In this paper, a new method for the estimation of the fundamental matrix is presented based L_∞ minimization framework. Experimental results and comparisons are also reported.

2 Optimization Algorithms

Given a pair of images, the fundamental matrix $\mathbf{F} \in \mathbf{R}^{3\times3}$ is defined as the matrix satisfying the relation

$$u'^T F u = 0, \forall u', u, \tag{1}$$

where $\mathbf{u'}, \mathbf{u} \in \mathbf{R}^3$ are the projections expressed in homogeneous coordinates of the same 3D point in the two images. The fundamental matrix F has seven degrees of freedom being defined up to a scale factor and being singular.

Fundamental matrix estimation non-optimal methods use some simplified error criteria in order to obtain an estimate, often in closed form. A classical example is the 8-point algorithm[7] or alternatively a minimal method[10],which was improved by enforcing the singularity of the fundamental matrix in the estimation process. These non-optimal schemes often serve as an initialization for a local method.

In [11], the following optimization criterion was analyzed:

$$\min \sum_i \frac{\left(\hat{u}'^T_i F \hat{u}_i\right)^2}{\left(F\hat{u}_i\right)^2_1 + \left(F\hat{u}_i\right)^2_2 + \left(F^T \hat{u}'_i\right)^2_1 + \left(F^T \hat{u}'_i\right)^2_2}, s.t. \det(F) = 0 \tag{2}$$

Before we continue, we need to introduce a concept due to Schur [1]. Let $M = \begin{bmatrix} A & B \\ B^T & C \end{bmatrix}$ be a symmetric matrix and suppose that $A \succ 0$. Then, the following are equivalent:

$$M \succ 0 \Leftrightarrow C - B^T A^{-1} B \succ 0 \tag{3}$$

The matrix $C - B^T A^{-1} B$ is called the Schur complement of M.

Let γ_i be an upper bound on the i th residual error. Using a Schur complement argument, the problem can be reformulated as

$$\min_{i=1,\cdots,N.} \sum \gamma_i, s.t. \begin{bmatrix} \left(F\hat{u}_i\right)_1^2 + \left(F\hat{u}_i\right)_2^2 + \left(F^T\hat{u}_i'\right)_1^2 + \left(F^T\hat{u}_i'\right)_2^2 & \hat{u}_i'^T F\hat{u}_i \\ \hat{u}_i'^T F\hat{u}_i & \gamma_i \end{bmatrix} \succ 0 \tag{4}$$

$$\det(F) = 0$$

The particular convex optimization problems where the objective function is linear and the constraints are of the form

$$\left\| A_i x + b_i \right\|_2 - \left(c_i^T x + d_i\right) \le 0 \tag{5}$$

are called SOCPs. Here, $A_i \in R^{n_i \times n}, b_i \in R^{n_i}, c_i \in R^n$, and $d_i \in R$. The SOCP problem is easily solvable using commonly available software packages SeDuMi.

The problems in geometric computer vision may be written in the following minimax form:

$$\min_x \max_i \frac{\left\| A_i x + b_i \right\|_2}{c_i^T x + d_i}, s.t. c_i^T x + d_i \ge 0 \tag{6}$$

By introducing an additional variable γ, this problem may be transformed into an equivalent problem of the form

$$\min_{\gamma,x} \gamma, s.t. \frac{\left\| A_i x + b_i \right\|_2}{c_i^T x + d_i} \le \gamma \quad and \quad c_i^T x + d_i \ge 0 \tag{7}$$

we multiply out the denominator of each constraint, obtaining the following more convenient form for the problem:

$$\min_{\gamma,x} \gamma, s.t. \left\| A_i x + b_i \right\|_2 - \gamma(c_i^T x + d_i) \le 0 \quad and \quad \gamma \ge 0 \tag{8}$$

with known $\mathbf{A_i, b_i, c_i}$ and $\mathbf{d_i}$, and a vector x of unknown variables and unknown γ_i.

The constraint $c_i^T x + d_i \ge 0$ is no longer needed since it is implied by the inequalities

$$\left\| A_i x + b_i \right\|_2 \le \gamma(c_i^T x + d_i) \text{ and } \gamma \ge 0. \tag{9}$$

The simplest way of searching over values of γ for the least value is via a binary search.[6]

The key idea of the L_∞ scheme is to replace the L_2 error norm with the L_∞-norm (i.e. minimax norm). The residual error in Eq. (4) is a non-linear but quasi-convex function. However, when summing errors for all point correspondences, i.e. many quasi-convex functions, as done in the standard bundle adjustment, one gets a multi-modal residual function with many local minima. To prevent such a sum, and keep the problem quasi-convex with the guaranty of a global minimum, the use of L_∞ norm was proposed. The error in Eq. (4) under the L_∞ norm is defined as $\gamma = \max \gamma_i$, γ_i and the problem of searching for unknown variables reads as

$$x^* = \arg\min_x \gamma = \arg\min_i \max_i \gamma_i \tag{10}$$

3   Experimental Evaluation

We carried out experiment with real data to show performance of the proposed SOCP solution. For solving the SOCP we use the publicly available toolbox SeDuMi .

In our experiments, three estimation methods were tested, denoted as NEPA, CFNS and $L\infty$.

NEPA(Normalized Eight-Point Algorithm) refers to the normalized algebraic least squares method of Hartley[7], which takes suitably normalized data as input to algebraic least squares and back-transforms the resulting estimate.

GFNS(the Constrained Fundamental Numerical Scheme) is new iterative method based on an approximate maximum likelihood estimate, and the iterative method is based on Newton-Raphson minimization technique[8].

The proposed method denoted as $L\infty$. The method is no need for normalization of the image coordinates.

Three method has been programmed and its accuracy analyzed in real images. Fig. 1 shows one of two images used to estimate the fundamental matrix. The fundamental matrix was determined with 13 pairs of manually selected points.

For easier comparison, we define the geometric error as the geometric distance between points and corresponding epipolar lines. Table 1 shows experimental results of three methods.

Table 1. Experimental results of three methods. Every cell shows the max, min, mean and standard deviation of the discrepancy between points and epipolar lines.

method	minimum	maximum	mean	stddev
CFNS	0.0534	1.6236	0.5076	0.3747
NEPA	0.0104	2.4784	0.6378	0.6293
$L\infty$	0.0205	0.8669	0.3782	0.2132

Fig. 1 shows $L\infty$ method experimental result, the test image(13 used point correspondences) with epipolar lines superimposed.

Experimental results show that the $L\infty$ minimization method gives better results than NEPA and GFNS, and the method is no need for normalization of the image coordinates. The method introduced into the $L\infty$ computation provides a marked improvement.

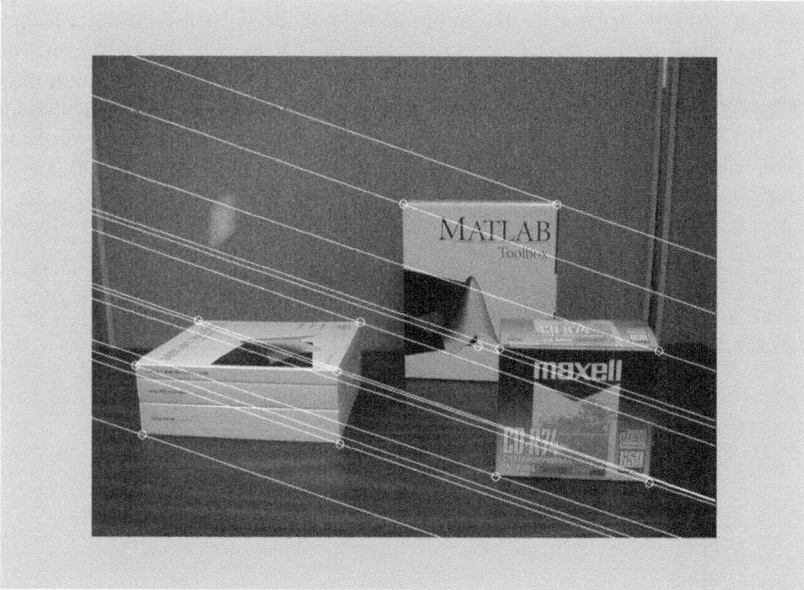

Fig. 1. Test image (13 used point correspondences) with epipolar lines superimposed

4 Conclusion

In this paper, the L-norm minimization can be used with success to estimate fundamental matrix. The approach discussed here uses Second-Order Cone Programming to obtain a global solution. A critical virtue of the L^∞ scheme is that the solution obtained is not only geometrically meaningful, but also globally optimal and hence unique.

References

1. Boyd, S., Vanderberghe, L.: Convex Optimization. Cambridge University Press, Cambridge (2004)
2. Hartley, R., Schaffalitzky, F.: L_∞ minimization in geometric reconstruction problems. In: Proc. IEEE Conference on Computer Vision and Pattern Recognition, vol. 1, pp. 504–509 (2004)
3. Kahl, F.: Multiple view geometry and the L_∞-norm. In: Proc. International Conference on Computer Vision (2005)
4. Ke, Q., Kanade, T.: Quasiconvex optimization for robust geometric reconstruction. In: Proc. International Conference on Computer Vision, pp. 986–993 (2005)
5. Sturm, J.: Using SeDuMi 1.02, a MATLAB toolbox for optimization over symmetric cones. Optimization Methods and Software 11-12, 625–653 (1999)
6. Lobo, M.S., Vandenberghe, L., Boyd, S.P., Lebret, H.: Applications of Second-Order Cone Programming. Linear Algebra and Its Applications 284, 193–228 (1998)

7. Hartley, R.I.: In defense of the 8-point algorithm. IEEE Trans. Pattern Analysis and Machine Intelligence 19(6), 580–593 (1997)
8. Chojnacki, W., Brooks, M.J., van den Hengel, A., Gawley, D.: A new constrained arameter estimator for computer vision applications. Image and Vision Computing 22(2), 85–91 (2004)
9. Hartley, R., Zisserman, A.: Multiple View Geometry in Computer Vision. Cambridge Univ. Press, Cambridge (2000)
10. Chesi, G., Garullli, A., Vicino, A., Cipolla, R.: Estimating the fundamental matrix via constrained least-squares: A convex approach. IEEE Trans. Pattern Analysis and Machine Intelligence 24(3), 397–401 (2002)
11. Zhang, Z.: On the optimization criteria used in two-view motion analysis. IEEE Trans. Pattern Analysis and Machine Intelligence 20(7), 717–729 (1998)

Attribute Reduction in Incomplete Information Systems

Shibao Sun[1,2,*], Jianhui Duan[1], and Dandan Wanyan[1]

[1] Electronic Information Engineering College,
Henan University of Science and Technology, Luoyang Henan 471003, China
sunshibao@126.com
[2] National Laboratory Of Software Development Environment,
Beijing University of Aeronautics & Astronautics, Beijing, 100191, China

Abstract. Through changing the equivalence relation of objects to reflexive and symmetric binary relation in the incomplete information system, a cumulative variable precision rough set model is proposed. The basic properties of β lower and β upper cumulative approximation operators are investigated. β upper, and β lower distribution consistent set are explored for defining β upper, and β lower distribution cumulative reduction. Finally, two attribute reduction approaches, such as β upper (β lower) distribution cumulative reduction, in the incomplete information system are given through discernible matrix and function. The example proves that the cumulative variable precision rough set model can effectively deal with information and fully maintain knowledge in incomplete information systems.

Keywords: Variable precision rough set, Incomplete information system, Decision table, Distribution cumulative reduction.

1 Introduction

Rough set theory (RST) has been proposed by Pawlak [1] as a tool to conceptualize, organize and analyze various types of data in knowledge discovery. This method is especially useful for dealing with uncertain and vague knowledge in information systems. Many applications of the RST method to process control, economics, environmental science, chemistry, psychology, conflict analysis and other fields can be found in [2, 3]. However, the classical RST is based on an equivalence relation and cannot be applied in many real situations. Therefore, many extended RST models, e.g., binary relation based rough sets [4], covering based rough sets [5, 6], and fuzzy rough sets [7, 8] have been proposed. In order to solve classification problems with uncertain data and no functional relationship between attributes and relax the rigid boundary definition of the classical RST model to improve the model suitability, the variable precision rough set (VPRS) model was firstly proposed by Ziarko [9] in 1993. It is an effective mathematical tool with an error-tolerance capability to handle uncertainty problem. Basically, the VPRS is an extension of classical RST [1-3], allowing for partial classification. By setting a confidence threshold,

---

* Corresponding author.

H. Deng et al. (Eds.): AICI 2011, Part III, LNAI 7004, pp. 587–594, 2011.
© Springer-Verlag Berlin Heidelberg 2011

$\beta(\beta \in [0,0.5))$, the VPRS can allow data noise or remove data errors [10]. Recently the VPRS model has been widely applied in many fields [11].

The key issues of the VPRS model mainly concentrate on generalizing models and reduction approaches under the equivalence relation. Reduction approaches, such as β-reduct [12], β lower (upper) distribution reduction [13] and reduction based on structure [14], etc, are under the equivalence relation. But in many practical problems, we need to generalize the VPRS model because the equivalence relation of objects is difficult to construct, or the equivalence relation of objects essentially does not exist. The ideas of generalization are from two aspects. One is to generalize approximated objects from crisp set to fuzzy set [15]; The other is to generalize the relation on the universe from the equivalence relation to fuzzy relation [15], binary relation [16], and covering relation [17, 18], etc. Mieszkowicz-Rolka and Rolka devoted to introduce the idea of the VPRS to fuzzy rough set to inquire into theory and application of fuzzy rough set [15]. Gong, et al., generalized the equivalence relation to the binary relation R on universe U in VPRS model, so that generalized variable precision rough set model was obtained [16]. Covering rough set model was obtained when the equivalence relation on the universe was generalized to cover on the universe in rough set model [19]. Zhang, et al., generalized the equivalence relation to cover on universe U in VPRS model such that we obtain two kinds of variable precision covering rough set models [17, 18]. Mieszkowicz-Rolka and Rolka gave the definition of variable precision rough fuzzy set model under the equivalence relation [20].

The classical rough set approach requires the data table to be complete, i.e., without missing values. In practice, however, the data table is often incomplete. To deal with these cases, Greco, et al., proposed an extension of the rough set methodology to the analysis of incomplete data tables [21]. The extended indiscernible relation between two objects is considered as a directional statement where a subject is compared to a referent object. It requires that the referent object has no missing values. The extended rough set approach maintains all good characteristics of its original version. It also boils down to the original approach when there is no missing value. The rules induced from the rough approximations defined according to the extended relation verify a suitable property: they are robust in a sense that each rule is supported by at least one object with no missing value on the condition attributes represented in the rule. Sun, et al. [22] have proposed a new VPRS model and a cumulative VPRS model based on transitive binary relation in the incomplete information system, the cumulative VPRS model maintains the monotonic property of the lower and upper approximation operators. But they only gave the definitions of the lower and upper approximation operators, and did not discuss the approaches of attributes reduction. Obviously, it will bring some difficulties for using these ideas to process information in fact. So, in this paper we will explore the approaches of attributes reduction of the cumulative VPRS model in the incomplete information system.

The paper is organized as follows. In Section 2, a general view of the VPRS approach and incomplete information systems are given. In Section 3, we explore two approaches of attribute reduction approaches in the incomplete information system. In Section 4, we present an illustrative example which is intended to explain the concepts introduced in Section 3.

2 Paper Preparation

Definition 1 [1]. An information system is the 4-tuple $S = (U, Q, V, f)$, where U is a non-empty finite set of objects (universe), $Q = \{q_1, q_2, \cdots, q_m\}$ is a finite set of attributes, V_q is the domain of the attribute q, $V = \bigcup\limits_{q \in Q} V_q$ and $f : U \times Q \rightarrow V$ is a total function such that $f(x, q) \in V_q$ for each $q \in Q$, $x \in U$, called an information function. If $Q = C \bigcup \{d\}$ and $C \bigcap \{d\} = \varnothing$, then $S = (U, C \bigcup \{d\}, V, f)$ is called a decision table, where d is a decision attribute.

To every (non-empty) subset of attributes $P \subseteq C$ is associated an indiscernible relation on U, denoted by R_P:

$$R_P = \{(x, y) \in U \times U : f(x, q) = f(y, q), \ \forall q \in P\}. \tag{1}$$

If $(x, y) \in R_P$, it is said that the objects x and y are P-indiscernible. Clearly, the indiscernible relation thus defined is an equivalence relation.

Similarly, decision attribute d is associated an indiscernible relation R_d:

$$R_d = \{(x, y) \in U \times U : f(x, d) = f(y, d)\} \tag{2}$$

Definition 2 [9]. Let X and Y be subsets of non-empty finite universe U, if every $e \in X$ then $e \in Y$, we call Y contain X, denoted as $Y \supseteq X$. Let

$$c(X, Y) = \begin{cases} 1 - |X \bigcap Y| / |X|, & |X| > 0, \\ 0, & |X| = 0, \end{cases} \tag{3}$$

Where $|X|$ is cardinality of set X.

Definition 3 [9]. Let S be a decision table, X is a nonempty subset of U, $0 \leq \beta < 0.5$ and $\varnothing \neq P \subseteq C$. The β lower approximation and the β upper approximation of X in S are defined, respectively, by:

$$\underline{P}_\beta(X) = \{x \in U : c([x]_P, X) \leq \beta\}. \tag{4}$$

$$\overline{P}_\beta(X) = \{x \in U : c([x]_P, X) < 1 - \beta\}. \tag{5}$$

Definition 4 [21]. An information system is called an incomplete information system if there exists $x \in U$ and $a \in C$ that satisfy that the value $f(x, a)$ is unknown, denoted as "*". It assumes here that at least one of the states of x in terms of P is certain where $P \subseteq C$, i.e. $\exists a \in P$ such that $f(x,a)$ is known. Thus, $V = V_C \cup V_d \cup \{*\}$.

Definition 5 [21]. For each $x, y \in U$ and for each $P \subseteq C$, $yI_P^* x$ means that $f(x,q) = f(y,q)$ or $f(x,q) = *$ and/or $f(y,q) = *$ for every $q \in P$. Let $I_P^*(x) = \{y \in U : yI_P^* x\}$ for each $x \in U$ and for each $P \subseteq C$. I_P^* is reflexive and symmetric but not transitive. We can define cumulative β lower and β upper approximation of X :

$$\underline{P}_\beta^*(X) = \{x \in U_P^* : c(I_P^*(x), X) \le \beta. \tag{6}$$

$$\overline{P}_\beta^*(X) = \{x \in U_P^* : c(I_P^*(x), X) < 1 - \beta\}. \tag{7}$$

where $U_P^* = \{x \in U : f(x,q) \ne * \ for$ at least one $q \in P\}$.

$\underline{P}_\beta^*(X)$ and $\overline{P}_\beta^*(X)$ satisfy the following properties:

① For each $X \subseteq U$ and for each $P \subseteq C$: $\underline{P}_\beta^*(X) \subseteq \overline{P}_\beta^*(X)$;

② For each $X \subseteq U$ and for each $P \subseteq C$: $\underline{P}_\beta^*(X) = U_P^* - \overline{P}_\beta^*(U - X)$;

③ For each $X \subseteq U$ and for each $P, R \subseteq C$, if $P \subseteq R$, then $\underline{P}_\beta^*(X) \subseteq \overline{R}_\beta^*(X)$. Furthermore, if $U_P^* = U_R^*$, then $\overline{P}_\beta^*(X) \supseteq \overline{R}_\beta^*(X)$.

3   Attribute Reduction in Incomplete Information Systems

Corollary 1. When $\beta = 0$, variable precision rough set model defined in formula (6) and (7) is equivalent to rough set model in incomplete information system [21].

Proof. In formula (7), $c(I_P^*(x), X) \le \beta$ is equivalent to $c(I_P^*(x), X) \le 0$, so $1 \le |I_P^*(x) \cap X| / |I_P^*(x)|$, such that $I_P^*(x) \subseteq X$, that is to say, $\underline{P}^*(X)$ is equivalent to $\underline{P}^*(X)$. Analogously, $\overline{P}_\beta^*(X)$ is equivalent to $\overline{P}^*(X)$.

Corollary 2. If an information system is complete, variable precision rough set model defined in formula (6) and (7) is equivalent to the classical variable precision rough set model.

Proof. $\forall x, y \in U$, $P \subseteq C$, $yI_P^* x$, then for every $q \in P$, we have (1) $f(y,q) = *$, (2) $f(x,q) = f(y,q)$ or $f(x,q) = *$. In a complete information system, we have $f(x,q) = f(y,q)$, so $I_p^*(x)$ is equal to $[x]$, such that formula (6) is equivalent to formula (4) and formula (7) is equivalent to formula (5).

Definition 6. Suppose that $S = (U, C \cup \{d\}, V, f)$ is an incomplete information system, for any $A \subseteq C$, $U / R_d = \{d_1, d_2, \cdots, d_r\}$, $j = 1, \cdots, r$.

A is called β upper distribution consistent set iff $\overline{A}_\beta^*(d_j) = \overline{C}_\beta^*(d_j)$;

A is called β lower distribution consistent set iff $\underline{A}_\beta^*(d_j) = \underline{C}_\beta^*(d_j)$.

Theorem 1. Let S be an incomplete information system, for each $A \subseteq C$, let

$$M_A^\beta(x) = \{d_j : x \in \overline{A}_\beta^*(d_j)\}, (x \in U_A^*). \tag{8}$$

$$G_A^\beta(x) = \{d_j : x \in \underline{A}_\beta^*(d_j)\}, (x \in U_A^*). \tag{9}$$

Then

(1) A is called β upper distribution consistent set iff $M_A^\beta(x) = M_C^\beta(x)$;

(2) A is called β lower distribution consistent set iff $G_A^\beta(x) = G_C^\beta(x)$.

Proof. (1) For each $x \in \overline{A}_\beta^*(d_j)$ iff $d_j \in M_A^\beta(x)$, and $x \in \overline{C}_\beta^*(d_j)$ iff $d_j \in M_C^\beta(x)$.

(2) Similar to (1).

Definition 7. Suppose that $S = (U, C \cup \{d\}, V, f)$ is an incomplete information system, $U / R_C = \{I_C^*(x) : x \in U_C^*\} = \{C_i : i = 1, \cdots, t\}$

$$D_1^{*\beta} = \{(I_C^*(x), I_C^*(y)) : M_C^\beta(x) \neq M_C^\beta(y)\}, \ x, y \in U_C^* \tag{10}$$

$$D_2^{*\beta} = \{(I_C^*(x), I_C^*(y)) : G_C^\beta(x) \neq G_C^\beta(y)\}, \ x, y \in U_C^* \tag{11}$$

Using $f_k(C_i)$ describe $f(a_k, C_i)$. Let

$$D_l^\beta(C_i, C_j) = \begin{cases} \{a_k \in A : f_k(C_i) \neq f_k(C_j)\}, (C_i, C_j) \in D_l^{*\beta}, \\ A, \qquad\qquad\qquad\quad (C_i, C_j) \notin D_l^{*\beta}. \end{cases} \ (l = 1, 2) \tag{12}$$

Then $D_1^\beta(C_i, C_j)$, and $D_2^\beta(C_i, C_j)$ are called β upper (β lower) distribution discernible attribute set of C_i and C_j. $\mathcal{D}_1^\beta = (D_1^\beta(C_i, C_j), i, j \leq t)$, and $\mathcal{D}_2^\beta = (D_2^\beta(C_i, C_j), i, j \leq t)$ are called β upper (β lower) distribution discernible attribute matrix of incomplete information system.

Theorem 2. Suppose that $S = (U, C \bigcup \{d\}, V, f)$ be an incomplete information system, for each $A \subseteq C$, then

(1) A is called β upper distribution consistent set iif for each $(C_i, C_j) \in D_1^{*\beta}$, $A \bigcap D_1^{\beta}(C_i, C_j) \neq \varnothing$;

(2) A is called β lower distribution consistent set iif for each $(C_i, C_j) \in D_2^{*\beta}$, $A \bigcap D_2^{\beta}(C_i, C_j) \neq \varnothing$.

Proof. (1) A is called β upper distribution consistent set. For $\forall (C_i, C_j) \in D_1^{*\beta}$, $x, y \in U_C$, let $C_i = I_C^*(x)$ and $C_j = I_C^*(y)$, then $M_C^{\beta}(x) \neq M_C^{\beta}(y)$. For $I_A(x) \bigcap I_A(y) = \varnothing$, then $a_k \in A$, $f_k(x) \neq f_k(y)$, that is $f_k(C_i) \neq f_k(C_j)$. So $a_k \in D_1^{\beta}(C_i, C_j)$ .that is $A \bigcap D_1^{\beta}(C_i, C_j) \neq \varnothing$.

On the contrary, if exists $(C_i, C_j) \in D_1^{*\beta}$ and $A \bigcap D_1^{\beta}(C_i, C_j) = \varnothing$, then $\forall x, y \in U_C$, $C_i = I_C^*(x)$ and $C_j = I_C^*(y)$. On the one hand, $(C_i, C_j) \in D_1^{*\beta}$, $M_C^{\beta}(x) \neq M_C^{\beta}(y)$; On the other hand, $\forall a_k \in A$, $a_k \notin D_1^{\beta}(C_i, C_j)$. So $f_k(C_i) = f_k(C_j)$, that is $f_k(x) = f_k(y)$. Then $I_C^*(x) = I_C^*(y)$. That is A is not β upper distribution consistent set.

(2) Similar to (1).

Definition 8. $\mathsf{D}_1^{\beta} = (D_1^{\beta}(C_i, C_j))$, and $\mathsf{D}_2^{\beta} = (D_2^{\beta}(C_i, C_j))$ $(i, j \leq t)$ are β upper (β lower) distribution discernible attribute matrix of incomplete information system. let

$$\begin{aligned} \mathsf{M}_l^{\beta} &= \wedge \{\vee \{a_k : a_k \in D_l^{\beta}(C_i, C_j)\} : i, j \leq t\} \\ &= \wedge \{\vee \{a_k : a_k \in D_l^{\beta}(C_i, C_j)\} : (C_i, C_j) \in D_l^{*\beta}\} \end{aligned} \quad (l = 1, 2) \quad (13)$$

Then M_1^{β} ,and M_2^{β} are called β upper (β lower) distribution cumulative discernible formulas respectively.

Theorem 3. Suppose that $S = (U, C \bigcup \{d\}, V, f)$ be an incomplete information system. Minimal disjunctive formulas of M_l^{β} $(l = 1, 2)$ is defined as:

$$\mathsf{M}_l^{\beta} = \bigvee_{k=1}^{p} (\bigwedge_{s=1}^{q_k} a_s) \ (l = 1, 2) \quad (14)$$

Let $B_{lk} = \{a_{l_s} : s = 1, 2, \cdots, q_k\}$, then $\{B_{lk} : k = 1, 2, \cdots, r\}$ is set of β upper (β lower) distribution cumulative reduction.

Proof. For any $k \leq p$ and $(C_i, C_j) \in D_l^{*\beta}$, we have $B_{lk} \cap D_l^{\beta}(C_i, C_j) \neq \varnothing$. B_{lk} is β upper(β lower) distribution consistent set. For M_l^{β}, if $B_{lk}' = B_{lk} - a_{l_s}$, where $s = 1, 2, \cdots, q_k$, then there exists $(C_i, C_j) \in D_l^{*\beta}$ such that $B_{lk}' \cap D_l^{\beta}(C_i, C_j) = \varnothing$. So B_{lk}' is not β upper(β lower) distribution consistent set. That is to say B_{lk}' is not β upper (β lower) distribution reduction.

β upper (β lower) distribution discernible formulas include all $D_l^{\beta}(C_i, C_j)$, so there does not exist β upper (β lower) distribution cumulative reduction.

4 An Example

The director wants to make an evaluation to students based on the level in Mathematics, Physics and Literature. However, there are some missing values as shown in Table 1.

Table 1. Student evaluations with missing values

Student	Mathematics	Physics	Literature	Global evaluation
1	medium	bad	bad	bad
2	good	medium	*	good
3	medium	*	medium	bad
4	*	medium	medium	good
5	*	good	bad	bad
6	good	medium	bad	good

For $\beta = 0.3$, Let $C = \{Mathematics, Physics, Literature\}$ be condition attributes and $\{Global\ evaluation\}$ be decision attribute. Let $bad = \{1, 3, 5\}$ and $good = \{2, 4, 6\}$, $U_C^* = \{1, 2, 3, 4, 5, 6\}$, $\underline{C}_{\beta}^*(bad) = \{1, 5\}$, $\overline{C}_{\beta}^*(bad) = \{1, 3, 4, 5\}$, $\underline{C}_{\beta}^*(good) = \{2, 6\}$, $\overline{C}_{\beta}^*(good) = \{2, 3, 4, 6\}$.

$M_1^{\beta} = P$. P is β lower distribution cumulative reductions of attribute set C.

From this example, we can see that the cumulative VPRS model in incomplete information system can effectively reduce database, roundly wide application range of the VPRS, and fully maintain information for database.

Acknowledgments. This work is partially supported by National Natural Science Foundation of China (60873108), Application Technology Research and Development Foundation of Luoyang(1101018A), Natural Science Research Foundation of Henan University of Science and Technology (09001172,13440072, 2009Y-016).

References

1. Pawlak, Z., Skowron, A.: Rudiments of rough sets. Information Sciences 177(1), 3–27 (2007)
2. Pawlak, Z., Skowron, A.: Rough sets: some extensions. Information Sciences 177(1), 28–40 (2007)
3. Pawlak, Z., Skowron, A.: Rough sets and boolean reasoning. Information Sciences 177(1), 41–73 (2007)
4. Zhu, W., Wang, F.-Y.: Binary relation based rough sets. In: Wang, L., Jiao, L., Shi, G., Li, X., Liu, J. (eds.) FSKD 2006. LNCS (LNAI), vol. 4223, pp. 276–285. Springer, Heidelberg (2006)
5. Zhu, W.: Topological approaches to covering rough sets. Information Sciences 177(6), 1499–1508 (2007)
6. Zhu, W., Wang, F.-Y.: On three types of covering rough sets. IEEE Transactions on Knowledge and Data Engineering 19(8), 10–41 (2007)
7. Qin, K.Y., Pei, Z.: On the topological properties of fuzzy rough sets. Fuzzy Sets and Systems 151(3), 601–613 (2005)
8. Wu, W.Z., Zhang, W.X.: Constructive and axiomatic approaches of fuzzy approximation operators. Information Sciences 159(3-4), 233–254 (2004)
9. Ziarko, W.: Variable precision rough set model. Journal of Computer System Science 46(1), 39–59 (1993)
10. Slezak, D., Ziarko, W.: The investigation of the Bayesian rough set model. International Journal of Approximation Reason 40, 81–91 (2005)
11. Tao, Z., Xu, B.D., Wang, D.W., Li, R.: Rough Rules Mining Approach Based on Variable Precision Rough Set Theory. Information and Control 33(1), 18–22 (2004)
12. Beynon, M.: Reducts within the variable precision rough sets model: A further investigation. European Journal of Operational Research 134, 592–605 (2001)
13. Zhang, W.X., Liang, Y., Wu, W.Z.: Information System and Knowledge Discovery. Science Press, Beijing (2003) (in Chinese)
14. Inuiguchi, M.: Structure-Based Approaches to Attribute Reduction in Variable Precision Rough Set Models. In: Proceeding of IEEE ICGC 2005, pp. 34–39 (2005)
15. Mieszkowicz-Rolka, A., Rolka, L.: Remarks on approximation quality in variable precision fuzzy rough sets model. In: Tsumoto, S., Słowiński, R., Komorowski, J., Grzymała-Busse, J.W. (eds.) RSCTC 2004. LNCS (LNAI), vol. 3066, pp. 402–411. Springer, Heidelberg (2004)
16. Gong, Z.T., Sun, B.Z., Shao, Y.B., Chen, D.G.: Variable precision rough set model based on general relations. Journal of Lanzhou University (Natural Sciences) 41(6), 110–114 (2005) (in Chinese)
17. Zhang, Y.J., Wang, Y.P.: Covering rough set model based on variable precision. Journal of Liaoning Institute of Technology 26(4), 274–276 (2006) (in Chinese)
18. Sun, S.B., Liu, R.X., Qin, K.Y.: Comparison of Variable Precision Covering Rough Set Models. Computer engineering 34(7), 10–13 (2008) (in Chinese)
19. Zhu, W., Wang, F.Y.: Reduction and axiomization of covering generalized rough sets. Information Sciences 152, 217–230 (2003)
20. Mieszkowicz-Rolka, A., Rolka, L.: Fuzziness in Information Systems. Electronic Notes in Theoretical Computer Science 82(4), 1–10 (2003)
21. Yang, X.B., Yang, J.Y., Wu, C., Yu, D.J.: Dominance-based rough set approach and knowledge reductions in incomplete ordered information system. Information Sciences 178, 1219–1234 (2008)
22. Sun, S.B., Zheng, R.J., Wu, T.T., Li, T.R.: VPRS-Based Knowledge Discovery Approach in Incomplete Information System. Journal of Computers 5(1), 110–116 (2010)

A Method of Uncertainty Measure in Set-Valued Ordered Information Systems

Yongqiang Yang and FuChang Ma

College of Computer Engineering, Taiyuan University of Technology, Taiyuan 030024
monsyang@163.com

Abstract. Through the development of set-valued information systems from models of single-valued information systems, we see there are important applications in the pattern recognition and intelligent decision-making. In this paper, we first introduce concept of dominance rough entropy in set-valued ordered information systems. When the average uncertainty quantity of rough set is measured in set-valued ordered information systems, we not only consider the number of distinguishable pairs of the elements on the universe, but also increase factor of rough degree. Furthermore, the average uncertainty quantity of rough set with respect to the dominance relation is defined. Finally, by use of a case, we prove that average uncertainty quantity of rough sets with respect to the dominance relation in a set-valued ordered information system drops monotonously with decrease of knowledge granularity. These results come up with a feasible method to acquire knowledge in set-valued ordered information systems.

Keywords: set-valued ordered information systems, dominance relation, uncertainty measure, average uncertainty quantity, rough degree.

1 Introduction

The theory of rough, put forward at the beginning of 1980s by Polish mathematician Pawlak [1, 2], was used for theory tool of data analysis. Having been developed in the 20 years, the theory successfully has applied in the field of knowledge discovery and great attention has been paid to in the international arena. At the present time, the theory has many important applications in the pattern recognition, intelligent decision-making and cognitive sciences. Rough set originally deal with data by data table. Data analysis based on rough set is generated from information systems which contain data about objects of interest, characterized by a finite set of attributes. However, the ordering of properties of the considered attributes plays a crucial role in the problems which are often to be solved. In this respect, the classical rough set theory does not pay attention to attributes with dominance relation. In order to deal with the problems, an extension of rough set theory, introduced by Greco, Matarazzo, and Slowinski [3–6], solves the ordering properties of criteria. The theory is called the dominance-based rough set approach (DRSA) [7–8], and has been researched so far.

The theory of entropy, defined by Shannon [9], is an effective tool to measure of the system uncertainty in many real situations. The theory of entropy is widely

H. Deng et al. (Eds.): AICI 2011, Part III, LNAI 7004, pp. 595–603, 2011.

applied in rough set and very reflects uncertainty of knowledge. Many authors [10-11] have make use of Shannon's theory to measure the uncertainty in rough set theory. Liang in [12-14] puts forward a new information entropy and meantime deduces many important properties of the entropy. Qian in[15] defines a new combination entropy and combination granulation which measure the uncertainty in an incomplete information system and establish some relevant concepts. Hu et al. [16] generalize Shannon's entropy to crisp ordinal classification and fuzzy ordinal classification. However, so far, how to measure uncertainty of rough set by entropy theory in set-valued ordered information systems has been rare.

In this paper, set-valued information systems based on dominance relation are discussed. The main research task is to introduce concept of dominance entropy in set-valued ordered information systems. However, the research is different from Shannon's entropy. We not only consider the number of distinguishable pairs of the elements on the universe, but also increase factor of rough degree when we measure the average uncertainty quantity of rough set in set-valued ordered information systems. Through calculation, we prove that average uncertainty quantity of rough sets with respect to the dominance relation in a set-valued ordered information system drops monotonously with decrease of knowledge granularity.

The paper is organized as follows: In Section 2, we review on rough set and Shannon entropy. In Section 3, we put forward a method of uncertainty measure in set-valued information systems based on dominance relation. In Section 4, the study case is given. Finally, we summarize this paper in Section 5.

2   Review on Rough Set and Shannon Entropy

In this section, we briefly review some basic concepts of rough set and Shannon entropy.

Definition 1. $S = (U, AT, V, f)$ is viewed as an ordered information system (OIS), if all condition attributes are criteria.

It is supposed that domain of a criterion $a \in AT$ is completely pre-ordered by an outranking relation $\succeq a$; $x \succeq_a y$ means that x is at least as good as (outranks) y with respect to criterion a.

Definition 2. Let $IND(R)$ be A binary indistinguishable relation, we denote

$$IND(R) = \{(x, y) \in U \times U | \forall a \in R, a(x) = a(y)\}$$

It can be obviously shown that $IND(R)$ is a binary indistinguishable relation on the set U.

We may view $U / IND(R)$ or U / R as a partition of U.

$$U / R = \{[x_i]_R | x_i \in U\}$$

According to classic rough set theory, a lower approximation and an upper approximation will be defined as follows.

Definition 3. Let $S = (U, AT, V, f)$ be information systems and $R \subseteq AT$, $X \subseteq U$, we denote

$$\underline{R}(X) = \left\{ x \in U \middle| [x]_R \subseteq X \right\}$$

$$\overline{R}(X) = \left\{ x \in U \middle| [x]_R \cap X \neq \phi \right\}$$

As follows, we will introduce the concepts of Shannon's entropy.

With the view of survey Shannon's entropy in a natural way, we view $[x_i]_R$ as the

partition of U/R .We may calculate probability $P([x_i]_R)$ of $[x_i]_R$ by $\left| [x_i]_R \right| / |U|$,

therefore Shannon's entropy is defined as:

$$H_B(U) = -\sum_{i=1}^{|U|} \frac{\left| [x_i]_R \right|}{|U|} \cdot \log\left(\frac{\left| [x_i]_R \right|}{|U|} \right)$$

3   Uncertainty Measure in Set-Valued Ordered Information Systems

In this section, we first introduce set-valued ordered information systems. In real issues, some of the attribute values of which we study objects are set-valued. The information system which is composed of the attribute values is a so-called set-valued information system.

Definition 4. Set-valued information system is a quadruple: $ZT = (U, A, V, f)$,

Where

U is a non-empty finite set of objects,

A is a finite set of condition attributes,

V is the set of condition attribute values

f is a mapping from $U \times A$ to V such that $U \times A \rightarrow 2^V$ is a set-valued mapping.

Definition 5. Let $ZTO = (U, A, V, f)$ be a set-valued ordered information system, $B \subseteq A$, we denote

$$R_{B\succeq} = \left\{ (y,x) \in U \times U \middle| y \succ_B x \right\} = \left\{ (y,x) \in U \times U \middle| f(y,b) \supseteq f(x,b) \forall b \in B \right\} \qquad (1)$$

If $(y,x) \in R_{B\succeq}$, then y dominances x with respect to B.

We may easily derive the following properties from the definition of $R_{B\succeq}$.

Property 1. Let $R_{B\succeq}$ be a dominance relation of set-valued ordered information systems, then

a) $R_{B\succeq}$ is reflexive ,transitive , asymmetric , so it is not a equivalence relation;

b) Given $B \subseteq A$ and $B = B_1 \cup B_2$, where attributes set B_2 according to decreasing preference, B_1 according to increasing preference.

$$[x]_{R_{B \preceq}} = \left\{ y \in U \middle| (x,y) \in R_{B \preceq} \right\}$$

$$= \left\{ y \in U \middle| f(y,b_1) \subseteq f(x,b_1)(\forall b_1 \in B_1) \quad and \quad f(y,b_2) \supseteq f(x,b_2)(\forall b_2 \in B_2) \right\}$$

$$[x]_{R_{B \succeq}} = \left\{ y \in U \middle| (y,x) \in R_{B \succeq} \right\}$$

$$= \left\{ y \in U \middle| f(y,b_1) \supseteq f(x,b_1)(\forall b_1 \in B_1) \quad and \quad f(y,b_2) \subseteq f(x,b_2)(\forall b_2 \in B_2) \right\}$$

As follows, but to simplify that we only discuss condition attributes with increasing preference.

Definition 6. Let $ZTO = (U,A,V,f)$ be a set-valued ordered information system and $Y \subseteq U$, $B \in A$, we define the lower and upper approximations of Y with respect to the dominance relation $R_{B \succeq}$ as follows:

$$\underline{R_{B \succeq}}(Y) = \left\{ y \in U \middle| [y]_{R_{B \succeq}} \subseteq Y \right\} \tag{2}$$

$$\overline{R_{B \succeq}}(Y) = \left\{ y \in U \middle| [y]_{R_{B \succeq}} \cap Y \neq \phi \right\} \tag{3}$$

In the following section, we will introduce the concepts of entropy in set-valued ordered information systems. Then an uncertainty measure in set-valued ordered information systems is studied. However, the study is different from Shannon's entropy. In the time of definition on entropy, we consider the whole number of distinguishable pairs of the elements on the universe and factor rough degree in set-valued ordered information systems.

As a rule, we cannot effectively distinguished the elements in an dominance relation class in set-valued ordered information systems, while the elements of different dominance relation classes can be distinguished each other according to rough set theory.

As far as the knowledge category of an approximation space $S = (U, R_{B \succeq})$, we exactly research on the whole number of distinguishable pairs of the elements on the universe U in set-valued ordered information systems. Based on this consideration as above, when we discuss the uncertainty of rough set in set-valued ordered information systems, the combination relation on pairs of the elements are considered.

On the other hand, in the classic rough set theory, the rough degree is used as measurement on the rough set. Therefore we introduce the rough degree which is measured in the rough set in set-valued ordered information systems.

Definition 7. Let $ZTO = (U, A, V, f)$ be a set-valued ordered information system and $C \subseteq A$, rough degree of the rough set $Y \subseteq U$ with respect to C is defined as follows:

$$\rho_{R_{C^\succeq}}(Y) = 1 - \frac{\left| R_{C^\succeq}(Y) \right|}{\left| \overline{R}_{C^\succeq}(Y) \right|} \tag{4}$$

Obviously, $0 \leq \rho_{R_{C^\succeq}}(X) \leq 1$.

Theorem 1. Let $ZTO = (U, A, V, f)$ be a set-valued ordered information system and $P, Q \subseteq A$, if $U / R_{P^\succeq} \subseteq U / R_{Q^\succeq}$, then $\rho_{R_{P^\succeq}}(X) \leq \rho_{R_{Q^\succeq}}(X)$ for $\forall X \subseteq U$.

From theorem 1, in the wake of knowledge classification becoming finer, the rough degree decreases.

Definition 8. Given a finite set Y and B dominance relation $R_{B^\succeq}$ on Y in a set-valued ordered information system, we calculate the average uncertainty quantity $TH_{\overline{B}}^{\succeq}(Y)$ of rough set Y with respect to the dominance relation $R_{B^\succeq}$ as follows:

$$TH_{\overline{B}}^{\succeq}(Y) = (1 - \frac{1}{|U|} \cdot \sum_{i=1}^{|U|}(1 - \frac{C_{\left|[x_i]_{R_{B^\succeq}}\right|}^{2}}{C_{|U|}^{2}})) \times \rho_{R_{B^\succeq}}(Y) \tag{5}$$

The average uncertainty quantity $TH_{\overline{B}}^{\succeq}(Y)$ of the dominance relation $R_{B^\succeq}$ on Y is called dominance rough entropy of the rough sets Y with respect to B in set-valued ordered information systems.

Proposition 1. Let $ZTO = (U, A, V, f)$ be a set-valued ordered information system and $P, Q \subseteq A$, we have

$$R_{P^\succeq} \subseteq R_{Q^\succeq} \Rightarrow TH_{\overline{P}}^{\succeq}(Y) \leq TH_{\overline{Q}}^{\succeq}(Y)$$

Obviously, we know $R_{P^\succeq} \subseteq R_{Q^\succeq}$ as above, that is classification of $R_{P^\succeq}$ is finer than that of $R_{Q^\succeq}$.

Moreover, the result indicate that average uncertainty quantity of rough sets with respect to the dominance relation in a set-valued ordered information system drops monotonously with decrease of knowledge granularity.

4 Case Study

In this section we will show how to compute average uncertainty quantity of rough sets with respect to the dominance relation in a set-valued ordered information system.

A set-valued ordered information system is taken on in Table1 , where

$$U = \{x_1, x_2, x_3, x_4, x_5, x_6, x_7, x_8, x_9, x_{10}\}$$

Table 1. A set-valued ordered information system

U	a_1	a_2	a_3	a_4
x_1	{1}	{2,3}	{2,3}	{1}
x_2	{1,2,3}	{1,2,3}	{2,3}	{1,2,3}
x_3	{1,2}	{2,3}	{2,3}	{1,3}
x_4	{1,3}	{2}	{2,3}	{1,2}
x_5	{2,3}	{2}	{2,3}	{2,3}
x_6	{2}	{1,2}	{1,2}	{2}
x_7	{1,2,3}	{1,2,3}	{1,3}	{1,2,3}
x_8	{2,3}	{1,3}	{1,2,3}	{1,2}
x_9	{3}	{2,3}	{2,3}	{2,3}
x_{10}	{1,3}	{1,2}	{2,3}	{1,2}

From Table 1, We may obtain that

$$f(x_2, a_1) = \{1,2,3\}, f(x_{10}, a_1) = \{1,3\}$$

Owing to $f(x_2, a_1) \supseteq f(x_{10}, a_1)$, we can conclude that the x_2 must be better than that of x_{10} with respect to a_1.

Then we can compute that:

Let $A = \{a_1, a_2, a_3, a_4\}$ then

$$[x_1]_{R_{A^\succeq}} = \{x_1, x_2, x_3\}, [x_2]_{R_{A^\succeq}} = \{x_2\},$$

$$[x_3]_{R_{A^\succeq}} = \{x_2, x_3\}, [x_4]_{R_{A^\succeq}} = \{x_2, x_4, x_{10}\},$$

$$[x_5]_{R_{A^\succeq}} = \{x_2, x_5\}, [x_6]_{R_{A^\succeq}} = \{x_6\},$$

$$[x_7]_{R_{A^\succeq}} = \{x_7\}, [x_8]_{R_{A^\succeq}} = \{x_8\},$$

$$[x_9]_{R_{A^\succeq}} = \{x_2, x_9\} \text{ and } [x_{10}]_{R_{A^\succeq}} = \{x_2, x_{10}\}$$

Let $B = \{a_1, a_2\}$ then

$$[x_1]_{R_{B^\succeq}} = \{x_1, x_2, x_3, x_7\}, [x_2]_{R_{B^\succeq}} = \{x_2, x_7\},$$

$$[x_3]_{R_{B^\succeq}} = \{x_2, x_3, x_7\}, [x_4]_{R_{B^\succeq}} = \{x_2, x_4, x_7, x_{10}\},$$

$$[x_5]_{R_{B^\succeq}} = \{x_2, x_5, x_7\}, [x_6]_{R_{B^\succeq}} = \{x_2, x_6, x_7, x_{10}\},$$

$$[x_7]_{R_{B^\succeq}} = \{x_2, x_7\}, [x_8]_{R_{B^\succeq}} = \{x_2, x_7, x_8\},$$

$$[x_9]_{R_{B^\succeq}} = \{x_2, x_7, x_9\} \text{ and } [x_{10}]_{R_{B^\succeq}} = \{x_2, x_7, x_{10}\}$$

Obviously, we may find $U/R_{A^\succeq} \subseteq U/R_{B^\succeq}$, namely, classification of $U/R_{B^\succeq}$ is coarser than that of $U/R_{A^\succeq}$.

Example   1.   Given   the   information   in   Table   1,   for   knowledge $A = \{a_1, a_2, a_3, a_4\}, B = \{a_1, a_2\}$,   one can obtain rough degree of $Y = \{x_2, x_5, x_7\}$

$$\rho_{R_{A^\succeq}}(Y) = 1 - \frac{\left|\underline{R_{A^\succeq}}(Y)\right|}{\left|\overline{R_{A^\succeq}}(Y)\right|} = 1 - \frac{3}{8} = 0.625$$

$$\rho_{R_{B^\succeq}}(Y) = 1 - \frac{\left|\underline{R_{B^\succeq}}(Y)\right|}{\left|\overline{R_{B^\succeq}}(Y)\right|} = 1 - \frac{3}{10} = 0.7$$

Example 2. (continue Example 1) Given the information in Table I, the average uncertainty quantity of $A = \{a_1, a_2, a_3, a_4\}, B = \{a_1, a_2\}$ are computed as follows:

$$TH_A^\succeq(Y) = (1 - \frac{1}{|U|} \sum_{i=1}^{|U|} (1 - \frac{C_{\left|[x_i]_{R_{A^\succeq}}\right|}^2}{C_{|U|}^2})) \times \rho_{R_{A^\succeq}}(Y)$$

$$= [1 - \frac{1}{10} \left[(1 - \frac{3}{45}) + (1 - \frac{0}{45}) + (1 - \frac{1}{45}) + (1 - \frac{3}{45}) + (1 - \frac{1}{45}) \right.$$

$$\left. + (1 - \frac{0}{45}) + (1 - \frac{0}{45}) + (1 - \frac{0}{45}) + (1 - \frac{1}{45}) + (1 - \frac{1}{45}) \right]] \times 0.625   =   0.01388$$

$$TH_B^\succeq(Y) = (1 - \frac{1}{|U|} \sum_{i=1}^{|U|} (1 - \frac{C_{\left|[x_i]_{R_{B^\succeq}}\right|}^2}{C_{|U|}^2})) \times \rho_{R_{B^\succeq}}(Y)$$

$$= [1 - \frac{1}{10} \left[(1 - \frac{6}{45}) + (1 - \frac{1}{45}) + (1 - \frac{3}{45}) + (1 - \frac{6}{45}) + (1 - \frac{3}{45}) \right.$$

$$\left. + (1 - \frac{6}{45}) + (1 - \frac{1}{45}) + (1 - \frac{3}{45}) + (1 - \frac{3}{45}) + (1 - \frac{3}{45}) \right]] \times 0.7   =   0.05444$$

respectively.

From Example 2, we may obtain $TH_A^\succeq(Y) \leq TH_B^\succeq(Y)$. Moreover, one may obtain that average uncertainty quantity of rough sets with respect to the dominance relation in a set-valued ordered information system drops monotonously with decrease of knowledge granularity.

5   Conclusions

In short, a set-valued information system, derived from models of single-valued information system, is a type of important information table. In this paper, we mainly deal with set-valued information systems based on dominance relation. While we introduce concept of dominance rough entropy in set-valued ordered information systems, we not only consider the number of distinguishable pairs of the elements on the universe, but also increase factor of rough degree. In addition, the average uncertainty quantity of rough set with respect to the dominance relation is defined. In conclusion, through a case, we prove that average uncertainty quantity of rough sets with respect to the dominance relation in a set-valued ordered information system drops monotonously with decrease of knowledge granularity. These results lay a certain amount of theoretic foundation for knowledge discovery in set-valued ordered information systems.

References

1. Pawlak, Z., Skowron, A.: Rudiments of rough sets. Information Sciences 177, 3–27 (2007)
2. Pawlak, Z.: Rough Sets: Theoretical Aspects of Reasoning about Data, System Theory, Knowledge Engineering and Problem Solving, vol. 9. Kluwer, Dordrecht (1991)
3. Greco, S., Matarazzo, B., Słowiński, R., Stefanowski, J.: An Algorithm for Induction of Decision Rules Consistent with the Dominance Principle. In: Ziarko, W.P., Yao, Y. (eds.) RSCTC 2000. LNCS (LNAI), vol. 2005, pp. 304–313. Springer, Heidelberg (2001)
4. Greco, S., Matarazzo, B., Slowinski, R.: Rough sets theory for multicriteria decision analysis. European Journal of Operational Research 129, 1–47 (2001)
5. Greco, S., Matarazzo, B., Słowiński, R.: A New Rough Set Approach to Multicriteria and Multiattribute Classification. In: Polkowski, L., Skowron, A. (eds.) RSCTC 1998. LNCS (LNAI), vol. 1424, pp. 60–67. Springer, Heidelberg (1998)
6. Greco, S., Matarazzo, B., Slowinski, R.: Rough sets methodology for sorting problems in presence of multiple attributes and criteria. European Journal of Operational Research 138, 247–259 (2002)
7. Dembczynski, K., Pindur, R., Susmaga, R.: Dominance-based rough set classifier without induction of decision rules. Electronic Notes in Theoretical Computer Science 82(4) (2003)
8. Dembczynski, K., Pindur, R., Susmaga, R.: Generation of exhaustive set of rules within dominance-based rough set approach. Electronic Notes in Theoretical Computer Science 82(4) (2003)
9. Shannon, C.E.: The mathematical theory of communication. The Bell System Technical Journal 27(3, 4), 373–423 (1948)
10. Düntsch, Gediga, G.: Uncertainty measures of rough set prediction. Aritificial Intelligence 106, 109–137 (1998)
11. Beaubouef, T., Perty, F.E., Arora, G.: Information-theoretic measures of uncertainty for rough sets and rough relational databases. Information Sciences 109, 185–195 (1998)
12. Liang, J.Y., Qu, K.S.: Information measures of roughness of knowledge and rough sets in incomplete information systems. Journal of System Science and System Engineering 24(5), 544–547 (2001)

13. Liang, J.Y., Shi, Z.Z.: The information entropy, rough entropy and knowledge granulation in rough set theory. International Journal of Uncertainty, Fuzziness and Knowledge-Based Systems 12(1), 37–46 (2004)
14. Liang, J.Y., Chin, K.S., Dang, C.Y., Yam Richard, C.M.: A new method for measuring uncertainty and fuzziness in rough set theory. International Journal of General Systems 31(4), 331–342 (2002)
15. Qian, Y., Liang, J.: Combination Entropy and Combination Granulation in Incomplete Information System. In: Wang, G.-Y., Peters, J.F., Skowron, A., Yao, Y. (eds.) RSKT 2006. LNCS (LNAI), vol. 4062, pp. 184–190. Springer, Heidelberg (2006)
16. Hu, Q., Guo, M., Yu, D., Liu, J.: Information entropy for ordinal classification. Science in China Series F: Information Sciences 53(6), 1188–1200 (2010)

Rough Kernel Clustering Algorithm with Adaptive Parameters*

Tao Zhou[1,2], Huiling Lu[1,**], Deren Yang[1], Jingxian Ma[1], and Shouheng Tuo[3]

[1] School of Science, Ningxia Medical university, Ningxia Yinchuan 750004
zhout123@gmail.com, lu_huiling@163.com
[2] Dept. Of Maths, Shaanxi University of Technology,Shaanxi Hanzhong 723000
[3] Dept. Of Computer, Shaanxi University of Technology,Shaanxi Hanzhong 723000

Abstract. Through analyzing kernel clustering algorithm and rough set theory, a novel clustering algorithm, Rough kernel k-means clustering algorithm with adaptive parameters, is proposed for clustering analysis in this paper. By using Mercer kernel functions, we can map the data in the original space to a high-dimensional feature space, in which we can use rough k-means with adaptive parameters to perform clustering in feature space. Efficiently. The results of simulation experiments show the feasibility and effectiveness of the kernel clustering algorithm.

Keywords: Rough Set, Kernel clustering algorithm, Rough clustering, Adaptive parameters.

1 Introduction

A cluster is a collection of data objects which are similar to one another within the same cluster but dissimilar to the objects in other clusters. The problem is to group N patterns into c desired clusters with high intra-class similarity and low inter-class similarity by optimizing an objective function. Clustering algorithms partition data into a certain number of clusters. Clustering algorithm [1][4] is a supervised pattern classification. We will look into clustering algorithms that are and driven solely by the information about the location of data in a Euclidean data space of dimension d. Patterns in the same cluster should be similar and the dissimilarity should be examinable in a clear and meaningful way. Rough set [2][3] is presented by Professor Z. Pawlak. It is an extension of set theory, mainly in the domain of intelligent systems. In Lingras' rough k-means clustering algorithm[5], each cluster has two approximations, a lower and an upper approximation. The lower approximation is a

* Sponsored by Ningxia Health Department Scientific Research Fund(2011033), Shaanxi Province Education Department Scientific Research Fund(2010JK466) and Ningxia Medical University Special Talent Scientific Research Start Fund, Ningxia Hui Autonomous Region Natural Sciences Research Fund(NZ11105).
** Corresponding author.

H. Deng et al. (Eds.): AICI 2011, Part III, LNAI 7004, pp. 604–610, 2011.

subset of the upper approximation. The members of the lower approximation belong to any other cluster. The data objects in an upper approximation may belong to the cluster. Since their membership is uncertain they must be a member of an upper approximation of at least another cluster.

Some clustering algorithms, include rough cluster algorithm, don't consider cluster sample characters, hence clustering performance depend on distribution of samples deeply, Tao Zhou[6] put forward kernel-based rough k-means clustering algorithm to resolve this problem. In rough k-means clustering algorithm [5], New centroids of the rough k-means algorithm depends on three parameters w_l, w_u and ε threshold. Experiment with various values of parameters is necessary to develop a reasonable rough set clustering. Tao Zhou[7] proposed an adaptive parameters, to select suitable combination coefficient about w_l, w_u and ε threshold. However, In rough cluster algorithm, In considering the distribution of the sample on the basis of further improving the performance of clustering algorithm is a problem. This paper put forward a novel clustering algorithm, rough kernel k-means clustering algorithm with adaptive parameters. By using kernel learning theory, firstly, we can transform these samples in the samples space to a high-dimensional feature space, and the data can be classified linearly (maybe usually nonlinear). Secondly, we can use adaptive rough k-means to perform clustering in feature space efficiently.

2   Related Basic Theory

2.1   Kernel Method

Kernel methods[8,9] are appellation of a serious advanced nonlinear data dealing technology, and using kernel map are their common characteristics. From idiographic operating, firstly, samples are mapped into feature space using nonlinear method; secondly, dealing with these samples in feature space in linear operating.

Kernel functions are nonlinear map function $\Phi : \Re^d \rightarrow F$ which for all pattern sets,

$$x_j \in \Re^d , \text{j=1,2,...,N,.} \Leftrightarrow \{x_1, x_2, ..., x_N\} \subset \Re^d .$$
$$\Phi(x_1), \Phi(x_2), ..., \Phi(x_N) \subset F$$

Here, $\Re^d$ is sample space .F represents a feature space with arbitrary high dimensionality, In feature space, kernels are often referred to as Mercer kernels or others.

2.2   Rough k-Means Algorithm

Calculation of the new means is important for rough k-means algorithm[5]. The means are calculated as follows:

$$\vec{m}_k = \begin{cases} w_l \cdot \sum\limits_{\vec{X}_n \in |C_k|} \dfrac{\vec{X}_n}{|C_k|} + w_B \cdot \sum\limits_{\vec{X}_n \in |C_k^B|} \dfrac{\vec{X}_n}{|C_k^B|} & \text{for} C_k^B \neq \phi \\[2em] w_l \cdot \sum\limits_{\vec{X}_n \in |C_k|} \dfrac{\vec{X}_n}{|C_k|} & \text{otherwise} \end{cases}$$

Where the parameters w_j and w_b define the importance of the lower approximation and boundary area of the cluster. The expression $|C_k|$ indicates the numbers of data objects in lower approximation of the cluster and $|C_k^B| = |\overline{C_k} - \underline{C_k}|$ is the number of data objects in the boundary area. If the upper bounder of each cluster were equal to its lower bound, the cluster will be conventional clusters. Hence, the boundary region C_k^B will be empty, and the second term in the equation will be ignored.

3   Rough Kernel Clustering Algorithm with Adaptive Parameters

3.1   Main Idea

Main idea about this algorithm is firstly, Given an unlabeled data set $X=\{x_1,x_2,\ldots,x_n\}$ in the d-dimension input space $\Re^d$,let $\Phi: \Re^d \rightarrow F$ be a nonlinear map function from input space to a high dimensional feature space F, differences of these samples are enhanced and these samples can be classified linearly (maybe close to linear).Object function is following:

$$J^\phi = \sum_{j=1}^{C}\sum_{l=1}^{N_K} \| \Phi(x_i) - m_j^\phi \|^2 = \sum_{j=1}^{C}\sum_{i=1}^{N_K} K(x_i,x_i) - \frac{2}{N_i}\sum_{k=1}^{N_j} K(x_i,x_k) + \frac{1}{N_i^2}\sum_{k,p=1}^{N_j} K(x_k,x_p)$$

Secondly, we can use adaptive rough k-means clustering algorithm to perform clustering in feature space. the algorithm in the high dimension feature space F iteratively searches for k clusters by minimizing the object function of the algorithm.

1) **Combination coefficient** w_l and w_u
In clustering early, means of one cluster is adjusted mainly depending on upper approximation data objects. Data objects in lower approximation only do some assistant adjustment role. Cluster centers will be find quickly in a wide region. Hence, the value of w_u should be bigger than w_l. With the growth of iterative number, the value of w_u will be decreased and the value of w_l will be increased.

In later of clustering, on the contrary, means of one cluster is adjusted mainly depending on lower approximation data objects. Data objects in upper approximation only do some assistant adjustment role. Cluster centers will be adjusted in a tiny region and cluster centoids should be more precise . Hence, the value of w_l should be bigger than w_u.

In order to realize the process named adaptive adjustment, We give a method and realize the process.

$$w_l = \cos^2 \left(\dfrac{w_l}{times^{\frac{1}{n}}} \right) \qquad w_u = 1 - w_l$$

Where ts iterative numbers, k, a, b are function parameters, $0 \le w_u , w_l \le 1$, when k=0, a=0.2, b=0.3, its function graph is shown in Fig 1.

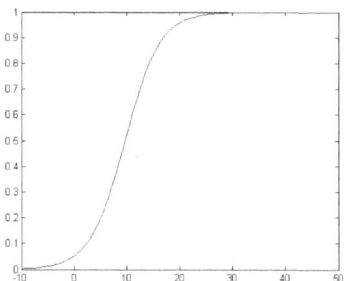

Fig. 1. Adaptive function diagram

2) ε Threshold

In clustering early, means of one cluster is adjusted mainly depending on upper approximation data objects. Data objects in lower approximation only do some assistant adjustment role. The value of ε is small, only do this, Most data objects are assigned to upper approximation and attend cluster centers adjustment. With the growth of iterative number, the value of ε will be increased.

In later of clustering, means of one cluster is adjusted mainly depending on lower approximation data objects. Data objects in upper approximation only do some assistant adjustment role. The value of ε is become big , Only do this, Most data objects are assigned to lower approximation and attend cluster centers adjustment.

In order to realize the process named threshold adaptive adjustment, We give a method and realize the process.

$$\varepsilon = \varepsilon + \frac{1}{times^n}$$

Times are iterative numbers and n is attenuation coefficient. Generally n=2.

3.2 The Algorithm Proceeds

1) Given an unlabeled data set in sample space $\Re^d$:{ $\vec{x}_1, \vec{x}_2, ..., \vec{x}_N$ }$\subset \Re^d$;

2) Given a kernel function Φ and map these samples into Hilbert space F: { $\Phi(\vec{x}_1), \Phi(\vec{x}_2), ..., \Phi(\vec{x}_N)$ }$\subset F$.

3) Initializing clustering centroids: $\vec{m_k^{\phi}} = \{\vec{m_1^{\phi}}, \vec{m_2^{\phi}}, ..., \vec{m_K^{\phi}}\}$, where K is number of class;

4) In kernel space, assigning each sample $\Phi(\vec{x_i})$ into up-approximation and low-approximation according to near distance principle

a) $d(\Phi(\vec{x_i}), \vec{m_k})$,calculating the distance between $\Phi(\vec{x_i})$ and clustering centroids $\vec{m_k}$,, k=1,2,...,K;

$$d_{i,h}^{\min} = d_{i,h}(\Phi(\vec{x_i}), m_h) = \min_{k=1,...,K}\{\Phi(\vec{x_i}), m_k\}$$

and assigning $\Phi(\vec{x_i})$ to up- approximation of $\vec{m_k}$, means $\Phi(\vec{x_i}) \in \overline{C_h}$;

b) the distance $d(\Phi(\vec{x_i}), \vec{m_k})$ between $\Phi(\vec{x_i})$ and $\vec{m_k}$ is less than $d_{i,h}^{\min}$ and $\exists \varepsilon$:

$$T = \{k : (d(\Phi(\vec{x_i}), \vec{m_k}) - d(\Phi(\vec{x_i}), \vec{m_h}) \le \varepsilon) \wedge (h \ne k)\}$$

Where: $\varepsilon = \varepsilon + \dfrac{1}{times^n}$

if $T \ne \phi$

then $\Phi(\vec{x_i}) \in \overline{C_t}$, $\forall t \in T$;

else $\Phi(\vec{x_i}) \in \underline{C_h}$;

5) Re-calculating clustering centroids $\vec{m_k^{\phi}} = \{\vec{m_1^{\phi}}, \vec{m_2^{\phi}}, ..., \vec{m_K^{\phi}}\}$ and object function J^{ϕ} ;

Because clustering center cannot calculated explicitly in feature space, calculation of cluster centroids is a puzzle question in this method. In this paper, we adopt following method that every sample can be assigned into up-approximation and low-approximation of each cluster centroids and Lingras algorithm is adopted to update cluster centroids, we can use following formulation to do this work:

$$\vec{m_k^{\phi}} = \begin{cases} w_l \cdot \sum\limits_{\Phi(\vec{X_n}) \in |C_k|} \dfrac{\Phi(\vec{X_n})}{|\underline{C_k}|} + w_B \cdot \sum\limits_{\Phi(\vec{X_n}) \in |C_k^B|} \dfrac{\Phi(\vec{X_n})}{|\overline{C_k}|} & for C_k \ne \phi \\[3mm] w_l \cdot \sum\limits_{\Phi(\vec{X_n}) \in |\overline{C_k}|} \dfrac{\vec{X_n}}{|\overline{C_k}|} & otherwise \end{cases}$$

Where:

$$w_l = \cos^2\left(\dfrac{w_l}{times^{\frac{1}{n}}}\right) \qquad w_u = 1 - w_l$$

6) repeat step 4 and step 5, until the value diversification of J^{ϕ} is very small.

4 Experiments

We generate 2 test samples: there are 200 samples in data set 1 and the distribution of the samples are two nested cycles. Fig 2 illustrates data set 1. There are 600 samples in data set 2 and the distributions of these samples are 4 cycles. Fig 3 illustrates data set 2. In table 1, we give out error clustering rate about k-means algorithm, rough kernel k-means algorithm and rough kernel k-means with adaptive parameter algorithm about these two testing sample respectively. Data set 1and data set 2 are not linearly inseparable data set, using k-means algorithm, cluster error rate is very high, and utilizing rough kernel k-means algorithm, Clustering performance is greatly improved and error clustering rate are reduced to 16.98% and 14.85%. in this algorithm, error clustering rate reach 5.68% and 9.46%,Experiment illustrate that rough kernel k-means with adaptive parameter algorithm can control error clustering rate effectively.

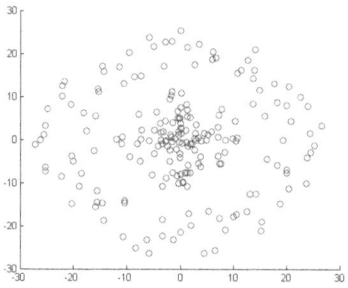

Fig. 2. Testing data set 1

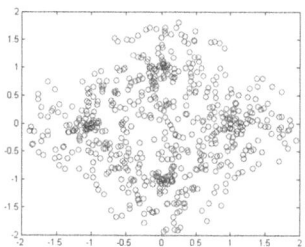

Fig. 3. Testing data set 2

Table 1. Comparing Experiment result

Samples	K-means (Error rate %)	Rough kernel K-means (Error rate %)	My algorithm (Error rate %)
data set 1 (2 nested cycles)	48.56	16.98	5.68
data set 2 (4 cycles)	51.23	14.85	9.46

5   Conclusions

Generally, the stability, precision and performance of clustering algorithm is depended on geometrical characteristics of the training data. If the difference is evidence and can be clustered easily. However in practical, this difference is not obvious among training data and even different samples in different are cross, traditional clustering algorithm based on distance can not resolve this problem. Kernel clustering algorithm can transform samples in original space into Hilbert space, the difference among samples can be preserved and even magnified, and therefore we can use k-means to do clustering in Hilbert space and get a better clustering performance. In this paper, we think different samples can have different affection about different clustering centroids, assigning each sample into up-approximation and low-approximation according to some principles. And updating clustering centroids according to the linear combination of up-approximation and low-approximation in adaptive strategy. Via experiment, we can know that this method has a better clustering performance and precision. Another merit is that it can restrain outlier role about clustering results.

References

1. Hansen, P., Jaumard, B.: Cluster analysis and mathematical programming. Math Program 79, 191–215 (1997)
2. Pawlak, Z.: Rough Sets theoretical Aspects of Reasoning About Data. Kluwer Academic, Dordrecht (1991)
3. Van Gestel, T., Baesses, B., Suykens, J.A.K., et al.: Bayesian Kernel based classification for financial distress detection. European Journal of Operational Research 172, 979–1003 (2006)
4. Xu, R., Wunsch II, D.: Survey of clustering algorithm. IEEE Transaction on Neural Networks 10(3), 645–678 (2005)
5. Lingras, P., West, J.: Interval set clustering of web users with rough k-means. Journal of Intelligent Information Systems 23(1), 5–16 (2004)
6. Zhou, T., Zhang, Y., Lu, H., Deng, F., Wang, F.: Rough Cluster Algorithm Based on Kernel Function. In: Wang, G., Li, T., Grzymala-Busse, J.W., Miao, D., Skowron, A., Yao, Y. (eds.) RSKT 2008. LNCS (LNAI), vol. 5009, pp. 172–179. Springer, Heidelberg (2008)
7. Zhou, T., Zhang, Y., Lu, H.: Rough k-means cluster with adaptive parameters. In: Proc. of 6th Inte. Conf. on Machine Learning an Cybernetics, Hong Kong, vol. 6, pp. 3063–3067 (2007)
8. Pozdnoukhov, A., Bengio, S.: Invariances in kernel methods: From samples to objects. Pattern Recognition Letters 7(10), 1087–1097 (2006)
9. Canu, S., Smola, A.: Kernel methods and the exponential family. Neurocomputing 69(7), 714–720 (2006)

Soft Sensor Modeling and Simulation Research of Flotation Cleaned Coal Ash of Slime

Ranfeng Wang

Mineral Processing Engineering Department,
Taiyuan University of Technology TaiYuan, China
wrf197010@163.com

Abstract. Realizes the flotation process cleaned coal ash soft Sensor is the key of flotation process automation. First introduction to least square support vector machines algorithm, subsidiary variable choice research on flotation process cleaned coal ash soft sensor is carried out, reasonable subsidiary variable is selected by experiment, soft sensor accuracy of coal change is proposed, experiment show that model accuracy is sensitive for coal change. This soft sensor model is help to flotation process automatic control.

Keywords: Flotation cleaned coal ash, Least square support vector machines, Subsidiary variable choice, Anthrax fluctuation.

1 Introduction

The flotation process has the serious misalignment, the close coupling and the big lag characteristic, is a physical chemistry synthesis reaction process, the ultimate objective is achieving the Quality assurance of flotation process product and the production rate maximization. Except development and the optimization in the flotation process equipment and the craft aspect, the flotation process automation is also realizes the above goal important condition and the method, the solution flotation process cleaned coal ash real-time examination is a key technology of realizing the slime flotation process automation, many domestic and foreign scholars launched study and have made certain progress and the progress [1, 2, 3]. Overseas have researched the measuring appliance of flotation cleaned coal ash examination, but because of the high price limits its application in the coal preparation plant. The domestic use the same principle the development measuring appliance, because of reliability, precision and security causes to be unable to promote in the coal preparation plant. The soft sensor theory and the technical rapid development and the application have provided the new mentality for the slime flotation cleaned coal ash examination. The soft sensor modeling based on the flotation process parameter Involves to the metalliferous ore flotation process present domestic and foreign research, the slime flotation process relatively are few. Based on support of the statistics theory ,vector return modeling technology by it to the small sample's serviceability, the most superior of overall situation and good model pan-ability becomes a kind of important modeling method in the soft sensor development, Natural can provide the worth trusted theory and the technical support for the flotation

H. Deng et al. (Eds.): AICI 2011, Part III, LNAI 7004, pp. 611–619, 2011.

cleaned coal ash soft sensor . Last square support vector machines operating speed to be quick, becomes the good technology which the statistics theory of learning and the support vector machines algorithm realized and obtained many research.

The paper take least square support vector machines modeling technology as the instruction, launches the subsidiary variable of the slime flotation cleaned coal ash soft sensor ,choices research and changes in view of the anthrax the soft sensor model the compatible research, provides the beneficial exploration and reference for the flotation cleaned coal ash soft sensor modeling.

2 Least Square Support Vector Machines Modeling Principle [4,5]

LS-SVM was increased the erroneous sum of squares item in the standard SVM objective function foundation , that between least square support vector machines (LS-SVM) and support vector machines (SVM) ,the main diversity is square item of errors as loss function, is not the insensitive loss function as the loss function. This then may transform the inequality constraint condition the equality constraint condition. In nonlinear system, Regards as the misalignment regression function is:

$$f(x) = w^T \phi(x) + b \tag{1}$$

And : $x \in R^n$, $y \in R$,

misalignment function $\phi(\cdot) :\ R^n \to R^{n_k}$.

The input space data will map the high Uygur feature space through the mapping function. For assigns the training data set $\{x_k, y_k\}_{k=1}^{N}$, LS-SVM May define the following optimized question, γ is regularization parameter.

$$\min_{w,b,e} J(w,e) = \frac{1}{2} w^T w + \gamma \frac{1}{2} \sum_{k=1}^{N} e_k^2 \tag{2}$$

s.t. $y_k = w^T \cdot \phi(x_k) + b + e_k$, k=1,,,n

Assigns the Lagrange function is:

$$L = J - \sum_{K=1}^{N} a_k [w^T \cdot \phi(x_k) + b + e_k - y_k] \tag{3}$$

In the above equation α is the Lagrange multiplier.

Again based on the KTT condition:

$$\frac{\partial L}{\partial w} = 0 \to w = \sum_{k=1}^{N} a_k \phi(x_k)$$

$$\frac{\partial L}{\partial b} = 0 \to \sum_{k=1}^{N} a_k = 0$$

$$\frac{\partial L}{\partial e_k} = 0 \to a_k = \gamma e_k \tag{4}$$

$$\frac{\partial L}{\partial a_k} = 0 \to w^T \cdot \phi(x_k) + b + e_k - y_k = 0$$

For $K=1,\ldots,N$, Eliminates w and e, then obtains the following equation equality:

$$\begin{bmatrix} 0 & 1^T \\ 1 & K+\gamma^{-1}I \end{bmatrix} \begin{bmatrix} b \\ a \end{bmatrix} = \begin{bmatrix} 0 \\ Y \end{bmatrix} \qquad (5)$$

In the equation equality:

$$1=[1,\ldots,1]^T, Y=[y_{1\ldots}y_N]^T, a=[a_{1\ldots}a_N]^T \qquad (6)$$

K is a Phalanx, Its i line of j row element is

$$K_{ij} = \phi(x_i)^T \phi(x_j) = k(x_i,x_j) \qquad (7)$$

k () is Kernel function. Further solves coefficient b and a through the use least squares method, finally obtained the LS-SVM model forecast output is:

$$y(x)=\sum_{k=1}^{N}a_k\phi(x)^T\phi(x_k)+b=\sum_{k=1}^{N}a_kk(x,x_k)+b \qquad (8)$$

3   Experimental Research on Flotation Process Cleaned Coal Ash Soft Sensor Modeling Subsidiary Variable Selection

3.1   Soft Sensor Modeling Performance Evaluation

For a forecast model, the key is obtaining the predicted value by the good effect, the evaluating indicator uses for to appraise the forecast model fit and unfit quality. The paper uses the mean square root error to weigh the system deviation. If the mean square root relative error value is small, the showing predicted value depending on the approximate real value, the forecast effect is good, and otherwise the showing forecast effect is bad.

The mean square root error definition is:

$$MSE = \frac{1}{l-1}(\sum_{i=1}^{l}|y_i - y_i^*|^2) \qquad (9)$$

Least square support vector machines algorithm to the system model parameter choice, the paper uses confirms (cross-validation) to make the parameter choice adjustment alternately. The cross-validation's basic philosophy is: Divides sample collection into two subsets oneself, with a group (training regulations) come the modeling, another group (test collection) uses in examining, then appraises the forecast performance according to the check result, and adjusts the related parameter, afterward carries on the same training and the alignment procedure again. When pan-wrong achieves the ideal value, and then obtains the corresponding parameter.

3.2   LS-SVM Model Structure Establishment and Simulation Confirmation

Subsidiary variable's determination is the question which the soft sensor modeling first needs to solve. The determination suitable subsidiary variable can guarantee that the soft sensor model can obtain to leads the variable the correct estimate. set condition flotation experiment data of the Zhangcun slime to divide into two kinds stochastically, kind of achievement training regulations, another kind of achievement test collection , carries on least square support vector machines soft sensor modeling, that uses the training regulations data to carry on the training, uses the test collection data to carry on the simulation contrast, finally obtains the good suitable flotation cleaned coal ash soft sensor model, then provides the basis for next step industry the modeling and simulation.

Table 1. Zhangcun Soft-Sensing Model Data Acquisition

Collectors	Frothers	Concent-ration	tailings Ash	Cleaned coal ash
1000	200	40	38.65	8.28
1000	200	70	52.38	8.96
1000	500	40	60.05	8.85
1000	500	60	66.74	9.72
1000	200	60	47.75	8.92
800	120	60	30.00	7.96
800	200	50	35.81	8.25
800	200	60	44.09	8.97
800	400	60	63.31	9.30
1000	400	60	65.28	9.13
1000	120	60	29.79	8.01
1000	500	70	68.55	10.32
800	400	50	58.93	8.85
1000	200	60	47.75	8.92
1000	200	50	44.39	8.64
1000	500	50	63.86	9.43
1000	300	60	56.65	9.06
900	120	60	29.92	7.98

Basis to flotation cleaned coal ash influence first uses collector and frother quantities, Concentration, the air input of Zhangcun flotation process data sheet Tab.1 as subsidiary variable, the cleaned coal ash as the leading variable carries on the LS-SVM simulation. And the first 12 data take the training regulations, latter 6 achievement as test collection, The optimization adjusts gam and the sig2 parameter value, gam parameter is Regularization parameter, is controls to the wrong assignment sample penalty degree adjustable parameter, sig2 parameter is RBF Kernel parameter, is controls bandwidth of "RBF_kernel". Penalty factor C and the Kernel parameters σ of standard SVM (radial direction base nuclear function) correspond. (In the later simulation the parameter significance is the same, the behind simulation no longer specially stated), Simulation result as shown in Fig. 1.With Tab.1, collector, frothers, the Concentration, the tail coal ash as the subsidiary variable carries on modeling with LS-SVM, and the first 12 data take the training regulations, latter 6 achievement test collection, Simulation result as shown in Fig.2.

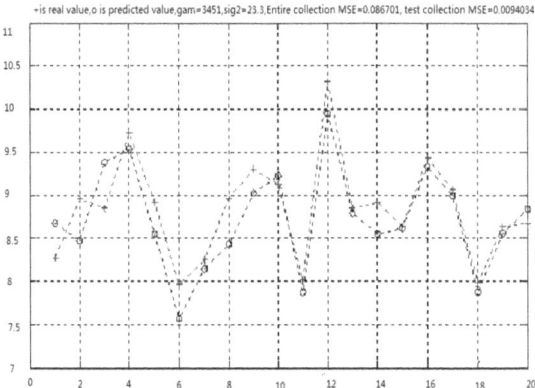

Fig. 1. Simulation about Collector, Frother and Concentration as Auxiliary Variable

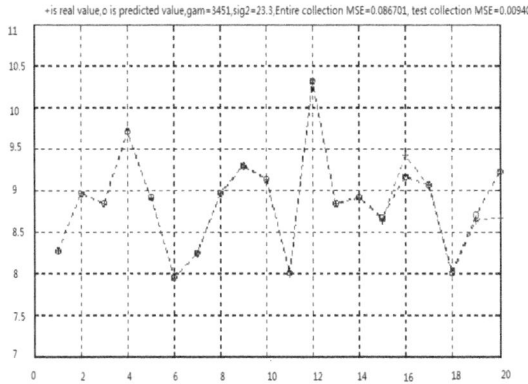

Fig. 2. Simulation about Collector, Frother, Concentration and Flotation Tailings Ash as Auxiliary Variable

Contrasts the above two charts to be possible to see, although Fig.1 tests the collection error slightly is smaller than Fig.2 test collection error, but its training regulations error actually compared to Fig.2 existence big error, this will cause its entire type collection error to be higher than Fig.2 entire type collection error directly. Between this phenomenon and the test collection data existence error may be possible has certain relations, therefore fit and unfit quality of evaluation model must make a balance at the test collection error and the entire type collection error two aspects. In summary, Fig.2 soft sensor modeling must surpass Fig.1. This also fully explained that in the soft sensor modeling choice of subsidiary variable has the very important function to the model return precision. May also see from the above two chart's contrast: The choice process observed value to leads the variable the return precision to be limited merely, investigates its reason to lie in lacks the separation result the attribute parameter. What because modeling forecast is the cleaned coal ash, the choice of nature subsidiary variable concentrates the flotation process tail coal quality which and the leading variable is closely linked to come up.

Regardless of the latter test collection error and entire type collection error all good in the former, soft sensor modeling surpass the former. Therefore, the subsidiary variable increases with the flotation process product nature related parameter are helpful to the enhancement return precision and the return stable uniformity. The different origin coal sample's empirical datum simulation result indicated: under the laboratory condition, uses the collector quantity, the frother dosage, the concentration, the tail coal ash pattern input to be possible to obtain the high model precision, namely the tail coal ash is very big to the soft sensor modeling forecast precision influence. Therefore may draw the conclusion: use the appropriate flotation tail coal ash to have the relevant sensor enormous to increase the flotation cleaned coal ash soft sensor modeling precision and extrapolation ability, in uses actually on flotation tail coal examination sensor, is the electro-optical principle sensor, by this achievement subsidiary variable, may obtain is similar to the tail coal ash test effect.

4   Modeling Accuracy Research on Coal Property Change

4.1   Model Accuracy Research on Different Mine Pit Coal

Under the laboratory condition, use the collectors quantity, the frothers dosage, the concentration, the tail coal ash be pattern's input, use the Zhangcun flotation process data as training set, separately use coal sludge flotation process data of mine 5# and 10# as the test set; after the LS-SVM modeling, separately examines two kind of typical operating modes, the LS-SVM model whether to be suitable and through the optimized model whether model parameter to be suitable.

The Zhangcun flotation process empirical datum as the training set- mine 5# slime flotation process empirical datum as the test set:

From the contrast of simulation experiments may see, if the coal property changes, regardless of how to adjust parameter: gam and the sig2 is unable to correctly predict the concentrations ash so that we must reject the old training set, establishes in view of the concrete coal property training set again, then adjust and optimize the new parameter in order to be able to satisfy the control system's request.

4.2   Model Accuracy Research on Different Coal Bed

Under the laboratory condition, uses the collectors quantity, the frothers dosage, the Concentration, the tailings ash be pattern's input, makes the training set by some mine 5# condition flotation process data, takes the test set with some mine 10# condition flotation process data, and optimizes and adjusts parameter: gam and sig2 with the LS-SVM modeling, with the optimized model examines compatibility of the identical mine pit different coal bed's coal sludge to the soft sensor modeling, that whether does the old model under the identical mine pit different coal bed condition can still maintain the same forecast precision.

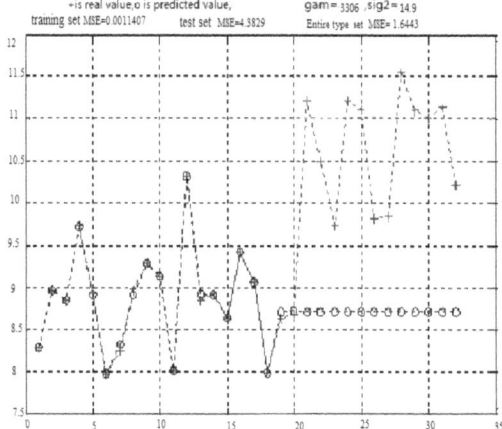

Fig. 3. Zhangcun(training set)-Mine 5#(test set)Simulation (original parameter)

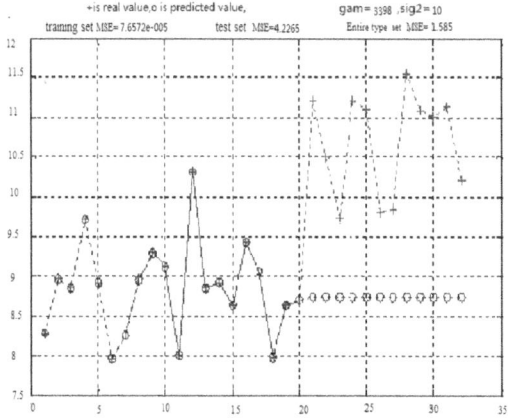

Fig. 4. Zhangcun(training set)- Mine 5#(test set) Simulation(parameter optimization)

The simulation result indicates that if the mining coal bed changes, merely depends adjusting parameter: gam and the sig2 is unable to achieve the requesting forecast precision of soft sensor modeling, therefore must reject the old training set, uses the new training set to carry on the training can satisfy control system's request.

The empirical datum research which paper used indicated: Different coal originates in the different mine pit as well as the coal of identical mine pit different coal bed ,needs to gather the data to establish the new soft sensor modeling, which can guarantee the model's forecasting precision. When design flotation concentrate's soft measurement system should consider that increases function that under the different coal situation the model to cut as well as increases the new soft sensor modeling to adapt the coal property's change.

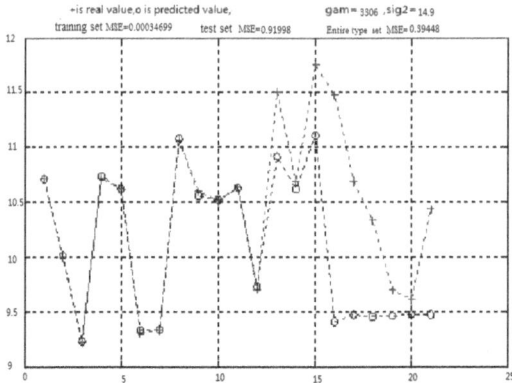

Fig. 5. Mine 5#(training set)-Mine 10#(test set) Simulation(original parameter)

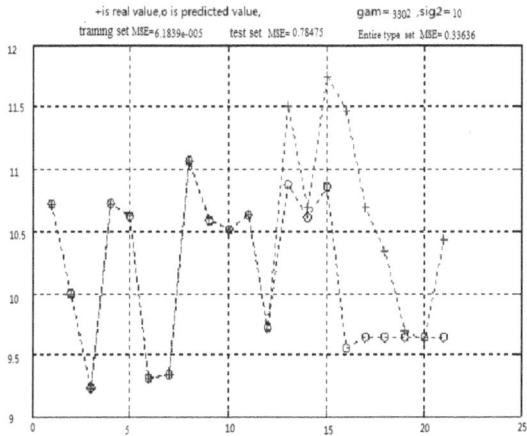

Fig. 6. Mine 5# (training set)-Mine 10#(test set) Simulation

5   Conclusion

Uses the different coal flotation process data, draws the conclusion through the simulation contrast: The collector quantity, the frother dosage, the density, the tailing's ash takes the subsidiary variable to be able to guarantee the flotation concentrate's ash model's forecasting precision. The simulation result that different coal influences the flotation cleaned ash forecast precision indicated: The different coal bed and the different coal to forecasting precious has very tremendous influence, in the scene soft sensor implementation it should increases entering the float coal archery target choice and the corresponding model cut mechanism, satisfies the scene to the flotation process ash forecast precision request. The simulation indicated that the LS-SVM soft sensor modeling may be used in the concentrate ash soft sensor modeling algorithm.

Acknowledgments. This work was supported by Natural Science Foundation of ShanXi Province (Item Number: 2009011034).

References

1. Kadlec, P., Gabrys, B., Strandt, S.: Data-driven Soft Sensors in the process industry. Computers and Chemical Engineering 33, 795–814 (2009)
2. Schladt, M., Hu, B.: Soft sensors based on nonlinear steady-state data reconciliation in the process industry. Chemical Engineering and Processing, 1–32 (2006)
3. Al-thyabat, S.: On the optimization of froth flotation by the use of an artificial neural network. China Univ. Mining & Technol. 18, 418–426 (2008)
4. Scholkopf, Burges, C., Smola, A.J.: Advances in Kernel Methods-Support Vector Learning. MIT Press, Cambridge (1999)
5. Suykens, J.A.K., Vandewalle, J., De Moor, B.: Optimal Control by Least Squares Support Vector Machines. Neural Networks 14, 23–35 (2001)

Support Vector Machines Based on Weighted Scatter Degree

A-Long Jin, Xin Zhou, and Chi-Zhou Ye

Dept. of Commu. & Inform. Eng., Nanjing Univ. of P. & T., Nanjing 210003, China
{along.jin,clsx524,chizhou.ye}@gmail.com

Abstract. Support Vector Machines (SVMs) are efficient tools, which have been widely studied and used in many fields. However, original SVM (C-SVM) only focuses on the scatter between classes, but neglects the global information about the data which are also vital for an optimal classifier. Therefore, C-SVM loses some robustness. To solve this problem, one approach is to translate (i.e., to move without rotation or change of shape) the hyperplane according to the global characteristics of the data. However, parts of existing work using this approach are based on specific distribution assumption (S-SVM), while the rest fail to utilize the global information (GS-SVM). In this paper, we propose a simple but efficient method based on weighted scatter degree (WSD-SVM) to embed the global information into GS-SVM without any distribution assumptions. A comparison of WSD-SVM, C-SVM and GS-SVM is conducted, and the results on several data sets show the advantages of WSD-SVM.

Keywords: Support Vector Machines, Scatter Degree, Hyperplane, Translation, Large Margin Machines.

1 Introduction

In the past few years, large margin machines have been specially valued. The most famous one, support vector machines (SVMs, also known as C-SVM) [1] founded upon statistical learning theory [2], has played an important role in many fields including classification, regression, image processing, and so forth [3, 4, 5]. For a binary classification task, C-SVM aims to construct an optimal hyperplane by maximizing the margin between two classes. However, the margin is merely determined by a number of critical points known as support vectors, whereas all other points remain unused. Therefore, C-SVM loses some robustness for discarding the global information of the data.

Recently, some new large margin machines have been proposed to pay more attention on the structural information than SVMs. They provide a novel view to construct such classifier that should be sensitive to the data distribution. Based on this view, a good decision hyperplane seems reasonable to lie closer to the class with smaller variance. By using extremal value theory in statistics, Feng and Williams proposed Scaled SVM (S-SVM) [6] and gave a theoretical translating distance in 1-D case. In [7], Liu and Ding proposed a method called General

H. Deng et al. (Eds.): AICI 2011, Part III, LNAI 7004, pp. 620–629, 2011.

Scaled SVM (GS-SVM) to generalize Feng's method to multi-dimensional case. However, it may be improper for GS-SVM to use Feng's method to calculate the translating distance, since Feng's conclusion is obtained under the case of uniform distribution. Besides, as GS-SVM translates the hyperplane according to the range of each class, it only takes the points with extreme projection distance into consideration. Therefore, it still loses some global information.

In this paper, we propose a simple method called WSD-SVM to embed global information into GS-SVM without any specific distribution assumption. In order to utilize global information, we define the scatter degree of data points in terms of the distance between them and weight each point in terms of its position. Our method has three steps. First, it uses C-SVM algorithm to obtain the hyperplane. Then it projects all data points onto the normal vector of the hyperplane and calculates the translating distance by evaluating the weighted scatter degree of each class on the projection. Finally, it translates the hyperplane according to the translating distance.

The rest of this paper is organized as follows: Sect.2 briefly reviews C-SVM and GS-SVM. Besides, related works are also presented in this part. Our proposed method will be introduced in Sect.3. After that, experimental results and analysis are given to support our method. Finally, Sect.5 summarizes the paper.

2   Background

2.1   Support Vector Machines

One of the most widely used models for Support Vector Machines is the Soft Margin Optimization algorithm (C-SVM) [1]. The Soft Margin method chooses a hyperplane that splits two classes as cleanly as possible, while still maximizing the distances to the nearest cleanly split classes. Given a dataset $\{(\mathbf{x}_i, y_i)\}_{i=1}^{l}$ with input data $\mathbf{x}_i \in \mathbb{R}^n$ and class labels $y_i \in \{+1, -1\}$, C-SVM is to construct a hyperplane to separate two classes, by optimizing such a primal problem:

$$\min \ \|\mathbf{w} \cdot \mathbf{w}\| + C \sum_{i=1}^{l} \xi_i^2$$

$$s.t. \ \begin{cases} y_i(\mathbf{w} \cdot \mathbf{x}_i + b) \geq 1 - \xi_i, \\ \xi_i \geq 0, \end{cases} \quad i = 1, 2 \ldots, l \tag{1}$$

where ξ_i are slacking variables, C is a regularization parameter to get the tradeoff between maximizing the margin and minimizing the training error. Usually, this optimization problem is transformed into its dual form, which also allows the use of kernel tricks:

$$\max \ -\frac{1}{2}\boldsymbol{\alpha}^T \mathbf{Q}\boldsymbol{\alpha} + \frac{1}{2}\mathbf{1}^T \boldsymbol{\alpha}$$

$$s.t. \ \sum_{i=1}^{l} y_i \alpha_i = 0$$

$$\alpha_i \geq 0, \quad i = 1, 2 \ldots, l \tag{2}$$

where the coefficients α_i are the solution of the dual problem, and $\mathbf{Q}$ is an l by l positive semi-definite matrix. The (i, j)-th element of $\mathbf{Q}$ is given by $\mathbf{Q}_{ij} = y_i y_j K(\mathbf{x}_i, \mathbf{x}_j)$ where $K(\mathbf{x}_i, \mathbf{x}_j)$ is called the kernel function.

2.2 General Scaled SVM

Due to the sparseness of $\boldsymbol{\alpha}$, only several critical points are taken into account, whereas all other points have no influence on constructing the decision hyperplane. Inspired by the observation, Feng [6] proposed Scaled SVM by taking the distributions of two classes into consideration in 1-D case. In [7], Liu has got a conclusion that translating (moving without rotation or change of shape) the hyperplane is independent from optimizing the dual problem in Eq.(2). Based on the conclusion, Liu proposed GS-SVM to generalize Feng's method to multi-dimensional case.

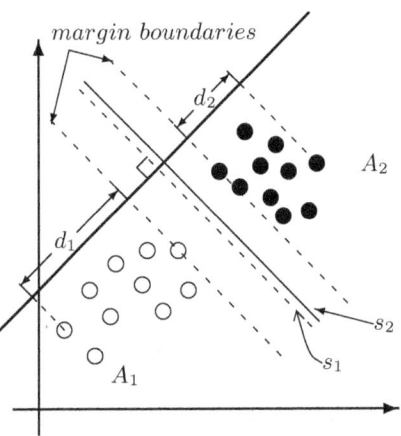

Fig. 1. An illustration of GS-SVM in 2-D. s_1 and s_2 are the hyperplanes obtained by C-SVM and GS-SVM respectively.

Assume two classes A_1 and A_2 are distributed in 2-D space, as illustrated in Fig.1. According to GS-SVM, the optimal decision hyperplane can be obtained in three steps:

1. Use the C-SVM algorithm to obtain the original hyperplane s_1.
2. Project all the points onto the normal vector of hyperplane and denote d_1 and d_2 as the distribution scales of A_1 and A_2 respectively.
3. Calculate the translating distance (Δ) and translate the original hyperplane to obtain the optimal one s_2, which lies closer to A_2 with smaller scale.

According to Feng's conclusion:

$$\Delta = \frac{\sqrt{d_2} - \sqrt{d_1}}{\sqrt{d_1} + \sqrt{d_2}} .$$

2.3   Related Work

A lot of works have been done, with the purpose of making use of the global information, to advance the performance of C-SVM. Shivaswamy *et al.* proposed a novel formulation to overcome the sensitivity that the solution obtained by SVMs is dominated by the directions with large data spread, and maximize the margin relative to the spread of the data [8]. Xiong and Cherkassky described a method named SVM/LDA, in which the global characteristics of the data is reflected by LDA while the local information is reflected by SVM [9]. Wang *et al.* proposed a new large margin learning model named probabilistic large margin machine, which make use of the global information by incorporating the prior probabilities and the distribution of each class into the decision hyperplane learning [10]. Huang *et al.* proposed a novel large margin classifier called the Maxi-Min Margin Machine, their model learns the decision boundary both locally and globally by estimating structure of each class [11]. In contrast to Huang's method, Yeung *et al.* determined the structure of data by using clustering algorithms, and made use of such structural information to construct the decision hyperplane [12].

3   Our Proposed Method

In GS-SVM, all the points are projected onto the normal vector of hyperplane obtained by C-SVM, and the translating distance is calculated according to Feng's conclusion by evaluating the scale of each class. However, it is improper for GS-SVM to use Feng's conclusion, since such conclusion is obtained under the case of uniform distribution, while the class distribution on the projection are unknown in GS-SVM. Besides, the scale (range) of a class cannot reflect the global characteristics of the data, sometimes may even play side-effects when constructing the decision hyperplane. For example, as illustrated in Fig.2, there are some points in 1-D space, the hyperplane h_1 is obtained by C-SVM. According to GS-SVM, the optimal should lie closer to A_1, since $d_1 < d_2$. Obviously, it is more reasonable to translate h_1 to get an optimal hyperplane h_2.

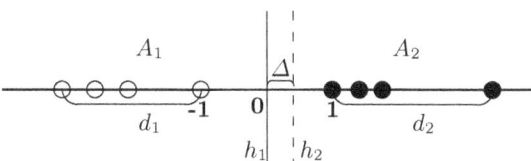

Fig. 2. A simple example in 1-D. h_1 is obtained by C-SVM, while h_2 is a better one.

Motivated by these facts, we want to recalculate the translating distance Δ in a new way, by which we can embed the global information into GS-SVM without any distribution assumptions. Due to projection in GS-SVM, all the works to calculate Δ are done in 1-D space, and no existing probabilistic model can be used. In such circumstances, we propose a novel method described as follows:

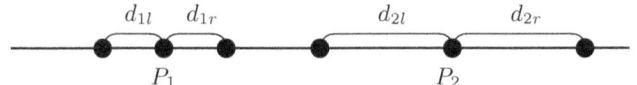

Fig. 3. An illustration of scatter degree of points.

3.1 Calculating Scatter Degree of Points

As described in GS-SVM, all points are projected onto the normal vector of the hyperplane obtained by C-SVM, it is hard for us to get any probabilistic information on the projection. In this way, we have to introduce a new measurement to estimate the local characteristics. As shown in Fig.3, it is clear that P_1 and P_2 have different local information. The most simple method to evaluate such difference is using the distance to the left and right neighbors of a point. Taking P_1 as an example, $d_{1l} + d_{1r}$ or $d_{1l}d_{1r}$ may be used to measure the local information, but these measurements are unapplicable in some cases, when $d = 0$ (overlap) or $d = \infty$ (no points in the side). Therefore, a good measurement not only reflects the local characteristics, but also should be applicable in those extreme cases. With such purpose, we set up a new model named scatter degree, as described in Eq.(3), to measure the local information:

$$sd = \frac{r}{2}(\frac{1}{d_l + r} + \frac{1}{d_r + r}) \tag{3}$$

where d_l and d_r stand for the distance to its left and right neighbors respectively. r is a constant used to overcome those extreme cases. Besides, sd is scaled to $(0, 1)$. For the convenience of calculation, we change the form of sd to Eq.(4):

$$sd = -\ln\frac{r}{2}(\frac{1}{d_l + r} + \frac{1}{d_r + r}) . \tag{4}$$

3.2 Calculating Weight of Points

As is known to us, translating the decision hyperplane a little away from the original position will make little influence on classifying those points far away from the margin boundaries, but will make great impact on those points on or over the margin boundaries. Therefore, it is reasonable to emphasize the points' position when constructing decision hyperplane. Unlike C-SVM which emphasizes only those Support Vectors, we take all points into consideration and weight each point in terms of its position. Obviously, data points closer to margin boundaries should have larger weight than those not. Based on these analyses, we weight each point as follows:

$$w = e^{-\alpha d} \tag{5}$$

where d is the distance between the point and the decision hyperplane, and α is a constant.

3.3   Calculating Δ according to Weighted Scatter Degree

As mentioned above, the scatter degree of a point stands for its local information, while the weight of a point denotes its importance according to position. We can combine these two facts to estimate the global information of a class:

$$SD = \frac{\sum_{i=0}^{l} sd_i \cdot w_i}{\sum_{i=0}^{l} w_i} \tag{6}$$

where sd_i and w_i is the i-th point's scatter degree and weight respectively, and l is the number of points in the class.

As illustrated in Fig.2, the hyperplane h_1 obtained by C-SVM falls in the middle of the maximal margin. According to Eq.(6), we have:

$$SD^- = \frac{\sum_{i=0}^{l^-} sd_i^- \cdot w_i^-}{\sum_{i=0}^{l^-} w_i^-} \tag{7}$$

$$SD^+ = \frac{\sum_{i=0}^{l^+} sd_i^+ \cdot w_i^+}{\sum_{i=0}^{l^+} w_i^+} \tag{8}$$

where SD^-, SD^+ represent the weighted scatter degree of A_1, A_2 respectively.

As a better hyperplane should lie closer to the class of smaller variance, we translate the hyperplane h_1 to get the new one h_2. Let the translating distance be Δ, as shown in Fig.2. After translating, we have:

$$
\begin{aligned}
SD^{-\prime} &= \frac{\sum_{i=0}^{l^-} sd_i^- \cdot (w_i^- \cdot e^{-\alpha\Delta})}{\sum_{i=0}^{l^-} (w_i^- \cdot e^{-\alpha\Delta})} \\
&= \frac{\sum_{i=0}^{l^-} sd_i^- \cdot w_i^-}{\sum_{i=0}^{l^-} w_i^-} \\
&= SD^-
\end{aligned}
\tag{9}
$$

Similarly,

$$SD^{+\prime} = SD^+ . \tag{10}$$

It is interesting to find that the global information of each class is independent of the position of the decision hyperplane.

Assume a new point M lies on hyperplane h_2. Obviously, M can be regarded to A_1, and can also be regarded as a member of A_2. Therefore, there is almost no effect on $SD^{+\prime}/SD^{-\prime}$ after the introduction of point M due to its duality.

When M is classified to class A_1, the weighted scatter degree of A_1 is

$$SD^{-\prime\prime} = \frac{sd_M^- \cdot w_M^- + \sum_{i=0}^{l^-} sd_i^- \cdot w_i^-}{w_M^- + \sum_{i=0}^{l^-} w_i^-} \tag{11}$$

where $sd_M^- = -\ln\frac{r}{2}\frac{1}{1+\Delta+r}$, and $w_M^- = 1$. As the value of Δ and r are small enough, we have $sd_M^- \approx r + \ln\frac{2}{r} + \Delta$.

When M is classified to class A_2, the weighted scatter degree of A_2 is

$$SD^{+''} = \frac{sd_M^+ \cdot w_M^+ + \sum_{i=0}^{l^+} sd_i^+ \cdot w_i^+}{w_M^+ + \sum_{i=0}^{l^+} w_i^+} \tag{12}$$

where $sd_M^+ = -\ln \frac{r}{2} \frac{1}{1-\Delta+r} \approx r + \ln \frac{2}{r} - \Delta$, and $w_M^+ = 1$.

As discussed above, we can get such relationship:

$$\frac{SD^{+''}}{SD^{-''}} \approx \frac{SD^{+'}}{SD^{-'}}. \tag{13}$$

By solving Eq.(13), we can get the translating distance:

$$\Delta = \frac{(R+S^+)S^-(1+\frac{1}{W^-}) - (R+S^-)S^+(1+\frac{1}{W^+})}{S^+(1+\frac{1}{W^+}) + S^-(1+\frac{1}{W^-})} \tag{14}$$

where $R = r + \ln \frac{2}{r}$, $S^+ = \sum_{i=0}^{l^+} sd_i^+ \cdot w_i^+$, $S^- = \sum_{i=0}^{l^-} sd_i^- \cdot w_i^-$, $W^+ = \sum_{i=0}^{l^+} w_i^+$ and $W^- = \sum_{i=0}^{l^-} w_i^-$.

4   Experiments

In this section, we first show the advantage of WSD-SVM on synthetic 2-D toy data sets. Then we compare WSD-SVM with C-SVM, GS-SVM on several real world benchmarks and give an intuitive approach to choose r and α. The training and testing of SVMs are accomplished by LIBSVM [13].

4.1   2-D Toy Data

As illustrated in Fig.4(a), the data set is generated under two Gaussian distributions: the negative class is randomly sampled from the Gaussian distribution

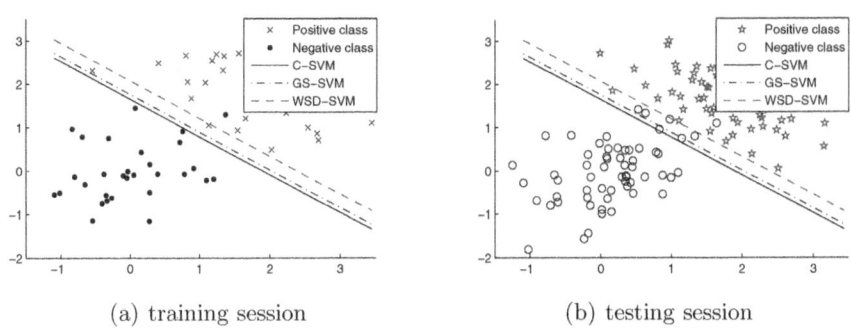

(a) training session   (b) testing session

Fig. 4. An illustration of toy data

with the mean $[0.2, 0.1]^T$ and the covariance $[0.5, 0.2; 0.2, 0.4]$, while the positive class is randomly sampled from another distribution with the mean and the covariance as $[1.7, 1.7]^T$ and $[0.4, -0.2; -0.2, 0.4]$. Training and testing sets consist of 30 and 60 data points respectively for each class. Fig.4(a) illustrates the hyperplanes obtained by C-SVM, GS-SVM and WSD-SVM. From Fig.4(b), we find that WSD-SVM achieves a better hyperplane by taking both the local and global information of the data into account when constructing the decision hyperplane. The classification accuracies of C-SVM and GS-SVM on the testing data are 94.17% and 95.83% respectively, while the accuracy of WSD-SVM is 98.33% with $r = 0.01$ and $\alpha = 1$. The improvement on accuracy shows the advantage of WSD-SVM.

4.2   Benchmarks

We also conduct a comparison of C-SVM, GS-SVM and WSD-SVM in both linear and Gaussian kernels on 8 standard data sets from UCI machine learning repository [14]. In C-SVM and GS-SVM, all the parameters are tuned via 10-fold cross validation. In WSD-SVM, we choose the same C and the width parameter as C-SVM, and then select the best r and α via 10-fold cross validation. The performance of these three methds in 10-fold cross validation is summarized in Table 1. Through the comparison, we show the importance and necessity of using global information when constructing the decision hyperplane.

Table 1. Comparisons of classification accuracies

data sets	linear kernel			Gaussian kernel		
	C-SVM	GS-SVM	WSD-SVM	C-SVM	GS-SVM	WSD-SVM
sonar	79.55	80.91	82.27	88.09	89.00	89.45
liver	67.95	69.10	69.33	71.57	72.43	73.62
heart	83.70	84.07	84.81	84.07	84.44	85.19
spect	**81.17**	80.81	**82.24**	**83.26**	82.90	**84.33**
breast	96.60	97.05	97.18	96.97	97.10	97.39
statlog	85.60	85.60	86.45	86.52	86.67	86.79
diabet	77.08	77.21	77.74	77.20	77.99	78.38
hepatitis	**80.50**	80.00	**84.50**	**83.50**	82.83	**86.00**

As shown in Table 1, WSD-SVM achieves a better performance in both linear and Gaussian kernels. It should be noted that, C-SVM surpasses GS-SVM on the performance of "spect" and "hepatitis" data sets. Taking "hepatitis" as an example to explain such phenomenon, there are 32 positive cases and 123 negative cases in "hepatitis", the global information may be misled by estimating the scales of classes in GS-SVM. On the contrary, WSD-SVM is still applicable to these unbalanced data sets.

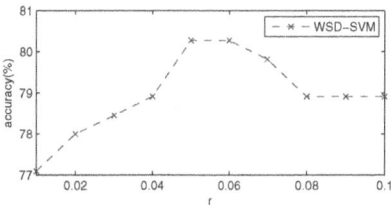 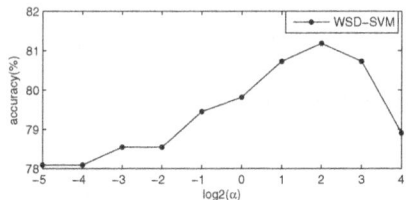

(a) Accuracy versus r with linear kernel (b) Accuracy versus α with linear kernel and and C=0.5, $\alpha = 1$ C=0.5, $r = 0.04$

Fig. 5. An illustration of the roles that r and α play

Besides, we notice the interesting roles that r and α play: we can transform Eq.(4) and Eq.(5) to:

$$sd = -\ln\frac{1}{2}(\frac{1}{1+\frac{d_l}{r}} + \frac{1}{1+\frac{d_r}{r}}) . \tag{15}$$

$$w = (e^{-d})^\alpha . \tag{16}$$

From Eq.(15), we can find that the scatter degree of a point will get insensitive to d_l and d_r as r increases. When r gets large enough, all the points will have the same scatter degree (local information). In other words, we discard the local information when constructing the decision hyperplane. On the contrary, when r is small enough, we will overvalue the importance of local information. We select "sonar" data as an example to show the relationship between r and classification accuracy in Fig.5(a). As illustrated in Fig.5(a), we know that r should be taken moderately.

Through the observation of Eq.(16) and Fig.5(b), we know that α indicates how much we value the importance of position. Similarly, we can come to the same conclusion that α should be taken moderately.

Finally, we should point out that the classification accuracies obtained by WSD-SVM may be not the best, since C and the width parameter are chosen the same as C-SVM. But if not so, the accomplishment of WSD-SVM would be more time-consuming.

5   Conclusion

Although support vector machines have been proven to be powerful both theoretically and empirically, it lose some robustness for discarding the global information. To solve this problem, one approach is to translate the hyperplane according to the global characteristics of the data. However, existing work of this approach can neither function without specific distribution assumption, nor take the global information into account. In this paper, we propose a simple but efficient method called WSD-SVM, which is based on weighted scatter degree. In this framework, WSD-SVM makes use of both local information and global information. Experimental results show that WSD-SVM advance C-SVM and GS-SVM on both toy data sets and real world benchmarks. In addition, WSD-SVM achieves good performance even when the data set is unbalanced. Throughout the paper, we evaluate the scatter degree only by two neighbors of a point, a few more points may be more suitable to estimate such local information. Besides, it may be interesting to find the relationship between r and α. A future investigation will focus on theoretical analysis on the generalization ability of WSD-SVM.

References

1. Cristianini, N., Shawe-Taylor, J.: An Introduction to Support Vector Machines and Other Kernel-based Learning Methods, 1st edn. Cambridge University Press, Cambridge (2000)
2. Vapnik, V.N.: The Nature of Statistical Learning Theory. Springer, Heidelberg (1995)
3. Gunn, S.R.: Support vector machines for classification and regression. Technical report, ISIS (1998)
4. Smola, A.J., Schölkopf, B.: A Tutorial on Support Vector Regression. Technical report, Statistics and Computing (2003)
5. Tong, S., Chang, E.: Support vector machine active learning for image retrieval. In: Proceedings of the Ninth ACM International Conference on Multimedia, pp. 107–118. ACM, New York (2001)
6. Feng, J., Williams, P.: The generalization error of the symmetric and scaled support vector machines. IEEE Transactions on Neural Networks 12, 1255–1260 (1999)
7. Liu, X., Ding, Y.: General Scaled Support Vector Machines. In: International Conference on Machine Learning and Computing (2011)
8. Shivaswamy, P.K., Jebara, T.: Relative Margin Machines. In: Advances in Neural Information Processing Systems 21 (2009)
9. Xiong, T., Cherkassky, V.: A combined SVM and LDA approach for classification. In: Proceedings of International Joint Conference on Neural Networks (2005)
10. Wang, D., Yeung, D., Tsang, E.: Probabilistic Large Margin Machine. In: International Conference on Machine Learning and Cybernetics, pp. 2190–2195 (2006)
11. Huang, K., Yang, H., King, I., Lyu, M.R.: Learning large margin classifiers locally and globally. In: Proceedings of Twenty-First International Conference on Machine Learning, pp. 401–408 (2004)
12. Yeung, D., Wang, D., Ng, W., Tsang, E., Wang, X.: Structured large margin machines: sensitive to data distributions. Machine Learning 68, 171–200 (2007)
13. Chang, C.-C., Lin, C.-J.: LIBSVM: a library for support vector machines (2001), Software available at http://www.csie.ntu.edu.tw/~cjlin/libsvm
14. Frank, A., Asuncion, A.: UCI Machine Learning Repository (2010), http://archive.ics.uci.edu/ml

ICESat-GLAS-Based Forest Type Classification Using SVM[*]

Licun Li and Yanqiu Xing[**]

Center for Forest Operations and Environment of Northeast Forestry University, Harbin
150040, China
lilicun628@126.com, yanqiuxing@nefu.edu.cn

Abstract. In order to study the forest classification effect of large footprint lidar date we used SVM(support vector machine) method to analyze the ICESAT-GLAS (Ice, Cloud and Land Elevation Satellite - Geoscience Laser Altimeter system) date in WangQing Bureau, Jilin province. In analysis we first used IDL to convert the ICESAT-GLAS original binary data into ASCII format. Then we got a waveform by using matlab software. After we were corresponded the waveform data to the field investigation data in 2006 and 2007, we could get the forest types of the waveform figure. Then waveform parameters were extracted. We applied of the SVM classification method to analyze 62 groups of training sample and established a classification model. After that we used another 62 groups of test sample to test the classification model, the result shows that the SVM classification method can better distinguish the broadleaved forest between the coniferous forest. And the classification accuracy is 82.26%.

Keywords: ICESat-GLAS, waveform parameters, SVM, forest type.

1 Introduction

Human activities make the carbon dioxide (CO_2) and other gases in atmosphere continue to increase, so that the environment around us has been taken place a series of changes [1]. Forest biomass above the ground has an important impact on decrease the carbon dioxide in atmosphere. The forest biomass above the ground is related to both the height and the type of forest [2]. In recent years, lidar remote sensing technique has been proved to be a very effective technique in estimation of canopy height [3]. But there were only a few papers used lidar data to class the forest types. This article will further study on how to apply of lidar data for forest type classification. SVM (support vector machine) is a kind of universal and effective machine learning methods which has been well use in many ways [4]. Such as handwritten digit recognition [5], classification of a monkey species [6], classification of College Students' Decision about Graduation. In this paper we applied of SVM

---

[*] This research is funded by the Natural Science Foundation of China (4087119), and Project of Foundation (Gram10) by graduate school of Northeast Forestry University (NEFU).
[**] Corresponding author.

H. Deng et al. (Eds.): AICI 2011, Part III, LNAI 7004, pp. 630–638, 2011.

method to classify the forest type by using the parameters extraction from ICESAT-GLAS waveform data. This paper would be useful to study forest structure and the change of carbon dioxide in the atmosphere.

2   Material and Methods

The status of study area, and the access of Lidar data and field survey data are depicted as follow.

2.1   Status of the Study Area

If you have more than one surname, please make sure that the Volume Editor knows how you are to be listed in the author index. In this paper, Wangqing Forest Bureau, Jilin province of china was selected as the study area. The forest locates in the cool temperate forest ecosystem in Changbai Mountains (43 ° 05'N ~ 43 ° 40'N, 129 ° 56'E ~ 131 ° 04'E), the total area of it is 304,000 hm^2. Ground elevation is 360 ~ 1477m, slope ranges from 0 ~ 45 °.A variety of plant species range in this region and the structure of the forest is very complex. Mixed forest is the major forest type in the Mountain areas. *Pinus koraiensis*, *Picea koraiensis*, *Abies nephrolepis* are the major .coniferous trees and *Quercus mongolica*, *tilia amurensis*, *Acer mono* are the major broadleaved trees in this area.

2.2   Access of Lidar Data

ICESat-GLAS is large footprint laser radar equipment in polar orbit, altitude 600 km, using for continuous observation of the world ground. GLAS includes a laser system to measure distance. In laser system Laser pulses at 40 times per second will illuminate spots (footprints) 70 meters in diameter, spaced at 170 meters intervals along Earth's surface. ICESat-GLAS provide a total of 15 kinds of date, GLA01\GLA02\...\GLA15. GLA01 is an altimetry data product record the full waveform data which are correspond to the ground surface features in laser footprint. GLA14 record the ground footprint location and elevation data which are correspond to waveform data. The study used GLA01 and GLA14 data. I downloaded the study area data from year 2003 to 2006. GLAS data was downloaded in the U S National Snow and Ice Data Center. (http://nsidc.org/data/icesat/data.html)

2.3   Field Survey Data

In September 2006 and 2007 in Wang Qing Changbai Mountains we used a pre-designed stratified random sampling method to investigate the GLAS laser footprint on ground. In investigation a total of 203 plots were selected. There are three kinds of forest types, namely, coniferous forest, mixed and broadleaved forest. In application of data we did not use the waveform data which had only one Gaussian curve waveform. Because only one Gaussian curve waveform data is only ground return data or that can not well distinguish the forest canopy return data with the ground return data. In investigation, we used GPS to local the position of laser footprints. Fig.1 shows the field survey point. Using Forest survey statistical theory we investigated the forest within the footprint on the plots effectively. First measure the slope of plots, we recorded it θ. Then we established a circular plot of 500 m² in horizontal projected. Then we record the vegetation distribution, forest types and vegetation cover in ICESat-GLAS footprint. We apply of the following methods to distinguish the plot forest type. When the coniferous forest volume is greater than or equal to 60% of the plot forest volume, we identified the plot forest type as coniferous. When the Broadleaved forest volume is greater than or equal to 60% of the plot forest volume, we identified the plot forest type as Broadleaved forest. Remain cases are mixed. In this paper I select 124 groups of data, the forest types is Broadleaved forest and coniferous forest. 62 groups of data were used as training sample to establish the classification model. The other 62 groups of data were used to test the model.

Fig. 1. Study area and the distribution of field investigation points

3 Support Vector Classification

SVM is a new method of machine learning which is developed basing on the statistical learning theory, in recent years this theory and algorithm have made rapid development. SVM classification method has applied to solve various practical problems, showing a lot better performance than the existing methods. C-SVC (support vector classification) is a classification method of SVM. C-SVC method is not only suit for the classification of linear separable problem, but also suit for the linear inseparable problem, so this paper applies of the C-SVC method.

3.1 C-SVC Algorithm

One: given a train set sample, T={$(x_1,y_1),(x_2,y_2),\ldots,(x_n,y_n)$}, x_i is n dimensional vector, $x_i \in R^n$, $y_i \in \{1,-1\}, i = 1,\ldots,n$

Two：select a appropriate kernel function K (x_i, x_j) and appropriate penalty factor c, construct and solve optimization problems

$$\min_a \frac{1}{2}\sum_{i=1}^{n}\sum_{j=1}^{n} y_i y_j a_i a_j \left(x_i \bullet x_j\right) - \sum_{j=1}^{n} a_j \qquad (1)$$

$$s.t. \sum_{i=1}^{n} y_i a_i = 0, 0 \le a_i \le C, i = 1,....,n \tag{2}$$

Then get the optimal solution $a^* = (a_1^*,...,a_n^*)$.

Three: calculate $w^* = \sum_{i=1}^{n} y_i a_i^* x_i$ and select a positive component a^* $0 < a^* < C$, then calculate

$$b^* = y_i - \sum_{i=1}^{n} y_i a_i^* (x_i \bullet x_j) \tag{3}$$

Structure differentiation hyperplane $(w^* \bullet x) + b^* = 0$, then solve the decision function

$$f(x) = \text{sgn} \left(\sum_{i=1}^{n} a_i^* y_i K(x_i, x_j) + b^* \right) \tag{4}$$

3.2 Kernel Function

In the step of C-SVC algorithm involved that the SVM classification method need use kernel function $K(x_i, x_j)$, and we use ten fold cross validation method to choose the kernel function. 10 fold cross validation is a common method of accuracy test. In this method first set the training data into 10 equal parts, then 9 parts of which will do the training in turn and the other group do the test. The best value of 10 times is the result of algorithm accuracy. There are four kinds of kernel function [8].

Linear kernel function $K(x_i, x_j) = x_i \bullet x_j$

polynomina kernel function $K(x_i, x_j) = [r(x_i \bullet x_j) + 1]^q$

radial basis kernel function $K(x_i, x_j) = \exp\{-\dfrac{|x_i - x_j|^2}{r^2}\}$

sigmoid kernel function $K(x_i, x_j) = \tan[r(x_i \bullet x_j) + a]$

4 Data Processing

In this section, we processed the ICESat-GLAS binary format data than got waveform. After that we extracted parameters from waveform.

4.1 ICESat-GLAS Date Processing

ICESat-GLAS waveform data is specifically defined in binary format, including the metadata information and data information. First, raw data format was needed to convert; we used IDL to convert the binary data into ASCII format data. In order to effectively compare the waveform data, we also standardized the waveform data, then using Gaussian filter to smooth ICESat-GLAS waveform. After the waveforms were smoothed, we made the original waveform curve into multiple Gaussian curves. Detail process in [3]. Fig. 2 is graphics obtained after deal with matlab software.

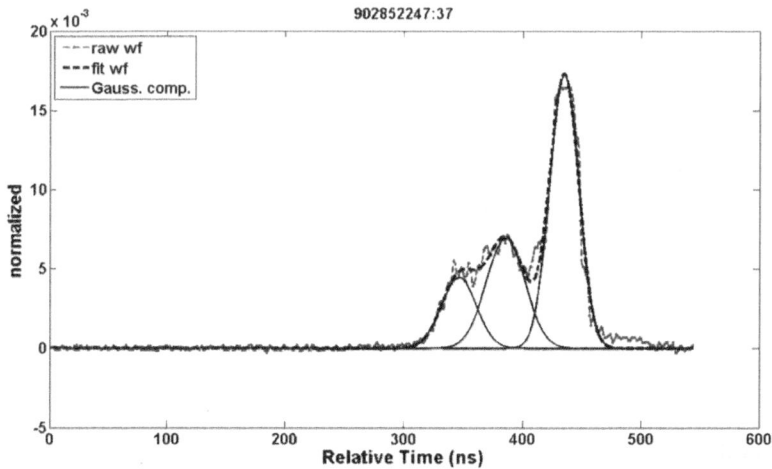

Fig. 2. Result of GLAS Waveform decomposition and Fitting

4.2   Waveform Parameters Extraction and Processing

From the physical sense, the different forest types have their own typical vertical structure and different typical LIDAR waveforms character. Moreover, from a mathematical point of view, echo waveform can be seen as a combination of several Gaussian curves, corresponding to different layers of the forest structure. Thus, by analyzing the corresponding Gaussian curves are expected to distinguish forest types. The vertical layers of coniferous tree is obvious more than the layers of Broad-leaved tree, so when lidar receive the energy from coniferous forest, the echo width is less than the Broad-leaved tree width. Thus, the slope of the Gaussian curve decomposition form waveforms of coniferous tree is larger than broad-leaved tree. Fitting the above analysis I extracted below reference points as described in this paper, extraction parameters diagram is shown as Fig. 3, t_1 is the effective echo time value of the first Gaussian curve, which is decomposition by the fitting waveform, t_2 is the time value corresponding to the peak of the first Gaussian curse, t_3 is the effective echo time value of the second Gaussian curve, t_4 is the time value corresponding to the peak of the second Gaussian curse, Q_1 is the energy value corresponding to the peak of the first Gaussian curse, Q_2 is the energy value corresponding to the peak of the last Gaussian curse. All parameters we extracted can be found in the files of the waveform generated.

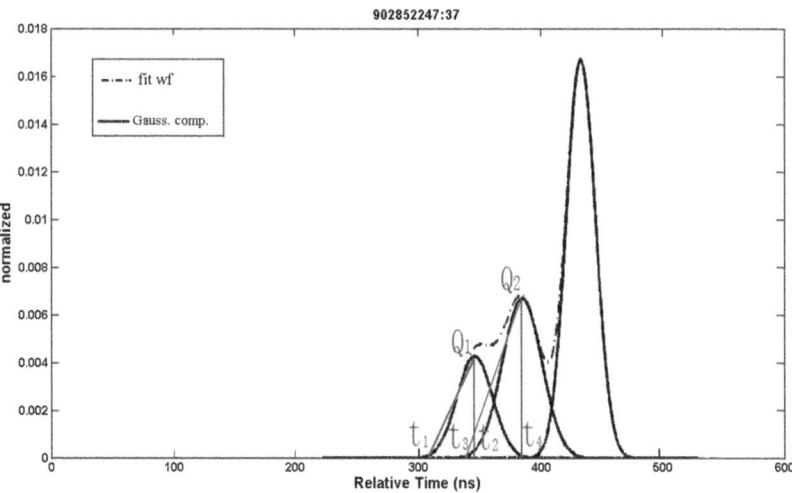

Fig. 3. Parameter extraction

When the original waveform curve was separated into many Gaussian curves. In Gaussian curve of i, assuming that Q_i is the standardized energy value of i Gaussian curve, t_{2i-1} is the effective echo time value of i Gaussian curve, t_{2i} is the time value corresponding to the peak of i Gaussian curve. We use formula 5 to calculate the slope of each Gaussian curve. The value of n is the number of Gaussian waveform curse besides of the last Gaussian waveform curse.

$$k_i = \frac{Q_i}{t_{2i} - t_{2i-1}} \tag{5}$$

We use formula 6 to calculate the mean slope of each Gaussian curve

$$\overline{K} = \frac{\sum\limits_{i=1}^{n} k_i}{n} \tag{6}$$

We use formula 7 to calculate standard root mean square error of slope of each Gaussian curve

$$\Delta K = \sqrt{\frac{1}{n} \sum\limits_{i=1}^{n} \left(k_i - \overline{k}\right)^2} \tag{7}$$

In this paper we apply of the following processed parameters, the value of $\overline{K}, \Delta K, \theta$, corresponding to each spot.

5   Result Analysis

We use C-SVC method to deal with the 62 groups of training samples, in C-SVC method we use ten fold cross validation to determine the kernel function. The result of ten fold cross validation is shown in Table 1. In Table 1 the best cross validation classification accuracy is 87.10%, so from Table 1 we can find that we should select Rbf as the kernel function in the classification method [9]. In Table 1 Poly is polynominal function, Rbf is radial basis function, Sig is sigmoid kernel function.

Table 1. Cross validation classification accuracy of different penalty parameter c and kernel function

c	0.01	0.1	1	10	100	1000
Poly	45.16	45.16	45.16	45.16	45.16	45.16
Rbf	74.19	74.19	83.87	87.10	77.52	77.52
Sig	74.19	74.19	74.19	74.19	74.19	74.19

We determine the value of penalty parameter c and kernel function coefficient r after we selected the Rbf kernel function. Table 2 shows that when $c=10$, $r=0.01$, the classification result is the best and the classification accuracy is 90.32%.

Table 2. Cross validation classification accuracy of different penalty parameter c and kernel function coefficient r

c / r	0.01	0.1	1	10	100	1000
0.001	74.19	74.19	85.48	82.25	83.87	79.03
0.01	74.19	74.19	87.09	90.32	82.25	82.25
0.1	74.19	74.19	85.48	87.09	79.03	80.64
1	74.19	74.19	74.19	79.03	75.80	75.80

When we select the Rbf kernel function, the value of $c=10$, $r=0.01$, we establish the classification model. The classification result when we built the model is shown in Table 3.

Table 3. The classification result of training data established model

Original Type	Divide forest type		Classification accuracy %	Total classification accuracy %	Kappa
	Broadleaved	Coniferous			
Broadleaved	44	2	95.65	90.32	0.7365
Coniferous	4	12	75.00		

Table 4. The classification result of the test data

Original Type	Divide forest type		Classification accuracy %	Total classification accuracy %	Kappa
	Broadleaved	Coniferous			
Broadleaved	42	4	91.30	82.26	0.5065
Coniferous	7	9	56.25		

Table 3 is the classification result of training data established model. Shown in Table 3, a total of training sample points is 62, 46 Broadleaved forest, 16 coniferous forest. The classification accuracy of broadleaved forest is 95.65% in which the number of correct classification is 44. The classification accuracy of coniferous forest is 75% in which the number of correct classification is 12. The total classification accuracy of training sample is 90.32%. The kappa coefficient is 0.7365. After we establish the classification model, we use the other 62 groups of test data to validation the model, the classification results shown in Table 4.

Table 4 is the classification result of test data. A total of 62 test sample points are Shown in Table 4, 46 Broadleaved forests, 16 coniferous forests. The classification accuracy of broadleaved forest is 91.30% in which the number of correct classification is 42. The classification accuracy of coniferous forest is 56.25% in which the number of correct classification is 9. The total classification accuracy of test sample is 82.26%. The kappa coefficient is 0.5065. Either in modeling or classification, the classification result of broadleaved forest is better than the classification result of coniferous forest when using the C-SVC method to classify the extracted parameters. There are two reasons why the classification accuracy of coniferous forest is not very high. First, although the broadleaved forest and coniferous forest have different, in many cases, the plots of each footprint has broadleaved trees and coniferous trees and the trees within the footprint is large difference between high and low which impact the vertical structure features distinction. Second we used the parameter θ to classification the forest types. The value of θ ranges from $0 \sim 45°$. When the slope angle increases, the ground return and the forest under the slope return information will mix, then the laser radar echo data will appear superimposed waveform. This will make Broad leave forest and coniferous forest return energy change, making the classification accuracy decline.

6 Conclusion

In this paper, we used C-SVC method to analyze the waveform parameters which extracted from ICESAT-GLAS. In this method we apply ten fold cross validation method for modeling and the model accuracy reaches 90.32%. When we used the other 62 groups of test data to test the model we get the classification accuracy of 82.26%. The classification result shows that C-SVC method can well distinguish broadleaved forest between coniferous forest. In further work we will apply of other methods to study on the waveform parameters extracting from ICESAT-GLAS and compare the classification accuracy of different methods.

Acknowledgments. The Fundamental Research Funds for the Central Universities (Grant: DL09CA08). And we would like to thank Ice Data Center for providing ICESat-GLAS data.

References

1. Pang, Y., Yu, X.F., Li, Z.Y.: Waveform Length Extraction from ICEsat GLAS Data and Forest Application Analysis. Scientia Silvae Sinicae 42, 137–140 (2006)
2. Nelson, Ranson, K.J.: Estimating Siberian timber volume using MODIS and ICESat-GLAS. Remote Sensing of Environment 113, 691–701 (2009)
3. Xing, Q., Wang, L.H.: ICESat-GLAS Full Waveform based Study on Forest Canopy Height Retrieval inSloped Area —A Case Study of Forests in Changbai Mountains, Jilin. Geomatics and Information Science of Wuhan University 34, 696–700 (2009)
4. Liu, G.Z., Shi, W.Z., Li, D.R., Qin, Q.Q.: Partially Supervised Classification of remote sensed Imagery using Suppor Vector Machines. Journal of Remote Sensing 9, 363–373 (2005)
5. Suykens, J., Vandewalle, J.: Least squares support vector machine classifiers. Neural Processing Letters 9, 293–300 (1999)
6. Zhang, Y., Feng, S.Q., Pang, D.Z., Tang, Q.: The Support Vector Classification Model of the Rhinopithecus Roxellanae Subspecies. Application of Statistics and Management 27, 211–215 (2008)
7. Xu, Y., Shi, L.K., Wang, H.M.: A Study of SVM Classification of College Students'Decision about Graduation. Journal of Shijiazhuang University 10, 34–41 (2008)
8. Lin, S., Xun, P., Liu, Q.: Traffic.: classification based on support vector machine. Application Research of Computers 25, 2488–2492 (2008)
9. Yang, J.Y., Zhang, Y.Y., Zhu, Y.S.: Classification Performance of Support Vector Machine with ε -Insensitive Loss Function. Journal of Xi'an Jiaotong University 41, 1315–1321 (2007)

Mine Working Face Gas Prediction
Based on Weighted LS-SVM

Tiezhu Qiao[1] and Meiying Qiao[2]

[1] Institute of Measurement and Control Technology Tanyuan University
of Technology Tanyuan, China
[2] School of Electrical Engineering and Automation Henan Polytechnic
University Jiaozuo, China
qtz2007@126.com, qiaomy@foxmail.com

Abstract. Because coal and gas outburst prediction are very complex. In recent years, using least square support vector machine (LS-SVM) time series forecasting model to predict mine working gas is proposed. However in the search support vector solution process, inequality constraints become equality constraints in the LS-SVM, its advantage is to improve the algorithm speed, at the same time the sparse of support vectors and robustness to model are loss. In this paper, weighted LS-SVM is proposed to improve sparse and robustness and its time series prediction model is used to analysis short-time mine working face gas emission. Under MATLAB2009b environment, using LS-SVM1.7 toolbox, specific algorithm model is established, further model is verified by Hebi 10th 1113 mine and gas outburst working face time series data. The results showed that: weighted LS-SVM can achieve a better short-time gas prediction than standard LS-SVM; meanwhile its model has a better robustness.

Keywords: weighted LS-SVM, MATLAB, working face gas, time series.

1 Introduction

The disaster caused by mine gas outburst is extremely serious, so its prediction has been widespread concerned around the world. With the development of computer technology and artificial intelligence, method for predicting the mine methane has also been greatly developed, such as the chaotic time series prediction, gray relational analysis, and neural network prediction and so on[1]. However, there are many complex factors which give rise to gas outburst. Furthermore, the data, which are used to predict emission, always contain a lot noise and have certain randomness. So it is very difficult to accurately predict gas outburst using these data [2-3].

This paper presents short-term time series gas emission prediction through using LS-SVM model, which is based on structural risk minimization (SRM) induction principle. Through the following steps to achieve this principle: (1) Input vector is mapped to high-dimensional feature space by utilizing non-linear transformation; (2) In this space, according to the linear decision rules set construct a structure with the formal hyper-plane model. (3) Select the best structure elements and the best function

H. Deng et al. (Eds.): AICI 2011, Part III, LNAI 7004, pp. 639–647, 2011.

of this element in order to minimize the error rate boundary [4]. From the above implementation process can be summed up the advantages of SVM as follows: (1) From low-dimensional space to high-dimensional space non-linear problem is transformed into a linear, and the calculation in the high-dimensional space has been simplified since the introduction of kernel function; (2) Algorithm eventually be transformed into a convex quadratic optimization problem, the final solution is the global optimal point, avoiding the disadvantages that the neural networks fall into local minima, but also to improve the generalization ability[4].

At the same time, the two drawbacks of LS-SVM are brought because of the algorithm improvements. First, the LS-SVM has lost the sparse and robustness of SVM; Second, the error square is as cost loss function in the LS-SVM, however only when the error variable is Gaussian distribution, this assumption is reasonable, if this condition is not satisfied, it will produce large errors [5-6]. In order to overcome these two drawbacks, weighted LS-SVM is proposed. In this paper weighted LS-SVM prediction model is established to analysis Hebi 10th mine gas time-series data. Under MALTAB2009b environment, using LS-SVM1.7 toolbox, which is developed by K. Pelckmans and J.A.K. Suykens et al., time series prediction model is build. The gas outburst time series data from the Hebi 10th mine 1113 working face is used to verify model. At the same time error indicators of weighted LS-SVM and standard LS-SVM are compared. The results showed that: weighted LS-SVM can achieve a better short-time gas prediction than standard LS-SVM, at the same time its model has a better robustness.

2   Basic Principle of LS-SVM and Weighted LS-SVM

LS-SVM is an improved SVM, and is proposed by J.A.K. SUYKENS and J. VANDEWALLE in 1999.It has been used to many engineering fields. LS-SVM retains structural risk minimization principles, and changes inequality constraints into the equation. Thus, the quadratic programming problems change into solving equations problem, which improve the speed of the algorithm.

Given a Training set of N data points (x_i, y_i), $i = 1, \cdots, N$, where $x_i \in R^m$ is the i-th input pattern and $y_i \in \{-1, 1\}$ is the i-th output pattern.

In this method, the input data are mapped into a higher dimensional feature space by using non-linear mapping $\Phi(x) = [\varphi_1(x), \varphi_2(x), \cdots \varphi_n(x)]$, and an optimal separating hyper-plane can be constructed in this space.

$$\sum_{i=1}^{N} \omega^T \varphi(x_i) + b = y_i \tag{1}$$

Optimal hyper-plane geometry as a measure of the standard optimal hyper-plane is will be determined by the maximum geometry interval. So that the problem can be transformed as follows.

$$\min \frac{1}{2} \omega^T \omega \tag{2}$$

The statement is hold in the linear separable case, in order to make the algorithm more fault-tolerant nature, the introduction of slack variables ζ_i and penalty factors γ. In the LS-SVM is used in second-order soft margin classification. Therefore, LS-SVM optimization problem become as follows.

$$\min\quad J(\omega,b,\zeta)=\frac{1}{2}\omega^T\omega+\frac{1}{2}\gamma\sum_{i=1}^{N}\zeta_i^2 \tag{3}$$

$$s.t.\quad y_i[\omega^T\varphi(x_i)+b]=1-\zeta_i\,(i=1,2\cdots n) \tag{4}$$

n is the number of samples in here.

One can using Lagrange optimization rule to solve the above problems, the introduction of Lagrange multipliers constructor as follows.

$$L(\omega,b,\zeta,\alpha)=J(\omega,b,\zeta)-\sum_{i=1}^{N}\alpha_i\{y_i[\omega^T\varphi(x_i)+b]-1+\zeta_i\} \tag{5}$$

α_i is Lagrange multipliers in here.

According to Kuhn-Tucker condition, one can obtain as follows

$$\frac{\partial L(\omega,b,\zeta,\alpha)}{\partial\omega}=0\rightarrow\omega=\sum_{i=1}^{N}\alpha_i y_i\varphi(x_i)$$

$$\frac{\partial L(\omega,b,\zeta,\alpha)}{\partial b}=0\rightarrow\sum_{i=1}^{N}\alpha_i y_i=0$$

$$\frac{\partial L(\omega,b,\zeta,\alpha)}{\partial\zeta_i}=0\rightarrow\alpha_i=\gamma\zeta_i \tag{6}$$

$$\frac{\partial L(\omega,b,\zeta,\alpha)}{\partial\alpha_i}=0\rightarrow y_i[\omega^T\varphi(x_i)+b]-1+\zeta_i=0$$

In order to solve the equations, some middle variables are introduced as follows [7].

$$Z=[\varphi(x_1)^T y_1;\cdots;\varphi(x_N)^T y_N],Y=[y_1;\cdots;y_N]\,\vec{1}=[1;\cdots;1],\ \zeta=[\zeta_1;\cdots;\zeta_N];$$

$$\begin{bmatrix} I & 0 & 0 & -Z^T \\ 0 & 0 & 0 & Y^T \\ 0 & 0 & \gamma I & -I \\ Z & Y & I & 0 \end{bmatrix}\begin{bmatrix} \omega \\ b \\ \zeta \\ \alpha \end{bmatrix}=\begin{bmatrix} 0 \\ 0 \\ 0 \\ \vec{1} \end{bmatrix} \tag{7}$$

The solution is also given by equation (8).

$$\begin{bmatrix} 0 & Y^T \\ Y & \Omega + \gamma^{-1}I \end{bmatrix}\begin{bmatrix} b \\ \alpha \end{bmatrix} = \begin{bmatrix} 0 \\ 1 \end{bmatrix} \tag{8}$$

Here, $\Omega = ZZ^T$ Mercer's condition can be applied to this matrix.

$$\Omega_{ij} = y_i y_j \varphi(x_i)^T \varphi(x_j) = y_i y_j K(x_i, x_j) \tag{9}$$

Given a kernel function, one can give the solution to determine the optimal classification surface by solving the linear set of Equations (7)-(9) instead of quadratic programming.

In the regression case, the objective function formula (4) is only rewritten as follows.

$$s.t. \quad y_i = \omega^T \varphi(x_i) + b - \zeta_i \, (i = 1,2 \cdots n) \tag{10}$$

n is the number of samples in here[8].

One can get the solution of least-squares regression equation by repeating the above calculation process.

$$\begin{bmatrix} 0 & \vec{1} \\ \vec{1} & \Omega + \gamma^{-1}I \end{bmatrix}\begin{bmatrix} b \\ \alpha \end{bmatrix} = \begin{bmatrix} 0 \\ Y \end{bmatrix} \tag{11}$$

Thus, the standard LS-SVM regression model can be drawn as follows.

$$y(x) = \sum_{i=1}^{N} \alpha_i K(x, x_i) + b \tag{12}$$

In order to improve the robustness and sparse of standard LS-SVM, a weight value v_i is multiplied to error variable in the standard LS-SVM. So the optimization problem can be written as follows:

$$\min_{\omega^*,b^*,e^*} J(\omega^*,e^*) = \frac{1}{2}\omega^{*T}\omega^* + \frac{1}{2}\gamma\sum_{i=1}^{N} v_i e_i^{*2} \tag{13}$$

$$s.t. \quad y_i = \omega^{*T}\varphi(x_i) + b^* + e_i^*, \quad (i = 1,2 \cdots N) \tag{14}$$

Note: the unknown variables with "*" are used in weighted LS-SVM optimization problem. When weighting coefficient is 1, the weighted LS-SVM becomes common LS-SVM.

The same construct Lagrange function to solve the above equation, and then eliminate the middle variables ω^* and e^*.

$$\begin{bmatrix} 0 & \vec{1}^T \\ \vec{1} & \Omega + V_\gamma \end{bmatrix}\begin{bmatrix} b^* \\ \alpha^* \end{bmatrix} = \begin{bmatrix} 0 \\ y \end{bmatrix} \tag{15}$$

Where $V_r = diag\ (1/\gamma_1, \cdots, 1/\gamma_N)$, the selection of the weight vector estimate is based on the following formula [9]:

$$v_i = \begin{cases} 1 & if\left|e_k/\hat{s}\right| \leq c_1 \\ \dfrac{c_2 - \left|e_k/\hat{s}\right|}{c_2 - c_1} & ifc_1 \leq \left|e_k/\hat{s}\right| \leq c_2 \\ 10^{-4} & other \end{cases} \qquad (16)$$

Where $\hat{s}$ is a robust estimates value of standard LS-SVM error, it is calculated as follows:

$$\hat{s} = \frac{IQR}{2\times0.6745} \qquad (17)$$

Where IQR the interquartile range of the error variable, this value is used to estimate how many error variables deviate from the Gaussian distribution. Since the cost loss function of the standard LS-SVM is set only error variable is the Gaussian distribution, then the weight vector is added in the formula (16) can increase robustness of the system. So even the error variable does not obey the Gaussian distribution, a better analysis results can be gained by using this model. Usually constant $c_1 = 2.5, c_2 = 3$, they can be gain from the density estimation of the error variable [9].

The radial basis function (RBF) is used in this paper, its expression as follows.

$$K(x, x_i) = \exp\left(-\frac{(x - x_i)^2}{\sigma^2}\right) \qquad (18)$$

The penalty factor γ and nuclear width σ^2 are two parameters which need to be adjusted in this model [5].

In this article 10 fold cross-validation commands in LS-SVM1.7 toolbox is used to determine these two parameters.

Wherever Times is specified, Times Roman or Times New Roman may be used. If neither is available on your word processor, please use the font closest in appearance to Times. Avoid using bit-mapped fonts if possible. True-Type 1 or Open Type fonts are preferred. Please embed symbol fonts, as well, for math, etc.

3   Prediction Model Algorithm Steps

Nonlinear time series prediction is currently based on the Takens' phase space reconstruction theory. The key of reconstruction phase space is how to determine the delay time τ and embedding dimension m . In this paper minimum differential Entropy ratio method is used to determine those two parameters [10-11].

Given a set of nonlinear time-series data $\{x_t\}_{t=1}^{n}$, firstly embedding dimension m and delay time τ can be determined by some method, Entropy ratio method is used in this paper. Then on this basis phase space can be reconstructed, LSSVM training and prediction are carried out in this space.

Reconstructed phase space as follows:

$$\left(X_1, x(t_{2+(m-1)\tau})\right), \left(X_2, x(t_{3+(m-1)\tau})\right), \cdots \left(X_{M-1}, x(t_n)\right) \tag{19}$$

Here $X_i = (x(t_i), x(t_{i+\tau}), \cdots x(t_{i+(n-1)\tau}))$ is the input of time series prediction model, and $x(t_{i+1+(m-1)\tau})$ is the output.

According to the Takens' phase space reconstruction theory, the state variables between exist function relationship.

$$x(t_{i+1+(n-1)\tau}) = f(X_i) \qquad i = 1, 2, \cdots M - 1 \tag{20}$$

Here $f(\cdot)$ is the state transfer function of the system, and this transfer function is one step time series forecasting model. Multi-step prediction model can gain by repeat these steps.

Robust weighted LS-SVM time series forecasting model algorithm steps are as follows:

- Processing the sample data, such as handling the exception samples, normalized samples. Gain the processed data samples $\{x_t\}_{t=1}^n$. According to minimum differential Entropy ratio method to gain the embedding dimension m and delay time τ. On this basis, using phase space reconstruction technique gain the sample data. Part of the samples as training samples, part of the sample as the test samples.
- Parameter initialization, according to training samples to adjust the standard LS-SVM algorithm model, where (γ, σ^2) is gained by the 10 fold grid search and cross-validation, here the search range is [0.1 10000; 0.1 10000].
- e_k is gained by using $e_k = \alpha_k / \gamma$, and $\hat{s}$ is gained from distribution of e_k. Weight vector v_k is calculated by e_k and $\hat{s}$, then robust weighted LS-SVM model can be obtained according to the formula (15).
- Train sample is used to train weighted LS-SVM. One step prediction model $\hat{x}(t_{i+1+(n-1)\tau}) = f(X_i)$ can be gained when end of the training [12].
- According to this prediction model can predict value $\hat{x}(t_{n+1})$ of $x(t_{n+1})$ time can be gained, repeat the above steps predict value $\hat{x}(t_{n+2})$ of $x(t_{n+2})$ time can be gained. Multi-step prediction can be gained by repeat multi step predict above step multi-step prediction model can be drawn.
- When the start points and predicted number are given, the regression model will give the prediction result. At the same time, the evaluation criteria, including of the root mean square error and maximum error percentage, will be given.

4   Example Analyses

In this paper, the gas outburst data is come from 1113 working face of the 10th mine in Hebi. The time series data are the percentage of gas emission concentration. These data are used for the learning samples and the training samples. KJ93 environmental monitoring system was used for monitoring Face tunneling head gas emission. The amplitude of the gas concentration is in the range of 0~4% using this system measurement.

There are 120 time-series data. Each interval between two points is 5 minutes. Embedding dimension and delay time are obtained by using minimum differential Entropy ratio method.

Fig. 1 shows the two parameters values in differential Entropy ratio map. Vertical axis is time-series differential Entropy rate, and two horizontal axes are respectively the embedding m and delay time τ. Minimum differential Entropy rate points corresponding to the two horizontal axes values are the optimal m and. In this example, "★" position show $m = 3, \tau = 1$.

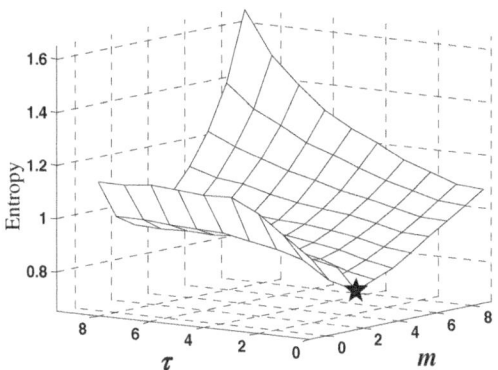

Fig. 1. Face gas time-series Entropy ratio

In the MATLAB2009b environment, LS-SVMlab1.7 package is used to compile the algorithm program. The model is trained by using given learning samples and training samples, then 20 point data will be forecasted through this learning machine, where each time interval is five minutes.

In this paper, Root Mean Square Error ($RMSE$) and Mean Absolute Percentage Error ($MAPE$) are used to evaluate the prediction results. The expression is as follows:

$$ RMSE = \sqrt{\frac{1}{l}\sum_{i=1}^{l}\left(\frac{Y_i^{'} - Y_i}{Y_i}\right)^2} \tag{21} $$

$$ MAPE = \frac{1}{l}\sum_{i=1}^{l}\left|\frac{Y_i^{'} - Y_i}{Y_i}\right| \tag{22} $$

Where $Y_i^{'}$ is the i-th predictive value. Y_i is the i-th true value. l is the predicted points number.

70 data points is selected as training samples. According to above algorithm step, 20 steps are predicted by using standard LS-SVM and the weighted LS-SVM, respectively. Coal and gas outburst time is included in the 20 points. Prediction results of LSSVM and weighted LSSVM are shown in Fig.2 and Fig.3.

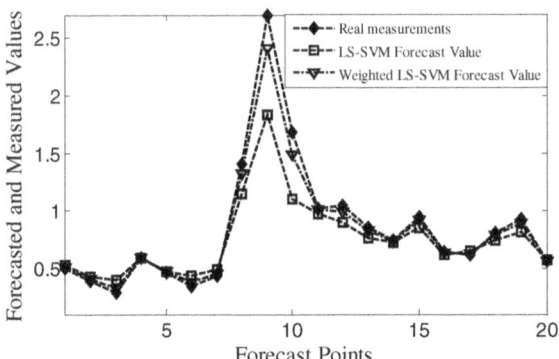

Fig. 2. Forecast curse of LS-SVM and weighted LS-SVM

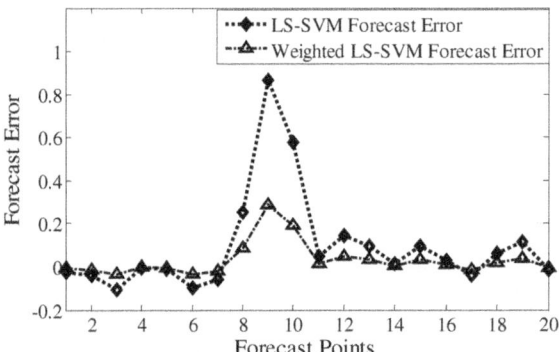

Fig. 3. Weighted LS-SVM and LS-SVM Forecast Error

Table 1. Error indicators comparison of two models

	RMSE	*MAPE*
LS-SVM	0.1678	0.1271
Weighted LS-SVM	0.0559	0.0424

Fig. 3 shows prediction error values at each point of the two models. Table 1 shows the predict effect evaluation index of two models.

5   Conclusions

In this paper, the basic theory of LS-SVM is discussed in detail based on the good generalization performance. Because of the two shortcoming of standard LS-SVM, a weighted LS-SVM is proposed in this paper. Under MALTAB2009b environment, using LS-SVM1.7 toolbox, which is developed by K. Pelckmans and J.A.K. Suykens et al., time series prediction model is build. The gas outburst time series data from the Hebi 10th mine 1113 working face is used to verify model. At the same error indicators of weighted LS-SVM and standard LS-SVM are compared. The results showed that: weighted LS-SVM can achieve a better short-time gas prediction than standard LS-SVM, at the same time its model has a better robustness.

Acknowledgment. The author would like to thank to Liu Yanwei providing the gas time-series data during writing the paper.

References

1. Cui, W.Z., Zhu, C.C., Bao, W.X.: Prediction of the chaotic time series using support vector machines for fuzzy rule-based modeling. Acta Physica Sinica 54(7), 2221–2230 (2009) (in Chinese)
2. Yang, M., Wang, Y.J., Chen, Y.P.: Improved differential evolution neural network and it s application in prediction of coal and gas outburst. Journal of China University of Mining & Technology 38, 439–444 (2009) (in Chinese)
3. Wang, G.H., Wang, J.G., Wang, H.F.: Prediction of coal and gas outburst based on neural network and grey theory. China Coal Bed Methane 16, 27–30 (2009) (in Chinese)
4. Vapnik (ed.), Xu, J.H., Zhang, X.G.:Trans. Statistical Learning Theory. Publishing House of Electronics Industry (2004)
5. Vapnik, V.N., Xu, J., Zhang, X. (translation): Statistical learning theory. Electronic Industry Press, Beijing (2004)
6. Deng, N.Y., Tian, Y.J.: Support Vector Machines - theory, algorithms and expansion. Science Press (2009)
7. Ji, L.L., Lin, Z.S., Wang, C.Y.: Experiments on nonlinear time series prediction with least square support vector regression machine. Journal of PLA University of Science and Technology (Natural Science Edition) 110, 92–97 (2009)
8. Suykens, J.A.K., Vandewalle, J.: Least squares support vector machine classifiers. Neural Processing Letters 9, 439–444 (1999)
9. Suykens, J.A.K., De Brabanter, J., Lukas, L., et al.: Weighted least squares support vector machines: robustness and sparse approximation. Neurocomputing 48, 85–105 (2002)
10. Gautama, T., Mandic, D.P., Van Hulle, M.M.: A differential entropy based method for determine the optimal embedding parameters of a signal. In: Proc. of the Int. Conf. an Acoustic, Speech and Signal Processing, Hongkong, pp. 29–32 (2003)
11. Guo, X.H., Ma, X.P.: Coal washery daily water consumption short-term prediction based on least squares support vector machines. Journal of China Coal Society 32, 1093–1097 (2007) (in Chinese)
12. Zhao, X.H., Wang, G., Zhao, K., et al.: On-line least squares support vector machine algorithm in gas prediction. Mining Science and Technology 19, 194–198 (2009) (in Chinese)

Multi-spectral Remote Sensing Images Classification Method Based on SVC with Optimal Hyper-parameters

Yi-nan Guo[1], Dawei Xiao[1], Jian Cheng[1,2], and Mei Yang[1]

[1] College of Information and Electronic Engineering, China University of Mining and Technology, Xuzhou, 221116 Jiangsu, China
[2] Department of Automation, Tinghua University, Beijing 100084, China
nanfly@126.com

Abstract. Traditional classification methods based on asymptotic theory for multi-spectral remote sensing images need the infinite training samples, which is impossible to be satisfied. And it has massive data information. Support vector classification(SVC) based on small samples overcomes above problems. However, the parameters determining its structure need to be optimized. For that, three optimization algorithms including genetic algorithm, particle swarm optimization and adaptive chaotic culture algorithm, are introduced to obtain optimal hyper-parameters of SVC model for multi-spectral remote sensing images. Experimental results compared with cross-validation method indicate that the computation time for classification by genetic algorithm is least and the generalization of genetic algorithm-based SVC model is best.

Keywords: SVC, optimization algorithm, hyper-parameters, remote sensing images, classification.

1 Introduction

Multi-spectral remote sensing images have high resolution, multi-band and massive data. How to accurately obtain the cultures in these images by the classification is the core of researches. Because the cultures in the multi-spectral remote sensing images are reflected by gray values, the values of different cultures in the same band or different band are different. This is the criterion for classifying different cultures. The feature vectors of each object are distributed in the same feature space. But different objects have different spectral and spatial information, so they distribute in different feature space. Therefore, the classification for remote sensing images is to partition different cultures by computers. Useful features are extracted through analyzing the spectrum and spatial information. Then these features are classified into non-overlapping feature space. At last, each image pixel are mapped into corresponding feature space[1].

In traditional classification methods for remote sensing images, minimum distance method[2] is easy to fall into local optimum because only the local characteristics are considered. But it has better performance for block objects. In maximum likelihood classification method[2], the probability distribution functions of each class are

H. Deng et al. (Eds.): AICI 2011, Part III, LNAI 7004, pp. 648–655, 2011.

needed to satisfy normal distribution. However, the selected samples may be deviate from normal distribution. Although the radial basis neural network[3] is good for classification of block object, it is not fit for the classification of confusion region. In view of above problems, different optimization algorithms are introduced to obtain optimal hyper-parameters of SVC model for multi-spectral remote sensing images in the paper so as to save computation time and improve the generalization of the model.

2   Least Square Support Vector Machine

Aiming at the non-linear classification problems, input feature space is mapped to the high dimensional feature space by special functions in support vector machine. Then the optimal liner classification hyperplane based on structural risk minimization is to be found in the high dimensional feature space. It corresponds to the non-liner classi-fication plane in input feature space. At last, the optimal liner classification hyper-plane is inversely mapped to input feature space. Least squares support vector ma-chine(LS-SVM) is an improved method based on the standard SVM. Least square error for liner system is used as loss function[4]. Then it is converted into an equality equation, shown as follows.

$$\min \quad \phi(\omega,b,e) = \frac{1}{2}\omega^T\omega + \frac{1}{2}\gamma\sum_{i=1}^{l}e_i^2$$

$$s.t. \quad y_i[\omega^T\varphi(x_i)+b] = 1-e_i \qquad i=1,\cdots,l \tag{1}$$

Lagrangian function is defined as follows.

$$L(\omega,b,e,\alpha) = \phi(\omega,b,e) - \sum_{i=1}\alpha_i\left\{y_i[\omega^T\varphi(x_i)+b]-1+e_i\right\} \tag{2}$$

According to the optimum condition, ω and ε are eliminated.

$$\frac{\partial L}{\partial \omega} = \frac{\partial L}{\partial b} = \frac{\partial L}{\partial e_i} = \frac{\partial L}{\partial \alpha_i} = 0 \tag{3}$$

$$\begin{bmatrix} 0 & -Y^T \\ Y & ZZ^T + \gamma^{-1}I \end{bmatrix}\begin{bmatrix} b \\ \alpha \end{bmatrix} = \begin{bmatrix} 0 \\ \rho_1 \end{bmatrix} \tag{4}$$

$$\begin{cases} Z = [\varphi(x_1)^T y_1, \varphi(x_2)^T y_2, \cdots, \varphi(x_l)^T y_l] \\ Y = [y_1, y_2, \cdots, y_l] \\ \rho_1 = [1,1,\cdots,1]^T \\ e = [e_1, e_2, \cdots, e_l]^T \\ \alpha = [\alpha_1, \alpha_2, \cdots, \alpha_l] \end{cases} \tag{5}$$

Here, $\Omega = ZZ^T = [q_{ij}]_{l\times l}$. According to Mercer conditions[5], the elements of the matrix are expressed as follows.

$$q_{ij} = y_i y_j \Phi(x_i)^T \Phi(x_j) = y_i y_j k(x_i, x_j) \tag{6}$$

Then the optimal classifier function is obtained.

$$f(x) = \sum_{i=1}^{l} \alpha_i k(x, x_i) + b \qquad (7)$$

Assuming the inner-product in the high dimensional feature space is expressed by kernel functions $k(x_i, x_j)$. In the paper, Gaussian radial basis function is used. Let σ be variance. According to LS-SVM model and kernel function, kernel parameter σ and regularization parameter γ are needed to be optimized.

$$k(x, x_i) = \exp(-\|x - x_i\|^2 / \sigma^2) \qquad (8)$$

3 Hyper-parameters Selection Method of Support Vector Classification Based on Intelligent Optimization Algorithms

The essence of SVC is an optimization problem. How to obtain optimal hyper-parameters is the key. So three optimization algorithms including genetic algorithm (GA), particle swarm optimization(PSO), adaptive chaotic culture algorithm (ACCA) are introduced in the paper.

3.1 The Fitness Function

The classification for remote sensing images is a multi-classification problem in fact. However, SVM is usually used to solve binary classification problems. So it is necessary to convert a multi-classification problem into many binary classification problems. Here, minimum output code(MOC) method is adapted because of its less computation complexity[6].Suppose there are C classes in the classification problem. $\hat{C}$ denotes the least binary bits for the number of required binary classifiers. In order to decrease computation complexity, there is no need to optimize hyper-parameters in each binary SVM classifier.Only $\hat{C}$ binary classifiers are optimized. The optimal hyper-parameters are shared by all binary classifiers.

According to LS-SVM model and kernel function, hyper-parameters including σ and γ are optimized. Let m be population size. The classification accuracy is used as the fitness function for optimization algorithms.

$$f(\gamma_i, \sigma_i) = \mathrm{AR}_{\mathrm{SVM}} \quad i = 1, 2, \cdots, m \qquad (9)$$

$$\mathrm{AR}_{\mathrm{SVM}} = \frac{1}{l} \sum_{i=1}^{l} H(\hat{y}_i, y_i) \qquad (10)$$

$$H(\hat{y}_i, y_i) = \begin{cases} 1 & \hat{y}_i = y_i \\ 0 & \hat{y}_i \neq y_i \end{cases} \qquad (11)$$

The accuracy rate(AR) is used as evaluation index of multi-classification SVM model obtained by MOC method. Suppose y_i is the actual value. $\hat{y}_i$ is the predictive output by model.l is the number of samples. $H(\hat{y}_i, y_i)$ denotes the classification result. 1 expresses the correct classification result.

3.2 The Evolution Operations in Different Optimization Algorithms

A) Genetic Algorithms

Genetic algorithm[6] is an optimization algorithm derived from natural selection and genetic mechanism. The optimal resolution is obtained by population-based evolution. Individual information is exchanged by crossover operator and mutation operator. The key of GA is how to express and evaluate each solution and how to achieve the selection, crossover and mutation operations.

Coding. Two parameters in LS-SVM model are formed into an individual in GA. Each individual is coded by two real-numbers, shown as $x = (\gamma, \sigma)$.

Selection Operator. Random rank selection combing with elitist preserved strategy is used as selection operator. Detailed selection operation is shown as follows:

Step1: The individuals with the largest or least fitness values are found from current population. If the best individual is better than the individuals in preserved set, it will be saved in preserved set. Then the worst individual in current population is substituted by the best individual in preserved set.

Step2: Aiming at any individual, N individuals are randomly selected from the population and compared with it. The individuals with less dominated individuals are preserved into the population in next generation.

Step3: Above steps are repeated for m times.

Crossover Operator. Arithmetic crossover operator is used. Two new individuals $x_a(t+1)$ and $x_b(t+1)$ are generated by linear combination with two individuals $x_a(t)$ and $x_b(t)$. Suppose $g \in (0,1)$ is constant.

$$\begin{cases} x_a(t+1) = g x_b(t) + (1-g) x_a(t) \\ x_b(t+1) = g x_a(t) + (1-g) x_b(t) \end{cases} \tag{12}$$

Mutation Operator. Non-uniform mutation operator is used. Taken γ as example, mutation operator is shown as follows. Here, γ and γ' denote the parameters before and after mutation. Suppose $[\gamma_{min}, \gamma_{max}]$ is the bound of this variable. $\Delta(t,e) \in [0,e]$ denotes stochastic number satisfying non-uniform distribution.

$$\overline{\gamma} = \begin{cases} \gamma + \Delta(t, \gamma_{max} - \gamma) & if \quad random(0,1) = 0 \\ \gamma + \Delta(t, \gamma - \gamma_{min}) & if \quad random(0,1) = 1 \end{cases} \tag{13}$$

B) Particle Swarm Optimization

Particle Swarm Optimization[7] is a random global swarm intelligent optimization technique derived from the simulation of birds movement. A particle is moved along with the possible solution direction via transfer information among particles.

Suppose $x_i(t) = (x_{i1}, x_{i2}, \cdots, x_{id}, \cdots, x_{iD})$ and $v_i(t) = (v_{i1}, v_{i2}, \cdots, v_{id}, \cdots, v_{iD})$ are the location and speed of ith particle. P_{lid} is the historical best location of ith particle. p_{gd} is the historical best particle in the whole population. The speed and location of a particle are updated as follows.

$$x_{id}(t+1) = x_{id}(t) + v_{id}(t+1) \tag{14}$$

$$v_{id}(t+1) = v_{id}(t) + c_1\beta_1(P_{lid} - x_{id}(t)) + c_2\beta_2(P_{gd} - x_{id}(t)) \tag{15}$$

Here, c_1 and c_2 are learning factor. β_1 and β_2 are uniform random number between 0 and 1. In order to avoid updated particles circulating beating in the search space, the bound of speed is given as $[-v_{max}, v_{max}]$. The bigger v_{max} is, the search ability is stronger. The smaller v_{max} is, the local search ability is better. If v_{max}, c_1 and c_2 have improper values, the particle will get away from the search space. So shrinkage factor are used to restrain such phenomenon[8]. Let w be inertial constant.

$$v_{id}(t+1) = \chi\{v_{id}(t) + c_1\beta_1(P_{lid} - x_{id}(t)) + c_2\beta_2(P_{gd} - x_{id}(t))\} \tag{16}$$

where $\chi = \dfrac{2}{|2 - o - \sqrt{o^2 - 4 \times o}|}, o = c_1 + c_2$. o is usually equaled to 4.1. So x is equaled to 0.7298. In this paper, PSO with shrinkage factor is adopted.

C) Adaptive Chaotic Culture Algorithm

In adaptive chaotic culture algorithm[9], implicit knowledge extracted from evolution process is used to guide the scale of mutation of chaotic mutation operator. Here, knowledge $Sk = [sp_1, sp_2, \cdots sp_{N_s}]$ expressed by bintree are extracted according to the distribution of individuals with largest fitness in each iteration.

$$sp_k = \frac{1}{2}(p_{best,j}(t) - p_{best,j}(t-1)), \quad j = \arg\max_{j=1,2,\cdots,n} \Delta l_j \tag{17}$$

$$\Delta l_j = \frac{f(p_{best}(t)) - f(p_{best}(t-1))}{p_{best,j}(t) - p_{best,j}(t-1)} \tag{18}$$

Here, sp_k is the split point. It divides the search space into two parts along the dimension with largest fitness gradient so as to shrink feasible search space. The scale of mutation is adaptively adjusted based on chaotic sequence according to current knowledge describing the dominant space.

$$c_{ij}(t+1) = \begin{cases} C_j(t) + (\overline{C_j}(t) - C_j(t))a_{ij}^l(t) & p_i(t) \notin \Omega_{k1}(t) \\ c_{ij}(t) + \exp(\dfrac{-\alpha t}{T}) \times (\overline{C_j^{K1}}(t) - C_j^{K1}(t)) \times a_{ij}^l(t) & p_i(t) \in \Omega_{k1}(t) \end{cases} \tag{19}$$

$$\begin{cases} \Omega_{k1}(t) : C_j^{K1}(t) = C_j(t-1), \overline{C_j^{K1}}(t) = sp_k \\ \Omega_{k2}(t) : C_j^{K2}(t) = sp_k, \overline{C_j^{K2}}(t) = \overline{C_j}(t-1) \end{cases}$$
$$\Omega(t-1) = \Omega_{k1}(t) \cup \Omega_{k2}(t) \tag{20}$$

$$a_{ij}^{l+1} = \mu a_{ij}^l(1 - a_{ij}^l), l = 0,1,2,\cdots Lm \tag{21}$$

Here, $\underline{C_j^K}(t), \overline{C_j^K}(t)$ denote lower and upper limits of the dominant space $\Omega_{k1}(t)$. $a_{ij}^l(t)$ is the value of Logistic chaotic sequence. Lm is the length of sequence. $\mu \in [3,4]$ is the chaotic factor. The ergodicity of a chaotic sequence is different when μ and Lm is different. Here, implicit knowledge is introduced to decide the value of μ.

$$\mu(t) = 3.5 + 0.5 \times \frac{\overline{c}_j(t) - \underline{c}_j(t)}{\overline{c}_j(0) - \underline{c}_j(0)} \tag{22}$$

Obviously, the possible value of $\mu(t)$ is between 3.5 and 4. When the span of current dominant space is shrunken, μ is smaller. It will decrease the ergodicity of the chaotic sequence and the complexity of computation in the algorithm.

4 Simulation and Analysis

In order to validate the rationality of SVC model with optimal hyper-parameters for remote sensing images classification problem, simulation experiments are done by matlab7.0. In multi-spectral remote sensing images, massive data information is contained. So the cultures are easy to be recognized. However, the redundant data increases the difficulty for image processing. Therefore, they need to be pre-processed. The processed original remote sensing images used in experiments are shown in Fig.1. Here, the size of each picture is 197×119.

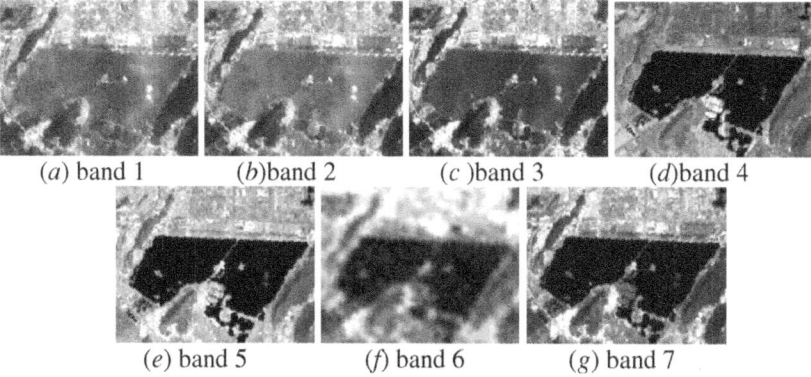

(a) band 1   (b)band 2   (c)band 3   (d)band 4

(e) band 5   (f) band 6   (g) band 7

Fig. 1. 7 bands of original remote sensing image

The parameters respectively used in GA-based LS-SVM, PSO-based LS-SVM and ACCA-based LS-SVM classification models are: $[\gamma_{min}, \gamma_{max}] \in [0.1,10]$, $[\sigma_{min}, \sigma_{max}] \in [0.1,10]$, m=20,termination iteration=100,Pc=0.8,Pm=0.03, $c_1 = c_2$=1.4962, inertia weight=0.7298, Lm=20, sample-selection proportion=0.2, knowledge influence proportion=0.1.

There are 7 classes cultures in the sample set. In each class, the training/test sample set respectively contains 10, 20 and 60 samples in three kinds of experiments. And the training sample set and test sample set has the same size. According to the training/test sample set, the performances of LS-SVM model with optimal hyper-parameters obtained by different optimization algorithms are shown in Tab.1. These results are mean after 10 times.

Table 1. Comparison of performance with different optimization algorithm

Number	Algorithm	Accuracy	Accuracy variance	Time	Time variance
10	GA	0.8871	1.84E-05	0.0680	6.85E-04
	PSO	0.8886	3.27E-05	0.0656	1.11E-03
	ACCA	0.8729	1.81E-04	0.7750	0.0961
	10-Cross-validation	0.8814	6.97E-04	0.0729	7.64E-04
20	GA	0.9043	9.39E-05	0.1648	4.93E-04
	PSO	0.8993	6.58E-05	0.2047	5.49E-03
	ACCA	0.8821	9.44E-05	0.6515	0.0439
	10-Cross-validation	0.9107	7.38E-04	0.1858	0.0034
60	GA	0.8514	3.63E-06	2.0142	0.0223
	PSO	0.8488	1.04E-05	2.4266	0.1703
	ACCA	0.8364	6.36E-05	2.8978	0.8020
	10-Cross-validation	0.8788	3.49E-04	2.8346	0.8635

From the Tab.1, we know that when the number of training samples contained in each class is 10, PSO-based model has the best accuracy and least running time. At the same time, GA-based model nearly has the same accuracy and running time with PSO. However, the accuracy and running time variance of GA-based model is least. These show that the accuracy and running time of GA method is more stable. Namely, the model performance is more stable. When the number of training samples contained in each class is 20, the cross-validation method has the best accuracy. GA-based model has similar accuracy to cross-validation. But its running time is the least. When the number of training samples contained in each class is 60, cross-validation has the best accuracy, whereas the running time is the largest. The accuracy of GA-based model is not as well as cross-validation. However, its accuracy and running time variance is the least. Namely, its performance is more stable. Therefore, it is obvious that GA-based model has better generalization and less running time.

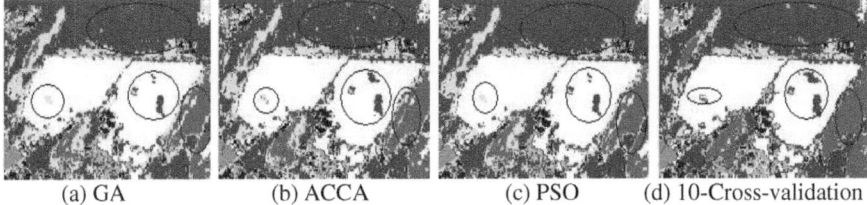

(a) GA   (b) ACCA   (c) PSO   (d) 10-Cross-validation

Fig. 2. Classification result based on different optimization algorithms

When the number of training samples contained in each class is 20, the classification results of LS-SVM model with optimal hyper-parameters obtained by different optimization algorithms are shown in Fig.2. It is obvious that the classification effect based on optimization algorithms are better than 10-Cross-validation as marked by black circle in Fig.2. Compared with Fig.1, we know that the GA-based LS-SVM model has better classification effect than other optimization methods.

5   Conclusions

Aiming at the multi-spectral remote sensing images classification, LS-SVM model with optimal hyper-parameters are given. Three kinds of optimization algorithms including genetic algorithm, particle swarm optimization and adaptive chaotic culture algorithm, are introduced to obtain optimal hyper-parameters of SVC model. optimization method based on optimization algorithm is proposed in this paper. Experimental results compared with cross-validation method indicate that the computation time for classification by genetic algorithm is least and the generalization of genetic algorithm-based SVC model is best.

Acknowledgment. This work is supported by National Natural Science Foundation of China under Grant No. 60805025, Natural Science Foundation of Jiangsu under Grant No. BK2010183, the China Postdoctoral Science Foundation Funded Project under Grant No. 20090460328 and the Qinlan Project of Jiangsu.

References

1. Zhou, F., Pan, H.P., Du, Z.S.: The classification of RBF neural network based on principal component analysis to multispectrum satellite remote-sensing images. Computing Techniques for Geophysical and Geochemical Exploration 30(2), 158–162 (2008)
2. Liu, Q.J., Lin, Q.Z.: Classification of remote sensing image based on immune network. Computer Engineering and Application 44(23), 24–27 (2008)
3. Tan, K., Du, P.J.: Hyperspectral Remote Sensing Image Classification Based on Radical Basis Function Neural Network. Spectroscopy and Spectral Analysis 28(9), 2009–2013 (2008)
4. Deng, N.Y., Tian, Y.J.: A new method of data mining: support vector machines. Science press, Beijing (2004)
5. Fang, R.M.: Support vector machine theory and its application analysis. China power press, Beijing (2007)
6. Guo, Y.-n., Xiao, D.-w., Yang, M.: Genetic algorithm-based support vector classification method for multi-spectral remote sensing image. In: Li, K., Fei, M., Jia, L., Irwin, G.W. (eds.) LSMS 2010 and ICSEE 2010. LNCS, vol. 6328, pp. 213–220. Springer, Heidelberg (2010)
7. Kennedy, J., Eberhart, R.C.: Particle swarm optimization. In: Proceedings of IEEE International Conference on Neural Networks, pp. 1942–1948 (1995)
8. Shi, Y., Eberhart, R.: Empirical study of particle swarm optimization. In: Proceeding of IEEE World Congress in Computation Intelligence, pp. 1945–1950 (1999)
9. Guo, Y.N., Xiao, D.W., Yang, M.: The Selection Method for Hyper-parameters of Support Vector Classification by Chaotic Cultural Algorithm. International Journal of Intelligent Computing and Cybernetics 3(3), 449–462 (2010)

Space Edge Detection Based SVM Algorithm

Fanrong Meng, Wei Lin, and Zhixiao Wang

School of Computer Science and Technology, China University of Mining and Technology
221116 Xuzhou, Jiangsu, China
mengfr62@163.com

Abstract. SVM algorithm has a great advantage when it deals with small sample data set. However, In the process of large sample data set classification, it always has to face to the problems of slowly learning and large storage space. This paper puts forward the process of space edge detection, designs and implements the space edge detection based SVM algorithm. The result of simulation experiments shows that the model can effectively reduce the SVM training set, improve the speed of SVM training, save the storage space and the accuracy of the classification also has a good performance.

Keywords: large data set, vector density, Space edge detection, SVM.

1 Introduction

SVM is by far the most successful implementation of statistical theory, the core of SVM is proposed since 1992, although the development time is very short, but because of its propose is based on statistical learning theory, which has a solid theoretical foundation, therefore supporting vector machine theory has made a great progress in recent years. The core idea of SVM is to find support vector to determine the optimal hyperplane. SVM training is essentially a process of solving a convex quadratic programming problem. Therefore, in solving the problems of small sample data classification, the SVM has a unique advantage. However, when the training sample is large, the training time will grow exponentially. In practice, it is difficult to avoid the large training data; it is an issue of the large sample training data. Therefore, the study of SVM algorithms to deal with the large-scale data sets is becoming one of the research focuses.

To resolve the difficulty of the SVM algorithms to handle large data sets, domestic and foreign scholars have made a number of studies. Reference [1] proposed the concentric hypersphere support vector machine HSVM. By using two sets of concentric hypersphere, the algorithm divides the vector space into multiple regions, and uses the restrictions to pick out some specific areas' samples to take the SVM training. However, the algorithm may ignore some specific support vector, lead the accuracy of the algorithms to drop. Reference [2] makes the vector space girdding. By calculating the distance between vectors within the grid, only leave part of the vectors to take the SVM training. But in the calculation of the distance between each space vector, the algorithm consumes the more time, reduces the efficiency of the algorithm. Reference [3] clusters the training samples, uses the cluster centers to take the first

H. Deng et al. (Eds.): AICI 2011, Part III, LNAI 7004, pp. 656–663, 2011.

SVM training, obtains support vectors, then all the samples whose cluster centers is the first time's support vector will be used to take a second SVM training The algorithm conducts the SVM training two times, and clusters the training data before the first SVM training, which make the algorithm efficiency and classification accuracy decline.

2 Principle of Edge Detection

2.1 The Edge of the Object

The main manifestation of the object's edge is the local characteristics' discontinuity. Edge often means the end of a region and the beginning of another region. The edge can outline the target object, contain a wealth of information. With the development of graphics technology, the object edge detection gradually evolved into the image edge detection.

2.2 Principle of Image Edge Detection

In the image processing, the edge is the region in which the image gray changes strongly, if a pixel fall on the edge of an object in the image, then its neighborhood will be changed with the gray value. Classical edge detection method is by adjusting the change of gray' first order or second order derivative to detect edges. Image gray's change uses gradient to represent. In the image, steep edge's gradient will be large; those areas in which gray changes flatly, the gradient value will be small; and those areas in which the gray is same, the gradient value will be zero. Through computing the gradient, the edge can be detected sensitively.

Gradient corresponds to the first order derivative, for a continuous image f(x, y), the gradient of f(x, y) is a vector, it can be defined as:

$$\nabla f(x, y) = [G_x \quad G_y]^T = [\frac{\partial f}{\partial x} \quad \frac{\partial f}{\partial y}]^T \tag{1}$$

Gx, Gy are respectively the x direction's gradient and y direction's gradient. The gradient amplitude $|\nabla f(x, y)|$ and orientation angle are:

$$|\nabla f(x, y)| = mag(\nabla f(x, y)) = (G_x^2 + G_y^2)^{1/2} \tag{2}$$

$$\phi(x, y) = \arctan(G_y / G_x) \tag{3}$$

Formula (2) and (3) show that the value of gradient is the increment at max change rate direction. For numerical images, gradient is achieved by the difference instead of the differential.

$$|\nabla f(x, y)| = \left\{ [f(x, y) - f(x+1, y)]^2 + [f(x, y) - f(x+1, y)]^2 \right\}^{\frac{1}{2}} \tag{4}$$

According to the theory of edge detection, the detection of vector space edge is proposed in this paper. Based on space edge detection, the vector located at the space edge can be selected. If uses this dataset instead of all data to take the SVM training, it will increase the processing speed of SVM and save the storage space.

3   Preprocessing of Edge Detection in Vector Space

In this paper, vector density is introduced to express density of the vector in the special space. Vector density is a regional concept. And it is meaningful within a certain space. Vector density is represented with ρ, m represents the number of the vector, and v is the volume. The calculated formula for the vector density is as follows.

$$\rho = m/v \quad . \tag{5}$$

3.1   Vector Space Gridding

Vector density is a regional concept. It is meaningful within a certain space. Therefore, vector space is divided into grids in this paper. The whole vector space is partitioned into multiple grids on the same size, and each volume of the grid is set the unit volume. The simplified calculating formula of the vector density is as follows.

$$\rho = m \quad . \tag{6}$$

where m represents the number of vector in the gird.

For ease to descript, this paper takes two-dimensional vector for example to introduce the process of girding. Two-dimensional space has two axes, axis X and axis Y. Xmin represents the minimum in all X data and Xmax represents the maximum; Ymin represents the minimum in all Y data and Ymax represents the maximum. Xscale represents the grid unit length in the X axis, and Yscale is that in the Y axis. From the original point (Xmin, Ymin) , and the step length Xscale, Yscale, the whole vector space is divided into a number of grid as $\left\lceil \dfrac{X_{max} - X_{min}}{X_{scale}} \right\rceil \times \left\lceil \dfrac{X_{max} - X_{min}}{X_{scale}} \right\rceil$. In order to prevent the case of Xmin=Xmax and Ymin=Ymax, we can add a step and the vector space will be divided into a number of grid as $\left\lceil \dfrac{X_{max} + X_{scale} - X_{min}}{X_{scale}} \right\rceil \times \left\lceil \dfrac{X_{max} + X_{scale} - X_{min}}{X_{scale}} \right\rceil$ .The restrictions of a point (x0, y0) belonging to the Grid(i, j) are formulated as (7):

$$X_{min} + i \times X_{scale} \le x_0 < X_{min} + (i+1) \times X_{scale}$$
$$Y_{min} + j \times Y_{scale} \le y_0 < Y_{min} + (j+1) \times Y_{scale} \quad . \tag{7}$$

3.2 Vector Density Calculation

After the vector space gridding, all of the space vector can be mapped to the grid. According to the formula of vector density, can get the vector density data sets .In Fig. 1, there are two types of vectors. After vector space gridding, vector density calculation, density matrix can be obtained.

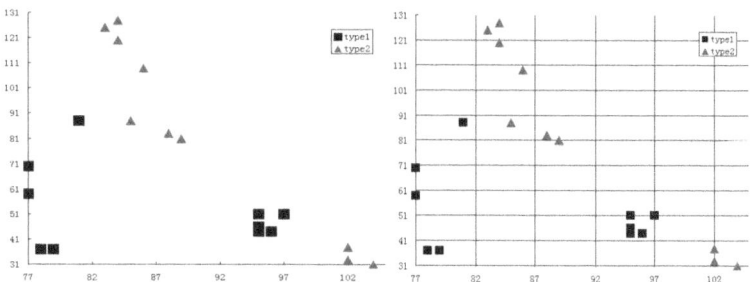

Fig. 1. Vector space gridding

In Fig. 1, the two-dimensional space is divided into grids, the density matrix of vector space are like this:

$$
\begin{pmatrix}
0 & 0 & 0 & 0 & 0 & 0 \\
0 & 0 & 0 & 0 & 0 & 0 \\
0 & 0 & 0 & 0 & 0 & 0 \\
0 & 0 & 0 & 0 & 0 & 0 \\
1 & 0 & 0 & 0 & 0 & 0 \\
0 & 0 & 0 & 0 & 0 & 0 \\
1 & 0 & 0 & 0 & 0 & 0 \\
1 & 0 & 0 & 1 & 1 & 0 \\
0 & 0 & 0 & 3 & 0 & 0 \\
2 & 0 & 0 & 0 & 0 & 0
\end{pmatrix}
\begin{pmatrix}
0 & 2 & 0 & 0 & 0 & 0 \\
0 & 1 & 0 & 0 & 0 & 0 \\
0 & 1 & 0 & 0 & 0 & 0 \\
0 & 0 & 0 & 0 & 0 & 0 \\
0 & 1 & 2 & 0 & 0 & 0 \\
0 & 0 & 0 & 0 & 0 & 0 \\
0 & 0 & 0 & 0 & 0 & 0 \\
0 & 0 & 0 & 0 & 0 & 0 \\
0 & 0 & 0 & 0 & 0 & 0 \\
0 & 0 & 0 & 0 & 0 & 3
\end{pmatrix}
$$

The left matrix is the type1's vector density, and the right one is the Type2's.

4 Vector Space Edge Detection

4.1 The Edge of Vector Space

The main performance of the vector space edge is vector density's discontinuity. In the given vector space region, the same type vector's density changes strongly, the region t is often the beginning or the end of the vector set. This region is called the edge of vector space. The edge of vector space is regional. In this area, the vector's density has changed. At one side of this region, vector density is large, this type vectors are large gathering. At the other side of the region, the density of this type vectors is very small, Or even zero.

4.2   The Method of Vector Space Edge Detection

Taking derivation on the image gray can quickly detect the edges of objects in the image. This article refers to this basic idea, take derivation on vector density to find out the vector space edge .This article uses gradient to descript vector density's changes. For a n-dimensional vector space, $\rho(x1, x2...xn)$ is the vector density in the Grid(x1, x2...xn), the gradient of the grid is a vector, is defined as

$$\nabla f(x_1, x_2...x_n) = [\frac{\partial \rho}{\partial x_1} \quad \frac{\partial \rho}{\partial x_2} \quad ... \quad \frac{\partial \rho}{\partial x_n}]^T \tag{8}$$

Gradient's amplitude $\left|\nabla f(x_1, x_2...x_n)\right|$ is defined as

$$\left|\nabla f(x_1, x_2...x_n)\right| = \sqrt{(\frac{\partial \rho}{\partial x_1})^2 + (\frac{\partial \rho}{\partial x_2})^2 ... + (\frac{\partial \rho}{\partial x_n})^2} \tag{9}$$

When $\left|\nabla f(x_1, x_2...x_n)\right|$ is larger than a given threshold, $Grid(x_1, x_2...x_n)$ is the edge of vector space. The vector in the grid is called as edge vector.

5   Space Edge Detection Based SVM Algorithm

Through the space edge detection, it's easy to find out the edge-vector-set in which the vector is located at the edge of the vector space. As the support vectors immediate impact the hyperplane and they always located at the vector space edge, so instead of all vectors, this article uses the edge-vector-set to take the process of SVM training. Compared with all vectors, edge-vector-set's size is smaller, so the Algorithm will significantly improve the speed of SVM training, save the storage space. Fig. 2 shows the process of Space edge detection based SVM algorithm.

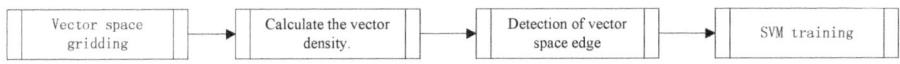

Fig. 2. The process of Space edge detection based SVM algorithm

5.1   The Description of Space Edge Detection Based SVM

Step1: vector space gridding, set the grid unit length. According to the introduction of section A of III, first set every axis's unit length, and then the whole vector space is divided into several equal size grid space.

Step2: Calculate the vector density. According to the vector density formula as $\rho=m/v$, calculate the vector density of each grid. Since this paper set the size of each grid to 1, Therefore, simplify the formula as $\rho=m$, so vector density of the grid equal to the number of vectors within the grid.

Step3: Detection of vector space edge. Reference to the idea of edge detection, take derivation on the vector density to find out the edge of vector space.

Step4: Through the detection of vector space edge, get the edge vector set.

Step5: Use the edge vector set instead of all vectors to take the process of SVM training, and then get the training model.

Step6: SVM parameter optimization. By cross validation and grid search algorithm, obtain the best SVM parameters.

Step7: Using the new training model to classify.

6 Simulations

Simulation's running environment is Window 7 operating system, cup is Intel core Duo. Using Java to program and the Java development environment is JDK 1.6, Eclipse. Using the interface provided by libsvm-2.89 [6] to do the SVM development. Simulation selects 2963 records from the UCI data set, all data is divided into two categories, 2155 and the other 808. Scatter plot of all data is showed in Fig. 3.

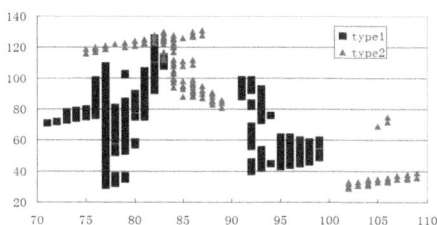

Fig. 3. The Scatter plot of all data

In the experiment, If the split step of the grid in the X axis and Y axis is set to 1. After space edge detection , edge vector set was obtained as shown in Fig. 4,After edge detection, the data in the data-intensive area has been deleted, leaving only the data at the edge of the area. The size of the data set reduced from the original 2963 to1446. Using the data in Fig. 4 to take the SVM training can significantly improve the training speed, save the storage space.

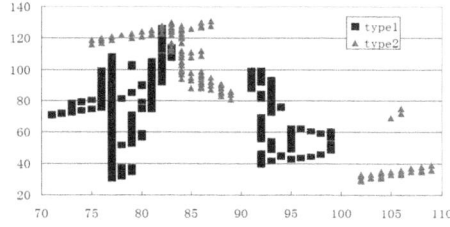

Fig. 4. After edge detection, obtained edge vector set

In the experiment, the results were obtained by adjusting the division step, in the gridding process of vector space. As shown in Fig.5, there is the SVM classification accuracy of ordinary SVM algorithm, SVM algorithm based on edge detection with grid area of 9, grid area of 4, grid area of 1, from left to right. Experimental results show that when grid area is increased to a certain extent, the classification accuracy of improved SVM algorithm will be close to the ordinary SVM algorithm. A theoretical analysis is made that when the grid is infinite, the SVM algorithm based on edge detection may translate into ordinary SVM algorithm; and while the grid is smaller, in the process of the space edge detection, some original support vectors may be ignored, which makes the decline of classification accuracy.

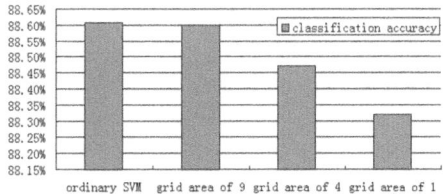

Fig. 5. The comparison chart of classification accuracy with different parameters

As shown in Fig.6, there are the SVM training time of ordinary SVM algorithm, space edge detection based SVM algorithm with grid area of 9, grid area of 4, grid area of 1, from left to right. Second was used as time unit. We can see that SVM training time is also reduced, with the decrease of grid area. This is because the smaller the grid, the higher the sensitivity of edge detection and the smaller the edge vector set, which makes the smaller the data set used by SVM training and the faster the SVM training speed will be.

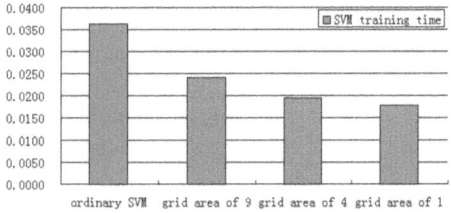

Fig. 6. The comparison chart of SVM training time with different parameters

As shown in simulation experiments, it can be seen that the Space edge detection based SVM algorithm can effectively compress the size of SVM training's dataset, markedly improves the operation efficiency of SVM algorithm, and with slightly effects of the final classification accuracy.

7 Conclusions

Up to now, Support Vector Machine is the most successful implementation in statistical theory, for its classification principle, which is of exceptionally advantage while dealing with the small data sets, but with long training time and slow processing speed in dealing with large data sets. In practical applications, large volume of data, mass data needs to be seen as an unavoidable problem, therefore, it has been becoming a research focus to find a SVM algorithm which can be fast processing of large data sets. In this paper, a Space edge detection based SVM algorithm was proposed, which can greatly improve the speed of SVM training, and ensures the classification accuracy of SVM algorithm will not drop too much. Experimental results show that the proposed algorithm has great effect on dealing with large data sets. However, the only drawback is that classification accuracy of the algorithm will decline slightly while improving the training speed, which will be one of the future directions of research.

References

1. Lang, J.: Research on Several Problems in Support Vector Machine and Support Vector Domain Description. XiDian University, Xian (2009)
2. Li, H., Wang, C., Yuan, B.: An Improved SVM: NN-SVM. Chinese Journal of Computers 26, 1015–1020 (2003)
3. Zhang, Z., Dong, C., Chen, Z., He, X.: Improved fast classifier based on SVM and density clustering. Computer Engineering and Applications 47, 136–138 (2011)
4. Wang, J., Neskovic, P., Cooper, L.N.: Selecting Data for Fast Support Vector Machines Training. Studies in Computational Intelligence, vol. 35, pp. 61–84 (2007)
5. Deng, N., Tian, Y.: A new method of data mining - support vector machine. Science Press, Beijing (2004)
6. Chang, C.C., Lin, C.-J.: LIBSVM A Library for Support Vector Machines [EB/OL]

Method for Determining Parameters of Posterior Probability SVM Based on Relative Cross Entropy

Qing-hua Xing, Fu-xian Liu, Xiang Li, and Lu Xia

Missile Institute of Air Force Engineering University, Sanyuan, 713800, China
liuxqh@126.com

Abstract. The technology of support vector machines (SVM) is being widely used in many research fields at present, but standard SVM does not provide posterior probability that is needed in many uncertain classification problems. To solve this problem, a probability SVM model is built firstly, then the cross entropy and relative cross entropy model for classification problems are built. Finally, the method for determining parameters of probability SVM model is put forward by minimizing relative cross entropy. Experiment results show that the method of determining model parameters is reasonable, and the posterior probability SVM model is effective.

Keywords: support vector machines, relative cross entropy, posterior probability.

1 Introduction

SVM [1,7] (Support Vector Machine) as a method of statistical learning theory has solved learning problems with finite samples, and is widely used in pattern recognition, data mining and many other fields. However, standard SVM only considers two extreme cases whose result belongs to some class with probability for 1 or 0, so it cannot provide posterior probability of what is needed in many uncertain problems of sample classification. Wahba [2] and Platt [3] had firstly introduced posterior probability in SVM to expand the capability for standard SVM. There are mainly two kinds of methods for determining posterior probability [4, 5]: the first one is the Bayesian framework theory which needs to calculate conditional probability density of every class firstly and then compute its posterior probability based on Bayesian theory; the second one is fitting posterior probability directly without calculating the probability density of every class. These methods are all the beneficial attempts of introducing the posterior probability into standard SVM. In this paper, a modeling method of posterior probability SVM based on relative cross entropy has been put forward. An optimization model has been constructed by using relative cross entropy as the objective function. The parameters optimal value of probability SVM model can be obtained by minimizing relative cross entropy. And the classification results of every SVM are given by probability in the method. Namely, categories of samples are determined by posterior probability, which can not only give a qualitative explanation but also give a quantitative evaluation.

H. Deng et al. (Eds.): AICI 2011, Part III, LNAI 7004, pp. 664–670, 2011.
© Springer-Verlag Berlin Heidelberg 2011

2 Posterior Probability SVM Model

The standard output value of SVM is [6]:

$$y = sign(f(x))$$
(1)

and $f(x) = (w^* \times x) + b^*$

In the equation above, w^* is the weight coefficient vector of optimal hyperplane and b^* is the threshold of classification.

The nearest sample point x (support vector) to hyperplane should satisfy $\|f(x)\| = 1$. So the sample points on the hyperplane should satisfy $f(x)=0$ and the other points should satisfy $f(x) = \pm r \cdot \|w\|$, where r is the distance between x and the hyperplane, and the sign means which side of the hyperplane it belongs to. In this way, the distance between the support vector and the hyperplane can be expressed as: $r_{sv} = 1/\|w\|$.

Therefore the distance between any sample point x and the hyperplane is: $r_x = f(x)/\|w\|$.

$$\text{then: } f(x)=r_x/r_{sv}$$
(2)

From Equation (2), $f(x)$ is the ratio of r_x to r_{sv}, which reflects the degree of a sample point belonging to certain class in the problem. Thus, the posterior probability model can be regarded as a function of $f(x)$ by which posterior probability of sample point can be measured.

Generally, the probability output function should satisfy the following requirements [2]: ① the range of the function value should be in [0, 1], ② the function must be monotonic. The contrastive analysis among several kinds of monotone functions used for the probability output function shows that, sigmoid function with two parameters (A and B) has a flexible function form in modeling on probability SVM [4] and presents better classification accuracy in practical application. Therefore, the sigmoid function with two parameters (A and B) is used as posterior probability SVM model.

For two kinds of classification problems, the posterior probability model of SVM can be given by use of the sigmoid function with two parameters (A and B):

$$P(y = 1 | f(x)) = \frac{1}{1 + e^{A \cdot f(x) + B}}$$
$$P(y = -1 | f(x)) = 1 - P(y = 1 | f(x))$$
(3)

In Equation (3), the modality of sigmoid function is controlled by parameter A and B, and $f(x)$ is the standard output value of sample x in SVM. Thus, it is obvious that after probability modeling on standard SVM, the class of sample x can be determined by the two equations above and the degree of a sample point belonging to certain class can be measured by the value of posterior probability which can also be called reliability. However, for standard SVM, the class of sample x is determined by Equation (1) with the presentation of $y=1$ or $y=-1$.

3   Method for Determining Model Parameters of Probability SVM Based on Relative Cross Entropy

After building the posterior probability model of sigmoid function according to the standard output $f(x)$ of SVM, how to determine the parameter A and B of the probability model? In the following, a method of minimizing relative cross entropy based on cross entropy is put forward in order to determine parameters in probability model (3).

3.1   Modeling on the Cross Entropy and Relative Cross Entropy for Classification Problem

Suppose that random variable x is from distribution $p(x)$. As $p(x)$ is unknown, it can be represented by distribution $q(x)$ which is known as some kind of parameter model. Define the cross entropy between $q(x)$ and genuine distribution $p(x)$ as:

$$- \int p(x) \ln q(x) dx \tag{4}$$

The cross entropy can get to the minimum only if $q(x)$ is equal to $p(x)$.

For two kinds of classification problems, assume $y=p(c_1|x)$ and $1-y=p(c_2|x)$. Namely, the output is t=1 when x belongs to c_1 and t=0 when x belongs to c_2. Then :

$$p(t \mid x) = y^t (1-y)^{1-t} \tag{5}$$

It is obvious that $p(t|x)$ obeys *Bernoulli* distribution. If the training sample (x_i,t_i) $(i=1,2,\ldots,n)$ is selected independently, the likelihood function of it can be described as $\prod_{i=1}^{n} p(t_i \mid x_i)$, that is:

$$\prod_{i=1}^{n} y_i^{t_i} (1-y_i)^{1-t_i} \tag{6}$$

Take the negative logarithm of the equation above, then:

$$E_1 = -\sum_{i=1}^{n} \left[t_i \ln y_i + (1-t_i) \ln(1-y_i) \right] \tag{7}$$

It can be proved that E_1 is the cross entropy between $y(x)$ and distribution of target t.

If $y_i = t_i$ is put into Equation (7), the minimum of E_1 can be got:

$$E_{min} = -\sum_{i=1}^{n} \left[t_i \ln t_i + (1-t_i) \ln(1-t_i) \right] \tag{8}$$

For the two kind problem, if t_i is 1 or 0, $E_{min}=0$ and if t_i is the successive value of (0, 1) , $E_{min} \neq 0$. Therefore, after Equation (8) is subtracted from Equation (7), a form of error function can be got as the following:

$$E_2 = -\sum_{i=1}^{n}\left[t_i \ln \frac{y_i}{t_i} + (1-t_i)\ln \frac{(1-y_i)}{(1-t_i)}\right] \qquad (9)$$

The error function, which can be called as relative cross entropy, is virtually a relative entropy between actual output y_i and theoretic output t_i. The smaller the error is, the closer E_1 is to E_{min} as well as $y(x)$ is to target t.

3.2 Method for Determining Parameters of Probability SVM Model by Minimizing Relative Cross Entropy

Suppose training sample set (x_i, y_i) $(i=1,2,...,n)$ is the training sample of SVM, and in order to calculate parameter A and B, another set of sample (f_i, y_i) $(i=1,2,...,n)$ can be considered as training sample, in which $f_i=f(x_i)$, $f(x_i)$ is the standard output of SVM and $y_i \in \{-1, 1\}$.

For the reason of avoiding over-fitting in using small data set to fit sigmoid function, noise is added into the original data set [3]. Namely, in the reconstructed training sample, the SVM output value of positive sample is $f(x_i)$ and the corresponding goal value $t_i=1-\varepsilon_+$. Also, the corresponding goal value of the negative one is $t_i=\varepsilon_-$.

There, $\varepsilon_+ = \dfrac{1}{N_+ +2}$ and $\varepsilon_- = \dfrac{1}{N_- +2}$ can be estimated by Bayes posterior probability. Then, a redefined training sample set (f_i, t_i) $(i=1,2,...,n)$, in which t_i is the goal value of $f(x_i)$ after adding noise, can be got. The equation is as follows:

$$t_i = \begin{cases} \dfrac{N_+ +1}{N_+ +2}, & y_i = 1; \\ \dfrac{1}{N_- +2}, & y_i = -1. \end{cases} \qquad (10)$$

Aiming at solving model p_i, namely computing parameter A and B in p_i and making the value of p_i as closer to t_i as possible, the relative cross entropy function of p_i and t_i can be constructed as follows:

$$E = -\sum_{i=1}^{n}\left[t_i \ln \frac{p_i}{t_i} + (1-t_i)\ln \frac{(1-p_i)}{(1-t_i)}\right] \qquad (11)$$

After minimizing relative cross entropy, parameter A and B of sigmoid function can be got. If the parameter A and B are expressed by the form of vector $Z=(A,B)^T$, the following equation should be minimized:

$$\min_{Z=(A,B)^T} F(Z) \qquad (12)$$

and: $F(Z) = -\sum_{i=1}^{n} \left[t_i \ln \frac{p_i}{t_i} + (1-t_i) \ln \frac{(1-p_i)}{(1-t_i)} \right]$,

$$p_i = \frac{1}{1 + e^{Af(x_i)+B}}$$

Use Newton iterative algorithm [3] to compute parameter A and B. The basic idea of the algorithm is:

Firstly, compute gradient $\nabla F(Z)$ and Hessian matrix $G(Z)$ of $F(Z)$ as follows:

$$\nabla F(Z) = \begin{bmatrix} \sum_{i=1}^{n} \frac{\partial F}{\partial p_i} \frac{\partial p_i}{\partial A} \\ \sum_{i=1}^{n} \frac{\partial F}{\partial p_i} \frac{\partial p_i}{\partial B} \end{bmatrix} = \begin{bmatrix} \sum_{i=1}^{n} (t_i - p_i) f_i \\ \sum_{i=1}^{n} (t_i - p_i) \end{bmatrix}$$

$$G(Z) = \nabla^2 F(Z)$$

$$= \begin{bmatrix} \sum_{i=1}^{n} p_i^2 f_i^2 (1-p_i) & \sum_{i=1}^{n} p_i^2 f_i (1-p_i) \\ \sum_{i=1}^{n} p_i^2 f_i (1-p_i) & \sum_{i=1}^{n} p_i^2 (1-p_i) \end{bmatrix}$$

For a given initial point Z^0 and parameter $\sigma \geq 0$, ensure that $H(Z^0) + \sigma I$ is positive definition.

Secondly, convert the calculating of the problem above into computing the following iterative equation:

$$[G(Z^k) + \sigma I]\delta^k = -\nabla F(Z^k)$$

If $F(Z^k) = 0$, end the calculation;

otherwise, select α^k successively from the sequence: $1, \frac{1}{2}, \frac{1}{4}, \cdots$. Namely, the first element of the sequence which satisfies

$F(Z^k + \alpha^k \delta^k) \leq F(Z^k) + 0.0001 \cdot \alpha^k (\nabla F(Z^k)^T \delta^k)$ can be considered as α^k. Suppose $Z^{k+1} = Z^k + \alpha^k \delta^k$ and continue the iteration.

In this way, the value of A and B can be got by the iterative calculation. Then, the posterior probability of sample x belonging to some class can be determined according to Formula (3).

4 Experimental Analysis

In this paper, the data of heart_scale, ionosphere_scale, liver-disorders_scale, and ijcnn1is are used in the experiments on probability SVM. The number of heart_scale sample is 260, which is made up of 120 positive samples, 140 negative samples and the data characteristic dimension of which is 13; the number of ionosphere_scale sample is 340, which is made up of 214 positive samples, 126 negative samples and the data characteristic dimension of which is 34; the number of liver-disorders_scale sample is 345, which is made up of 150 positive samples , 195 negative samples and the data characteristic dimension of which is 6; the training sample and testing sample are separated in ijcnn1 experiment which is made up of 35001 training samples, 91701 testing samples and the data characteristic dimension of which is 22. The results of data classification based on probability SVM model and standard SVM are shown in Table 1.

Table 1. The correctness of sample classification based on different methods

Method Sample	Standard SVM	Probability SVM of minimizing relative cross entropy	
	Classifying correct rate	Classifying correct rate	Parameters
heart_scale	85.3846%	86.1538%	A=-1.81391, B=-0.0998787
Ionosphere_scale	94.7059%	95.2941%	A=-7.33835, B=5.21406
liver-disorders_scale	60%	68.1159%	A=-4.16529, B=1.29649
Ijcnn1	91.0906%	92.3785%	A=-1.36896, B=-0.700627

From Table 1, it is obvious that the classification results of probability SVM are better than those of standard SVM.

5 Conclusion

For solving uncertain problems of sample classification, classification results are often required to be exported by the form of posterior probability, however, it cannot be realized by Standard SVM. Therefore, in this paper, based on cross entropy theory, a method of minimizing relative cross entropy is used to build posterior probability SVM model directly. In terms of this method, not only the classification precision of SVM is improved, but also the credible degree of which class the sample belongs to is provided. Experiment results show that the classification accuracy can be effectively improved by probability SVM based on minimizing relative cross entropy.

References

1. Song, N.-H., Xing, Q.-H.: Multi-class Classification of Air Targets Based on Support Vector Machine. Systems Engineering and Electrics 28(8), 1279–1281 (2006)
2. Wahba, G.: Support Vector Machines, Reproducing Kernel Hilbert Spaces and the Randomized GACV. In: Advances in Kernel Methods Support Vector Learning, pp. 69–88. MIT Press, Massachusetts (1999)
3. Platt, J.C.: Probabilities for Support Vector Machines and Comparisons to Regularized Likelihood Methods. In: Advances in Large Margin Classifiers, pp. 61–74. MIT Press, Massachusetts (2000)
4. Zhang, X., Xiao, X.-L., Xu, G.-Y.: Probabilistic Outputs for Support Vector Machines Based on the Maximum Entropy Estination. Control and Decision 21(7), 767–770 (2006)
5. Wu, G.-W., Tao, Q., Wang, J.: Support Vector Machines Based on Posterior Probability. Journal of Computer Research and Development 42(2), 196–202 (2005)
6. Lin, H.T., Lin, C.J., Weng, R.C.: A Note on Platt's Probabilistic Outputs for Support Vector Machines. National Taiwan University, Taipei (2003)
7. Wen, C.-J., Zhang, Y.-Z., Chen, C.-J.: Maximum-Margin minimal-Volume Hypershere Support Vector Machine. Control and Decision 25(1), 79–83 (2010)
8. Ma, Y.-L., Pei, S.-L.: Study on Parameter Optimization Algorithm for SVM Based on Improved Genetic Algorithm. Computer Simulation 27(8), 150–152 (2010)

Author Index